Aluminum Currents

Aluminum Currents

ISBN 978-1-945307-38-6
Book designed by Rodney Schroeter

Copyright © 2024 Rodney Schroeter,
and All Other Copyright Holders

The Silver Creek Press is:
Rodney Schroeter
PO Box 334
Random Lake WI 53075-0334
SchroeterRodney@gmail.com

Your Editor and Publisher has made every effort to include only material he has the authority to use. If you find any item(s) herein that you believe you have the rights to, which you have not granted permission to reprint, please contact the Publisher (above).

My thanks to Barry, Christie, and Ian Johanson
for launching my Current career.

My First Ten Years of Editing
The Plymouth Review Current

Edited by
Rodney Schroeter

Silver
Creek
Press

2024

Up Front Stuff

This book is about *My* First Ten Years of editing The Current; not *The* First Ten Years.

I did not originate The Current.

By the spring of 2014, my IT (Information Technology) career of over two decades had been over for about a year. I was looking for a different direction, some means of utilizing my long-time writing abilities and my newly-developing book design skills.

I'd applied to The Plymouth Review for (if memory serves me right) a graphic design position, where I could use Adobe InDesign and Photoshop. I didn't get that position, but the people at The Review kept my application and resume, and contacted me several months later for something else.

The position I was offered included:
• Attending and reporting on four meetings each month (school board, village board, town board).
• Composing newspaper pages (at first, the obituaries; then the sports pages; then news pages).
• (Later on) Assisting with the design of advertisements.
• (Mainly, and the focus of this book) Editing and composing The Current.

Abbey Harvey had been working at The Review, where she had originated The Current a little over three years previously.

Because Ms. Harvey intended to pursue new opportunities, I was called in for an interview. Apparently, I showed some promise, as I started in April, 2014.

The Current is a free monthly paper, financed by the ads. It is inserted in The Plymouth Review, usually the first week of the month; additional copies are distributed in the Plymouth (Wisconsin) and thereabouts region; the current month's issue is also posted online.

I struggled with that first issue. I couldn't come up with an image to put on the cover (and was finally given one by publisher Barry Johanson). And panic set in when I had used up all my gathered content, and found this big, white gap covering several pages. I finally filled it with a public-domain story by Thomas Thursday, an author I considered witty and hilarious.

I finished composing my first issue (the May 2014 edition), handed it over for Barry to look over, and headed south to the Windy City Pulp and Paper Convention. While at that show, I received a phone message from Barry, telling me how pleased he was with what I'd done.

But stepping into Ms. Harvey's shoes was a challenge. A somewhat painful challenge.

It taught me that, in a situation like that, sometimes it's best not to try getting into those shoes, but to get (or completely fabricate from scratch) an entirely different pair of shoes. Not that one should go too radically afar, and try wearing something like gloves on one's feet; best to stay with shoes. But shoes that fit. Shoes that one can actually walk and eventually run in.

In other words: Instead of trying to simply continue what The Current had been, I gradually made it my own.

There were several ways I did that:

— I leveraged my knowledge of movies. Highlights of movies scheduled on Turner Classic Movies for the coming month soon became a regular, prominent feature in each issue. (For obvious reasons, no examples of that column appear in this book.)

Surprisingly and encouragingly, people giving me in-person feedback on The Current name that column, and my additional comments on other movies, as their favorites.

— I feature a lot of art. But instead of modernistic piles of garbage, or trendy blank canvases, I include what I term in my mind "art for farmers."

I certainly do not mean that in the sense of a contemptibly-titled series of books, "Art for Dummies." I grew up on a farm, and realize that farmers are no dummies (or they are not farming for long). Farmers need to be *reality-oriented,* something modern anti-art most definitely *is not.*

I have been to auctions and estate sales of many local farmers. I have noticed one thing: There are always framed pieces of art—reality-oriented art—that had been hanging for years on farmhouse walls.

I more often need look to the past, if I want to find art that speaks to reality-oriented minds (whether on isolated farms or in the hearts of vast megalopolises). But not exclusively. You'll discover in this book, two contemporary artists whose work deals with real-life values.

— I feature pro-freedom articles. This, too, brings me favorable comments from readers. *Most* readers. But it has enraged a small minority who passionately hate freedom; hate the unique form of human consciousness that gives rise to freedom and rights; and ultimately hate human life itself. I encourage those people to indulge their rage by repeatedly head-butting the brick wall of reality as they clamor for my cancellation.

But until I am canceled, I intend to keep constructing issues of The Plymouth Review Current.

For another ten years, and beyond?

We'll see.

Rodney Schroeter
Spring, 2024

— Book covers, unless otherwise indicated, are from Barnes & Noble, BN.com

— All fine art images by James Bama are Copyright © the estate of James Bama

— Images marked "HA.com" are imaged by, and courtesy of, Heritage Auctions, HA.com

— Most (but unfortunately not all) uncredited photos herein are by Rodney Schroeter.

— The book reviews by Beth Dippel are reprinted here with permission from Beth Dippel. At the time those reviews were published, Beth was Executive Director at the Sheboygan County Historical Research Center.

— Internet links given in articles may or may not still work. In assembling this book, when a non-functioning link was found, it was removed.

— Unless otherwise noted, images accompanying PulpArtists biographies are from the PulpArtists.com website, where you can find hundreds of entries written by David Saunders. The PulpArtists biographies in this book are reprinted with David Saunders' permission.

— Your Editor and Publisher has made every effort to include only material he has the authority to use. If you find any item(s) herein that you believe you have the rights to, which you have not granted permission to reprint, please contact the Publisher (see Copyright page). (Yes, I know. It bears repeating.)

— Award-winning science teacher Larry Scheckel has been answering high schooler's questions for over 40 years. He has collected some of these questions into several books. His "Ask A Science Teacher" excerpts from these books are reprinted here with the author's permission. His email is Lscheckel@charter.net; his website is larryscheckel.com

2014

May
2014

Cover photo: Vulture, by Larry Stone
Reading, Books and More by Patti McKenzie: Spelling: A lifelong skill that will serve you well
I Ate At... by Richard J. Baumann: Greg's Tap, Adell
White's Wine by David White: Comic books and thoroughbreds, inspired by wine
Bring a world-class chef into your kitchen by Rodney Schroeter: Joël Robuchon
Like Father, Like Daughter by Mark Walters: Living on the ice in late April
Emily Stone: Turkey vultures play role in food chain
The Science in Science Fiction: Hal Clement and the heavy world of Mesklin
Hello and welcome, from the Editor
The Incomparable Hildegarde: from Adell to fame, by William & Joy Wangemann
The Mailboxes of Libbie Nolan
Dance studio welcomes new owner, by Eric Mathes
Stories from the past: Fall of the Wise, by Thomas Thursday

The Mailboxes of Libbie Nolan

The Wisconsin Writers Association is a statewide organization the helps amateur and professional writers of all kinds.

I'm likely to write more about WWA in future columns: About how there are local WWA charter clubs; how WWA conducts conferences; the contests sponsored by WWA, with cash prizes.

But for now, I'd like to focus on one WWA member I recently met, and just one aspect of her work. Her name is Elizabeth Faulkner Nolan, but she goes by "Libbie."

I've been a member of the WWA for only five years. A lot of people have been members for far longer. But Libbie has (I think) everyone else beat. She was around when the organization was formed, in 1948.

Libbie is now 97. Her eyesight has diminished somewhat, her hearing has faded a little. But her mind? Ever hear the expression, "Sharp as a tack"? That phrase was invented precisely for someone who has the quick wit, humor, and memory that Libbie still enjoys.

One of Libbie's life accomplishments was a series of drawings for the Wisconsin Regional Writer, published for several decades by WWA. From the 1960s through the 90s, she drew an interesting mailbox for most covers of this quarterly publication. At first, she drew mailboxes she observed personally. But as the covers became more popular with WWA members, people would send her photos of creatively crafted mailboxes from around the state.

Desserts from Joël Robuchon

Desserts from the 16-course tasting menu at Restaurant Joël Robuchon, Las Vegas. Green chartreuse sabayon, topped with herb sherbet and a hazelnut praline.

Raspberry dome on mascarpone, with red fruit coulis and Calpico Jelly.

The SCIENCE in SCIENCE FICTION
by Rodney Schroeter

Hal Clement and the heavy world of Mesklin

Let's start with a simple science fact: You would weigh less standing at the Earth's equator, than you would at the North or South Poles.

Why is that?

It's because, as the Earth spins, centrifugal force pushes things away from the center of spin. On a spherical object like Earth, the farther you are from the axis, the greater the centrifugal force, because you're traveling faster around that axis.

Granted, the difference between your weight at the pole and at the equator would be very small. About half a percent. So, if you weigh 100 pounds at the North Pole, you would weigh (let me get the calculator out here) 95.5 pounds at the equator.

Earth is not a perfect sphere. It actually bulges slightly at the equator, because of centrifugal force.

But Saturn bulges even more. First, because it's not a rocky planet. It's made up of gasses and, probably, liquids further toward its core. In fact, if you had a pail of water large enough to drop Saturn into it (now if that doesn't boggle your mind, I don't know what will), Saturn would float in the water!

(So if you ever read a science fiction novel where the hero flies to Saturn, and lands on a solid surface, and sees interesting rocks, mountainous terrain, etc., you're entitled to shout, in your most derisive voice, "BO—gus!!")

The second reason Saturn bulges so much is because, large as it is, it's spinning around once every ten hours (compared with 24 hours for Earth). Now, the faster a planet would spin, the stronger the centrifugal force is at the equator.

There's another important factor. Density. That's simply how much stuff is packed into a given area. Fill up a suitcase with those styrofoam peanuts used for shipping material. You can lift that up just fine; it's not very dense. Now fill the same suitcase with rocks. Much denser!

Much... heavier.

If the Earth were made up of solid lead, we would all weigh much more. (And if you can figure out roughly how much more, please send your solution in to the Current — see our e-mail on page 2.)

If you're with me so far, please take a deep breath, because we're about to take a step farther out. Maybe... quite a large step. Perhaps... one giant leap.

Imagine a world that's very dense. So dense that, if it did not spin, you would stand on its surface and weigh seven hundred times what you weigh on Earth. Or, using Earth's gravity as a unit of measure that we humans can relate to, we'd use the term "700g."

You certainly wouldn't last long on such a planet. 700g would crush your soft tissues and your bones.

But the world of Mesklin, created by author Hal Clement, does indeed spin (or rotate). This super-dense planet spins so fast, that its rotation ("day") is only about fifteen minutes. When you watch the sun rise on Earth, you know it's going to be another 24 hours before it rises again. On Mesklin, you'd see a star-rise every fifteen minutes!

Standing at either pole of Mesklin, you'd be totally flattened by 700gs. Drop a marble (if you could), and it would fall 700 times faster than you're used to.

But as you walk toward the planet's equator, you'd suffer less g force, and weigh less.

Now, can you imagine how strong the centrifugal force would be on a planet spinning so fast? It's enormous. Strong enough to make the planet really bulge out at the equator, making it look like a thick pancake. And strong enough that, by the time you reach the planet's equator, you'd only ("only!") experience 3gs.

Weighing three times what you're used to will not kill you (right away!), but it will slow you down plenty. If you'd like to experience what that's like, load up a backpack with twice your own weight and carry it around for awhile. See how soon you say, "That's enough of that experiment."

Hal Clement (May 30, 1922 – October 29, 2003) set his science fiction novel, *Mission of Gravity,* on the planet Mesklin. When *Mission of Gravity* was published in 1953, Clement's SF career was over a decade old; his first published story ran in the June 1942 issue of *Astounding Science Fiction.*

If you're looking for big, bloody wars between humans and aliens, blasters shooting and bodies blowing up, look elsewhere. When human and alien species meet in a Hal Clement story, it's typically peaceful and mutually respectful.

The stories of Hal Clement are essentially benevolent. Contrast that with so many of today's blood-drenched, malevolent-toned series where you must kill to survive.

But conflict, suspense, stress, urgency, and excitement are found aplenty in Clement's work. In *Mission of Gravity,* the ship from Earth, carrying a crew, has a problem. And the beings living on Mesklin, cautious but excited to meet another sentient race, are willing to help.

What kind of life form could live in Mesklin's super-high gravity? The "Mesklinites" are small, compact, many-legged creatures that resemble foot-long centipedes, built strongly enough to withstand high g.

Clement was especially good at building plot events around misunderstandings between human and alien races. Misunderstandings caused by assumptions. Clement took his readers through the minds of his human characters, but gave insight into the thought processes of the aliens as well. So the reader sees the human species from the perspective of an alien, and gains a fresh perspective on human nature.

Here's an example of human vs. alien outlook. The humans have an all-terrain vehicle they drive on Mesklin (remember how hard walking in 3g would be) and want to travel some distance. One of the small Mesklinites says it would take a long time for it to get there. The human, trying to be helpful, lifts the Mesklinite from the ground, and sets it on the vehicle. The man doesn't understand how terrifying it is for the alien to be off the ground at all. In such high gravity, a fall of a few inches is enough to splatter them.

In the course of the book, the humans succeed in getting the Mesklinites to "think outside of the box," and consider life-enhancing practices they otherwise never would have considered, given the conditions on Mesklin. And the Mesklinites return the favor. Cultural exchange at its finest!

You'll notice I give very little of the story away. I believe that not knowing too much about a story makes the reader's discovery of that story more of a delight.

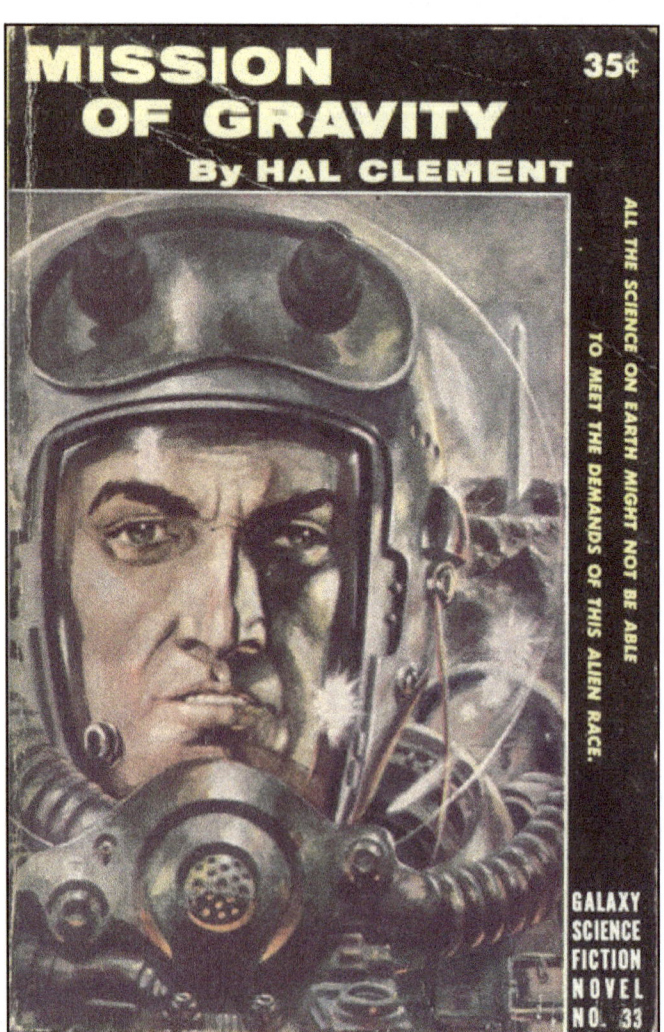

Early paperback edition of *Mission of Gravity* by Hal Clement. Cover painting by Wallace Wood.

Mission of Gravity will engage and entertain a reader willing to put a little extra effort into his or her reading. The reader will better understand Earth and its gravity (through the description of a very different planet), and human psychology (through the workings of an alien mind). The reader will enjoy a benevolent collaboration between two thinking species and share the problem-solving challenges that threaten them.

Now *that's* good science fiction.

Books by Hal Clement (not a complete list)

Most of these are not in print, but are available at very reasonable prices in the used-book marketplace. Check a local used bookstore, eBay, Amazon, or bookfinder.com.

Needle (1950)
Iceworld (1953)
Mission of Gravity (1954)
Star Light (1971) (sequel to Mission of Gravity)
Still River (1987)
Fossil (1993)
Half Life (1999)
The Essential Hal Clement, three volumes
Heavy Planet (2002), (a collection of all the Mesklin stories)
Noise (2003)

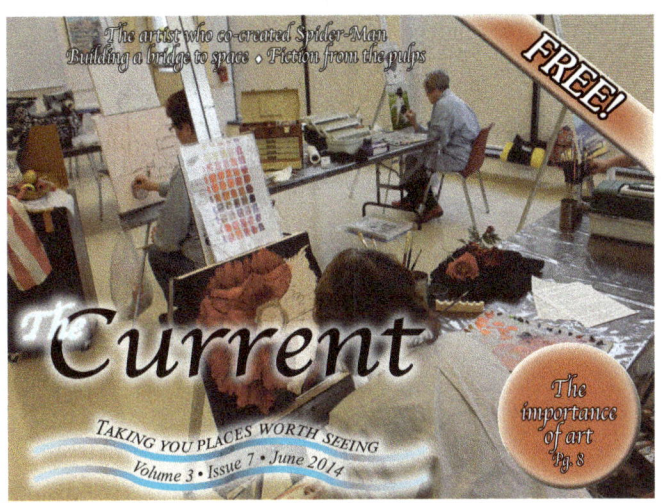

Vegetable rolls, served at Restaurant Guy Savoy at Caesar's Palace, Las Vegas.

June
2014

Cover photo: Art Class at the Plymouth Arts Center
The Importance of Reading, Editorial
I Am That Baby!
Reading, Books and More by Patti McKenzie: Reading: it's not just for the school year
Steve Ditko: co-creator of Spider-Man
When Things Go Wrong, by William & Joy Wangemann
The importance of taking art seriously (discussion with Kitty Lynne Klich and Lori Beringer at the Plymouth Arts Center)
Emily Stone: Birds can fly because they take themselves lightly
I Ate At... by Richard J. Baumann: The Black Dog Bistro, Rhine Center
White's Wine by David White: Trading a Desk Job for One in the Vineyards
Bring a world-class chef into your kitchen by Rodney Schroeter: Guy Savoy
The Science in Science Fiction: Building a bridge from Earth to space
Discover the world of pulp fiction
Like Father, Like Daughter by Mark Walters: Shultz Lake visit the best week of the year

'I am that baby!'

I write a column for the Random Lake *Sounder* called "What We Were Reading," in which I quote a few paragraphs from the Random Lake papers of 25, 50, and 75 years ago.

For a 2011 column, I presented the following piece, in full, from the April 23, 1936 paper:

A two-week old baby girl was left on the kitchen table at the home of Mr. and Mrs. Ed Bruesewitz, Silver Creek Sunday evening, with a note as follows:

"Here is a little baby for you to keep. This baby is two weeks old, it was born April 4. I am not married and can not aford to suport it as I have to work for a living and I am sure that you can give it a bet-

High school yearbook photos of (left) Val Bruesewitz, and Eugene Wettstein (right), from 1954 and 1952 Kiel yearbooks. — From the Kiel Public Library

ter home then I can. So please keep her and take good care of her and do not try and find out where she comes from and where I am as it will do no good. Feed her every 3 hours giving her 1/2 milk and 1/2 water and wash out her mouth with sugar water to get rid of that white stuff or else see a doctor about it. And as for the name that you will have to pick yourself as I did not have her baptized yet. You will have to have that done. Now be sure and take good care of her."

Mr. and Mrs. Bruesewitz left their home at 8 o'clock in the evening, which they spent with their neighbors, Mr. and Mrs. Henry Hannert. They returned at about 11:45 when the child was found, dressed in shabby clothes and placed in a clothes basket belonging to the Bruesewitz home.

At present the babe is being cared for by Mr. and Mrs. Bruesewitz who will continue to do so until authorities have completed a thorough investigation.

"Interesting?" The word is hardly adequate.

Long-time Silver Creek resident Delmar Schroeter said that the Bruesewitz home, a stone house, no longer stands. A house later built on the site was occupied for many years by Leroy and Gloria Goehring.

As I scanned subsequent issues of the Random Lake paper on microfilm, I watched for any follow-up details on the baby in the basket. I found none.

Eddie's Meat Market, 617 Fremont Street, Kiel, 1950s. "Eddie" was Ed Bruesewitz who, with his wife in 1936, discovered a baby left on the kitchen table of their Silver Creek home. — From the Kiel Public Library

In 1956 we moved to Ca. hoping it would help my Mom's asthma. This is where I've stayed, watching a city of 12,000 grow to over 200,000 in those 55 years.

The reason your parents don't recognize the name Wettstein is probably because they're from Kiel.

My cousin married Clem Schladweiler. I believe one of his brothers was at Risse Hardware Store. Can't remember which one.

Two of my cousins, Margie Murphy & Darlene Eischen live in Random Lake.

As to my letter. You are welcome to print it if you wish. I have nothing to hide. I'm sorry I don't have any pictures of the house in Silver Creek.

It was nice to hear from you.

Val Wettstein

On May 19, *Sounder* editor Gary Feider e-mailed me that their office had received an envelope, addressed to me. I picked up the letter, opened it in my car, and started reading. The question marks of curiosity floating about my head soon burst into exclamation points.

I excitedly returned to the *Sounder* office, and shared the letter with the staff:

May 13, '11
Mr. Schroeter,

Have you ever read a story in the paper from years ago & wondered how it ended? I thought I'd let you know how mine ended, seeing you ran the letter about the 2 week old baby being left on the kitchen table at the home of Mr. & Mrs. Edwin Bruesewitz in April 1936.

This is the kind of story that most journalists can only dream of.

After a trial year they adopted me. They thought they couldn't have children after losing a daughter at birth. They were blessed with a son 2 years after my arrival.

I was so blessed. Wonderful parents & brother & relatives on both sides who accepted me as family. I had a wonderful childhood & have had a neat life.

I married the boy across the street & we have 5 children. I lost my husband to cancer 16 years ago. All my children & grandchildren live close by.

At 75 yrs. old I can still take care of myself. My health could be better but could also be worse so can't complain. God has blessed me in so many ways.

So there you are! In case you had a moment of wondering "What happened to that little baby?" She's alive & well in S. California that has been home for 55 years. I am thankful I grew up in beautiful Wis. among such great people.

Sincerely,
Val Rae Wettstein

I replied to Ms. Wettstein, asking for further details and for permission to print her letter.

Her follow-up letter is dated May 30, 2011:

Dear Rodney,

I received your letter. I am flattered you want to know more about my life but I'm afraid you'll be disappointed. You see, I didn't grow up in Silver Creek. My parents lived on a farm when I came along & I have no idea where it was. I do remember a house made of stones & cement. It had a sunken living room, which I thought was neat. We moved a lot. From Silver Creek we went to Batavia, then to Kiel. I was in kindergarten to 3rd grade there, 4th & 5th in St. Johns Lutheran school, while living in West Bend. 6th thru high school back in Kiel where my Dad had a meat market called Eddie's Market.

I received this letter minutes before I chaired a panel at the Random Lake Area Historical Society. With the panel's topic being the history of Silver Creek, I opened the session by reading Val's letter aloud, to an amazed audience.

Per long-time Silver Creek resident Dean Risse, the brother of Clem Schladweiler would have been Al Schladweiler, who operated a machine repair shop at the corner of State 144 and County DE.

If you ever need to do research on Kiel, Wisconsin, you will find a wealth of information at the Kiel Public Library on 511 Third Street. Dozens of loose-leaf binders, compiled by Edwin Majkrzak, bring Kiel's history excitingly to life with facts, figures, and photos.

Val's father, Edwin E. Bruesewitz, was born June 7, 1908, in the Town of Scott, the son of Mr. & Mrs. August Bruesewitz. On June 28, 1930, he married Miss Irene Ehnert of New Fane. "A meat cutter all his life, he operated a meat market in Kiel for 15 years," states his obituary.

Eddie's Meat Market was located at 617 Fremont St., Kiel, and operated from the 1940s to 50s. This was not the first purpose for this building. An 1899 photo shows it as the office of the Kiel *National Zeitung,* a German-language newspaper published from 1893 to 1918. A 1907 photo describes the building as "Dr. Nauth's Office," and a 1941 photo as "Huberty's Grocery." In the early 1950s, Bruesewitz sold his business and it became Benke's Meat Market.

The "boy across the street" whom Val married was Eugene Wettstein, born March 24, 1934. He and Val were married on Jan. 18, 1958, in Kiel.

Eugene's senior class photo in the 1952 Kiel yearbook appears with the comment, "The Shiek of Araby, that's me."

Val was in the 1954 Kiel graduating class. Accompanying her yearbook photo is the quote, "Here's to the girl with the heart and the smile, who makes the grind of life worth while." For the class will, Val "wills her all around popularity to all Kiel High School students." The class prophecy for Val predicted: "Owner of Queaky Cat and Dog Food Co. — manufacturer of good food for famous cats and dogs."

Yes, I have often "read a story in the paper from years ago & wondered how it ended," as I spend bleary-eyed hours at the microfilm machine. I am very grateful to Val Rae Wettstein, for contacting me over a distance of half a continent, and three-quarters of a century, to let me know what happened to that baby left on the kitchen table in a house that once stood across the street from where I now live. Her story and letters sent me on a trail that gave me a taste for what researchers go through.

My thanks to Val for allowing me to share her letters.

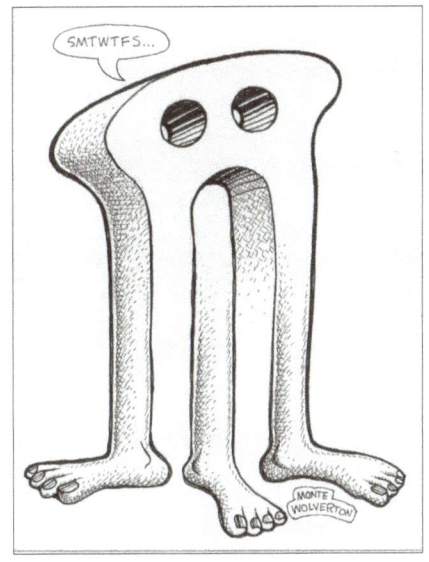

July 2014

Cover photo: Chef Prepares Special Dinner at The Blind Horse, Kohler
Why Silent Movies?
Emily Stone: Dragonflies
The Magic of Radio, by William & Joy Wangemann
White's Wine by David White: America's unquenchable thirst for wine and exploration
I Ate At... by Richard J. Baumann: Koehring's Grand Central House, Kiel
5-course wine-pairing meal at the Blind Horse
Highlight on Wisconsin Writers: Jim Landwehr
The General, starring Buster Keaton
Basil Wolverton Meets Buster Keaton

Great Comic Artists series: Basil Wolverton

Basil Wolverton (1909 to 1978) started his career in comic books not long after comic books, as we know them, began—in the 1930s.

Basil described himself as a "Producer of Preposterous Pictures of Peculiar People who Prowl this Perplexing Planet" (alliteration was a favorite technique in the comics he wrote).

The two most popular characters he created in the 1940s are Spacehawk and Powerhouse Pepper. The first was science-fiction-adventure; the second, a wacky humor strip about a good-natured, super-strong character. Anthologies of both characters have been published over the years. A thick book collecting all the Spacehawk stories, in full color, was published in 2012.

While the comics publishers were headquartered in New York City, Basil chose to live in Vancouver, Washington. Timely Comics, which would later become Marvel, ran the Powerhouse Pepper stories that Basil wrote, drew, and lettered, as well as other humor stories. Basil was very prolific during his cartooning career, working for various comics publishers.

In 1946, cartoonist Al Capp ran a contest in his newspaper strip, Li'l Abner. The world's ugliest woman, Lena the Hyena, appeared in the strip—sort of. Every time the character was shown, the big block letters "CENSORED" appeared where her face would have been. Supposedly, she was just too ugly for publication in a newspaper.

But Capp asked readers to submit a drawing of what they imagined Lena looked like. About half a million entries were sent in, seven of them from Wolverton.

Judges Boris Karloff, Salvador Dali, and Frank Sinatra picked one of Basil's submissions as the winner. The image of Lena was published not only in the Li'l Abner strip, but in the October 28, 1946 issue of Life magazine. Life subsequently published a number of caricatures drawn by Basil.

In the 1950s, Basil did stories for SF/horror comics. Also published

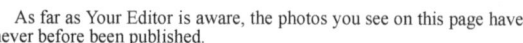

**World Premiere!
Exclusive to The Current!
First-ever publication
of these historic photos!**

As far as Your Editor is aware, the photos you see on this page have never before been published.

That's amazing, considering their historical significance. They represent a unique meeting of two giants of American popular culture.

In 1926, Buster Keaton was shooting what many would consider to be his greatest film, *The General*, on location in Oregon. Aspiring cartoonist Basil Wolverton, living in Washington state, would have been about 17 at the time.

Whatever the circumstances, Basil knew about production of the movie, traveled to Oregon to visit the set of *The General*. What happened during that meeting? How long did Basil stay on the set? I wish there were a detailed account of that meeting. But even Monte Wolverton, the son of Basil, knows little about the story behind these photos.

I am extremely pleased to publish these photos, access to which I gratefully acknowledge my friend, Monte Wolverton. For this issue of The Current, I've written a little about Buster Keaton, Basil Wolverton, and silent movies. I hope you find something of interest in some or all.

Clockwise, starting upper left: Buster Keaton and film crew; Basil Wolverton; on the set of *The General* (note cameramen, lower right); Keaton. — Photos on this page courtesy of Monte Wolverton.

was a booklet, Common Types of Barflyze, which contained grotesque drawings of people who hung around bars too long, drank too much, and showed the effects thereof. Barflyze was reprinted in the 1970s.

Most non-comics-collectors see his work and ask, "Did he work for Mad magazine?" He did. Not as regularly as "The Usual Gang of Idiots," but enough that he could be considered a "Mad artist."

In the 1960s, Basil's work appeared on Fink buttons, Topps Ugly Stickers, Nutty Initials, and various novelty items. People growing up at that time recognize the style, even though they might not know the name.

In the 1970s, DC Comics introduced Basil's work to a new generation of comics reader when they published his drawings on the covers of Plop! comics.

All his life, Basil tried but was unable to break into writing and drawing a newspaper strip. Among his many original drawings that exist, and are bought and sold among collectors at ever-rising prices, there are many sample strips he did, with the intent of trying to sell a newspaper syndicate one idea or another. One of the most amazing examples of this goal of Basil's is a set of four daily strips featuring Mickey Mouse! If I remember correctly, Walt Disney studios was looking for the right artist for a Mickey newspaper strip in the 1930s. Basil did not get that job. It boggles the comic art historian's mind to think what could have been. Instead, the artist hired to draw Mickey's adventures was Floyd Gottfredson, who did such a good job for many decades, that his work is being reprinted today in hardcover.

In the 1970s, I wrote to Basil. His son, Monte, wrote back that his father was unable to reply to mail as a result of a stroke. I've known Monte ever since. He's a graphic designer and artist. His work has similarities with his father's, but Monte has developed his own personal style and gone in his own direction.

Further research (and believe me, *this* kind of research can be hugely enjoyable):

Google and/or search eBay on: Basil Wolverton (combined with: Plop, Mad, Life, Nutty Initials); Topps Chewing Gum.

One of the many caricatures Basil Wolverton did. *Who is this?* The first person to correctly identify the subject of this drawing will receive a copy of Barflyze, by Basil Wolverton. HINT: He was a regular actor on a TV show several decades ago; however, most people have heard his voice and never seen his face. Send name, mailing address, and whether you want your name published if you win, to [The Current].

August
2014

Cover photo: Hay Bales in Your Editor's Back Yard
Which One is Mel Blanc?
Harold Lloyd: Two masterpieces
Emily Stone: The Babes of Summer
Bring a world-class chef into your kitchen by Rodney Schroeter: Pierre Gagnaire
The Science in Science Fiction: Space Colonies
White's Wine by David White: At wine-focused restaurants, embracing the unknown
I Ate At... by Richard J. Baumann: Whispering Orchards Café
Like Father, Like Daughter by Mark Walters: Back to the Flambeau!

Which one... ...is Mel Blanc?

Caricature by Basil Wolverton, run in last month's Current. Who does it portray? Mel Blanc.

Guesses sent in to The Current included:
A. Eddie Cantor
B. Harold Peary
C. Mel Blanc (correct)
D. Willard Waterman (born in Madison, Wisconsin, by the way)
E. Jerry Colonna

Your Editor (left) meets Pierre Gagnaire (right) in 2010. — Photo by Pierre Gagnaire staff.

September 2014

Cover photo: At the 4-H Cat Show
How I Made a Comic Book:
- Human Interest Stuff
- Albert Payson Terhune
- William Messner-Loebs
- The Wisconsin Writers Association
- The Weirdo

Emily Stone: What can be said in defense of a swarm of mosquitoes?
I Ate At... by Richard J. Baumann: Courthouse Pub, Manitowoc
4-H cat show winners
White's Wine by David White: Embracing The Rhone Rangers
The Science in Science Fiction: Ringworld by Larry Niven
Like Father, Like Daughter by Mark Walters: Prepping a young lady for the hunting season

Above: Clarifying Self, by Jon Wos. In the artist's words, it shows "the fact that a clearer view of yourself leads to a clearer view of life." – Courtesy of the artist

October 2014

Cover photo: Michael Perry at Barnes & Noble, Appleton
Editorial: An abundance of opportunities
Dick Tracy: Morality in black & white
The vision of artist Jon Wos
I Ate At... by Richard J. Baumann: LaClare Farms, Pipe WI
Adventures Out There: Teaching the beauty of nature, by Anna Maria Hansen
Natural Connections by Emily Stone: We still look to nature for insights on how to fly
Echoes of our past by William & Joy Wangemann: Made in Sheboygan
White's Wine by David White: Life is richer with wine: The 'magical' connections we make
Meet a world-class chef in person: Kohler's Food & Wine Experience
Like Father, Like Daughter by Mark Walters: Father & Daughter Mississippi duck hunt

Dick Tracy:
Morality in black & white

Chester Gould was 31 years old in 1931, when he convinced editors at The Chicago Tribune to distribute the newspaper strip that would make history. That strip was *Dick Tracy.*

The Tracy strip has come under attack throughout its history for its violence. No one familiar with the strip would deny it has violent events. Not always, of course; there are tender, even humorous moments among its good characters, of which the strip has many.

This is not exactly the same article I wrote years earlier, with the same title.

But I will attempt to make the case here that the Tracy strip, despite its violence, promotes a *morally healthy* approach to life. This is in contrast to the complete lack of morals found in many violent forms of entertainment available today. I contend that the values found in Tracy, if taken seriously, would lead to a complete rejection of the criminal life, violent or otherwise.

You see, "violence" is not the issue. Violence is only one form of initiating force against another person(s). The important distinction here is initiatory force (starting it) and retaliatory force (reacting to the initiated force to stop or contain it).

Here is how initiating force is presented in the Tracy Strip. It forms a kind of progression:

• It comes in many forms. Some do not involve violence at all; a stealthy theft, for example, with no physical attack or harm done. Whatever the form, it is presented as evil in the Tracy strip.

• Evil is a matter of choice. (A person has free will; this theme runs throughout the history of the strip.) Therefore, evil is not done by accident or innocent ignorance. (Hold that last thought.)

• Evil comes in degrees. For lesser evils, a character can make amends, show he has changed, and reform. That must be done by *choice*. For the severest of evils, deliberately taking an innocent life, no amends are possible; you can't bring the victims back.

• What are the ultimate results of choosing evil? One or more of the following: unhappiness; a fear-ridden, neurotic life; no self-esteem; loss of one's values; the death of others; injury and death for oneself.

• Choosing "just a little evil" does not bring "just a little" destruction. Getting involved in evil to any degree puts the person choosing to do so at risk for total destruction. "Just a little evil" leads to further and deeper involvement with evil, engulfing the person entirely.

• Conclusion for the Tracy reader: There are degrees of evil, and a person can back up and start fresh if he chooses to do so, and it's not too late. But the choice to commit evil by initiating force, even "just a little," is a clear-cut, black-and-white, either-or choice. The choice to retain one's integrity, or to commit evil against another person, is a choice every person faces, every day.

To support this, Chester Gould used a variety of characters:

• There is the villain thoroughly committed to evil, to the point of complete destruction. The strip is famous for its grotesque crooks. Some of them made readers downright sick. The villains that weren't outright hideous looked like dopes. Even some of their names are telling: Pruneface. Shakey. Wormy. Itchy. Zero Nought. Flyface.

No rational reader would look at one of these villains as a role model.

I believe Gould intended his hard-core villains to be visual metaphors for their evil. But that doesn't mean he considered anyone who was less than physically perfect to be evil. Far from it. The Tracy strip is populated with completely virtuous people like Frizzletop, who had lost an arm early in World War II, and Steve the Tramp, who lost a leg and an eye. Both these characters were physically incomplete, but morally intact. (More on Steve in a moment.)

• There is the person who's never been involved with crime before, who meets one of these villains, and thinks he can somehow benefit from the evil, without becoming or considering himself evil. Events in the Tracy strip show repeatedly, tragically, emphatically, that this is a false belief.

"I'm not a crook. I just sell these car stereo systems that this guy supplies me with. I don't ask questions about where they come from." Or, "Hey, this crook needs help. I'll hide him or help him, and get some money from him. I'm not a crook myself." Sometimes, a character like that learns better in the Tracy strip, before it's too late. Sometimes, it *becomes... too late.*

• The person with a *lack of purpose.* This leads to self-destruction, whether turning to crime out of boredom, or getting involved in drugs. Characters like this are typically young, because few are able to survive this attitude into adulthood. (Each person must *choose* his purpose(s), and then set goals accordingly.) In contrast, there are many positive characters who do choose purposeful action. An example is Junior Tracy and his friends, who start the "Crime Stoppers" club. They succeeded in stopping several characters' petty evils, reversing the course they were on, and helping them lead happy, purposeful lives.

Nellie, one of the best examples in the history of the Tracy strip, of a character getting involved with evil through innocent ignorance. (The villain shown in panel 2 is 88 Keyes.) Right: Nellie makes a choice. (I usually loathe spoilers, but I will assure you: Nellie is *wrong;* she's about to find out that the death of everyone in the car is *not* the "only way out.") Panels taken from *The Complete Dick Tracy,* Volume 8, published by IDW Publishing.

A few years later, I purchased a 1943 original daily strip from this, one of my favorite Tracy sequences. Watch for the article, "The Crook in the Corn Sheller."

• The person who has never chosen evil, but is tied to someone who has. Time and again, we see the tragedy, loss, and suffering of such people.

• The person who gets involved with evil through innocent ignorance. Again, sometimes they are able to separate themselves from the situation, when they realize what's happening; other times, not. (See the panels here with Nellie.)

• The person who once chose evil, but who chooses to reform. Steve the Tramp is the greatest, most inspiring example I can think of, in Tracy's history, of a bad character who turned good. When first introduced in 1932, Steve was a child-abusing criminal. After spending years in jail, on his release in the late 1930s, his reform was complete. Readers saw the difficulties (the suspicion and mistrust) faced by an ex-con who truly wants to go straight.

Does the above sound like the kind of material that you would enjoy? Is it something you'd give to a young son or daughter, or other young relative? (You might have to read it for yourself, to determine that.)

If your goal is to encourage reading in young people, I can assure you that the Tracy strip is exciting. Gould never seemed to repeat himself, when it came to specific events. But the theme in Dick Tracy, as I've described above, remained constant, up to his retirement from the strip in 1977 (at age 77!).

And if the kids find it as exciting? You might decide, as I have, that despite all the violence the strip is notorious for, Dick Tracy sets a good example for his readers.

Fortunately, we have the sixteen volumes of *The Complete Dick Tracy* available to us, with more coming. Together, they reprint the Tracy strips from 1931 to 1956. Twenty-five years' worth! But I warn you: Reading these books can become terribly habit-forming. You might decide to read one of these books for a few minutes before bed, but you could end up reading far longer than that.

What do you think? We'd love to hear from you. Pro *or* con! When corresponding, please let us know if it's OK to print your name and town.

Which volume to start with?

If I've convinced you to try reading Dick Tracy for the first time, you might ask: Where should I start? Should I begin with the first strips, in 1931? Or what?

I recommend that you start out running. The early strips are all right. I believe that, once you're hooked on Tracy, you'll want to read them all, eventually.

But the dark days of World War II produced some of the most intense villains and story lines.

I've printed panels from Volume 8 of *The Complete Dick Tracy*, and if I had to recommend one volume to start with, that would be it. It features Pruneface on the cover, and also features 88 Keyes (and Nellie), and (ugh!) Mrs. Pruneface. Highly recommended.

Tracy, newspaper strips, etc.

I tried to focus on one aspect of the Tracy strip here. Entire books can be written about the strip and its history. One thing Gould did was to incorporate technology into the strip. He gave Tracy the 2-way wrist radio. Some people think Gould went a little too far with science and technology when, in the 1960s, Gould gave Tracy the magnetic air cars, and took Tracy too the moon.

That's right! Tracy and his crew made it before Neil Armstrong did. And did you know they found a civilization of beings on the moon?

Did you know Junior Tracy married a woman from the moon? Believe it or don't, she was called the "Moon Maid," and had insect-like antennae sprouting from her forehead.

There was a time when comic strips were so good, they actually helped sell the papers they ran in. I'm living proof of that. I discovered Dick Tracy through various books that collected the strips, and liked them so much that I started reading *The Chicago Tribune* on a regular basis. I even subscribed to it! I remember enjoying columns by Mike Royko, Andrew Greeley, Gene Siskel (all now gone), and Charles Krauthammer (I'm glad he's still around). I even had a few letters to the editor printed.

After Gould retired from the strip in 1977, I met the writer who was assigned to the strip: Max Allan Collins. He authored many mysteries and crime thrillers, and a series of graphic novels, *The Road to Perdition,* which was made into a movie with Paul Newman.

Some historians of newspaper comics believe the newspaper strip has declined in quality over the decades. There has certainly been a decrease in the number of daily continuity strips. I don't understand that, because there are many TV series that are continual, week to week, and offer story lines that are sophisticated and complex.

Cartoonists (including Chester Gould) had for many years complained that the comic strip has shrunk in size on the newspaper page; they continued to shrink.

The Complete Dick Tracy is being published by IDW Publishing. Their web site: idwpublishing.com.

Bryan Voltaggio, giving a demonstration for the Kohler Food and Wine Experience in 2010. At top is a mirror, which shows the chef's work area. Attendees are also able to see the chef's activities on two large projection screens for demonstrations taking place on the Main Stage. Voltaggio was a contestant on Season 6 of Top Chef.

Your Editor has always thought the Flatiron Building looked pretty cool, ever since he saw photos of it as a kid. He had the opportunity to travel to Manhattan this past August, and took the above photos. It was designed by architect Daniel Burnham of Chicago, to fit an oddly-shaped lot at the intersection of Fifth Avenue and Broadway.

Meet author Michael Perry

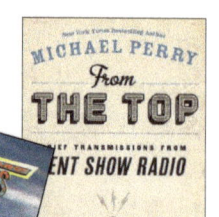

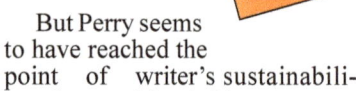

Michael Perry was born in 1964 and grew up on a farm in northern Wisconsin. He went to school, intending to become a nurse. But somewhere along the way, he was able to make a living by writing.

Being able to support oneself through writing is not as common as you might think. Your Editor, working with and meeting writers for many years (some through the Wisconsin Writers Association), knows that even published authors usually have to rely on a day job, or a spouse that has steady work.

But Perry seems to have reached the point of writer's sustainability, where writing is his career.

The books by Perry that most caught the attention of Wisconsinites first, were those he wrote about his childhood on the farm in the past, and his current life as a gentleman farmer (my term, not his).

Many Current readers will identify with what Perry writes about. I recently listened to the audiobook of Coop. A Year of Poultry, Pigs, and Parenting (2009), wherein he described the hay harvest process.

But wait. Why read about something you're already all too familiar with?

Let me ask you another question, and I'll try to connect the two.

There are lots of good paintings of flowers. But if you can look at a real bouquet of flowers, or a nice photo of flowers, why would anyone waste all those hours creating a painting of flowers? Further, why would anyone look at that painting?

As I understand it, an artist helps you to learn to see a flower, with a painting of a flower. The artist, if skillful enough, is selective in what he/she paints. The painting of the flower is stylized, with the most essential elements included, and the irrelevant parts thrown out.

I believe the same can be said about writing. Good writing.

When I listened to Coop, and heard the sequence about making hay, it was a process I was well familiar with. Yet Perry, with his craftsmanship of the English language, was able to describe haying in a stylized way, which helped me contemplate the process with a fresh perspective.

One of Perry's books is Population 485: Meeting Your Neighbors One Siren at a Time, released in 2002. The title refers to Perry's decision to join the local fire department and ambulance crew when he moved back to his home town.

It's hard not to relate to that book, for people who live within the distribution area of The Current. Even if you've never served on a volunteer fire department, you are likely to have participated at one time or another in fire department picnics, appreciation dinners, fund-raising events and other activities.

There is a lot of laughter in Perry's work.

But his books also have their share of sadness. Along with the achievement and enjoyment of values in life, comes the loss of values. Perry addresses that.

Some other books by Perry:

Off Main Street: Brainstormers, Prophets, and Gatemouth's Gator (2005), a collection of essays.

Truck: A Love Story (2006). Woven through the multi-colored strands of rural life anecdotes, Perry recounts his project of restoring an International Harvester pickup truck that had been sitting in his yard for years.

Visiting Tom: A Man, a Highway, and the Road to Roughneck Grace (2012). Wit and wisdom resulting from Perry's visits with a man in his 80s.

From the Top: Brief Transmissions from Tent Show Radio (2013). I am not familiar with Tent Show Radio, but I hope to be, soon.

Perry's newest book, released this past September 2, takes him in a different direction as a writer. It's called The Scavengers, and is intended for a teen readership. However, Perry assured an audience at the Barnes & Noble store in Grand Chute (near Appleton), that he also wanted it to appeal to adults.

(The photos accompanying this article were taken at that appearance on September 15.)

Perry made the point that, as a father of two girls, he's seen a lot of movies and read a lot of books for kids. In the best of them, he told the audience, there is always another level that allows the adults to enjoy them, as well.

In this regard, Perry told the audience of a unique review of The Scavengers, which was done by a mother and daughter team. He described the following, which is taken from his web site, and links to the actual review:

"Wow. This review of The Scavengers is like none other I've ever received. Favorite part? Where the young person rolls her eyes and says, 'I think it's easier for kids.' I almost cut the passages she's referring to because I worried they'd be too tough. But at the last minute I decided young readers are inquisitive and tenacious and would hang in there. Thanks for proving me right, Stella. And thanks to parents everywhere who read with their children–mine did, and it changed my life."

Perry's web site is sneezingcow.com (a reference to something you don't want to be standing behind; we old farm kids need no further explanation, ain't it?). Under "Events," you'll find where Perry will make appearances. (If you didn't yet read my remarks on the etiquette of meeting authors, in the September issue of The Current, you might find that helpful.)

Your Editor assures you, from personal experience (hearing him twice): Perry is a very entertaining speaker and very considerate.

But then, why not check out his web site, see where he's scheduled to appear, and discover that for yourself?

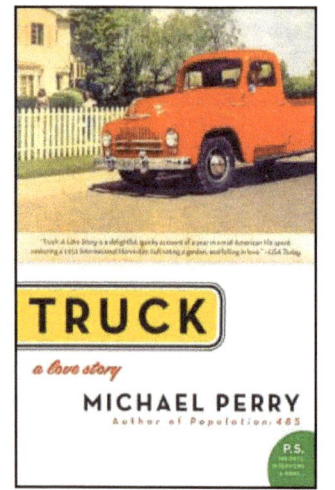

The Current

TAKING YOU PLACES WORTH SEEING
Volume 3 • Issue 12 • November 2014

New contest: Design a solar sail!

Silent movie reviews for November

An Iron Chef comes to Wisconsin Pg 10

November
2014

Cover photo: Geoffrey Zakarian at the Kohler Food & Wine Experience
Editorial: "Intellectual" is not a dirty word
Silent movies in November
Natural Connections by Emily Stone: Blue jays: beautiful and intelligent marauders
Echoes of our past by William & Joy Wangemann: 'Number, please?'
Meet one of Wisconsin's most prolific authors! [Jerry Apps]
My 4-decade mission: Find that POW! by Morreen O'Reilly-Mersberger
I Ate At... by Richard J. Baumann: Homefront Restaurant & Bar, Random Lake
White's Wine by David White: Beaujolais: The Greatest Secret in Wine
Bring a world-class chef into your kitchen: Geoffrey Zakarian
The Science in Science Fiction: Sailing on the Sunlight
Like Father, Like Daughter by Mark Walters: Food plots, bow hunts
The Feast of Talent
Rick Siegler's pride and joy: a wine-glass stern boat, by Barry Johanson

Chef Staphanie Izard, winner of season 4 of Bravo's Top Chef, seems to have as much fun as the people she signed her book for at the Kohler Food & Wine Experience.

December
2014

Cover photo: Dale Van Minsel and his photography
Editorial: Our contest: Design a solar sail! **(We received no entries)**
Great movies in December **(The first TCM Highlights column)**
Natural Connections by Emily Stone: Passenger Pigeons and Lyme
Echoes of our past by William & Joy Wangemann: History Unread
Something for the engineers!
Stevie Nicks and Mabel Normand
White's Wine by David White: A Napa Valley tech entrepreneur is revolutionizing customer service
I Ate At... by Richard J. Baumann: Urbane, Sheboygan
Jams, Jellies & More
The photographic art of Dale Van Minsel
The Science in Science Fiction: Dragon's Egg
Like Father, Like Daughter by Mark Walters: Deer camp with Selina
Making Spirits Bright
r04040: My monkey died as he lived, by Bill Lueders
He cooks at home!
From pulp to film: Lady in the Lake
Follow-Up: Michael Perry

Something for the engineers!

In the last issue of The Current, I wrote about Dr. K. Eric Drexler, and quoted a couple of paragraphs from his book, *Radical Abundance: How a Revolution in Nanotechnology Will Change Civilization*.

I wrote about Drexler in the context of solar sails, but that's not the main subject of *Radical Abundance*. The book's subject is nanotechnology.

The prefix "nano" literally means "one billionth," but the term "nanotechnology" basically means technology at a very small level—in fact, at the level of manipulating atoms and molecules.

While the skeptic will respond, "Yeah, right!" to the very idea, Drexler not only makes the case for the feasability of such technology, but demonstrates the several ways in which it is already becoming a reality.

I am only half-way through this book, and found one aspect of it of great interest. I've always been interested in Science. One of my past careers was a seven-year stint as a Science teacher in North Dakota; six of those on a small American Indian reservation near the Canadian border (hello, all you former students from the Turtle Mountains); and one year near Minot (greetings, those of you from Surrey). I educated myself in the space sciences as I taught the same in my 7th and 8th grade classes. After raising funds, I took some students to an L5 Society Conference on Space Development, where they met Dr. Drexler (see, this rambling paragraph is not off-topic) and others (but yes, I should write about that separately).

I've also long been interested in philosophy. One aspect of philosophy is epistemology, which addresses the nature and validity of knowledge.

So science and epistemology came together in the first part of *Radical Abundance,* when Drexler analyzes the difference between scientific research, and engineering.

That difference is, simply (and this is in my own wording, based on my understanding of epistemology): scientific research is inductive, while engineering is deductive.

The thought processes go in two different directions (though not exclusively). Induction is a process of looking at particular things, and then coming to a generalization. You study all the specific facts, and come up with a basic law. Galileo wasn't just sitting around, doing nothing, when he had an insight and shouted, "I just figured something out!" He performed many, many (way more than many) experiments, took measurements, and came up with several mathematical formulae that would describe how something would fall the same way, given the same circumstances.

Deduction is taking a general law, and applying it to a specific circumstance. For example, once the inductive process resulted in a particular formula, people could use that formula to accurately shoot a cannonball. Plug the numbers (distance, angle of the cannon, how much force, weight of the ball), and take care of any other factors, and you'll hit the target.

Drexler does not use the terms "induction" and "deduction," but the concepts are there. He discusses several differences in methodology between the two, and points out that projects like sending manned craft to the moon were accomplished by engineers, not scientists.

Certainly, the engineers relied on what the scientists, for decades, even centuries before, had discovered, and built up as a foundation.

But the differences between science and engineering, and how their methods are different—yet complementary—makes for fascinating reading.

The whole science / engineering topic, however, is introductory. The real substance of this book is the nanotechnology. To get a feel for how radically (or fundamentally, or basically) the author claims civilization would be changed if this technology came about, he suggests that a factory the size of your garage could house all the assembly equipment needed to manufacture a car.

This factory would need to be fed raw materials—metals. And they wouldn't have to be new metals, either. Scrap would do. The nano-machines would be able to remove the rust and other impurities.

We've heard, for decades, about the crisis of shortages, of one kind or another. Energy shortages. Resource shortages. Well, if this book's author is on the right track, we can forget about shortages of resources. We'll have exactly the opposite "problem"—too much of any given good will be available to us.

This is a truly fascinating book. If you know a young person going into the sciences or engineering (and that covers a lot of territory), this book makes a great gift.

Who knows, I might have even more to report to readers of The Current, as I finish the 2nd half of the book.

Wisconsin author Michael Perry reads all about himself in the October issue of The Current.

2015

January
2015

Cover photo: Kids at a Head Start Class
Editorial: Education and Freedom
Great movies in January
Echoes of our past by William & Joy Wangemann: Prohibition arrives
Natural Connections by Emily Stone: Where are the loons?
White's Wine by David White: With Priest Ranch, Craig Becker Is Betting on Honesty
I Ate At… by Richard J. Baumann: Butternut Café, Greenbush
Spaceport Sheboygan
For 50 years, kids have been getting a Head Start
Like Father, Like Daughter by Mark Walters: Mississippi River duck hunt
Modern silent movies
Buster Keaton meets Dick Tracy?
Bring a world-class chef into your kitchen: Hubert Keller
The Job Seekers Network Group
Big Eyes: The Movie…. The Artist…. The Gallery….

After seeing the Tim Burton movie, Big Eyes, I enthusiastically contacted the California gallery that handled Margaret Keane's work. I received permission to run one of her paintings (the person from the gallery even emailed me an image). Contacting people like this for inclusion of material in The Current was making me feel like a big wheel.

Glass works from Jon Wos

As well as being a fine painter, Jon Wos also works with glass.

Spaceport Sheboygan

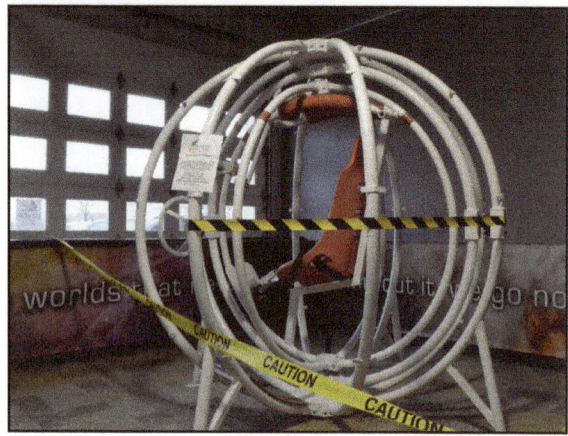

The spaceport has since closed its physical facility, but personnel continue to provide educational activities.

February 2015

Cover photo: Sundogs. Photo by Fred Niffenegger.
Great movies coming up
Natural Connections by Emily Stone: Lamar Buffalo Ranch: "We got the tablets here."
White's Wine by David White: 3 Wine Trends to Watch for in 2015
I Ate At... by Richard J. Baumann: Lake Church Pub & Grill, Belgium
Everett Raymond Kinstler: "Doomed to be an artist"
The roots of Little Orphan Annie
Church bells ring again in Falls, by Jeff Pederson
A bell from Germany
"You are Warbucks!"
Like Father, Like Daughter by Mark Walters: A place called Buckskin

The original painting of this portrait of Herbert Kohler, by Everett Raymond Kinstler, can be viewed in the lower level of the Kohler Design Center.

In 1941, Kinstler did the sketch at right of his friend, Jim Bama. At the time, both boys were 15 years old. Both would become successful commercial illustrators; both would move into a career in the fine arts. The sketch appears in the incredible book, shown at left: Everett Raymond Kinstler, The Artist's Journey through Popular Culture—1942-1962.

A bell from Germany

On March 14, 1812, Johann Gotthelf Risse was born in Germany.

Risse came to America and settled in Wisconsin. He was one of the founding members of the St. Paul's Evangelical and Reformed Congregation (later, St. Paul's United Church of Christ) of Silver Creek, which first assembled in 1868. In 1872, a brick church was dedicated.

In 1873, Risse returned to Germany. He undoubtedly visited his family mansion, which is pictured in the St. Paul's Diamond Jubilee booklet, published in 1943. But his main purpose was to procure a top-quality bell for the new church building back in his new home.

Risse purchased the bell at his own expense for the church, at a cost of $500. To put that sum into perspective, roughly that same amount could have constructed two of the stone homes that were then built in Silver Creek.

The bell was manufactured by the Bochumer Verein Gusstahlfabrik. Engraved on it is, "Gott Mit Uns! [God be with us!] J. Gotthelf Risse 1873." It's estimated that another $500 (or more) was required to ship the bell from Germany to America.

After bringing a lightning-caused fire under control, firefighters worked to save the historic bell of St. Paul's United Church of Christ. — Photo by Nancy Schroeter

The bell that Gotthelf Risse traveled to Germany to have manufactured. It now rests on a platform next to Risse's grave (the tree trunk with the scroll, at right) in the Silver Creek cemetery. The keys once adorned the steeple, serving as a lightning rod, on St. Paul's UCC, Silver Creek.

The Diamond Jubilee booklet states, "The distinctly clear, musical, ringing tones which emanate from this bell and which carry for miles around have been marveled at by many musicians who have a keenly trained ear for resonance, sound, and pitch." That is the sound Silver Creek residents heard for over a century.

On May 20, 2004, lightning struck the church and started a roof fire. Local fire departments responded immediately, but it was soon obvious that the church would be a total loss.

As the fire was contained to the doomed building, some firefighters, having grown up in Silver Creek, were well aware of the historical significance of the church bell, and considered possible means of salvaging it. Some thought there was little hope for a rescue, but a group of firefighters quickly devised a plan, and with the right equipment, the bell was removed intact.

The bell now rests on a platform at the Silver Creek cemetery, next to the sculpted tree-trunk gravestone of Gotthelf Risse (1812-1901), the man who brought the bell from Germany and gave it to his church in his chosen home of Silver Creek.

"You are Warbucks!"
My favorite Little Orphan Annie sequence of all time

I've read many sequences from *Little Orphan Annie*, reprinted in books and magazines. The one that stands out in my mind as a shining representative of what the strip is all about is from 1931. It's reprinted in IDW Publishing's Volume Three of *Little Orphan Annie*. They've called that volume "And a Blind Man Shall Lead Them," but in my mind, I've always called it, *"You are Warbucks!"*

The following panels are from the above-mentioned Volume Three, and are presented here for review purposes. There are panels, sometimes several pages, being left out to summarize this sequence.

Oliver "Daddy" Warbucks has lost his fortune. He and Annie are living in a modest place, each working to earn enough money to get by; each spiritually unconquered by misfortune.

Warbucks gets a job driving a truck. A kid runs into the street in front of him.

Warbucks is blinded by the accident. He's known by hospital staff only as "Oliver" as he slowly recuperates. Flop-House Bill, seeing how dejected this newly-blinded man is, introduces himself.

His first day out of the hospital, Warbucks wanders the streets, thinking, "Guess I'm lost—I must have missed a turn some place—but what difference does it make where I am—one place is as good as another—but I've got to get some place soon—

"That doctor was a fine chap—he gave me a few dollars to eat on, but that's about gone now—I wonder about that chap, Flop-House Bill—he sounded like a man who could give me some sound advice—"

The next two panels are examples of the sheer benevolence that abounds in the Annie strip. (There are malevolent characters, as well.)

Bill, glad to see the man he took a liking to, leads Warbucks into a room that has three pictures hanging on the wall... pictures of *Oliver Warbucks!*

Harold Gray's artistic style is simplistic enough that you might be fooled into thinking (if you're not familiar with it) that it has the emotional range of stick figures. But look at Warbucks' body language in the next four panels (I'm sure you can come up with your own descriptions for these).
  Panel 1: desperation.
  Panel 2: shock.
  Panel 3: reflection.
  Panel 4: speculation.

Warbucks considers what Bill has told him, and makes some choices.
The chair represents a petty obstacle that reminds him of his blindness.
What to do with such obstacles? Why, exactly what he *does*.

Bill now knows who his guest is. *But what has changed?* Warbucks still has the same beard, dark glasses, and clothing he had moments before. Is it the way Warbucks *stands,* that makes Bill realize, *"You are Warbucks!"*?

Flop-House Bill has found Oliver Warbucks. And Oliver Warbucks has found... *himself.*

The sequence represented by the previous panels took several *weeks* to tell through the daily Annie newspaper strips. As you can probably guess from the last panel shown above, what I've shown you here is only the *beginning* of an even larger-scale story of Oliver Warbucks building himself back up to his former stature.

While he was blind, he didn't want to be a burden to Annie; thus, Annie does not know, during this time, what has happened to him. Rest assured, they are reunited.

JOHN: I've been cheated!
MARSHA: How's that, John?
JOHN: Well, when I saw that sign over there, I got so excited, that I picked up the first big stick I could find, and started threshing around every tree and bush in this whole rest area, and would you believe it? I couldn't find a single rattlesnake!
— Photo taken somewhere in Montana

March 2015

Cover photo: Grand Opening, Random Lake Area Historical Society Museum
Great movies coming up
Newspaper continuity strips: A sad decline
Natural Connections by Emily Stone: The Tribes wake trilling
White's Wine by David White: Delectable: A Wine App That Could Revolutionize Drinking
I Ate At... by Richard J. Baumann: Racer's Hall, Plymouth
Coffee, breakfast, history, or all three?
How a real capitalist thinks and operates
Our Wisconsin: A magazine for Wisconsin readers & writers
Like Father, Like Daughter by Mark Walters: Arctic deer hunt
Ambigrams

A few things you should know about the Moon

Suppose you're ready to call it a day. You look forward to a good night's sleep.

To help you relax into a state of calmness, you pick up the book you're reading. Ah, yes, reading something soothing focuses the mind. It helps reduce the amplitude of those alpha waves, so they don't bounce around the occipital lobes so frantically, as they do during daytime and wakefulness. You know that, after a few pages, you'll be drifting off into peaceful slumber.

You begin where you left off:

> Rock Tumblr stood stock still. He had stealthily progressed through the dark, dank, dingy, damp, dusty, drippy dungeon. He had avoided all the heinous death-traps, passing the stomach-wrenching remains of several poor unfortunates who had not been so cautious, or lucky, or both.
> He realized that he now stood on a trap-door!
> Before Tumblr could leap to the side, and most likely onto another trap, the trap-door fell open.
> Down plunged Rock Tumblr!
> Suddenly, he was engulfed in icy water that was blacker than midnight!
> Black as was the water, something even more ominously inky approached him. Its bulk grew. Two glowing, baleful eyes opened!
> It was a gigantic octopus!
> Rock Tumblr whipped out his knife from its scabbard. But almost instantly, every part of his body was covered and held immobilized by the octopus' ten tentacles—

You leap from your bed, throw the book on the floor and stomp on it, cursing the author for the uneducated fool that he is. (Or was, as the case may be.)

An octopus with ten legs! An unforgivable insult to your intelligence! How ***dare*** he! (Or she.) (As the case may be.)

Well, I know just how you feel, when that happens. But it's happened to me so often, that I can restrain myself from stomping on the book. (That, and the fact that the book might be worth some money.)

The two panels heading this article are from the 1955 comic book, *Love Secrets*.

Why in the world would Your Editor be reading a romance comic from the 1950s? Well... I'll explain another time. The present article is intended to address a few scientific principles, a few things you should know about the moon, whether you're drawing it, writing about it, or just see something like the above panels.

A crescent moon

The above two panels are intended to show a night scene.

As I'm about to explain, that's obviously impossible.

Or maybe it's not so obvious. Maybe the artist lived all his life in New York City, and never saw the moon close to the horizon.

An artist needs to get into the habit of carefully *observing* things. Everything. In the case of this moon, we can chastise the artist as Sherlock Holmes chastised Watson: "You see, but you do not observe."

As we observe the Sun and Moon from Earth, there are a few principles we have learned. And we could have observed the following even if we lived thousands of years ago, and didn't know the Earth was round, without knowing exactly what the Moon is, and so forth. Here's what we would actually *see:*

— When the Moon is in a crescent phase, its outward curve points at where the Sun would be.

— The slimmer the crescent Moon is, the closer it is to the Sun.

— (Implied by the previous observation) If the moon is a very thin crescent, it will be low on the horizon (never high in the sky), and it will be either shortly after the Sun has set, or before the Sun has risen.

— When the Moon and Sun are in the sky at the same time, and they are very close to each other, the brilliance of the Sun makes it (usually) impossible to see the Moon.

Put all of these observations together, and we conclude about the situation in these two panels:

— The sun is in the direction that the arrow points, shown in the panel here.

— The sun is high in the sky. It is not night-time at all.

— The moon would likely not be visible, because of the brilliance of the sun.

Conclusion: These two panels are an impossibility. Q.E.D.

The full moon

People over the ages have also observed a few facts about the full moon.

The page shown here is from a 1955 comic called *Lovers.* There's nothing particularly wrong with it, other than the Moon's size. The moon, full or otherwise, would never appear as large as it does here, but let's ignore that.

What time of night would this be? It would either have to be shortly after sunset, or shortly before sunrise.

Why? The careful observer would know that:

— The more full the Moon is, the farther away it is from the Sun.

— A full Moon rises just as the Sun sets, is visible throughout a clear night, and is highest in the sky around midnight.

Conclusion: If any of the following happen as you're watching a movie or reading a story:

— A full Moon appears on the horizon in the middle of the night...

— A full Moon appears on the horizon at one point of the story (time of night not specified), and a few hours later, the Moon is still hovering just over the horizon...

...As with a crescent moon with its horns pointing downward, you now have the full knowledge to shout out, "Bogus!"

Nearly everything in this book has been laid out differently from its original publication.

Not so, with the next page. It is presented slightly smaller, but otherwise as it was first published.

My approach to composing the page was to make the visuals as symmetrical as possible; and then put in blocks of text in different orientations. My intent was that the text blocks could be read in any order, each saying something about the page's subject.

I printed the page for Display Ads to approve. They eyed it very dubiously, and insisted it be shown to the newspaper's owners for approval.

The owners looked it over (also seemingly with some misgivings), but ultimately gave it their OK. I recall one owner remarking something like, "Leave it to Rodney to come up with something like that."

By David Langdon.
— From his website

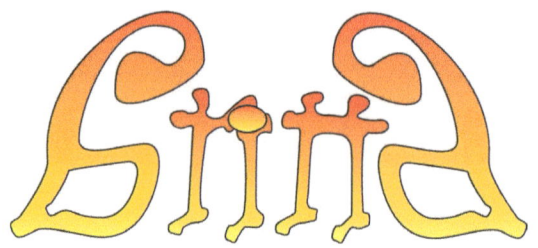

Your Editor's attempt at an ambigram. What does it say?
The names of my twin nieces: Anna and Britta

Arts

The Current March 2015. Page 8

by Rodney Schroeter for the Current
Wordplay by John Langdon.

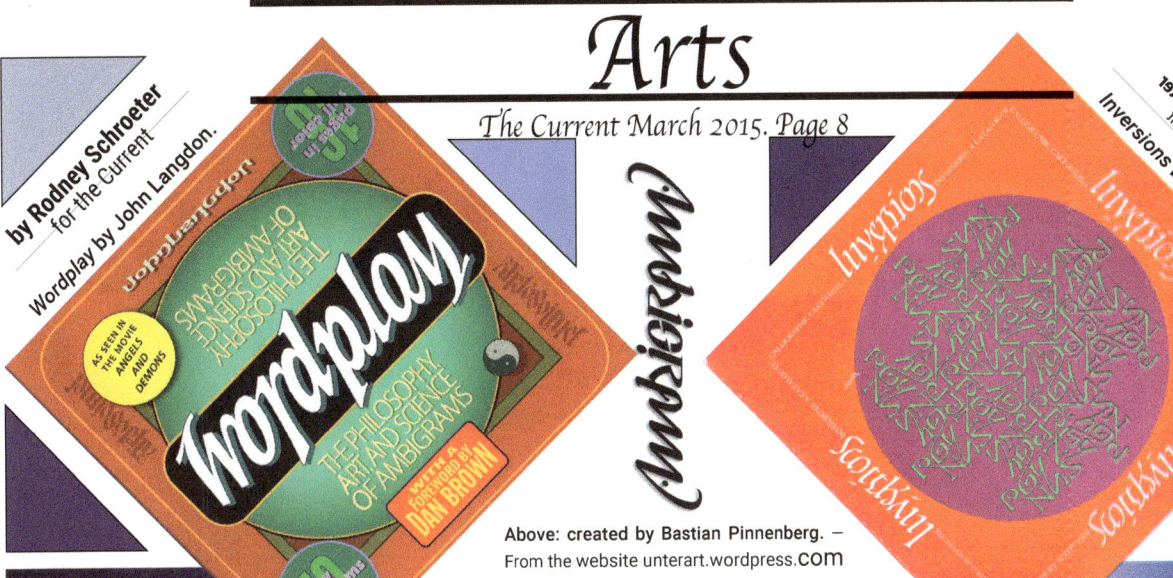

Above: created by Bastian Pinnenberg. — From the website unterart.wordpress.com

Inversions by Scott Kim. by Rodney Schroeter for the Current

By David Langdon. — From his website

I first heard of ambigrams (though they were not called such) in a 1979 issue of *Omni* magazine. *Omni* was thick, slick, and devoted to science fact and science fiction.

On the Games page in *Omni*, readers were introduced to "designatures," imaginative and symmetrical uses of typography (the form of letters) by Scott Kim.

The editor of *Omni's* Games page, Scot Morris, challenged readers to come up with their own designatures. And readers rose to the challenge.

One person who saw the 1979 issue of *Omni* was John Langdon, who describes his surprise in his book, *Wordplay*.

Langdon was surprised because he and Bob Petrick had been doing the same types of designatures (or ambigrams, or upside-down-words) for some years. Until *Omni's* article, they'd been unaware that anyone else had been doing something similar.

Besides a wealth of creative typography, including sixteen pages of color, *Wordplay* contains some very interesting insights from author John Langdon. It gives a fascinating account of how he started doing creative typography.

Wordplay is in print, in a second, revised edition.

Langdon describes in *Wordplay* how he met Dan Brown, author of *The Da Vinci Code*. Brown asked if Langdon could create an ambigram of the title of another of Brown's books, *Angels and Demons*.

Langdon writes that it was a difficult task. But one reason he kept trying was Langdon's interest in M. C. Escher, who'd done a work called "Circle Limit IV," which is a tesselation (a design of interlocking shapes) of angels and devils.

Langdon successfully created the logo, which was used on the cover of the first edition of *Angels and Demons*.

Above: creator not specified. — From multiple websites

From *Wordplay*, by John Langdon:
"Some words almost beg to be ambigrams (but not enough!). Some words may look daunting, but then yield to my coercion with little resistence. Some prove to be impossible, either for years, or perhaps even forever."

Moral: If you try your hand at creating an ambigram, and it doesn't work out at first, you're not alone.

Created by "Splarka." — From Wikipedia

Created by Punya Mishra. — From the website planetperplex.com

By Scott Kim. — From his website

The grand-prize winner of the *Omni* competition was Chuck Krausie, whose designature spelled "LIFE" in one orientation, and "DEATH" when it was turned 180 degrees.

A couple of years ago, I was asked to do a promotional flyer for the Wisconsin Writers Association. I thought the words "life" and "death" would figure nicely into what the flyer wanted to say. So I found Chuck Krausie's phone number, called him, and asked for permission to use his creation.

He told me, to the best of my recall, that the design was in use all over, and that I should feel free to use it.

As they say on *Storage Wars*, "This is the *Wow!* factor."

Jef Raskin (hey, a book that you keep turning upside-down ought to have a backword, right?). I've read elsewhere that Hofstadter is credited with coining the term "ambigram." Kim does not use the term; "ambigram," he calls them—the title of the book—inversions.

Scott Kim's book, *Inversions*, was first published in the early 1980s. It's not in print, but can be easily found

Kim's book has an article on different kinds of symanalytical. It's very very interesting. The applications of the principles Kim discusses go far beyond creative typography, having implications for other areas of life. There are lots of helpful diagrams. Kim also writes about the process of creating ambigrams. I'll have to read that in careful detail.

Kim writes, "I hope that these examples will encourage you to go exploring on your own."

Now, that's the statement of a true educator. So it's no surprise that his book has exercises for teachers. But if you can't find the book, you need only check his web site. In the Ambigrams section, you'll find a link to Classroom Activities for Teachers.

Kim's website also has several thought-provoking essays on education.

When I contacted Kim to ask permission to use his work, he wrote me: "To get your readers involved, I suggest you invite readers to make their own ambigrams, on a theme of interest in your local area, and print the interesting entries in your paper."

What do you think, Dear Reader, of *that* idea?

By David Langdon. — From his website

From Barnes & Noble

By Scott Kim. — From his book, *Inversions*

The web page of John Langdon: www.johnlangdon.net

This madness continues on page 13

The web page of Scott Kim: www.scottkim.com

Long, long ago, I tried creating an ambigram of my name.

It was shortly after the appearance of the *Omni* magazine. I was teaching on a small reservation in North Dakota, editing a little newsletter for the Middle School. (Hm... do I hear the term deja vu echoing somewhere?)

That's about all I can tell you. I can't show you, because I... I... can't find it.

It's somewhere around here. Maybe I'll find it someday.

But just recently, I tried an "oscillation" or "paradigm shift" style of ambigram. It's shown here. Or there. Somewhere around here.

What does it say? I wanted it to spell both names of my twin nieces, without rotating it. If you can't read it...it's a dismal failure.

This was the first coherent thing I accomplished in Adobe Illustrator, after reading the first book on that program that made sense to me.

life

Created by Chuck Krausie.

I recall contacting every creator named here, asking permission to run his/her ambigram. I talked with Chuck Krausie on the phone. He assured me it was OK to use this one.

—— By Scott Kim, from his book, Inversions ——

Both *Wordplay* and *Inversions* show sketches the authors/wordsmiths made, as they puzzled through the process of creating ambigrams/inversions.

I always find it interesting to see artist sketches. It's a way to gain insight into the artist's thought processes.

I once had the chance to ask comic artist Will Eisner, "Have you ever done a preliminary sketch and then done the finished work, only to find that there's something you did in the preliminary, that you just can't seem to carry over into the finished work?"

His reply: "All the time."

I asked him this because I'd experienced this situation myself. At the time, I was writing and drawing comics as a hobby.

There are varieties of ambigrams. I believe I have examples of each of these, so rather than struggling with the terms below, trying to visualize them, see if you can find the example(s).

As categorized on John Langdon's web site:
Symmetrical ambigrams:
• Rotational. Turn them 180 degrees, and they say the same thing.
• Bilateral or mirror image. Hold it up to a mirror, and it will look the same as in a book.
• Chains (rotational or bilateral). A word repeated, linked together, forming a circle or spiral.

Asymmetrical ambigrams:
• Symbiotograms. It's one word, but when turned 180 degrees, it's a different word. Perhaps even its opposite.
• Figure/ground relationships. The positive space of the letters form one word; the negative space between the letters form another.
• Oscillations (I've also seen the term "paradigm shift" used). The word is ambiguous, and can be read more than one way. My attempt at an ambigram would fall under this category.

Mathematics

Victoria **Dance** **mozart**

onomatopoeia

As press time nears, I received another yet another ambigram book: *Ambigrams Revealed: A Graphic Designer's Guide to Creating Typographic Art Using Optical Illusions, Symmetry, and Visual Perception*, by Nikita Prokhorov. As the long subtitle indicates, this 2013 book contains sketches and some commented upon contributions like Scott Kim, John Langdon, Morris, and some (with explained "how to" in certain ambigrams.

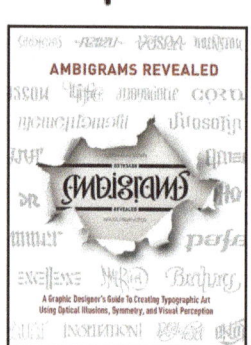

It's not surprising that both John Langdon and Scott Kim have found influence in the work of M. C. Escher.

I would have like to have featured an example or two of Escher's art here. However, I found the web site of M.C. Escher Company B.V., in the Netherlands, which holds the copyrights of Escher's work. His work seems not to be in the public domain, and since press time for this issue rapidly approaches, I didn't think there was time to seek permission to use any of his images. But maybe sometime soon...

In the meantime, please see: mcescher.com

By John Langdon, from his book, Wordplay

April 2015

Cover photo: Bare Trees
Great movies coming up
The quest for Hitchcock's autograph
Natural Connections by Emily Stone: Awakening
White's Wine by David White: Investing our hearts in champagne
Plymouth's Sharon earns prestigious skiing award, by Matt Kraus
I Ate At... by Richard J. Baumann: P.J. Campbell's at the Depot, Plymouth
Like Father, Like Daughter by Mark Walters: Wet weekend for a deer hunt
Giving freedom a chance
Hammer and anvil

Two Giants

One might think the "big picture" of this 150-page graphic narrative is the sum of historical events leading up to the Civil War.

But I don't think so. I believe the "big picture" here is the portrayal of two big men who changed the course of history.

What makes a person "big" in that sense? I believe it's because of "big" ideas. Ideas that are so fundamental, that they made a difference that still affects us today, and will affect the thoughts and lives of people on into the future.

The Hammer and the Anvil, by writer Dwight Jon Zimmerman and artist Wayne Vansant, is the story of two big men in history, operating in two very different worlds, who decided to change the world in at least one sense.

This book uses a clever technique to tell two stories. The biography of each man is told in a different monochromatic color. The parallel stories unfold in shades of blue and brown, until... well, until something *wonderful* happens.

My thanks to Author Zimmerman and artist Vansant, who kindly gave The Current permission to use excerpts from *The Hammer and the Anvil.* Quotes and images accompanying this article, unless otherwise stated, are from that book, and are Copyright © by the author and artist.

Abraham Lincoln

It was Abe Lincoln's mother who taught him to read and enjoy books. She passed away when Abe was 9. But a year later, when Abe's father remarried, Abe received further encouragement to read and learn when his new step-mother brought with her a trunkful of books.

Abe's half-sister would later recall: "Abe was not energetic except in one thing, he was active and persistent in learning—read everything he could."

Lincoln's father held Abe's book-learning in contempt. The father hired out the son to area farmers to work, but kept the money, giving young Abe a taste—but only a taste—of what it was like to be a servant with no choice. It was not, by any means, the equivalent of slavery. But when one of his no-pay jobs took him and a companion on a 2400-mile journey to New Orleans and back, Abe encountered slavery for the first time. He did not like what he saw, as shown on page 29, here, where Lincoln is visible in all 4 panels.

Frederick Bailey / Frederick Douglass

"Of my **father** I know **nothing.** Slavery had no recognition of fathers... That the **mother** was a slave was enough... By its **law** the child followed the condition of its mother."

So Frederick Douglass wrote of his early life, when his last name was Bailey.

Bailey was born about a decade after Lincoln. (The exact date is not known.) His mother, with whom he had little contact, died when he was about 7.

Bailey, born a slave, grew up on a 200-acre plantation whose master was "not a humane slaveholder." Despite this, Bailey's early life was relatively free of brutality. He became friends with the owner's youngest son, and was present during the son's tutelage. Bailey listened to, watched, and benefitted from those lessons, which included the art of speaking properly (diction).

In the mid 1820s, Fred Bailey was shuffled back and forth between owners. "Slaves were property. That meant the Bailey slave family was going to be split among the [plantation owner's] heirs along with the livestock, wagons, and furniture."

He received kind treatment at one home in Baltimore, where he was given the task of supervising and befriending the family's son. When the mother, Sophia Auld, taught him to read, the father, Hugh Auld, became enraged, saying, "If he learns to **read** the Bible, it will forever **unfit** him to be a **slave!** He should know nothing but the will of his **master,** and learn to **obey** it."

"You are wrong to do this, master," Bailey thinks in the privacy of his own mind, as shown on page 26 of the book.

One goal: But how to reach it?

"**Abolitionists, united** in their desire to end slavery, were **divided** in how to accomplish it."

Some of the greatest conflicts, in reality and in fiction, are between two or more people (or movements, or schools of thought, etc.) who agree on the *goal.* But the *means* of getting to that goal...? That's where the conflict arises.

Suppose you're born into a situation that you see must be changed. Can that change be made *right away*—or must it be brought about *in steps?* That conflict runs throughout the rest of *The Hammer and the Anvil,* the second chapter of which opens by setting some historical context as Lincoln and Bailey are young adults.

Fred's owner "decided he would earn some money by **leasing** Fred to a man **skilled at breaking the will** of troublesome slaves. In the **seven-mile walk** to his new master's house, Fred Bailey had much to think about."

The new master beat Fred regularly, but Fred ultimately stood up to him, in an inspiring scene I'll allow the reader to discover.

"One way or another, I'm going to be free!" thinks Fred. In 1838, he took the most danger-fraught option, but the only option he had, to that

Quotes from this book are Copyright © by author Dwight Jon Zimmerman

freedom. He escaped to the North with help from a free black woman who would later become his wife.

Boarding a train that will take him North, wearing a sailor's uniform, Bailey is asked for ID papers he does not have, but he's prepared. He offers a slip of paper with a $20 gold piece. The conductor winks and says, "You're all right, sailor."

Usually, one associates taking a bribe or "looking the other way" with *corruption*. Here, it's done (*possibly;* we don't know what went through the conductor's mind) through *virtue*. (Elsewhere in this issue of The Current is a similar example of how "looking the other way" resulted in escape from oppression.)

Settling in New Bedford, Massachusetts, Frederick changed his last name to Douglass. He was in a free area, but escaped slaves could be captured and returned to their owners; the law did not protect them.

The book makes an interesting point that affirms certain economic views held by Your Editor:

Narration: "In the South, Fred had been taught that slavery was the **foundation** of all **wealth** and social standing. And so the sights of New Bedford came as a great surprise."

Douglass to friend: "I assumed everyone here would be poor. But, Nathan, I find here among **all** classes more **wealth** than I thought possible! Even here, where **laborers** live, houses are more **elegant** and have more **comforts** than many slaveholder houses in **Talbot County**."

Nathan: "And **not just here,** Frederick, but **throughout** the north."

Douglass became involved with abolitionist organizations. Giving lectures about life under slavery, and denouncing it, Douglass sounded a little too educated to be credible. When doubt is expressed about him ever being a slave, Douglas whipped off his shirt and showed the audience the scars on his back. "The audience was **horrified**. This was their first look at the **brutality** of **slavery** in the flesh."

To further convince people, Douglass decided to write his life story. *Narrative of the Life of Frederick Douglass* became a best-seller when published in 1845. (The book is easily available, in many editions, including e-book.) His former "owners" in the South were not amused, and swore they'd capture Douglass. Douglass fled the country, taking a ship to Great Britain.

He traveled to and lectured in England, Ireland, and Scotland. Several friends gathered $700 and sent it to his former "owner" to purchase Douglass' freedom. (I like to imagine that check reaching out and slapping its recipient in the face.)

Douglass returned to America, and started his own newspaper. He became what I would call an "intellectual activist." He realized that ideas matter, that they change history. He counted on reasoned, rational arguments to persuade people of the truth.

And as a person who took ideas seriously, Douglass was himself was open to rational, logical argument. He'd come to believe that America's Constitution allowed for slavery. But Garrit Smith, a member of the National Liberty Party, challenged him: "Frederick, there is not one pro-slavery line, **not one line** that, justly interpreted, contributes to the **upholding** of slavery. In fact, I would say the Constitution promotes the **anti-slavery** cause. The Constitution needs to be administered only **according to its principles**. Doing so will cause a speedy **overthrow** of the whole system of American slavery."

So Douglass, being a man of honesty and integrity, researched the issue for himself. He concluded that he'd held a mistaken viewpoint and so admitted, "By **condemning** the Constitution, I have been arguing on the slaveholders' side."

Several achievements and talents and disappointments of Abe Lincoln that readers might not be familiar with are given. Elected to the Illinois state legislature in 1834, he decided that he should know something about the law. He purchased books and studied on his own. Lincoln is shown putting a lot of effort and work into his learning.

Lincoln was asked to run for President, against Stephen A. Douglas. The debates between the two are legendary. On one page, with words and pictures, this book summarizes the results of the election, where four men were running for President. The reader easily grasps the voting results, sees how Lincoln won the vote, but also how the majority of the country was not behind him.

With Lincoln's election, several states seceded, and one nation became divided into two.

The Hammer and the Anvil uses a very clever technique to tell the parallel but separate stories of Abraham Lincoln and Frederick Douglass: Each is depicted in a monochromatic color—blue for Douglass, brown for Lincoln.

I hate spoilers, but I'll give away one of the surprises in this book.

Lincoln and Douglass met on several occasions. On their first meeting, the world quite literally changes in a way you can see on the pages reproduced here. Two monochromatic worlds turn into full color!

This was not the only meeting between these two intellectual and

Unyielding

Artwork from this book is Copyright © by artist Wayne Vansant moral giants. In a development with an interesting Wisconsin connection, Lincoln asked Douglass to return to the White House:

"Lincoln had written a reply to a letter from Charles Robinson, the editor of a Wisconsin newspaper called The Green Bay *Advocate*. Robinson supported Lincoln but wanted to know how the President would react to the political pressures. Lincoln's response was an attempt to appease both sides. But before he sent it to Robinson, who would surely publish it in his paper, Lincoln wanted Douglass to read it."

And when Douglass did read it, Lincoln asked if he should send it.

"**Certainly not,**" Douglass replied.

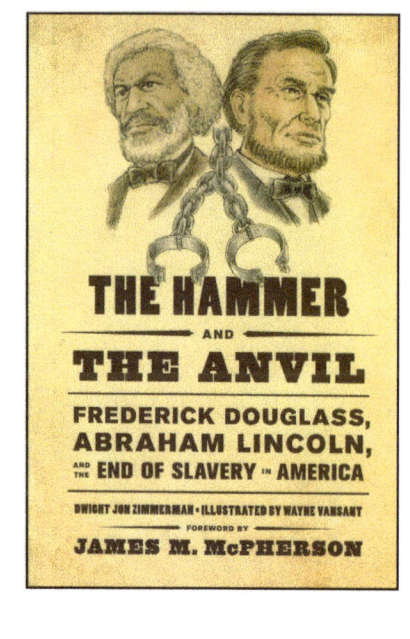

"It would be given a broader meaning than you **intend** to convey," Douglass explained. "It would be taken as a complete **surrender** of your anti-slavery policy."

Lincoln did not send the letter.

Also during this second meeting, Lincoln (facing re-election and fully expecting to be voted out of office) asked Douglass for help with a plan, the exact nature of which I'll let the reader discover. But Douglass' reaction:

"Lincoln's words stunned Douglass. It revealed to Douglass the depth of the president's moral conviction to end slavery."

"Moral conviction." Now that's a good summary of what this book is all about.

More about Wayne Vansant

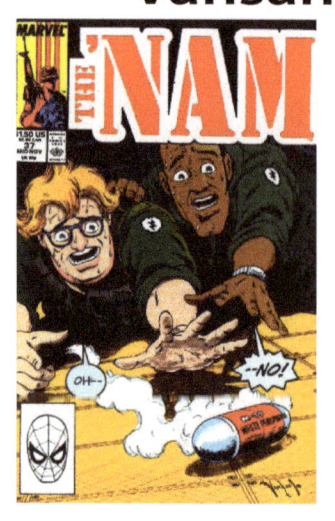

Vansant drew many interior stories for *The 'Nam*, a Marvel series in the 1980s and 90s. For whatever reason, he was not assigned to draw many covers, but one of them is shown here.

Wayne has created a number of historical graphic novels, doing both the writing and illustration: *The Battle of the Bulge, Normandy, Gettysburg, The Red Baron, Bombing Nazi Germany,* and *Grant vs. Lee*.

He has had two volumes published of a planned trilogy about Katusha, Girl Soldier of the Great Patriotic War.

You will be seeing more of Wayne's work in a future issue of The Current.

Thanks to Wayne for allowing The Current to print examples of his artwork from *The Hammer and the Anvil.*

Cover art by Wayne Vansant. – Copyright © Marvel Entertainment

More about Dwight Jon Zimmerman

Zimmerman has been a writer and editor at Marvel Comics and Topps Comics.

He's written a number of historical books. With Wayne Vansant as illustrator, he wrote *The Vietnam War: A Graphic History.*

He collaborated with Bill O'Reilly to write *Lincoln's Last Days,* the young-adult version of *Killing Lincoln,* by O'Reilly and Martin Dugard. *Lincoln's Last Days* was awarded the Branson Stars and Flags Grand Prize in 2013. (Zimmerman had received the same award the previous year for his book, *Saga of the Sioux.*)

I thank Dwight for kindly granting permission to print excerpts from *The Hammer and the Anvil*

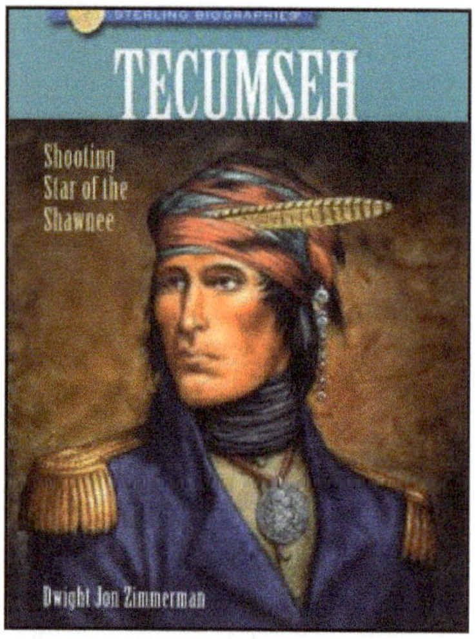

One of Zimmerman's books. – From Barnes & Noble

Giving freedom a chance

John Riordan lives in Belgium, Wisconsin (Ozaukee county). Forty years ago this month, he made a choice—and took actions—which have led some to call Riordan the "Oskar Schindler of the Vietnam War."

Riordan was the subject of a segment on CBS's *60 Minutes* last year. Now, he's written of how he struggled with difficult decisions, how he carried through on those decisions, and how they changed his life—and the lives of over a hundred people.

It's not the kind of situation that many people who've lived in America most of their lives can fully grasp:

You're living in a city, or near one, where life is normal. Civilized. Free of fear. *But...*

...there are rumors that the Invaders are coming.

Most people around you go about their daily lives, unconcerned. So things must be normal, right?

A few people are packing up. Before leaving, they urgently recommend that you do the same.

Government officials smile, hold their hands out, and say, "Everything's fine. No need to worry."

You then hear the Invaders are only a few hundred miles away. Heading your way. The last you'd heard, they'd been over a thousand miles from you.

You carefully study the people around you. Some are outwardly calm. Some are plainly worried. Some don't know what to expect. Even if the Invaders did come, what would happen? Some people consider the Invaders to be conquerors; others think they're liberators. Is the fear that seems to appear in more and more eyes a justified fear of the Invaders' true identity, or is it simply a fear of the unknown?

You decide you're going to leave.

You're not telling anyone that. But it's impossible to hide it. The people close to you, whom you work with, know you're leaving. They say nothing. But as you gather your things, prepare to walk out the door, you look up at them.

You think: I am able to leave. They cannot.

They could be in great danger.

But there's nothing you can do.

Or is there?

A few months ago, I received an advance reading copy of a book, *They Are All My Family,* written by John P. Riordan and Monique Brinson Demery. It was addressed to me in my capacity as editor of The Current.

I see John nearly every month, at the Town of Belgium meetings in Ozaukee County. He sits near the back of the town hall, an enigmatic smile fixed on his face. After calling me "Mr. Sounder" for a couple of years (because I cover Town of Belgium for the Random Lake Sounder), he finally learned my real name, probably because I now hand out copies of The Current after each meeting.

That's why John asked his publisher to send me the advance reading copy. The final book is now available; I received a copy the day before I started this article. It looks great!

Briefly: In 1975, John worked for First National City Bank (FNCB) in Saigon, South Vietnam. The North Vietnamese were getting closer and closer to Saigon.

In early April, New York bank officials ordered John to close the Saigon branch and get out of the country.

As John made preparations, he looked at his co-workers.

John Riordan in Vietnam, 1968. — Photos from the book, *They Are All My Family*, courtesy of the publisher

The staff of First National City Bank, Saigon branch, outside the building for the branch opening in 1972.

There was nothing he could do for them.

Or was there?

You would not easily confuse John Riordan with Sylvester Stallone or Arnold Schwartzenegger. However, *They Are All My Family* tells of suspense and courage that is in many ways more exciting than even the best action-thrillers of those two mega-stars. More exciting—because it's real life.

They Are All My Family tells what happened when John made one choice that changed everything. That choice? He concluded: "Yes. Yes—there *is* something I can do."

Dishonesty as official policy

As the Communist North Vietnamese army advanced into South Vietnam, U. S. executives of companies having branches in Vietnam became concerned. But they could not express that concern openly. Officials of both the U. S. and South Vietnamese governments would not admit there was anything wrong. Riordan shows this by describing how he was ordered to appear at the U. S. embassy by ambassador Graham Martin, early in April.

Martin didn't like the fact that Riordan was about to close FNCB's office and leave Saigon. "I want you to cancel that plane," Martin told Riordan.

But Riordan wouldn't be intimidated. "I've been ordered by FNCB New York to close our Saigon branch. I'm closing it. The plane is arriving here tomorrow. I am going to be on it."

Riordan describes the reaction: "Martin's face puffed red and radiated anger. If the American banks left, it would look terrible for him. Martin's story was that everything was going to be fine. Nobody should panic. He gave me a long glare, throwing daggers with it, but the effect bounced right off me, which must have made him even angrier."

Martin then pantomimed washing his hands. "That's what I feel about you guys. I wash my hands of you. I don't give a [expletive deleted] what happens to you. You will get absolutely no support from me, or the United States government."

"[I]n every account I have read of those final weeks in Saigon," Riordan writes, "Ambassador Martin comes across as someone who refused time and time again to face reality." And, "I had an embassy that was feeding me false information, and on purpose."

What about the Vietnamese?

As John made preparations to leave Saigon, he couldn't help thinking about those he would have to leave behind. Friends. Co-workers.

"If Martin had such a problem with Americans leaving, how would the South Vietnamese ever get out of their own country?" John writes. "What was the right way for America to leave the country we had fought so hard to keep free? We couldn't underwrite their struggle forever, but it didn't feel right to abandon such a vulnerable ally."

John writes, "To come right out and ask the staff if they wanted to leave would be illegal. Under current South Vietnamese rules, it would be treason. We ran the risk of offending someone loyal to the faltering government, someone who would inform on us."

"[I]t was verey clear that [the embassy] was not going to risk upsetting the South Vietnamese government by advocating the departure of its citizens..."

When one courageous private individual planned to fly children out of Vietnam, at his own expense, the main obstacle was—you guessed it: Ambassador Martin. Why? Because such an operation would make Martin look bad.

John had little choice at that point. He was told by his bosses to get out.

He got out. Alone. He flew to Hong Kong.

Alone was not enough

But after thinking and talking about the situation, John realized he'd have to go back and help his co-workers get out of the country. "It was the right thing to do," he writes.

The choice was especially difficult, because returning to Vietnam would be direct defiance of the orders he'd received from FNCB executives. But he returned in the third week of April.

"Some of the Vietnamese confessed to me later that I was the last person they had expected to see back," he writes. "I was definitely not thought of as the kind of guy who would risk his job and his life, to come back and help staff members he had only worked with for two years. But the rush back to Saigon to help the staff seemed like a natural instinct to me."

The bank staff was not so large. But when some asked that John help members of their family to leave as well, John agreed the families should not be broken up. (Some families were split, however. And when some relatives refused to go, some staff chose to stay behind, as well.)

Riordan describes a suspenseful four days of driving multiple times to the airport, to see his co-workers and their families safely flown out of the country.

But wait. Not just any citizen could leave Vietnam. How did John get them all past the official paperwork? By naming each one as being a relative.

Were officials suspicious? Most likely. One remarked to John that he had a pretty large family. On the second or third day that John brought in a load of "relatives" to the airport, an American official told him, "You look very familiar." John writes, "I thought that was probably going to be it for me, surely the game was up, but to my great relief, he just smiled and passed me on."

(Elsewhere in this issue of The Current, there is a similar example of how "looking the other way" resulted in escape from oppression.)

From April 22 through 25, John got over a hundred people through the system, to the airport, and out of the country. On the 26th, John himself flew out.

On April 30, the Communist flag was raised at Saigon's presidential palace.

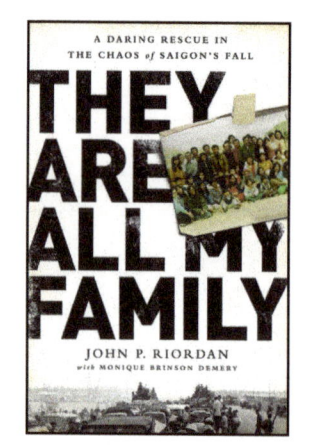

Life after escape

John no longer had a job with the bank. But 106 people no longer had a home.

But when John contacted bank executives to face the music, the music he heard was unexpectedly reassuring. FNCB execs not only approved of what John had done, but gave support to the refugees. The same New York bank vice presidents who'd told John to get out of Vietnam now sent him a telex of praise and congratulations.

"FNCB loaned every employee half a year's salary with no interest rate," he writes. "That made it possible for many of the staff to get on their feet. The bank also reimbursed tuition for any college or continuing education classes. There was never squabbling over which profit center was going to pick up the costs. Everyone at the bank was in this one together."

One last major confrontation

Once John was back at FNCB's head office in New York City, he "ran into George Vojta. It had been Vojta who had told me that under no circumstances was I to go back to Vietnam." Undoubtedly, Vojta had taken great heat from his management when John's defiant actions had first been discovered. "I was still tense about running into Vojta, whom I had so blatantly defied."

What was said and done, in that confrontation? It's a highlight of the book.

But I'll let readers discover it for themselves.

Lives affected

In **They Are All My Family**, several people tell how their lives were affected by John Riordan's decision to help them escape from Vietnam.

The publishers of the book have kindly granted The Current permission to run the following three statements:

In the years since the 1975 escape from Vietnam, several reunions have been held, this one in 2013 in Long Island, New York.

When I look back upon my life, I often wonder if the fortune teller I met as a 16 year old girl really had the ability to predict the future or was it all happenstance and coincidence. My present self would say neither. My present self would say that things happen because of the warm hearts of kind and caring people like Mr. John Riordan. He and the people at Citibank changed the fate of [106] of their employees and the generations to come. My husband and I are forever grateful for the opportunity that has been given to us and the smile on our children's and grandchildren's faces are a constant reminder of that generosity.

Bui Thi Bich Lien

After 39 years, thinking of my unexpected and sudden journey to escape from the Communist regime, I feel so lucky to have joined FNCB (now called Citibank) and very thankful to the bank and its employees who helped us to evacuate from Vietnam and resettle in the US. Among the benefactors from Citibank, I am deeply grateful to Mr. John Riordan, whom we call Papa John. John risked his life by returning to Saigon to help us safely get out of Vietnam in the nick of time. He gave me and my family the opportunity to seek freedom and prosper in the free land of the United States. This story is dedicated to John Riordan as my special thanks to him.

Xuan Nhan

Still available from Barnes & Noble and other booksellers.

My husband and I are so grateful that we were rescued. We establish our family in the land of opportunity and freedom. My son is thirty years old, a successful entrepreneur and married. I am looking forward to the expansion of the future generations of my family. We are so grateful for John he is truly a hero for my entire family as well as many more families. John Riordan is the proof that one man's actions can positively affect the lives of many.

Truong Le Khanh (Helen)

John Riordan's story on YouTube!

Google the following search words, and you should find a 13-minute segment which first aired on *60 Minutes*, CBS, on July 20 2014:

youtube john riordan 60 minutes vietnam

The Current

Taking you places worth seeing
Volume 4 • Issue 6 • May 2015

What you collect is who you are pg. 9 & beyond

FREE!

Movies
Art
Dining
Macrocosms & Microcosms

May 2015

Cover photo: What you collect is who you are
Great movies coming up
National Nurses Week in May
Big Eyes: The book, the movie
Natural Connections by Emily Stone: The Wolves of Isle Royale and Michipicoten Island
White's Wine by David White: In Its Greatest Moments, Wine Provides An Idealized Reality
I Ate At... by Richard J. Baumann: Brown Baer, Elkhart Lake
Buttons...!?! You collect what?!?
Report: Windy City Show
Like Father, Like Daughter by Mark Walters: Canadian fly-in fishing on Shultz Lake
Shotgun Lovesongs by Nickolas Butler: Book Review by Cara Scofield

I purchased this original gag drawing. It had no caption. Can you think of one?

The Current

TAKING YOU PLACES WORTH SEEING
Volume 4 • Issue 7 • June 2015

FREE!

The Art of James Bama pg. 12

Movies * Arts * Dining * Futures past & pasts to come

Win a DVD! See pg. 14

June 2015

This was the first time I used the centerspread as one layout, or "double truck," a practice I would continue.

Cover photo: Your Editor's Front Yard
Steamboat Bill, Jr.
Great movies coming up
Natural Connections by Emily Stone: Broad-winged Hawk
I Ate At... by Richard J. Baumann: Red Cabin At Green Acres, Fond du Lac
White's Wine by David White: Worry About Wine, Not Arsenic
Recipes from world-class chefs
Coakley's Crazy Cookie Corner by John Coakley: Applesauce, oatmeal, hickory nut, all fruit mix and honey cookies
The Art of James Bama
Who Is Doc Savage?

Cowboy from Kaycee, oil painting by James Bama

July 2015

Cover photo: Wings and Wheels, Sheboygan County Memorial Airport
Great movies coming up
Mary Poppins Comes to Random Lake
Natural Connections by Emily Stone: Orange Chicken
I Ate At... by Richard J. Baumann: Two Area Coffee Shops
Coakley's Crazy Cookie Corner by John Coakley: Hickory Drops
The Rahr-West Art Museum, Manitowoc
Wings and Wheels
Follow-Up: Michael Perry
Why does college cost too much? Ask Karl Marx, by Bonnie K. Snyder

August 2015

Cover photo: Gessert's Ice Cream and Confectionery, Elkhart Lake
Great movies coming up
Ant-Man
A Night Out at the Movies: The Window
Real-Life Values from Fantasy? Harry Potter's Lessons for Muggle Politicians, by Ari Armstrong (excerpt from his book, Values of Harry Potter)
Natural Connections by Emily Stone: Monarch Caterpillars
Coakley's Crazy Cookie Corner by John Coakley: Honey & Oats
Getting a Perspective on Movie Posters
Movie Posters
Forward to the Past! (Random Lake Historical Society Museum)

September 2015

Cover photo: Honest Tea at the Local Piggly Wiggly

Great movies coming up

A Night Out at the Movies

Natural Connections by Emily Stone: The Corn Belt Tightens the Belt on Monarchs

I Ate At... by Richard J. Baumann: The Elkhart Inn, Elkhart Lake

Coakley's Crazy Cookie Corner by John Coakley: Sticky Hickory Coconut Macaroons

White's Wine by David White: With Wine, Endless Treasures Await

Like Father, Like Daughter by Mark Walters: Challenges on the Hunt

Sputnikfest

Planning on Building a House? Consider a Dumbwaiter

A History of Honest Tea

Life history of a tea company, told in "graphic narrative" format. Honest Tea was discontinued in 2022.

Planning on building a house?
Consider a dumbwaiter

If you're designing your ideal home, consider a feature that's very uncommon in house plans. Once you see how useful a dumbwaiter is, you'll wonder why most homes don't have them.

The "dumb" in "dumbwaiter" doesn't refer to it being stupid. Rather, in means "silent." It actually means a "silent waiter." It's also been referred to as a "lazy waiter," but let's dispense with the derogatory terms, and think of it as a "labor-saving waiter," even a "back-saving waiter."

Despite what you might have seen on old Three Stooges episodes, a dumbwaiter is not intended for people to ride in. But it will spare you the safety risks and strain of carrying heavy items up and down the stairs.

Dumbwaiters are available in manual and motorized form. When I designed a home for my wife and me, I chose to keep it simple and had a manual one installed. I didn't want to maintain a motor. After nine years of use, ours still works fine.

My manual dumbwaiter is operated by pulling one of two ropes. One rope brings the dumbwaiter cart up; the other brings it down.

I say "bring" instead of "send," because I prefer to load the dumbwaiter wherever the payload is, and then go to the floor to which I want to bring the payload. I pull on the rope until the cart is at my level, and I unload.

In contrast, if I were upstairs and wanted to send the cart to the basement, I could do that — but I'd better listen closely for the cart to hit the springs at the very bottom, and hope the cart wasn't damaged by sending it down too fast. No, it's "bring" not "send," for me.

Pulling the rope takes very little physical effort. For a 100-pound payload, you need not be strong enough to directly lift 100 pounds. That's partly because of the large pulley wheel at the top of the dumbwaiter shaft, translating motion into lift. It's also partly because of the counter-balancing weight that slides up as the payload cart is brought down; or down as the cart is brought up.

What should you consider when designing a house with a dumbwaiter?

Make a list of your anticipated routines of carrying something from one place to another within the home, which involves more than one floor. List each action. An example could be:

44

- Basement: Carry toolbox from southeast corner workbench corner to stairs.
- Stairs: Carry toolbox from basement to ground floor.
- Hallway: Carry toolbox from stair door to garage door.
- Garage: Load toolbox into car.

Prioritize your various routines: Which will you do most frequently?

The above is important, because it will help you plan the following:

- Where in the house should the shaft be located?
- What floors will it access? (Ours goes from basement, to ground floor, to 2nd floor.)
- What weight capacity is needed? This affects the construction of the shaft.
- How will the cart be oriented? Will it have to be loaded on one side, but unloaded on another?

Installing a dumbwaiter doesn't require out-of-the-ordinary construction skills. At least, our manual model didn't. The builder of our house had never installed one before. It arrived as a kit, with full instructions and the promise of phone support if it was needed. It wasn't needed. Our builder installed it perfectly.

The practical value of a dumbwaiter is obvious. Climbing or descending stairs while carrying something with both hands, you can't hold onto the safety rail. That's just asking for trouble.

The dumbwaiter can save time, and wear and tear on your body. You could make five trips from your car to the basement, carrying something downstairs each time. Or you could make five trips from the car to the dumbwaiter, walk downstairs with both hands free, and bring the dumbwaiter down.

Knowing I would load and unload boxes from the car, I situated our dumbwaiter shaft just a few steps from an entry to the garage. That has proven to be very convenient, because it makes loading things into and out of the car easier.

Visitors to our home are amazed by the dumbwaiter's practicality. Yet, as I say in my opening, they're not common. The amazed remark I hear most is, "I just never thought of something like that!"

The cart is ready to move payload. Pulling the left rope raises the cart; pulling the right rope lowers it.

Well, here's your chance. Think about it!

The brand of dumbwaiter we went with is called Silent Servant. It's designed for both residential and commercial use. For more information, their website is:

silentservant.com

The doors to the dumbwaiter shaft can be any style. The upstairs room has some rustic elements, so antler handles and dark wood were selected (left). For the ground floor, light wood matching the rest of the floor with steel handles (center). For the basement, we didn't install handles (right).

October 2015

Cover photo: Vladimir Kush and (Superimposed) One of His Paintings
Great Movies Coming Up
Vladimir Kush: Metaphorical Realist
The Baby Who Lived: How Energy Saved My Friend's Son, by Alex Epstein
Natural Connections by Emily Stone: Borealis
Coakley's Crazy Cookie Corner by John Coakley: Lemony Chocolate Chip Cookies

I Ate At... by Richard J. Baumann: Woodland Creek Supper Club, New Prospect
Road America: It don't git no better than this! Claude Ingrassia

November
2015

Cover photo: Not All Heroes Have Big, Bulging Muscles
Great Movies Coming Up
Bullying Causes Teen Suicide... ...but What Causes Bullying? by Dr. Michael J. Hurd
Natural Connections by Emily Stone: Clay-colored sparrow returns
Like Father, Like Daughter by Mark Walters: A day in the life of an outdoor adventures writer
White's Wine by David White: Looking For a Wine List Bargain? Go Off the Beaten Path
Coakley's Crazy Cookie Corner by John Coakley: Banana Maple Hickory Bread
I Ate At... by Richard J. Baumann: After Burners, Sheboygan County Airport
The Girl on the Cover
The 2015 Kohler Food & Wine Experience
Cosplay at the Comicon

The 2015 Kohler Food & Wine Experience

Rob Hurrie, chef and co-owner of The Black Pig in downtown Sheboygan, gave a demonstration of how to use three types of Wisconsin cheese in three simple preparations.

Members of America's Test Kitchen (Christopher Kimball, Bridget Lancaster, and Jack Bishop) have appeared at the Kohler Food & Wine Experience in the past. This year, the three stars of this popular show gave demonstrates to a large crowd at the Stella Artois tent. Audience members could view the stovetop action in the mirror, above, or on large projections screens at each side of the stage.

Can't see from way in the back of the tent? No problem! Gigantic TV screens make sure you miss nothing.

Father/daughter team of Jacques and Claudine Pépin not only demonstrated how combining and cooking ingredients can lead to joyful eating; their own personal chemistry in working together warmed and entertained the audience.

One dealer's setup at the Grand Rapids Comic Con

The Current

Taking you places worth seeing
Volume 5 • Issue 1 • December 2015

FREE!

What's she painting? Look inside!

The Life and Adventures of Santa Claus

December
2015

Cover photo: Elizabeth Carr Whitmore Participates in "Paint the Town"
Great Movies Coming Up
The Life and Adventures of Santa Claus, by L. Frank Baum (excerpts)
Memories of JFK, by Sue Mroz
James Bama's Santa Claus
Making Spirits Bright
I Ate At... by Richard J. Baumann: Home!
Coakley's Crazy Cookie Corner by John Coakley: Soft Chew Cookies

James Bama's rendition of Santa

49

2016

January 2016

Cover image: Albert Payson Terhune's Dog Stories
Great Movies This Month
Merlini of the Movies
And the winner is — Ricky Klas! by Sue Mroz
Natural Connections by Emily Stone: We are surrounded by minerals taken for granted
The Throwback by Albert Payson Terhune
Coakley's Crazy Cookie Corner by John Coakley: Peanut butter coconut cookies
I Ate At... by Richard J. Baumann: Roadside Bar & Grill, Plymouth
White's Wine by David White: Fake Wines Take a Toll on Everyday Consumers
Terhune books published locally (by Your Editor, of course

February 2016

Cover image: Albert Payson Terhune's Dog Stories
Great Movies This Month
Freedom of Opportunity, Not Equality of Opportunity, by George Reisman
New Year's Eve dinner at the Blind Horse
Truffle dinner at the Lake Park Bistro
Falcon Java Roost percolates, by Jeff Pederson
Port Exploreum — a community jewel by Sue Mroz
Natural Connections by Emily Stone: Virtual Exhibit
Coakley's Crazy Cookie Corner by John Coakley: Super Chocolate Chip Cookies
I Ate At... by Richard J. Baumann: St. John the Baptist Catholic Church, Plymouth
Echoes of our past by William & Joy Wangemann: A Glance Back
Telepresence Success Stories, by Jacquelyn Bengfort

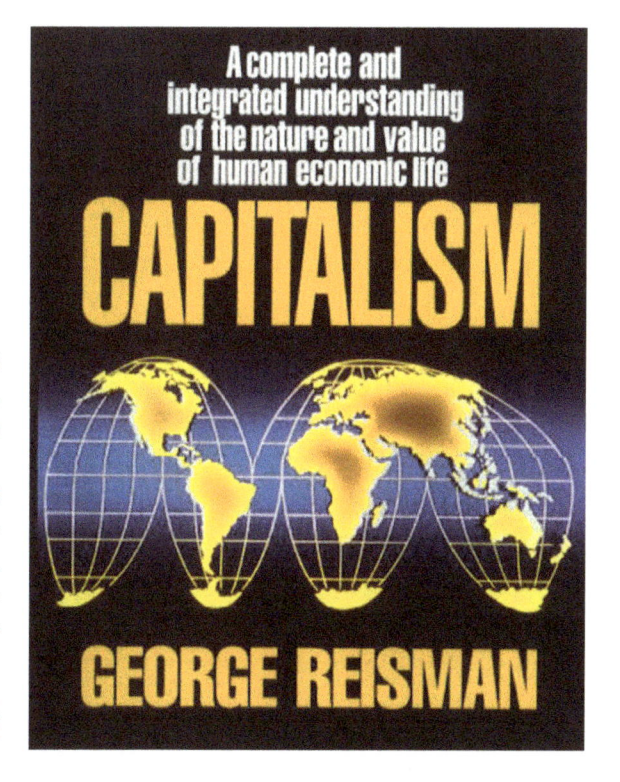

I consider George Reisman to be one of the greatest economists living during my lifetime. Undoubtedly, his greatest work is a mammoth book, titled simply Capitalism.

He has also written numerous short articles and recorded many lectures, which any advocate of freedom should become familiar with. A long lecture, Capitalism: The Cure for Racism, is available online. I consider it outstanding, and can't recommend it strongly enough.

I had the pleasure of meeting him in 1991, when he gave a talk at Madison: The Toxicity of

Environmentalism.

I received permission to run his article, Freedom of Opportunity, Not Equality of Opportunity. I suspected ideas expressed therein would step on some toes, and I was correct. I several times lamented in print that I did not receive feedback for The Current. This time around, I got it aplenty. One highly unpleasant phone conversation with a particularly deranged person convinced me to end future conversations as soon as I saw them going in that direction.

Dr. Reisman's website is capitalism.net

Lower left: A New Year's Eve dinner at the Blind Horse, Kohler; photo by Rodney Schroeter. *Upper right:* The 13th annual Truffle Dinner at the Lake Park Bistro, Milwaukee; photo courtesy The Bartolotta Restaurants.

Super Chocolate Chip Cookies
By John Coakley

Ingredients
- 1 cup soft butter
- ¾ cup packed brown sugar
- ¾ cup granulated sugar
- 3 eggs
- ¼ cup honey
- 1 tsp. vanilla extract
- 3 cups all-purpose flour
- 1 tsp. baking soda
- ½ tsp. baking powder
- 1 tsp sea salt
- 2 cups old-fashioned oats
- 1 cup chopped hickory nuts
- 1 cup all fruit mix
- 1 cup coconut flakes
- 2 cups semi-sweet chocolate chips

Directions
1. Mix butter, sugars, eggs, honey and vanilla together until nice and creamy.
2. In a separate bowl, stir the rest of the dry ingredients until well blended.
3. Add dry mixture (a small amount at a time) to the wet mixture. Mix at various speeds until everything comes together.
4. Cover and refrigerate overnight.
5. Line cookie sheets with parchment paper.
6. Place tablespoon-sized dough balls two inches apart on the parchment.
7. Bake at 350° for approximately 9 minutes.
8. Cool on wire cooling racks.

Try a warm one of these with coffee and see if you have the will power to quit after eating just one cookie. I couldn't, and I have diabetes. Blood glucose elevated but it was worth it. Crazy as I am, I only did this once. This recipe is one of my greatest accomplishments. I don't know if I can top it next month, but it won't be for lack of trying.

Until next time, have a happy!

Crazy Coakley

The Current

Taking you places worth seeing
Volume 5 • Issue 4 • March 2016

FREE!

Culture * Dining * Cookies
Motivational running

March 2016

Cover image: Your Editor's Front Yard
Free Movies on the Internet
Great Movies This Month
What happened to Roscoe Arbuckle?
From couch potato to ultra marathoner, by Sue Mroz
A Dozen Great Apps for Children Learning Math, by Daniel Wahl
Natural Connections by Emily Stone: Secrets of a busy night revealed
I Ate At... by Richard J. Baumann: Five Pillars, Random Lake
Coakley's Crazy Cookie Corner by John Coakley: Caramel Apricot Cookies
Book Signing in Beaver Dam

Several people provided feedback to the previous month's article by George Reisman. The compliment at right makes up for any number of unpleasant phone conversations with psychotics. The main reason I never reprinted more articles by Dr. Reisman is their length.

Did my reprinting of his article result in "an otherwise unexplained surge" in his sales? If so, I have contributed to the advancement of civilization (or to the slowing of its decline).

from George Reisman

Thank you for the copies of The Current. I'm very happy with the way my article appeared. If you want to reprint any more of my articles, please let me know. Meanwhile, I can't help wondering if your reprinting has contributed to an otherwise unexplained surge in my sales. The last few Mondays in particular have been very strong.

Economist George Reisman wrote the article here under discussion, published last month.

What happened to Roscoe Arbuckle?

Typically, people who hear about Roscoe "Fatty" Arbuckle also hear something else—that he was involved in some kind of scandal, for possibly attacking and murdering a woman.

(He was called "Fatty" in his movies, but he hated that name; thus, I will use it as little as possible.)

To learn about Arbuckle, I read a couple of books: *Frame-Up!* by Andy Edmonds, and *The Day the Laughter Stopped* by David Yallop. (I consider the latter to be the better-researched.)

So here's what happened in 1921. While spending a weekend in San Francisco, Roscoe held a party in a suite of three adjoining hotel rooms. He was acquainted with some of the people who dropped in on this party; others, not. Two of the latter were Virginia Rappe, an actress, and her friend, Maude Delmont.

In the course of the party, Virginia became ill. Arbuckle discovered her vomiting, and tried to determine how seriously ill she was. He was alone in the room with her for a short time. She became incoherent and hysterical. The other party guests were summoned. The hotel detective, and finally a doctor, were called.

Several days later, Virginia died. Maude Delmont accused Arbuckle of raping her, and causing the internal injuries she later died of. Arbuckle was arrested.

The first trial ended in a deadlock, after the jury deliberated for forty-four hours. For most of that time, only one juror had insisted on Arbuckle's guilt. By the end, two people voted "guilty," ten "not guilty."

A second trial was held. Perhaps believing that the facts were obvious, Roscoe's defense team did not make as strong a case as they had the first time. The jury was again deadlocked, ten to two—but now, the majority voted "guilty."

For the third trial, Roscoe's defense team was very thorough. They made every fact known. The jury went to the deliberation room and unanimously concluded "Not guilty," *in one minute*. But the jury did an unusual thing. They spent five more minutes in the deliberation room, composing the following statement:

> Acquittal is not enough for Roscoe Arbuckle. We feel that a great injustice has been done him. We feel also that it was only our plain duty to give him this exoneration, under the evidence, for there was not the slightest proof adduced to connect him in any way with the commission of a crime. He was manly throughout the case and told a straightforward story on the witness stand, which we all believed. The happening at the hotel was an unfortunate affair for which Arbuckle, so the evidence shows, was in no way responsible. We wish him success and hope that the American people will take the judgment of fourteen men and woman who have sat listening for thirty-one days to evidence, that Roscoe Arbuckle is entirely innocent and free from all blame.

"Fourteen men and women"? A jury has only twelve members. Here's the explanation, from Wikipedia: "After the reading of the apology statement, the jury foreman personally handed the statement to Arbuckle who kept it as a treasured memento for the rest of his life. Then, one by one, the entire 12-person jury plus the two jury alternates walked up to Arbuckle's defense table where they shook his hand and/or embraced and personally apologized to him. The entire jury even proudly posed in a photo op with Arbuckle for photographers after the verdict and apology."

This Arbuckle portrait hangs in Your Editor's home office.

Wow. Sounds like Roscoe Arbuckle was ready to start afresh, and continue creating movies that made millions who loved him laugh. You'd think, right?

But less than a week later, the newly formed Hays Office banned him from the movies.

Not because he was guilty, but because he was associated with scandal.

Roscoe "went underground." For the next ten years, he made a living by directing others—under a phony name—and not appearing before the camera.

After those ten years, after films had started to talk, Roscoe was at last allowed to make movies again. He appeared in six short comedies. He was happily looking forward to doing something he loved, and making at least a partial comeback.

Also from Wikipedia: "Arbuckle had finished filming the last of the two-reelers on June 28, 1933. The next day he was signed by Warner Bros. to make a feature-length film. That night he went out with friends to celebrate his first wedding anniversary [to his second wife] where he reportedly said: 'This is the best day of my life.' He suffered a heart attack later that night and died in his sleep. He was 46. His widow Addie requested that his body be cremated as that was Arbuckle's wish."

I hope, by this point, you're asking, "How could this happen? How could his life be ruined by a blatant falsehood?"

I'll explain this to the best of my understanding, by telling of several people in Roscoe's life. Some are heroes. Some, villains. Heroes or villains? By what standard? See if you can tell.

First, the villains:

Maude Delmont
The person who claimed that Roscoe had physically assaulted Virginia Rappe, leading to charges of murder (reduced by a preliminary investigation to manslaughter) against Arbuckle. Edmonds writes that Delmont "had an extensive police record up and down the California coast. By 1921, at least fifty counts had been filed against her on crimes ranging from bigamy to fraud, racketeering to extortion. She was known in Los Angeles and San Francisco as a professional correspondent: a woman hired to provide compromising pictures to use in divorce cases or for more unscrupulous purposes such as blackmail."

Matthew Brady (and the goons working for him)
"Within twenty-four hours of Roscoe Arbuckle's arrest on the charge of murder, the district attorney, Matthew Brady, was aware that the testimony of his star witness was riddled with lies. Yet he pursued Arbuckle through the courts of San Francisco for eight months." (Yallop, 10) This was not a man of integrity who was simply mistaken about the facts. This was a man for whom reality was negotiable—facts were whatever he wanted to make them appear, to the public. Why did he want to destroy Arbuckle? Would it lead to greater political power—the governorship of California? Did he simply hate Arbuckle, because of his great success? Whatever his motives—it doesn't matter. He attempted to destroy a man's life (quite literally) by faking reality, but ultimately, reality asserted itself.

(And if you're interested in a modern-day example of unjust persecution, see Dinesh D'Souza's recent book, *Stealing America*.)

The involved editors, writers, and owner of the Hearst papers

To a certain extent, William Randolph Hearst must be held accountable for the content of his papers. An owner has such a responsibility. But for the writers and editors more directly involved, nothing but moral condemnation is in order. Reality was of no concern to them; whipping up a frenzy against Arbuckle was. Again, their motivation—whether they simply wanted to sell more papers, or they genuinely believed Arbuckle and the Hollywood he stood for were morally corrupt—is not important. The fact that they printed unchecked assertions against Arbuckle, or did not print facts that indicated his innocence, or doctored photos to present a distorted view of reality (see Yallop's book, the photo section)—they tried to assert, or believe in, or promote the unreal, the untrue.

Gosh, I'm so glad that kind of slanting doesn't exist in today's reporting, when it comes to political/philosophical issues. Aren't you?

People who mindlessly join a moral crusade

Note, "mindlessly." A moral code, if based on reality, is a necessity for human life; and a moral crusade based on a rational code of ethics can only do good, so long as it doesn't advocate, or actually engage in, the initiation of force.

A moral code which ignores reality, however, is destructive to human life.

In the Arbuckle case, I'm talking about members of various groups claiming to represent a certain moral view, who demanded censorship, or the destruction of the entire film industry, or other violations of individual rights (e.g., Prohibition). The advocacy of any moral view (even if it is false) violates no individual's rights;

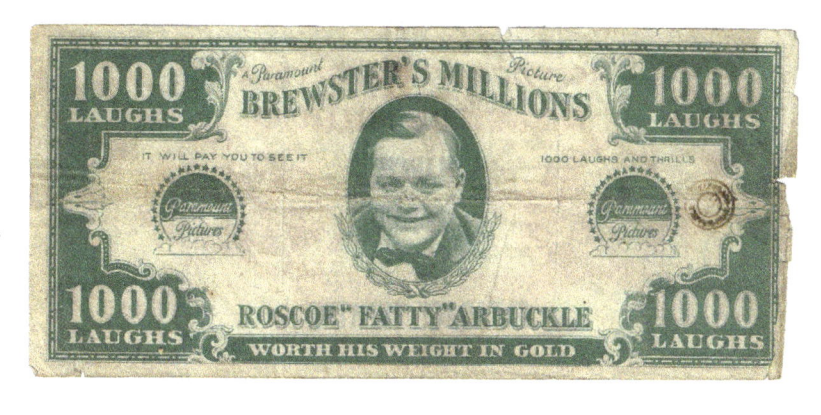

This promotional item (which is the size of real money) for one of Arbuckle's films might be about all you and I will ever know about the movie. It was released in 1921, when Arbuckle's popularity was at its highest. But this was also the year Arbuckle was struck by the scandal. There are no known copies of Brewster's Millions, so it is considered a "lost" film.

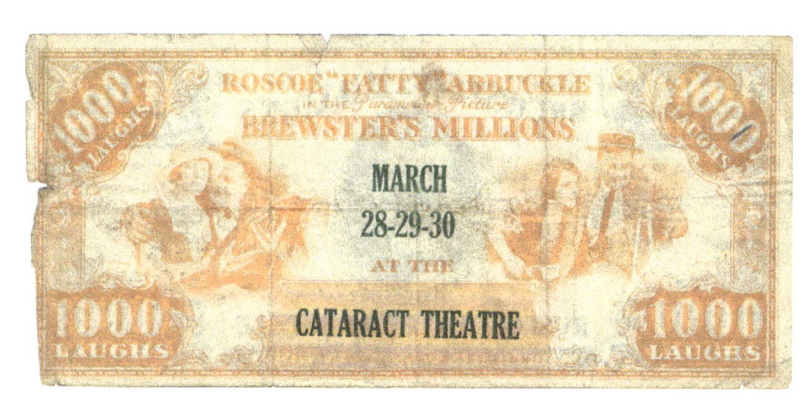

the initiation of force, to mandate a moral code (even if it is true), negates both rights and morality.

This type of destructive evil—holding a moral view mindlessly, shunning any need for a rational foundation—is perfectly represented by one juror at Roscoe's first trial. She voted "guilty" throughout the jury's deliberation. Did she interpret the facts differently? Did she look at the evidence, and just come to a different conclusion? Did she merely make an honest mistake?

Yallop, page 240: "Not only was Mrs. [Helen] Hubbard convinced of his guilt, but she refused to discuss the evidence and told the others that she intended to vote guilty 'until hell freezes over.' When August Fritze, the foreman of the jury, and the others began to discuss the case, she put her hands to her ears, to avoid hearing the discussion... She refused to look at the exhibits. She refused to read the trial transcripts."

Watch for this deadly pattern, when reality is ignored: "I want it to be true; thus I believe it to be true; *thus it is true.*"

Will Hays, and those who gave him power

This includes all the scared little people who believed that a form of "self censorship" would appease those immoral crusaders who were clamoring for the destruction of rights. These moral

The lie...

From The Seattle Star, September 17, 1921. The cartoon is credited "From the Denver Post." It's my understanding that Arbuckle was never in a jail cell during his entire ordeal. So why portray him this way? Is an image like this dishonest? Have you seen examples of images like this?

The truth...

"Exonerated of manslaughter." From an unidentified newspaper.

The reality...

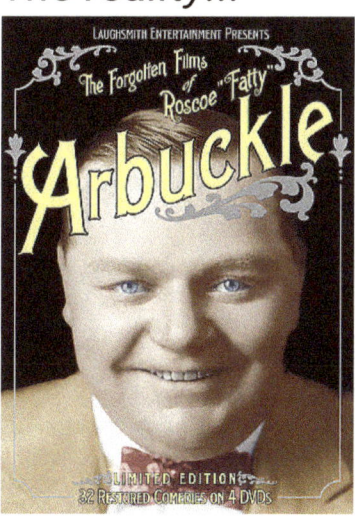

This smiling photo, on the cover of a 4-DVD set published by Laughsmith, shows Arbuckle's true personality. This excellent set features over 30 Arbuckle films, most of them short (and many of them sharp and clear). It's out of print, but can be found on eBay for a reasonable $20 or less. – Image from Barnes & Noble cowards thought that using Roscoe as a scapegoat would make it safe for their own miserable existences. But every time you throw a piece of your rights away to an enemy, hoping he'll be satisfied and not come back, you find that the gesture of surrender only makes him hungrier. I wish people like this would first study history, and then have the honesty and courage to face facts.

Then, there are heroes in this story:

Zey Prevon

This woman was present at the party where the whole thing started. She refused to sign a false statement, at the behest of Brady and his henchmen, despite the incredible pressure they put on her (if you're euphemistic enough to call her false imprisonment and forcible isolation as "pressure"). For a good example of her moral strength, her dedication to the truth, see the excerpts from her grand jury testimony in Yallop, 162-173.

August Fritze, jury foreman at the first trial

In his words, the prosecution's case was "an insult to the intelligence of the jury. They asked us to substitute conjecture for facts. Human liberty and American rights should depend, not upon guesses of anybody, but upon evidence." (Yallop, 244) Right on! Here's someone who understood that an innocent person's life and liberty are not trivial things.

Lee Dolson, juror at Roscoe's second trial

Lee would not surrender his "not guilty" vote. But wait—another juror also voted for acquittal; was he not also a hero? No, because this person said he'd change his vote to "guilty," if Dolson would (Yallop, 248). Far from being a hero, I count this other juror as a petty villain. He did not use his independent judgement, based on the facts, to make his choice. Rather, he surrendered his mind.

Minta Durfee, Buster Keaton, and others who lent moral support

Some of Roscoe's fair-weather "friends" disassociated themselves from him, for fear of being targets of the same irrational condemnation he was suffering. But there were those who refused to compromise, when it came to truth and justice. These true friends did what they could to stand by Roscoe. Minta physically stood with him during his trials, despite the fact that their marriage was failing. Keaton gave Roscoe work, such as an all too brief appearance as a woman in a store, in his 1925 feature, Go West.

Roscoe died young—46. And what of Matthew Brady? I, who value justice, wish I could report that he was voted out of office and, since he had no skills of any use on a free market, and he couldn't find anyone evil enough to give such an evil man charity, he became a homeless, wandering, drunken bum, staggering through back alleys, pawing feebly through trash cans for bits of organic material to consume, being constantly beaten up by purposeless hooligans who possessed the same level of moral depravity that he had. But no such luck. He lived an unfortunately long life, active in politics to the end.

From the 1916 short film, Fatty and Mabel Adrift, one of Arbuckle's finest. At right is Mabel Normand. You can find this for free viewing on the Internet.

If you value honesty, Dear Reader, be true to reality. If you value justice, look at the facts and don't evade them, when it comes to judging other people. You'll be in good company—you'll deserve to stand with the heroes I've mentioned above. And you'll help to identify, and fight, all those villains who have contempt for honesty and justice.

Arbuckle's own words

[**Editor's note:** This is an excerpt of a much longer statement by Arbuckle, which appeared in the Dec. 31, 1921 issue of Movie Weekly. This was a few weeks after Arbuckle's first trial. Though he writes here of difficulties faced, he would soon face many more.]

I knew when I went on the witness stand that my cross-examination was going to be as rigid as it could be made, but I had no fear, for I was telling nothing but the truth. I know that the lawyers tried many times to catch me on details, but they couldn't, because everything I said was true, and there was no need to remember what I had said the first time.

No man can do any more than to tell the truth, and it was the truth I told on the witness stand.

A great many very harsh and unjust things have been said about me since this affair began and they have hurt me very much. I have always had many friends, but I found when this trouble came, who my real friends were.

It has hurt me deeply to think that the people to whom I have tried to give good clean enjoyment for so many years could turn on me and condemn me without a hearing. I suppose every man accused of crime must expect that, but it didn't make it any easier for me.

I have been very grateful to the other people who refused to believe that I was guilty merely because I was accused of crime. There have been many of them. I have received many many letters and telegrams from people all over the country, assuring me that they believed in me, and I am glad to know that I have these real friends.

If everything is straightened out at last and I am cleared of all the charges, I hope that these friends will be as ready to welcome me back on the screen as I shall be glad to get back. I like to make people laugh and enjoy themselves. It pleases me because children are amused at my pictures, and I have always tried very hard not to do anything in any picture that would offend or be bad for the children.

One really good thing has come out of all this trouble. It has been the means of reuniting my wife and myself after five years of separation. We are happy to be together again, and we have discovered that the things that kept us apart were very unimportant after all.

Mrs. Arbuckle has been wonderfully loyal to me during all this trouble. She came all the way across the continent to be with me, and every minute she has stuck by me. Her faith and love, and the faith and love of her mother, who is like a mother to me, have been my greatest helps all these long hard weeks.

While, through the technicalities of the law, I have not been legally acquitted of the charge of manslaughter in connection with the death of Virginia Rappe, I have been morally acquitted.

After the organized propaganda, designed to make the securing of an impartial jury an impossibility and to prevent my obtaining a fair trial, I feel grateful for this message from the jury to the American people. This comes, too, after hearing only part of the facts, as the efforts of the District Attorney succeeded, on technical objections, in excluding from the jury the statements from Miss Rappe to several people of high character, completely exonerating me.

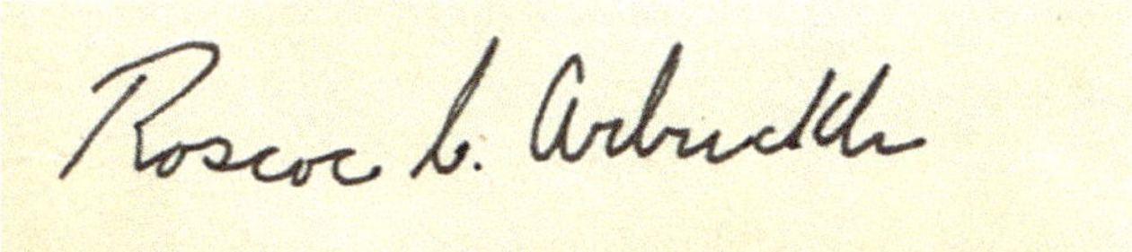

Roscoe C. Arbuckle

In the rest of this statement, Arbuckle gives a detailed account of his side of what happened. It can be found at: www.public.asu.edu/%7Eialong/Taylor28.txt

Above: A signature Your Editor acquired. It was cheap, likely because it wasn't signed "Fatty" (which Arbuckle hated). If it's not authentic, that could also explain its cheapness.

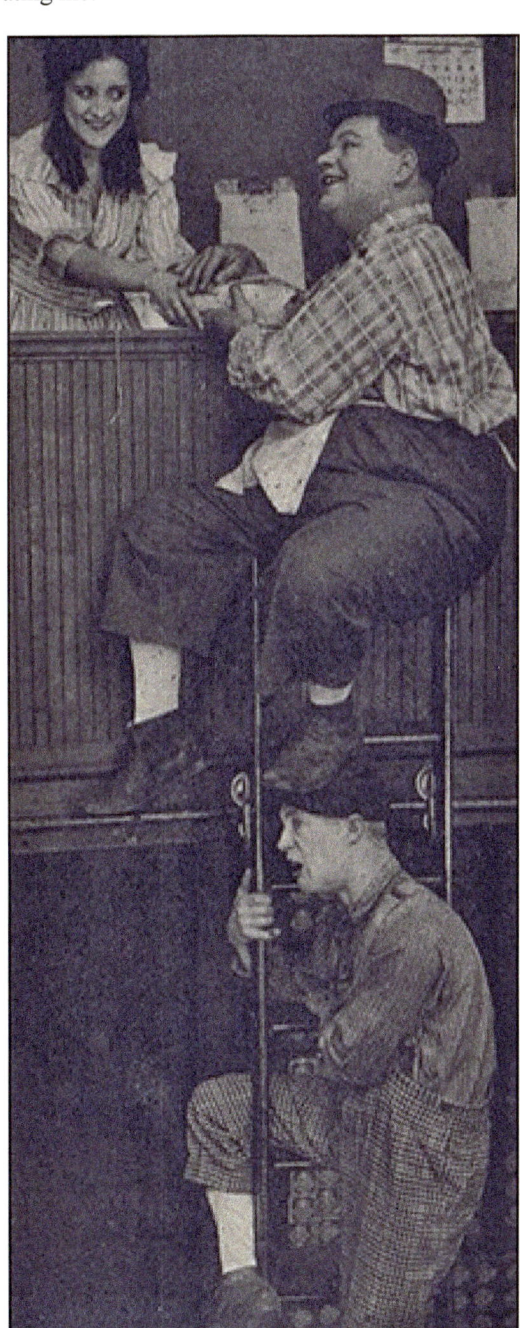

The most *ridiculous* crossword puzzle *ever?*

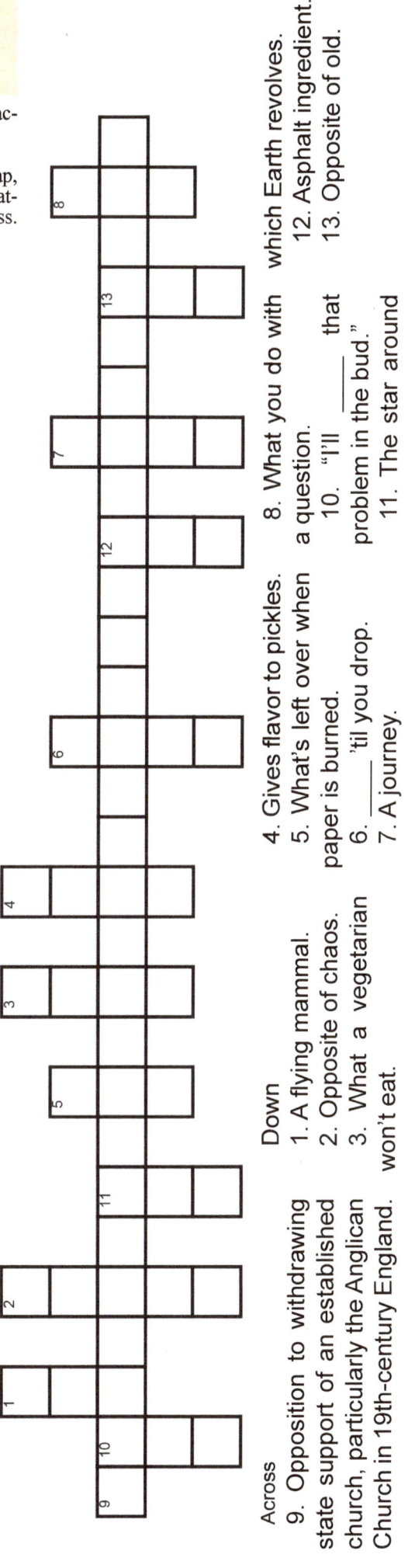

Across
9. Opposition to withdrawing state support of an established church, particularly the Anglican Church in 19th-century England.

Down
1. A flying mammal.
2. Opposite of chaos.
3. What a vegetarian won't eat.
4. Gives flavor to pickles.
5. What's left over when paper is burned.
6. ___ 'til you drop.
7. ___ A journey.
8. What you do with a question.
10. "I'll ___ that problem in the bud."
11. The star around which Earth revolves.
12. Asphalt ingredient.
13. Opposite of old.

57

April

2016

Cover image: The Sagrada Familia, Barcelona, Spain. Photo taken 2011 by Tot conflueix / All's connected

Great Movies This Month

Antonio Gaudi—A Brief History, by Max Abroad

I Ate At... by Richard J. Baumann: "Pic A Deli"-Generations, Plymouth

Coakley's Crazy Cookie Corner by John Coakley: Crazy Raisin Cranberry Cookies

Echoes of our past by William & Joy Wangemann: Politics

New tapas menu at the Blind Horse

Dale Van Minsel Photography Exhibition

The Current is on Facebook!

From Homelessness to Happiness: The Story of Tom Richardson's Life-Changing Idea, by J.A. Windham

Fritz Lang's flight for life

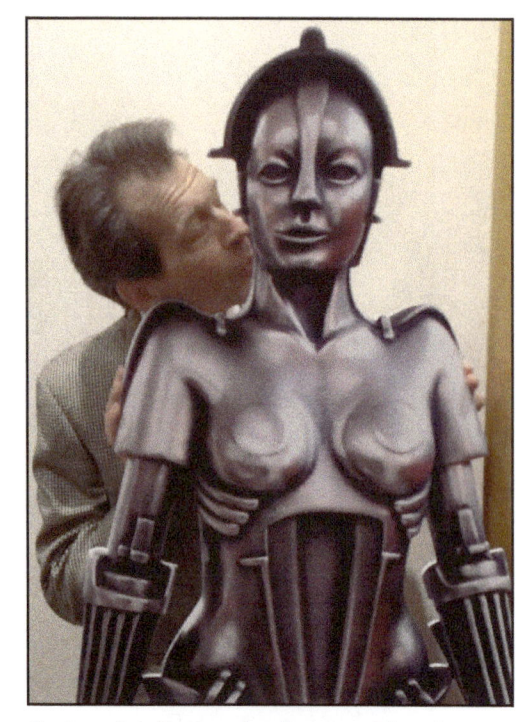

Cartoonist Batton Lash gave The Current permission to run this photo of him, showing loving affection for this replica of a robot from one of the movies listed in this issue. (Do you know which one?) Batton is the creator of "Wolff & Byrd, Counselors of the Macabre," a series featuring two lawyers who take on supernatural clients. Search the Internet for his name to find out more.

Antonio Gaudí

A detail of the exterior, the Sagrada Familia. – Photo by Poniol60

The Sagrada Familia viewed from Casa Milà, Barcelona, Spain, taken 2009 – Photo by Bernard Gagnon

Casa Milà, Barcelona. – Photo by Paolo da Reggio

Gaudí's "El Capricho", in Comillas (Cantabria, Spain). – Photo by Tirithel

All photos of Gaudí's work were found on Creative Commons.

Here's what started it all!

The fact that Turner Classic Movies has scheduled this documentary this month started Your Editor on a research binge that led to the inclusion of photos and articles on Spanish architect Antonio Gaudi in this issue.

The documentary was released as a single disk some years ago. The version shown here is a more recent, 2-disk edition from The Criterion Collection. The first disk has the original 72-minute, 1984 film. The second disk has documentaries and other short films about Gaudi.

To prepare for this issue's publication, I viewed both disks. It's a great set. But there's a paradox here.

Just watching the original documentary, you won't learn much at all about Gaudi's life, but you will see much of his work. The film has almost no narration. No explanations. It opens with some horrific paintings. Were they painted by Gaudi? Did they inspire him? It's a mystery. You see impressive rock formations. I know from the other documentaries on Disk 2 that their shapes inspired Gaudi; but would you conclude that from just seeing Disk 1's main documentary? I'm not sure.

So, while the documentary shows you much of Gaudi's work, you will learn little about the man himself.

But maybe that's OK. Maybe it will serve to draw you in, catch your interest, make you decide to learn more.

Heck, if the cover of this issue served that purpose, it's a success.

An even more ridiculous crossword puzzle than the one we featured last month!!

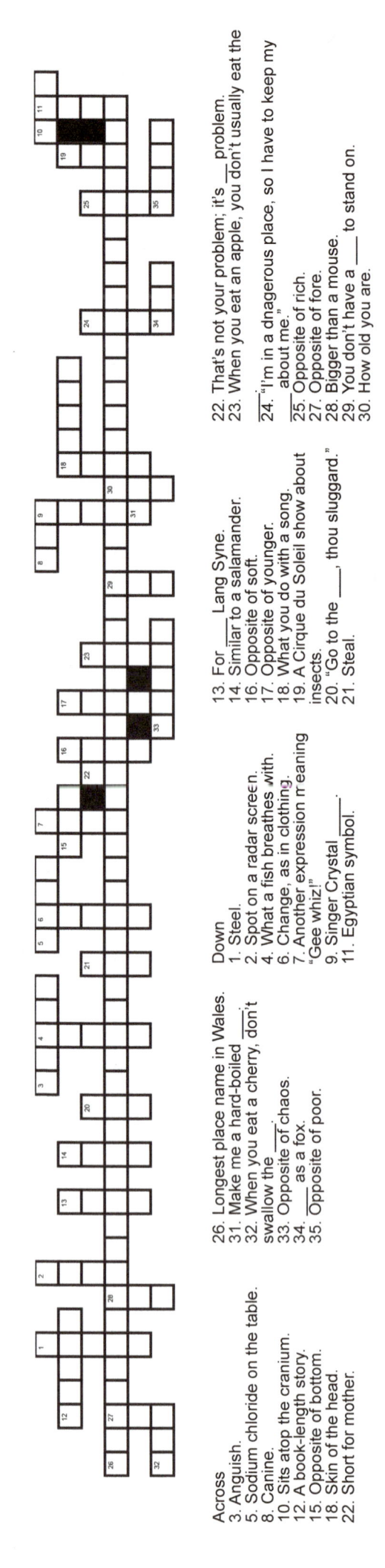

Across
3. Anguish.
5. Sodium chloride on the table.
8. Canine.
10. Sits atop the cranium.
12. A book-length story.
15. Opposite of bottom.
18. Skin of the head.
22. Short for mother.
26. Longest place name in Wales.
31. Make me a hard-boiled ___.
32. When you eat a cherry, don't swallow the ___.
33. Opposite of chaos.
34. ___ as a fox.
35. Opposite of poor.

Down
1. Steel.
2. Spot on a radar screen.
4. What a fish breathes with.
6. Change, as in clothing.
7. Another expression meaning "Gee whiz!"
9. Singer Crystal ___
11. Egyptian symbol.
13. For ___ Lang Syne.
14. Similar to a salamander.
16. Opposite of soft.
17. Opposite of younger.
18. What you do with a song.
19. A Cirque du Soleil show about insects.
20. "Go to the ___, thou sluggard."
21. Steal.
22. That's not your problem; it's ___ problem.
23. When you eat an apple, you don't usually eat the ___.
24. "I'm in a dnagerous place, so I have to keep my ___ about me."
25. Opposite of rich.
27. Opposite of fore.
28. Bigger than a mouse.
29. You don't have a ___ to stand on.
30. How old you are.

Best of Show!

Readers of The Current have seen numerous examples of the art of Jon Wos in the past two years; some of his wine-related paintings have accompanied the "White's Wines" columns.

The 10th annual "Art in the Garden" show was held at the Hilton Garden Inn, Oshkosh, this past April 9 and 10, where visitors had a chance to vote on their favorite pieces entered.

Voted "Best in show" was Jon's painting, "Who Is Li Hu?" shown here with the proud artist himself (taken *before* Jon knew the painting would win this award).

Li Hu was one of Jon's painting instructors.

(The photo of the child right behind Jon is not his work.)

The Current

TAKING YOU PLACES WORTH SEEING
Volume 5 • Issue 6 • May 2016

FREE!

*Dining * Cinematic arts * The Pollard Family Motivational culinary arts*

May
2016

Cover image: Robert Irvine, Disney California Adventure Food and Wine Festival, April 2, 2016

Best of Show!

Great Movies This Month

Ben Franklin's 5 Tips for Making Americans Better Writers, by Annie Holmquist, intellectualtakeout.org

From starving artist to celebrity (George Pollard), by Sue Mroz

Nan Pollard, Illustrator, by Ross Pollard

Natural Connections by Emily Stone: False Morels

I Ate At... by Richard J. Baumann: Some Places That Weren't Very Good (And which will remain anonymous)

Coakley's Crazy Cookie Corner by John Coakley: Breakfast Delights

Routinely achieving the impossible

Routinely achieving the impossible

Your Editor was fortunate enough to attend Robert Irvine's presentation on April 2 at Disneyland, as part of the Disney California Adventure Food and Wine Festival.

Chef Irvine did a TV show called "Dinner Impossible" for The Food Network. In each episode, he was given a ridiculously difficult challenge (like cooking dinner for numerous guests in a hotel constructed entirely of ice; or cooking a *vegetarian-only* meal for dozens of hungry cowboys).

Then, he moved on to "Restaurant Impossible." On this show, he walks in to a restaurant that has requested his help, because it's on the verge of financial failure. With little time (48 hours) and little money ($10,000), he and his team redesign the look and atmosphere of the restaurant; teach the staff how to create delicious, economical meals; help the owners understand the financial aspects of a restaurant; and—most importantly—get owners and workers to all re-examine and reject the failure-oriented attitudes that brought the business to its present state.

One of Irvine's favorite approaches to a problem lacks a great deal of subtlety. He sharply asks his design team: "Didn't I tell you I don't want that wall there anymore?" When they hem and haw and try to explain why the wall is needed where it is, Irvine walks out and, with a grim expression, selects a sledge hammer from the tool truck. A few seconds after his return to the restaurant, when things have quieted down, Irvine tells his staff, who have their hands to their foreheads and their eyes closed, "Now you *have* to get rid of that wall!"

Chef Irvine has been a contestant and judge on other shows on The Food Network; for example, Worst Cooks in America. Irvine lost one season of that show to Chef Anne Burrell and, per their agreement, Irvine had his hair dyed the same color as Burrell's.

At one point during his presentation at the Disney California Adventure Food and Wine Festival, Irvine asked the audience if there were any questions. Your Editor was first with his hand up.

Question: You sometimes get pretty frustrated, pretty angry, on your shows, but you still have an overall positive attitude. How do you hold onto that, despite all things that happen on your shows? Is that a choice you've made, or is it part of your nature?

Robert Irvine: That's a great question.

I have literally 36 hours to change somebody's life. I walk in, and have no knowledge. And that's the truth. I walk in, you tell me the story of your life, and it's up to me to decide which way I go with your restaurant, and with your relationship.

So in real time, that's about 22 minutes of real time, on a show that's 42 minutes. So on the show level you'll see maybe three minutes of that [anger and frustration]. It's my responsibility, when you call me for help, to make sure I leave you better than when I came to you. We are 84% successful with the restaurants after one year after we have taken over. Which is a huge success, when you think we've finished our thirteenth season, 165 restaurants. [Applause from audience]

Irvine's Staff: And, by the way, still the number one show in the history of the Food Network. Yes!

Robert Irvine: The demeanor, when everything's falling apart—your family, your house, your mortgage, somebody's going to take your house, your business, and you have no money—they're already [experiencing] every emotion you can imagine. Frustrated. Angry. They're sad. Everything's falling apart and I'm the guy that has to keep it together.

When I get frustrated, it's real frustration. I don't hide it. Because I can't. I'm not that way. I tell you as it is, because I believe that if you listen, we can actually change your life.

Those that listen—and one thing we don't like, right, is change. We hate it. Big companies, little companies, mom and pop operators, they hate change. And I'm the guy that's going in there with a big stick and saying, *"Change! Change! Change!"* And some do, and they'll be more successful, and those who don't, go back to their old ways, and some of them get a brand new restaurant two weeks later.

So. Calm. I was in the military. I'll talk about the military in a minute. But I was in the military for many, many years. Under pressure, that's what you're supposed to do. Remain calm. Sometimes it's very difficult, but we do. Because we're trained that way.

Crazy Coakley's Cookie Corner

Breakfast Delights
By John Coakley

Ingredients
- 3 cups all-purpose flour
- 2 cups rolling oats
- 1 tsp baking soda
- 1 tsp sea salt
- ½ tsp cinnamon
- 1½ softened butter
- ½ cup honey
- 3 eggs
- 1 cup light brown sugar, packed
- 2 cups granulated sugar
- 2 tsp vanilla extract
- 1½ pounds bacon
- 1 tbs bacon fat
- 1 generous cup hickory nuts
- 1 cup sweetened dried cranberries
- 1 cup semi-sweet chocolate chips

Directions
1. Mix first five ingredients in a bowl and set aside.
2. In a large bowl, mix next eight ingredients until well blended.
3. Add dry ingredients to wet mixture a little at a time.
4. Stir in cranberries, hickory nuts and chocolate chips. Dough will be hard to work with, but it will be well worth it.
5. Refrigerate until cold.
6. Make 1-inch balls and place on parchment-lined cookie sheets. Press balls to ½ inch rounds, two inches apart.
7. Bake at 350° for 9 to 10 minutes.
8. Cool on a wire rack until firm.
9. Now have breakfast.

The reason I called these cookies Breakfast Delights is they have bacon, eggs, and flour that makes bread that makes toast. With a cup of coffee you have a complete breakfast that is sweet, delicious and decadent.

The idea for this recipe is from my crazy brain. Most of the people that tasted my delights liked them.

If you like the bacon flavor you can add more bacon and fat to taste.

With coffee, I thought they were very good. Next month's cookie might be more outlandish yet. Until then...

Have a happy!
Crazy Coakley

June

2016

Cover image: Morel Dinner, Lake Park Bistro, Milwaukee
Great Movies This Month
Hunter finds his own way, by Jeff Pederson
Dear attorneys general: Conspiring against free speech is a crime, by Glenn Harlan Reynolds
Suing Oil Companies for Free Speech = Censorship, by Michael J. Hurd
A Morel Meal
Echoes of our past by William & Joy Wangemann: Early Harbor
Natural Connections by Emily Stone: Tree Frogs Trilling
I Ate At... by Richard J. Baumann: Marytown Tap, New Holstein
Coakley's Crazy Cookie Corner by John Coakley: Peanut Butter Bars
100 Shadows (Publisher reprinting all original Shadow pulp novels)
Gibson (main writer of The Shadow) Meets Houdini
Two other Gibson books

From the Morel Dinner: Fried soft-boiled egg with sauteed morels, asparagus, morel cream and brown butter vinaigrette. – Designed by Adam Siegel, Executive Chef

The Current

Taking You Places Worth Seeing
Volume 5 • Issue 8 • July 2016

FREE!

Arts * Dining * Cultural trends   Movies: Bridge of Spies * The Martian

July 2016

Cover image: Mill Pond Park, Waldo; sculpture by Tristan Preder
Great Movies This Month
He Volunteered to Go to Auschwitz, by Lawrence W. Reed, FEE.org
An interview with David Aaron Gray, producer, Operation Auschwitz, conducted by Wojciech Wybranowski, moviepilot.com
A Mini-Renaissance in Film? by Andrew Bernstein, theobjectivestandard.com

Modern Movies: Some Random Shots
Visiting with Mario Andretti, by Gina Steinhardt
Coakley's Crazy Cookie Corner by John Coakley: Cookies Hawaiian
I Ate At… by Richard J. Baumann: This time, you choose!
"The Martian" and the Earthlings, by Robert Tracinski
Natural Connections by Emily Stone: The Nature of My Garden
Hollywood Baroque, by Robert Tracinski
Behind the Bridge…

He Volunteered to Go to Auschwitz

by Lawrence W. Reed
FEE.org

In this great mortuary of the half-living—where nearby someone was wheezing his final breath; someone else was dying; another was struggling out of bed only to fall over onto the floor; another was throwing off his blankets, or talking in a fever to his dear mother and shouting or cursing someone out; [while still others were] refusing to eat, or demanding water, in a fever and trying to jump out of the window, arguing with the doctor or asking for something—I lay thinking that I still had the strength to understand everything that was going on and take it calmly in my stride.

That was on a relatively good day at the infamous Auschwitz concentration camp in 1942, in the words of the only known person to have ever volunteered to be a prisoner there. His name was Witold Pilecki. His story is one of history's most amazing accounts of boundless courage amid bottomless inhumanity.

Powerful emotions gripped me when I first learned of Pilecki and gazed at his picture. I felt rage toward the despicable regimes that put this honorable man through an unspeakable hell. I welled up with admiration for how he dealt with it all. Here you have a story that depicts both the worst and the best in men.

Olonets is a small town northeast of St. Petersburg, Russia, 700 miles from present-day Poland. It's where Witold Pilecki was born in 1901, but his family was not there by choice. Four decades earlier, when many Poles lived under Russian occupation, the czarist government in Moscow forcibly resettled the Pileckis in Olonets for their part in an uprising.

For the first time since 1795, Poland was reconstituted as an independent nation at the conclusion of World War I, but it was immediately embroiled in war with Lenin's Russia. Pilecki joined the fight against the Bolsheviks when he was 17, first on the front and then from behind enemy lines. For two years he fought gallantly and was twice awarded the prestigious Cross of Valor.

To label Pilecki a "hero" seems hopelessly inadequate.

In the 18 years between the end of the Polish-Russian war in 1921 and the beginning of World War II, Pilecki settled down, married, and fathered two children with his wife, Maria. He rebuilt and farmed his family's estate, became an amateur painter, and volunteered for community and Christian charities. And, after extensive officer training, he earned the rank of second lieutenant in the Polish army reserves. He probably thought his days of mortal combat were over.

Hitler and Stalin secretly agreed in August 1939 to divide Poland between them. On September 1, the Nazis attacked the country from the west, and two weeks later, the Soviets invaded from the east. The world was at war again—and so was Pilecki.

An overwhelmed Warsaw surrendered on September 27, but Polish resistance never ceased. Together, Pilecki and Jan Wlodarkiewicz cofounded the Secret Polish Army (Tajna Armia Polska) in early November. They and other elements of a growing underground movement carried out numerous raids against both Nazi and Soviet forces. In September 1940, Pilecki proposed a daring plan that in hindsight appears nearly unimaginable: he would arrange to be arrested in the hope that the Nazis, instead of executing him, might send him to the Auschwitz camp where he could gather information and form a resistance group from the inside.

If he could survive arrest, Pilecki figured, Auschwitz would likely be where the Nazis would incarcerate him. It was nearby, and many Polish resistance fighters were imprisoned there. It wasn't yet the death camp for the Jews of Europe that it would soon become, but there were murmurings of executions and brutality that the Polish resistance wanted to investigate so that they could inform the world.

On September 19 in Warsaw, Pilecki kissed his beloved wife and two young children goodbye (both of whom are still alive today). Equipped with forged identity papers and a new name, he walked into a Nazi roundup of some 2,000 civilians. Two days and a few beatings later, he was Auschwitz inmate number 4859.

Viktor Frankl, himself an Auschwitz survivor and author of the powerful 1946 book Man's Search for Meaning, had men like Pilecki in mind when he wrote:

"Fire can only be met with fire."
– Quote by and photo of Pilecki from moviepilot.com

The way in which a man accepts his fate and all the suffering it entails, the way in which he takes up his cross, gives him ample opportunity — even under the most difficult circumstances — to add a deeper meaning to his life. It may remain brave, dignified and unselfish. Or in the bitter fight for self-preservation he may forget his human dignity and become no more than an animal. Here lies the chance for a man either to make use of or to forgo the opportunities of attaining the moral values that a difficult situation may afford him. And this decides whether he is worthy of his sufferings or not.

Fired by a determination that almost defies description, Pilecki made the most of every opportunity that his 30-month imprisonment at Auschwitz presented. Despite bouts of stomach ailments, typhus and pneumonia, lice infestations, backbreaking toil hauling rocks, extremes of heat and cold, and relentless hunger and cruelties at the hands of German guards, he formed an underground resistance group, the Union of Military Organization (Zwiazek Organizacji Wojskowej, ZOW). His initial reports of events and conditions within Auschwitz were smuggled out and reached Britain in November 1940, just two months after his detention began. Using a radio transmitter in 1942 that he and his fellow ZOW conspirators built, he broadcast information that convinced the Western Allies that the Nazis were engaged in genocide on an unprecedented scale. What became known as "Witold's Report" was the first comprehensive account of the Holocaust from a first-hand witness.

"The game which I was now playing in Auschwitz was dangerous," Pilecki later wrote. "This sentence does not really convey the reality; in fact, I had gone far beyond what people in the real world would consider dangerous." That too is an understatement. He was surrounded by a camp staff of 7,000 Nazi SS troops, each of whom possessed life-and-death power over every inmate. It was a hell on earth—one where no moral rules applied.

More than two million people died at Auschwitz. As many as 8,000 per day were gassed with the deadly chemical Zyklon-B, while others died of starvation, forced labor, disease, or through hideous "medical" experimentation. Smoke from the ovens that burned the corpses could be seen and smelled for miles. Pilecki saw it, wrote about it, broadcast news of it, and even prepared for a general uprising of inmates against it—all under the noses of his captors.

By spring 1943, the Germans knew full well that there was an extensive resistance network in Auschwitz. Many ZOW members had been found out and executed, but Pilecki's identity as the ringleader hadn't yet been discovered. Then, on the night of Easter Sunday, 1943, Pilecki accomplished what only 143 other people in the history of Auschwitz ever could. He escaped, bringing with him incriminating documents that he and two fellow inmates had stolen from the Germans.

If this were the end of the story, Witold Pilecki would already be a major figure in the history of World War II. Incredibly, there's still more to tell — and it's every bit as stunning as what you've read so far.

Avoiding detection, Pilecki made his way from Auschwitz to Warsaw, a journey of some 200 miles. There, he reestablished connections with the underground in time to assume a commanding role in the Warsaw Uprising, the largest single military offensive undertaken by any European resistance movement in World War II.

For 63 days, fighting raged in the Polish capital. No one came to the rescue of the brave Poles—not even the Soviet Army, which halted its advance just east of the city and watched the slaughter like vultures overhead. Warsaw was demolished, the rebellion was put down, and Pilecki found himself in a German POW camp for the remaining months of the war. If the Nazis had realized who he was, summary execution would surely have followed quickly.

Still, there's more.

Germany's surrender in May 1945 resulted in the immediate liberation of its prisoners. For Pilecki in particular, it meant a brief respite from conflict and confinement. Stationed in Italy as part of the 2nd Polish Corps, he wrote a personal account of his time at Auschwitz. But as the summer turned into fall, it was becoming apparent that the Soviets were not planning to leave Poland.

In October 1945, Pilecki accepted yet another undercover assignment—to go back to Poland and gather evidence of growing Soviet atrocities. This he did, marking him by the pro-Soviet Polish puppet regime as an enemy of the state.

In May 1947—two years to the day after Nazi Germany capitulated—Witold Pilecki's cover was blown. He was arrested and tortured for months before a sham public trial in May 1948, where he was found guilty of espionage and given a death sentence.

According to IMDB.com, the movie Operation Auschwitz is currently "in production."

His last words before his execution on May 25 were, "Long live free Poland!" He was 47.

Are you wondering why you've never heard of this man before?

For decades, information about Pilecki was kept hidden by the leaders of the postwar, Soviet-installed regime. They couldn't recount his anti-Nazi activities without completing the story and telling of his anticommunist work as well. With the release in recent years of previously classified or suppressed documents, including Pilecki's own reports in their entirety, his superhuman exploits are finally becoming known around the world. (At this writing, American film producer David Aaron Gray is working on a movie about Pilecki's life, slated for release in 2016.)

Polish author and translator Jarek Garlinski, in his introduction to *The Auschwitz Volunteer: Beyond Bravery* [Pilecki's 1945 Auschwitz account] summarizes the extraordinary character of Witold Pilecki:

Endowed with great physical resilience and courage, he showed remarkable presence of mind and common sense in quite appalling circumstances, and a complete absence of self-pity. While most inmates of Auschwitz not slated for immediate death were barely able to survive, he had enough reserves of strength and determination left to help others and to build up an underground resistance organization within the camp. Not only that, he managed to keep a clear head at all times and recognize what he needed to do in order to stay alive.

Pilecki's reports from the death camp, Garlinski wrote, were more than indispensably valuable for intelligence purposes. They also represented a "beacon of hope" — demonstrating that "even in the midst of so much cruelty and degradation there were those who held to the basic virtues of honesty, compassion, and courage."

The Current

TAKING YOU PLACES WORTH SEEING
Volume 5 · Issue 9 · August 2016

Movies * Art * Dining — Worlds within Words

FREE!

August 2016

Cover image: Mill Pond Park, Waldo; sculpture by Tristan Preder
Great Movies This Month
"You, Too!" Here's one logical fallacy to watch out for
2016: the "Year of the 1%" or the Year Poverty Fell to a New Low? by Chelsea German, HumanProgress.org

Natural Connections by Emily Stone: A Change of Plans
Solomon Kane's Homecoming, by Robert E. Howard
I Ate At... by Richard J. Baumann: Jay Lee Inn, Elkhart Lake
Movie Posters
Echoes of our past by William & Joy Wangemann: The Sheboygan Quarry
PulpArtists by David Saunders: Anton Otto Fischer

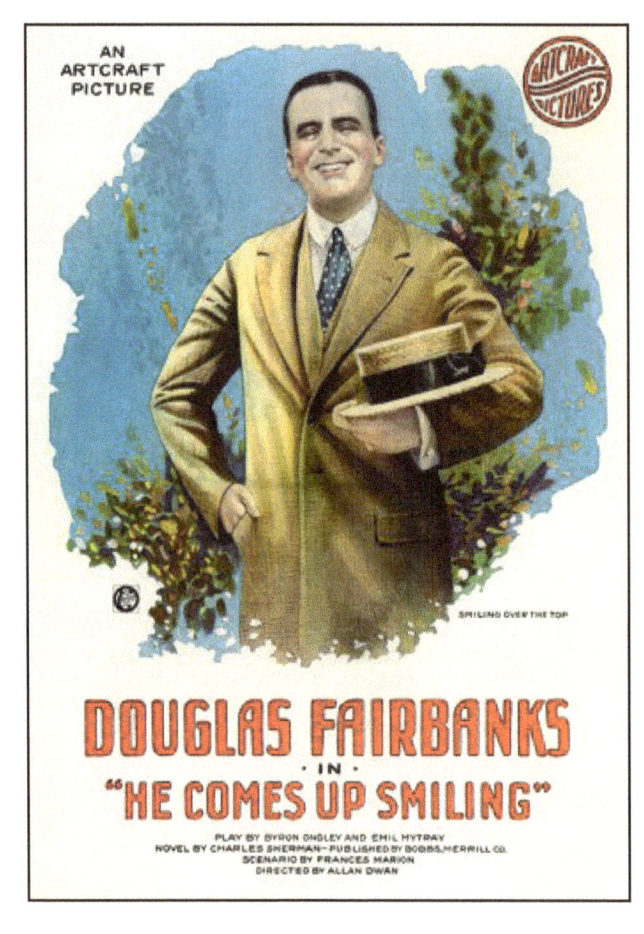

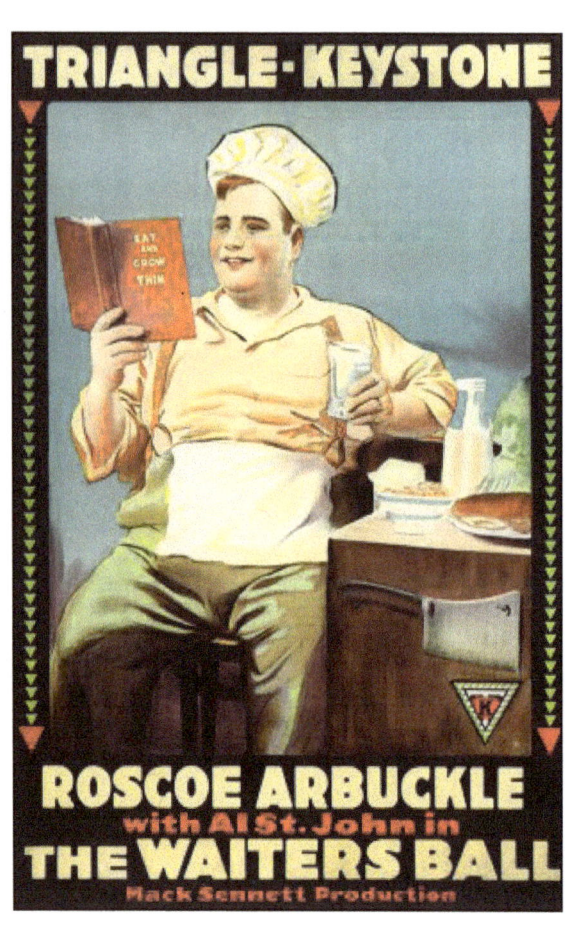

— Movie posters from HA.com

66

An origin story

David Saunders has created an online reference work of hundreds of artists who have worked for the pulps.

A "pulp" is a comic book-sized magazine, popular in the first half of the 20th Century. They usually had colorful, painted, eye-catching covers.

Most illustrators would seek out a diversity of work. Not only would they create work for the pulps, but they would seek work from higher-paying magazines, like *The Saturday Evening Post.* Many artists, growing in their skills and confidence, broke into the world of fine art, painting according to their own personal visions, in contrast with the demands of an art director.

With Saunders' permission, The Current features in this issue one artist from this project—Otto Anton Fischer—in this issue. We might run other artists in the future. Why?

First, the artwork is great to look at, especially if we run it in color.

Second, because the artist's life story has something to offer each of us, whether it's a successful career struggle or an example of how one person faced and overcame a difficulty.

Finally, illustration as you see it here is scarce in today's culture. (The range of subjects illustration is used for has narrowed; much work is done for science fiction, for example.) To view this wealth of American art and culture, we have no choice but to look to the past.

David Saunders' pulpartists.com

ANTON OTTO FISCHER: OCEANIC HORIZONS

Anton Otto Fischer was born on February 23, 1882 in Regensburg, Bavaria, Germany. In 1887 at the age of five he became an orphan. He was raised in a Christian charity asylum and although he wanted to be a painter, he was educated for the priesthood. In 1894 at the age of twelve he was sent to a monastery for priest training. He ran away from the monastery and lived with an uncle in Munich. In 1897 at the age of fifteen he left his uncle's home with the warning to never come back.

For the next five years he sailed as a deckhand on a Dutch merchant ship, a Norwegian lumber bark, a Swedish steamer, and a German trawler. In 1902 he jumped ship in New York City and applied for U.S. citizenship, after which he sailed as a merchant marine for another three years. He saved his earnings with the intention to eventually afford art school training.

In 1905 he worked in New York City as a studio assistant and model for the celebrated illustrator and cartoonist, A. B. Frost (1851-1928).

In October of 1906 he traveled to Paris, where he studied at the Academie Julian.

In 1908 he returned to New York City.

In 1909 he studied with Howard Pyle in Wilmington, Delaware. Other artists that studied with Pyle included N. C. Wyeth, Thornton Oakley, Harvey Dunn, Gayle Hoskins, and Henry C. Kiefer.

Howard Pyle was an enlightened teacher with a spiritual vision that great American art was more likely to grow from commercial illustration in the service of American industry, than from imitating European Art. Pyle was raised as a Quaker and adopted the Swedenborgian faith, which emphasized loving acts of charity. He encouraged his students to follow a wholesome family life, to marry and settle down to hard-working careers as professional illustrators.

In 1910 Anton Otto Fischer returned to New York City and opened an art studio at 15 West 29th Street, from which he sold illustrations to *The Saturday Evening Post, Metropolitan Magazine, Cosmopolitan,* and *Harper's Weekly.*

His artist circle included John Sloan (1871-1851), Art Young (1866-1943), and William Balfour Ker (1877-1918), all of whom worked as newspaper cartoonists and illustrators. On March 25, 1911 the Triangle Shirtwaist Factory infamously burned and killed 146 garment workers, most of whom were ladies between the ages of 16 and 23. In support of the victims he and his socially-conscious friends donated paintings to sell at auction at the Rand College of Social Science, a school for workingmen based on Ruskin's College at Oxford.

William Balfour Ker was married to Mary "May" Ellen Sigsbee Ker. She was also an artist, and they had both been pupils of Howard Pyle when they married in 1899. She was born February 26, 1876, the daughter of Rear Admiral Charles D. Sigsbee, who was in command of the battleship Maine when it blew up in Havana Harbor at the start of the Spanish American War in 1898. Her grandfather was General Henry Hayes Lockwood, a founder of the U.S. Naval Academy. Her family lived at 529 West

112th Street, on Riverside Drive near Columbia University. Their son, David Ker, was born November 9, 1905. On July 28th, 1911 she divorced her husband. Two months later, on October 2, 1912, she married Anton Otto Fischer, who legally adopted and raised her son. They moved to a farm on Bushnellsville Road in Shandaken, NY, from which he continued to sell freelance illustrations to magazines.

In 1914 he became a naturalized U.S. citizen and their daughter Katrina Sigsbee Fischer was born.

During the Great War he was thirty-six years old. He did not serve in the military. He painted recruitment posters for the U.S. Coast Guard.

In 1920 he and his family moved to 164 Elmendorf Street in Kingston, NY.

He painted covers for pulp magazines, such as *Everybody's Magazine, Munsey's, The Popular, Argosy, Top-Notch, Short Stories,* and *Sea Stories.*

The Great Depression ruined the advertising industry and brought hard times to mainstream magazines, which were forced to cut costs. Many artists were forced to look for alternative sources of income, such as pulp magazines, but the fact that Anton Otto Fisher continued to regularly appear in *The Saturday Evening Post* throughout the 1930s indicates the extent of his popular appeal.

In 1940 he and his family moved to Woodstock, NY.

During WWII he was commissioned by the U.S. Coast Guard as a Lieutenant Commander. He again painted inspiring patriotic recruitment posters [Editor's note: See one of these on page 2], but along with these assignments he also shipped out on convoy duty in the North Atlantic aboard the Coast Guard cutter Campbell.

One night while celebrating his sixty-first birthday below deck with crew members, the lookout swept the sea with a searchlight and sighted a German U-Boat at close range. The alarm was sounded and the birthday cake was forgotten as the artist rushed to the ship's bridge to sketch the engagement. According to the ship's officer, "The submarine was rammed and blasted, time and again, by all the guns we could bring to bear. Without time to fire back, the submarine was raked by rapid fire, as well as by our heavier guns, for two brief minutes. Every one of the men on her decks were swept off by our fire while she sank. We hit the jackpot this time, but we were close to being a dead duck ourselves, if there had been another submarine present, we would have been finished."

After the war Anton Otto Fischer wrote his autobiography *Foc'sle Days: A Story of My Youth,* published by Scribners in 1947.

During his forty-five years with *The Saturday Evening Post* he painted a dozen covers, as well as over four hundred story illustrations, the last of which appeared in 1956.

He was widely regarded as America's finest illustrator of adventurous seascapes.

In 1959 he suffered a heart attack, which forced his semi-retirement from painting.

On November 3, 1960 his wife died at the age of eighty-four.

In his later years he followed Yankee baseball and made savvy stock investments that made him a millionaire.

Anton Otto Fischer died in his home in Woodstock, NY, at the age of eighty on March 26, 1962.

© David Saunders 2012

David Saunders is pleasantly surprised to receive an award intended, as PulpFest's website states, "to recognize his substantial service to the pulp community over the years."

Solomon Kane's Homecoming
by Robert E. Howard

The white gulls wheeled above the cliffs, the air was slashed with foam,
The long tides moaned along the strand when Solomon Kane came home.
He walked in silence strange and dazed through the little Devon town,
His gaze, like a ghost's come back to life, roamed up the streets and down.

The people followed wonderingly to mark his spectral stare,
And in the tavern silently they thronged about him there.
He heard as a man hears in a dream the worn old rafters creak,
And Solomon lifted his drinking-jack and spoke as a ghost might speak:

"There sat Sir Richard Grenville once; in smoke and flame he passed.
"And we were one to fifty-three, but we gave them blast for blast.
"From crimson dawn to crimson dawn, we held the Dons at bay.
"The dead lay littered on our decks, our masts were shot away.

"We beat them back with broken blades, till crimson ran the tide;
"Death thundered in the cannon smoke when Richard Grenville died.
"We should have blown her hull apart and sunk beneath the Main."
The people saw upon his wrist the scars of the racks of Spain.

"Where is Bess?" said Solomon Kane. "Woe that I caused her tears."
"In the quiet churchyard by the sea she has slept these seven years."
The sea-wind moaned at the window-pane, and Solomon bowed his head.
"Ashes to ashes, dust to dust, and the fairest fade," he said.

His eyes were mystical deep pools that drowned unearthly things,
And Solomon lifted up his head and spoke of his wanderings.
"Mine eyes have looked on sorcery in dark and naked lands,
"Horror born of the jungle gloom and death on the pathless sands.

"And I have known a deathless queen in a city old as Death,
"Where towering pyramids of skulls her glory witnesseth.
"Her kiss was like an adder's fang, with the sweetness Lilith had,
"And her red-eyed vassals howled for blood in that City of the Mad.

"And I have slain a vampire shape that sucked a black king white,
"And I have roamed through grisly hills where dead men walked at night.
"And I have seen heads fall like fruit in a slaver's barracoon,
"And I have seen winged demons fly all naked in the moon.

"My feet are weary of wandering and age comes on apace;
"I fain would dwell in Devon now, forever in my place."
The howling of the ocean pack came whistling down the gale,
And Solomon Kane threw up his head like a hound that sniffs the trail.

A-down the wind like a running pack the hounds of the ocean bayed,
And Solomon Kane rose up again and girt his Spanish blade.
In his strange cold eyes a vagrant gleam grew wayward and blind and bright,
And Solomon put the people by and went into the night.

A wild moon rode the wild white clouds, the waves in white crests flowed,
When Solomon Kane went forth again and no man knew his road.
They glimpsed him etched against the moon, where clouds on hilltop thinned;
They heard an eery echoed call that whistled down the wind.

Public domain. First published in Fanciful Tales, Fall 1936

Editor's Note: Robert E. Howard (1906-36) was a prolific writer, despite his tragically short life-span. He created Conan the Barbarian, a character many people today are familiar with, because of several Conan movies. A movie was also made of Solomon Kane in 2009. Howard himself was the subject of a movie, The Whole Wide World, based on the memoirs of a teacher who dated him in the mid 1930s.

The Current

TAKING YOU PLACES WORTH SEEING
Volume 5 • Issue 10 • September 2016

FREE!

Movies
Art
Dining
The cosmos

Preview: Kohler Food & Wine Experience

September 2016

In the years since this photo was taken, this structure seems to have been razed. Or otherwise absconded with.

Cover image: Somewhere in the Hinterlands of Washington County.
Great Movies This Month
Stop Hitting the Snooze Bar on Life, by Kirk Barbera
To Win Your World, Risk It All, by Kirk Barbera
Threshold to Host Showcase of Authors in West Bend
Jack Davis
I Ate At... by Richard J. Baumann: Twisted Restaurant & Bar, Sheboygan Falls
Natural Connections by Emily Stone: Mud and Water Daughter
New book by Emily Stone
Stone Wins Writing Awards
Meet a world-class chef in person
PulpArtists by David Saunders: Gloria Stoll Karn

Anita Page, who appears with Buster Keaton in Free and Easy. If you ever send a photo for a movie star to sign, someone who is no longer very famous, you KNOW he/she appreciates hearing from you, when he/she sends your photos back, nicely signed, AND includes an EXTRA photo or two. That's just what happened when I contacted Anita Page back in... back in... now, WHAT year was that?

David Saunders' pulpartists.com

GLORIA STOLL KARN: LOVE AND CRIME

Gloria Maria Stoll was born November 13, 1923 in the Bronx. Her mother was Anne Vera Finamore Stoll and her father was Charles Theophile Stoll. Gloria was their only child. Her father was a WWI veteran and had been awarded the Distinguished Service Cross as well as the Croix de Guerre. He was a commercial artist and a graphic designer working in advertising. They lived at 2083 Davidson Avenue.

When the Great Depression came the father's advertising company closed and the family moved to 4136 Forty-Seventh Street in Sunnyside, Queens.

In 1936 she was among the first students to attend LaGaurdia High School of Music & Art.

In 1938 her father died unexpectedly of a cerebral hemorrhage. Her mother found work as head of the statistical typing department at Universal Pictures in the RCA Building in midtown.

In 1940 after highschool graduation she was awarded a scholarship to the Display Institute, but quit after a few disappointing months of labor. She then found work as a secretary at an insurance company.

One fateful day in April of 1941 she impulsively threw away all of her student artwork. The janitor rescued her portfolio from the incinerator room and showed it to another tenant in the building who happened to be the pulp artist, Rafael DeSoto. DeSoto asked to meet the discouraged seventeen-year-old art student, and inspired her to become a commerical illustrator.

With DeSoto's introduction she sold her first freelance story illustration to a Popular Publication pulp magazine. From 1941 to 1949 she sold story illustrations and cover paintings to All-Story Love, Detective Tales, Dime Mystery, Love Novels, Love Short Stories, New Love, Rangeland Romances, and Romance Western.

She and DeSoto shared a sixth floor skylit art studio at 28 West 65th Street. While earning her living as an illustrator she also continued to study anatomy, etching, watercolor and lithography at evening art classes at the Art Students League and the Society of Illustrators. She had one painting class with Harvey Dunn.

Her pulp artist career abruptly ended when she married Fred Karn on November 13, 1948. They moved to Pittsburgh, PA, where he worked as a scientist for the Bureau of Mines in coal-to-oil research. They have three children and seven grandchildren.

She continued to paint and to make etchings. In the 1950s she began to teach her own art classes. Her work has been exhibited at the Carnegie Museum of Art, the Brooklyn Museum's National Print Annual, and the Pittsburgh Watercolor Society's International Exhibition. Her work is in the permanent collections of Yale University, the Carnegie Museum of Art, Westinghouse Corporation, the Speed Art Museum, the Brooklyn Museum of Art, the Pittsburgh Department of Education. She is listed in Who's Who in American Art.

© David Saunders 2009

Photos from the artist's website, used with the artist's permission

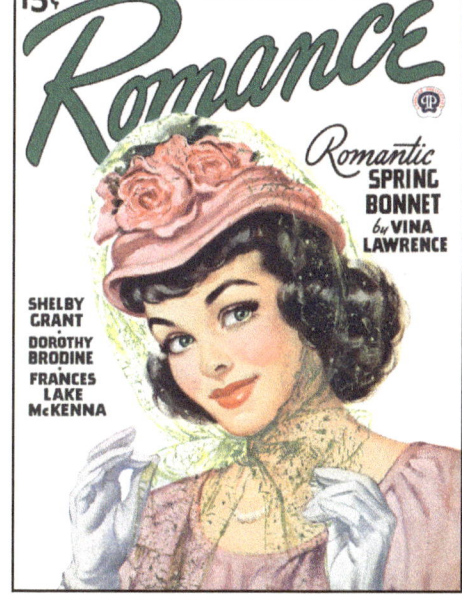

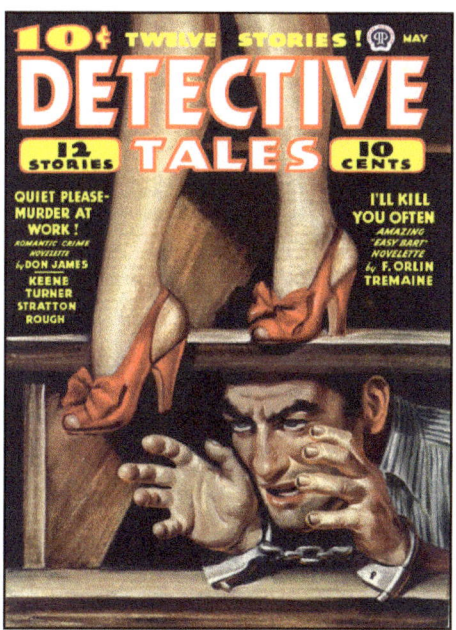

GLORIA STOLL

The pulp fiction magazines died out by the 1950s. So it's understandable that most of the artists who worked for the pulps are no longer with us.

This is the second in a series of pulp artists, taken from David Saunders' website with his kind permission. Browsing a long list of names, my attention was caught by a woman's name.

At the top of the article, the date of Gloria Stoll Karn's birth was given as 1923, but it didn't have— *wait!* Did that mean she's—

I found she has a website, and an e-mail, but... (learned later) not having a computer of her own, she doesn't often check her e-mail.

I sent her a letter, along with several issues of The Current.

And she called me!

We had a very pleasant conversation.

Photos accompanying this article are from Gloria's website, and are used with her permission. Visit her website, click the "Pulp Covers" tab, and you'll see lots more of the covers she did in the 1940s.

Gloria told me of the incredible incident involving Rafael DeSoto, a very prolific and highly regarded pulp artist (see David Saunders' article for details).

Back when there was big demand for illustrators, an artist often got his/her start by doing illustration work, taking an assignment from an art director, submitting several preliminary sketches to the art director for approval, then creating a large, finished work from the approved prelim. Many artists dreamed of the day when they could make a living by drawing or painting what they wanted to create. A few succeeded in doing that (James Bama is one). Some realized that goal on retirement.

I told Gloria that, as much as I like pulp art in general and hers particularly, that I also wanted to feature some of her own personal work. Thus we have "The Gift," a work she did in 2005, based on her own goals and vision. Readers of The Current might be treated to other examples of her work in the future.

Note, 2024: Fired up after talking with Gloria, I devoted the whole centerspread to her. I sent copies to Gloria, and received a very nice voicemail (unfortunately, auto-erased later by the phone app), telling me how surprised and pleased she was with my coverage.

While Gloria was still living, she was recognized by the Norman Rockwell Museum, which features her life and work on their website.

Gloria was one of a few people to whom I regularly mailed The Current. In mid-2022, I received a call from one of her daughters, telling me Gloria had passed away.

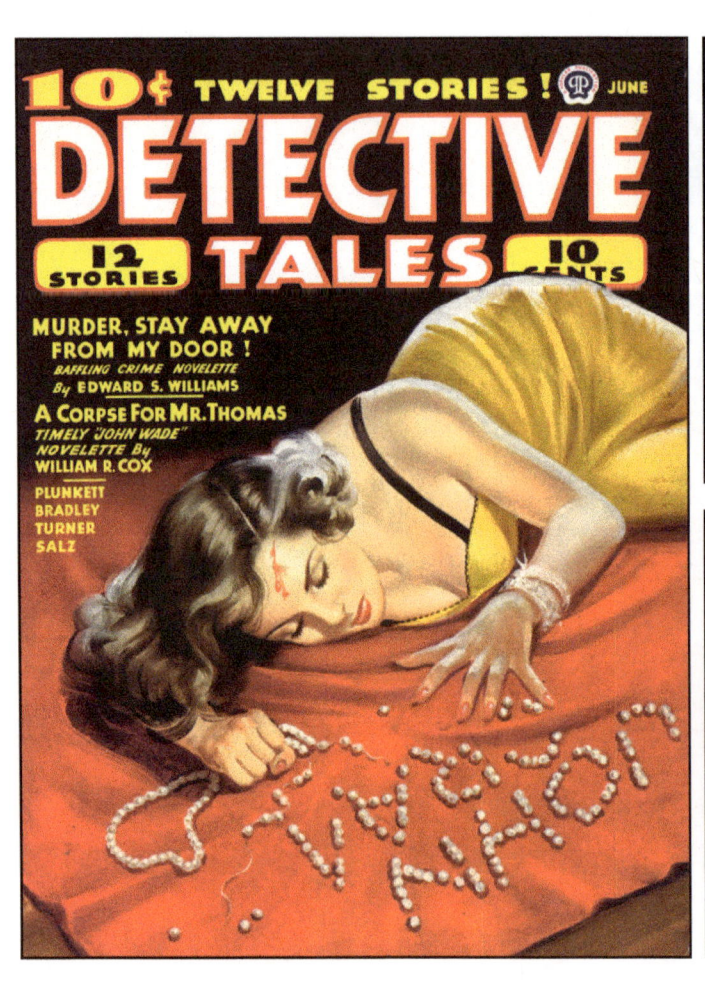

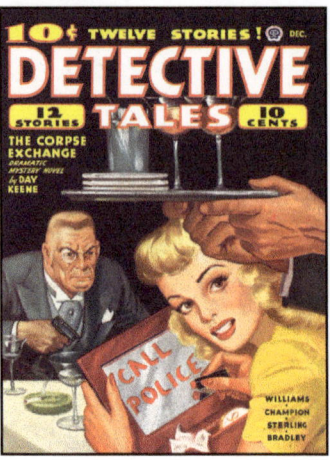

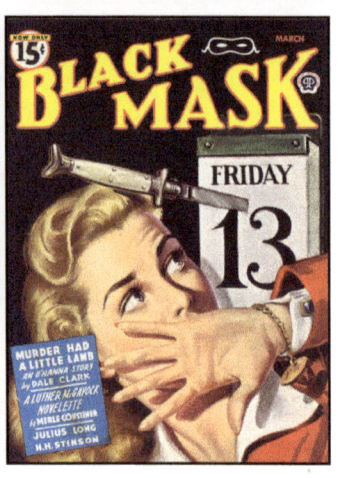

Gloria Stoll Karn comments on her pulp paintings

"In a field dominated by men, it was unusual for a woman to be painting covers for pulp magazines in the 1940s. As a free-lance artist, I often traveled New York subways carrying wet canvases to Popular Publications. Starting in my teens, ideas for romantic scenes came easily as the influence of Hollywood's "boy meets girl" movies was significant. It was also during the time of WWII when uniformed men provided a valiant and romantic presence.

"Noteworthy is the fact that pulp artists were required to come up with ideas for the magazine covers which reflected the general flavor of the stories within. Moving on to painting covers for mystery and detective magazines involved a radical conceptual switch. It was a surprise when I came up with gruesome ideas and concluded that, within the human psyche, there is a shadow side of which we are often unaware. I am grateful that my work struck a balance which uncovered the dark side within along with the light side depicting the joys of romance."

The Current

TAKING YOU PLACES WORTH SEEING
Volume 5 • Issue 11 • October 2016

Arts, Movies, Thrilling escapes, Dining

FREE!

A version of the book, released in conjunction with the film. – From IMDB.com

October 2016

Cover image: Photo by Steve Wilkens
Great Movies This Month
Introduction to the Book, I Am a Fugitive From a Georgia Chain Gang, by the Rev. Vincent G. Burns
Introduction to the Introduction
I Ate At... by Richard J. Baumann: Bread & Bean Eatery, Sheboygan Falls
Jerry Apps, Wisconsin Author
PulpArtists by David Saunders: Roy G. Krenkel
At Theaters Now...

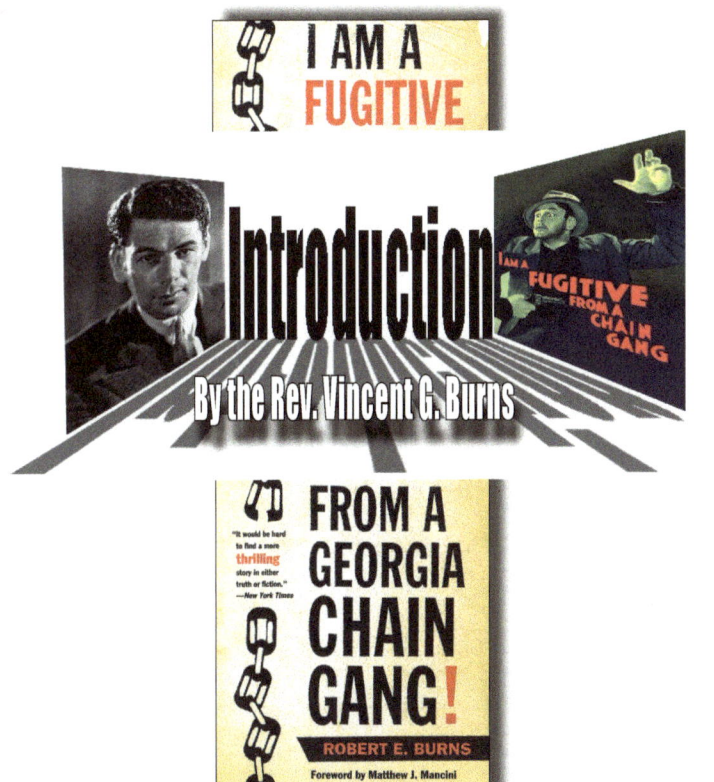

This issue reprinted the long introduction from the book at left. It was the basis for a superb 1931 move with Paul Muni in the starring role.

Drawing by Roy G. Krenkel, from Your Editor's collection.

The Current

TAKING YOU PLACES WORTH SEEING
Volume 5 • Issue 12 • November 2016

FREE!

Master Chefs visit Sheboygan County

November
2016

Cover image: Aarón Sánchez, Amanda Freitag, and Spike Mendelsohn, Kohler Food & Wine Experience

Great Movies This Month

Stanley Kubrick and Emilio, excerpt from Stanley Kubrick and Me, by Emilio D'Alessandro with Filippo Ulivieri

Natural Connections by Emily Stone: Mount Telemark

I Ate At... by Richard J. Baumann: River Wildlife, Kohler

Ask a Science Teacher, by Larry Scheckel: Do Migrating Birds Get Jet Lag?

Tat's Us! by Patti Brethouwer

The Kohler Food & Wine Experience

Breast Cancer Detection: A New Era, by Aurora Health Care

PulpArtists by David Saunders: Ernest Chiriacka

Something to get you thinking about the holidays: an exercise in texture techniques by Mike Hinge, apparently from late 1960 / early 1961. Hinge (1931 – 2003) was born in New Zealand, but became a commercial illustrator / graphic designer in the USA.

You could easily be mystified, looking at this drawing. Nobody is in plain sight, but there are many figures peeking and sneaking between the seats and from the alcoves. What's going on? The answer was on the back of the artwork: This is a convention of private detectives.

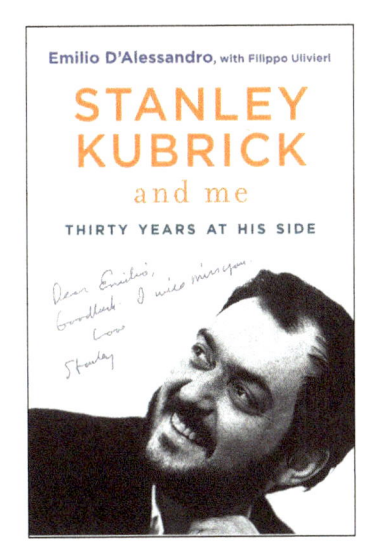

Your Editor contacted Filippo Ulivieri in Italy to seek and receive permission to print an excerpt from this book in this issue. Ulivieri requested and received two copies of the published paper. Much information is available at: www.emiliodalessandro.it/english/

Jon Wos, whose artwork has appeared in several past issues of The Current, poses with 11 paintings he created. This was at the Richeson School of Art & Gallery, 557 Marcella Street in Kimberly, Wisconsin (just east of Appleton).

First column of the series!

Ask a Science Teacher

By Larry Scheckel

Q: Do migrating birds get jet lag?

A:

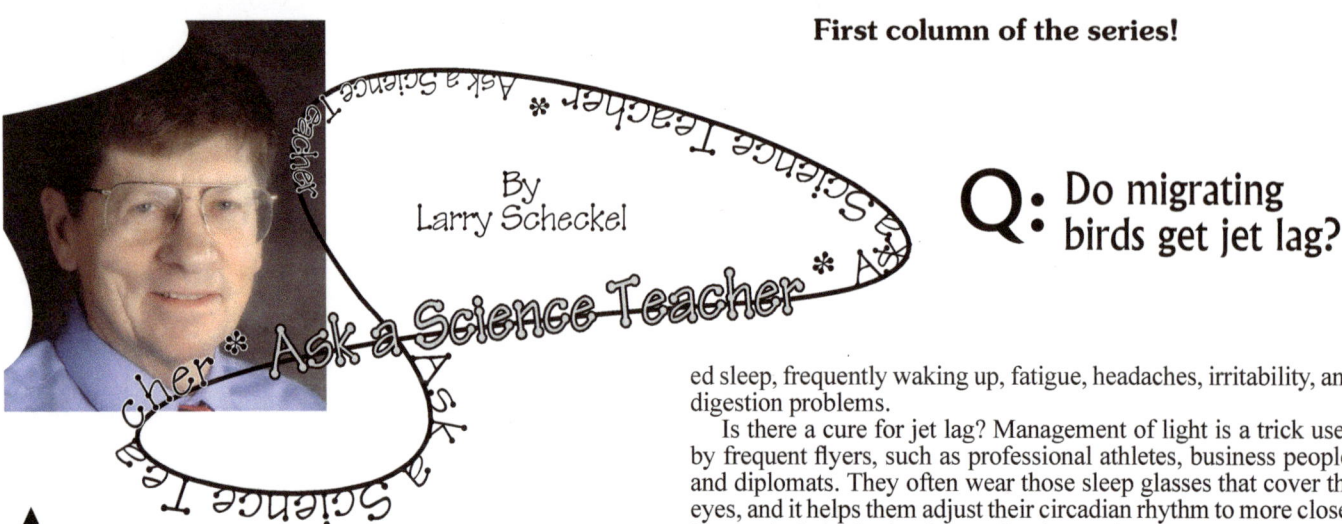

No, birds don't seem to be bothered by jet lag. Jet lag is caused by passing rapidly through time zones. Birds tend to fly between breeding grounds in the north and wintering grounds in the south, most often staying in the same time zone. And if they do cross time zones, they might take several days, if not weeks, to do so.

One could speculate that birds are immune to jet lag because they don't have to put up with lost luggage, extra charges for suitcases, seats made for a butt that is 12 inches wide, seats that recline into your chest, airline food, airport delays, cancelled flights, crying babies in the seats ahead and behind, and overhead bins that are so full they may burst open and conk you on the head.

Birds don't fly from Chicago to Beijing or New York to Australia in one day. They don't really stretch their physical limits unless they are forced to, such as flying over a large body of water. If birds get tired, they land, feed, rest, and continue the next day.

Going east is more difficult on the body than traveling west. Moving east means the body clock has to be advanced. That's harder than going west, where the time zones dictate less advancing of the body clock. Moving east across seven or more time zones, such as flying from Chicago to Rome, or Minneapolis to Oslo, causes the most problems for American travelers.

The medical profession even has a medical term for jet lag, called *circadian dysrhythmia*. The body's clock, or circadian rhythm, gets out of step as it experiences patterns of daylight and darkness different to which it is accustomed. We all have a natural pattern of eating, sleeping, working, and that steady pattern is disturbed.

The most common trouble is getting to sleep if going east, and waking up early if flying west. Difficulties may include interrupted sleep, frequently waking up, fatigue, headaches, irritability, and digestion problems.

Is there a cure for jet lag? Management of light is a trick used by frequent flyers, such as professional athletes, business people, and diplomats. They often wear those sleep glasses that cover the eyes, and it helps them adjust their circadian rhythm to more closely match their destination. Adjusting eating times and amounts, and exercise routines are helpful to many. Fortunately, jet lag only lasts a few days, at most.

Around 2,000 bird species migrate, out of a total of 10,000 bird species. Most fly in flocks, and larger birds, such as geese, travel in the familiar V formation to conserve energy.

The Arctic Tern does one of the longest migrations, flying from its Arctic breeding grounds in the far north to its Antarctic non-breeding places in the far south. The Arctic Tern sees two summers a year and more daylight than any other bird.

Hummingbirds fly very large distances, usually at night. They land in the morning, eat and rest for a few days, then continue on. They fly at night to avoid predators and to prevent overheating by taking advantage of the cooler nights.

The famous song, "When the Swallows Come Back To Capistrano," celebrates the cliff swallows that return each year to the old Spanish Mission at San Juan Capistrano, just south of Los Angeles, California. These mud-nest builders winter in Argentina and fly 6,000 miles to return to the Mission, arriving on March 19, St. Joseph's Day. They fly back south to Argentina, leaving on October 23, St. John's Day.

If you visit the Great Stone Church at San Juan, look for the swallows and their mud nests. It is the oldest building in California, erected in 1782. Beautiful grounds, many artifacts, a most peaceful place.

Did you hear about the two birds migrating south, flying over Camp Randall Stadium at UW-Madison? The football game below was between the Badgers and the Ohio State Buckeyes. The one bird asked, "Who do you think will win that game down there?" His aviating buddy, winking mischievously, replied, "Well, I don't know, but I just put everything I had on the Buckeyes."

David Saunders'

pulpartists.com

ERNEST CHIRIACKA: "DARCY"

(1913-2010)

Anastassios Kyriakakos was born in New York City on May 11, 1913. His parents were Greek immigrants, Portia and Herakles Kyriakakos. They came to America in 1907 from the mountain village Xero Cambi in the Sparta region of Greece. Anastassios was their third child. The family lived at 42 Madison Street in the Lower East Side. His father was a peddler and laborer.

Ernest Chiriacka is the transliterated English equivalent of Anastassios Kyriakakos. The familiar form of the name Anastassios is "Tassi," which sounds like the English name "Darcy."

In 1927, as an industrious teenager, he painted signs for local stores, and was hired to work at a professional sign painting shop.

In 1932 he studied drafting, lettering, and illustration at the Mechanics Institute on 20 West 44th Street, which is the city's oldest tuition-free evening school for college-level technical training.

He worked for two years at a display company and studied advanced illustration with Harvey Dunn at the Grand Central School of Art. He married his wife Katherine in 1937 and they moved to an apartment in Brooklyn.

In 1939 his first published story illustrations appeared in Street & Smith's pulp magazine *Love Story*.

He sold freelance pulp covers for *Ace-High Western, Adventure, Big Book Western, Black Book Detective, Detective Fiction Weekly, Dime Western, Exciting Detective, Fifteen Western Tales, 44. Western, G-Men Detective, New Detective, Phantom Detective, Rodeo Romances, Star Western, Sweetheart Stories, Ten Detective Aces, 10-Story Western, Texas Rangers, Thrilling Mystery, West,* and *Western Aces*.

According to Harry Steeger, owner of Popular Publications, "I like Chiriacka's pulp covers, because when his women are screaming, they almost look like they might be laughing!"

His pulp covers were usually left unsigned, and he used a variety of psuedonyms, such as Acka, Darcy, and A.D. He is given printed credit as "Ernest Chiriacka" on the contents pages of only a few Ace Magazine titles.

He was not eligible for military service in WW2, because of a pre-diabetic health condition, so he was among the few professional pulp cover artists to remain fully active during the war years, and as such his work was in great demand.

In 1950 he joined the American Artists Agency and began a successful career as a slick magazine illustrator for *American Magazine, Colliers, Coronet, Argosy, Saturday Evening Post,* and *Esquire,* where his pin-up calendar art brought him his greatest renown.

In 1952 he and Katherine moved to a splendid mansion in Great Neck, Long Island, where they raised their two children, Leonard and Athene.

He painted many paperback covers up until 1965, and then retired from commercial illustration to concentrate on painting visionary landscapes of the Old West, which have continued to attract appreciative collectors at fine art galleries around the world.

Ernest Darcy Chiriacka died peacefully, surrounded by family and friends, at his home in Great Neck, NY, at the age of ninety-six on April 26, 2010.

© David Saunders
2009

A few years ago, Your Editor bid on two paintings by Chiriacka at an online auction. I watched as the first piece soared above and beyond my modest bid. When final bidding started on the second piece, I figured "Forget about it," expecting the numbers to once again leave my bid in the dust. But no. Nobody bid above me. I got it. *I got it!* And here it is, in all its rough glory. Chiriacka initialed it "E.C." in the upper left area. (By the way, does anyone recognize this from a book they have?) – HA.com

Chiriacka signs something for an eager fan, who is hovering over him like some kind of vulture and— hey, *wait* a minute, that's Your Editor!

Two unidentified young ladies, thrilled to meet a living legend. The woman at right is Athene, Ernest Chiriacka's daughter, who accompanied Chiriacka on his trips.

77

Editor's Notes:

Saunders is perhaps too modest to mention the fact that, through some incredible detective work on his part, he "discovered" Ernest Chiriacka to be the uncredited artist of many pulp covers, and that Chiriacka was still alive when he made this discovery. Saunders wrote up this process of discovery, which reads like a detective mystery. It was published in Illustration magazine. Saunders also conducted a lengthy interview with Chiriacka.

Because of Saunders' efforts to identify him, Chiriacka was invited to be the Guest of Honor at the 2005 Windy City Pulp and Paper Show. Those in charge of that show baked a large cake, with images of pulp covers Chiriacka had done; one photo here shows him enjoying a piece.

Chiriacka also appeared at the 2006 PulpCon in Dayton, Ohio, and at 2006's Windy City show.

An explanation of two terms in Saunders' article: a "pulp" was a magazine printed on coarse, *pulpy* paper, and had nothing to do with the type of fiction printed on it. A "slick" was printed on (are you ready for this?) *slick* paper. (Some magazines used both slick and pulp paper in the same issue.)

Thus, Saunders' statement that Chiriacka became a "slick magazine illustrator" does not mean that Chiriacka was a "slick illustrator" (though the word "awesome" would be appropriate); rather, that Chiriacka was an illustrator for "slick magazines."

Kohler Food & Wine Guest Chefs

Spike Mendelsohn

Aarón Sánchez

Amanda Freitag

Chiriacka did the cover for this 1940s pulp, and I asked him to sign it. I didn't read "Heads for Homicide" inside this issue, so I don't know what's going on here... but you have to admit, a scene of a guy carving fake shrunken heads is hilarious. (It's *not*?) When I asked Chiriacka to sign it, he said, "Oh, I remember that guy. That was Louie the Jerk!" (Chiriacka, and other illustrators, relied on models for their work. Was he speaking of the *character* he painted, or his *model*?)

Nice story-telling on this Chiriacka cover. The robber (see his mask?) was tricked by bags of nuts and bolts, so he's planning revenge. I'm not a weapons expert, so I have to ask: Is that how you load this gun? – HA.com

78

The Current

TAKING YOU PLACES WORTH SEEING
Volume 6 • Issue 1 • December 2016

FREE!

Glass sculpture by Dale Chihuly

* Culture * Movies * Arts * Dining * Travel *

December
2016

Cover image: The Gallery Featuring Dale Chihuly at the Aria, Las Vegas

Rovings and Ravings

Great Movies This Month

Malthusian Theory Is History, by Rob Tracinski

Inferno and the Overpopulation Myth, by Jonathan Newman, mises.org

PulpArtists by David Saunders: Julius Erbit

The Value of Reading a Biography

Echoes of our past by William & Joy Wangemann: Sheboygan River Was I-43 of its Day, from Fruit to Furniture

The story of Gyp

Ask a Science Teacher, by Larry Scheckel: Are there scientific achievements that were overlooked and didn't get a lot of attention?

I Ate At... by Richard J. Baumann: Hub City Family Restaurant, Plymouth

Art by Chihuly

In Theaters Now...

Enjoying a special meal

Glass sculptures by Dale Chihuly

Something for the Holidays...

This drawing is by Mike Hinge (can you find his name?), and was probably done in the early 1960s. I don't know if it was published. A humor magazine called Help! was published that same time, and cartoons would often incorporate the word "Help!" into the drawing, so that's a possibility.

Art by Chihuly

The Gallery Featuring Dale Chihuly (now closed) rested at the foot of skyscrapers. LEFT: In the background is the Aria, part of the City Center complex that was built in the past decade. RIGHT: The 37-story Veer Towers lean slightly. That was deliberate. Don't let any cab driver tell you the construction crew had too much to drink the night before they were built.

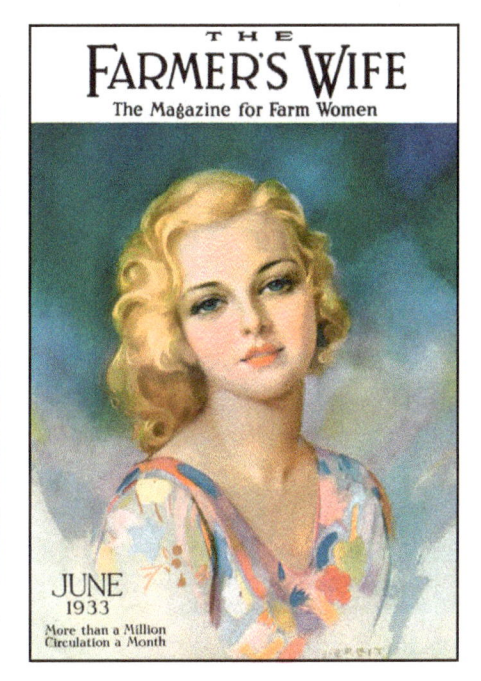

Cover art by Julius Erbit

Art by Kuster

Two courses at Restaurant Guy Savoy, Las Vegas. ABOVE: Chef Julien Asseo prepares "Salmon Iceberg." After resting on the block of pink Himalayan salt at right, it is seared on each side on the block of dry ice. BELOW: "Colors of Caviar," with caviar hidden between the top two layers.

Some people, driving I-43 just north of State 28 at Interstate speeds, catch a glimpse of these glass pieces and think they are by Dale Chihuly.

They are actually the work of Robert Kuster.

Kuster was commissioned by the CEO of Acuity to create seven glass spheres for the company's corporate headquarters. Installation was completed in 2004.

The set was named "The Seven Sisters," after the star cluster Pleiades that leads Orion in the winter sky. A PBS documentary, "The Seven Sisters, A Creation in Glass," was televised in 2005.

Two more spheres were added only recently, as the building undergoes expansion, but the set is not being renamed "Nine Sisters" (because the Pleiades actually has more than seven stars, and... well, that's a long story).

Thanks to Paul Miller, Communications Manager at Acuity, for allowing me to photograph the Kuster spheres, and for providing interesting information on them.

2017

January 2017

Cover image: Your Editor's Side Yard
Great Movies This Month
The Career and Art of Steranko
Making an Investment in Live Entertainment, by Jim Steranko
Films that influenced Steranko
Natural Connections by Emily Stone: Have You Ever Smelled a Garter Snake?
Echoes of our past by William & Joy Wangemann: Sheboygan's Horrific Winters
Feedback to Think About (objecting to previous month's pieces on overpopulation)
Excerpt from The Ultimate Resource, by Julian Simon
Ask a Science Teacher, by Larry Scheckel: Did an Advanced Technological Civilization Live Here on Earth or Visit the Earth a Long Time Ago?
I Ate At... by Richard J. Baumann: Gosse's at the Northwestern House, Sheboygan
PulpArtists by David Saunders: Norman Saunders
It's More than Makeup...

David Saunders compiled this book, a tribute to his father's life and career.

February 2017

Cover image: Truffles in Milwaukee / Truffles in Kohler
Great Movies This Month
Fake News?
Annie Sets an Example
New Year's Eve Dinner at the Blind Horse, Kohler
Truffle Dinner at the Lake Park Bistro, Milwaukee
PulpArtists by David Saunders: Nina Albright
Natural Connections by Emily Stone: Science of Nature Has Great Stories for Children to Enjoy
I Ate At... by Richard J. Baumann: City Club Tavern & Grill, Plymouth
Ask a Science Teacher, by Larry Scheckel: Why Is There That Big E on the Top of Eye Charts?
Echoes of our past by William & Joy Wangemann: Playing the Name Game

The Current

TAKING YOU PLACES WORTH SEEING
Volume 6 • Issue 4 • March 2017

FREE!

Model Sheboygan Museum Railroad

*Trains of thought * Train Movies * Train Novels*

March 2017

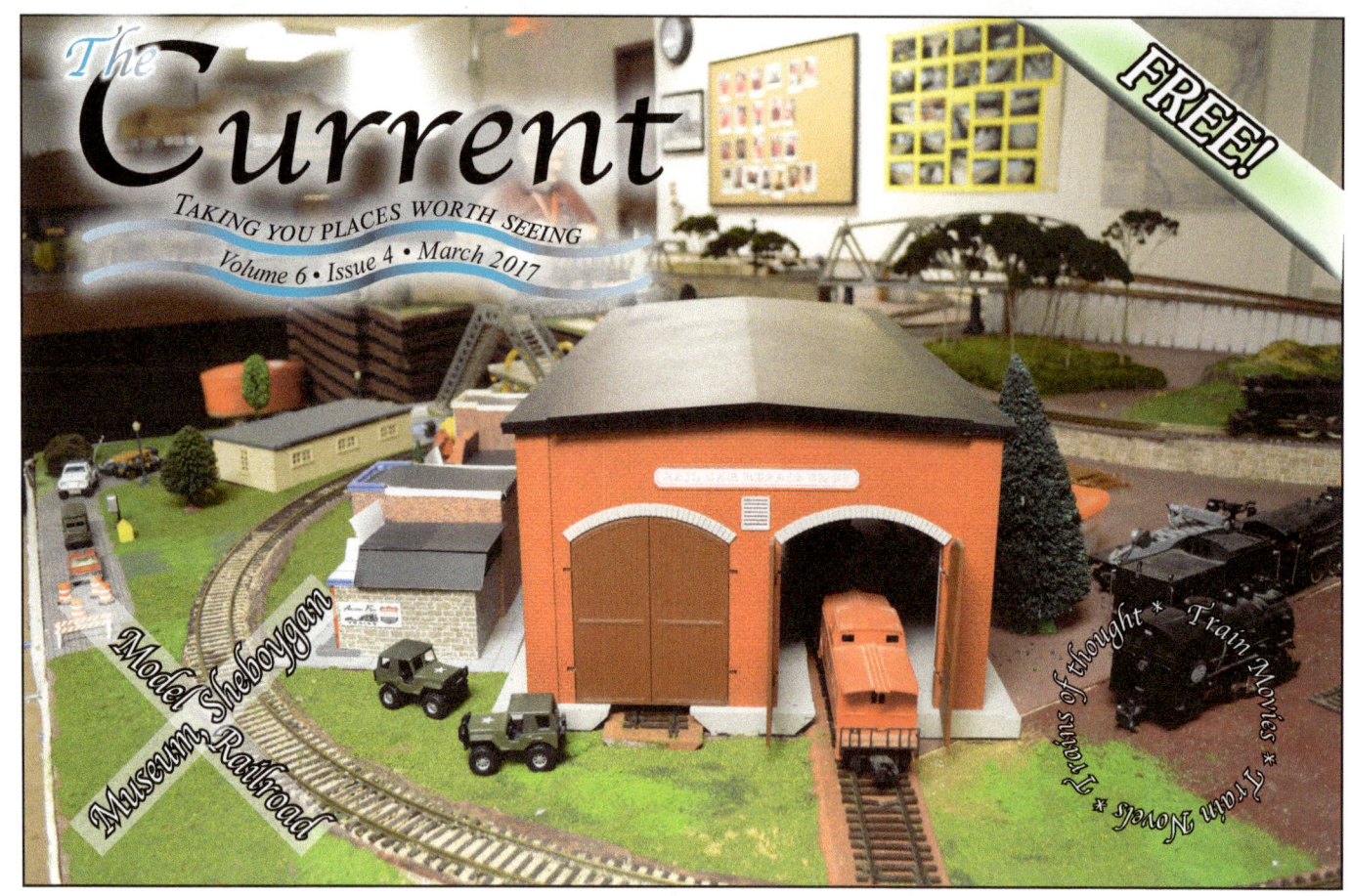

This was the first issue produced using printing facilities other than that owned by The Review.

Cover image: The Sheboygan Railroad Museum

Great Movies This Month

Science Without Numbers, by Robert Tracinski

The New York Times Thinks You're Too Dumb to Understand Numbers, by Robert Tracinski

PulpArtists by David Saunders: Walter Baumhofer

I Ate At... by Richard J. Baumann: St. John the Baptist Church, Plymouth

The Incomparable Hildegarde, by Gary Feider

Ask a Science Teacher, by Larry Scheckel: What is the "God Particle"?

The Sheboygan Railroad Museum

The Greatest Train Novel Ever? (Atlas Shrugged)

The Greatest Railroad Magazine Ever? (Railroad Stories)

The Greatest Railroad Movie Ever? (The General)

Feedback to Think About (objecting to Rob Tracinski's two articles in this issue)

Whooper Whereabouts

Nearly 40 years ago, Your Editor purchased this publicity photo, signed by Alfred Hitchcock and Gregory Peck (looks like he was in a hurry to sign his name) (and the cigarette looks fake). A "publicity photo" was not used in the movie, but often taken on the set. The film being made here was Spellbound. The actress in the center is Ingrid Bergman. The story of the film involved psychoanalysis, and featured dream sequences painted by Salvador Dali. – Scan by Rodney Schroeter

The Incomparable Hildegarde

by Gary Feider
Special to the Current

Editor's Note: The following appeared in The Random Lake Sounder's editorial section of April 16, 1992, and is printed here with permission.

The most famous entertainer to come from the Village of Adell was inducted into the Wisconsin Performing Artists Hall of Fame on Sunday in Milwaukee.

Of course, we're talking about the Incomparable Hildegarde. She delighted the nearly 1,800 in attendance at the Performing Arts Center in Milwaukee with an uninterrupted 90-minute reprise of her dynamic show, "Hildegarde! Alive at 85 Plus."

Few of today's Adell residents can recall ever seeing this star on the village streets. She was born there as Hildegarde Loretta Sell—in what is now Schwab's Scooter Bar on Maine Ave. Her family moved to New Holstein shortly thereafter, and 12 years later they moved to Milwaukee.

New York impressario Gus Edwards convinced her to shorten her name around 1930. Walter Winchell eventually added the famous adjective. The Incomparable Hildegarde is listed under "I" at the Actors Equity headquarters. Her rise to fame includes many interesting stories. King Gustave of Sweden had come to the Cassanova Club in Paris to hear Hildegarde sing. She had been fired the night before, but the king insisted that she be rehired. From that point on her career soared.

The Incomparable Hildegarde is 86 years young, and we wish her all the best.

Come to think of it, wouldn't a "Hildegarde Street" be a nice addition to the Village of Adell map? She's a star worth singing about!

The Incomparable Hildegarde, born in Adell. The village of Adell is currently considering renaming a street after her, putting up a sign to honor her, or both. – Public domain photo from Wikipedia

Some people have their acts together, and a very clear sense of priorities. Painting by Walter Baumhofer. – This and other images for this article: HA.com

David Saunders used the image from the first Doc Savage pulp for this thick, detailed book about Baumhofer. – From David Saunders' Pulpmags.com

Walter Baumhofer: Doc Artist

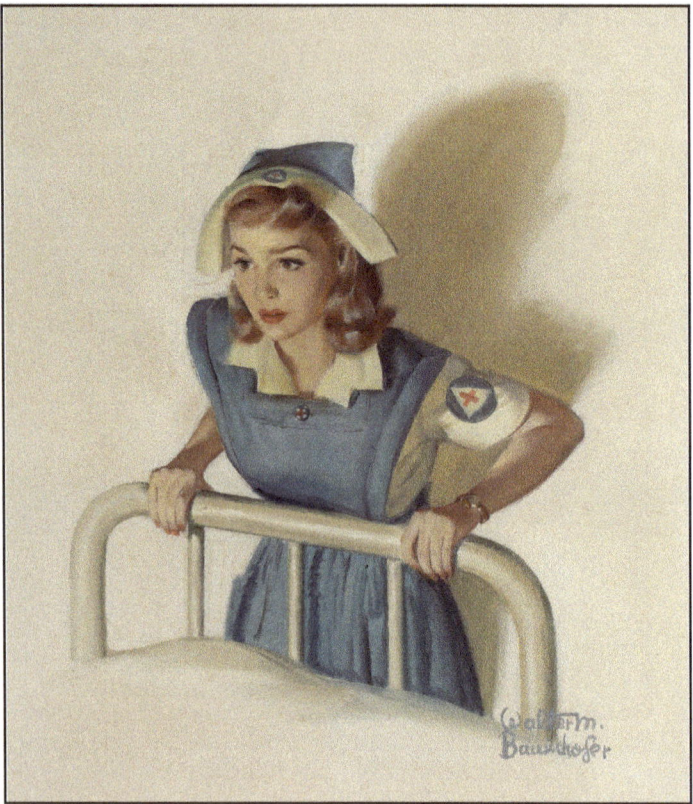

(1904-1987)

Walter Martin Baumhofer was born November 1, 1904 in Brooklyn. His parents were German immigrants, Marie and Henry Baumhofer. They had two sons, Richard and Walter. They lived at 92 Ralph Avenue. The father was a clerk at a local coffee company.

In 1918 his father lost his job and was hired as the janitor of an apartment building at 1498 Bushwick Avenue, where the family was able to live rent free. When tenants needed a plumber, he would hire a local one, named George Gould, who lived two doors away at 1502 Bushwick Avenue. That plumber's twelve-year-old son was John Fleming Gould, who became Walt's best friend. They went to school together.

In 1919, at the age of fourteen, he accidentally blew three fingers off his left hand while handling a live round of ammunition, which was a relic of the Great War. The accident left him unfit for manual labor, so he began to seriously pursue a career as an artist. He graduated high school in 1922 and was given a scholarship to attend Pratt Institute. John Gould joined him there one year later. They both studied under Dean Cornwell and H. Winfield Scott.

In 1925, while still an art student, he began his career by drawing pen & ink story illustrations for *Adventure* magazine. His painting teacher, H. Winfield Scott, convinced him to think more ambitiously about working for the pulps, and to submit unsolicited cover paintings instead of waiting for more drawing assignments. Baumhofer followed his advice and in 1926 sold his first pulp cover to Clayton Publications for *Danger Trail*.

In 1930 he married his wife, Alureda, whose nickname was "Pete."

He quickly became the top cover artist. He created the first covers of *Doc Savage*, *The Spider*, and *Pete Rice*.

In 1937 he joined the American Artists agency and began to sell freelance illustrations to slick magazines, such as *American Weekly, Colliers, Cosmopolitan, Country Gentleman, Esquire, Liberty, McCall's, Redbook,* and *Woman's Day*.

During WWII he was thirty-nine years old and missing three fingers, so he was exempt from military service.

In 1945, the Baumhofers moved to 56 School Street in Northport New York, on Long Island, where they lived for the rest of their lives.

In the 1950s, he worked for men's adventure magazines, such as *Argosy, Outdoor Life, Sports Afield,* and *True*.

After he retired from freelance magazine illustration, he stayed very busy painting and exhibiting portraits, landscapes, and scenes of the Old West at fine art galleries nationwide.

In 1978, he was thrilled to be "rediscovered" by enthusiastic fans of pulp magazines. He was a guest speaker and the Guest of Honor at several conventions. He was also featured and interviewed in several fanzines.

Walter M. Baumhofer died at age eighty-two on September 23, 1987.

© David Saunders 2009

Painting by Walter Baumhofer.

April 2017

Cover image: Work Area
Great Movies This Month
Echoes of our past by William & Joy Wangemann: Snow Me The Way To Go Home Like In The Old Days Enlightenment Values In Your Life
Ask a Science Teacher, by Larry Scheckel: If There Is No Air in Space, What Caused Air to Form on the Planets and Why Can't We See Air?
Mystery Science Theater 3000
I Ate At... by Richard J. Baumann: Schwarz's Supper Club, New Holstein
Two Books On The Methodology Of Science
Natural Connections by Emily Stone: Needle Ice a Result of Unsettled Weather Patterns
PulpArtists by David Saunders: Casimir B. Mayshark
The Hindenburg

David Saunders' pulpartists.com

CASIMIR B. MAYSHARK: AVIATION ARTIST

(1912-1978)

Casimir Benton "Duke" Mayshark was born Casimir Mieczyslaus Mayshark, Jr., on January 3, 1912 in Sacramento, California. His father, Casimir Mieczyslaus Mayshark, was born in 1881 in Poland and came to the U.S. in 1893 and settled in San Francisco, California.

The family name Mayshark is an English transliteration of the Polish name in the Cyrillic alphabet, so U.S. immigration officials had to assign approximate phonetic equivalents. Other members of the same family who came to the U.S. were assigned various names of similar sounds, such as "Maycherczyk," "Marzajek," "Majchrzak," and "Mazureck."

The father was a commercial artist in the advertising industry of San Francisco. It was the father's second marriage, the first one having ended unhappily, after he deserted his wife and two sons in Missouri.

The mother, Oreon Gracie Page, was born in 1875 in Mississippi, so she was six years older than her husband. She was also an artist. She designed and decorated Art Nouveau china. It was also her second marriage, the first one having ended after one year, when her husband, Percy Frank Wilson (1878-1906), the city editor of the Memphis News Scimitar, died of typhoid fever on January 15, 1906. After his death she lived with her parents in El Paso, Texas, where she operated a private art school.

In 1908 she advertised her classes in the local newspaper. By 1910 she had moved to Los Angeles, California, where she met and married Casimir Mieczyslaus Mayshark on May 7, 1910. They had two children, Casimir Mieczyslaus Mayshark, Jr., (b. 1912), and his younger brother, James Page Mayshark, born June 5, 1913. The family lived at 278 29th Avenue in San Francisco.

On May 25, 1913 *The San Francisco Call* reported in the Art Notes column by Porter Garnett, "Casimir M. Mayshark has recently shown a landscape at the Bohemian Club. This is the first easel picture that Mr. Mayshark, who has specialized in scenic decoration in European and Eastern theaters, has exhibited here. It arrests the attention immediately by its personal quality, its quietness and its altogether delightful color."

In 1913 the San Francisco Sketch Club organized a poster contest to commemorate the city's patron saint, Saint Francis. On November 1, 1913 *The San Francisco Call* published the results of the contest. Casimir M. Mayshark was listed as an entrant but failed to win the $500 prize, which went to the NYC artist Adolph Treidler (1886-1981).

In 1914 Casimir M. Mayshark, with his wife and two sons, moved to El Paso, Texas, where they lived with the mother's family and the father worked as a manager of the Tuttle System outdoor advertising agency.

In 1915 Casimir M. Mayshark, with his wife and two sons, moved to the East Coast to pursue his career as a Commercial artist in New York City. The family lived at 24 Van Dyke Place in Summit, New Jersey. The father commuted by ferry boat to NYC, where he worked as a freelance commercial artist.

On September 12, 1918 during the Great War Casimir M. Mayshark registered with the draft board. He listed his occupation as Poster Designer. He was recorded to be of medium height, slender build, with blue eyes and brown hair. He was thirty-six, married and supporting two young sons, so he was not selected for military service.

In 1919 the father deserted the family and was never heard from again. Casimir, Jr., was age seven and James was age six. After the marriage was legally dissolved, Casimir Mieczyslaus Mayshark, Jr., was renamed Casimir Benton Mayshark.

The mother and two sons moved to Chatham, New Jersey, where they lived at 222 Hillside Avenue. She supported the family as a commercial artist designing decorative wall paper for a manufacturer.

The father had moved to Atlantic City, NJ, where he worked as a sign painter.

On September 15, 1920 Casimir M. Mayshark addressed the 11th Annual Convention of the Outdoor Advertising Association, held in Cleveland, Ohio. His lecture topic was "Color in Outdoor Advertising."

In 1925 Casimir M. Mayshark married his third wife, Jesse Whitney. She was born in 1889 in New Hampshire. They lived with her brother's family at 54 Turner Street in Boston, Massachusetts, where he worked as an Interior Decorator. They had two children, Cyrus, born August 3, 1926, who grew up to become an author, and Mary, born May 5, 1928, who grew up to become Mrs. Mary Mayshark Perkins.

In 1929 the father, Casimir M. Mayshark, lived with his third wife and two children at 54 Conant Street in Roxbury, MA, but the following year he again deserted his third wife and two children, after which that marriage was legally dissolved.

In June of 1930 Casimir Benton "Duke" Mayshark graduated from Chatham High School. He had always liked to draw, but by high school he had become interested in a career as a commercial artist.

In 1931 he attended the University of Alabama, where he completed his freshman year. The Great Depression brought hard times to most American families, which made college difficult to afford. By 1932 his younger brother, James Mayshark, had graduated high school with a promising record in football and a dream to play in college, so Casimir Benton "Duke" Mayshark entered the work force instead of returning to Alabama after his freshman year. His brother became a star player with the Mountain Hawks of Lehigh University in Bethlehem, PA.

In 1932 C. B. Mayshark began to work as a commercial artist in NYC publishing and advertising. He attended night school art classes at the Art Students League at 215 West 57th Street, where his best teacher was Morris Kantor (1896-1974).

In 1934 C. B. Mayshark painted covers for the pulp magazines *Sky Birds* and *Flying Aces.* He also drew pen-and-ink interior story illustrations for these two titles. In addition, he wrote several descriptive articles about his cover paintings, which were featured inside the magazines. He signed his work for pulp magazines "C. B. Mayshark" and "C.B.M."

The 1940 NYC Business Directory listed the art studio of C. B. Mayshark at 15 West 51st Street, between Fifth and Sixth Avenues.

In 1941 he was hired as a staff artist at the James M. Mathes Advertising Company in the prestigious Chanin Building, at 122 East 42nd Street, where Street & Smith, Ideal Publishing, and Decker Publications also had offices. While working at the advertising company he met Helen Lucille Dunaway. She was born December 30, 1919 in Yonkers, New York, and was a graduate of Smith College. She worked as a clerical secretary at J. M. Mathes.

By 1941 his estranged father, Casimir M. Mayshark, had moved to San Diego, California, where he worked as a draftsman for the Simpson Construction Company at the San Diego Naval Training Station. He lived in a lodging house at 432 F Street.

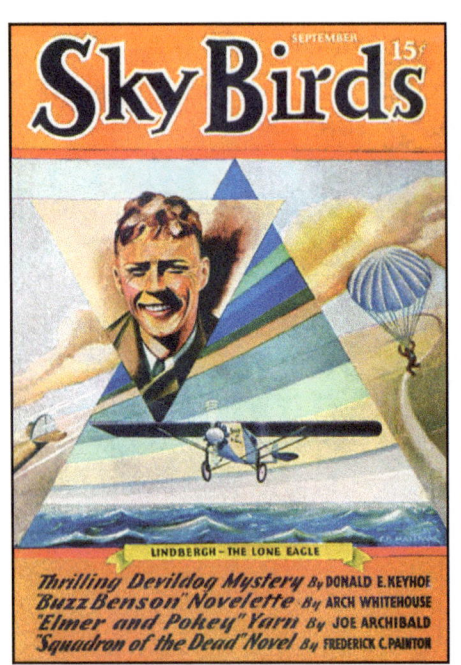

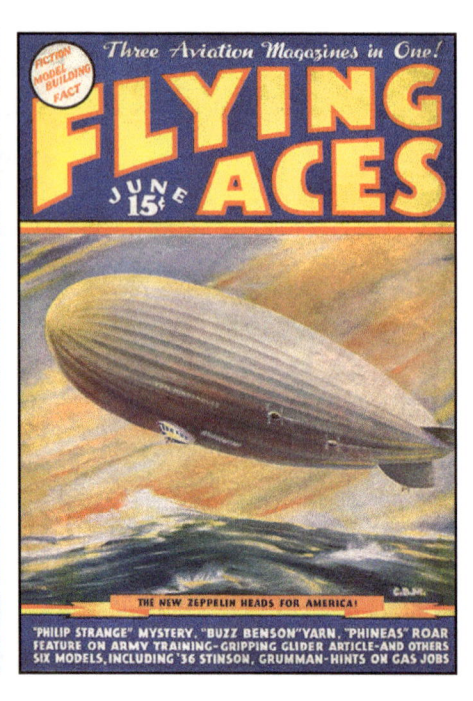

In 1943 Casimir Benton Mayshark was drafted. Before entering service he married Helen Lucille Dunaway. They eventually had three children, Joseph (b. 1944), Cassandra (b. 1946), and Sanford (b. 1951). The family lived in Forest Hills, Queens, NY.

During WWII C. B. Mayshark served as a Second Lieutenant in the Army Air Corps, 17th Bomber Wing, Second Air Corps, Radio Division. He was stationed at an air base in Idaho, where he painted a mural in Building 23 of the air base. He was not sent overseas.

His younger brother, James P. Mayshark, served as a Captain in the Army Tank Corps and was wounded in North Africa.

On 1943 nationwide newspapers covered the poignant story of his mother, Mrs. Oreon Page Mayshark, and her remarkable experience as she sat in a Times Square movie theater and watched a wartime newsreel with dramatic battle scenes, and suddenly recognized her son as he was wounded in combat.

After the war, C. B. "Duke" Mayshark started Mayshark & Keyes Advertising Art Company with a partner, Bill Keyes. The company grew successful during the post-war years.

His brother, James P. Mayshark, became a salesman of Pneumatic tools and moved to Buffalo, NY.

In 1950 C. B. Mayshark sold his share in the business to his partner and retired to Santa Fe, New Mexico, where he designed and built the family home.

In 1952 he was appointed Director of the New Mexico State Tourist Bureau, of the State Department of Development, under Governor Ed Mechem.

In 1954 that political appointment ended, after which C. B. Mayshark started Mayshark Lithographing Company, which printed jobs for the public, but also won contracts to print posters for the New Mexico State Tourism Bureau.

In 1962 Casimir B. Mayshark's mother, Oreon Gracie Page Mayshark, died at the age of eighty-seven in Santa Fe, where she had lived with the family.

In 1962 C. B. Mayshark closed the printing company when he was appointed Administrative Assistant for New Mexico Governor Jack Campbell.

In 1964 C. B. Mayshark became Executive Secretary to the Governor of New Mexico, in charge of Promotion of Business and Tourism with national advertising campaigns, New Mexico Magazine, and the organization of the New Mexico State Exhibition at the 1964 World's Fair in NYC.

The father, Casimir Mieczyslaus Mayshark, returned to San Fransisco, where he lived at 715 Clementina Street, and continued to work as a Commercial Artist, until he died at the age of eighty-four on November 5, 1965.

In 1966 C. B. Mayshark was the Director of the New Mexico Department of Development.

In 1968 C. B. Mayshark retired from New Mexico State politics and concentrated on making art. His work was exhibited at the University of New Mexico, St. John's College in Santa Fe, and the University of Hawaii.

C. B. "Duke" Mayshark (age sixty-six) and his wife, Helen Lucille Mayshark (age fifty-eight), were fatally injured in an automobile accident in Albuquerque, NM, on September 28, 1978.

© David Saunders 2015

Two Books on the Methodology of Science

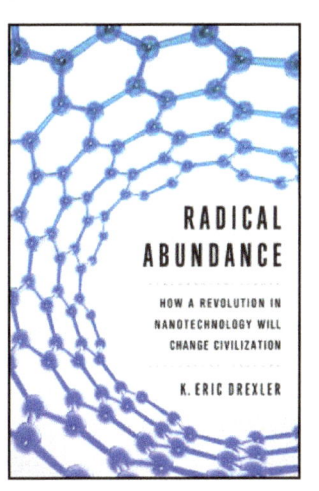

Images from Barnes & Noble, BN.com

Interested in how scientists conduct their craft?

The Logical Leap by David Harriman explores the role that induction plays in scientific discovery, and uses the work of Galileo as a prime example.

"Induction" is the process of looking at many specific things or actions, and drawing a generalization from your observations. It's a process people perform all the time.

The *"Radical Abundance"* in Drexler's title refers to a mind-boggling implication of the field of nanotechnology—the ability to manipulate things on a very small, even molecular level. If this technology becomes available, it would be possible to manufacture just about anything so cheaply and so plentifully, that the resulting abundance would, Drexler believes, truly change civilization.

(This, by the way, is an example of "deduction," of taking a general principle or basic fact, and applying it in a more specific way.)

While that's the thesis of the book, Drexler explores something else of interest. He spends some chapters exploring the difference in methodology between scientists, who discover natural laws, and engineers, who apply those laws. If you know any students planning to go into engineering or the sciences, but are not sure what direction they really want to take, this book could help them with that choice.

Last month, we ran this 1921 Country Gentleman cover (yes, farmers *are* capable of being gentlemen—or gentlewomen; I know quite a few of them). I didn't know the term for the special, double-slatted stick the clown is about to use. Well, leave it to amateur popular-culture historian, bon vivant, man-about-town and artiste extraordinaire William F. Messner-Loebs to know the technical name for that tool. It's a "slap stick," which led to the term "slapstick comedy." (We will run an outstanding example of Messner-Loebs' work in a near-future issue of The Current.) – Scan by Rodney Schroeter

The Current

Taking you places worth seeing

Volume 6 • Issue 6 • May 2017

FREE!

Movies ◆ Art ◆ Dining ◆ Tools that Feed the World

May
2017

Cover image: Gibbsville Implement, Waldo
Great Movies This Month
PulpArtists by David Saunders: Alex Schomburg
Follow-Up: Casimir B. Mayshark
Natural Connections by Emily Stone: Just Take Two Willows and See Me in the Morning
Book Review: On Tyrrany, by Barry Johanson
I Ate At... by Richard J. Baumann: Quit Qui Oc Golf Course, Elkhart Lake
Echoes of our past by William & Joy Wangemann: Remembering Is the Key to a True Memorial Day
Ask a Science Teacher, by Larry Scheckel: Why Are Some Elements Radioactive?
Thought-Provoking Comics by Steve Ditko
WisconScene Festivals in the Weeks Ahead

Alex Schomburg: Gold in Pulps & Comics

David Saunders' pulpartists.com

Above three images from HA.com. Painting of Marvel's "big three" at right sold at Heritage for nearly $42K.

(1905-1998)

Antonio Alejandro "Alex" Schomburg was born May 10, 1905 in Puerto Rico. His father, Guillermo Schomburg, was born in 1845 in Puerto Rico of German ancestry. His mother, Francisca Rosa, was born in 1875 in Puerto Rico. His parents had seven children, one daughter and six sons, of which Alex was the youngest. The fourth-born son, August Schomburg, also became a pulp artist. The father was a civil engineer and land surveyor.

The Schomburg family were rather prosperous. They lived in an upper class coastal neighborhood at 50 Calle San Sebastian, San Juan, PR. They spoke English fluently. The family also had a second home in Aguadilla, PR, where another pulp artist, Rafael M. DeSoto, was born in 1904. The two artists knew each other as children and remained in contact throughout their remarkably parallel lives.

In 1917 at the age of twelve Alex Schomburg moved to New York City to join his older brothers. They lived in Harlem at 630 West 124th Street, which is near Broadway. Alex attended public school, while his older brothers earned their livings in various creative trades.

In 1923 all four brothers started their own freelance art studio, with Fred Schomburg as the manager and salesman, William Schomburg as a clerk, and August and Alex as the artists. They built window displays, lettered signs, and illustrated song slides for theater organists.

That same year Rafael M. DeSoto followed the adventurous example of the Schomburgs and also moved to NYC. Although he could only speak a few words of English. He was encouraged by their example to seek success as an artist in New York City.

In 1928 the Schomburgs sold their business to a manufacturer of slides, and the company then hired Alex Schomburg to work for them.

On November 7, 1928 he married Helen Scott, born 1904 in Northern Ireland of English ancestry. They moved to 1240 Walton Avenue in the Bronx. They raised two children, Diana and Richard.

In 1929 he joined the National Screen Service Company as a staff artist, where he helped to produce movie trailers for fifteen years.

In his free time he also created freelance illustrations. His first published assignments appeared in *Popular Western, Popular Detective, Radio Craft, Sky Raiders,* and *Thrilling Adventures.* At that same time his brother, August Schomburg, developed his own significant career as a top cover artist for *Flying Aces* magazine.

Alex Schomburg sold his first science-fiction magazine cover in 1939. According to the artist, "One day the publisher asked me to do an illustration for *Thrilling Wonder Stories.* I had always been interested in science fiction and they liked the way I handled the art work. I enjoy reading the story as much as doing the illustrations. In my opinion an illustration is very important. For instance, give the same story to two different persons... then ask them to picture a certain scene. You can bet they'll be entirely different."

He created interiors and cover paintings for *Startling Stories, Fantastic Story, Dynamic Science Fiction, Science Fiction Quarterly,* and *Thrilling Wonders Stories.*

From the late 1930s to the late 1940s, he created over five hundred covers for comic books, including Captain America, The Human Torch, Sub Mariner, Black Terror, and The Green Hornet.

He left the comics industry in the 1950s and concentrated on illustrating books and science fiction magazines, as well as the Winston Science Fiction series for young readers.

According to Stan Lee, "Alex Schomburg was totally unique. I remember hearing Timely Comics publisher Martin Goodman tell me time and again how great a cover illustrator Alex was, and how he wished we had more like him. He was the only artist I knew able to combine strong, dramatic layouts, and exciting superhero action with a simplistic, almost cartoony style of execution. One could never be sure if Alex was an illustrator who approached his work like a cartoonist, or a cartoonist who chose to render his artwork like an illustrator. Despite the quantity of work we gave him, despite the care and effort that went into every Schomburg cover, I cannot remember Alex ever being late with any illustration. He was as reliable as he was talented."

His son married and moved to Hillsboro, Oregon. After retiring from illustration the Schomburgs moved to Oregon to live near their son's family.

Alex Schomburg died in Beaverton, Oregon at the age of ninety-two on April 7, 1998.

© David Saunders 2009

Follow-up

Last month's PulpArtists featured the work of Casimir B. Mayshark.

While at the pulp fiction convention near Chicago, in late April, I examined over 200 lots to be sold at the show's auction. One lot was a stack of six issues of Sky Birds, all from 1935, and all with covers... *by C. B. Mayshark!*

Interesting coincidence!

Or... (shudder) *was* it a coincidence?

I decided to get them, if the bidding didn't go too high.

But this was an auction where two super-excellent condition Shadow pulps went for $750 each. (My friend heard someone, looking over the auction items earlier, say he was going to bid, and keep bidding, until he got those specific issues. And he did.) Would the bidding on these six pulps fly as high as the sky birds shown on the covers?

Well, I got them, scanned them, and here are the covers. Do you recognize two of them from last month's issue?

Interestingly, I found that artist Mayshark was familiar with the subjects he painted. Inside each issue, he wrote a page or two about the man or machine (or both).

My, How Times Have Changed

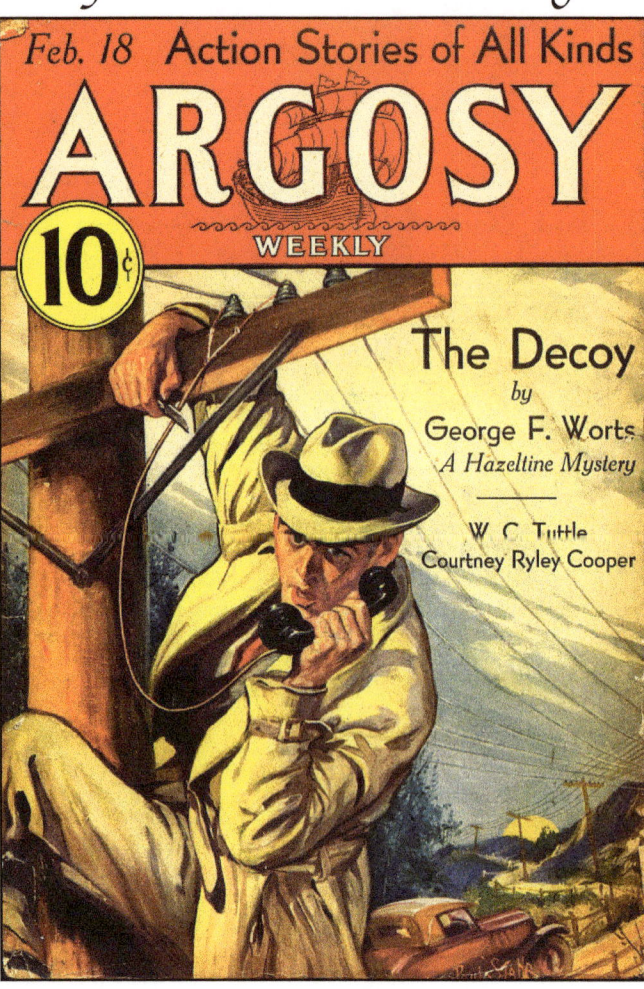

This is one of my favorite pulp covers.
You're out driving at night on a country road, and you have to make a phone call. What do you do? Today, you pull off to a safe side spot (that is, if you have any sense), whip out the cell phone, and make the call. What could be simpler?
But in the 1930s, when this cover (painted by Paul Stahr) was published, you didn't have that luxury. You parked, got this handset out of the glove compartment, crawled up the telephone pole, attached the headset wires (I hope you knew what you were doing with that), and made your call.
This illustration was for "The Decoy," by George F. Worts. The character shown making the call is Gillian Hazeltine, who appeared in many stories in the 1920s and 30s. What kind of career did this man have, who was involved in dozens of action-packed, pulse-pounding, edge-of-death dramas? Was he a private detective? A G-man? A bounty hunter?
Not quite. Gillian Hazeltine was *a laywer*.

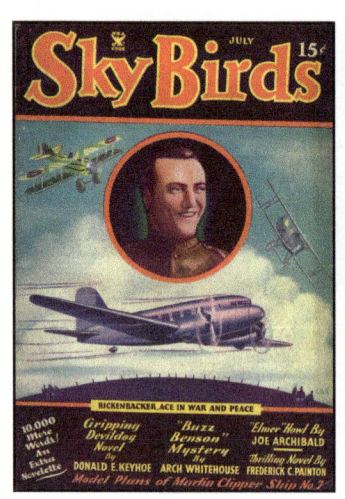

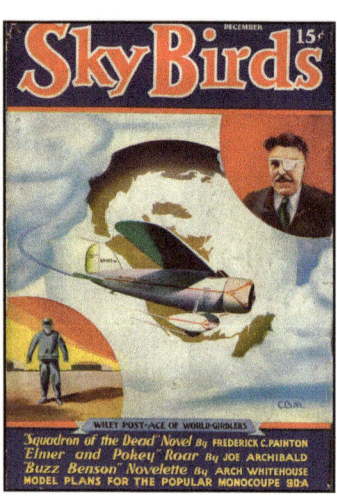

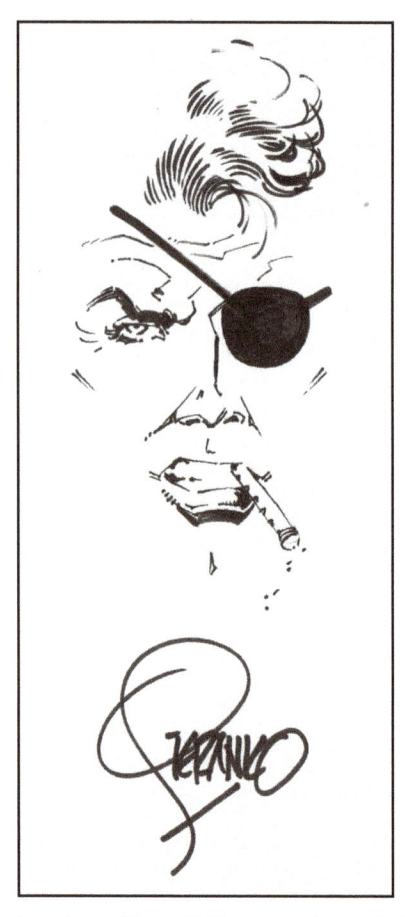

One of two drawings Your Editor purchased directly from Steranko at the recent Windy City pulp show: Nick Fury, Agent of S.H.I.E.L.D. A visually stunning survey of his work can be found at thedrawingsofsteranko.com
– TM and © Marvel Comics

Q: Why are some elements radioactive?

By Larry Scheckel

Ask a Science Teacher

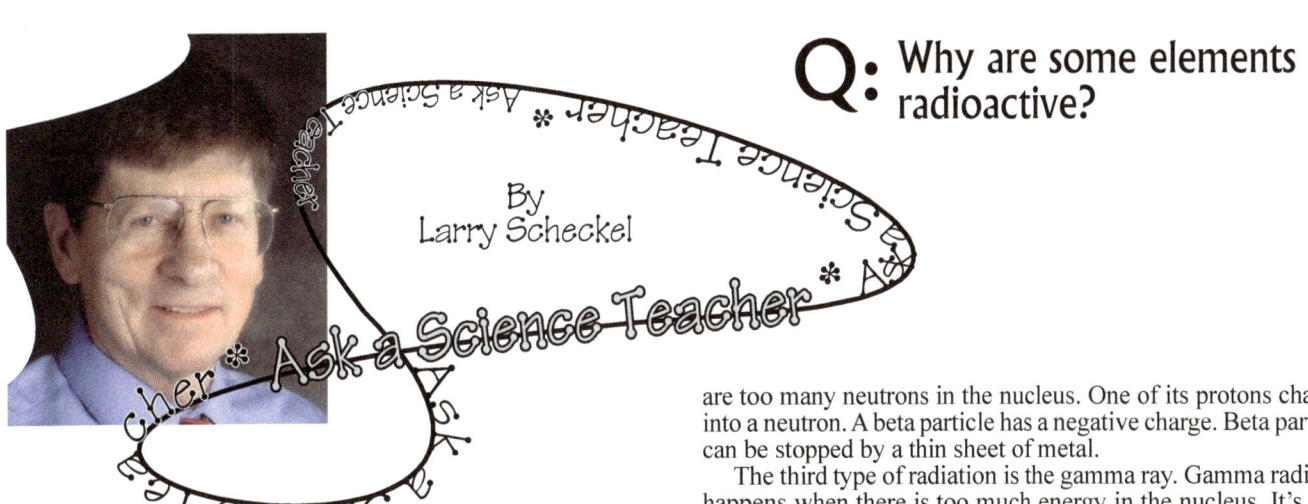

Some elements are radioactive because they are unstable. Atoms have a central core called the nucleus. The nucleus is made up of protons, with a positive charge, and neutrons that do not have a charge. They are neutral, as the name implies. Orbiting the nucleus are tiny negative electrons.

In that nucleus are those protons, all with a positive charge. Protons repel protons, as "like" charges repel. The nucleus wants to fly apart. But those neutrons prevent that from happening. The neutrons stick to the protons using a fundamental force called the strong nuclear force. The neutrons prevent the protons from flying apart.

There are two competing forces at work. One pulling and one pushing. For most atoms, there are just enough neutrons to keep the nucleus stable. But for some atoms, such as uranium and plutonium, the ratio of neutrons to protons is out of whack.

Nature wants the radioactive atom to become stable, so it throws off some pieces of itself. This ejection, or throwing off, is called radioactivity. There are three kinds of radioactivity depending on what is thrown off.

An alpha particle is ejected when there are too many protons in the nucleus. It is made of two protons and two neutrons. It's a massive particle, as particles go, and carries a positive charge. It can't travel very far and can be stopped by an inch of air or a piece of paper. Harmless outside the body, but deadly if it gets inside a person.

A beta particle is an electron ejected from an atom when there are too many neutrons in the nucleus. One of its protons changes into a neutron. A beta particle has a negative charge. Beta particles can be stopped by a thin sheet of metal.

The third type of radiation is the gamma ray. Gamma radiation happens when there is too much energy in the nucleus. It's not a particle but a wave, much like a light wave or a radio or television wave, but at a much higher frequency or vibration rate. Gamma rays can be stopped by thick metal, deep water, several feet of soil, or a lead shield.

All three of these types of radiation can be dangerous because that pack a terrific wallop due to their high speed. The kinetic energy of these particles is sufficient to smash apart chemical structures in the human body. A strong dose can damage DNA and cause cancer. A really, really robust attack can burn the skin, destroy blood cells, and kill within minutes.

We get hit by radioactive particles all day and every day. They are in such small amounts that they don't do much harm. People do have to be careful about radiation. There is an insidious nature to radiation. Certain kinds of radioactive particles can be absorbed and our body will treat them just like chemicals that we are used to.

Radioactive Iodine-131 replaces the regular iodine in the thyroid. Cesium-137 and Strontium-90 replaces calcium in the bone. Plutonium239 replaces iron in the blood and bone marrow.

There are a number of good ways that science has used radiation. These include X-rays, carbon dating, nuclear power plants, and to kill germs. Radiation therapy is one of the most common treatments for cancer. It uses high-energy particles or waves, such as x-rays, gamma rays, electron beams, or protons, to destroy or damage cancer cells.

Like many things in life, there are pluses and minuses. Radioactive elements can kill or cure.

Send questions and comments to: lscheckel@charter.net

June
2017

Cover image: At the Blind Horse Restaurant
Great Movies This Month
Dinner at the Blind Horse, Kohler
Food Trucks at the Blind Horse
Plymouth Artist's Work Featured in Guidebook
Camo Quilts
Logic in Your Life
I Ate At... by Richard J. Baumann: The Hub, Plymouth
PulpArtists by David Saunders: Louis G. Schroeder
Ask a Science Teacher, by Larry Scheckel: Is There Any Science Connected with Tecumseh's Curse?
Natural Connections by Emily Stone: Snapping Turtles Bring With Them Prehistoric Memories
Echoes of our past by William & Joy Wangemann: Phones Once Only Made Calls with No Manual!
Life on the Frontier (William Messner-Loebs)

Logic in your Life

Think of some fact. Anything you're confident is true.

How do you know it's true?

I don't mean, how you would defend that fact, arguing with someone else. I mean, how would you validate it, prove it, to yourself?

Why is this important?

I could fill this entire issue of The Current with answers to that. Instead, let's move forward, and see if the real-life examples given here demonstrate how this is important.

What is logic?

The human mind operates in a certain way to gain knowledge. Logic is a part of the process—the methodology—of putting things together to form knowledge. Knowledge doesn't come automatically. You have to work for it. Logic is the set of thinking tools telling you when you can be certain of something; when there's some doubt; when you've made an error and how to correct it.

Logical fallacies

Some people are not aware of any methodology in their thinking. But anyone who is conscious, and mentally capable to the point where they can use language, can learn to understand the logical processes they use every day.

A number of logical fallacies have been identified over the years. Some were identified by Greek philosophers over 2000 years ago. Some are so common, that as soon as you learn to identify them, you will realize that they are everywhere.

More important, if you come to see that a logical fallacy is wrong, you can prevent it from happening in your own thinking. By doing that, you will gain greater control, greater power, over your own thinking, and your life.

Example: What's the error here?

Does the following sound plausible?

A TV commercial of over 30 years ago (mind you, this is from memory, and none of these are exact quotes) showed a bored man eating a slice of pizza. The narrator asks, "How's your pizza?" The man shrugs as if to say, "It's OK." The narrator says, "Did you know your pizza is made with casein?" The bored man shows a glimmer of interest. Narrator: "And did you know that casein is an ingredient in *glue?*"

The man eating the pizza leans forward in horror and asks, *"Ga-LUE???"*

The narrator continues: "Well, our pizza isn't made with that stuff, so it's much better..." Etc.

Here's another example.

From the Internet (vigorously re-worded, so as not to be plagiarism):

Lots of so-called "vanilla" ice cream doesn't have any real vanilla in it. Instead, an artificial flavor called piperonal is used.

Well, you know what?! Piperonal is an ingredient in **lice killer!** How d'ya like *that!!* Eating ice cream is like eating lice killer.

Uncovering the fallacy

You probably don't like the thought of eating glue, right? In fact, it might make you gag. And eating (or would it be drinking?) lice killer? I didn't think so.

Even if you've never heard of logical fallacies, you can think this through.

Try to think of something similar, in pattern, to the above two examples, which is obviously false. If you can, you've found at least a clue that something's wrong with these arguments.

Here's an example. Suppose a co-worker gets a cup of water from the water cooler, and gently sips it.

(Now please don't do this for real; this is only a theoretical example for educational purposes.)

Suppose you stop ped in your tracks and pointed at the water cup in horror and disgust.

"Ugh!" you tell your co-worker. "You—you're drinking—gag—choke—*water?"*

"Yeah!" the co-worker retorts. "So?"

"Well!" you say, with a superior tone. "Water is an ingredient in—*raw sewage."*

Pretty good, huh? You've just proven that water is not good to drink.

Only... only... that is obviously untrue. Water *is* good to drink. Not only good, but somewhat vital.

This is important! You've gone through some kind of thinking process—and you've hit the Brick Wall of Reality. You realize, even without advanced training, that something's wrong.

The fallacy of Division

"Division" is a fallacy where you start with a group, made up of units. Or an assembly, made of pieces. Or a mixture, made of ingredients.

You can find characteristics of the group, assembly, or mixture.

Example: That football team is the best in the county.

Example: The brain is capable of thinking.

The fallacy of Division is the belief that, if it's true of the whole, it's going to be true of each individual unit or part.

Example: That football team—*as a team*—is the best in the county. You cannot assume that each individual player is the best in the county.

Example: The brain—as a whole—is capable of thinking. You cannot assume that one neuron firing can be called "thinking."

The fallacy of Composition

"Composition" works in the opposite direction as Division. It assumes that a characteristic of one part will also apply to the whole.

To use my example of the brain, certain philosophical scoundrels will say, "One neuron firing—that's just an electrical impulse. It's not thinking at all. Well, the brain is just a collection of neurons firing, so how can you say that the brain is doing any thinking?"

And the football example? Find the greatest quarterback in the county; the greatest halfback; etc. Now put them all together. Can you, with any confidence, say they're going to form the greatest *team* (whole) in the county?

Composition is not always fallacious. If you have a machine made of 100 parts, and every part is made of gold, it is perfectly logical to say the machine (as a whole) is made of gold.

Now, if you said, "Every one of these 100 parts that make up this machine is light, therefore the whole machine will be light"...

Bzzzt!!

Logical fallacy.

The two examples, with the pizza and ice cream, are a combination of the two fallacies. Its pattern is:
- The whole (glue) is disgusting to eat.
- Casein is a part of the whole (glue).
- Casein is a part of another whole (pizza).
- Conclusion: Pizza made with casein is disgusting to eat.

More to come

I plan to highlight different logical fallacies in the future. You can help me by e-mailing me to tell me if this article is helpful to you. Questions and challenges are always welcome. Does anything need clarification?

Sources

There are many sources, if you're interested in learning more about logical fallacies. Many of them are free, online.

E-Books. Search for "logical fallacies" on your e-reader. There are many available for free (and a few for 99¢). I found *Forty Two Fallacies,* by Dr. Michael C. LaBossiere, which I've been consulting.

Audio lectures. A great learning tool if you do a lot of driving. One of the best I've listened to is *Introduction to Logic* by Leonard Peikoff. It's a 27-hour, 10-unit course that covers the fallacies but also goes into other aspects of logic. I believe this is available online for free.

Online sources. Plentiful information is available. Just search.

Parting shot

You know there is a need of more logic when you Google "casein ingredient cheese" to research this article, and see, among the results, the following two headings:

Cheese really is crack. Study reveals cheese is as addictive as drugs ...

No, cheese is not just like crack | Science News

Cover art by Louis G. Schroeder.
Short Stories was a long-running pulp. For much of its run, a red circle was incorporated—in some cases, as the sun—into the cover design. This made it easier for readers to recognize, as it would stand out on a newsstand from dozens of other titles on display. Editors looked for artists who could convey a very basic situation at a quick glance, with further story elements revealed on closer inspection. Here, the man's snow-blindness might not be the first thing you notice.

What does *this* old-style phone remind you of? I immediately thought of a Topps Ugly Sticker ("Artie") from 1965, designed by Basil Wolverton and painted by Norman Saunders (faithful readers of The Current will recognize both names). – Photo of phone by Biswarup Ganguly. Sticker image from normansaunders.com

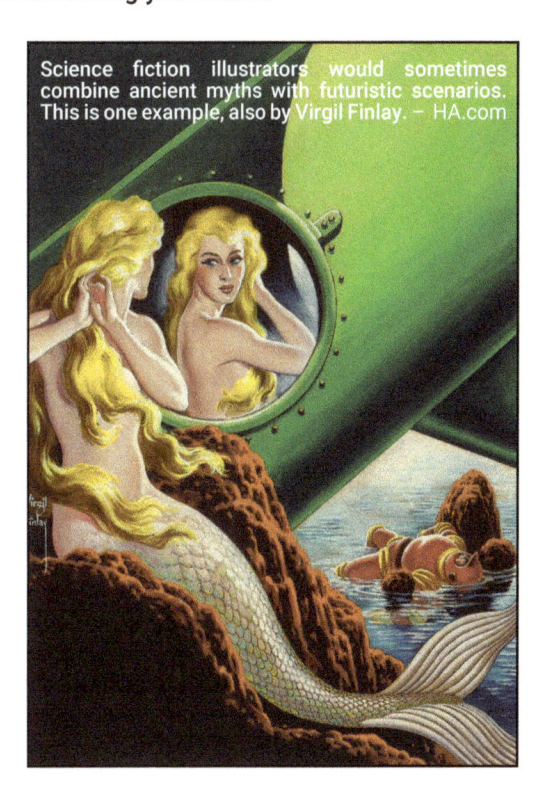

Science fiction illustrators would sometimes combine ancient myths with futuristic scenarios. This is one example, also by Virgil Finlay. – HA.com

The Current

July 2017

Cover image: Whinemaking at SoLu Estate, Cascade
Great Movies This Month
It's More than Wine at SoLu
PulpArtists by David Saunders: Modest Stein
What Did Dick Tracy Think of "Modern Art?"
Influential Books
Logic in Your Life
Coin Box Telephone, by Lou Bulebosh
Going Back in Time—Things to Jog Your Memory, by Lou Bulebosh
Echoes of our past by William & Joy Wangemann: Summertime Memories Are Warm and Pleasant
Ask a Science Teacher, by Larry Scheckel: What is the Proof that the Earth Orbits the Sun?
Don't Demonize Capitalism—It's Making the World a Better Place, by Marian L. Tupy, HumanProgress.org
Natural Connections by Emily Stone: Oh Say Can You See by the Fireflies' Night Light
Mumbling, Muttering, And Meandering in Modern Movies
I Ate At... by Richard J. Baumann: Big Al Capone's, Pipe, Wisconsin

Q: What Is the proof that the Earth orbits the Sun?

By Larry Scheckel

A: It seems so obvious to us today in our modern times, but the Earth orbiting the Sun is a relativity new idea, only about 500 years old. Prior to about 1500 the majority of mankind held that the Sun moved around the Earth (this is called the geocentric model of the Solar System). The sun-centered, or heliocentric, idea can be credited to Nicolaus Copernicus (1473-1543).

Is there a way that we can prove to ourselves that the Earth indeed orbits the Sun? Yes, there is, but it takes a year of patience and careful observation. Let's look at the Astronomy Made Easy or the Astronomy For Dummies books and see what they say.

Over the course of one year, the patterns of stars in the sky will change. On any particular night, some constellations of stars will appear on one side of the sky and others will appear on the other side. Then those constellation of stars will disappear and the original stars will return. The heavens rotate over the course of one year. It seems like the stars are set on a giant bowl and we are inside the center of that bowl.

But even though the stars look like they're attached to the inside of a giant bowl, most are at very different distances from Earth. Some are quite close, some are very far away, relatively speaking.

Over the course of one year, many of the stars will move relative to each other. Find two stars that are very close to each other. It's best if one star is slightly brighter or a different color than the other. It is possible to note, over a period of one year, that the two stars get closer to each other, seem to merge together, and then move apart.

At the end of the year they will be back where they started. This is because the Earth moves around the Sun in a near perfect circle, so that six months from your first observation, you are viewing the stars from a slightly, but observably, different angle.

This stellar parallax observation can only be explained if the Earth is orbiting a "fixed" point, in this case, the Sun.

Simply put, parallax is the apparent change in position of objects due to a change in observation location. You can easily experience an example of parallax by holding your thumb out in front of your face at arm's length. Using just your left eye, look at where the thumb lines up with some object in the distant background such as a door frame or a tree outside. Now look with just your right eye. Notice the thumb moved. That's parallax, since your two eyes are at different locations.

The ancient peoples claimed that if the Earth is moving around the Sun then the stars should shift their positions due to this orbital motion. They should have been able to see this stellar parallax phenomena. In reality, it wasn't seen because it is too small to be easily seen.

It wasn't noticed until 1838, and then only with a telescope, long after astronomers agreed the Earth goes around the Sun.

So we can just forget about picking out two stars in the nightly heavens and taking a year to observe their position. Astronomy Made Easy and Astronomy For Dummies are very fine books, but on this idea, they do not make a good case. We probably can make better use of our time.

Yet, stellar parallax is the best scientific proof that planet Earth orbits the Sun.

Send questions and comments to: lscheckel@charter.net

Szukalski's comments on his portrait of Copernicus:

"Mikolaj Kopernik's family hailed from the Polish village Koperniki, where prospered many families that cultivated and harvested dill, so indispensable in the pickling of cucumbers. The German-English 'dill' is called in Polish 'Koper,' therefore the name of Kopernik means a 'diller.'

"From the attic of his provincial confinement to oblivion he boldly dismissed the whole motley crowd of good and evil demons that so confounded our mutual ancestors, thus freeing pure science from the tyranny of shamanist anti-reason. Then he correlated the brilliance of man's mind with the radiance of the all-causing sun. At the same time he recognized the affinity between his heart and the heartbreak world, thus populating an aimless universe with divinely human purpose.

"Though a mere earthling he rearranged the then-existing interplanetary chaos according to his own logos. Singlehandedly, he stopped the idle wanderings of the errandless sun by hitching it to the immovable post of rationalist consistency and by—demoting the self-obsessed Earth to mere spinning around it, despite the promised eternal damnation."

– Image provided by and Copyright © 2017 ARCHIVES SZUKALSKI; printed with permission.

The project by Szukalski for the Monument of Copernicus. The youth who dared single-handedly to stop the sun and spin the earth with the other quadrillions of planets and stars, to circle around it. – Image provided by and Copyright © 2017 ARCHIVES SZUKALSKI; printed with permission. A poster of this work can be seen at szukalski.com/posters.htm

Who was..... Szukalski

Glenn Bray has been a friend of mine for four decades. Through him and his wife Lena, I've discovered artists I otherwise would never have heard of.

Bray discovered Stanislaus Szukalski, originally from Poland, living in California. The details of Szukalski's life are too incredibly detailed to even try summarizing here; the website below gives some background.

What's relevant here is that Bray recognized Szukalski as a genius, and worked as much as possible with Szukalski while the artist was alive, to preserve and promote his work.

Bray published two books of Szukalski's work. In the early 1990s, he worked with the Polish Museum of America, in Chicago, to display a large selection of work, including cast bronzes of his sculptures. (I was fortunate enough to attend that exhibition.)

In 1983, I visited with Glenn and Lena. They took me to visit Szukalski, then age 90, who signed his print of Copernicus for me (an image of which is on the previous page). Not only did Szukalski create fantastic drawings and sculptures, he created his own penmanship. Can you read it? If not:

"To dear Rodney Schroeter who is on his way to meet a better Destiny from S. Szukalski, Aug. 1983"

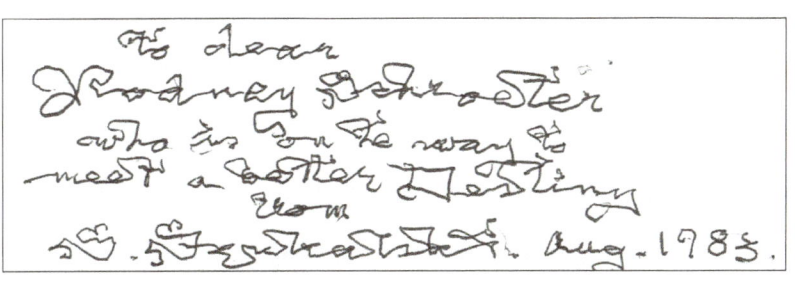

**Want to learn more about Szukalski?
See szukalski.com**

Influential Books

A few years ago, members of the public were invited to list books that had been influential in their lives.

The following list was taken from the Library of Congress website. So far as can be discerned, the list itself is in the public domain.

How many have you read? What's in *your* library?

Ayn Rand, "The Fountainhead"
Kurt Vonnegut, "Slaughterhouse-Five, or The Children's Crusade: A Duty-Dance with Death"
Laura Ingalls Wilder, "Little House in the Big Woods"
Joseph Smith, "The Book of Mormon"
Willa Cather, "My Ántonia"
Alex Haley, "Roots: The Saga of an American Family"
Ayn Rand, "Anthem"
Alice Walker, "The Color Purple"
John Steinbeck, "Of Mice and Men"
John Steinbeck, "East of Eden"
Sylvia Plath, "The Bell Jar"
Tim O'Brien, "The Things They Carried"
Bob Woodward and Carl Bernstein, "All the President's Men"
Arthur Miller, "Death of a Salesman"
Arthur Miller, "The Crucible"
Ernest Hemingway, "The Old Man and the Sea"
Ken Kesey, "One Flew Over the Cuckoo's Nest"
Hunter S. Thompson, "Fear and Loathing in Las Vegas: A Savage Journey to the Heart of the American Dream"
Ernest Hemingway, "The Sun Also Rises"
John F. Kennedy, "Profiles in Courage"
Stephen King, "The Stand"
Larry McMurtry, "Lonesome Dove"
Judy Blume, "Are You There God? It's Me, Margaret"
Howard Zinn, "A People's History of the United States"
James Fenimore Cooper, "The Last of the Mohicans: A Narrative of 1757"
Robert A. Heinlein, "The Moon Is a Harsh Mistress"
Wilson Rawls, "Where the Red Fern Grows"
Madeleine L'Engle, "A Wrinkle in Time"
Frank Herbert, "Dune"
Thomas Pynchon, "Gravity's Rainbow"
Simone Beck, Louisette Bertholle and Julia Child, "Mastering the Art of French Cooking"

Kate Chopin, "The Awakening"
Shel Silverstein, "The Giving Tree"
Milton Friedman, "Capitalism and Freedom"
Milton Friedman and Rose Friedman, "Free to Choose: A Personal Statement"
Ralph Waldo Emerson, "Nature"
Napoleon Hill, "Think and Grow Rich"
John Kennedy Toole, "A Confederacy of Dunces"
Robert Penn Warren, "All the King's Men"
Robert M. Pirsig, "Zen and the Art of Motorcycle Maintenance: An Inquiry into Values"
Ayn Rand, "Atlas Shrugged"
Harper Lee, "To Kill a Mockingbird"
Mark Twain, "The Adventures of Huckleberry Finn"
Thomas Paine, "Common Sense"
Harriet Beecher Stowe, "Uncle Tom's Cabin; or, Life Among the Lowly"
The Federalist: "A Collection of Essays, Written in Favour of the New Constitution"
Upton Sinclair, "The Jungle"
J. D. Salinger, "The Catcher in the Rye"
John Steinbeck, "The Grapes of Wrath"
Alcoholics Anonymous: "The Story of How More Than One Hundred Men Have Recovered from Alcoholism"
Ray Bradbury, "Fahrenheit 451"
F. Scott Fitzgerald, "The Great Gatsby"
Louisa May Alcott, "Little Women, or, Meg, Jo, Beth, and Amy"
Margaret Mitchell, "Gone With the Wind"
Theodore Geisel (Dr. Seuss), "The Cat in the Hat"
Rachel Carson, "Silent Spring"
Henry David Thoreau, "Walden; or, Life in the Woods"
Jack Kerouac, "On the Road"
Betty Friedan, "The Feminine Mystique"
L. Frank Baum, "The Wonderful Wizard of Oz"
Herman Melville, "Moby-Dick; or, the Whale"
Dale Carnegie, "How to Win Friends and Influence People"
Joseph Heller, "Catch-22"
Walt Whitman, "Leaves of Grass"
Benjamin Spock, "Baby and Child Care"

This 1953 pulp reprinted Anthem, a short novel used in many classrooms.

Your Editor's pick for Most Important Book Published During His Lifetime is on this list. Which one do you think it is?

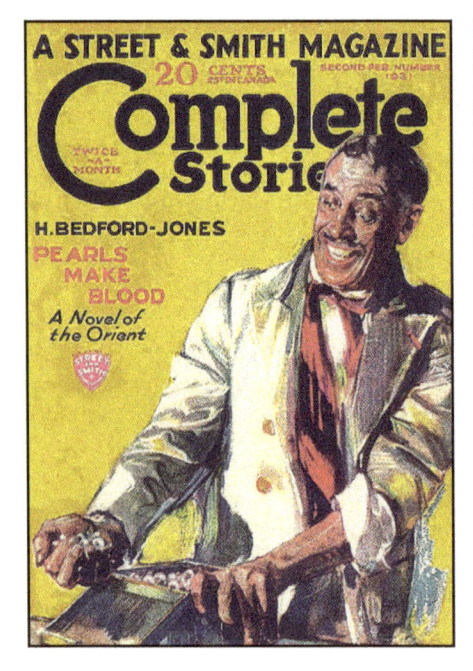

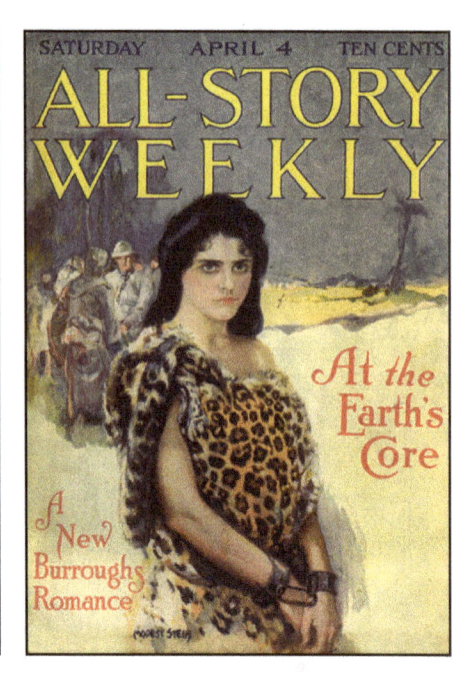

Covers by Modest Stein

The Plymouth Review Current

TAKING YOU PLACES WORTH SEEING
Volume 6 • Issue 9 • August 2017

FREE!

"Hello World!"

Meaningful Movies • Great Art & Literature • Fine Dining • Hatchlings

August
2017

Cover image: Dad's Hatchery
Great Movies This Month
Logical Fallacies Poster from yourlogicalfallacyis.com
The Man Who Laughs: The Book. The Movie. The Audiobook. The Critique.
Ask a Science Teacher, by Larry Scheckel: How Risky is Driving a Car?
I Ate At... by Richard J. Baumann: Siebkens Resort, Elkhart Lake

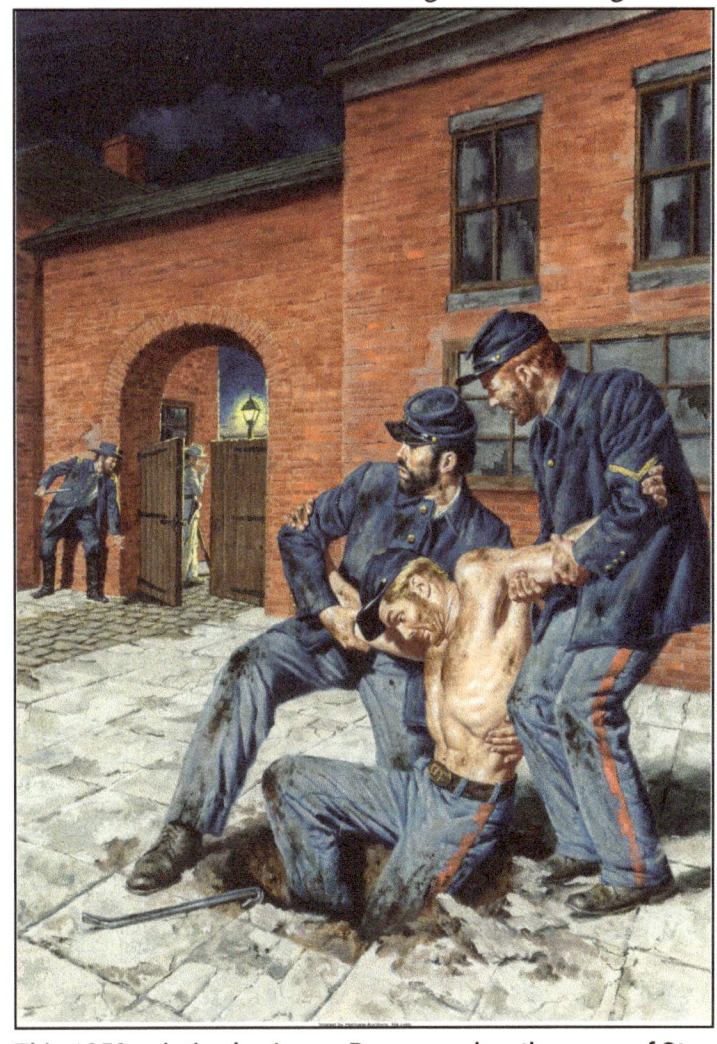

This 1959 painting by James Bama, used on the cover of Stag magazine, sold recently for $1,625. – HA.com

September
2017

Cover image: The Big Cheese Festival, The Blind Horse Restaurant
Great Movies This Month
Kohler Food & Wine Experience Preview
Feel Like Dancin'?
The Big Cheese Festival

Possible Dreams: Happy Movies (Hidden Figures)
Summer Kitchen Pantry Restoration, by Barry Johanson
Attractions en Route: 12 Along-the-Way Wisconsin Hot Spots to Hamilton Wood Type & Printing Museum
Echoes of our past by William & Joy Wangemann: A Stroll Through Neighborhoods of the 1950s
Watching Destination Moon with Someone Special [Robert A. Heinlein] in the Audience
Ask a Science Teacher, by Larry Scheckel: What Is a "Fermi question"?
Logic in Your Life
Movie Posters
I Ate At... by Richard J. Baumann: The Gravel Pit Sports Bar & Grill, Kiel
PulpArtists by David Saunders: Earle K. Bergey
Natural Connections by Emily Stone: Tiny Wasps Crucial to Big Farms

October
2017

Cover image: Flight for Life at the Silver Creek Centennial
Great Movies This Month
Hard Hat Harmony
Logic in Your Life
Natural Connections by Emily Stone: Horror Story Plots in Pretty Places
Ask a Science Teacher, by Larry Scheckel: Why Do Giraffes Have Long Necks?
PulpArtists by David Saunders: Henry Enoch Sharp
I Ate At... by Richard J. Baumann: Bummy's Haus, Howards Grove
Possible Dreams: Happy Movies (The Tiger and the Snow)
Dark Wings of the Shadow, by Will Murray
Why Schools Should Teach Rational Discourse, by Annie Holmquist, IntellectualTakeout.org
Echoes of our past by William & Joy Wangemann: During the Depression, People Danced the Night, and Their Cares, Away

The Plymouth Review Current

Taking You Places Worth Seeing
Volume 6 • Issue 11 • October 2017

FREE!

Movies • Art • Practical Thinking Skills • Fine Dining
Autogyros

Possible Dreams: Happy Movies

My pick this time around is The Tiger and the Snow, from 2005, directed and co-written by Italian filmmaker Roberto Benigni.

When talking about Benigni, it is nearly impossible to not mention his most famous film: Life is Beautiful (1997). Sometimes I'm surprised by how many people haven't seen something. With this film, I'm surprised in conversations by how many people *have* seen it.

A brief description of Life is Beautiful would not make one think, "Now *there's* a Happy Movie." In it, a husband, wife, and their 4-year-old child are put into a World War II concentration camp.

With a setting like that, a movie that is all fun and games would be offensively grotesque. Appropriately, it does have its share of horrors. In contrast, the uplifting, happy part of the movie is the process of Benigni using his genius again and again to protect his son. He protects the boy physically, of course, but just as importantly, *psychologically*.

The Tiger and the Snow takes place in 2003, with the background of a quite different war. As with many of Benigni's films (including Life is Beautiful), his lead co-star is his real-life wife, Nicoletta Braschi.

We're introduced to Benigni's obsession with a woman. He dreams of marrying her. We're not even sure she's real—until he sees her and follows her. He even talks with her, but she wants nothing to do with him.

Braschi's character works with an Iraqui professor. Both go to Baghdad, Iraq, on business.

And then, Operation Shock and Awe begins.

Benigni hears that Braschi has been hurt in the bombing. A wall fell on her.

He *must* get to her.

But when he tells airport personnel, "I want a ticket to Baghdad," they look at him as if he's crazy. Baghdad is being *bombed*. Incoming flights have all been *canceled*.

His method of reaching Baghdad is sheer genius. The way it's told is movie-making at its best.

It seems insane for Benigni to be so passionately focused, so intent on getting to Baghdad, to help a woman who doesn't seem to return any feeling for him. That might mystify you. Don't worry, you didn't miss anything. Benigni's intensity, his unwavering, uncompromising focus which he never gives up, this use of his free will to direct every thought and action to preserve the one thing he selfishly values the most in life, makes this a refreshingly life-affirming Happy Movie, and Benigni's character a true hero.

Once he reaches Baghdad, the news is not good. Braschi is

alive. But comatose. In a hospital staffed by one overworked young doctor, whose most hopeful comment to Benigni is, "She is alive."

Still, Benigni will not give up.

Parts of this story are not explained until the last few moments of the film. Some of the mystery of Benigni's obsession become clear. Or clearer. There are unanswered questions... Are they—? Will they—? Or am I missing something, even after seeing the movie three times?

Despite the lingering mysteries, the ending of this film is one of the most satisfying I have ever seen. It deserves a Grand Champion-level "Happy Movie" award.

Note: The original language for both movies described here is Italian. Some such movies imported into the US are dubbed with English. That can work OK, but you cheat yourself by not hearing the inflection and tone of the original actor's voice.

Roberto Benigni, desperately explaining to his transportation that the leisurely pace being set is inadequate for his need to reach Baghdad and save the woman he loves.
– From The Tiger and the Snow, imdb.com

By Henry Enoch Sharp, from 1951. Artists were fortunate to get cover painting assignments, because they paid better than interior, black & white drawings like this. But then, there were many more opportunities to do b&w pieces than covers.

November
2017

Cover image: Alex Guarnaschelli Smiles at the Kohler Food & Wine Experience
Great Movies This Month
Possible Dreams: Happy Movies (Sunrise)
Kohler Food & Wine Experience Highlights
Once in a Lifetime, by Paul Mueller
Christmas 2014, by Annie Mueller
Book: The Art of the Pulps
I Ate At... by Richard J. Baumann: Dragon Buffet, Plymouth
Echoes of our past by William & Joy Wangemann: Gales of November
Natural Connections by Emily Stone: Dances with Wolves Brightens the Day
Ask a Science Teacher, by Larry Scheckel: What Is Laughing Gas?

Richard Blais holds an item he had cooking in an immersion circulator (silver pot in front of faucet). He explained how he'd attached a hamburger patty to a bone (because meat is just better when it has a bone in it, he said), and had it cooking in a vacuum bag, a technique called sous vide ("under vacuum"). Those sitting in the central front row got cold feet when Blais brought out a canister of liquid nitrogen.

Stephanie Izard told her audience how she'd opened her third restaurant in the Chicago area—Duck Duck Goat, which features "Reasonably authentic" Chinese cuisine. Izard and Blais competed against each other in the 2008 season of Bravo's Top Chef. Each made it to the final episode and... Izard won.

Kohler Food & Wine Experience Highlights

During her presentation, Alex Guarnaschelli encouraged audience members to ask questions. Here is one.

Your Editor: What is your next planned career milestone that you'd care to talk about?

Alex Guarnaschelli: [Repeats the question, so that everyone in the huge Stella Artois Tent can hear.] [pause] [with some exasperation] Jeez, I'm stressed out. [Audience laughter] I've had a restaurant, Butter, in Manhattan for sixteen years. I only have one restaurant. My joke is, I have one restaurant, and my goal is zero. I definitely want to have a kind of green market, related by season, little store. And I want to just stand in there and make stuff. And have people come and buy and eat it. So, that in New York City, is very difficult to do. Because rent is brutal.

Your Editor [rudely interrupting]: It's not too hard here. [Smattering of audience laughter]

Alex Guarnaschelli [casting a Funny Look at Your Editor]: It's not too hard here? I have a ten-year-old who's not going to like what you just said. [getting back on topic] So that's definitely something I want to do. The other thing is definitely Iron Chef has come back. So I'm hoping you all watch it? That's something— [Torrent of audience applause] That's something—I know it's kind of funny—I practice a lot for that. I do practice a lot. And that's really very time-consuming, because I really like to win, because I'm super-competitive. Like, psycho-competitive. So those are my two things that I'm leaning towards. A good season of Iron Chef where I crush everybody [audience laughter], and some type of concept where I can cook what I want to cook every day. I've stood at a lot of stoves and I've cooked a lot of chicken breasts. I'm very happy about that. But I really want to just go to the market—I hate to sound hokey, but—put the stuff in the basket and cook it.

[Note: When Your Editor visited New York City a couple of years ago, one of the few restaurants accepting his dining reservation requests was Guarnaschelli's restaurant, Butter. **It's a great place!**]

At left is Chef Adam Siegel, Executive Chef / Managing Partner of the Bartolotta Restaurants in Milwaukee; at right, Chef Aaron Bickham, also of the Bartolotta Restaurants. At the Kohler Food & Wine Experience, these two chefs demonstrated to an audience of 40 how to make a traditional fondue. Audience members were able to sample the result, and take home the fondue's recipe. Chef Siegel kindly permitted us to print that recipe here.

Roth Grand Cru Fondue
Recipe by Adam Siegel

Serves 4-8 as an appetizer or main course.

   2 lbs Roth Grand Cru, small diced
   1 qt + 1 cup heavy cream
   12 egg yolks
   Salt to taste

1. In a heavy stainless steel pot, combine the cheese and quart of cream. For best results let the cheese sit in the cream for up to 4 hours on top of the stove. This allows the cheese to soften. (If the oven is on, that's even better; the indirect heat will gently help the process.)
2. Turn the heat on to medium low, constantly stirring with a wooden spoon.
3. Cook until completely melted, about 9-15 minutes.
4. Slowly add in egg yolks, constantly stirring. Simmer until thickened—thick enough to coat the back of the spoon. This can sometimes take another 10 minutes.
5. Remove from the heat and add the remaining cream.
6. Season to taste.
7. Serve with boiled potatoes or sauteed vegetables or mushrooms. This goes great with a variety of combinations. Also great with pasta, risotto or polenta.

Richard Blais pours the liquid nitrogen.

The Current
Plymouth Review
TAKING YOU PLACES WORTH SEEING
Volume 7 • Issue 1 • December 2017

FREE!

Fine Art ◆ Science ◆ Movies ◆ Local Dining
The Christmas Spirit ◆ Kestrels

December
2017

Cover image: Kestrel Chicks, About Two Weeks Old. Photo by Paul Mueller.
Great Movies This Month
Weinberg Tales
I Ate At... by Richard J. Baumann: The Fork & Dagger Ale Haus, Kiel
Ask a Science Teacher, by Larry Scheckel: How Come I Can See Lightning a Long Time before I Hear the Thunder?
PulpArtists by David Saunders: Rudolph Zirm
The Arbitrary and the Burden of Proof
Echoes of our past by William & Joy Wangemann: Letters to Santa from Yesteryear
The Art and Career of Will Eisner
The Christmas Spirit, by Will Eisner
If You Build It, They Will Come, by Paul Mueller
Scientific Poetry by Paul Kosir
Natural Connections by Emily Stone: We Are Surrounded by Minerals Taken for Granted

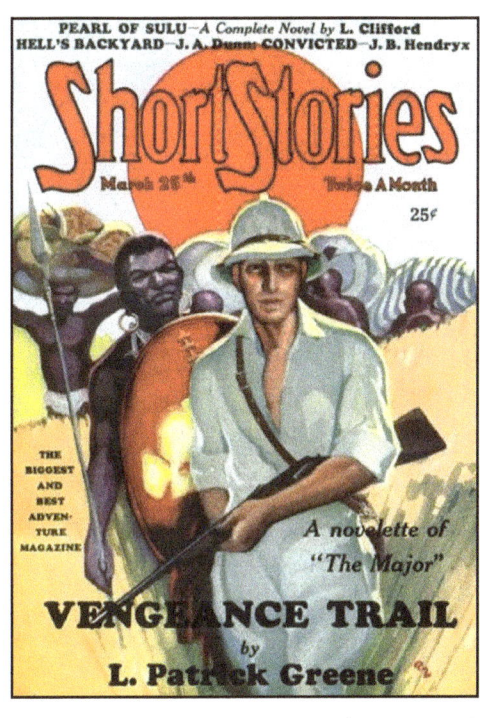

Author Lewis Patrick Greene (1891-1971) lived for several years in Africa, and later in life said, "Dealing almost entirely with natives, I learned to speak their language and came to admire them. They taught me many things that were good for a youngster to know." This attitude carried over into his fiction. Whereas some writers portrayed African natives as sub-human stereotypes (and flaunted profound ignorance about that continent), Greene portrayed natives as fully human, in the setting of a realistic Africa. 1933. Cover art by Rudolph Zirm.

Weinberg Tales

What a book about collecting can say to a non-collector

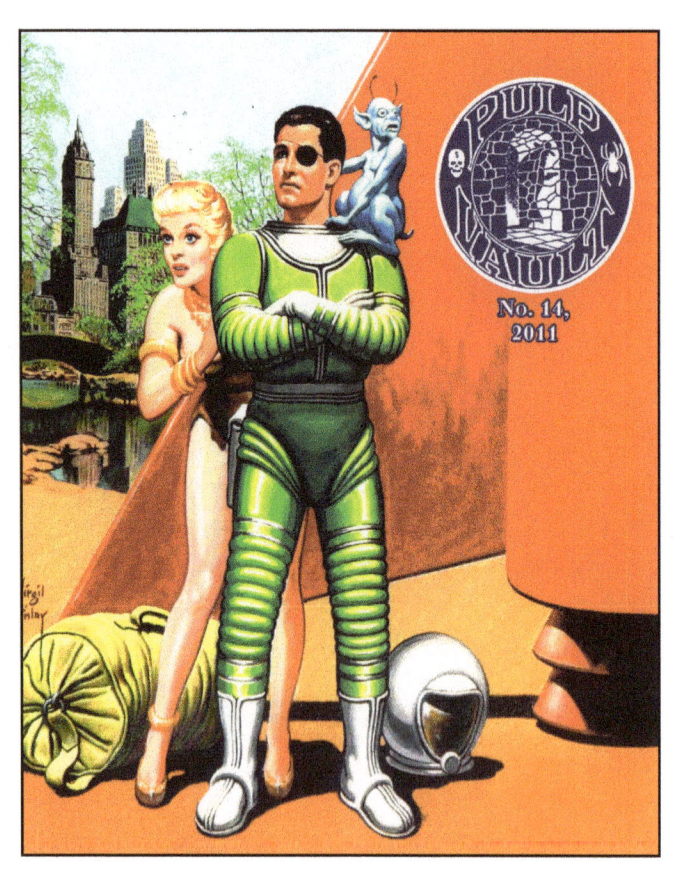

This 2011 issue of Pulp Vault featured a previously-unpublished painting by Virgil Finlay (1914-1971) on its cover. – Cover image Copyright © Lail Finlay

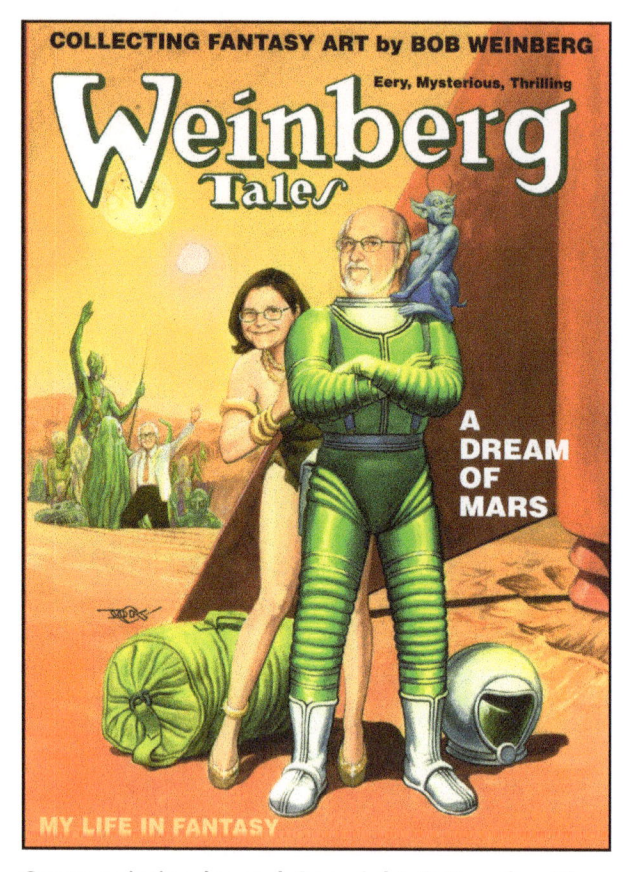

Cover painting by and Copyright © Douglas Klauba, based on the Finlay painting at left. This book collects a series of essays on how Bob and Phyllis Weinberg assembled a massive private collection of science fiction and fantasy art. – Published by American Fantasy Press and Tattered Pages Press, www.americanfantasypress.com.

Weinberg Tales starts with this introduction:

"I own one of the finest collections of original science fiction and fantasy art in the world. My collection is particularly nice in regards to the first Golden Age of SF, the late 1930s and early 1940s. I own approximately 100 pieces by Virgil Finlay, including over 20 color originals. I also have twenty Edd Cartier's, about an equal number of Hannes Bok pieces, and twenty or so pieces by Lawrence Sterne Stevens.

"It's taken me nearly forty years to assemble my collection. During that time I was involved with many of the major deals involving art in the science fiction field. I've bought and sold hundreds of paintings and black and white originals. I never cheated anyone and by and large, I feel I treated just about every collector I dealt with, with respect. No one was ever cheated by me in dealing for art, and my word was and is my bond.

"How I amassed approximately four hundred originals by many of the top artists in the SF and fantasy fields is the subject of these articles. I started with nothing, not one piece of art, nearly four decades ago. It took me years to accumulate my collection. It's a long, complicated story, and involves many well-known figures in the science fiction collecting field. I hope it proves to be of some use for collectors to come. I know I could have used some help during my years and years of building my collection."

Robert Weinberg died in fall of 2016. Several of his friends, and his wife Phyllis, compiled this book which chronicles his adventures in collecting original artwork.

It's a book that would obviously appeal to other collectors.

You wouldn't expect non-collectors to get any value from it,.

So, assuming all you non-collectors will never read this book, I'll tell you what I took away from it.

Weinberg first describes setting his goal, making his decision, to collect SF and fantasy art.

He then tells how he decided to achieve this goal. One thing he did was to "network," though I don't think he ever used that word. It's something job-seekers are advised to do. Motivational speakers, encouraging those looking for work, or to make that next big move in their careers, emphasize the importance of developing a network of diverse people, keeping in touch with them, and most importantly, letting everyone in that network know what the person is looking for.

That is exactly what Weinberg did.

Time after time, example after example, Weinberg describes how he set the groundwork for future opportunities. As described in the quote above, he did so with respect and honesty. A job seeker or other professional, desiring to build a network, is also advised to treat people with respect and honest; few people will want to help you if you act like a jerk (except for other jerks; and what value can they offer?).

One great value a book like this offers: "Example after example." It's fine for someone to tell you to establish a network and make it grow. Good advice, but can you take that general statement and translate it into practical, real-life actions? Maybe. Or maybe it's helpful to see example after example of how someone else did it—even if the specifics (collecting art) are nothing you'd ever engage in.

All the examples of Weinberg's networking, establishing relations with people and letting them know what he's looking for, is like working the land and planting the seeds. Instead of seeds, Weinberg prepared the soil for *opportunities*.

The next phase is to be ready, when those opportunities presented themselves. He needed the background education to recognize that they were opportunities. He needed to be ready and willing to act. To seize those opportunities.

The opportunities he describes are incredible.

If you're able to look beyond the specifics of collecting art, it's plain that his approach can be used for nearly any kind of long-range goal.

Changing careers.

Meeting substantial, long-lasting friends.

Realizing a goal that is much more than just a "hobby" (like climbing Mt. Everest).

Learning a skill you've always wanted to acquire, that is not directly involved with your current line of work.

Turning that skill, interest, or hobby into your career.

Bob Weinberg's book tells of:

1. Setting the goal (and refining it as needed).
2. Creating the necessary conditions for opportunities.
3. Recognizing opportunities and acting on them.

(Repeating this cycle as necessary.)

Anyone can offer you advice in that summary form. But it lacks the emotional impact of reading example after example, which this book offers.

Maybe you know of other books where the author describes the steps he/she took to achieve a long-term goal.

If you do, would you like to tell us about them?

The Arbitrary and the Burden of Proof

"There are too many people living on this planet."

Does that statement contain a logical fallacy?

How could it? The person is just stating a fact. Or wait—*is it* a fact?

Someone is asking you (telling you? *ordering* you?) to accept something as true, with a simple statement. If no support, evidence, or justification for the statement is given, the logical fallacy consists of what is *not* there, rather than what *is* there.

When someone makes a claim, it is perfectly reasonable to say, "You made the claim. Now back it up. The burden of proof is on *you* to support or prove it."

Without any supporting evidence, a claim like the above should be considered *arbitrary*.

There is no need to try refuting an arbitrary claim. (In some cases, that's impossible; an example is given later.) But when you see or hear an arbitrary statement, it *is* necessary to identify it—in your own mind, for sure; to others, if appropriate.

Be sure it's arbitrary

Always ask questions for clarification. Never assume you understand a person's views, based on a simple statement. Especially if they're provocative or controversial, ask:

"Why do you say that?" (It doesn't have to be any fancier than that.)

Now, if the other person elaborates with a series of facts, figures, reasons, etc., that's something you can evaluate. You have the basis for a conversation which will possibly contribute to your knowledge.

Sometimes there is no time to justify your statements. I've heard of authors who have spent months, even years, writing a book that takes a particular viewpoint. The book could spend hundreds of pages supporting, leading up to, and confirming that viewpoint. Authors being interviewed on radio or TV are sometimes faced with a host who says, "Now your book has just been published, and you make a claim that has startled some people. What is it?" (The host then leans over and whispers, "You have 15 seconds.")

A culture of the arbitrary

Pumped gas, lately? Been assaulted by one of those gas-pump TV channels? The kind that give you "sound bytes" that are so quick, they don't even leave an aftertaste in your mind?

And what about the TV news? As the 2- or 3-person comedy team flits from one item to another, spending 15 to 30 seconds per topic as the same 5-second video loop keeps repeating, do you ever feel a sense of incompleteness? That uneasy "I think I missed something" feeling?

News shows, and so much else in our culture, continues to "dumb down" (something The Plymouth Review Current refuses to do). News and other topics sometimes become superficial. Claims are made on one side or more. Evidence? Support? *Reasons?* There's no time for that.

That doesn't necessarily mean the evidence, support and reasons *aren't* there. Again: Be sure it's arbitrary.

Arbitrary vs. arbitrary

If someone makes a statement in a conversation, there's a very simple way to find if it's arbitrary, and it's even possible to retain your cool politeness. State the negative of the original statement.

Someone tells you, "There are too many people living on this planet." You reply, "There are *not* too many people living on this planet. Now, I realize that my statement has just as much validity as yours—that is, no validity whatsoever. But they do cancel each other out. So the net result is zero. And that's exactly what the two statements add up to. *Zero!*"

If he opens his mouth, but can't think of what to say, encourage him with: "Now, if you have *reasons* for that statement, I'm all ears."

And if he doesn't give you any reasons? You're entirely justified in treating the statement as if nothing has been said.

Because....

The burden of proof is on he who makes the claim.

This is a very basic principle in human thought.

"Prove it's not true!"

Suppose someone makes a statement. You ask for evidence. His reply: "Prove it's not true!"

What then?

Are you going to gather evidence to prove it's not true?

You shouldn't. What he's asking is impossible. If something does not exist, there can be no evidence pointing to the fact that, "This thing does not exist."

This is a logical result of the Burden of Proof principle.

No, wait. *Correction.* It's the other way around. The fact that something's non-existence provides no evidence against it, leads to the Burden of Proof principle. (Sorry; I know that's a hard sentence to digest.)

The Burden of Proof principle applies widely to human thought. *Very* widely. Anywhere you need to determine what is true.

One example is the idea that a person is guilty until proven innocent.

A society that ignores this principle would collapse into barbarism. If some little girls point at an elderly woman and say, "She's a witch!", imagine the nightmare results if the Inquisitors say, "Now, old woman, prove that you are *not* a witch!"

Similarly, if someone pointed to you and shouted to everyone else, "He's a murderer!" (and supposing you are in fact innocent), and you were then told, "Prove it's not true!", you couldn't do it, no matter how innocent you are. Your act of murder is non-existent; there is nothing in reality, no clue, that would result from the non-existence of that murder.

Living in a non-arbitrary world

If people understood logical thinking enough to identify and reject the arbitrary, life would be quite different. For example:

• When you ask someone to justify a statement, they do so. They don't hide behind a shrug and a smirk and say, "Well, I have a right to my opinion."

• People would be more careful about making claims. Anticipating the need to justify their claims, they'd be ready to defend their positions. People would understand it's foolish to spout off statements without understanding them, to some degree.

• Disagreements or misunderstandings would be addressed with reasoned arguments, not with fists or guns. That doesn't mean everyone will always agree on everything, but—sometimes that's *OK*, right?

• Having some understanding of a viewpoint's basis gives a person confidence in that viewpoint; a sense of "I can defend my view with facts. It's more than just a baseless opinion." In contrast, a person holding a viewpoint shallowly, without a foundation, often becomes irritated, defensive, even violent, when challenged.

Don't think that kind of social change is impossible. It's always been happening throughout history, and it's always *(always)* based on some aspect of philosophy. Change the overall philosophy, and you change a culture.

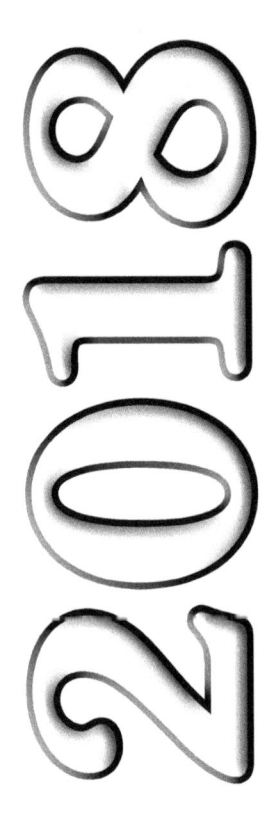

2018

The Plymouth Review Current

Taking You Places Worth Seeing
Volume 7 • Issue 2 • January 2018

FREE!

Movies • Art • Dining (Local and Otherwise) • Practical Logic • Bread

January
2018

Cover photo: Bread Cart at Restaurant Guy Savoy, Las Vegas

Great Movies This Month

PulpArtists by David Saunders: Virgil Finlay

Natural Connections by Emily Stone: Hibernating Bears May Look Asleep, But They Are Still Alert / Let Sleeping Bears Lie

I Ate At... by Richard J. Baumann: Cheese Counter Dairy Heritage Center, Plymouth

Recipes from World-Class Chefs

Ask a Science Teacher by Larry Scheckel: What Are Some Science Predictions that Did Not Come True?

In Principle, by Steve Ditko

Logic in Your Life: Principles, Double Standards, and Slippery Slopes

Once in a Lifetime, by Paul Mueller: Ospreys

Eating Out—Way Out

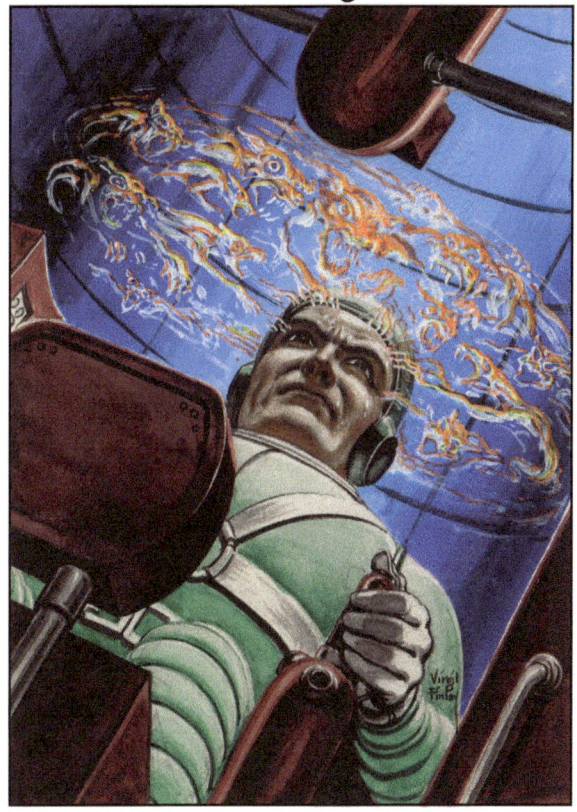

Friends, do tasks you perform routinely demand every bit of your concentration? If so, you know how annoying distractions are. For instance, when navigating a space ship with thousands of passenger lives depending on your undivided attention, you don't have the luxury to be distracted by those pesky space gremlins that sneak. That's why doctors recommend TANST (There Ain't No Such Thing) to help you concentrate on the task at hand. – Art by Virgil Finlay; HA.com

Seneca Seasons:
A Farm Boy Remembers

In Seneca Seasons, Larry Scheckel takes us to his boyhood days, growing up with eight siblings on the family farm in the hill country of southwestern Wisconsin. With both humor and grace, he shares his memories of seasonal farm life and the one-room country school out on Oak Grove Ridge, which was the social heart of the community, from the basket social to the Christmas program and the end-of-the-year school picnic. Join Scheckel on his nostalgic and evocative journey back to a simpler time when life revolved around family, farm, Church, and seasons.

This is what Larry has to say about this memoir: "All the events in the book really happened, but the mind is not a video camera, so my stories are only as accurate as my memory. This memoir is a collection of impressions that still linger in my heart.

"When I was 18 years old, I left the farm and joined the Army. I was sent to Fort Leonard Wood, Missouri, in October 1960. After that, I often visited, but never again worked on the farm.

"Our Crawford County farm was located in the middle of Seneca Township. Called the Driftless area, it was roughed up by the glaciers 10,000 years ago. Hill country is where farmers plow the narrow ridge hilltops and the coulee bottoms. People think that all farm country is flat, and a lot of it is. If you look at a plat book or county road map of Iowa, you will see roads that are straight lines. That is flat country. But if you glance at a road map of Crawford County, the roads look like spaghetti on a plate. The roads follow the ridge tops and are so crooked they could run for Congress, as we often joked.

"Most families on Oak Grove Ridge were either German, Norwegian, Irish or English. The Scheckels were German. People celebrated their heritage by keeping traditions alive. The Norwegians made their lefse flatbread and lutefisk and sent their children to Norwegian language summer schools. Germans were fond of their wurst sausages and ale beers. The Irish celebrated their music, St. Patrick's Day, and their Catholic heritage.

"Saints and sinners lived on Oak Grove Ridge. Most attended a church of their chosen religion. The Scandinavians gravitated to the Lutheran Church. The Irish were partial to the Catholic faith. The Germans practiced both.

"Most people behaved themselves. Some drank more than they should. A few farmers treated their spouses and children harshly. Most people stayed married to the same mate their entire life. Divorce was a rarity.

"Nobody thought they were better than anybody else. Arguments and feuds rarely occurred. Everybody just tried to get along and get ahead. Farmers helped other farmers, especially if one was injured or sick. Late-summer threshing crews bound neighbors together. The sense of community was strong.

"The Oak Grove District #15 one-room country school was a focal point that drew all families together three times a year. Appropriately, it sat on a hill in the middle of Oak Grove Ridge. The children of those farmers mingled, worked together, learned together, and played together. Kids talked. There were few family secrets.

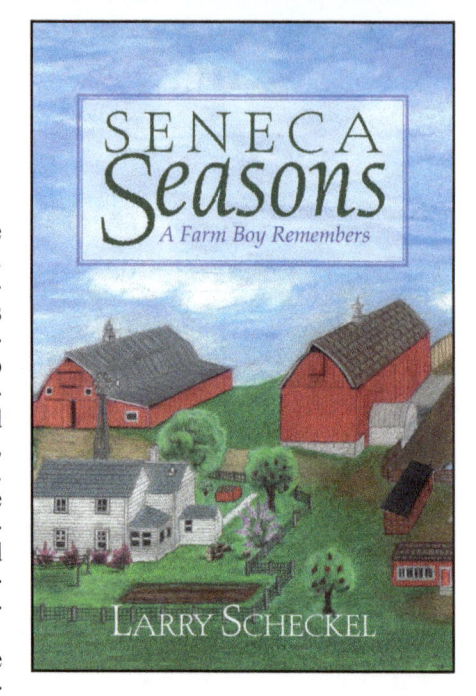

"Perhaps there were easier places to grow up in America in the 1940s and 1950s, but I'd pick the 238-acre farm on Oak Grove Ridge. The lessons learned from Dad, Mom, my brothers and sisters, the one-room country school, and St. Patrick's Catholic Church have lasted me a lifetime.

"This narrative means to capture a slice of a unique era in Wisconsin history. It was the age when horses were supplanted by tractors and when a threshing band was replaced by the combine. Through all these changes, though, the beat of the heartland, of its simple people and their direct ways, has remained ever the same. In the end, that is why that farm on Oak Grove Ridge has never stopped calling me home."

Dining Out— *Way* Out

My wife and I go to Las Vegas for two main reasons: the shows (mostly Cirque du Soleil), and the restaurants.

Gambling? Not much. The last few times, I gambled *once*.

This past November, we ate at three special restaurants. Descriptions in quotes are taken from the menus. Don't worry if you don't know what some of the terms mean; I don't, myself.

A lot of items are shown for a single meal, but: Portions are usually quite small (you can leave after a 17-item sampling menu feeling quite satisfied, but nowhere near as bloated as with a typical Thanksgiving dinner); and what is shown was for two people.

Restaurant: *Twist*

Location: The Mandaran Oriental
Chef: Pierre Gagnaire

Pierre Gagnaire owns several restaurants in the world, but Twist is his only one in America.

Gagnaire competed on the Japanese Iron Chef TV show. Search the 'net for "Gagnaire Iron Chef French Castle" and you should be able to find this on YouTube; it's an inspiring 2-part battle taking place in a French Castle. You'll know you have the right video if it starts with Chairman Kaga, looking reflectively out the window of a speeding train. (Joel Robuchon is one of the judges on this episode.)

At the end of 2015, Gagnaire was voted by his peers as the "Best Chef in the World."

Talking to one of the restaurant's managers, I told him I consider Chef Gagnaire to be "a Thomas Edison of cuisine." The manager looked surprised and said, "I've never heard

Chef Gagnaire; his book, 175 Home Recipes with a Twist.

that. I think—I think *I'll* use that!"

Gagnaire lives in France. He visits Twist several times each year. Chef Frédéric Don is the Chef de Cuisine at Twist.

1. Diners receive several pre-meal treats. I can't remember what these were.
2. "Pierre's Salad. Bouquet of Fresh Herbs and Salad, Tartare of Fruits and Vegetables, Seasonal Dressing, Three Slices of Artisinal Cheese." Salad is in a thin, crispy bread shell; breaking this into flaky parts provides the croutons.
3. "Beignet of Langoustine. Caramelized Onions, SWA Spice; Pascaline of Raisins, Beurre Fondue and Cauliflower Sommites; Bisque: Green Lentils from Puy en Vilais, Heart of Palms; Spicy Tartare, Savoy Cabbage and Mango." This serving could also be called "Langoustine Four Ways." (Langoustine is a crustacean, larger than a shrimp.)
4. "Hudson Valley Foie Gras, Two Ways." Bottom left: "Seared Foie with Red Marmalade." Bottom right: "Natural Terrine, Dulcey Chocolate, Fig Paste, Beetroot Syrup and Cabbage Gelèe." (Gelèe is French for jelly.) Center: "Butter brioche and red tuille" (a tuille is a thin wafer).
5. Palate cleansers. Sorbet, fruit, and a tiny beet.
6. Prime beef. The long item is a crispy potato roll with some bits of Iberico ham.
7. "Wild European Turbot. Roasted and Finished in a Beurre Nantais, Globe Artichoke Purée and Dry Grapes." Three small dishes at top, left to right: "Pomme Fondante stuffed with Braised Beef Cheek," "Carrot and Coconut Foam," "Fregola Pasta and Prawns."
8. Desserts. (Remember, these are quite small portions.) Top center: "Latour. Manjari Chocolate Biscuit, Cheesecake and Praline Mousseline, Hazelnut Crunch, Blackcurrant Sorbet, Sicilian Pistachio, Hazelnut, Almonds." Grand Dessert (the other 5 dishes): "Raisins and Aloe Vera with Licorice Kaffir Lime Vodka Coulis, Basil Lime Sherbet. Coconut Panna Cotta with Elderflower Cream, Frozen Heering Pineapple. Apple Tatin with Calvados Caramel Sauce, Vanilla Ice Cream. Manjari Parfait, Almond Nougatine, Bitter Chocolate Foam. Grand Marnier Hibiscus Gelée, White Almond Paste."
9. And when the meal is complete, you get more free treats. The one at right, I believe, was in honor of our anniversary.

Sadly, Twist closed during the "pandemic" and never re-opened. Chef Gagnaire has restaurants in other parts of the world.

Restaurant: *Guy Savoy*

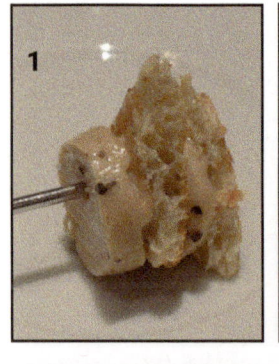

Guy Savoy; a "Best of" book.

Location: Caesar's Palace
Chef: Guy Savoy

Chef Savoy lives in France. Chef Julien Asseo is the head chef at the Las Vegas restaurant; a brief interview with him appeared in the December 2016 issue of The PRC.

Several little pre-meal treats are served: 1. A tiny sandwich with foie gras; 2. a teeny-weeny hamburger; 3. spiced mango soup.

4. (See cover.) The bread cart is—well, is "impressive" an exaggeration?

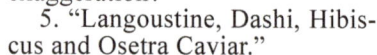

5. "Langoustine, Dashi, Hibiscus and Osetra Caviar."

The cheese cart: 5. The server describes each (soft, hard; cow's, sheep's or goat's milk) and you can select a slice of any that sound interesting. All are French. 7. Our cheese selections.

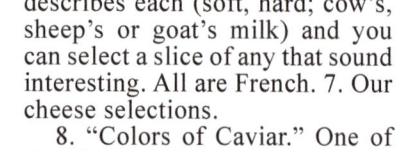

8. "Colors of Caviar." One of the dishes this restaurant is famous for. Atop several layers of whipped vegetables is a dollop of caviar, which is all but invisible, as it was covered by a layer of sabayon sauce. A metal spoon will react with the caviar and affect its flavor; so as shown here, a mother of pearl spoon is used.

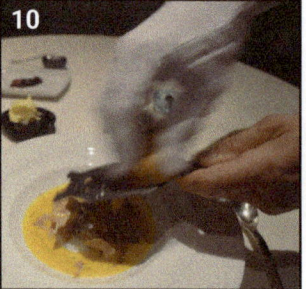

Pumpkin soup with white truffles: 9. With the lights of Vegas in the background, the pumpkin soup is about to be ladled out. Just to the left tip of the soup bowl is a portion of a white truffle which cost the restaurant $3000 per pound. 10. Faster than the eye (or camera) can follow, the server shaves several slices of white truffle onto the pumpkin soup.

11. "Salmon 'Mi-Cuit.'" Osetra Caviar atop salmon, with a caviar / Beurre Blanc sauce.

12. "Crispy line-caught French Sea Bass with delicate spices."

13. A refreshing palate-cleanser. (Uh oh... what was it?)

14. Dessert: "Carrot and Orange." That's not an actual carrot. Both items on the plate are made of a carrot-orange fondant. Both flavors could be tasted in this refreshing combination. *Very* special.

15. Dessert: Chocolate variations.

16. Selections from the dessert cart include a pineapple lollipop.

Restaurant: *Joel Robuchon*

Location: MGM Grand
Chef: Joel Robuchon

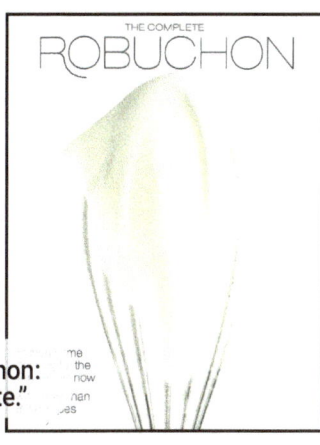

Two books by Joel Robuchon: A "Best of" and a "Complete."

Chef Robuchon also lives in France. As with the two chefs above, this restaurant in Las Vegas is his only one in the United States.

As with many other chefs, I first heard of Robuchon through the Japanese Iron Chef TV show. He appeared as a guest, though not as a contestant, on several episodes.

About the restaurant's head chef, a recent magazine article said: "At just 29, [Christophe] De Lellis is quite possibly the city's youngest Executive Chef, working at arguably one of the best restaurants in the world."

Alex Guarnaschelli (who appeared on the front cover of last November's PRC) wrote in her book, Old-School Comfort Food:

"Cooking is a lifelong learning process. Whether cooking at home or becoming a chef, don't forget to be patient. Consider this:

"In 1983, my parents took me on a trip to Paris. The second night, we ate at Chef Joel Robuchon's famous restaurant Jamin. At that time, Robuchon had been cooking for twenty-plus years and was considered the most important chef in Paris. As we ate our appetizers, we didn't utter a word. There were flavors so pure and so complex that speaking and eating at the same time was out of the question. My father turned to the waiter and exclaimed: 'This is some of the best food I have ever eaten in my life!' The water tilted his head slightly in my father's direction and responded: 'Yes, and in another ten years he will almost be a really great chef.' "

In the late 1980s, Chef Robuchon was named, by a French culinary organization, "The Chef of the Century."

(His restaurant is right next to the Cirque du Soleil show KA. If you plan a trip to Las Vegas, KA is the Cirque show (out of seven the city offers) I'd recommend the most highly.)

I opted for the 17-course tasting menu, while my wife ordered a la carte.

1. View of the restaurant from the corner where we sat.
2. Tiny appetizer.
3. A little butter and olive oil, for your bread?
4. And here comes the bread cart. Selections include milk bread, bread with saffron, rosemary, basil, bacon; traditional French breads, and more.
5. "Oscetra caviar served atop of king crab in a gelèe dotted with cauliflower puree.
6. Daikon radish soup, with caviar and herbs.
7. Left: "Shaved white truffles and potatoes with olive oil, topped with carpaccio of foie gras." Right: "Duo of beetroot and apple, young shoots of herbs served with green mustard

sorbet."

8. "Scottish salmon with a wasabi creme fraiche layered with oscetra caviar."

"Celariac served al dente as tagliatelle with comte cheese sauce. (No photo; didn't turn out.)

9. "Frog leg fritter with black and white garlic puree." One of the most delicious items I've ever eaten.

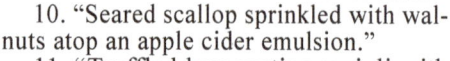

10. "Seared scallop sprinkled with walnuts atop an apple cider emulsion."

11. "Truffled langoustine ravioli with simmered green cabbage."

12. "Delicate cream of pumpkin with mimolette cheese and white truffles."

13. "John Dory fish fillet with tempura of shiso leaf on delicate squid ink risotto."

14. "Lobster wrapped in spinach served atop Malabar pepper sauce."

15. "Grilled matsutake [mushroom] with duck foie gras in crispy gyoza and celery foam."

16. "Venison fillet and foie gras 'Rossini' style, vintage port reduction." Robuchon's mashed potatoes are legendary.

17. Filet mignon. The thin, translucent tuille is made of pepper.

18. Three pre-desserts. Center: "Shaved ice with hibiscus syrup." The two leaves: "Raspberry-cherry blossom compote" and "Earl Gray tiramisu with mascarpone."

19. Grand dessert: "Smooth hazelnut milk chocolate cremeaux with coffee chantilly and praline ice cream." (This looked like a little terrarium in a glass. Everything in it was edible; rock, "dirt," butterflies, twig, moss.)

20. A little cake in honor of our anniversary.

21. The dessert cart. The server names every item on it.

22. Our selections from the dessert cart. (This photo almost became our cover for this issue.)

Chef Robuchon passed away in August, 2018.

February 2018

Cover photo: Your Editor's Front Yard
Great Movies This Month
Delving into the Mind of Alfred Hitchcock
One Take
I Ate At... by Richard J. Baumann: The Wisconsin Room, The American Club, Kohler
Ask a Science Teacher by Larry Scheckel: Are Baseballs Juiced Up?
Natural Connections by Emily Stone: Some Marvels of a Three-Dog Day
Once in a Lifetime, by Paul Mueller: Sturgeon
PulpArtists by David Saunders: W. B. Grubb

The Plymouth Review **Current**
TAKING YOU PLACES WORTH SEEING
Volume 7 • Issue 3 • February 2018

FREE!

Movies • Art • Alfred Hitchcock • Dining
Thinking Skills • Astrophysics

One Take

Here's how part of a movie is made.

The film camera starts recording. Some plaque identifying the film, scene, and take are shown. The director says, "Action!"

The actor is looking down at his soup. He looks up, then leans back in his chair, frowning.

"Cut!"

This little snippet will be edited along with many other little snippets. The final result is a continuity where one actor is shown (and maybe says something); another is shown, reacting and maybe responding. They go back and forth, with "cuts" between the two actors.

Let's imagine a scene where a secret agent has to climb all the steps of the Lincoln Memorial. Suppose the director, to emphasize how many steps there are, decided to follow the actor as he climbed the steps. He calls "Action!" before the actor takes the first step; keeps the camera tracking the actor; calls "Cut!" when the actor reaches the top step.

That step-climbing sequence would be said to be "one continuous take."

The longer a director plans for one continuous take, the higher the chances that something—anything—could go wrong, and the whole thing has to be photographed over again.

In 1948, Alfred Hitchcock decided to try something different. He made Rope, a movie based on a play. It was his first Technicolor movie, but it was very different in another way. He wanted to make it seem like a play, with events happening in real time. He also wanted to do one continuous take.

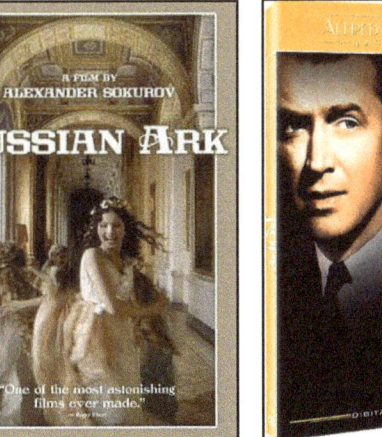

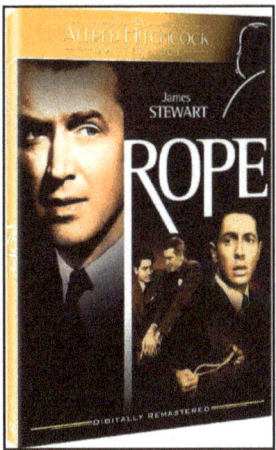

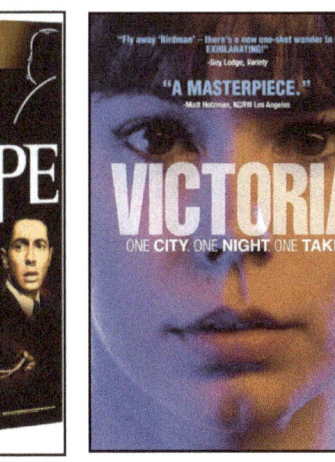

– DVD cover images from Barnes & Noble, BN.com

But he was limited. He couldn't just start the movie camera, tell the actors to get going and keep going for over an hour. Hitchcock was limited by the length of film in the movie camera. A reel of film only lasted about ten minutes.

Yet, Hitchcock worked within those limits. He made Rope by doing a series of long, continuous takes, transitioning the different parts by focusing (for example) on someone's back, at which point the reel of film would end; then, again focusing on the same person's back, the next reel of film would start, and the actors would go into action for the next ten minutes.

Rope is a very different type of film. There is no general agreement as to whether it's any good. Pamela Hutchinson of The Guardian calls Rope "My favourite Hitchcock film." Roger Ebert wrote in 1984 that Rope was an experiment that "didn't work out."

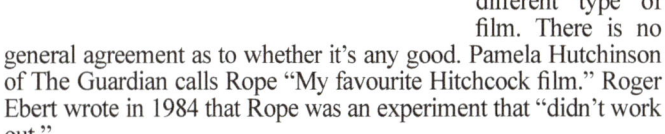

What advance in technology would make it possible to do an entire feature-length movie in one take? Digital film, where the film camera's images are saved to a hard drive instead of being saved on exposed film.

A 2002 film, Russian Ark, did just that. It's a hard film to categorize, but I consider it a fantasy. Two narrators wander through the Winter Palace in Saint Petersburg. Time periods change as they go from room to room, touring the museum.

It's about 90 minutes long, and was done in one take.

A documentary (called In One Breath) on the DVD version that I have is just as fascinating as the actual film. It tells how any interruption or critical error in the process would have made it necessary to start filming from the beginning. Indeed, that happened! They had three failures, causing them to start from scratch. And the film producers only had a limited number of hours to work in the museum.

But they finally succeeded. As stated at Wikipedia, "The film displays 33 rooms of the museum, which are filled with a cast of over 2,000 actors and three orchestras." The film's climax is a magnificent ballroom dance.

Can you imagine the planning needed to accomplish this? As the camera crew moved from one room to another, whatever actors and props had to be in place and ready to go.

Russian Ark is a film that's **highly recommended.**

The 2014 film Birdman, starring Michael Keaton, was constructed to look like it's one continuous take. But it's not.

The 2015 German film, Victoria, is one uninterrupted take. It's a staggering 138 minutes. A notable achievement, to be sure, but is the movie any good? Sorry—I can't make a recommendation. I started watching it, could not relate to the characters, and didn't watch the whole thing. Victoria is available on Netflix.

I'm sure we'll see other movies made in one continuous take. They will need to be judged like any other movie, however. Is it a work of cinematic art, or is it just a stunt?

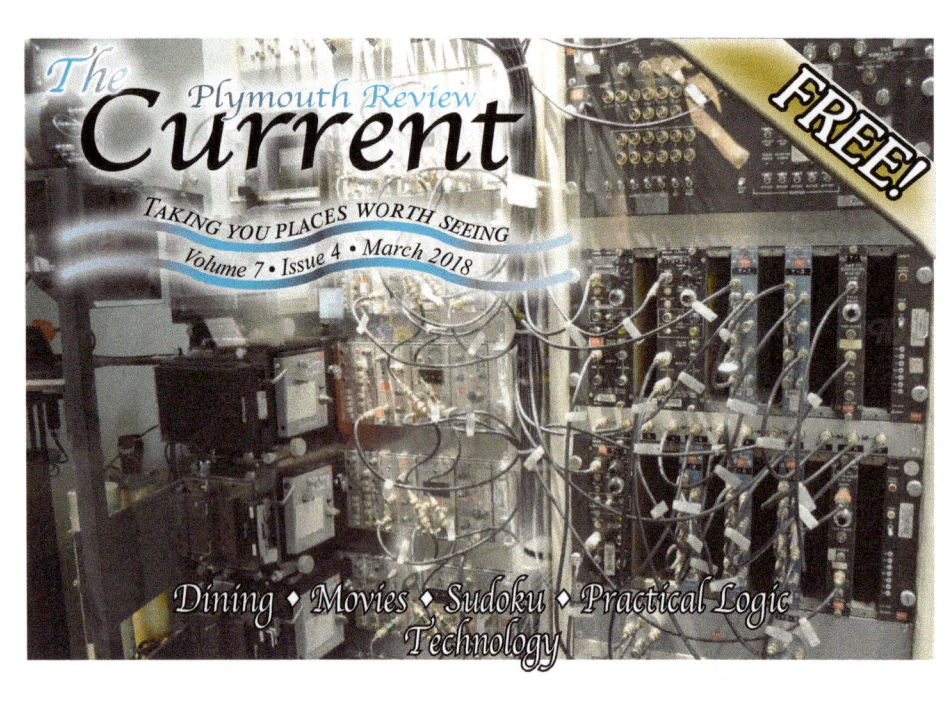

March
2018

Cover photo: National Atomic Testing Museum, Las Vegas
Great Movies This Month
PulpArtists by David Saunders: Wallace Wood
Logic in Your Life: Principles: An Integrated View of Life
Ask a Science Teacher by Larry Scheckel: Why Doesn't the Earth Have More Craters, Like the Moon?

Blind Horse: "Culinary Star of the Year"
Once in a Lifetime, by Paul Mueller: Going West
I Ate At... by Richard J. Baumann: Yummy Bones BBQ, Port Washington
Natural Connections by Emily Stone: Grouse Drumming Is More Like Something Felt Than Heard

Drawings by Wallace Wood. See PulpArtists. – both HA.com

The Atomic Testing Museum

The National Atomic Testing Museum is a short distance off the main Las Vegas strip.

Here is the museum's own description, from its website:

"The National Atomic Testing Museum (NATM) is a national science, history and educational institution that tells the story of America's nuclear weapons testing program at the Nevada Test Site. The Museum uses lessons of the past and present to better understand the extent and effect of nuclear testing on worldwide nuclear deterrence and geo-political history. It provides collection-based exhibits and learning activities for greater public understanding and appreciation of the world in which we live. Its collections and activities are inseparably linked to serve a diverse public of varied ages, backgrounds and knowledge.

"The National Atomic Testing Museum is one of a handful of private national museums and showcases some of the rarest of artifacts relating to the nation's atomic testing program. Nowhere else can you see a large nuclear reactor that was used in the development of the nuclear rocket and the first air-to-air missile, Genie. Personal atomic weapons that were developed to use in place of conventional weapons such as the Backpack Nuke and the Davy Crockett Weapon System (recoilless gun) are placed throughout the 8,000 square feet of museum exhibits.

"From Atomic Age culture to the scientific and technological advances, the Museum highlights 70 years of nuclear testing. The end of the Cold War is depicted through a piece of the Berlin Wall complete with the celebratory graffiti painted by Berliners when the wall came down. Two pieces of the World Trade Center signify the beginning of the Global War on Terror and how the Museum today plays a role in the training of first-responders from across the nation who come to learn about the nuclear materials terrorists might use."

Among museums and similar attractions in Las Vegas, the NATM is one of the highest rated by those posting reviews online.

nationalatomictestingmuseum.org

Mike (right) had actually worked with the atomic testing program in the 1960s. He walked through the museum, answering questions and relating stories of his experiences. A *very* interesting person! Behind him is the Ground Zero Theater.

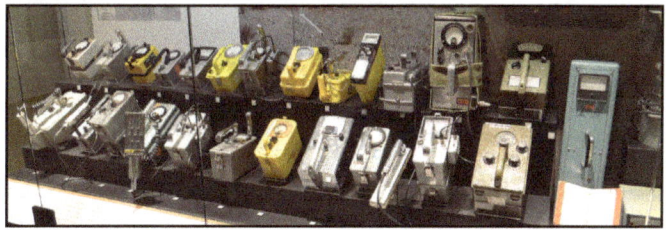

David Saunders'
pulpartists.com

Wallace Wood: Best of the Best

(1927-1981)

Wallace "Wally" Allan Wood was born June 17, 1927 in Menahga, Minnesota. His father, Max Glenn Wood, was born 1901 in Minnesota. His mother, Alma Lalli, was born 1895 in Minnesota of Finnish ancestry. They married in 1924. They had two children. His older brother Glenn was born in 1925. They lived on a farm in Becker, Minnesota.

In 1933 at the age of six he had a dream about finding a magic pencil that could draw anything.

His father was a farmer, as was his father before him. When the Great Depression brought hard times, many farmers looked for work as migrant laborers. Max Glenn Wood became a logger and traveled to wherever they were hiring. He eventually became a gang foreman. His family followed and relocated to towns across Minnesota, Michigan and Wisconsin, but his father often worked at remote logging camps for a month at a time. During these absences his mother was head of the family. Such long absences strained their marriage.

By 1943 his older brother was studying engineering in an Oregon college, while he and his mother had moved to Minneapolis. In June of 1944 he graduated Minneapolis West High School. Afterwards his parents formally agreed to lead separate lives.

That fall he joined the Merchant Marines. His training was in New York City's Sheepshead Bay. He sailed around the world during wartime on a fuel tanker. Mercifully, the ship was never attacked.

In the fall of 1945 after WWII had ended he returned to Minneapolis, where he worked at a funeral home as an embalmer undertaker.

On February 11, 1946 he enlisted and served in the Army Airborne 11th Paratroopers. His basic training was at Fort Benning, Georgia. He was stationed at an airbase in occupied Japan.

In 1947 after honorable discharge he returned home and enrolled in the Minneapolis School of Art on the G.I. Bill.

In August of 1948 he moved to New York City and lived on West 97th Street. To make ends meet he worked as a bus boy in a restaurant. In his spare time he looked for work as a pen and ink artist in the New York publishing industry. He also took classes in lettering, drawing and anatomy three nights a week at the Hogarth School of Art, which was founded one year earlier by Burne Hogarth, who drew the newspaper comic strip *Tarzan*. The school was on East 23th Street near 2nd Avenue. It was a trade school, originally called the Cartoonists and Illustrators School.

He gradually found a wide range of low-paying entry level jobs in New York City's busy comic book industry. That fertile commu-

117

Wood illustration from Galaxy magazine, late 1950s, illustrating a story by Clifford Simak, who lived part of his life in southwest Wisconsin. The story was "Crying Jag," about a race of aliens (one of which is at left) that gets intoxicated by listening to other species' troubles. This alien met a farmer (second from left) who had a *lot* of troubles (one sometimes suspects farmers, like *any* business owners, have *more* than their fair share of troubles), so the alien was able to get very, *very* intoxicated. But in this future society, this was against the law, so the robot patrol squad is here coming to arrest the alien. Why was all this illegal? Aw, you'll have to read the story to find out.
Simak often featured robots in his short stories or novels. His most famous books are Way Station (about an old farm in Wisconsin that's used as a kind of truck stop for aliens traveling through the galaxy), and City (about a future when people stopped living in crowded cities; where dogs learned how to talk; where robots and dogs formed friendships; where a wandering genius taught ants how to use wheeled carts). In Simak's stories, contact between aliens and humans was usually a benevolently rational event, not a lethally warlike disaster. Some conflicts would sometimes arise, as conflicts happen even when both parties are rational.
– HA.com

nity soon brought him into contact with many inspired artists, such as Will Elder, Harvey Kurtzman, and Will Eisner.

He rented a studio on 64th Street and Columbus Avenue. According to Jules Fiefer, "It was in a very slummy Upper West Side. It was an artist's and writer's ghetto. Just a huge room where the walls were knocked down, dark, smelly, roach-infested, and all these cartoonists and writers bent over their tables." Among his neighborhood acquaintances were Ken Battefield, Allen Anderson, and Norman Saunders.

By 1950 he began to draw comic pages for pulp magazines, such as *Six-Gun Western, Fighting Western,* and *Leading Western,* all of which were produced by Trojan Publishing Co. under the art direction of Adolphe Barreaux, an historic figure in early American comic books. Wood went on to draw interior pen and ink story illustrations for pulp magazines *Planet Stories, Avon Fantasy Reader, Science-Fiction Stories,* as well as an important series of work for the digest-sized pulp magazine *Galaxy Science Fiction.*

On August 28, 1950 he married Tatjana Weintraub, who was born 1928 in Germany. They moved to Rego Park, Queens, NY.

In 1952 he was a founding artist of *Mad Magazine* along with Harvey Kurtzman and Will Elder.

In May of 1953 he and his wife moved back to Manhattan to live on West 74th Street near Columbus Avenue.

In 1962 he was hired for a freelance job to illustrate an inspired story by Woody Gelman at Topps Bubble Gum to create the preliminary designs for the landmark set of trading cards, *Mars Attacks.* The approved drawings were refined by Bob Powell and painted by Maurice Blumenfeld and Norman Saunders.

Throughout the 1960s, Topps continued to routinely hire Wally Wood to contribute to many subsequent projects, such as *Comic Book Foldees (1964), Ugly Stickers (1965), Wanted Posters (1966), Crazy Little Comics (1967),* and *Nasty Notes (1968).*

During the 1960s he also drew freelance illustrations for men's magazines, such as *Fury, Dude, Gent, Nugget,* and *Playboy.*

His legendary career is wide-ranging, prolific, and mind-boggling. His inspired work for comic books have earned him many honors and tributes, but according to the artist, "I don't worry about words, like whether I'm an illustrator or cartoonist or whatever. I'm an artist. I do it for a living. I don't make any great distinctions between fine art and commercial art either. After all, they sell those fine art paintings."

On March 30, 1963 his father died in Minnesota at the age of sixty-two.

In 1966 he and Tatjana divorced. His second marriage to Marilyn Silver also ended in divorce. His third marriage to Muriel Van Sweringen ended in separation.

Although he had two step-children in his second marriage, and three step-children in his third marriage, Wally Wood had no biological children of his own.

In the late 1960s he created Sally Forth, a comic strip for the Vietnam era servicemen's periodicals Military News and Oversees Weekly.

On November 7, at the age of 1972 his mother died in Minnesota at the age of seventy-seven.

He suffered from depression, chronic headaches, alcoholism, and kidney failure. In 1978 he had a stroke and lost the vision in his left eye.

According to Harvey Kurtzman, "Wally had a tension in him, an intensity that he locked away in an internal steam boiler. I think it ate away his insides, and the work really used him up. I think he did some of the finest work that was ever drawn, and I think it's to his credit that he put so much intensity into his work at great personal sacrifice."

According to Will Elder, "There was a quiet warmth about Wally that I liked. He was very unpretentious. He actually projected himself through his work. I felt that he could only exemplify himself through his art. There was a need of showing his sensitivity through his work, since I don't think Wally had the personality to show it any other way."

Wally Wood died from a self-inflicted gun shot in Los Angeles, CA, at the age of fifty-five on November 3, 1981.

© David Saunders 2012

Wood did a lot of work for comical cards in the 60s. He would draw crazy creatures in pencil (top), and another artist (in this case, Norman Saunders) would create a finished image (above; from the Ugly Stickers series). – Top: HA.com; bottom: from normansaunders.com

Wood was commissioned to create this image for the cover of the Overstreet Price Guide for comic books in the late 1970s. It was meant to evoke his work for EC Comics' science fiction titles, which Wood illustrated in the 50s. – Imaged by and courtesy of Heritage Auctions, HA.com

Ever visit **Hurley, Wisconsin**?

The **Iron County Historical Museum** has a small display dedicated to Wallace Wood! Why? Because he and his brother went to school there, for a short time.

Here are two photos provided by staff at the ICHM; an exterior shot of the building, and the collection of Wallace Wood material the museum has (this photo taken by Delores Genisot, one of the museum's volunteers). The exhibit, normally in a display case, can be found on the museum's second floor, in the Photo Room.

The ICHM in Hurley is open Mondays, Wednesdays, Fridays and Saturdays, from 10 to 2. It is housed in the former Iron County courthouse, and features three floors of exhibits. Hand-crafted rag rugs, runners and placemats are made and sold in the museum's weaving room.

Address: 303 Iron St, Hurley, WI 54534 (715) 561-2244
https://www.hurleywi.com/events/iron-county-historical-museum/

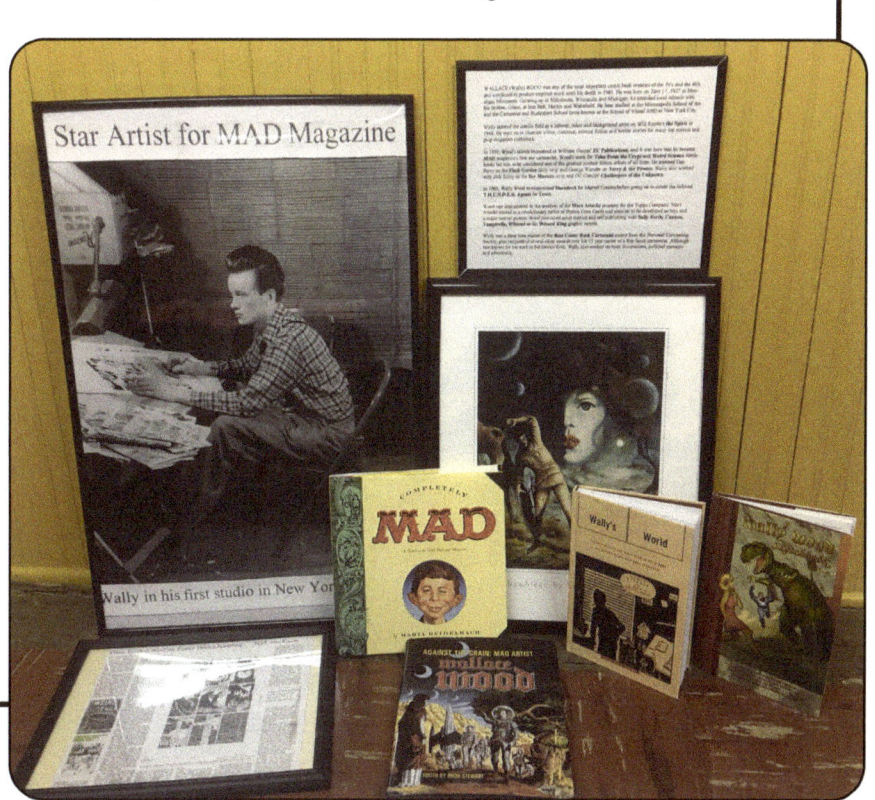

119

April
2018

Cover photo: Oaks, Inc. Candy Store, Oshkosh
Great Movies This Month
Photo: Mural of Musicians, Oshkosh
PulpArtists by David Saunders: Chester Bloom
It's Not Fair, by Steve Ditko
The Road to Polvenon, by Amy J. Heyman
Ask a Science Teacher by Larry Scheckel: Can a hole be drilled all the way through the Earth?
I Ate At... by Richard J. Baumann: D.E. O'Malley's, Plymouth
Natural Connections by Emily Stone: 'Monkeys' of the North drill for themselves to the benefit of others
Logic in Your Life: Contradictions
Once in a Lifetime, by Paul Mueller: Prairie Chickens
Two recent sources on Frederick Douglass

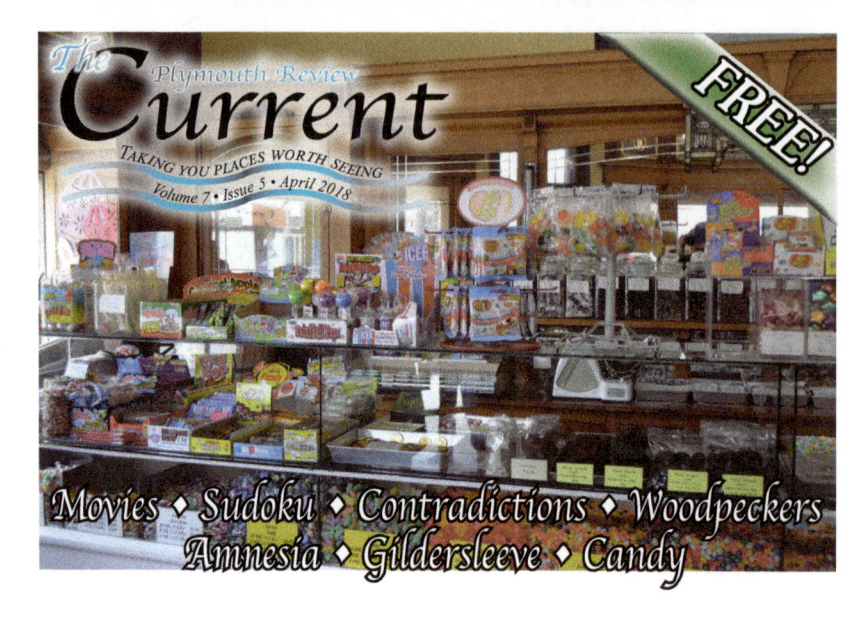

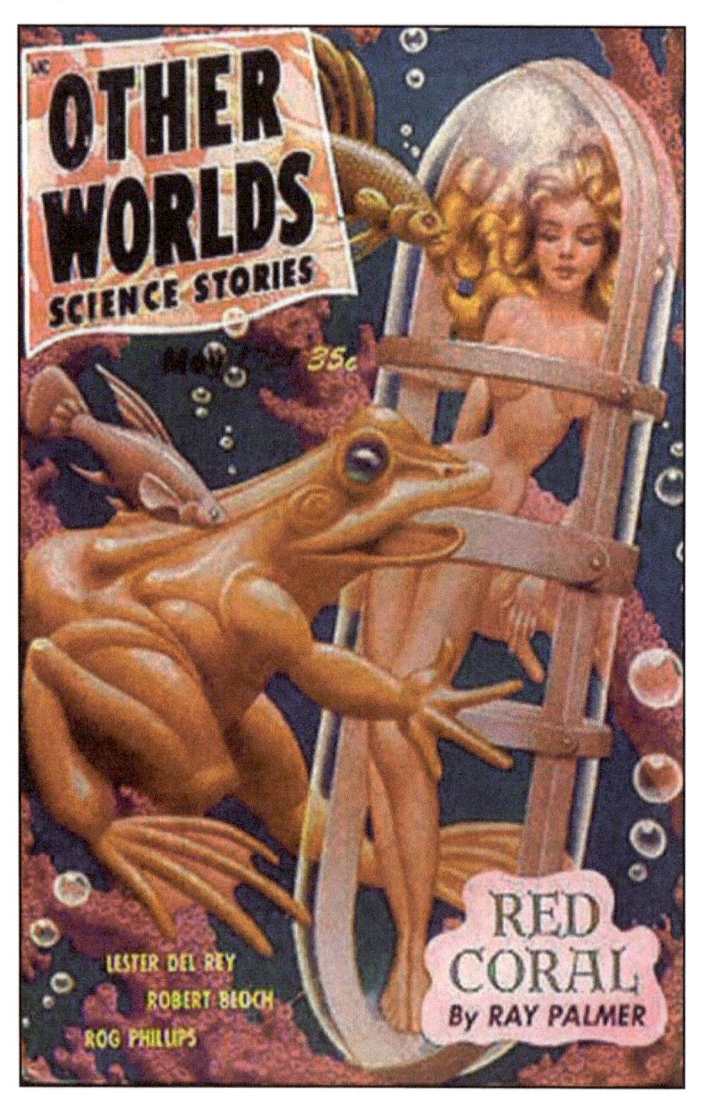

Cover painting by Hannes Bok. Robert Bloch and Ray Palmer both had ties to Wisconsin.

The Plymouth Review Current

TAKING YOU PLACES WORTH SEEING
Volume 7 • Issue 6 • May 2018

FREE!

Dr. Kildare ◊ Movies ◊ Perry Mason ◊ Boston Blackie ◊ Dining
Sudoku ◊ The Saint ◊ Beautiful Art ◊ Bulldog Drummond ◊ Masks

May 2018

Cover photo: Mask by Hannes Bok
Great Movies This Month
Articles and full-page house ad opposing newsprint tariff
Top-Selling Book Series
$30K for a Magazine?? Well... Almost
Once in a Lifetime, by Paul Mueller: A Bird of a Lifetime
The Work of Robert E. Howard
Echoes of our past by William & Joy Wangemann: City's Blue Collar Reputation Started with Barrels of Smoked Fish / Prange's Was at the Beating Heart of Sheboygan County
Natural Connections by Emily Stone: Wilderness Medicine Is Mostly About Realistic Risk Management
I Ate At... by Richard J. Baumann: A Second Look at Various Places
Ask a Science Teacher by Larry Scheckel: Why Do People Say Our "Fate Is in the Stars"?
PulpArtists by David Saunders: Hannes Bok
Your Editor to Give Presentation on Pulps at the Random Lake Library
The Pulp Roots of these Characters:
  • Dr. Kildare
  • Boston Blackie
  • Bulldog Drummond
  • The Saint
  • Perry Mason

1947 illustration accompanying "The Case of the Crying Swallow," a Perry Mason short story in American Magazine. By an incredible coincidence (or *was* it coincidence?), Your Editor saw the original painting of this work at the recent Windy City Pulp and Paper show. The painting did not have the lettering. – Public domain image from Wikipedia

$30K for a magazine??
Well... *almost*

Your Editor had a table at the Windy City Pulp and Paper (WCPP) show, selling books he's published and giving out copies of The Plymouth Review Current to anyone coming near.

Next to us was a dealer from England. Walking by one of his displays, I recognized a copy of a very special pulp—the October 1912 issue of The All-Story. According to The Art of the Pulps, "In 2006, a copy in apparent fine condition sold for $59,750, a record for a pulp magazine."

Why is it so valuable?

It has the first appearance of Edgar Rice Burroughs' character, Tarzan.

Not only that. Typically, a novel-length story was serialized; portions would run over several issues. Breaking that pattern, this first Tarzan story was published complete in this issue.

The dealer next to us had this pulp priced at $30,000. And they sold it!

I talked with the dealer, who gave me the following background:

The pulp was among some donations given to a charity shop (we in the States call them "thrift stores"). A staff member thought it might be valuable, even worth as much as $100. The shop submitted it to a small auction house in England.

The dealer next to us was the highest bidder, at $17,000 (most of which went to the charity shop). He displayed it at this pulp show, priced it at $30,000, and sold it to a buyer for $25,000. (People like to haggle on prices; it's always nice to save $5,000, right?)

Clearly, the character Tarzan is a part of our culture.

Another character that's stayed with us is Conan the Barbarian. Ever see those Conan movies with Arnold Schwarzenegger? I saw the pulp with Conan's first appearance—the Dec. 1932 issue of Weird Tales—sell at one of WCPP's auctions for $2,000. Not as high-priced as the Tarzan one, but still impressive.

Conan's creator, Robert E. Howard, was an excellent writer, and produced a surprising volume of material. But he was a troubled young man, and took his own life at age 30. A 1996 movie—The Whole Wide World—was based on the memoirs of Novalyne Price, a schoolteacher who befriended Howard late in his life.

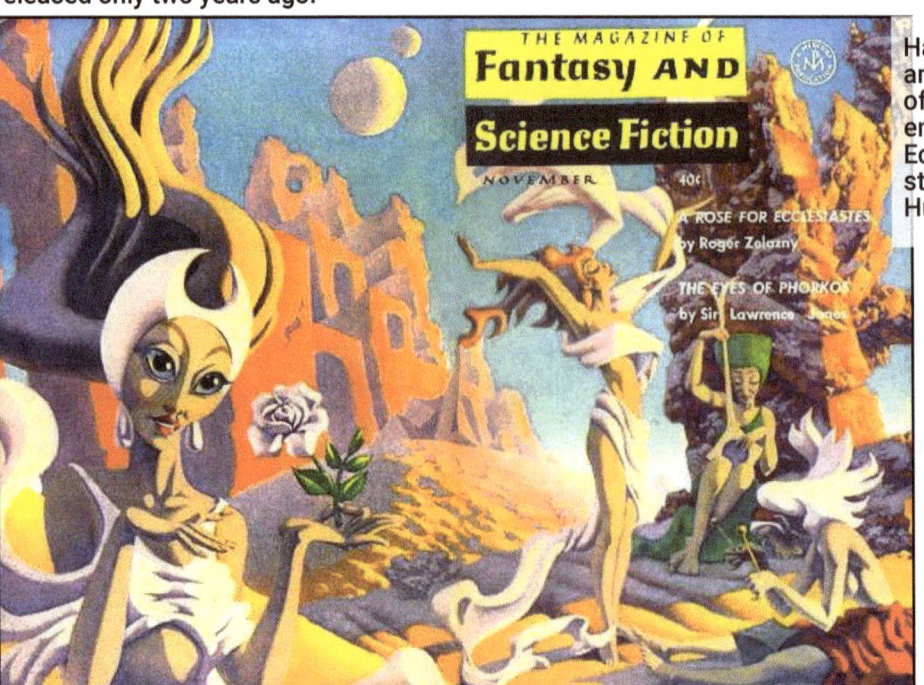

The October 1912 issue of The All-Story magazine introduced a character who is still familiar to many people throughout the world. The first movie made about him was a silent version in 1918; the most recent film chronicling his exploits was released only two years ago.

Hannes Bok did this famous wrap-around cover for the Nov. 1963 issue of The Magazine of Fantasy and Science Fiction, illustrating "A Rose for Ecclesiastes" by Roger Zelazny. The story was nominated in 1964 for the Hugo Award for short fiction.

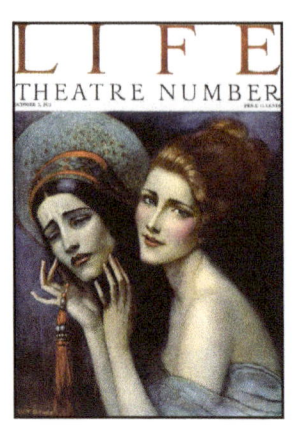

Hannes Bok created the mask on our cover, but it resembles masks created by W. T. Benda. This 1922 magazine's cover painting is by Benda.

The Plymouth Review Current

TAKING YOU PLACES WORTH SEEING
Volume 7 • Issue 7 • June 2018

FREE!

Galileo • Sports Pulps • Fine Movies • Heliocentric Theories • Great Dining
Harriet Tubman • Frederick Douglass • Profundity with Clarity • CYMK+

June 2018

Cover photo: Ink at Badger Tag, Random Lake
Great Movies This Month
I Ate At... by Richard J. Baumann: Cabaret Supper Club
Ask a Science Teacher by Larry Scheckel: Why Was Galileo Famous?
Natural Connections by Emily Stone: Wisconsin Born Upon Rock of Ages
Logic in Your Life: No Argument at All
Echoes of our past by William & Joy Wangemann: State Hated War, aut Fought Hard
'Critical Thinking'—Everyone Talks About It; No One Seems to Know What It Means, by Daniel Lattier, IntellectualTakeout.org
Once in a Lifetime, by Paul Mueller: Out Behind the Barn
Want to Learn More about the PULPS?
PulpArtists by David Saunders: Robert Savon Pious

Boxer Joe Louis, painted by R. S. Pious.

July 2018

Cover photo: 2nd Annual Native American Artifact Show, New Holstein
Great Movies This Month
Once in a Lifetime, by Paul Mueller: Almost Fooled—and a Road-Killed Red Tail Hawk
Ask a Science Teacher by Larry Scheckel: Why Do Wires Spark when You Plug Something In?
I Grew Up in a Communist System. Here's What Americans Don't Understand About Freedom, by Carmen Alexe, FEE.org
I Ate At... by Richard J. Baumann: Chris & Sue's, Plymouth
Five reasons we should still read Cicero today, by Paul Meany, FEE.org
Natural Connections by Emily Stone: Protective Clothing, Vigilance Best Defense against Ticks
Spitting on the Torch
PulpArtists by David Saunders: George Rozen

David Saunders' pulpartists.com

GEORGE ROZEN: DEFINING THE SHADOW

(1895 – 1973)

George Jerome Rozen was born October 16, 1895 in Chicago. His parents were Mary and Vaclav James Rozen, who had both immigrated in the 1860s from Bohemia (the Czech Republic). The father was a saloon keeper. There were six children in the family, including George's twin brother, Jerome. The twins were the youngest. The Rozen family lived at 1317 West 18th Street.

In 1899, the Rozens left the Chicago tenements and moved to Arizona for the health of their eldest son, James (16), who had contracted tuberculosis. They lived at 824 West Birch Avenue in Flagstaff. The father found work as a house carpenter for a building contractor. In 1902 brother James died from TB.

In 1910 the Rozens moved back to Chicago and lived at 1616 Washington Avenue. The father worked at a carpentry shop. The three older sisters worked as secretaries, and the 15 year old twins attended high school.

After the twins graduated high school in 1914 the Rozen family returned to Arizona, where the father found better opportunities to work as a house carpenter. George found work as a telegrapher at Western Union, while Jerome began to take classes from a local art teacher.

In 1918 during the Great War, George was drafted into the Army and was assigned to the Telegraphy Signal Corps, where he worked as an instructor, stationed at an Army training base in

Michigan. During his induction he was recorded to be five-eight, slender build, with fair complexion, blue-grey eyes and reddish blonde hair.

After the war George Rozen was discharged as a Sergeant. He returned to his job at the Flagstaff Western Union and joined the National Guard. Meanwhile, his brother Jerome Rozen had decided to pursue a career in art and attended the Chicago Art Institute. Jerome graduated in 1923 and was hired as an art instructor at the school. When he began to earn good money as an illustrator, George decided to give up telegraphy and to instead follow in his brother's footsteps. He enrolled in the Chicago Art Institute, and even took one class that was taught by his brother.

While in art school George met his wife to be, Clara Ellen Mason. She was born on October 15, 1902 in Indiana. They married on December 19, 1927 and moved to New York City in 1930. They rented an apartment for $50 a month at 2725 Morris Avenue in the Bronx. They had no children.

His first published assignments were covers and interior pen & ink story illustrations for Fawcett magazines, *Battle Stories, Triple-X Magazine,* and *Modern Mechanix.* He was soon painting covers for *College Stories, The Popular, Top-Notch, War Birds, Wild West Weekly,* and *Western Romances.*

In 1931 he suddenly replaced his brother Jerome as the cover artist for Street & Smith's The Shadow Magazine. George Rozen became The Shadow's most renowned cover artist, while his brother branched out into the more prestigious fields of advertising and slick magazines. During the Great Depression George Rozen was content to work for pulp magazines, such as *War Aces, War Stories, Western Aces, Western Trails, Doctor Yen Sin, Phantom Detective, Popular Detective, Thrilling Adventures, Thrilling Ranch Stories,* and *The Shadow,* which became the world's top selling pulp magazine with two-hundred-and-fifty-thousand bi-weekly sales.

By 1938 George Rozen was prosperous enough to leave NYC and move to East Williston, NY, on Long Island, where they happened to live on 10 Shadow Lane. The artist worked from a home studio located on the second floor.

On April 23, 1938 a traffic accident killed Jerome Rozen's wife and left Jerome in the hospital for ten months. During the recuperation, his two children, Helen (13) and Jerome (10), lived with George and Ellen on Long Island, until their father's recovery permitted him to re-

George Rozen's cover for The Shadow were often allegorical. Years later, editors asked subsequent artists to portray more action and fight scenes. – Center image HA.com; others from pulpartists.com

sume parental responsibilities.

During the Second World War George Rozen was too old for military service, but he remained busy producing pulp covers, such as *Argosy, Army-Navy Flying Stories, Captain Future, Giant Western, Masked Rider, Mystery Magazine, The Rio Kid, Range Rider, Six-Gun Western, Ten Detective Aces, 10-Story Detective, Thrilling Adventures, Thrilling Western, Western Aces, West,* and *Wings.*

After the war his illustrations appeared regularly on paperbacks from Popular Library and Ace Double Books.

In 1954 at age 59 he retired from freelance illustration and moved to Willowtree, Arizona, a small town near his boyhood home in Flagstaff.

On November 5, 1958 his wife, Clara Ellen (Mason) Rozen, died at the age of fifty-six in Arizona.

Because of his military record as an instructor and a member of the National Guard, George Rozen applied for a job teaching art at Veterans Affairs. His application was accepted, but instead of a local job, he was assigned to teach art classes at Wright-Patterson Air Force Base in Ohio, so at the age of sixty-three, he left Arizona and moved to 3015 East 5th Street in Dayton, Ohio, where he taught art classes for ten years, until his retirement at age seventy-three in 1968.

George Rozen died at age seventy-seven on July 14, 1973, while recovering from arterial surgery at a hospital in Dayton, Ohio.

© David Saunders 2009

SPITTING ON THE TORCH

Freedom! Wahooooo! That's what we're celebrating this month.

And to prove it? We're going to shoot off lots of *fireworks!*

All right. *Nothing wrong* with fireworks, when handled properly. But your celebration shouldn't end there.

How does one celebrate freedom?

My suggestion: First understand what it is, and what's necessary for it to exist. You won't learn all that here, but I might be able to point you in some different directions, where you can discover it.

Loving freedom passionately

I suspect some people take freedom for granted. They consider it a given; something that just exists; something we'll always have.

For such a person, the concept of freedom doesn't inspire much passion. How could it, if one believes there is no danger of losing it?

The people most passionate about freedom are those who either do not have it, or those who realize they truly *are* in danger of losing it.

A contemporary example is found in Carmen Alexe's essay, elsewhere in this issue.

Looking back in years, to the beginnings of this country, we can find many impassioned writings promoting freedom, from those who considered it a life-or-death issue to be free. Using Enlightenment philosophy as a basis, they drew up a plan for this country's formation. (The thesis that America is based on the Enlightenment is put forth in The Ominous Parallels, by Leonard Peikoff. It is a thesis I agree with. Read that book for yourself and give us your thoughts.)

As I wrote a few months ago, slavery contradicted the principles of individual rights and freedom this country was based on. That contradiction ultimately split the nation with a near-fatal wound.

A person subjected to the horrors and degradations of slavery, who is then fortunate enough to escape it, is likely to value, to savor, freedom with great passion. It would be inspiring to read whatever she writes about her struggle to be free, and her joy in living as a free person.

What if such a person goes farther with his thoughts and writings? He not only condemns slavery—or any assault on individual rights—and defends freedom; he delves into how freedom is inherent in human nature. He explores the psychological and moral basis of freedom, showing how it is necessary for a person to live—as a person.

Reading such work would inspire the reader, motivate him to recognize it as a precious value.

Further, that work would help the reader understand what, exactly, freedom is; why human beings, by their nature, need it; and what is necessary to maintain it.

Let me tell you about just one such man. I discovered him and his work a few short years ago, though I'd heard his name for decades. That is:

Frederick Douglass

Sure, I'd probably heard of Frederick Douglass way back in grade school. I might have mixed him up with Stephen Douglas, who didn't seem to be one of the good guys in history.

I was dramatically introduced to the life and ideas of Frederick Douglass by a "comic book" / "graphic novel," The Hammer and the Anvil. I reviewed this book in the April 2015 issue of The PRC (I'm sure you still have that issue on your shelf). It was written by Dwight Jon Zimmerman; illustrated by Wayne Vansant.

I can't recommend this book highly enough. It portrays the lives of Douglass and Abraham Lincoln; their ideas, the history of the times, and their contributions to history.

A few months ago, the periodical The Objective Standard featured some articles about Douglass, and a speech he himself wrote, The Self-Made Man.

Also a few months ago, a book written by Timothy Sandefur was published—Frederick Douglass, Self-Made Man. Not an exhaustive biography, this book explores Douglass' view of what it means to be "self-made."

I came to consider Frederick Douglass an heroic figure in American history. Right up there with many of the Founding Fathers.

Douglass' home in Washington, DC

Fact 1. My wife was asked to speak at a nurse convention in Washington, DC. She asked if I'd like to come along.

Fact 2. The house Frederick Douglass lived in the last years of his life, still stands—in Washington, DC. It is a national park, open to the public.

When those two facts collided in my brain, a bell went off.

As we planned our 48-hour trip, we purchased tickets online to tour the Douglass house. They cost the princely sum of $1.50 each.

On the morning of Sat., June 23, a cab picked us up at our hotel. We gave the driver our destination. As we twisted around the narrow streets, the driver remarked, "We're really getting into the—" (he paused for an instant) *"historic area, now."*

The ranger at the visitor's center who took our tickets was not familiar with The Objective Standard, so I gave her a copy. To my surprise, she'd never heard of The Plymouth Review Current, either, so I gave her a copy of that, too.

After the tour, we returned to the visitor's center. I showed heroic restraint by buying only two books (there were dozens). Oh, I also bought an uncirculated 2017 quarter with Douglass on the back. Oh yeah, I also bought a little bust of FD. (I wish a life-size one, like that in his house, were available somewhere.)

How Douglass benefits us all

Douglass, and other intellectuals who discover and/or write about philosophical/political principles that enhance human life, perform an invaluable service to the layman (one who is not a full-time intellectual).

The layman might not have the time or knowledge to figure these principles out, and explore them in depth. However, the layman owes it to himself to have *enough* knowledge and reasoning skills to be able to *evaluate* what the intellectual presents.

The intellectual ought to be able to make ideas clear and understandable to the layman.

(Some intellectuals write only for other intellectuals. Such specialization can be useful, but it has little impact on a culture.)

Some intellectuals, such as Frederick Douglass, can be thought of as a torch-lighter, offering light by which the layman can see and comprehend the ideas the intellectual is trying to present.

The spitters

Unfortunately, some people (both intellectuals and laymen) hate the light of human thought and understanding. They'd rather spit on the torches that others light.

One person can light a torch. Frederick Douglass, it could be argued, lit many of them. The fact that books and speeches he wrote are still available, indicates the light he

A few photos from Your Editor's tour of the home of Frederick Douglass.

offered mankind still shines, for those who choose to open their eyes.

"Now, come on," you might say. "Who are you talking about here? We live in much more enlightened times than people did in the 1800s, when slavery existed. Who, besides fringe lunatic hate groups, would be spitting on Frederick Douglass' torch?"

Excellent question.

During our guided tour of Douglass' home, the ranger explained that, even when Douglass was a free man in the north, even when slavery had been officially ended, Douglass sometimes could not eat at certain inns, or sleep at certain hotels. Jim Crow laws, you see. Or, where Jim Crow was unable to spread his foul wings, likely just plain, ignorant bigotry.

Yes, society today is so much more enlightened, and would not perpetuate such ignorance today, right?

So, that evening of June 23, as I was glowing inside from the tour of the Frederick Douglass home and the freedom-illuminating torch that Frederick Douglass had lit for me, I saw on the news:

Sarah Sanders, the White House Press Secretary, was asked to leave a restaurant in the DC area. Reason? She works for the current administration.

August 2018

Cover photo: Cattle Egret, Photo by Annie and Paul Mueller

Great Movies This Month

Once in a Lifetime, by Paul Mueller: Almost Fooled—and a Road-Killed Red Tail Hawk

Feedback to Think About (taking issue with Carmen Alexe's article, July issue)

Editor's Thoughts (on the above)

2016: the "Year of the 1%" or the Year Poverty Fell to a New Low? by Chelsea German, HumanProgress.org

I Ate At... by Richard J. Baumann: Carole's Cafe, Plymouth Sesquicentennial, Jeff-Leen Farm

Ask a Science Teacher by Larry Scheckel: What Is the Universe Made Of?

PulpArtists by David Saunders: Clinton Pettee

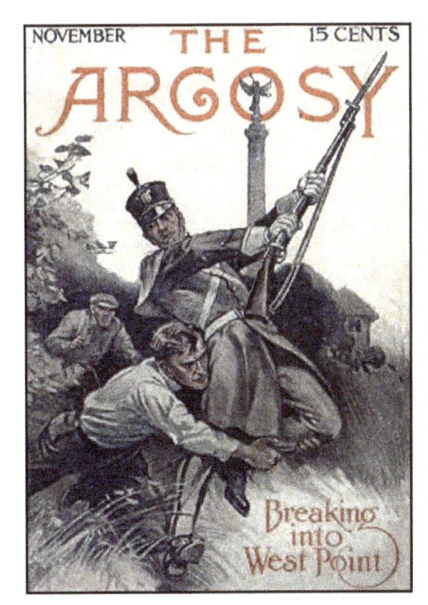

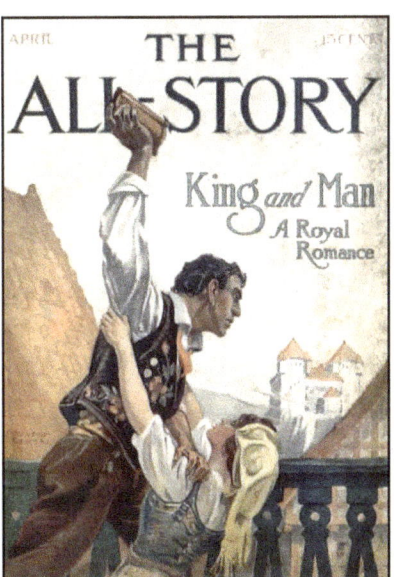

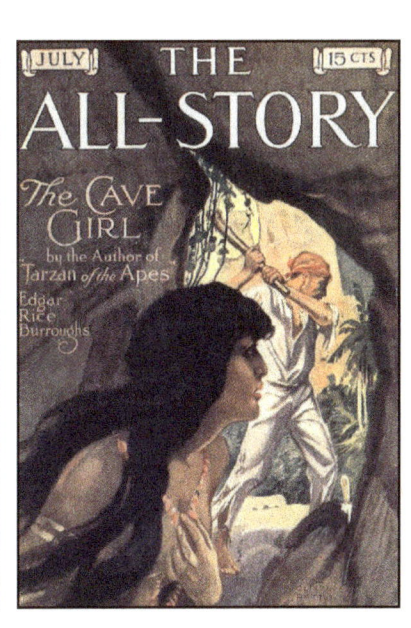

Pulp covers by Clinton Pettee from 1912 and 1913, at the time he illustrated one of the most famous pulp covers of all time (the first Tarzan).

Ask a Science Teacher

By Larry Scheckel

Q: What is the universe made of?

A: Everything we see and touch, and yes, the air that we breathe, is made of atoms. Atoms are composed of protons, neutrons, and electrons. The protons and neutrons are stuck together into the nucleus and the nucleus is surrounded by orbiting electrons. It's the planetary model of the atom, analogous to our eight planets orbiting the sun. A somewhat more accurate model is one that has a dense nucleus core surrounded by a cloud of electrons. The term "element" is used for atoms with a given number of protons

All the elements, some 118 of them, are composed of various numbers of these building blocks. Hydrogen, the most plentiful element, consists of one proton and one electron. Helium has two protons, two neutrons, and two electrons. Carbon has six protons, six neutrons, and six electrons. The heavier, more massive elements, keep building up the number of protons, neutrons, and electrons. Uranium, one of the most massive elements found in nature, has 92 protons, 92 neutrons, and 92 electrons.

Some new findings turned up about 30 years ago. Only about 5 percent of the universe is made of atoms. Most of the universe seems to be missing, 24 percent is cold dark matter, and 71 percent is dark energy.

Astrophysicists do not know the whereabouts of this missing matter. Brown dwarfs, black holes, and undiscovered particles are good candidates. Until they find it, it really doesn't matter. (Pun intended).

That leaves us to concentrate on the atoms that we encounter in everyday life; atoms we can see, touch, and atoms that excite our sense of smell, taste, and hearing. The elements are arranged in a meaningful way on the Periodic Table.

Let's look at some interesting facts about the elements. Helium is lighter than air and so it's perfect for filling party balloons. Hydrogen is an even lighter gas than helium. But hydrogen is explosive and if a hydrogen balloon got close to the lit candles on a birthday cake, that could be a disastrous party.

Oxygen is necessary for life on Earth, but about one percent of the sun is oxygen. Carbon is found in diamonds, graphite, coal, crude oil, and you and me. Carbon-12 (6 protons, 6 neutrons) is the most common form. But Carbon-14 (6 protons, 8 neutrons) is radioactive and is useful in finding the age of formerly living things.

A small amount of carbon in living things is of the Carbon-14 variety. The amount of Carbon-14 in our environment remains constant as new Carbon-14 is being created in the upper atmosphere by cosmic rays.

Living things ingest materials that contain carbon, so the percentage of Carbon-14 in living things, such plants and animals, remain the same as the percentage of Carbon-14 in the environment. Once an organism dies, the Carbon-14 is no longer replaced. The percentage of Carbon-14 begins to decrease at a constant rate. By measuring the percentage of Carbon-14 in the remains of the plant or animal, scientists can estimate when that organism lived and died.

For example, if the amount of Carbon-14 in a dead plant or animal is half the natural concentrations of Carbon -14, a researcher would estimate the organism died 5,730 years ago, which is the half-life of Carbon-14. (A "half-life" is the time it takes half a radioactive substance to decay.) If the amount of Carbon-14 remaining is one-fourth the usual concentration, then the plant or animal is twice 5,730 years, or 11,460 years old. Carbon-14 acts as sort of atomic clock.

One of the most amazing Carbon-14 dating projects was the Dead Scrolls that were discovered in 1946 and 1947 by Bedouin shepherds in the Qumran Caves in the Judean Desert along the Dead Sea. The Dead Seas Scrolls were written on animal hides and papyrus, both living materials before being put into use.

The accuracy of Carbon-14 dating was confirmed by the naming of people, dates, and cities, that occurred at the time of the writing, which ranged from 3 centuries BCE to one century CE.

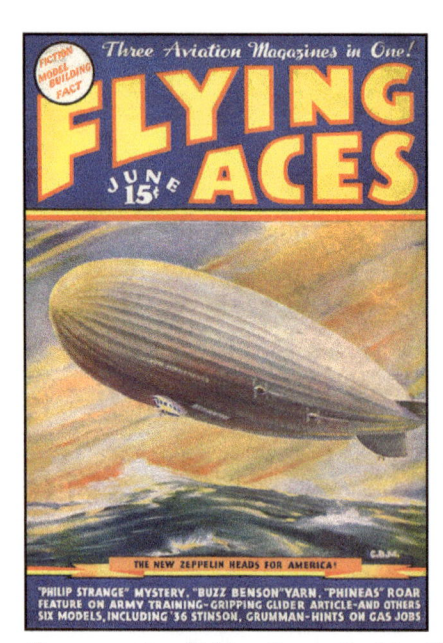

If you want a lighter-than-air ship, fill it with the lightest of all elements: Hydrogen. Makes sense, right? The problem is... it reacts rather violently with oxygen, if there is a flame or spark. At left: the cover of a 1936 pulp, painted by Casimir B. Mayshark, showing the German airship Hindenburg. At right, the same ship's demise in 1937. – Pulp scan by Rodney Schroeter; photo by Sam Shere (no Copyright restrictions)

The Current
Plymouth Review
TAKING YOU PLACES WORTH SEEING
Volume 7 • Issue 10 • September 2018

FREE!

Joel Robuchon • Meaningful Movies • Great Local Dining
Steve Ditko • Wildlife Adventure • Lives Well Lived • Caviar

September 2018

Cover photo: Caviar Appetizer Designed by Joel Robuchon

What's That? You Say You've Never Seen Iron Chef Japan?

ICJ: How Fanatical Can You Get?

Great Movies This Month

Joel Robuchon, French chef, dead at 73, by the Associated Press

Alex Guarnaschelli on Robuchon

Steve Ditko 1927-2018: An Independent Mind, by Nick Caputo

Ask a Science Teacher by Larry Scheckel: What Is the Meaning of "A Life Well-Lived"?

"A Life Well-Lived"?

I Ate At... by Richard J. Baumann: Old Plank Farm, Plymouth

Once in a Lifetime, by Paul Mueller: One more Time

A Plea for Free Speech in Boston, by Frederick Douglass

PulpArtists by David Saunders: Jerome Rozen

Your Editor Meets Albert Einstein

Jerome Rozen painted the cover for this early (1931) issue of The Shadow. Jerome's brother, George, would soon regularly paint covers for this pulp title.

ICJ: How fanatical can you get?

Chiharu Katsuyama, Sakai's restaurant manager, posed very formally when I asked if I could take his photo.

Your Editor meets Hiroyuki Sakai

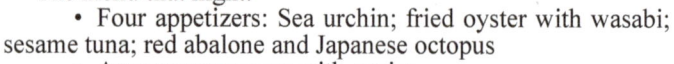

The video guy (I never got his name) was a little more casual.

I'd watched Iron Chef Japan (ICJ) for two years when I heard that Hiroyuki Sakai, the Iron Chef who cooked in the French tradition, would help re-open the restaurant of a friend in New Orleans, in March, 2006.

How *fan*-atical a *fan* was I for ICJ?

I made a reservation for the dinner and bought two airline tickets to New Orleans.

This was not long after Katrina. My wife and I saw abandoned, water-wrecked cars as the cab drove us to our hotel.

The restaurant was Stella!, and the chef was Scott Boswell. (Sadly, that restaurant closed a few years ago.)

Sakai and Boswell collaborated on the meal.

Sakai's restaurant manager was on hand. A very formal man, he assisted in serving the dishes (wearing cotton gloves).

Also present was a small film crew. I pretended they weren't there as the camera focused on me, tasting the sea urchin flan. If anything from that event has ever been televised, I never saw it.

The menu that night:
- Four appetizers: Sea urchin; fried oyster with wasabi; sesame tuna; red abalone and Japanese octopus
- Asparagus mousse with caviar
- Truffle-scented foie gras croquette
- Turtle and shark fin soup, "Iron Chef Style"
- Scallop with Chinese cabbage
- Cucumber popsicle with blood orange-mint sauce
- Grilled American Kobe beef strip with Japanese mountain yam and tempura
- Chilled pineapple bisque, frozen vanilla bean parfait
- Dark chocolate espresso pate, smoked Viking sea salt, Meyer lemon souffle

(Another article in this issue explained that I first heard of Chef Joel Robuchon on the Japanese TV show, Iron Chef.)

David Saunders'

GEORGE ROZEN: DEFINING THE SHADOW

(1895-1987)

Jerome George Rozen was born October 16, 1895 in Chicago. His parents were Mary and Vaclav James Rozen, who had both immigrated in the 1860s from Bohemia (the Czech Republic). The father was a saloon keeper. There were six children in the family, including Jerome's twin brother, George. The twins were the youngest. The Rozen family lived at 1317 West 18th Street.

In 1899, the Rozens left the Chicago tenements and moved to Arizona for the health of their eldest son, James (16), who had contracted tuberculosis. They lived at 824 West Birch Avenue in Flagstaff. The father found work as a house carpenter for a building contractor. In 1902 brother James died from TB.

In 1910 the Rozens moved back to Chicago and lived at 1616 Washington Avenue. The father worked at a carpentry shop, the three older sisters worked as secretaries, and the 15 year old twins attended high school.

After their graduation in 1914 the Rozen family returned to Arizona again, where the

Ah, the wild, wonderful, wacky world of advertising.

father had better business opportunities in the home building industry. George found work as a telegrapher at Western Union, while Jerome began to take classes from a local art teacher.

In 1918 Jerome was drafted into the Army for the World War and was stationed in France. He was recorded to be five-ten, slender build, with fair complexion, blue-grey eyes and reddish blonde hair.

After the armistice in 1919 he was at liberty to visit the Louvre Museum in Paris. After returning home he decided to attend the Art Institute of Chicago. He graduated in 1921 and by 1923 he was hired as an art instructor. During one semester he even taught his twin brother, George, who had decided to follow Jerome into commercial art.

While in art school Jerome met his wife, Della K., of Chicago. They married in 1923 and moved to New York City and rented an apartment for $56 a month at 181 West 238th Street in the Bronx, which was on the southern edge of scenic Van Cortlandt Park. Their daughter Helen was born in 1925 and their son Jerome Jr.

was born in 1928.

Jerome Rozen rode the local IRT subway every day twenty-six stops straight south to his art studio in Manhattan's Flatiron District at 163 West 23rd Street.

His first published assignments were interior pen and ink story illustrations for Fawcett's *Triple-X Magazine.* His first pulp covers were for *Battle Stories, Complete Stories, Over The Top, The Popular Magazine, War Birds,* and *Western Story.*

In 1931 he painted the four earliest original pulp magazine covers for *The Shadow,* but starting with the January 1932 issue he was suddenly replaced by his brother George, who went on to become *The Shadow's* more renowned cover artist, while Jerome branched out into the more lucrative and prestigious fields of advertising and slick magazine illustration. He worked for such magazines as *Country Home, Boy's Life, Good Housekeeping, Liberty, Pictorial Review, Redbook,* and *The Saturday Evening Post.*

When the George Washington Bridge opened in 1931 the Rozens moved to New Jersey, because properties were nice and it was a better place to raise kids. They bought a home at 150 Rockwood Place, Englewood, which was only six blocks from the bridge's exit ramp. Each day Della drove Jerome to a bus stop at the entrance to the bridge where he caught the bus over to the 181st Street IRT subway stop, and then rode down to 23rd Street. In this way his subway commute was seven stops shorter than before.

During the morning rush hour on April 23, 1938, while driving her husband to the bus stop, a truck loaded with clams and oysters was sideswiped by a bus and knocked onto its side, blocking all traffic in both directions. Mrs. Rozen hit the overturned truck and four other cars piled up behind her. Only the Rozen car was seriously damaged. Patrolman Royal Slaughter was first on the scene, because he had been a passenger of the bus that caused the crash. He administered first-aid to the Rozens and then called an ambulance. Della Rozen died in the hospital the next day. Jerome Rozen sustained severe injuries that required six months of hospital care and left him with permanent physical disabilities, most noticeably in his left leg. During the recuperation, his two children went to live with George and his wife on Long Island, where daughter Helen (13) and son Jerome (10) stayed for ten months before Jerome's recovery permitted him to resume parental responsibilities.

By 1942 Rozen had been out of the fast-paced slick magazine market for four years. He was finally able to re-start his career by painting pulp covers for *Western Aces, Mystery Magazine, Ten Detective Aces, Wings, Thrilling Adventures,* and *10-Story Detective.*

During the Second World War Rozen was too old and unfit for military service, but he still contributed to the war effort by creating many patriotic posters and magazine advertisements. The most poignant of which was a poster to avoid unnecessary driving, which is painted in the likeness of his beloved wife, Della Rozen.

After the war his illustrated advertisements for the Pennsylvania Railroad, C&O Railroad, and Shell Oil appeared regularly in national magazines such as *Boy's Life, Look,* and *Life.*

In 1948 he remarried. His second wife was Doris Spiegel.

In 1965 at age 70 Jerome Rozen retired.

In 1978 he was rediscovered by fans of pulp magazines and was commissioned to recreate several of his long-lost classic pulp paintings.

Jerome Rozen died at age of ninety-one in Englewood, NJ, on July 10, 1987.

© David Saunders 2009

Traveling by train *can be* this restful.

(Not Phantom) Detective Work

If you can think of a better incentive for building a time-travel machine than this photo, let us know!

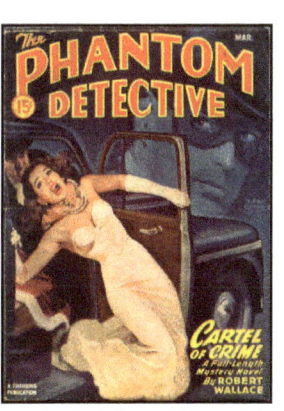

Enjoying a comic book. What year is this endearing photo from? Your Editor did some extensive research and detective work (about *five minutes'* worth) and found the cover from the March 1947 issue of Phantom Detective (right) to match the cover at the lower right corner in the photo. Pulps and comics were (comics still are) dated two to four months *ahead of* their actual newsstand shelf life, so this photo was almost certainly taken in the November 1946 to January 1947 range. This photo shows *four* types of popular reading of the time: Comic books in the center; pulp magazines at the right; slick magazines at left (nice supply of True Confessions, there); and newspapers at lower left. — Image found various places on the Internet; no Copyright notice or name for the puppy-dog found

Q: What Is the Meaning of "A Life Well-Lived"?

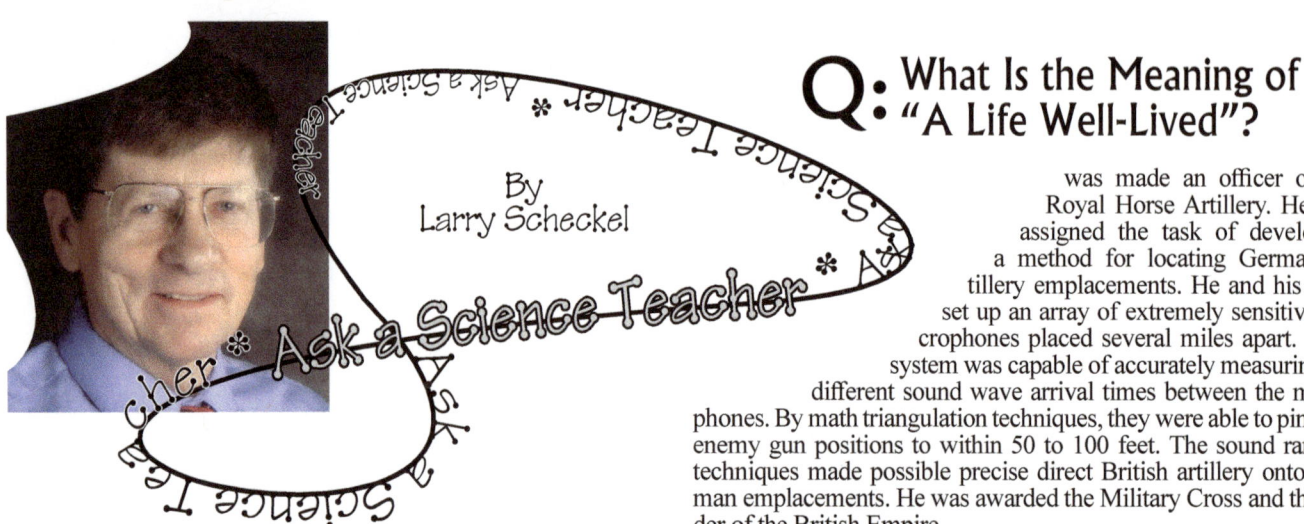

By Larry Scheckel

A: If you asked a dozen people that question, you would probably get a dozen different answers. I suppose it would be someone who contributed to the general well-being of people and to our planet Earth. Someone who followed the Golden Rule and a person who did their best to follow the Ten Commandments.

Let's look to the scientific community for one example. William Lawrence Bragg (1890-1971) was an Australian-born British scientist who used X-rays to discover how matter is put together.

His father, William Henry Bragg, was a British-born scientist and mathematician. He graduated from Trinity College and won an appointment to a teaching post at the University of Adelaide, in South Australia in 1885.

In 1889, William Henry Bragg met and married a skilled water-color painter, Gwendolen Todd. They had 3 children over the years, the oldest being William Lawrence Bragg, born in 1890. When young William Lawrence was growing up, his father experimented with the newly discovered X-rays. The manner in which X-rays pass through a material can reveal its atomic structure.

When young Bragg broke his arm in a tricycle accident, the father X-rayed his son's arm. This was some years before X-rays were routinely used in the medical profession.

The family moved back to England in 1908, and young Bragg entered Trinity College, graduating with high honors in 1911. All the while he worked with his father on X-rays striking materials. They were able to calculate the position of atoms in a crystal.

WWI interrupted the work of both father and son. Young Bragg was made an officer of the Royal Horse Artillery. He was assigned the task of developing a method for locating German artillery emplacements. He and his team set up an array of extremely sensitive microphones placed several miles apart. Their system was capable of accurately measuring the different sound wave arrival times between the microphones. By math triangulation techniques, they were able to pinpoint enemy gun positions to within 50 to 100 feet. The sound ranging techniques made possible precise direct British artillery onto German emplacements. He was awarded the Military Cross and the Order of the British Empire.

On September 2, 1915, while engaged with German forces on the Western Front in France, William Lawrence Bragg received word that his brother was killed in the ill-fated Gallipoli Campaign. A few days later he received a message that both he and his father had been awarded the Nobel Prize. It was the first and only time in history that a father-son team won the Nobel Prize.

After WWI, both Braggs returned to university teaching and research. In 1921, William Lawrence married Alice Hopkinson. They had four children. Alice Hopkinson was elected Mayor of Cambridge and served as National Chairman of Marriage Guidance, among other roles.

The elder Bragg died in 1942 and his son worked on sound ranging problems for the British Navy during WWII. After the war, William Lawrence Bragg ran the Cavendish Lab at Cambridge University and oversaw the work of Watson and Crick, who discovered the double-helix nature of DNA in 1953. William Lawrence earned every high science honor that can be bestowed on any scientist. In addition to his 1915 Nobel Prize, Bragg received both the Copley Medal and the Royal Medal of the Royal Society.

William Lawrence Bragg is just one example of a life well-lived; a dutiful son, who worked closely with his father, a soldier who served his country in two World Wars, who married an accomplished person in her own right. They were parents of four successful children who made their parents proud.

A recommended good read – William and Lawrence Bragg, Father and Son: The Most Extraordinary Collaboration in Science, by John Jenkin.

"A Life Well-Lived"?

Elsewhere in this issue, Larry Scheckel addresses the question, "What is 'a life well-lived'?"

As his opening paragraph says, ask a dozen people on what constitutes "a life well-lived," and you'll likely get a dozen different answers.

How one answers that question depends on a number of prior questions. A few of those are:

To whom does your life belong? (You? Society? A higher power?)

Who ought to decide your life's purpose, goals, and actions? (You? Society? A higher power?)

If *you* are the one to properly define your life's purpose, then the extent of your success in achieving that purpose is the degree to which your life is "well-lived."

But let's think about two people whose lives we are honoring in this issue of The PRC: Joel Robuchon and Steve Ditko.

Do we consider their lives to have been "well-lived" by the fact that they contributed so much (in different ways) that has been appreciated by other people?

Suppose Joel Robuchon developed his cooking techniques, but never shared them.

Suppose Steve Ditko drew comics, but kept them to himself.

Suppose each man was satisfied with his achievements. Each would be happy, satisfied with life. Would those be two lives well-lived?

To each of those men, yes. If his life belonged to *him,* if *he* were the one setting his purpose and goals, then his own long-range happiness and satisfaction would be the measure of how well-lived each life has been.

In a social system of individual rights (capitalism), most producers choose to trade what they create for income. Every unit of income going to the producer/seller represents some benefit perceived by the consumer/purchaser. To the extent that benefit is objectively life-enhancing, to that extent the purchaser's life is enhanced; and to that extent "society" is improved.

It's perfectly fine for a producer to be gratified that his creation enhances someone else's life. But I believe it's damaging to one's psychology if the satisfaction or (especially) *praise* of others is used as one's *primary* source of self-esteem.

First comes the creation of the good or service, and everything leading up to it: rational thinking, choices, skills, education, and how well it reflects his purpose and goals. *That* is a genuine source of self-esteem.

(I find it haunting to think the substance abuse, or even suicide, of certain celebrities is *possibly* a result of having great numbers of other people holding them in high esteem... but failing to learn how to esteem themselves and their own achievements.)

The contributions of Joel Robuchon and Steve Ditko have enhanced many others. Their achievements are known world-wide.

But imagine the following:

- A farmer who looks with satisfaction at his well-kept buildings, his fertile land, and his healthy animals.
- An auto enthusiast who's taken what most people would consider a pile of junk, and refurbished it into a shiny, fully operational vintage car.
- A software developer who perfects a routine to perform a useful function. It makes one little task easier for hundreds or millions of users, but the developer is the only one who will ever know the difficulty, inventiveness, and perhaps even sheer genius of the code behind that routine.
- A homeowner with a successful garden and/or beautifully landscaped yard that nobody else sees.

Articles—even entire books—are written in praise of the achievements of Joel Robuchon and Steve Ditko. That's because achievements like theirs are meant to be shared on a wide basis.

But what of the examples listed above? Wide-scale public recognition for their achievements is unlikely.

And—*so what!?*

If each person sets his/her own life goals; if each person establishes the standards of his/her own success in life; then it's a personal, not a public matter. If that person achieves long-range satisfaction and happiness, *that* is a life well-lived, even if the rest of society, or the entire universe, doesn't know or care about those achievements.

So while we at The PRC share with you some achievements of Joel Robuchon, Steve Ditko, the many people who created writing or artwork for the pulps, those who made scientific discoveries, those whose thinking benefited our lives in numerous ways...

...we also urge you to pause, sit quietly, and contemplate your own personal achievements, or to define (or re-define) your purposes and goals.

We know nothing of your achievements. (Unless you put them in writing and send them in; we *love* that kind of mail!!)

You know of your achievements. And about those, it's *your* thoughts that count. *You* are the best judge of whether you are living "a life well-lived."

To suppress free speech is a double wrong. It violates the rights of the hearer as well as those of the speaker.

Frederick Douglass

October
2018

Cover photo: The Jeff-Leen Farm's 150th Birthday
Great Movies This Month
I Ate At... by Richard J. Baumann: Nap's Place, Plymouth
Natural Connections by Emily Stone: Bats Aren't Blind, and Other Facts of Life
Ask a Science Teacher by Larry Scheckel: Why Don't We Have a Moon Colony Yet??
A City on the Moon...? WHY??
Happy 150th Birthday to Jeff-Leen Farm
Letter to the Editor (general praise for The PRC)
PulpArtists by David Saunders: Jules Cannert
Once in a Lifetime, by Paul Mueller: So Close to Home — Who Would'a' Thought?
Stop-Motion Animation Lives On!
Destinations Wisconsin: American Science & Surplus
Playing Cosmo Detective

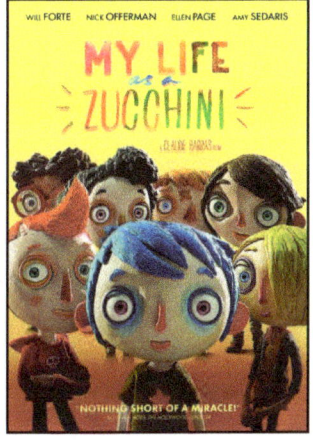

Stop-motion animation is alive and well in these films! Isle of Dogs; My Life as a Zucchini.

Playing Cosmo Detective

One way you could estimate the date of the photo would be to find an expert on fashions, and have him/her give you an estimate based on the clothing.

But if that's not *precise* enough, you could ask, "What month and year is that issue of Cosmopolitan the one sister is holding?"

Let's rotate it, to see it better. Then, we look for an image of that cover. That might not be so easy. Much of the cover is obscured. And you'll have to find a place online showing all Cosmo covers. And you'll need a general idea of the year, or you'll waste hours. (For example, it's safe to assume this wasn't the 1950s!)

But here it is. Cosmopolitan, December, 1916. Another success story.

— Photos and detective work courtesy of Your Editor's Wife

Your Editor's wife found this photo of her grandfather's sisters. How would you determine *what year* this photo was taken? (Hint: If you read last month's issue of The PRC thoroughly, you'll have one idea.)

November 2018

Cover photo: Fabio Viviani at the Kohler Food & Wine Experience

Great Movies This Month

The Big Red One: The Greatest War Movie Ever Made?

PulpArtists by David Saunders: Howard V. Brown

Eight of the Best Views in

Milwaukee, by Kristen Finstad, Associated Press
Once in a Lifetime, by Paul Mueller: The Parade Never Ends
Forty Ways the World Is Getting Better, by Marian L. Tupy, HumanProgress.org
I Ate At... by Richard J. Baumann: Rumors, Plymouth
Feedback to Think About (objecting to human exploration and settelement of space)
Ask a Science Teacher by Larry Scheckel: What will happen if another asteroid strikes the earth?
Follow-Up: Isle of Dogs
Natural Connections by Emily Stone: The Strange Ways by which Mushrooms Can Save the World

THE BIG RED ONE
THE GREATEST WAR MOVIE EVER MADE?

The Big Red One begins with an ending. A real-life ending that happened a century ago this month.

An American sergeant staggers through a smoking landscape desolated by war. Out of the haze charges a horse that nearly tramples him. ("Horses can go mad during war as well as men," he's later told.)

He hears a voice speaking German. The sergeant kills the German.

Finding an allied trench, the sergeant learns the Armistice has been signed; the war was over several hours before he killed the German.

The Big Red One (TBRO) was written and directed by Samuel Fuller (1912–1997). The director presented the studio with a 3-hour film. But executives would not release it at that length.

The movie was edited down to just under two hours and released in 1980.

I saw it then. I was impressed. I told at least one acquaintance I thought it was the best war movie I'd ever seen, and he thought the same.

After Fuller's death, Richard Schickel, film historian and movie critic for Time magazine, began a project to restore as much of the deleted material as possible. TBRO (The Reconstruction) is about 47 minutes longer than the original release. The 2-disk set now available contains the reconstructed movie, and several documentaries, including how the reconstruction was accomplished.

The longer version is "about 90 percent of the film Sam [Fuller] intended, as close as humanly possible," commented Schickel. "There's some footage that is completely lost, things that would have been nice to have, close-ups and reaction shots."

After the WWI incident described above, the film transitions to the sergeant in WWII. (Of all the times I watched this, I never caught that his name is Sgt. Possum—which must carry some kind of symbolism.)

The movie is episodic. For some, that's a complaint; for others, it genuinely reflects a soldier's wartime experience. Some highlights:
- The constant presence of children (something Fuller comments on in a documentary). A girl swipes the sergeant's helmet and returns it with flowers woven into the netting. "The Krauts are going to see that a mile away," he's told. "I like it," he replies, looking the little girl in the eye and putting it on.

Photo signed by Lee Marvin, from The Big Red One. – HA.com

- The cast. Lee Marvin plays Sgt. Possum. Mark Hamill (yes, *Luke Skywalker!*) plays a soldier under his command.
- Soldiers hiding from a convoy of German tanks by digging holes in the ground and letting the tanks ride over them.
- A woman about to give birth, and the only soldier who's consider "qualified" is one who once *thought about* being a medic.
- The soldiers coming across a monument, dedicated to those who've died in war. The soldiers think it's recent. Sgt. Possum says it's from WWI. "But the names are the same," a soldier says. "They always are," Possum replies.
- The D-Day beach landing. One review I found said this was the best portrayal of that event until Spielberg's Saving Private Ryan.
- The liberation of a concentration camp, and all its horrors. Mark Hamill's character is psychologically and emotionally complex; he's unable to kill, until this powerful moment. It prompts one to ask what would have happened to the world, to history, if the National Socialist (Nazi) movement had not been fought and defeated.
- The perfect esthetic closure of the movie's ending, taking Sgt. Possum back where this story started. In more ways than one. And yet... with a big, important *difference.*

Some scenes in TBRO are unforgettable. Many are not pleasant. That's war. That's the movie. It's not for the little ones.

Fuller directed (in some cases also wrote) many films. One of his last was considered too controversial by studio executives, and it was never released in the theaters. White Dog (1982) has a message so clearly, unmistakably anti-racist, that the modernist, deliberately inverted mis-perception interprets as racist. Look it up. Racist? *I don't think so,* to put it mildly. (I first saw it on Cable TV. It's available on home video.)

Trailers for The Big Red One can be found on the Internet, including on YouTube.

Also worthwhile is The Typewriter, The Rifle & the Movie Camera, a documentary available on the 'net (but not included in the 2-disk Reconstruction set).

Amanda Freitag at the Kohler Food & Wine Experience. Attendees could view her demonstration on-screen, or above in mirrors.

Marcus Samuelsson (right) talks about cooking fish at the Kohler Food & Wine Experience.

December
2018

Cover image: *Breaking Through,* Copyright © Bryan Larsen
Great Movies This Month
Painter Bryan Larsen on His Artwork and Ideas
I Ate At... by Richard J. Baumann: Camp Dundee Bar & Grill, Campbellsport
Once in a Lifetime, by Paul Mueller: The Deer of Sheboygan County
PulpArtists by David Saunders: Morr Kusnet
Natural Connections by Emily Stone: Little Birds with Hot-Rod Engines
Ask a Science Teacher by Larry Scheckel: Can You Kill Somebody by Dropping a Penny off the Top of the Empire State Building?

Painter Bryan Larsen on His Artwork and Ideas

I recently had the great pleasure of speaking with Bryan Larsen about his work, how he became a painter, who and what inspires him, and why his subjects always look so beautifully purposeful. Mr. Larsen's work can be seen and purchased through the Quent Cordair Fine Art gallery in Napa, California. His painting, Liberty, adorns the cover of [the Summer 2012] issue of *The Objective Standard*.

— Craig Biddle

This interview was first published in **The Objective Standard,** *Summer, 2012. The PRC thanks Craig Biddle, Editor in Chief of TOS, for granting permission to reprint this interview, which is Copyright © The Objective Standard.*

theobjectivestandard.com

https://theobjectivestandard.com/2012/05/bryan-larsen/

Craig Biddle: Thank you for joining me, Bryan.

Bryan Larsen: My pleasure.

CB: Many of our readers are already fans of your work, others are likely to become fans over time, and I suspect all will enjoy hearing about how you create such beautiful paintings, what inspires you, and how you became an artist. Let's begin with this last point: How did you get into art? And why did you choose painting as a career?

BL: I've been drawing and painting since before I can remember. My parents were very supportive of that, so I got a lot of practice and encouragement, and I had a ready supply of paper, crayons, and pencils.

As far as painting for a living, I went to college on an illustration scholarship, but I never really thought I would do it for a living. I always assumed it would be an auxiliary to whatever my line of work was. I didn't think you could make a living as an artist. I'm glad I turned out to be wrong.

I chose painting over some of the other mediums because it offers a lot of flexibility and a lot of permanence. You have access to a broad range of colors and techniques; it's more affordable than many of the other mediums; it's easy to make reproductions of. I think it's something a lot of artists gravitate to because it's simple and inexpensive from the production side.

CB: Perhaps it's simple for someone with your skill! And I gather, given the scholarship for illustration, that you had acquired substantial skill even prior to college. Tell me about your schooling and how you transitioned to painting for a living.

BL: Well, it gets a little complicated there. I was good at art in high school, and Utah has what it calls a Sterling Scholar program—it's a statewide competition for scholarships in various disciplines.

My art teacher encouraged me to enter that, and I ended up getting a scholarship to an illustration program at a state college in Utah. It was a pretty decent program. The complication arose when the instructor I really liked, the one who seemed to really know what he was doing, retired, and simultaneously I ran out of money.

So I left the program, moved back to Salt Lake City, and started working as a cabinetmaker. My dad was always into woodworking, so I knew a bit about it. And then I got married and worked while my wife went to school.

My other love, while I was in school, was mathematics and design. So when my wife finished school, I went back to be a mechanical engineer. I always thought that would be fun. So I had two years of illustration education and then the rest of my college was in engineering.

About three years into that program, I was painting in my spare time, and I sold my first painting. I had never really considered fine art as a career option before that, but the sale opened up the possibility, and I decided to take a stab at it.

It was a rocky start, but in retrospect I had it pretty easy. The Cordair gallery was willing to take my work, even though I didn't have a large portfolio, a degree, or any real references. My boss at the cabinet shop was also supportive. I must have quit four or five times to paint full-time, and when money got tight he was always willing to let me come back. It certainly didn't hurt that my wife was working, too. Eventually art sales picked up, and I was able to reach that tipping point where I was consistently making as much painting as I had been at the shop. I never looked back.

CB: Have you ever worked in other mediums or art forms, such as sculpture or music?

BL: My mom was a piano teacher, and I played the piano. But I don't think my understanding of music runs deep enough to create music.

I do enjoy sculpture quite a bit. But I think complicated themes are more difficult to tackle in sculpture. You only have a few things to work with—the gesture, the figure, and maybe the interaction between figures. You don't have the benefit of using backgrounds, different color schemes, or different times of day to support the composition like you do with paint.

Sculpture is also very expensive on the start-up side. Even if you work in clay, you have to be able to pay to have the casts made. I didn't have the option of doing that at the beginning. I did a lot of sculpture in high school and college, but when I was doing art on my own, in my spare time before I started selling paintings, there was no way I could afford to pursue it.

You have to have space, too. You have to be able to make noise. So in some ways I moved into painting because it was so simple on the production side—although I find it interesting that a lot of the things I'm drawing and painting these days seem like themes that are simple and figurative and could work well as sculptures.

Maybe, one of these days, when I have the time, I'll go back to sculpture. I think it's beautiful; a lot of my favorite artists are sculptors.

CB: You've done some still-lifes, for instance *The Art of Precision*, and some cityscapes, such as a couple in the series *Among the Clouds*, but you focus primarily on painting human figures in various contexts and environments. Why is this?

BL: I think even with still-lifes and cityscapes and landscapes, the thing that interests me—in both the things that I do and other artists' work—is the human element.

The reason I would do a cityscape instead of a landscape would be the human creativity and design and intelligence behind the city. I find that interesting. The same with the still-lifes I have done—the objects in The Art of Precision are the tools of a creative human mind; they're not just objects.

The still-lifes and the landscapes I've done are sort of paintings of people; it's just that the people aren't in the paintings. And I guess I just find it easier to identify with images of people. I find them fascinating and beautiful, and it's what I've been drawn to all along.

There are a lot of amazing still-life and landscape painters. When I do them, they tend to be more scholastic. I'm learning to paint them so that they can be backgrounds or backdrops for figures.

The simplest answer, though, is that I find the people,

the figures, more interesting and more telling. They're more difficult and more challenging to paint as well—and I like that aspect.

CB: Who are some of your favorite painters and why?

BL: That's a big question. I guess it depends on the genre. As far as figure painters are concerned, William-Adolphe Bouguereau is an amazing figure painter. I like him mostly for his technique. His subjects weren't always the most compelling, but they were always beautiful. I think there are very few people who would argue that he wasn't one of the best, if not the best, figure painter who ever lived. He was certainly the most prolific. If I were ever to aspire to someone's technique in painting a figure, it'd probably be his.

Alma-Tadema is another Victorian painter. What I like about him is his attention to detail. He painted amazing scenes of Roman baths and people looking over vistas at huge, man-made edifices of marble or down at ships. The figures are beautiful. So I admire that attention to detail and his work ethic—he was prolific.

There's a story about him that I love. When he was starting out, a critic said that his marble looked like blue cheese, and, instead of being offended by that, he took it to heart. And he ended up working like crazy on painting marble. From then on, almost every painting he painted had marble in it, and these days he's renowned for being one of the best painters of marble who ever lived. I admire that ability to take criticism and turn it into a strength.

CB: A new twist on the "when life gives you lemons" cliché. . .

BL: Yes, when life gives you lemons, you build a giant lemonade empire . . .

CB: And when life gives you blue cheese, you learn how to paint marble perfectly.

BL: Yes, I love that. I also love that he wasn't concerned with painting what the critics thought was popular. He was a Victorian painter, but toward the end of the Victorian era the impressionists started to take hold, and critics started to like what they were doing. But he painted what he liked and was popular with a lot of regular people. I think this is important because he was painting things that mattered to people other than just art critics. And I like that about him.

CB: So do I, being a regular person.

BL: Yes. If you can understand it and it looks like something you think is beautiful and worth aspiring to, that's what I like. And he was good at that.

As far as other painters who did figures, there's a gentleman named Jacob Collins who works in New York. Like Bouguereau, his subject matter isn't always the most exciting. He paints a lot of what you would call academic or academy-style paintings that are nudes reclining—not really the most interesting settings or subjects, but, again, incredibly beautiful.

The reason I like him is because he's an absolute master at painting the figure and he's one of the artists who has decided it's his mission to bring back that kind of classical skill or technical ability—that attention to detail—which has really been lost for a long time.

Although he doesn't paint many interesting subjects himself, he has done all the work to figure out how to do it, how to paint in that kind of amazing, realistic, representational style. And, like I said, he's dedicated his career to rediscovering those techniques, adding to it as best he can using modern understanding of light and color, and then passing that on to his students—some of whom I think will end up painting really amazing paintings. I think he's great.

Other inspirations include Maxfield Parrish. He is sometimes dismissed as an illustrator, but I think his artistic vision and talent are amazing. His paintings were among my favorites when I was a kid. They still are.

There's also John Berkey, who paints really loosely; but I've always been a sci-fi fan, and he paints scenes of starships and planets in a way that's very mysterious and artistic. There's a part of me that really likes his work, too.

CB: I'll have to look him up. I've never heard of him.

BL: Not a lot of people have, I guess. He was an illustrator. But he was a very talented one, and I think he had a great sense of composition. His scenes are grand and awe-inspiring. His sense of design was amazing—he pulled it off in the style of an old master painter, but painting in the 25th century.

CB: How do you choose subject matter for a painting? What's your process there?

BL: I'm drawn to a few different things. Human achievement is always something I'm really interested in, especially groundbreaking new ideas that change the way people live. I like working with subjects such as Galileo and Newton, because they were working at a time when science was simpler and a lot of what they did was visual. You could see what they were doing, so it makes for a great composition.

I'd love to do a painting of Turing and his early computer. I have a friend who's a neuroscientist, and I'm trying to figure out how to turn that into a painting. It's hard because

The title of this Bryan Larsen painting is "Free Will." Quent Cordair Fine Art (see elsewhere for website) offers this image as limited-edition prints ranging in size from 48 inches to 72 inches in width. A very well-defined thought process obviously went into the *creation* of this work; the start of a clearly-defined approach to life can be formulated by *contemplating* it. — Used here with permission of the artist, Bryan Larsen. Copyright © Bryan Larsen.

a lot of the innovation that happens now is stuff that's subtle and unseeable, and thus it's hard to make it visually striking.

I've always loved architecture. My dad was a draftsman and a huge fan of Frank Lloyd Wright. For as long as I can remember, he had a huge poster of the mile-high skyscraper at his office, and I always loved Wright's buildings. I also always loved seeing people in environments that they created themselves. I still find that fascinating. I love doing paintings of the human form juxtaposed over the beauty of geometric surroundings they've created for themselves.

I'm also really drawn to the concept of aspiring to do what your heroes have done and take it another step beyond. So I've done a lot of paintings with children aspiring to do great things. They seem to have the purest form of hero worship. For them, there are no limits; and if something has been done, there's no reason why you can't do something twenty times more difficult.

Once I have a subject in mind, it's just a matter of trying to figure out a way to make it work in a simple composition, finding a model that fits the part and going from there.

CB: So you start out with a theme in mind, then you look for a model and a scene that can convey that?

BL: Most of the time it works that way. For a long time, I would actually do careful drawings trying to work out the exact pose and the interaction between the figure and the background. Eventually I realized that a lot of times the relatively crude sketches I would do beforehand would have problems. I'd try to put a real person into that pose and it looked unnatural. Or, because people's proportions are different, it was not possible for them. Sometimes there are other issues. The end result is that I would often change the pose entirely once I had the model in front of me.

So these days, I'll usually have the basic idea and a really rough sketch. Then I'll find a model who I think fits the idea and then sit down with the model for a few hours and try different poses and interactions, trying to figure out what looks right and feels natural. Then I'll do sketches based on that.

I've also found that a lot of times out of those brainstorming sessions with the models, I'll stumble across poses that I hadn't thought of before that suddenly strike me as interesting—or I'll get an idea while the model is there and try something else. So, especially recently, I have had a few ideas develop simply out of brainstorming sessions. Most of the time the idea comes first, but there are times when a pose suggests something that I hadn't thought of yet and the painting evolves from there.

CB: One of the things I love about your work is that the subjects in your paintings always look purposeful, even when they're just sitting or relaxing. For instance, in both *The Letter* and *Deliberation*, the woman is sitting and not engaged in any physical activity beyond that, but she's clearly up to something mentally—she's clearly, well, as the title of *Deliberation* says, deliberating. There seems to be something going on in the minds of all your subjects; they appear to be active mentally even if not physically. Do you intentionally portray your subjects this way, always with purpose?

BL: Absolutely. That's what makes them more interesting to me than landscapes. It's not just the fact that they're beautiful people; what's beautiful to me is their capacity—the things they can do, the things they think, the things they can create, and their appreciation for beauty in others.

To me, it would be less interesting to paint a person doing nothing or thinking nothing—even if they were really beautiful. It would be like painting a beautiful mountainside. It's beautiful, and there's value in that, but it's so much more interesting to have something else going on that's uniquely human and purposeful and didn't just happen by accident.

CB: This aspect of your work is obvious in some paintings—for instance, in *Young Builder* the girl is reaching up to place another block on her skyscraper. In that case, her purpose is clear in the physical action she's taking. But you accomplish this even in the drawings and paintings where people are not physically acting. You accomplish it in their countenance and body language. How do you go about that? What methods or techniques are involved?

BL: Well, doing a painting as opposed to a photograph accomplishes a little of that, because the details that an artist decides to include in a painting can't help but reflect what the artist thinks is important.

I know that I have a tendency to pull out geometric and architectural forms and figures rather than drapery, but you mentioned *Deliberation*, and that kind of ties back into what we were talking about before. That was one of those poses where I had brought in a model for something else completely, and as we were working through some different poses, I caught her in a moment of trying to decide what to do next. That struck me as really interesting. The pose and her facial expression said a lot about what she was thinking.

So when I was looking back through the reference photos I had taken, that one jumped out at me even more than the ones I had taken for the painting I had intended to do. The idea evolved from there.

So that's a situation where I saw something in the model that hadn't occurred to me to do before, and it turned into a new painting.

CB: A beautiful one, at that.

BL: Thanks!

CB: You seem also to have a great fondness for people engaging in feats of engineering and production. In addition to *Young Builder*, several others are in this vein—*Motive Force* and *First Heat* come to mind. Tell me about your inspiration here.

BL: I've been drawn to engineering and architecture all along. Motive Force and First Heat were, for anyone who has read Ayn Rand, obviously inspired by Hank Rearden and Dagny Taggart. But engineering and the sciences in general inspire me because they're such obvious examples of physical things that have been brought about only because of what people can dream up and figure out and make work.

To me they are as great an example of human achievement as an athlete; they're as beautiful as the human figure, so it makes sense to me to mix the two together. And as I mentioned earlier, I like to paint people in the background that they created for themselves rather than paint them wandering through a landscape, no matter how beautiful that is. Manmade environments are more interesting to me.

If I hadn't been a painter, I would have been a mechanical engineer. I'm amazed by the things that people do in these disciplines, so it makes sense that I think they are important enough to paint.

CB: As happy as I am that you're a painter, I'm curious as to what you would have created as a mechanical engineer.

BL: [Laughing] I was always interested in outer space, so Elon Musk and SpaceX are things I follow closely—with a tiny bit of jealousy in the "what if I had gone that route" sense.

CB: It's that one-life problem . . .

BL: Exactly.

CB: Once you've selected your subject and you know what you want to paint, how, generally speaking, do you go about creating a painting—what's involved in the mechanics

---

See and hear Bryan Larsen talk about his art:
https://www.youtube.com/watch?v=7sLI0G44sJA
or search the 'net for:
**TOS-Con 2019:
Optimism in Visual Art with Bryan Larsen**

Quent Cordair Fine Art
offers quality prints
by Bryan Larsen
and many other fine artists
www.cordair.com

of the process?

BL: To simplify the whole process: The first thing is to have the idea. Then I need to find a model; sometimes it's really important to find out who the model is—he or she may have to fit a certain profile. Other times, it doesn't matter. But I'll often start with three to twenty photos of the model and a dozen photographs of different backgrounds and textures and things that are going to be in the picture. Then I'll sit down and do a compositional drawing to scale.

Once I have that, and I think all the proportions are right, I transfer that to the canvas. There are a few ways to do this. For instance, I can use a grid system to manually enlarge the image onto the canvas. Some artists use a projector. These days, I've found it's really handy to have a drawing blown up on a large-scale Xerox machine. I'll cover the back of the enlarged copy with oil paint, fix it to the canvas and trace over the drawing. It works just like carbon paper.

But one way or another, I'll transfer that drawing to the canvas, and from there it depends on the composition. If the lighting is really extreme, if the colors are going to be bright and difficult, sometimes I'll do an underpainting or study to help me figure out the lighting.

Most of the time, once I have the overall composition figured out, I dive right in—referring back and forth to the different pictures and trying to keep a general image in my head of what I want the overall relationships to be.

Again it depends on the complexity of the painting, but if it's simple I'll start with a figure, because it's the most interesting. I usually paint the face first and then all the other flesh tones. If the composition's very complicated, I'll start with the background—just to make sure that by the time I get to the figure, I can adjust the colors and the flesh tones to make them work with the background.

So most of the time I'll work in a one-pass sort of way, painting one thing until it's finished—a face, an arm, a dress, a building, the sky. Then, when I have everything there, every once in a while there'll be something that obviously doesn't fit or needs to be adjusted. I'll adjust how light or dark it is, or adjust the colors to make them play well together.

CB: And you work exclusively in oil, right?

BL: Yes, it's my favorite medium. It allows an amazing amount of flexibility for reworking and refining to get things exactly the way you want them, and it can produce an incredible range of colors.

CB: What's your favorite part of the process?

BL: As I'm working, the entire canvas is sketched out, everything's there, and I'm dropping these bits and pieces in their finished state, but they exist in a vacuum—just a face floating in space, then an arm—and it can be disconcerting. There's a lot of second-guessing that goes on there; you have to trust what you know from past paintings and the reference material. But there's always an enormous sense of justification or relief when you fill in the final bit of blank canvas and the whole thing comes together.

CB: You astonish yourself once again?

BL: Well, if you've ever painted a room and you've masked everything off with tape and you know all the lines are straight, and the molding is straight, and everything's perfect, but the tape is all there and you can't really tell if the paint job is good. As soon as you pull down the masking tape and put in the furniture, it all comes together and works as one unit.

That's a really gratifying moment with a painting because the month or two months of work that you've done finally pay off.

I also enjoy seeing a finished painting again several months after finishing it and sending it off. When I first finish a painting, I have been looking at it far too long to be objective about it. But after a nice break I can appreciate it for what it is. That's a great feeling.

CB: I'll bet it is.

I understand you produce commission works as well as speculative pieces. Who are some of your commission clients, if that's OK to discuss, and what kinds of works have you produced for them?

BL: My biggest client by far has been BB&T, a bank headquartered in Winston-Salem, North Carolina. Until about two years ago, its CEO was John Allison, who many Objectivists will be familiar with.

He's an amazing person. I met him briefly at a conference one year and was very impressed by him and was quite excited when, through the Cordair gallery, he approached me about using *Heroes*—the painting of the Apollo rocket launch with the father and son—on the cover of the bank's annual report.

I was obviously going to say, "Yes," and that was great. The next year, they used *Young Builder*. The third year they decided to commission an original painting to use on their annual report. And every year since then, including these past two years, when they've had a new CEO, they've continued to do that.

That's been a really fun project every year. They always want something interesting and achievement-oriented, the exact sort of thing I love to paint, and they've been very easy to work with. The bank's corporate symbol over the past few years has been a lighthouse, so I've done a lot of seascapes with figures, with a lighthouse prominently featured in the background.

I also did a big commission for an architectural firm called The Durango Partners. That was a really fun commission, too. They wanted me to paint an architect looking across a bay at a newly completed house, which they wanted to be his masterwork. He's standing with the blueprints draped over a rock in front of him. We ended up calling the piece *Breaking Through*, in reference to both the career of the architect and the way the house seemed to be breaking out of the cliff face.

The really fun part of that commission was designing the house. I must have done fifty different elevation views before we found something they liked.

I have done a number of simpler portrait commissions and things like that as well.

CB: Where can people see your works—especially those that are for sale?

BL: If they want to see originals, the only place is the Quent Cordair Fine Art gallery in Napa, California, which has a number of my originals as well as prints of paintings that have already sold. They've done an amazing job representing me, to the point where I can't even keep them supplied let alone think about selling things anywhere else.

CB: Nice problem!

BL: It is. It's a really good problem. They're amazing people, too. And they have quite a few originals there, as well as prints. Their website is **www.Cordair.com**. All the originals, as well as anything they offer prints of, are shown on their website.

I also maintain a website of my own at **www.bryanlarsen.com**. I try to keep that updated. There are links there to a blog where I occasionally post images of paintings in progress or art-related stories that I find interesting. My wife helps me manage that, and she has a great eye for interesting web stories.

Aside from those two online sources and the gallery, you'll have to stumble on someone who owns a piece.

CB: If someone wants to commission you to do a painting or portrait, how should he contact you?

BL: The best way is to call the Cordair gallery. They're really great at working out all those details, and then I can concentrate on what I do and not worry about the business side of things.

CB: What are you working on now?

BL: Right now, in fact today, I will probably finish the last few details on a painting of Justice, which I've been working on as a sort of companion piece to Liberty, which I painted a few years ago. I'm pretty excited about it. Images of it [are] up at the Cordair website.

CB: Well, I look forward to seeing Justice, and I appreciate you taking time to talk to me.

BL: Again, my pleasure.

A Moment of GLORY

Sgt. William Harvey Carney was a member of the all-African American 54th Regiment Massachusetts Volunteer Infantry, featured in the movie Glory. I have not seen that film (but fully intend to), so I don't know if Carney is mentioned or featured in it. (He is not listed as a character in the film on **imdb.com**, the Internet Movie Database.)

According to Wikipedia, Carney "was awarded the Medal of Honor for grabbing the U.S. flag as the flag bearer fell, carrying the flag to the enemy ramparts and back, and singing 'Boys, the old flag never touched the ground!' While other African Americans had since been granted the award by the time it was presented to Carney, Carney's is the earliest action for which the Medal of Honor was awarded to an African American."

Per Wikipedia, the inscription on Sgt. Carney's medal, awarded May 23, 1900, reads: "When the color sergeant was shot down, this soldier [Carney] grasped the flag, led the way to the parapet, and planted the colors thereon. When the troops fell back he brought off the flag, under a fierce fire in which he was twice severely wounded."

From The United States Service Magazine, 1864: "As our forces retire, Sergeant Carney, who has kept the colors of his regiment flying upon the parapet of Wagner during the entire conflict, is seen creeping along on one knee, still holding up the flag, and only yielding its sacred trust upon finding an officer of his regiment. As he enter[ed] the field-hospital, where his wounded comrades are being brought in, they cheer him and the colors. Though nearly exhausted with the loss of blood, he says, 'Boys, the old flag never touched the ground.'"

Sgt. William Harvey Carney (1840-1908) with his Medal of Honor. Photo taken later in Carney's life. – Photo by James E. Reed

LEFT: Posed photo of Sgt. William Harvey Carney, taken about 1864 by John Ritchie. RIGHT: Sheet music based on a quote from Sgt. Carney. – Public domain images from Wikipedia

Who saw Your Editor mentioned on the *Svengoolie* show on Me TV? I tagged along on my wife's business trip to Washington DC back in June. A time frame of only 48 hours to run around town allowed me two mandatory objectives: A visit to the Frederick Douglass home (written up previously in The PRC) and a visit to this Albert Einstein statue. I wore my Svengoolie shirt for the photo, sent it in, and on Aug. 25, Sven aired it. I wanted to visit the statue because, 30+ years ago, I showed a film on the statue, its creator (Robert Berks), and its assembly, to my North Dakota Science students, seeing the film 6 times that day. — Photo by Your Editor's Wife

By Larry Scheckel

Ask a Science Teacher

Q: Can You Kill Somebody by Dropping a Penny off the Top of the Empire State Building?

A: It's one of those classic urban legends. A person stands on the observation deck of the Empire State building. Makes a wish and throws a penny over the barricades to the street below. The penny falls and kills a pedestrian on the sidewalk below.

We assume that the penny will fall faster and faster (accelerate) under the influence of gravity. Such is not the case. As the penny falls faster and faster, it encounters more air resistance, more drag. It's running into an increasing amount of air molecules. The faster the penny falls, the greater the air resistance it experiences, and so at some certain maximum velocity of the penny, the drag force becomes equal and opposite to the downward pull of gravity. When the two forces are balanced, the penny no longer accelerates. Instead it falls at a constant speed, called the terminal velocity, all the way to the ground.

Pennies are flat, so they experience a lot of air resistance. Pennies are light, so it doesn't take much drag to counteract their weight. Pennies achieve their terminal velocity after only about 50 feet of descent. After that point, they flutter to the ground at a mere 25 mph. A conk on the head by a penny off the Empire State Building, a fall of 1250 feet, will get your attention, but no medical attention needed.

It would be a vastly different story if the penny did not fall in air, but rather in a vacuum. If there were no air, a falling penny would accelerate to a speed of over 200 mph by the time it reached the ground, or your head. At that speed, it might very well damage your skull, but it wouldn't cause death.

It's a different story if a falling ballpoint pen hits you on the noggin. If someone tossed a ballpoint pen off the top of the Empire State Building, it could kill. Depending on their design, a pen could spin, flutter, or shoot down like an arrow. In the case of "shoot down like an arrow," it could reach a speed of 200 mph. When it hits the skull, it will hit a small area with a lot of momentum. It would insure an ambulance call, perhaps the Last Rites, maybe a closed coffin.

There's a reason why areas beneath construction sites are roped off or have covered walkways. The workers wear hard hats. A nut or bolt, weighing 2 ounces (57 grams), dropped several hundred feet can do major damage to the cranium. It could be lethal. It would "ring your bell" if you wore a hard hat, but you would be able to return to hearth and home.

Mythbusters tested out the idea of the penny drop in an episode that aired on October 17, 2003. They constructed a gun that could fire a penny at 65 miles per hour. It's the very maximum speed at which a penny dropped from the top of the Empire State Building would hit the ground and far faster than the calculated 25 mph. They fired the penny into a ballistics dummy. It caused only slight damage. They then shot each other with the gun. It stung, but it didn't really do any harm.

From Wikipedia Commons. – Photo by Smithfl (photo has been doctored)

From Wikipedia Commons. – Photo taken in 2012 by Sam Valadi

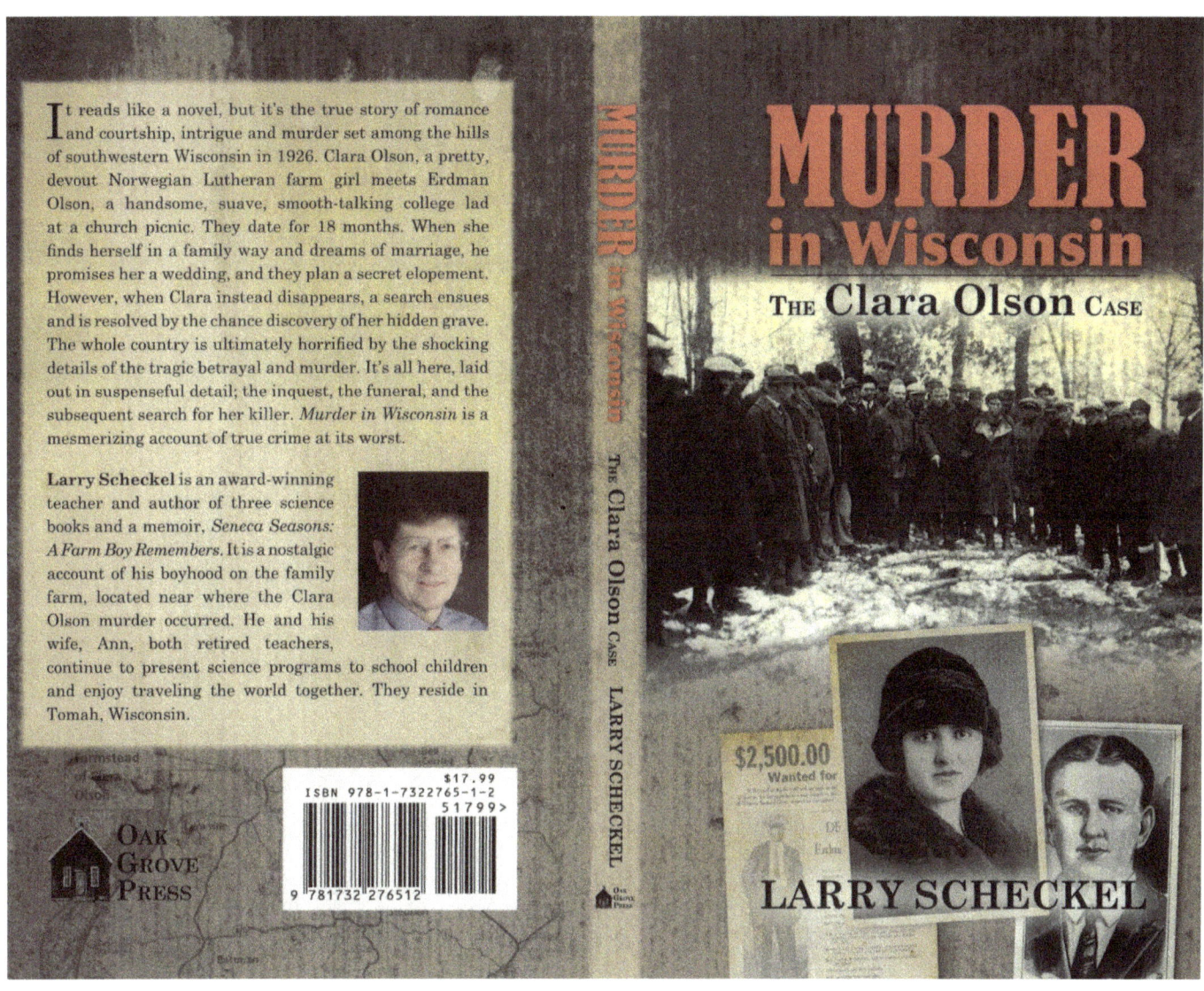

NEW BOOK by Larry Scheckel: Released this past September [2018], Murder in Wisconsin documents the true story of the 1926 killing of Clara Olson. This murder took place just a few miles from the farm Scheckel grew up on. – Scan provided by the author

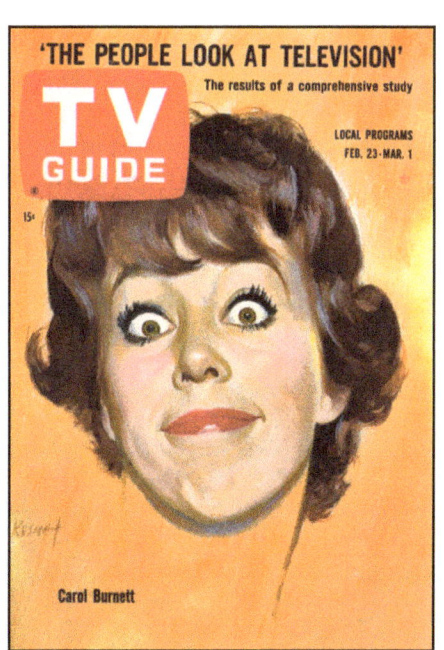

Examples of cover art by Morr Kusnet. – From PulpArtists.com

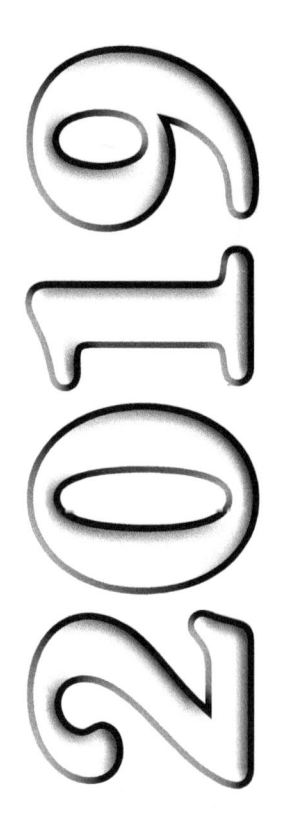

2019

The Current
Plymouth Review
Taking you places worth seeing
Volume 8 • Issue 2 • January 2019

This issue: Tributes to home cooks, chefs, and bakers

FREE!

January
2019

Cover photo: Your Editor in 4-D
Great Movies This Month
Rendez-Vous, A New French Restaurant in Sheboygan
The Rendez-Vous Tasting Menu
New Year's Eve Dinner at the Blind Horse
Little Pink House
Ask a Science Teacher by Larry Scheckel: What Sports Projectile Moves the Fastest?
IJ Helps WI, by Conor Beck, IJ.org
Ready to Roll: Nine Lessons from Ending Wisconsin's Home-Baking Ban, by Jennifer McDonald, IJ.org
Once in a Lifetime, by Paul Mueller: So Many Birds So Close to Home!
Sticks Nix Hick Pix headline explanation
Infinity Covers
2001: A Space Odyssey — Synopsis in 8 Sentences

This promotional comic book tells a story of how Surge milk machines are the best choice for farmers. It's an example of an "infinity cover."

This is one of the most famous newspaper headlines of all time. It's from July, 1935.

Translation (arranging the syntax somewhat):
People in rural areas (Sticks)
are not attending (nix)
movies (pix)
depicting rural people as hicks (hick).

Or, to put it plainly: People living in rural areas do not react favorably to movies depicting people living in rural areas as hicks, rubes, clods, dolts, country bumpkins, hayseeds, yokels, apple-knockers, stump-jumpers, backwoodsers, clover-kickers, yahoos, bog-hoppers, and other terminology like that there.

(I'll admit I had help with that one. For an hilariously long list of such terms, see the Dictionary of American Regional English; search for "Names and nicknames for a rustic or countrified person.")

In one scene of the film Yankee Doodle Dandy, actor James Cagney is relaxing in a hammock, reading a paper with this headline (with *one* error—can you spot it?). He explains the headline's meaning to a group of young hippies.

2001: A Space Odyssey — Synopsis in 8 sentences

1. Aliens visit Earth and find a species verging on extinction.
2. The aliens decide, "These creatures have potential, so let's advance them along a little, so they survive."
3. The aliens decide, "Let's check back on them when they're advanced enough to reach the moon."
4. Many years later, that species (mankind) discovers evidence of aliens on the moon.
5. Their discovery sets off a signal aimed at Jupiter.
6. To find out who/what the signal was aimed at, a manned spaceship is sent to Jupiter.
7. At Jupiter, aliens show one man many things, but the man cannot understand what he sees.
8. The aliens decide, "Let's advance this guy along a little."

Alien thoughts translated into English from their native language, courtesy of The Plymouth Review Current.

Little Pink House

The cover for Little Pink House presents two images.

One is a calm but apprehensive woman sitting on the porch of her home.

The other is a nightmarish scene of a backhoe poised to destroy a lone, pink house.

Little Pink House is a 2016 movie based on Jeff Benedict's 2009 book of the same title. (From descriptions of the book I found, researching this article, I'll be reading it.) It tells the real-life battle of Susette Kelo to keep her home when local government first tries to buy it, then decides to take it by force, so that a private company (lured with economic development money), can build on the property, thus increasing the tax base and enriching the municipality's coffers.

Paramedic Susette Kelo (pronounced KEY-low) buys a modest home in New London, Connecticut. She remodels it and paints it pink.

A certain public-spirited woman works with local and state governments, encouraging a pharmaceutical company to build a plant in her community of New London. The site of the proposed plant has all these houses on it. But that should pose no problem.

Interestingly, the state's governor is never named. More interestingly, the public-spirited woman's real name (and the real name of the college she was president of) are not given. In the film, her name is Charlotte Wells. (Her real name can be found with a little Internet research.)

As Wells spouts standard politically-correct buzz-phrases ("Your community needs this and your city wants it"), a front company is formed to buy up houses: the New London Development Corporation (NLDC).

Some people decide to sell.

Kelo and a few others do not.

"If you don't sell now, they can acquire your property through other methods," these hold-outs are ominously told.

Now, any "true story" film dealing with multiple parties interacting over several years is very likely over-simplified. (One good reason to get the book.) Often, such films are hard to follow. (I find events in war movies especially difficult to keep track of.)

Little Pink House does a great job of presenting the essentials, linking them together, allowing the viewer to grasp them. Titles identify people and give dates of events.

Kelo is contacted by the Institute for Justice (IJ). According to its website, IJ "litigates to limit the size and scope of government power and to ensure that all Americans have the right to control their own destinies as free and responsible members of society."

IJ takes her case.

"This Institute for Justice," Charlotte Wells asks someone over the phone. "Do we need to be concerned?"

Yes. Oh, yes. IJ *gives* them cause for concern. But for Susette Kelo to help her own cause, IJ tells her, she has to speak in front of the public, something she is not, as presented in the film, great at. But her virtues of honesty and valuing her own property come through, loud and clear, and her message has widespread appeal.

"I just know that we should be able to keep our homes," she says. Simple as that.

Charlotte Wells' and the governor's increasingly blatant strong-arm tactics become increasingly unpopular.

This is *not* a story about the evils of "greed," a highly over-misused word. "Greed" is essentially wanting more. As such, it's neither good nor bad. It's *how* one decides to acquire more that can be good or evil. By buying, improving, and defending her own home and property, Susette Kelo was every bit as "greedy" as the government officials who wanted to confiscate residents' homes and the pharmaceutical company that wanted the government's economic incentives.

This *is* a story of the unholy alliance between business and government. You've likely heard it said that big business is "too powerful." But what kind of power is that? In a fully free society, initiation of force is banned from public interaction, and the government's

146

job is to prevent or stop initiated force. In a society where business and government are mixed, the government initiates force to *stop* a business from operating (from selling baked goods, for example; see elsewhere in this issue), or initiates force to *help* a business (offering "economic incentives" expropriated from taxpayers; removing obstacles like Susette Kelo's house).

In a free society, the "power" of big business is the power of persuasion. A business could offer any astronomical amount of money—billions and billions—for Susette Kelo's home. She would be free to refuse it.

In a mixed alliance of business and government, where government initiates force in the form of eminent domain, she is not free to refuse it.

This *is* a story of how "the public good" is used to destroy the rights of individuals.

"This whole plan is for the greater good," a lawyer representing NLDC tells Scott Bullock, IJ attorney. "Why don't you see that?"

"Some of the worst acts in history were justified because they were in pursuit of a greater good," Bullock replies.

This is beyond belief to the NLDC attorney, who sputters incredulously.

Some people truly believe the "public good" takes precedence over individual property rights, and would say Kelo should have willingly sacrificed her values for the sake of the "greater public good."

Readers familiar with my writings on movies know that I give away precious little—sometimes *nothing*—of the story. I understand that can be frustrating. But I consider the process of discovery, of surprise, to be one of the most enjoyable things about viewing a film (or reading a book).

With Little Pink House, however, not only have I already given away the essentials of the story; I will tell you exactly how it ends! And I bet you'll still want to see it.

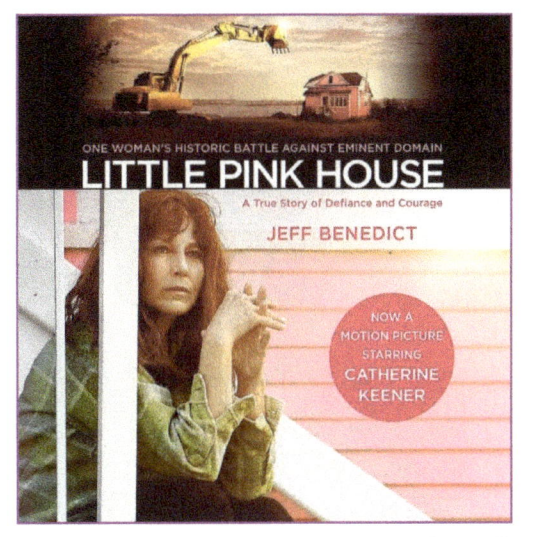

The Little Pink House story, written by Jeff Benedict, is available as both a book and audiobook. The home video of the film seems to be out of print, but is easily found on eBay. — Barnes & Noble, BN.com

In 2005, the Supreme Court (Kelo vs. City of New London) rules against Kelo, 5-4. Justices John Paul Stevens, Anthony Kennedy, David Souter, Ruth Bader Ginsburg and Stephen Breyer rule in favor of eminent domain. Dissenting are Justices William Rehnquist, Clarence Thomas, Sandra Day O'Connor, and Antonin Scalia.

Kelo watches as a part of her life, her little pink house, is razed. (She was not the only person who did not want to move; others see their own lives torn apart as their homes are demolished.)

The film gives several follow-up events.

The pharmaceutical company never builds anything on the confiscated property. The land from which homes had been cleared by government force became a dump.

The governor served two terms in prison for several charges of corruption.

"Dr. Charlotte Wells went on a national speaking tour, lecturing on behalf of the poor and disenfranchised." Right. After declaring a long-term war on same.

And the most interesting end title of the film: "The Supreme Court decision was the most widely-hated decision in modern history."

End of story?

Not... *quite*.

What followed were laws enacted by several states (including Wisconsin) in response to outrage over the concept of eminent domain. (Some will say "outrage over the *abuse* of eminent domain." I think it's the *existence* of eminent domain.)

The fact that the pharmaceutical company never built anything shouldn't matter. Even if a manufacturing complex had been built, had created jobs, and had enriched the local government, the question to ask is:

Should eminent domain be used for the benefit of a private company?

But *then* the question should be shortened:

Should eminent domain be used?

February
2019

Cover photo: Your Editor Ponders What to Do with Two Truffles

Great Movies This Month

Ask a Science Teacher by Larry Scheckel: Why do we have time zones and daylight savings time?

Cooking Truffles

Black Truffle Dinner at the Lake Park Bistro

Logic in Your Life: What's the Principle?

PulpArtists by David Saunders: Robert A. Graef

Once in a Lifetime, by Paul Mueller: Common Critters with Not-So-Common Colors

The Art of James Bama

Mr. Happy Cook, by Richard J. Baumann: Adult Sandwiches

Best Views in Wisconsin, by Mariah Haberman: Gibraltar Rock State Natural Area (Lodi)

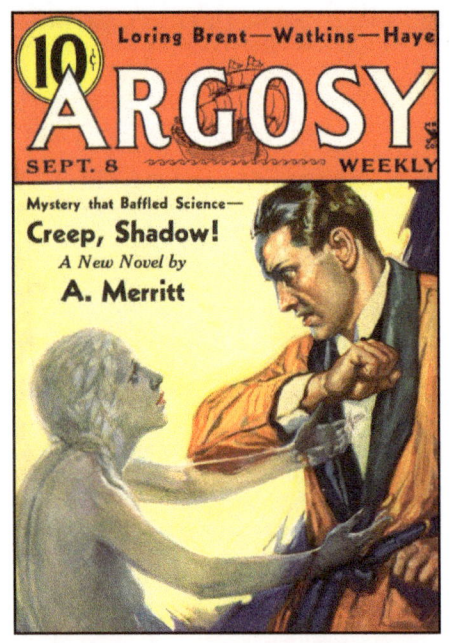

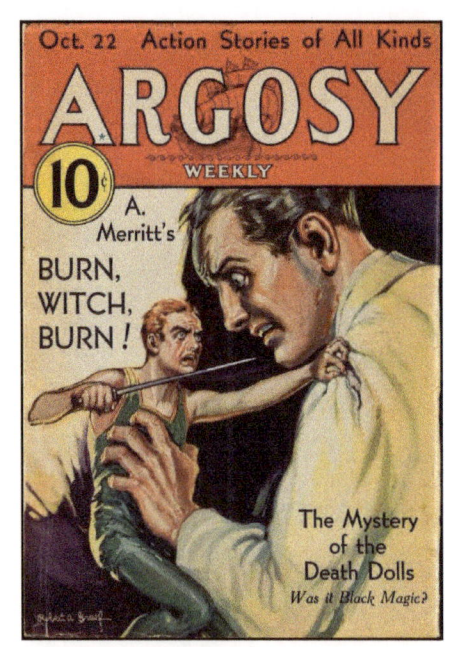

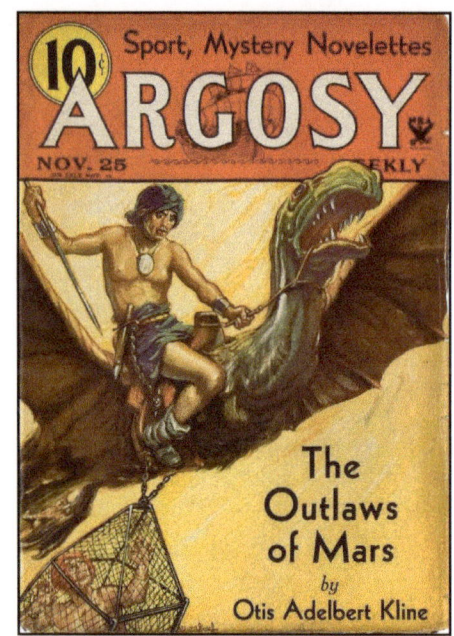

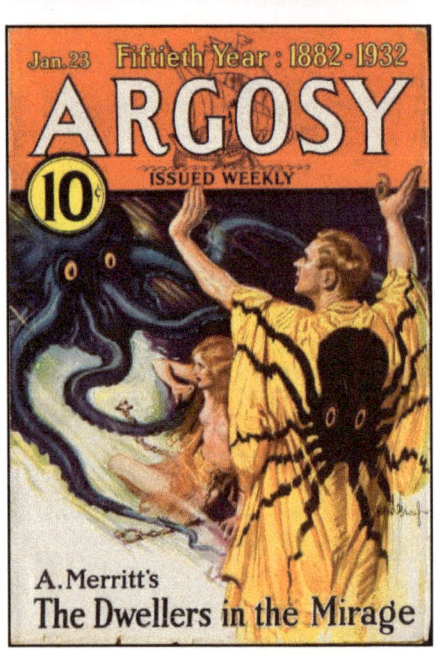

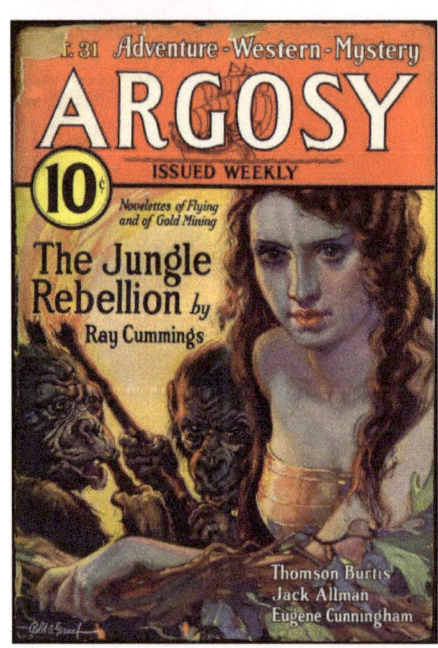

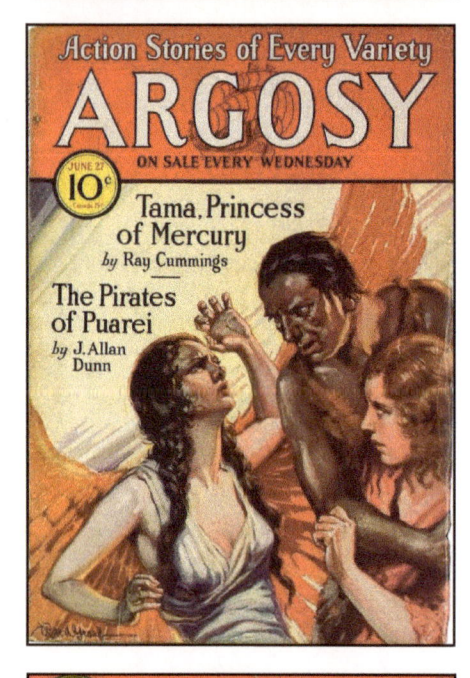

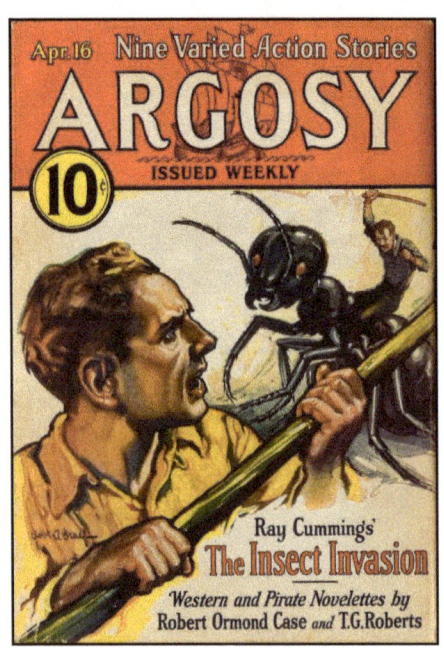

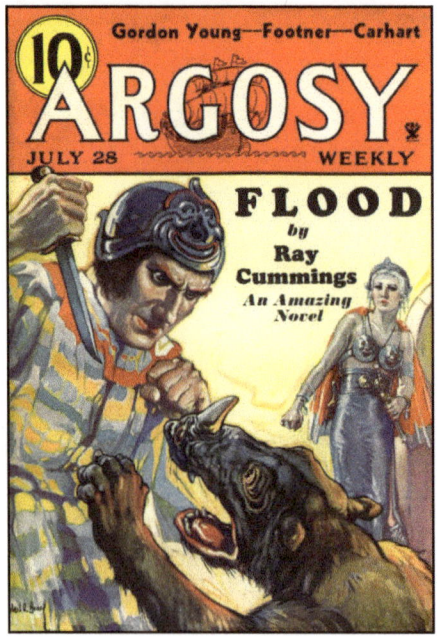

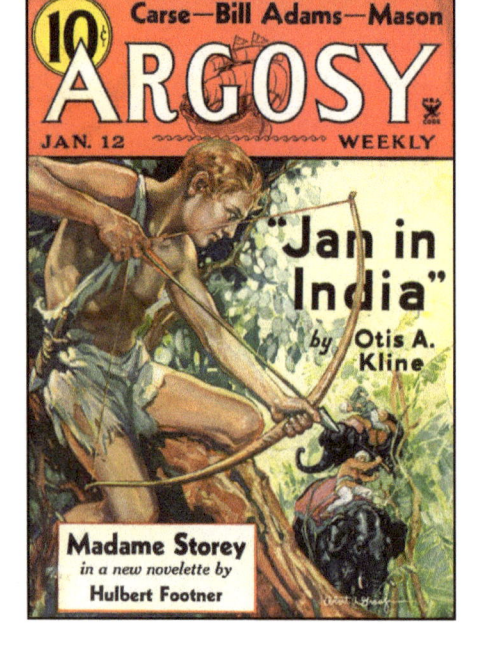

Covers featuring art by Robert Graef.

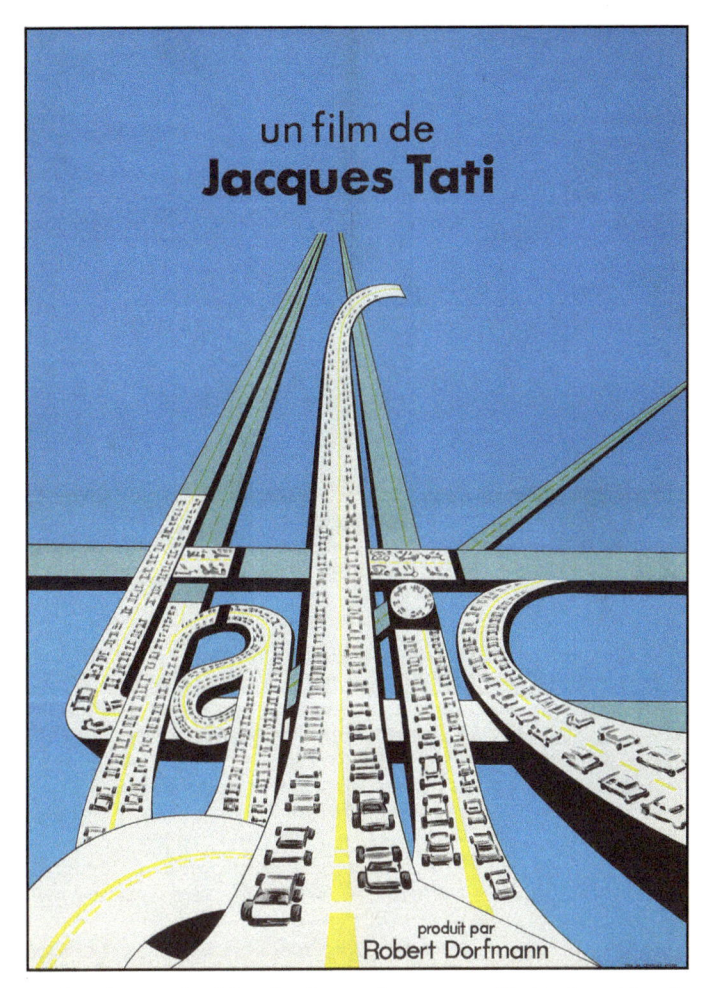

We're always looking for inventive uses of lettering. Here's a *fantastic* example! The movie Traffic, by Jacques Tati, is as brilliant as this poster. — HA.com

The Bells of Saint Mary's, paperback cover, 1966. Oil on paper. 18.5 x 13.5 in. Sold, 2017 auction, $6,000. Used on a Bantam paperback book cover. — HA.com

March
2019

Cover photo: Freaktoyz, Sheboygan
Best Views in Wisconsin, by Mariah Haberman: Wyalusing State Park (Prairie du Chien)
Great Movies This Month
Ask a Science Teacher by Larry Scheckel: What makes a boomerang come back when you throw it?
Mr. Happy Cook, by Richard J. Baumann: Good Bye Winter
Restaurant of the Month, by Amanda Weber: Heavenly Soups

PulpArtists by David Saunders: Richard Lillis
Supreme Court Strikes Down Excessive Fines, by John Kramer, IJ.org
Natural Connections, by Emily Stone: Frumpy Beaver, Elegant Swan Have Much in Common
New Bouguereau Exhibition at Milwaukee Art Museum Explores Artist's Popularity in Gilded Age America, Milwaukee Art Museum press release
Logic in Your Life: Divisiveness

Divisiveness

We hear it from many sources. People say it as if it's self-evidently true. No controversy. No doubt.

"This country is divided."

And who's causing this divisiveness?

You'll get a thousand answers. The President. The former President. This side. That side. This group. That group.

OK, that's not very helpful, but we should also ask: What are we divided *about*?

Here again, a thousand answers. Racism. Income inequity. Immigration. Policies of this party. That party. This group. That group.

In past articles, I've written about finding basic principles in the midst of specific, complicated situations. I'm going to try applying that approach to this question.

You see, I think I have a good, useful answer as to *what* we're divided *about*.

Sure, I could blurt it out right here. But I'm not going to.

What if I took you on a little journey of discovery? What if I spent this article, and the next two, leading you through certain pathways, so that you could very possibly reach some of the same conclusions I have reached? What if you could *discover* them—on your own?

This and the next two articles are for those who have felt satisfaction and pride in creating something. For those who open a newspaper and say, "I designed that ad." For those who look at a house and think, "I helped build that." Or a model battleship, thinking, "I put that together."

If all goes well with these articles, you just might end up thinking, "I had a little help, but *I discovered that principle.*"

You will know the pride that comes, not only having *created* something, but *discovering* something.

To understand the Present, look to the Past

We're in the midst of the present. We could simply study everything we can about present times. And sure, we'd learn something useful about our present divisiveness.

But that might not be enough. What if we look to the past? Ah! We might be able to put the present into better perspective. Compare today's divisiveness with that of other times.

There is another possible benefit. A big one. We could find situations in history where there was great divisiveness, and... we can see how things turned out.

If we can learn something helpful, we should look at history. Even if it makes us uncomfortable, and more than a little apprehensive about our own future.

For example...

Let's look to this country's early history. It was the first country to base its existence on individual rights, the idea that each individual existed for his own sake, and not out of duty to any monarch, or to "society."

(This is an oversimplification. Ancient Greece had high regard for the individual, and the United States owes much to that culture.)

But individual rights were not implemented consistently. There were contradictions.

One of the worst, most divisive contradictions in this country's existence (as I've written in past columns) was slavery. I believe understanding each side—those who supported slavery, and those who fought it—will help us better understand today's divisiveness.

Arguments against slavery

I'm reading and taking notes on a book edited by C. Bradley Thompson: Anti-Slavery Political Writings, 1833-1860. The book contains essays by Frederick Douglass (one of my personal heroes), Harriet Beecher Stowe, Abraham Lincoln, and others whose names might be less familiar to non-historians.

Complementing this book, I listened to a series of three lectures by Thompson: American Slavery, American Freedom, which can be downloaded at estore.aynrand.org.

In the preface, the editor writes that the book has three purposes: "first, to present the best writings and speeches of the most influential antislavery thinkers, activists, and statesmen in the years between 1830 and 1860; second, to demonstrate the range of theoretical and political choices open to antislavery advocates during the antebellum period; and finally, to introduce students to the general problem associated with reconciling theory and practice."

As the United States grew in size and maturity, it became more obvious that slavery was incompatible with the nature of this country. It was a basic, or *fundamental* contradiction.

Take the various articles in the book, Anti-Slavery Political Writings, 1833-1860, and boil them down. Get to the essential, the fundamental point. What is it?

It's one answer to the question: "Who owns a person?"

The abolitionists all agreed on one basic moral principle: It is wrong for one person to own another.

You own your life. I own mine.

That's it.

Of course, there is a long history, interesting and important, of the development of the concept of rights; of how individuals should treat each other; what any one person is "owed." The concept didn't just appear. It developed. Grew. Is still growing.

There are other questions, such how rights are violated. How to untangle the issue of individual rights in complex situations.

All details we can't touch on here. So let's stick to the basic principles, and look at the opposite answer to "Who owns a person?"

Who could possibly defend slavery?

This is the kind of question I'd expect from the typical, honest person in the street. Most people, hearing evil spouted, will turn away in disgust, and not want to think too much about it.

But just as doctors have to study smallpox in order to rid the world of it, I think those same honest people have to turn back and face that evil to understand it. Introducing a weaker version of smallpox into the body helps that person resist the actual disease. Understanding evil will help one stand up to it. Understanding the evil *in principle* will help a person recognize it when it comes along in a new and different form.

One way advocates of slavery got around the "Who owns a person?" question was to claim, "Slaves aren't persons."

OK, how would you answer that? Just think about it a bit. Look at the world around you. If you're educated enough to read and pick up this newspaper, you'll soon enough understand that it's easy to prove that's wrong. If someone claims it's a matter of one race being human, and one race being less than human, your own observations will show you that belief to be ridiculously false.

As I've written before, this kind of thinking doesn't take any PhD-level education. All that's required is good, honest common sense. Your observations will show that all races have both geniuses and fools; productive people and parasites. You'll see, if you're honest, that achievement is an individual matter. That you can't just lump individuals of one race together and say, "Human," and call individuals of another race "Non-human."

(To me, it's just common sense. But I also realize people believe all kinds of things for which there is no basis—psychic powers, astrology, haunted houses, etc.)

Yes, you and I have the advantage (if we take it) of historical perspective. But what about someone living during slavery? Can they be excused for greater ignorance?

Not in the final analysis. For at least one big reason: It was illegal in slave states to teach slaves to read.

If slaves were less than human, would they even have the *ability* to learn how to read? Have you heard of any conspiracies, lately, of subversive farmers trying to teach the cows or chickens they have penned up, to read?

Being able to read—having a conceptual consciousness—is one basis for being a person. A person with rights. A person whose life belongs to that person, and to no one else.

A principled approach would be: "If a person, by his nature, owns his own life, then that applies to every person." An unprincipled approach would be: "Some do, and some don't."

An anthology of abolitionist writings. — From Barnes & Noble, bn.com

Harriet Beecher Stowe, one of the writers appearing in the above book. What book is she most famous for? — Public domain photo from Wikipedia

Descending deeper

Now we're going to look into the face of even greater evil.

One advocate of slavery was George Fitzhugh. The title of one of his books is very revealing: Sociology for the South; or the Failure of Free Society (1854).

Some people in the 1800s likely thought, "Look, I'm not a slave. So it's not my problem."

That's not a practical view. If you're not willing to fight injustice when it affects others, you allow that injustice to spread until it does affect you.

(And by "fighting," I don't mean with physical weapons, and I don't mean you should fight the whole war. "Fighting" in this sense means standing up for what you believe is right, in whatever way is appropriate and possible for you. It could mean discussing the subject; writing letters to newspapers; writing articles; etc.)

George Fitzhugh made slavery *everyone's* problem. He advocated that slavery be applied to *all* races. So you see, if you ignore justice and say, "Not my problem, man," the evils you pretend don't exist have a way of knocking on your door, saying with an wicked grin, "Got a problem for you, man."

"Nineteen out of twenty individuals have a natural and inalienable right to be slaves," Fitzhugh wrote.

Get that? A *right* to be a slave? A perfect example of a contradiction!

Said Fitzhugh: "If Yankees were caught young they could be trained, domesticated & civilized to make 'faithful and valuable servants.'"

Since this is an attack on the very founding principles of America, it's no surprise that Fitzhugh said, "The Declaration of Independence is exuberantly false, and aborescently fallacious." (I couldn't find a definition for "aborescently," but I think we get his drift.)

"Liberty is an evil which government is intended to correct. This is the sole object of government." Know of any modern-day politicians who'd agree with Fitzhugh on that?

And: "Slavery is a form, and the very best form, of socialism." Yes, Fitzhugh was very consistent. Much of his thought anticipated Karl Marx by several decades.

Can't we compromise?

Every time you hear how divided our country is (which is often), you usually hear pleas for compromise.

But when it comes to basic, very fundamental principles, compromise is the last thing you want to do.

When you ask, "Is it right for one person to own another?", what kind of compromise between Yes and No is conceivable?

Would it be a "compromise" to have allowed the southern states to retain slavery, while the north outlawed it? Not at all. That would be a concession that slavery is OK, sometime. It would be a total moral surrender to the principle of slavery.

I return to C. Bradley Thompson's book, Anti-Slavery Political Writings, 1833-1860. In it are found passionate, uncompromising, principled arguments against this abomination. There was divisiveness between those who supported slavery and those who opposed it; that divisiveness was over opposite sides of a fundamental principle.

But within the abolitionist movement, there was also divisiveness, of another sort: How to eradicate slavery. Immediately? Gradually? How?

There was disagreement about the *how* of ending slavery. There was no compromise, however, on the view that it *should* be ended. I believe without that uncompromising fidelity to moral principle, slavery could have lasted longer, or still exist today.

Slavery was ended, but not before a terrible Civil War. Which leads one to ask, with some trepidation: Is the divisiveness we now face serious enough that another civil war is possible? Or can we learn enough from the past to avoid that tragedy?

What kind of divisiveness *do* we face today?

Tune in next issue. I'll have some thoughts.

This William-Adolphe Bouguereau painting sold at a Heritage auction in 2012 for a cool $1,762,500.00 (plus, presumably, a few bucks for shipping). — Above, HA.com; others Public Domain Images

Complete works!
www.bouguereau.org/
View over
500 paintings
by this incredible artist!

The Milwaukee Art Museum hosted a display of art by Bouguereau in 2019.

The Plymouth Review **Current**
TAKING YOU PLACES WORTH SEEING
Volume 8 • Issue 5 • April 2019

FREE!

Divisiveness ◆ Destinations Wisconsin ◆ Sudoku (4 Levels) ◆ Movie Posters
Richard Baumann: Cakes & Caseroles ◆ The Batmobile

April
2019

Cover photo: Batmobile Used in Tim Burton's 1989 Batman Movie, Smithsonian National Museum of American History, Washington, DC
Best Views in Wisconsin, by Mariah Haberman: Holy Hill National Shrine of Mary, Help of Christians (Hubertus)
Great Movies This Month
Green Book—Great Movie
Mr. Happy Cook, by Richard J. Baumann: It's Just April
PulpArtists by David Saunders: Harvey Dunn
The Wisconsin Restaurant Association Presents New Regional Awards
An Evening of the Classics:
Ask a Science Teacher by Larry Scheckel: Can People Just Burst into Flames?
Movie Posters
Divisiveness: Split Country, Split City

Opening comments

Attempting to summarize vast historical, global events in a short article like this (well, some would consider it short) can be perilous.

How do you do justice to so many events, relationships, causes and effects? It's like fitting a car into your back pocket.

Readers who are well-versed in the historical details of the subject that follows: Please read this charitably and try to overlook the oversimplifications. In contrast, if I have any actual facts incorrect (through error or omission), please drop us a note or e-mail. We do value factual accuracy.

Germany divided

When Germany was defeated in World War II, part of it was occupied by the Soviet Union (this eventually became East Germany), and part was occupied by Britain, the US, and France (West Germany).

The Soviet Union had fought with the Allies to defeat the National Socialists (Nazis). But as we soon found out, contrary to the ancient proverb, the "enemy of our enemy" is not necessarily our friend. As freedom in West Germany allowed human activity and life to flourish, the Soviet Union imposed its totalitarian philosophy on East Germany: "Property and industry was nationalized in the East German zone. If statements or decisions deviated from the described line, reprimands and (for persons outside public attention) punishment would ensue, such as imprisonment, torture and even death." (Wikipedia)

For awhile, it was possible to travel somewhat freely between East and West Germany. In a period of about a decade, over 3 million people left East Germany and never came back.

If the "means of production" had already been seized, you'd think East Germany would have everything it needed to create the worker's paradise it was supposed to be, and nobody would miss those 3 million people. But even communists had to face the fact that human minds have something to do with that "means of production." And people fleeing en masse from a communist country makes communism look bad. Solution: Stop people from leaving by brute force.

So the Soviet-controlled East German government erected, piecemeal, an "inner German border" between the two countries, trying to stop citizens from fleeing. But the "brain drain" continued as East German citizens could still move from East to West to a limited extent. Oppression of these people increased. By the early 1960s, the inner German border was fortified with wide ditches, barbed wire, lookout towers, booby traps, and minefields.

As this wide border was built, if your home was in its path, or too close, it would be torn down (something advocates of eminent domain would be perfectly comfortable with). An East German farmer's field was cut in half? Too bad. He could now work only the part within East Germany, and then, only during the daytime, as armed guards watched and made sure he didn't do anything subversive out in what was left of "his" field.

Thousands of East Germans living too close to the border were forcibly cleared out and settled elsewhere, in a program charmingly named "Operation Vermin." A few lucky ones escaped to

The Reichtag Parliament building in West Berlin on Sept. 5, 1961. The building gutted by fire in 1933 is being rebuilt. Barbed wire in front belongs to fence around Soviet War Memorial which was surrounded with the wire by British troops after the closing of the sector border to prevent possible demonstrations by West Berliners. — AP photo the West.

Berlin divided

Berlin, capital of Germany, was in the middle of the Soviet-occupied East Germany. The city, as the country, was cut into East and West sections.

By the early 1950s, the inner German Border pretty effectively stopped East Germans from escaping to the West. But within Berlin, movement between East and West was still relatively free. And West German citizens could travel between Berlin and West Germany, even though they had to pass through East Germany (with many restrictions and much checking of credentials—"Your papers, please!").

This comparative freedom within Berlin rankled the totalitarians. When you advocate complete subservience to the state, you can't allow all these individuals, each with his own thoughts, each with her own goals, to brazenly decide where to go and what to do.

These totalitarians clamped down on all that chaotic freedom by building another barrier, separating East Berlin from West Berlin. This destructive construction started in August, 1961, and extended into 1962. The wall was constantly "improved" over the years to become two barriers, with a "death strip" between the two.

(Neither national nor city borders were uniform. There were concrete or brick walls in some places; barbed wire or fences in others; anti-tank devices; or combinations thereof.)

"In an October 1973 order later discovered by researchers, guards were instructed that people attempting to cross the Wall were criminals and needed to be shot: 'Do not hesitate to use your firearm, not even when the border is breached in the company of women and children, which is a tactic the traitors have often used.'" (Wikipedia)

"If an escapee was wounded in a crossing attempt and lay on the death strip, no matter how close they were to the Western wall, Westerners could not intervene for fear of triggering engaging fire from the 'Grepos,' the East Berlin border guards. The guards often let fugitives bleed to death in the middle of this ground, as in the most notorious failed attempt, that of Peter Fechter (aged 18). He was shot and bled to death, in full view of the Western media, on 17 August 1962." (Wikipedia)

Yep. Real nice guys. Not!

One country again

Last issue, I wrote how slavery divided America. Abolitionists agreed *that* slavery should be abolished, but did not agree on *how*— whether it should be done immediately, or in phases, and what to do with the former slaves.

Before the demolition of the Berlin Wall, some worried about how an East and West Germany, disunified for so many years, could come together. I was shocked to learn that British Prime Minister Margaret Thatcher (about whom I'd heard so many positive things) said to Soviet President Gorbachev, "We do not want a united Germany. This would lead to a change to postwar borders and we cannot allow that because such a development would undermine the stability of the whole international situation and could endanger our security."

But reunification (or "die Wende" as some prefer, which approximately translates to "the turning point" or "turnaround"—that has a nicer ring to it, don't you think?), while presenting challenges, has produced no disaster. Free people, to the extent they value and understand freedom, can deal with such complexities.

The nature of this split

In last issue's article on Divisiveness, I wrote about a split in America, coming about because two sides could not compromise on a moral principle: whether every individual human being has the right to life and liberty. There was no "coming together" of those who said Yes to that principle, and those saying No.

That split—the divisiveness, taking sides, and resulting ugly war—came from within.

Germany's split is quite a different story. In the early part of the 20th Century, the country's culture started going mad, leading to World War I (the war that was so horrible, it would convince people to never fight wars again), and then World War II (see why history is important?). After the second war, those who conquered Germany split it up. So this country's split was imposed by outside forces.

And there was no war between the two sides.

A different kind of split, yes. But still one that can teach us something about divisiveness.

East and West. What was the difference?

East vs. West

Professor Hope Harrison, of George Washington University, wrote, "The [Berlin] wall symbolized the lack of freedom under communism. It symbolized the Cold War and divide between the communist Soviet bloc and the western democratic, capitalist bloc."

Now would be an excellent time to define communism and capitalism. But I'll wait. See next issue's article.

A resident of a building in East Berlin looks longingly across the Wall into West Berlin. — AP photo

East Berlin laborers work on the "Death Strip" which communist authorities created on their side of the border in the divided city on Oct. 1, 1961. A double barbed wire fence marks the border, with West Berlin at right. In this view of the area on September 23 laborers level rubble of houses which, just days before, stood on the site close to the border. Buildings along the 25-mile dividing line were evacuated and razed by Berlin reds to eliminate one means of escape used by East Berliners to jump to the west. — AP photo

A section of what's left of the Berlin Wall, on display at the Smithsonian National Museum of American History in Washington, DC. "Freiheit" is German for "Freedom."

Welsh historian Jan Morris wrote: "Traveling from west to east through [the inner German border] was like entering a drab and disturbing dream, peopled by all the ogres of totalitarianism, a half-lit world of shabby resentments, where anything could be done to you, I used to feel, without anybody ever hearing of it, and your every step was dogged by watchful eyes and mechanisms."

Kate Connolly, writing for The Guardian, in a piece looking back 25 years after Germany's "turnaround," says, "...life expectancy has risen considerably in the east since reunification..." That's interesting. It's significant (and positive) from a certain moral/political perspective. (A rise in human life expectancy is not held as a positive value by everyone.)

An essay written in 1960 by Indian economist Bellikoth Ragunath Shenoy, Ph.D (1905–1978), entitled "East and West Berlin: A Study in Free vs. Controlled Economy," is prefaced with the statement, "Shenoy contrasts the results produced in the two halves of Berlin, one under communism and the other capitalism, to show planning is not required for growth."

There's that communism/capitalism comparison again.

"The contrast between the two Berlins cannot miss the attention of a school child," Shenoy writes. Some of the contrasts he makes (remember, this is 1960, prior to the Wall):

East: Much rubble and damage from WWII is still in evidence. "[B]uildings here are generally grey from neglect, the furnishings lack in brightness and quality, and the roads and pavements are shabby."

West: "Rebuilding is virtually complete in West Berlin." "[T]he shopping centers radiate boom conditions."

East: Mass transit predominates. "The new phenomenon of workers owning cars, which West Berlin shares with U.S.A and many parts of Europe, is unknown in East Berlin."

West: Highways are "jammed with prosperous looking automobile traffic."

East: "The food shops in East Berlin exhibit cheap articles in indifferent wrappers or containers and the prices for comparable items, despite the poor quality, are noticeably higher than in West Berlin. Walking into a restaurant in East Berlin, one finds the same contrast."

West: "The departmental stores in West Berlin are cramming with wearing apparel, other personal effects and a multiplicity of household equipment, temptingly displayed. Nothing at all comparable is visible in East Berlin."

East: "Visiting East Berlin gives the impression of visiting a prison camp." People there "show an unwillingness to talk to strangers, generally taking shelter behind the plea that they do not understand English."

West: People are cordial, willing to talk when approached.

East: "The flow of traffic, human and financial, is pre-dominantly one way, from East to West Berlin."

West: No such movement, the opposite way.

Are you seeing a trend here? I suspect you do, as you are a sharp, intelligent, perceptive reader.

Tune in next issue!

Note: The movie Bridge of Spies, starring Tom Hanks, depicts the beginnings of the Berlin Wall.

David Saunders'
pulpartists.com

HARVEY DUNN: AIMING FOR A HIGHER LEVEL

(1884-1952)

Harvey Thomas Dunn was born March 8, 1884 on his parents' homestead near Manchester, South Dakota. His father was Thomas Dunn, a farmer, and his mother was Bertha Dunn, a farmer's wife. He had an older sister and a younger brother. They lived in a sod house on the prairie of Red Stone Valley. He worked as a plowboy until he was 17 and remained a large and powerful man throughout his life.

From 1901-02 he studied at South Dakota Agriculture College, in Brookings, where his art teacher encouraged him to attend the Art Institute of Chicago, which he did from 1902-1904. He then studied with Howard Pyle for the next two years at Chadds Ford, PA, and Wilmington, DE. He was deeply influenced by Pyle's philosophy of art and life. He was a Christian Scientist.

In 1908 Harvey Dunn married Johanne "Tulla" L. Krebs of Wilmington, DE.

In 1911 Howard Pyle received several mural commissions, and in preparation traveled to Italy to study the masters, but he tragically died in Florence. Afterwards, Harvey Dunn moved to Leonia New Jersey to establish his own art studio from which he sold illustrations to *The Saturday Evening Post, Harper's, Red Book, American Legion Monthly, Collier's,* and *Scribner's* magazines.

He also painted pulp covers for Street & Smith's *The Popular Magazine,* a twice monthly pulp magazine of manly adventure fiction "for the common man."

In 1915 he opened the Leonia School of Illustration.

During WWI, Dunn was one of only eight official war artists of the American Expeditionary Forces (AEF). After the war, he moved to Tenafly, NJ.

From 1926 to 1942 he taught at the Grand Central School of Art, which held classes on the top floor of the actual terminal building. Students rode a special elevator located on track 23 to the sky-lighted 7th floor. The Grand Central Terminal was the heart of America's modern streamlined industrial commerce. This setting inspired Dunn's students to consider the power of their own commercial work to elevate mass media to a higher level of art, by generously filling their work with the power of their unique inner spirit. Among his many pupils were pulp artists Lyman Anderson, Ernest Chiriacka, John Clymer, Dean Cornwell, Curtis Delano, Don Hewitt, Norman Saunders, Amos Sewell, Gloria Stoll, and Herbert Morton Stoops. Dunn believed the purpose of illustration was to set the stage for the reader's imagination. He would often select a scene that was not described in detail in the text, in order to concentrate on depicting the mood of the story instead of the details. Dunn's approach to painting was to first establish the darker tones that provide base color values and contrasts and then build up to the light tones. Figures started with the heads, and the heads had to remain the most interesting elements in the final painting.

> Lyman Anderson, Ernest Chiriacka, John Clymer, Dean Cornwell, Curtis Delano, Don Hewitt, Norman Saunders, Amos Sewell, Gloria Stoll, Herbert Morton Stoops are mentioned as pupils of Dunn. Three of these illustrators have been featured previously in The PRC. *Which three?*

After WWII, Dunn only taught occasional seminars. He was the President of the Society of Illustrators, and he used that platform to vigorously attack changes in the publishing industry that threatened to destroy the noble humanist traditions of illustration art. Dunn could see that the need of corporate mass marketing to control a unified media message would soon destroy the classic era of freelance illustration by stifling the voice of the artist's individual creativity. Up until then magazines had used art editors to make curatorial selections from trusted artists, but that cordial relationship ended when art editors were replaced by art directors, or as Dunn called them, "art dictators!," whose prescribed assignments were best fabricated by anonymous graphic studios. "If I can't sign my own name on a painting, why would I bother to paint it! I'd rather quit the business and paint landscapes. If you ever amount to anything at all, it will be because you are true to that deep desire or ideal which made you seek artistic expression." — Harvey Dunn

He died of cancer at age 68 on October 29, 1952.

© David Saunders 2009

HARVEY DUNN

Front cover art for Outing Magazine, May 1908. Sold at auction in 2009 for just under $66K. — HA.com

Front cover of The Country Gentleman magazine, January 28, 1922. Painting sold at auction in 2010 for over $8K. The Country Gentleman carried mostly articles oriented toward farm life, but also featured fiction. — HA.com

> "If you ever amount to anything at all, it will be because you are true to that deep desire or ideal which made you seek artistic expression."
> — Harvey Dunn

Lincoln Surveying the Landscape, painted in 1929. Sold at auction for $35K. — HA.com

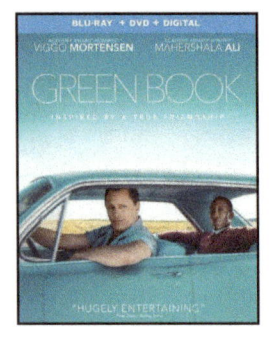

The movie Green Book (left) deals with real-life pianist Don Shirley. At right are some of Dr. Shirley's albums.

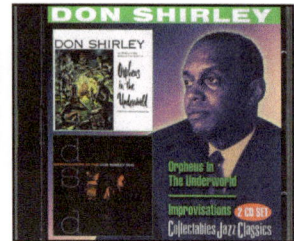

The Plymouth Review Current
TAKING YOU PLACES WORTH SEEING
Volume 8 • Issue 6 • May 2019

FREE!

Divisiveness • Sudoku • Art • Planet Stories • Bratwurst • Classical Conditioning
Strange and Interesting Things • Community Events • Sunsets

May
2019

Cover photo: Batmobile Used in Tim Burton's 1989 Batman Movie, Smithsonian National Museum of American History, Washington, DC
Best Views in Wisconsin, by Mariah Haberman: Buena Vista Park (Alma)
Great Movies This Month
Mr. Happy Cook, by Richard J. Baumann: It's that Time Again (for Bratwurst)
Ask a Science Teacher by Larry Scheckel: What is Conditioned Response by Pavlov?
Art in the Garden (Oshkosh)
SCHRC book reviewed: *From Bootlegging to Brothels, Sheboygan County Vice during the 1920s and 1930s*
Spring Art Tour
What Happens When an MBA Student Raised in Communist China Reads Hayek, by Barry Brownstein
Resources for Further [pro-freedom] Reading
Divisiveness: What Divides Us?
PulpArtists by David Saunders: Allen Anderson
The Human Freedom Index (excerpt)

During the recent Windy City Pulp and Paper Show, we caught up with David Saunders, whose biographies of pulp artists have appeared in these pages for about three years. Here, he shows his appreciation for fine reading.

In our March issue, we took a brief look at how slavery divided this country. With no compromise possible between the views that a) it is acceptable for some people to enslave other people; and b) that each person has rights which forbid slavery, the country split up and erupted in war.

In our April issue, we looked at a country and city forcefully split in two. Germany and Berlin were split between East and West, the first under control of the communist Soviets, the second under other countries. Some historians characterize this split as communism vs. capitalism.

In our country today, there is much divisiveness. That is—many cultural commentators and politicians say there is. And they keep accusing each other of creating more divisiveness.

Which makes me wonder how much divisiveness there actually is. Hearing over and over, "There's so much divisiveness!" and then thinking, "Yeah, I guess there is"—you're really cheating yourself out of actual knowledge, with that "thinking" pattern.

How would you measure divisiveness? Is it even possible? Elsewhere in this issue, we feature articles describing an attempt at measuring freedom within a given country. So maybe divisiveness can be measured. But who's doing that?

Can we look at present times and compare them with other events in history? Oh... yeah... I *did* that, with the article on slavery. (Sneaky, ain't I?)

We're not fighting a civil war. Yet. Let's hope never.

No one's seceded from the Union. Yet. Though some Californians have proposed it.

All right, so we have a vague, general idea (if even that) of the *degree* of divisiveness we're seeing. So just *what* is it that we're divided *about?*

Immigration? Racism? I'd like to write about both of those important topics in a future issue. I do believe they *contribute* to the level of divisiveness. But they don't get to the root, or fundamental cause of things. I'm looking for the one point of divisiveness that explains the many points of divisiveness, if there is such a thing in this case.

I'm going to call it the Master Divisiveness Issue. MDI.

I have an idea of what that MDI is. It's difficult to find, because very few people talk about it. Amazing! People talk about almost anything. All body functions. Every physical cruelty, real or imagined. But this issue is not named often enough. If it were named, I think things would make a whole lot more sense.

Last issue, I quoted an article by Indian economist Bellikoth Ragunath Shenoy, Ph.D (1905–1978). Here's another paragraph from his 1960 work, "East and West Berlin: A Study in Free vs. Controlled Economy":

"For an explanation of the contrast of the two Berlins, we must look deeper: the main explanation lies in the divergent political systems. The people being the same, there is no difference in talent, technological skill and aspirations of the residents of the two parts of the city. In West Berlin efforts are spontaneous and self-directed by free men, under the urge to go ahead. In East Berlin effort is centrally directed by Communist planners, who do not lack in determination for speedy progress; the urge to progress is particularly strong, if only to demonstrate the potentialities of communism to foreign visitors to the two Berlins. The contrast in prosperity is convincing proof of the superiority of the forces of freedom over centralized planning. It is difficult to resist the inference that workers in East Berlin, deprived of the incentives of full property rights over the fruits of one's effort, are loath to put in their best."

Good observations. I'm not disparaging what Shenoy writes. But what word is present, above? And what word is missing?

Even in the Human Freedom Index—certainly, a valuable and important work—there is one important word used only once, and then, only in a contradictory way.

I'm convinced too many people are afraid of this word. Even many who support it don't dare say it.

I dare.

It's *capitalism.*

All right. So does the MDI boil down to communism vs. capitalism, as some quotes from last month's article suggest? I don't think so. Now, I was recently astounded to read a thread at the bottom of a news show suggesting that the main issue in the coming presidential election was going to be "socialism vs. capitalism." I think a thorough dialogue on that topic is needed.

But—hey, wait. Just a minute. If we're going to use these terms, we should know precisely what they are. (Have you seen those videos where university students say, "I'm for socialism," and when asked what socialism is, don't have an answer?)

The following are distilled from several sources each. Don't agree with these definitions? You know how to contact us.

Slavery. A system where one individual legally owns and coerces another individual. The owner may or may not have the legal authority to physically abuse the slave, even to the point of death.

Communism. A system where individual interests are surrendered to the

What Divides Us?

"commune" or "community" (however that is defined).

Egalitarianism. A result of communism. The theory that all individuals should have, or be rewarded, equally, even when some individuals create or produce more than others.

Socialism. A social system based on public ownership of the means of production.

Capitalism. A system based on private ownership of the means of production.

Fascism. A system based on private ownership of the means of production, with a centralized government controlling every aspect of that means of production.

Statism. A system based on state/government control of social and economic activity. This higher-level concept includes communism, socialism, and fascism.

Careful! The phrase "means of production" is used several times. If you're on one side of this Master Divisive Issue, you might not want "means of production" clearly understood; if you're on the other side of the MDI, you *must* clearly understand it.

To understand principles like this, it helps to get very basic. Therefore:

You decide one morning, "I'm going to collect sticks," and act accordingly. What is the "means of production"? Your choice and your freedom to act on it.

Under communism and egalitarianism, you'd divide the gathered sticks equally (by force or voluntarily), with every member of the community (however you define that: a local hippie commune; the village; the nation-state; the world).

Under slavery, socialism, or fascism, personal choice is abolished, and isn't a factor. You're directed to gather sticks (or not) by the authorities. You're told when, where, and for how long to gather them. Their distribution would be determined by the rulers. The authorities' orders and your actions in following orders are the "means of production."

In all examples, you are part of the "means of production." So the most important, basic, fundamental question, on which there is no compromise, is:

Who owns your mind and your body?

Slavery. The slave-owner owns you.

Communism. The commune owns you.

Socialism. Here's where understanding "means of production" is important. Some socialism advocates say, "We're only talking about public ownership of factories, machines, and land. You own yourself." As written last month, East Germany and East Berlin had a problem. Once they nationalized the factories, machines, and land, the *people,* while they were still free, fled from East to West, leaving no human *minds* to operate the factories, etc. The East German authorities then turned their country and city into prison camps. If that is the nature of socialism, it is a system where society in general owns you.

Capitalism. You own your life, mind, and body.

I believe the Master Divisive Issue is: you own your life vs. someone else owns your life.

Or: individual rights, with the individual's life and happiness its own justification vs. the individual is a means and justification to some other ends.

Or: capitalism vs. statism.

If you've read any of my past articles, you might know what's coming next.

You should *not* believe what I've said here, simply because I've said it. If you have a good background in history, politics, and economics, you might have a good basis for evaluating what's in this article. But if you're just starting out, here's my advice:

Don't accept any of it. But *understand* it. In the years ahead, observing developments in this country and around the globe will give you a better basis to say whether I've identified the MDI or not. (You might discover some other divisive point I'm not aware of. I'd love to hear about it.)

I've been especially skimpy on my description of capitalism. If what I have said intrigues you or outrages you...

If you believe there is such a thing as "crony capitalism"...

If you believe "wage slavery" exists under capitalism...

If you believe lobbyists, or special-interest groups, or political favors for one sector of the economy, are part of capitalism...

If you believe that pure capitalism leads to depressions or inflation or widows and orphans starving in the street...

If you look at the definition of capitalism, and only part for fascism, and see "private ownership," and think, "Hey, capitalism and fascism are the same!" (I've actually seen it claimed that Nazi Germany was "capitalist," which is one of the most offensive falsehoods I can imagine)...

...then I challenge your misunderstandings, and urge you to discover what capitalism truly is.

Suppose you conclude my MDI identification is correct. You must still choose which side of the issue you're on. There's no compromise here. Either you as an individual own your life, mind, and body—or you don't. Whichever side you're on, you need to be able to defend it. That will require self-education on your part.

There are those who believe that the individual's right to life, liberty, property, and the pursuit of happiness is a part of the individual's nature.

There are those who believe the individual should give up liberty and the pursuit of individual happiness; that property should be communally owned.

Which side are you on?

An introduction to *The Human Freedom Index*

The 2018 edition of The Human Freedom Index (HFI) is a 400-page analysis and rating of freedom for most countries of the globe.

It was published by the Cato Institute (Washington, DC, USA), the Fraser Institute (Vancouver, British Columbia, Canada), and the Friedrich Naumann Foundation for Freedom (Berlin, Germany).

The Index is available free, for browsing online or downloading to your own computer. To find it, go to cato.org and search on "freedom index."

How does one measure something like freedom? To get an idea, please see "Defining and Measuring Freedom." This is one of several excerpts which the Cato Institute kindly granted The PRC permission to run.

Of 162 countries for which a Human Freedom Index was calculated, these are the top (most free) 20:
  1 New Zealand
  2 Switzerland
  3 Hong Kong
  4 Australia
  5 Canada
  6 Netherlands
  6 Denmark
  8 Ireland
  8 United Kingdom
  10 Finland
  10 Norway
  10 Taiwan
  13 Germany
  14 Estonia
  15 Luxembourg
  16 Austria
  17 United States
  17 Sweden
  19 Malta
  20 Lithuania

And these are the lowest (least free) 20:
  143 Zimbabwe
  144 Gabon
  144 Cameroon
  146 Saudi Arabia
  147 Chad
  147 Mauritania
  149 Myanmar
  150 Ethiopia
  151 Congo, Dem. Rep. of
  152 Central African Republic
  153 Iran
  154 Burundi
  155 Algeria
  156 Egypt
  157 Sudan
  158 Libya
  159 Iraq
  160 Yemen, Republic of
  161 Venezuela
  162 Syria

Collecting Planet Stories

This past April, the 19th annual Windy City Pulp and Paper Convention was held in Lombard, IL.

One special event at the show was a celebration of Planet Stories (PS), a pulp first launched 80 years ago. Beginning with the Winter 1939 issue, it lasted 71 issues, the last published in Summer 1955. (By the 1950s, the pulp format of magazine had pretty much vanished from the newsstands.)

Covers for all 71 issues can be seen at philsp.com/mags/planet_stories.html

A panel on PS consisted of Ed Hulse, Walker Martin, and Garyn Roberts. Panelists commented on writers, artists and editors of PS, and collecting it.

Roberts commented on his long-time friendship with writer Ray Bradbury. "In 2003, there was the 50th anniversary of Fahrenheit 451. A lot of people love that story. Probably about one out of ten people really understand it correctly. But Ray was a great guy."

Roberts said PS was "space opera," but said it was fun, and said he'd make no apologies for enjoying it. He gave Star Wars as a modern-day example of space opera.

"There is Bradbury in [Planet Stories] that has never been reprinted," Roberts said, which drew some excited interest from the audience.

(Editor's note: Some authors, such as Ray Bradbury, had their stories first printed in the pulps. Years later, publishers looking for material would search the pulps for stories they could reprint in hardcover or paperback form. Many authors had only a fraction [or none] of their writings reprinted. A few, like Bradbury, or Louis L'Amour, or Edgar Rice Burroughs, became so popular that publishers would search the pulps for anything that author had ever done. For fans of such authors, a non-reprinted story is a great find.)

Roberts said pulpgen.com contains many free stories from PS.

Hulse emphasized (and Roberts readily agreed) that PS was not exclusively space opera. "Planet is one of the most fun pulps to collect," he said. "First of all, it's 71 issues. It's not an impossible dream to collect [a whole run]," in contrast to some titles that ran hundreds or thousands of issues.

Hulse said, "To tell us a little more about the adventures of putting Planet sets together, I will defer to the master collector, Walker Martin."

Martin said he had two complete sets of PS. "And one set has to be the world's worst condition set of Planet Stories, and the other set has to be the world's best condition set.

"How this all came about was, in the 1970s, when I first started collecting pulps, I started collecting everything. Mystery pulps, adventure, western, science fiction—everything except the romance pulps. Now, I had a wife, children, mortgage, car. So I didn't have a lot of money. I'd buy pulps in almost any condition to get a complete a set. My first set of Planet Stories was the world's worst set. It was brittle, brown. They had covers, but when I would read them, pulp flakes and shreds would fall all over my lap.

"Well, toward the end of the 70s, I hurt my back. I couldn't go to work. All I could do was lie flat on my back in bed, so I read Planet Stories. Well, as I read the magazines, and went through the set, for the three weeks I was immobile, the magazines just about disintegrated, right on my side of the bed. My wife, after awhile, started to notice this. Things came to a head when, one night, I heard her screaming upstairs, howling, and all I could understand from the words she was saying was something about, 'Those dang Planet Stories.' So she actually told me it was either the Planet Stories, or her. Well, after thinking about it for awhile—"

The audience broke into laughter.

"—I did choose her, and I sold my collection of Planet Stories to a friend who gave me a fairly decent price. I think he gave me a thousand bucks. For 71 beat-up issues, 20 years ago, that was really a good price. So off they went.

"But needless to say—and this has happened several times with me—I started immediately missing my set of Planet Stories. They were gone, I really wanted them back. I've done this with several other titles. Any time I sell something, I want to start rebuilding. And that happened with Planet Stories. So I was looking for how I could get a complete set again. Not just scattered issues, but a complete set. I never found one.

"Until the Frank Robinson auction, a few years ago. I was friends with Frank. I knew the conditions of his Planet Stories was white paper, glossy covers, full spines. In other words, they look like they're freshly off the newsstand, even though these are 70 year old magazines. So when the auction came off, I sent in my bid, thinking, 'How much do I have to bid to get this Frank Robinson set, which had to be the best-condition set in the world?' I figured, $100 an issue isn't going to do it. So I had to bid $200 an issue. For 71 issues, that's $14,000. I got it.

"So when my Planet Stories arrived, I opened up the box, and these are 70 year old magazines, but that smell that wafted out of that box was of newsstand-fresh magazines. We've all had that experience when we open up a box of brand-new magazines. They have a certain smell. A certain scent.

"So I quickly grabbed one of my favorite issues—I hadn't read one in 20 years—ran upstairs, threw myself on the bed, flat on my back, took the magazine out of the plastic bag, started to read this copy, which was a thing of beauty...

"And I made the horrifying discovery that I could not read that magazine because it was so pretty.

"I was afraid I was going to wreck it! I was going to do it harm. It was a beautiful thing! So I carefully put it back in the bag, went downstairs, and said, 'OK, what am I going to do now?'

"I had to contact my friend, go back over to his house, and see if he still had that first set I'd sold him 20 years ago. Well, he opened up his closet, and there was my old set of Planet Stories, still in the same box, looking even worse than when I had them, and of course he charged me twice what I'd sold them to him for."

(Uproarious laughter from the audience)

"So there I am with the Planet Stories, going home... I don't tell my wife... I take one out, I go upstairs, I lie flat on my back, and the flakes are falling all over. And all I heard late that night when my wife got into bed was screaming about the Planet Stories being back again.

"I swore I would never sell them again, so to this day, I still have two sets. The worst set, and the very best!"

(Audience applause)

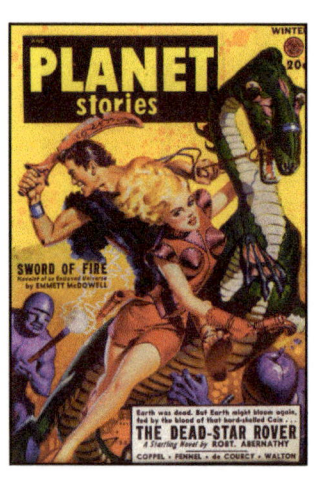

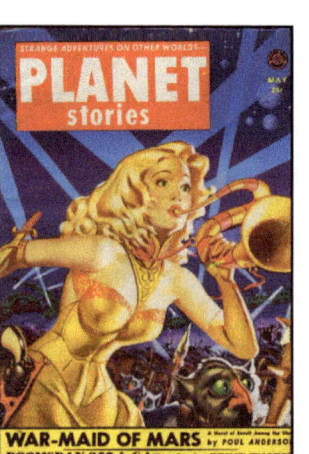

The Planet Stories panel at the recent Windy City pulp show. Left to right: Ed Hulse (publisher, writer), Walker Martin (collector), and Garyn Roberts (university professor, author).

June
2019

Cover photo: Batmobile Used in Tim Burton's 1989 Batman Movie, Smithsonian National Museum of American History, Washington, DC
Best Views in Wisconsin, by Mariah Haberman: Devil's Lake State Park (Baraboo)
Great Movies This Month
Human Trafficking
The AFI's Top 100
PulpArtists by David Saunders: Ilo Kopland
SCHRC book reviewed: *Sheboygan County's Native American Past: From the Archives*
Ask a Science Teacher by Larry Scheckel: Why Do We Have Two Eyes and Two Ears?
Morel Mushroom Dinner
Mr. Happy Cook, by Richard J. Baumann: Gini's Dirt Cake
Test Your Skills at Allegory

Two cover paintings by Ilo Kopland.

Human Trafficking

Part I
It's Happening. Here.

"I am forever grateful to the kids at South High who opened my eyes."

When Detective Tamara Remington came to Sheboygan 13 years ago and became school liaison officer at Sheboygan South High, she heard an outrageous story from some students.

They told her of a house in the heart of Sheboygan: "You can go inside and pick from pictures of young girls, runaways from Appleton, Sheboygan, Milwaukee — you can pick which one you want, and if you want her drugged or not."

It was hard to believe. But investigation showed it was all too true.

(The house in question has since been torn down.)

This is an example of sex trafficking. This crime, this modern-day slavery, is happening here, in Wisconsin, in Sheboygan county.

It's hard for some people to believe. Or — worse — some *refuse* to believe it. "Oh, that's a big-city problem. A Milwaukee problem. Maybe even Green Bay. Not in *our* town. Not *here.*"

But sex trafficking has officially been documented in all 72 Wisconsin counties.

"Sex trafficking" involves a trafficker (or pimp) forcing, defrauding, or coercing a person into a sex act with a customer.

(There is also "labor trafficking," which is using force, fraud, or coercion to make a person work. Labor trafficking accounts for 20 per cent of all trafficking, and deserves its own, separate discussion and articles.)

To better understand *trafficking*, it must be sharply distinguished from two other concepts people might confuse it with: prostitution and human smuggling.

Prostitution involves consenting adults, but it is illegal in many states.

Human smuggling is a chosen, non-coercive arrangement to pay a smuggler to transport one or more persons across a border. The crime is that of entering a country illegally.

Human trafficking can involve crossing national or state borders, but it often does not.

One additional distinction is needed. If a minor is involved in a commercial sex act, it is considered trafficking, even if force, fraud, or coercion are not present.

Remington is part of the Federal Task Force for the Eastern District of Wisconsin (which includes Fond du Lac and Sheboygan counties, extending southward to Kenosha county). The task force meets regularly at the Milwaukee court house. They have identified over 30 violent pimps (or traffickers) in the Eastern District, with "two-thirds of the traffickers having their hooks into kids and community in Sheboygan."

While Milwaukee county has the most documented cases of trafficking, Sheboygan is tied with Racine county as having the second-most cases in Wisconsin.

That single statistic, however, is misleading.

"I don't think it's happening more in Sheboygan than elsewhere," Remington says. "I think Sheboygan is ranked so high because of all the good things happening here. All of our deputies, our city police, our dispatchers, they're all trained to be aware. Having the support of Sheriff Cory Roeseler, and Chief of Police Christopher Domagalski. And District Attorney Joel Urmanski takes every single human trafficking case that we present. He's not afraid. These are difficult, challenging, very time-consuming cases. He's just fearless. So while Sheboygan county's number of reported cases are up there, that doesn't mean it's happening more than elsewhere."

Several programs in the county have aided in discovering trafficking cases. (See Part IV.)

Remington finds the public's willingness to gain awareness on the topic encouraging. But there is still much information that needs to get out there. There are still myths needing to be replaced with facts.

> Information for this series of articles was taken from a presentation by Detective Tamara Remington of the Sheboygan Police Department; and from several websites, including the Wisconsin Department of Justice's website on human trafficking, which is https://www.doj.state.wi.us/ocvs/human-trafficking
>
> **The Human Trafficking Hotline is 1-888-373-7888**

For example, sex trafficking is not confined to back alleyways, or to the seedier parts of towns. Nor do those involved slink about only under cover of night. Trafficking can be happening in any type of neighborhood, and the majority of cases Remington has dealt with happened in broad daylight.

Some will say, "I don't believe we have modern-day slavery. I don't see people in chains and shackles and cages in Sheboygan."

But traffickers gain the trust of their victims over periods of weeks, months, even years, in a process called "grooming." The chains and shackles then applied are unseen, in the form of manipulative drug addiction, and sometimes brutal beatings and gang rapes. (See Part III.)

The Midwest is a hub for trafficking. But why?

The basic, paradoxical answer: Those perpetrating this evil rely on a virtue.

"Midwesterners are trusting, you're nice, you're people-pleasers, you have a great work ethic," Remington says. "Now, I'm not telling you to go out and be mean jerks, or to raise your kids to be jerks. But we could all benefit by being less trusting. You can start with your social media. Do you really need 857 friends? We need to consider that, and be careful on social media. Everybody. That's where most traffickers look for recruits."

"This topic is one that's very important, very close to my heart," Remington says. "I want people to know this. Not to scare them, but to give simple tips that we can use to stay safe, and to raise the awareness that this problem is everywhere."

Remington admits this is not the prettiest topic to hear about or think about. Yet, her talks draw large audiences. People come to hear about human trafficking, to become the alert eyes and ears ready to detect its presence, which is the key to its prevention.

"There are so many positives about Sheboygan county," she says. "I'm so proud of Sheboygan county."

Part II
Who's at Risk? Rethinking Your Preconceptions

Before she became a member of the Sheboygan Police Department 13 years ago, Detective Tamara Remington had her own preconceptions about sex trafficking.

"When I worked in the San Francisco Bay area, I had cases involving Asian gangs," she says. "There were some human trafficking cases. But even as a police officer, I thought that human trafficking is an international problem. I started to better understand trafficking, its magnitude, and that it's going on domestically, because of the types of cases I worked on when I came to Sheboygan."

So Remington understands if people have misconceptions about this subject—a subject she admits is not pleasant. But she is continually encouraged by the large number of people attending her public talks, which indicates people want to understand the problem and do something about it.

One of several actual cases Remington uses to inform and raise awareness took place in Sheboygan: the Jason Guidry case.

"This case challenges us to re-think who the traffickers are, who the victims are, who you think their families are," Remington says.

The traffickers

The terms "pimp" and "trafficker" mean essentially the same thing: people who sell humans for sex or labor purposes.

What do pimps look like? Movies sometimes portray them dressed like royalty gone mad, with outlandish fur and leather clothing, elaborate hats, glittering gold and diamond jewelry. This version likely drives (or is chauffeured in) a large, luxury car whose interior is decorated with the same exotic flair as the pimp's attire.

One place they will dress this way is at a pimp convention. The Players Ball is an annual convergence of pimps, held in Chicago and other cities.

"It's like the Emmys or the Grammys gone wrong," Remington says. "They give awards to the biggest, baddest pimp."

But in the real world, away from the fantasy land of pimp conventions, traffickers look like anyone else. They can be men or women (despite the generic use of "he" that follows), and of any ethnic background.

Pimps are very good at communicating with each other, Remington says, and gives another discouraging fact: Milwaukee is known as the "Harvard of pimping," where pimps come from all over to learn the trade.

Remington identified three types of pimp: the Romeo (or finesse), the bone-breaker, and (a relatively recent development) the CEO

A "Romeo" pimp is so named by being a master of psychological manipulation through sweet-talking cajolery. Jason Guidry was one. He was a good-looking slick talker. Remington says, when he was arrested, "An officer warned me, 'Hey, Remington, be careful. After spending a few minutes with him, I want to take him to lunch or dinner.' He was that slick."

The "bone-breaker" (or "gorilla") pimp exerts power through brutal physical abuse and terrorizes with the threat of more of the same.

The "CEO" pimp defrauds the victim into believing he is arranging a legitimate business relationship, often posing as a modeling photographer or a music producer.

"There are more Romeo pimps in our area than bone-breakers," Remington says. "Though Romeo pimps are bad enough."

The victims

Remington says people might think victims of sex trafficking are trouble-makers. Misfits. Kids living in poverty. Kids from a big city.

The reality? "Jason Guidry had a 'stable' of six beautiful young ladies," she says, including "a straight-A student, a cheerleader, a softball star. Some of the best and brightest."

In her experiences in Sheboygan county, she's seen victims ranging in age from two to 72, and everything between. "Men, women. Boys, girls. All ages, all races, all sizes, all shapes. Males and females."

Victims come from a range of income levels; from rural or urban areas.

Out of this diversity of backgrounds, they had one thing in common. Vulnerability.

"All of us as human beings are vulnerable at some point in life, right?" Remington asks her audiences. "That's one thing I hope will challenge you to re-think who the victims are."

Sometimes Remington is asked, "What's wrong with the victims? Are they dumb? Do they want to be in this situation? They must, because there's the door, they can leave, or they can scream for help."

The trafficker uses certain methods to gain control of a victim; other methods to retain that control.

The parents

Some people ask, "Who are their parents? They must be terrible people."

"Again, I challenge you to re-think your preconceptions," Remington says. "Some of these parents are terrible; they're selling their kids off for their own next fix of dope. However, some of the parents are wonderful. Having worked many of these cases, I've met many survivors of human trafficking, and they are some of the best and brightest. And their families, some of them are wonderful people. I hope the community, hearing these cases, will think twice about judging the families."

When one 14-year-old girl went missing, "her mom was out there on the streets, looking for her daughter, and was on the verge of getting fired because she'd missed so much work. We eventually recovered the girl in Milwaukee."

In another case, the father saw a sex ad for his missing daughter and pretended to be a customer. "I would not recommend that," Remington warns. "That was very daring, very dangerous. She was being held by a gorilla pimp. A bone-breaker. We have the escape on video, and it is chilling. Terrifying."

Part III
How Does it Happen?

Riddle: What's easy to get into, but hard to get out of?
Answer: A habit.

On a darker note, that is also true of "The Life," or "The Game"—two euphemistic terms for sex trafficking.

How do traffickers (or pimps) recruit their victims? How do they keep the victims enslaved? It turns out this waking nightmare can be very easy to walk into; and heart-breakingly, sometimes mind-breakingly difficult to walk away from.

Awareness of these techniques will hopefully prevent more victims from entering this lifestyle.

Easy to get into

It can begin with one simple action. Getting into a car. Going to a party. Sipping a drink containing "something extra."

Real-life scenario: Three girls are walking. A nice car pulls up. The driver is unknown to the girls. He gives the girls some cash, smiles, says "Get yourself some burgers," and drives off. The girls get their burgers. An hour later, the car comes back. "Hey, girls, get in the car," the driver says. None of the girls thinks that's a good idea. "Hey, come on," the driver says, "I'm the cool guy that got you those burgers. Get in." Not one girl wants to. They each know they shouldn't. But because they "owe" him for the burgers, they get into the car.

Real-life scenario: Two girls are walking. A nice car pulls up, driven by a young, beautiful, bi-racial woman. The driver makes friendly conversation and suggests the girls get in the car. Neither of the walking girls thinks that's a good idea. "Oh, I see," the driver says scornfully, "you're racist." Well, those two girls will show her they're not racist! They get into the car.

Real-life scenario: A lone girl is walking. A nice car pulls up. A man is driving. A pretty, teen-age girl leans out the passenger window and says, "Hey, you're too beautiful to look sad and lonely. Come on in for a ride. We'll go get something to eat and cheer you up." Astonished that the girl in the car knew she was feeling sad and lonely, the walking girl gets into the car.

What could happen, once someone steps into that car?

In the last scenario, the driver ordered the food, handed it to the teenager in the passenger seat, who in turn passed a burger and soda to their new friend in the back seat.

The food had been drugged.

When the girl in the back seat regains consciousness, she finds she's lost several days; she's been pumped full of drugs; she's addicted and will do anything for her next fix.

Anything.

Three tactics are used in the above scenarios to convince the victim to take that first unknowing step into sex trafficking.

Debt bondage, paradoxically, relies on the victim's sense of fair play. "He did something for me; now I have to do something for him."

An accusation of unearned guilt can catch a person off-guard, overriding one's better judgment.

A vulnerable person can be especially receptive to, and cooperate with, anyone extending an act of kindness. How did the teenager know the walking girl was sad and lonely? She and her pimp (the driver) had likely tried the same line with several other girls, who'd told them to buzz off (but who, unfortunately, failed to note the license plate and call the police). After several tries, they'd likely find someone who's sad and lonely.

Pimps driving a slick car often have an attractive, teen-age girl or boy in the passenger seat, offering anything to get someone into the car. Variations on this theme include, "Hey, you're beautiful! I love your hair. You want to go to the beach? Want a ride? Breakfast? Some weed? Booze? Whatever you want, we'll get it for you."

"Promise her Heaven, you can take her to Hell," is how Detective Remington puts it. Remington has worked on sex trafficking cases in Sheboygan county for over a decade.

Grooming

In Remington's talks to communities about sex trafficking, she tells how traffickers patiently comb social media for kids and adults who are vulnerable, or who tell the world they want something they can't have. In a process called "grooming," the trafficker builds online relationships built on deception, wearing a false face of trust and support.

"I want to go on a shopping trip to Mall of America, but my parents won't take me," one girl complained on social media. A trafficker and his "stable" of girls took her on a shopping trip of a lifetime, but then made it known that she owed them. (Debt bondage.)

"I want a tattoo so bad, but mom won't let me have one," a 13-year-old girl lamented online. "Hey, baby, we'll get you a tattoo," a Sheboygan pimp promised her. But it wasn't a colorful rose, or an elegant Asian character. It branded the 13-year-old as the pimp's property.

Traffickers spend months, even years, building online relationships of trust with people all too willing to share personal information about themselves, their families, and where they live. That time is well spent for the pimp, because success results in control over a human being, which the trafficker can sell for sex over and over again.

Jason Guidry, a Sheboygan trafficker behind bars for the next two decades, found six young ladies through social media who were down on their luck. One had lost her job; one, her apartment; one was fighting for custody of her child. Guidry swooped down and became a knight in shining armor to the six women. "Hey, I'll help you find a job. I'll give you shelter. I'll help with your child." He helped them when no one else would.

A master manipulator, he promised each of the six he would marry her.

Pimps also search for victims of past abuse. "I do appreciate the Me Too movement," Remington says. "But at the same time, we have to be careful about what we post online. If we post publicly that we've been previously sexually molested, that's going to attract the attention of pimps."

Hard to get out of: invisible chains

The slick, sweet-talking "Romeo" or "finesse" pimp can brainwash a victim into complete submission, convincing the victim that having sex with strangers ten to thirty times a day or night is something the victim owes the pimp. It can take months to undo such brainwashing, for victims fortunate enough to be rescued.

For victims not so willingly cooperative, other methods keep them enslaved.

If a person has no previous drug habit, that person will almost surely have one on falling prey to a trafficker. Threatening to withhold the drug to an addict is a powerful form of bondage.

The "CEO" type of pimp, promising a career in modeling or in music, has applicants fill out detailed applications, then tells the applicant, "Now you're going to have sex with these men." When the applicant refuses, the CEO pimp replies, "Yes you are. You filled out this form. If you don't do what we say, we'll hurt (or kill) your family, brother, sister, your pet."

The "bone-breaker" or "gorilla" pimp uses sheer brute force and gang rapes, and the threat of more of the same, to keep his or her stable of victims subdued.

Detective Remington offers this sobering fact: "Once you enter The Life, your life expectancy is seven years. So prevention is the key."

Part IV
What can one do?

"How can I help?"

The answer is sometimes quite simple. To illustrate, what would you do in this—

Real-life scenario: You're a motel manager. A very good-looking man pays for room 15. His one request that the room never be entered by motel staff makes you suspicious at first, but his gentlemanly manner reassures you. As weeks go by, you notice a lot of visitors enter room 15. You never enter the room, as requested, but while cleaning rooms on either side, you occasionally hear a woman screaming for help. You feel you should do something, and knock on room 15. The well-educated man answers, suavely stepping into the hall to offer a calm explanation which, the more he talks, the more plausible it sounds. You decide there's no cause for concern and take no action.

Or do you?

The key word here is "decide." The slick-talking man above was a trafficker of the "Romeo" or "finesse" variety, an expert at using manipulation to recruit his victims, keep them enslaved, and placate suspicious people who notice too much and get too curious.

After this trafficker's arrest, Remington learned the pimp had forcibly taken the young woman from Sheboygan to a Milwaukee motel room. During the seven months she was kept there, the trafficker brainwashed her, promising to marry her and warning, "You're going to jail if we're caught, because you're the one having sex with customers." The situation began under violent duress. It mutated into willing cooperation by the victim.

"It took seven or eight months to undo the brainwashing she was subjected to, while imprisoned in that motel room," Remington tells audiences at her talks on trafficking.

The motel manager's lack of action, however one chooses to judge it, gives one answer to the question, "What can one do?"

That answer: Choose to be aware, and don't allow anyone to override your judgment.

Recognizing the signs

What do you watch for? Remington draws attention to the Wisconsin Child Sex Trafficking and Exploitation Indicator and Response Guide, which she tells audiences has an 80 per cent accuracy rate. The Indicator is reproduced on pages 12-13, and can be found online at dcf.wisconsin.gov/files/aht/pdf/indicatorguide.pdf.

"This flowchart has really prevented a lot of kids from falling through the cracks," Remington says. Effective state-wide as of May, 2017, Sheboygan county led the way by adopting it four years earlier.

The chart has three risk levels: At Risk, High Risk, and Confirmed. It is recommended that local law enforcement, or Child Protective Services, be contacted if three or more items are present from the At Risk category; or if one or more items from the High Risk or Confirmed category are present.

One At Risk item is, "Child has possession of money, electronics, or other material items that are unexplained, unusual, or out of the ordinary for that child (e.g., nails, hair, clothing, shoes)." Remington says pimps often groom their victims by giving them something exciting, like a new cell phone, and then use the phone's GPS to monitor the child's location.

An Internet search on the phrase "evidence of sex trafficking" will bring lists of warning signs from many organizations throughout the world.

Programs that help

Remington tells her audiences of several programs that fight trafficking, or help its victims.

Sheboygan Safe Stay is a partnership program between city of Sheboygan places of lodging and Sheboygan county law enforcement. All city hotels and motels participate and cooperate, learning to be on the alert for suspicious, possibly criminal activity. Owners and employees are educated as to what to watch for. (Had events in the "real-life scenario" opening this section happened at a Sheboygan lodging, they would have surely been reported to law enforcement, because of this training.)

Ending the Game (endingthegame.com) is a nation-wide educational organization that holds classes locally (with Wisconsin contacts in Appleton, Brookfield, Green Bay, Milwaukee, Neillsville, and Sheboygan) and publishes research articles. Its website says it is a "'coercion resiliency' curriculum that reduces feelings of attachment to traffickers and/or a lifestyle characterized by commercial sexual exploitation, thereby reducing the rate of recidivism among sex trafficking survivors. Ending The Game is designed to educate and empower survivors of commercial sexual exploitation and trafficking by providing a structure and framework to uncover harmful psychological coercion (a.k.a. 'The Game') that victims may have been subjected to during or before their exploitation experience."

The Rose Home established in Green Bay by Eye Heart World is a rehab home for young women who have been rescued from trafficking.

Convergence Resource Center (convergenceresource.org), per its website, is a Milwaukee "faith-based, community service, non-profit organization that provides ancillary support for men and women rebuilding their lives after trauma with an emphasis on justice involv[ing] women and female survivors of human trafficking." Co-founder and co-CEO Dr. Debbie Lassiter comes to Sheboygan regularly to provide services for trafficking survivors and high-risk girls. Dr. Lassiter is one of Wisconsin's few trainers for Ending the Game facilitators, one of several programs CRC offers.

SOLACE Support Line is one CRC-offered service: (414) 797-3047.

Restoration Bags are backpacks for trafficking survivors, prepared by various organizations nation-wide. Local organizations active in this project include Love INC of Sheboygan county (loveincsheboygancounty.org) and Freedom Cry (freedomcryinc.org). Bags include new clothing, hygiene and comfort items. Remington says some bags include a teddy bear or other stuffed animal. At first, she wondered why, but she has sometimes seen these prized stuffed animals in the protective possession of recovering victims she follows up with.

Prevention

"The majority of recruiting happens via social media," Remington says, and urges people to be cautious when online.

While online, she says, we have to be careful about what we post. Pimps are looking for people who are victims of past abuse. If we are posting that we've been previously sexually molested, that's the number one thing they're looking for—prior trauma or abuse."

When in groups, have a plan that avoids leaving someone behind, alone or with strangers. If the group is confronted with a suspicious situation, such as getting into a stranger's car, or going to a hotel room for a party, or answering questions with personal information, be assertive and (again) don't surrender your own judgment—show that you value your own life and safety, and that of your friends, by saying, "This is not a good idea." *And say it with conviction.*

Above all, if you are an adult with a child in your life, do what you can to ensure that child is comfortable talking to you about his or her concerns.

Big Brothers Big Sisters of Sheboygan County (bbbssc.org) is currently working with Remington to develop methods to mentor children and provide much-needed positive role models.

"I want to make sure that every kid in Sheboygan county has a trusted adult," Remington says, because without that, traffickers are all too willing to fill that void.

TEST YOUR SKILLS AT ALLEGORY

This pulp cover is part of a presentation I give on pulps. Most recently, I gave this talk in Plymouth (thanks, ladies, you were a great audience). This cover generated a lot of interest when I asked, "What do you think this represents?"

The cover date is January, 1919. What historical event happened shortly before that?

A few thoughts below.

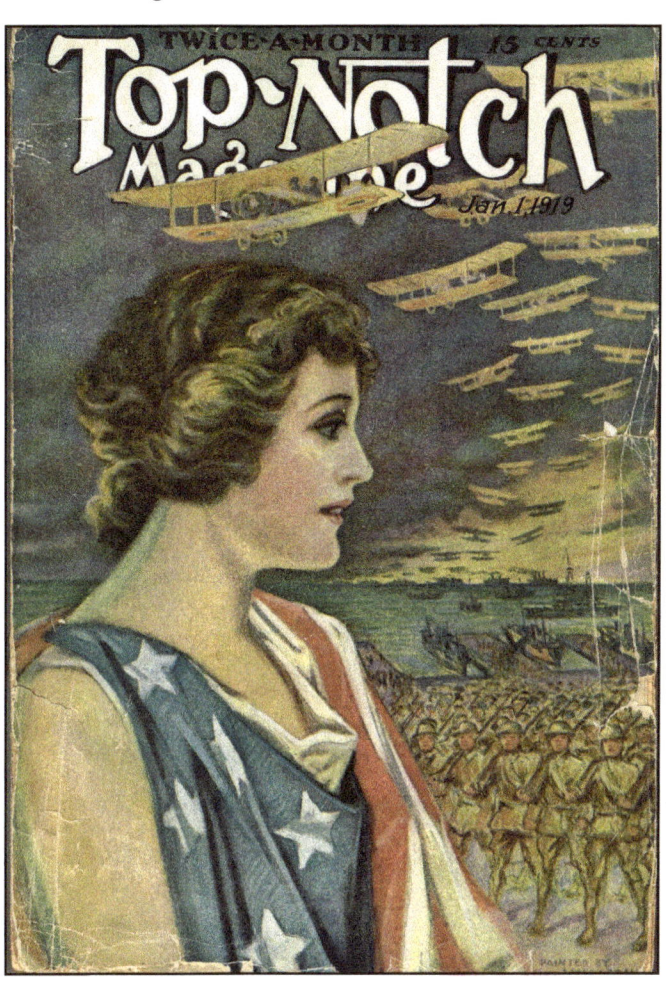

The woman is Columbia. She and Uncle Sam were symbols of America. Interestingly, Wikipedia says, "While the figure of Uncle Sam represents specifically the government, Columbia represents the United States as a nation."

An Armistice was signed on November 11, 1918, in Europe. That would be about the time this pulp was being produced.

Characters in stories of the 1920s or 30s sometimes mention fighting in The Great War, meaning the 1914-18 war. Few people would have thought of adding a "I (one)" at the end of "World War," because it was also referred to as "The War to End All Wars." Optimists thought this particular war was so horrifying, so devastating, that civilization had learned its lesson, and would never fight another. Well, by the late 1930s, the unsettling truth became more and more evident.

The cover shows Columbia glad to see her boys coming home from across the ocean (or "Over There," as George M. Cohan put it).

Showing biplanes flying in from the ocean was definitely more symbolic than realistic.

While they are not visible on this cover (an artist doesn't always have room for everything), many American women served in Europe, providing medical aid or assisting the war effort in other capacities.

165

July
2019

Cover photo: Conservatory at the Bellagio, Las Vegas
Best Views in Wisconsin, by Mariah Haberman: Granite Peak at Rib Mountain State Park (Wausau)
Great Movies This Month
Mr. Happy Cook, by Richard J. Baumann: National Hot Dog Month
Ask a Science Teacher by Larry Scheckel: Can chocolate kill a dog?
Free Markets Increase Trust Among People, by Marian L. Tupy, HumanProgress.org
From Names to Faces
Jazz & Blues Crawl
It's Now Legal to Grow Your Own Food in Florida, by Andrew Wimer, IJ.org
Glory Returns to Big Screen for its 30th Anniversary
PulpArtists by David Saunders: Herbert Morton Stoops
SCHRC book reviewed: *Riding on the Electrics: The Story of the Milwaukee Northern Sheboygan's Interurban Link to the Rest of the World*

Watching Over Them, done by Herbert Morton Stoops for calendar publisher Brown & Bigelow Company. – HA.com

Who Goes There, World Peaceways advertisement, 1939. The original painting measures 34 x 36 inches, and sold for $13,750 at auction. – HA.com

Riding on the Electrics

Book review by Beth Dippel
for The Plymouth Review Current

Interurban/train guru Peter J. Fetterer has authored another volume on a once-popular mode of transportation. Many of us have heard stories from our parents and grandparents about their trips aboard the interurbans, yet we tend to know relatively little about the industry. Fetterer does a great job in *Riding on the Electrics,* providing a fun and accurate introduction to the business.

The Milwaukee Northern interurban line was once Sheboygan's link to the rest of the world. Early in the 20th century, it offered travel adventures and trade advantages the city and its neighbors had never known.

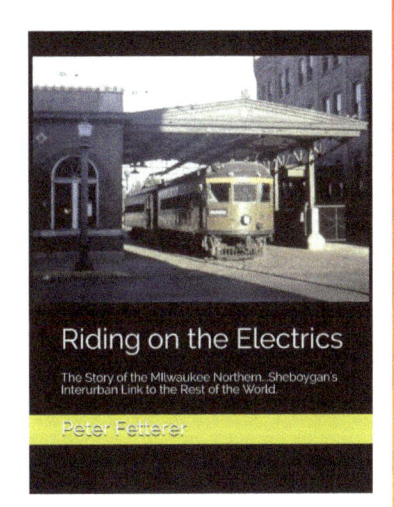

It provided frequent, timely service that was relatively inexpensive and comfortable. It opened up new vistas for travelers and new markets for area manufacturers, merchants and farmers. And it put Sheboygan on the map as a modern, progressive, up-with-the-times city.

There was a time when you could board an interurban car early on a Sunday morning in Sheboygan, transfer to another car in Milwaukee, enjoy a Cubs or White Socks game in Chicago, and be home again by sundown. Or, if you were really adventurous, you could ride connecting interurban lines to Indianapolis, Detroit, or almost all the way to New York City.

The Milwaukee Northern was incorporated in 1905. One of its founders was from Sheboygan, another from Elkhart Lake. The first of the big Northern cars arrived in Sheboygan on September 21, 1908.

Over the years, the Northern offered services that ranged from speedy limited-stop cars to comfortable parlor chair cars to local cars that stopped at any crossing where passengers were waiting or farmers had milk they wanted to ship to Milwaukee.

But it didn't last … it couldn't last. The same people who rode the interurban lines gradually fell in love with the freedoms that automobiles offered. The same businesses that shipped products, produce, milk and beer on the interurban found trucks more convenient. Cities, states and the federal government built thousands of miles of new streets and highway for cars, buses and trucks. Interurban companies simply could not compete with them.

Ridership declined. Schedules were reduced. Freight shipments decreased. Revenues fell. Maintenance was deferred. Stations closed. And finally, on Sunday night, Sept. 22, 1940, thirty-two years and one day after the first Milwaukee Northern car arrived in Sheboygan, the last of the big interurbans pulled out of its depot, turned south on 8th St. and disappeared forever into the night.

Filled with maps, stories, news clippings and photos, Fetterer's book gives us a clear, engaging picture of the interurban running between Milwaukee and Sheboygan. It's a story everyone can enjoy. *Riding on the Electrics* is a 95 page volume which sells for $15.00. It can be purchased at the Sheboygan County Historical Research Center, 518 Water Street, Sheboygan Falls, WI or online at schrc.org/buy.

Lake Shore Limited parlor car joined the MN fleet serving Sheboygan in 1923. Built by the Niles Car Co. as #10 in 1907, it became TM #98 after a rebuild in 1928. It was scrapped in 1935. — Don Ross collection. Permission for SCHRC to use in promotional items.

Construction of the new MN depot by the Jacob Van Doeselaar Co. of Sheboygan began in August 1924. Later that year the WP&L, while upgrading its tracks on 8th St., added sidings that served the station. — Sheboygan Press Collection/SCHRC

An Art Deco female prop figure designed by Gilbert Adrian for the film Ninotchka, circa 1939. For a photo of where it appeared in this great Greta Garbo film, see the next page. — HA.com

Ask a Science Teacher
By Larry Scheckel

Q: Can chocolate kill a dog?

A: Will your pooch flop over dead if it eats the ears off the chocolate Easter bunny?

It depends.

It depends on what kind of chocolate Rover scarfed down, how big Rover is, how much is eaten, and Rover's breed. Chocolate contains theobromine.

You and I can process or metabolize theobromine quite easily, but for dogs that process is much slower. Large amounts of chocolate for a smaller dog, eaten rapidly, can literally mean "dog gone." Toxic levels of theobromine can build up in the dog.

Small amounts of chocolate will give a dog an upset stomach, perhaps with vomiting and diarrhea. The first sign of theobromine poisoning from chocolate is hyper activity such as panting, whining, and muscle twitching. A big dog can tolerate some chocolate without any ill effects. Large amounts of chocolate for any dog can bring on irregular heartbeat, internal bleeding, muscle tremors, and seizures, and a heart attack. It's the rapid heart rate that can deliver the fatal blow.

Not all chocolates are created equal. Cocoa, cooking chocolate, and dark chocolate contain the highest levels of theobromine. Milk chocolate and white chocolate have lower levels. An ounce of dark chocolate may be enough to poison a 44-pound dog.

The usual treatment for theobromine poisoning is to induce vomiting as soon as possible. If you take Spot to the veterinarian, that's what they will do.

If you can get a few teaspoons of hydrogen peroxide down the affected pooch, that will induce vomiting. Hydrogen peroxide is cheap and available in any department store or drug store.

Getting a dog to eat a small amount of activated charcoal can be helpful. Theobromine binds to charcoal and keeps it from entering the blood stream. Activated charcoal is used in bar soap and in filters for fish aquariums. Keep Fido hydrated by providing plenty of water.

Theobromine is an alkaloid, and is in the same family as caffeine that stimulates the central nervous system and cardiovascular system. It causes elevated levels of blood pressure.

A vet at the clinic can give a dog that is in really bad shape, shots of anti-convulsants, if the dog is having seizures.

All these problems can be avoided if people make sure that their dog does not have access to chocolate, keeping it in a high cupboard so the dog can't jump up and grab it. Giving chocolate to a little kid? Give him/her just a wee bit at a time so a begging or grabbing dog or generous tyke limits the amount any dog can ingest.

A few chocolate sayings: Chocolate makes everyone smile, even lawyers. In the beginning, the Lord created chocolate, and he saw that it was good. Then he separated the light from the dark, and it was better.

David Saunders'
pulpartists.com

Herbert Morton Stoops: Painter of Power

(1887-1948)

Herbert Morton Stoops was born May 28, 1887 on a ranch in Logan City, Utah. His father was Philip Dexter Stoops, born 1850 in Pennsylvania. His mother was Eliza Janet Stoops, born 1858 in Ohio. His parents married in 1886. He was the firstborn of their five children. His father worked as a ranch hand, but eventually became an ordained Presbyterian Minister.

In 1910 the family lived at 126 East 2nd South Street in Logan City, which is seventy miles from Yellowstone Park.

After finishing high school he was sent to Utah State College, where he took art classes and graduated in 1905 at the age of 18. Soon after that his father died.

He first drew illustrations for a local newspaper, but soon moved to 428 Broderick Street in San Francisco, where he worked as a staff artist for *The San Francisco Chronicle* in 1910. He later worked for the *San Francisco Examiner*.

In 1914 he moved to Chicago to study at the Art Institute, while working as a staff artist for *The Chicago Tribune*.

In 1915 he joined Officer's Training at Fort Sheridan in Illinois. During the Great War, he served in France as a first lieutenant, 6th Field Artillery, First Army Division. He was a physically powerful man, who was prone to giving his friends heartfelt bear hugs. After the war he moved to New York City and married Elise Borough.

During the 1920s he illustrated interior stories for *Colliers, Liberty, Cosmopolitan, McCall's,* and *Ladies Home Journal.* He painted his first magazine covers for *The American Legion Magazine.*

In 1935, Stoops began to paint covers for *Blue Book,* which was one of the more literary pulp magazines.

He spent his summers painting in a rustic stone house that he built on Mason's Island, CT.

Some of his interior illustrations for *Blue Book* are signed with an assumed name that reflects his WWI experiences in France, "Jeremy Cannon."

His loose and vigorous Impressionist style of painting had a marked influence on many younger pulp artists, such as Charles DeFeo, A. L. Ross and H. W. Scott.

In January 1947 he began a fascinating project with *Blue Book* to paint a memorial cover for each of the forty-eight United States. Unfortunately, he died before he could complete the series.

After a long period of failing health and several weeks of illness, Herbert Morton Stoops died in his art studio residence on 42 Barrow Street in New York City's Greenwich Village on May 19, 1948, only a few days before his sixty-first birthday.

© David Saunders 2009

Surprise! Didn't think it was this tall, *did* you? Statue sold for $7,500 at auction. — HA.com

August 2019

Cover photo: Milwaukee Art Museum

How to Read this Issue...

Great Movies This Month

Mr. Happy Cook, by Richard J. Baumann: Toe-Mah-Toe Toe-May-Toe

SCHRC book reviewed: *Plymouth, Wisconsin*

Ask a Science Teacher by Larry Scheckel: What Are Some Unscientific Claims About Race?

Across Wisconsin, Recent Rises in Hate, Bias Incidents Spark Concern, by Mukhtar Ibrahim, Wisconsin Center for Investigative Journalism

Bonfires of Bigotry: The Sources of Our Present Anger, by Jeff Minick, IntellectualTakeout.org

Big Rise in Interracial Marriage Since "I Have a Dream" Speech, by David M. Simon, HumanProgress.org

Things Are Looking up Across the Board: US Race Relations Are Getting Better, by Marian L. Tupy, HumanProgress.org

So What's the Answer?

Is it Racism If...?

PulpArtists by David Saunders: James Reynolds

This 1914 image was James Reynolds' first published pulp cover.

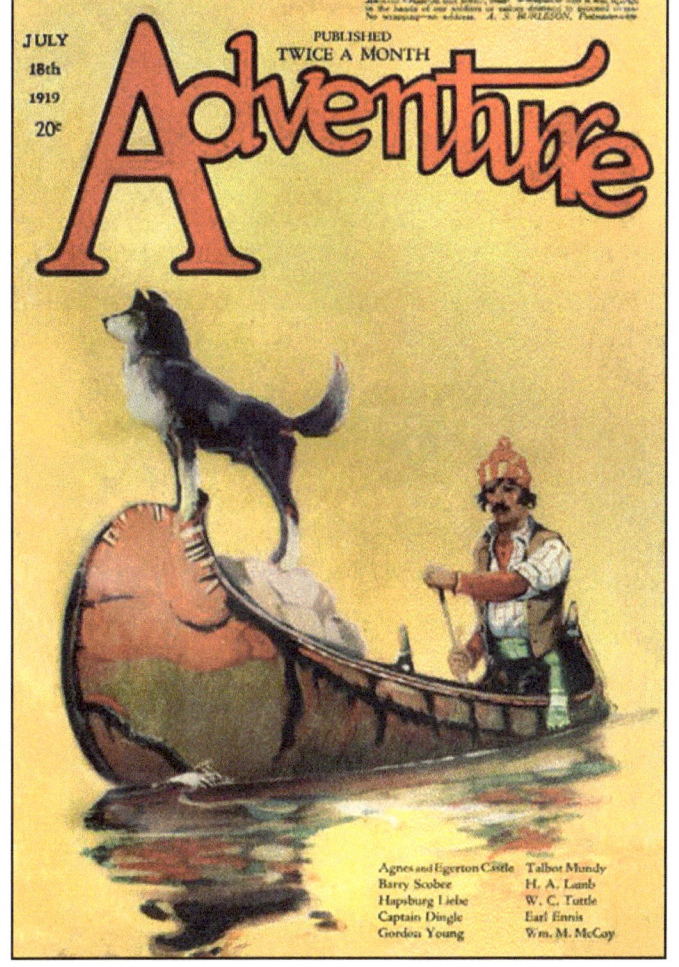

People sometimes ask Your Editor, "Why are pulps so interesting?" Instead of a lengthy explanation, a cover like this (by James Reynolds) will sometimes answer that question quite adequately.

How to read this issue...

Aside from the usual delightful features, we have a theme in this month's PRC. If you so choose, this article will act as your guide for this theme.

Some months ago, I read an article by Dee J. Hall, of the Wisconsin Center for Investigative Journalism. Listing topics the WCIJ covered, Hall wrote WCIJ had "cover[ed] the rise of hate and bias in Wisconsin..."

That statement suggests hate and bias have increased in Wisconsin. Right away, I asked myself, "How did they measure that? What is that conclusion based on?" So I looked up the article referred to.

If you haven't yet read **"Across Wisconsin, recent rises in hate, bias incidents spark concern,"** written by Mukhtar Ibrahim (starting on page 8), please do so now.

Well. What do you think? Does the article support the claim, "Hate and bias have increased in Wisconsin"?

But wait. Here's someone coming to a different conclusion. If you haven't already read **"Bonfires of bigotry: the sources of our present anger,"** written by Jeff Minick (page 9), please do so now.

So, the two articles seem to contradict each other. The WCIJ article gives examples of "hate and bias," and concludes, per its title, there are "recent rises in hate, bias." In Minick's article, the author does not personally encounter examples of "racial inequality, sexual bias, bigotry, and intolerance," and thus concludes the prevalence of such attitudes has been exaggerated.

But I consider both of these articles to be based on a single logical fallacy, and therefore, both of their conclusions are questionable at best.

(And some of you out there might have thought I only run articles I fully agree with. Not so!)

I have no reason in the world to deny that each anecdote of "hate and bias" in Ibrahim's WCIJ article actually happened. I view the perpetrators of those or similar incidents with contempt.

Nor, on the other hand, could I reasonably doubt that Minick, in his personal experience, has *not* encountered hate and bias on a large scale.

Both articles, however, are examples of the Anecdotal Fallacy. Several specific events (or non-events) are documented, and that is given as evidence that they are happening in general; or on a wide scale; or "have increased."

But this is not valid. Ibrahim, in his WCIJ article, comes close to admitting so, when writing under the heading, "No reliable data," "There are no reliable data on the number or rate of hate crimes in the United States, according to the investigative news nonprofit ProPublica."

And yet... WCIJ concludes (and claims it has documented) "the rise of hate and bias in Wisconsin."

OK, it is now time to ask: What kind of data *would* make a plausible case, indicating whether racism is increasing or decreasing over a given time? Or how prevalent racism is?

(I'm now leaving the terms "hate and bias" behind as being too imprecise.)

The next article to read would be **"Big Rise in Interracial Marriage Since 'I Have a Dream' Speech,"** by David M. Simon (page 12).

Instead of supporting his view by quoting experts (the Argument from Authority fallacy) or by using the Anecdotal Fallacy, Simon uses cold, hard facts to support his conclusion that "race relations in the United States have made almost unfathomable progress" in the past 50 years. True—he's using only one aspect of society to support his claim. But I agree with him that it's a very important aspect.

Does he support his case with reliable evidence?

Are there additional ways to measure the rise or fall of racism, over time?

Please now read the article, **"Things are looking up across the board: US race relations are getting better,"** by Marian L. Tupy (starting on page 12).

Again, does the author support his case with reliable evidence?

To answer the question, "How prevalent is racism in our country?", the articles by Simon and Tupy are only beginnings. Much more documentation and study are needed. But they are starting points.

Then, Your Editor's thoughts can be found on page 14.

You'll also want to be sure to read Larry Scheckel's column, "Ask a Science Teacher," which makes a great addition to this issue's theme.

Dealing with the theme of racism reminds me of growing up on the farm when, just as you start cleaning out the gutters, the barn cleaner chain breaks. No way to avoid it: You have to reach in and get your hands dirty. But it's the only way you're going to fix things, so you can ultimately get rid of what's in the gutter.

So what's the answer?

OK, so you agree racism is a bad thing, and want to know what you can do about it.

(I make that statement with confidence. The Plymouth Review Current does not appeal to irrational people. Readers of The PRC are of above average intelligence, and of high moral integrity. If, by some insane chance, you *are* a person who believes racism is valid, good, or workable—tear up this paper. Never pick up another. *Be off with you!*)

One of the finest single essays I've ever read on racism was written in 1963 by Ayn Rand. The essay, "Racism," can be found online.

Her first three paragraphs:

"Racism is the lowest, most crudely primitive form of collectivism. It is the notion of ascribing moral, social or political significance to a man's genetic lineage — the notion that a man's intellectual and characterological traits are produced and transmitted by his internal body chemistry. Which means, in practice, that a man is to be judged, not by his own character and actions, but by the characters and actions of a collective of ancestors.

"Racism claims that the content of a man's mind (not his cognitive apparatus, but its *content*) is inherited; that a man's convictions, values and character are determined before he is born, by physical factors beyond his control. This is the caveman's version of the doctrine of innate ideas — or of inherited knowledge — which has been thoroughly refuted by philosophy and science. Racism is a doctrine of, by and for brutes. It is a barnyard or stock-farm version of collectivism, appropriate to a mentality that differentiates between various breeds of animals, but not between animals and men.

"Like every form of determinism, racism invalidates the specific attribute which distinguishes man from all other living species: his rational faculty. Racism negates two aspects of man's life: reason and choice, or mind and morality, replacing them with chemical predestination."

Also from this article by Rand:

"Historically, racism has always risen or fallen with the rise or fall of collectivism. Collectivism holds that the individual has no rights, that his life and work belong to the group (to "society," to the tribe, the state, the nation) and that the group may sacrifice him at its own whim to its own interests. The only way to implement a doctrine of that kind is by means of brute force — and statism has always been the political corollary of collectivism."

And:

"Individualism regards man — every man — as an independent, sovereign entity who possesses an inalienable right to his own life, a right derived from his nature as a rational being. Individualism holds that a civilized society, or any form of association, cooperation or peaceful coexistence among men, can be achieved only on the basis of the recognition of individual rights — and that a group, as such, has no rights other than the individual rights of its members."

There's an important point implied by the above paragraphs.

Hate is *not* a necessary result of racism. A person can honestly love all races, and still be racist.

Per Rand's essay: "Racism claims that the content of a man's mind (not his cognitive apparatus, but its *content*) is inherited; that a man's convictions, values and character are determined before he is born, by physical factors beyond his control."

Whenever you hear of "Race X values," that's exactly what Rand was talking about—"the doctrine of innate ideas." You can have a completely benevolent view of all races, and still believe this. But it would still be a false belief.

Another thing. Some people truly believe the following:

1. A person of Race X being racist toward a person of Race Y is racism.
2. However, a person of Race Y being racist toward a person of Race X is not racism.

Racism is racism. In either direction. A thing is what it is. A is A.

Building on the above view of racism, collectivism, and individualism, but adding detailed economics dynamics, economist George Reisman wrote a long essay, "Capitalism: The Cure for Racism." This is available as a 99-cent ebook from Amazon. A video of Reisman giving this entire speech (it's long!) is available free on C-Span's website.

Another essay by Reisman is "Education and the Racist Road to Barbarism." This piece is easily found online, free.

Maybe this talk about collectivism and individualism is a little too abstract. Let's use some theoretical examples to see how each of those relates to our topic.

For a collectivist:

* You meet a person for the first time.
* Looking at the person, talking with him, you discover several groups he is part of. Those include race, gender, country of origin, state of origin, age, political views, philosophical orientation, career, and others.
* In evaluating a person's character, you've built up a hierarchy of which group(s) you believe are important, and which are not. An unimportant group might be age. If the person is 30 years old, you could realize that will tell you nothing about his political views or career.
* Race, on the other hand, is very important to you. You believe that race is a strong factor in determining any individual's personality. You identify the person you meet as belonging to Race X.
* You review in your mind the characteristics you know about Race X.
* As you get to know this person better, things could develop differently. For example:

a) Every time this person shows what you believe is a "Race X quality," a bell rings in your mind and the word "CONFIRMED" lights up. Whenever this person contradicts a "Race X quality," you consider it insignificant, shove it to one side in your mind, and forget it. By the time you know this person better, you think, "Yes, this person displays Race X qualities."

b) Any time this person contradicts a "Race X quality," you grow more irritated. Enraged, you conclude, "He's a traitor to his race!"

For an individualist:

* You meet a person for the first time. You remind yourself:
* You've never met her before. You know nothing about her.
* This person is unique. She's the only one of her there is. She's a microcosm of her own.
* Her race, age, gender, nationality—things she had no choice in—do not define her.
* What does define her? Her ideas, her thoughts, her choices.

All this is fine, for one's own development. But how does one deal with *others* who are racist?

You can first (if you choose) try showing how any irrational ideas (including racism) are detrimental to human life, including the one holding those ideas. (That's the whole point of the articles by Rand and Reisman, mentioned here.)

If that doesn't work? Make it known (as I did in the second paragraph of this article) that, in every way possible, you won't deal with them, support them, or give them any kind of legitimacy.

David Saunders'
pulpartists.com

JAMES REYNOLDS: ARTISTIC ADVENTURE!

(1884-1956)

James Walter Reynolds, a pulp magazine illustrator, is not to be confused with Harold James Reynolds (1891-1957), a travel-book illustrator and set designer, or James Elliott Reynolds (1926-2010), a fine art painter of the Old West.

James Walter Reynolds was born August 18, 1884 in Chicago. His father, Frank Reynolds, was born in 1853 in New York of Irish ancestry. His mother, Fannie Moran, was born in 1853 in Illinois of Irish ancestry. His parents married in 1884 and had three children, James (b. 1884), Frank (b. 1886), and Adelaide (b. 1889). The family lived at 552 North Clark Street in Chicago. The father was a finisher at a brass factory.

The children all attended public schools in Chicago, and after each child completed the eighth grade, they left schooling and entered the work force.

In June of 1897, at the age of thirteen, James Reynolds began to work as a paper puller in a Chicago book bindery. Two years later, his younger brother, Frank Reynolds, began to work at a printing shop, while their younger sister became a clerical secretary when she turned thirteen.

By 1906, at age twenty-two, James Reynolds had become interested in an art career, and began to take evening classes at one of Chicago's excellent art schools, while he continued to work at the book bindery.

By 1913, at the age of twenty-nine, he sold his first pulp cover painting to the Ridgway Company of New York City, which published his painting on the January 1914 issue of Adventure Magazine.

In 1915 the artist left Chicago and moved to New York City, where he opened an art studio in the Arcade Building at 1947 Broadway, and sixty-sixth street. His monthly rent was $22.50. He proceeded to show his portfolio to the art editors at various NYC publishing houses, and soon sold a cover to The Argosy.

In 1918 during the Great War, James Reynolds, age thirty-four, was drafted for military service. He was recorded at the time to have been five-foot-three, 114 pounds, with a ruddy complexion, brown eyes, red hair, and a "U" shaped scar on the top of his head. His brother, Frank Reynolds was also drafted and served overseas.

The war ended with the declaration of armistice on November 11, 1918, after which both brothers were discharged from the Army. Frank Reynolds returned to Chicago, where he started the Reynolds & Eby Printing Company at 508

South Dearborn Street, while James Reynolds resumed his career as a magazine illustrator in NYC.

Over the next fifteen years James Reynolds painted covers for pulp magazines, such as *The Frontier, Lariat Stories, Short Stories, Star Magazine, The Thrill Book, West, Western Story,* and *Wild West Weekly.*

He also drew pen-and-ink interior story illustrations for *Physical Culture, Everybody's Magazine,* and *Boy's Life.*

James Reynolds also illustrated several novels, such as "Apache Gold" by White Birch from H. K. Fly in 1919, "Laramie Holds The Range" by Frank Spearman from Scribner's in 1921, and "The Bar 20 Rides Again" by Clarence Mulford from the A. L. Burt Publishing Company in 1925.

Starting in 1925 James Reynolds was listed for three years as an illustrator of fiction stories in Lee & Kirby's annual nationwide directory of artists.

On April 17, 1927 the artist's sister, Adelaide Reynolds, died at the age of thirty-eight in Wheatland, Montana.

By 1930 James Reynolds was still renting his same space in the Arcade Building, a massive tenement of office studios, whose long list of tenants included George Gross, Richard Lillis, and Rafael DeSoto.

In 1933 at the depth of the Great Depression, James Reynolds left the field of magazine illustration and moved back to Chicago, where he lived with his elderly parents at 6640 North Maplewood Avenue, and worked as a staff artist at his brother's printing shop.

On September 31, 1938 the artist's father, Frank Reynolds, died at the age of eighty-five.

On September 10, 1940 the artist's mother, Fannie Moran Reynolds, died at the age of eighty-seven.

After the deaths of his parents, James Reynolds was age fifty-five, unmarried, with no children, and ready to turn over a new leaf, so he left Chicago and moved to Madison, Nebraska, where he worked as an artist for Earl John Moyer (1893-1962), a State Court Judge, the president of the Nebraska State Bar Association, director of the Madison Savings & Loan Company, prominent Republican politician, and board member of the State Racing Commission.

On April 26, 1956 the artist's brother, Frank Reynolds died at the age of sixty-nine in Chicago. He was survived by his wife, Addah May Seely Reynolds (1897-1995), three children, Mary (b.1934), Shirley (b.1938), and James (b.1932), and six grandchildren.

James Reynolds died at the age of seventy-two in Madison, Nebraska, on October 8, 1956.

© David Saunders 2019

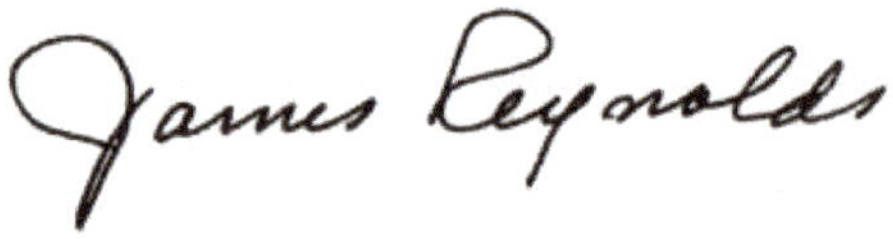

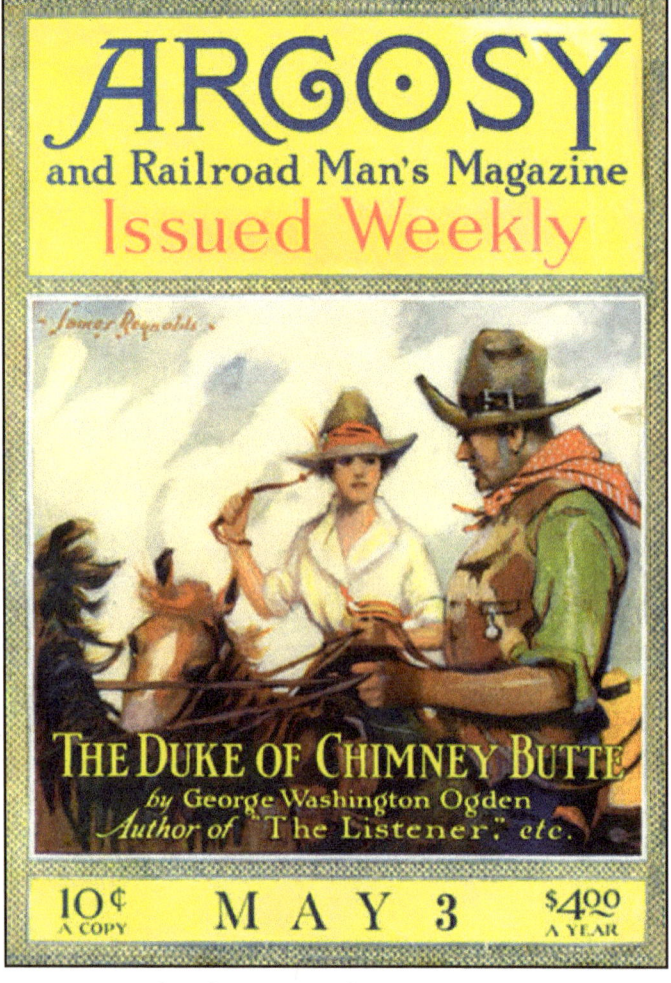

These were published so long ago, that there were no railroad women at that time.

The Plymouth Review Current

TAKING YOU PLACES WORTH SEEING
Volume 8 • Issue 10 • September 2019

FREE!

Jon Wos paints Cheyenne • Norman Rockwell paints Plymouth
Restaurant of the Month • Electricity • Smiles

September
2019

Cover photo: Jon Wos at TOS-Con, Park City, Utah
Great Movies This Month
SCHRC book reviewed: *The Ultimate Sacrifice: Sheboygan County's World War II Casualties*
Restaurant of the Month, by Amanda Weber: Las Brisas, Sheboygan
Ask a Science Teacher by Larry Scheckel: Why Is Electricity So Deadly?
'The truth!'
The Anti-Capitalist Ideology of Slavery, by Phillip W. Magness, American Institute for Economic Research
Capitalism: Who Are the Real Beneficiaries? by Mark Perry, American Enterprise Institute
PulpArtists by David Saunders: Norman Rockwell

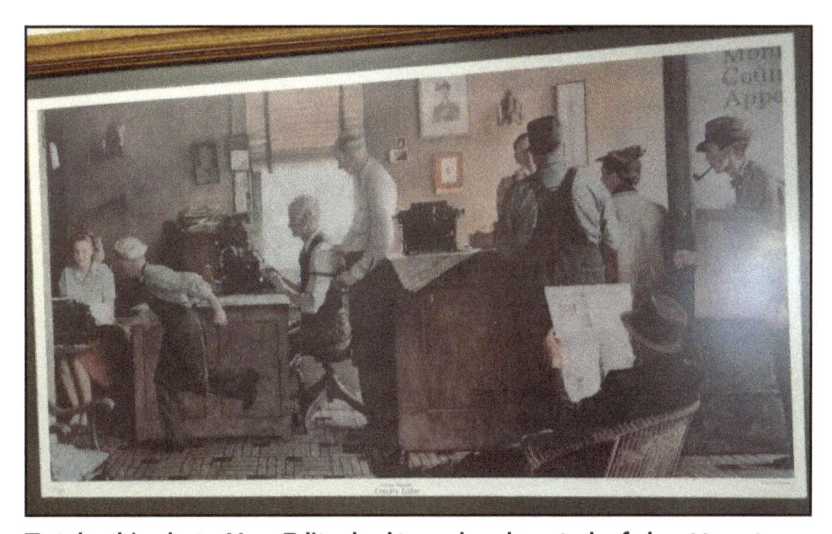

To take this photo, Your Editor had to make a long trek of about ten steps, from his work station to where this Norman Rockwell print is prominently displayed in The Review's composition room. "Country Editor" is from 1946. Rockwell painted himself (far right) entering the frantic environment of a small-town newspaper office.

Jon Wos appeared at TOS-Con this past August, sponsored by Quent Cordair Fine Art. Set up outside the Cordair "pop-up" gallery, he drew his friend Ryan Murphy in pastel (top photos) and Cheyenne Biederman (cover photo). Jon was not finished with the portrait of Cheyenne by the end of the conference, so he took it home to complete it. The finished piece (left) was received from Jon just days before The PRC went to press. — Pastel drawings courtesy of Jon Wos.

Bryan Larsen (right) contemplates the December 2018 issue of The PRC, which carried his work on its cover. Your Editor was present when Wos and Larsen met in-person for the first time, and heard each express admiration for the other's work, a moment destined for 21st-Century art history.

(From Jon's website, **www.wosart.com**)

Jon Wos was born in Lena, Wisconsin in 1981. He was diagnosed at birth with Osteogenesis Imperfecta, a congenital condition that is manifested by weak bones, leaving people who have it very susceptible to fractures. Though this condition limited his physical ability, it heightened his sensitivity to the world around him, and, out of his love of creation, Jon began drawing as a very young child. His artistic expression blossomed as he grew older, and by the age of 11, he was painting with oils. At 16, he started working with glass.

When Jon was a sophomore in college, he won a $10,000 grand prize in a national competition for disabled artists. In 2005, Jon graduated from the University of Wisconsin-Oshkosh, receiving a Bachelor of Fine Arts with an emphasis in drawing, painting, and sculpture.

Mr. Wos has exhibited his various pieces of artwork throughout North America, including the Kennedy Center for the Performing Arts in Washington D.C., the Chicago Cultural Center, and the Joseph D. Carrier Gallery in Toronto, Ontario, Canada. In addition, Mr. Wos's work is held in such public collections as the University of Wisconsin-Oshkosh and Ripon College in Wisconsin, and MacMurray College in Illinois.

Quent Cordair Fine Art
offers original art and quality prints
by Jon Wos
and many other fine artists
www.cordair.com

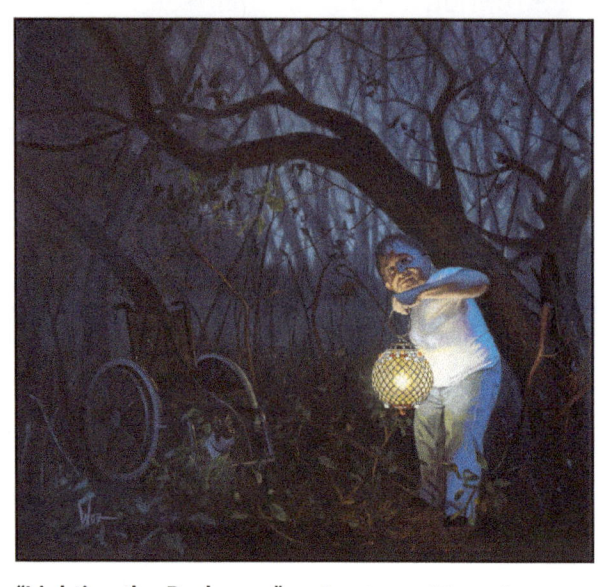

"Lighting the Darkness". — Courtesy of the artist

David Saunders' pulpartists.com

NORMAN ROCKWELL: PART OF AMERICAN HISTORY

1894 - 1978

Norman Perceval Rockwell was born on February 3, 1894 in New York City. His father was Jarvis Warren Rockwell and his mother was Nancy Mary Hill. He and his older brother, Jarvis, were their only two children. His father was a salesman. They lived in a four-family brownstone at 789 St. Nicholas Avenue in the Harlem district of Manhattan.

In 1903 the family moved to Mamaroneck, NY, in Westchester County, where they lived in various boarding houses. A high school art teacher inspired him to become an artist. He began to take Saturday art classes at The New York School of Art. During his Sophomore high school year he quit school and enrolled in the National Academy of Design. In 1910 he began to study at The Art Students League.

In 1911 his family moved to New Rochelle, where he opened a shared art studio and sold freelance illustrations to magazines, such as *Country Gentleman*, *Literary Digest*, and *Life*. In 1912 at age eighteen he was hired to work as the art director of *Boy's Life*.

From 1915 to 1916 he sold pulp magazine covers to Street & Smith's *The Popular Magazine*.

In 1916 at age twenty-two he sold his first cover to *The Saturday Evening Post*. This was the start of a long relationship with the magazine, which would soon earn him around $40,000 annually. He married Irene O'Connor in 1916.

From 1917 to 1918 he served in the U.S. Navy.

In 1923 he went to Paris to study at the Academie Colarossi, where he seriously studied the avant-garde art of Picasso and Matisse. He then returned to New York to resume his career, but continued to follow developments in modern art. He revisited Paris in 1927, and he moved into the Hotel Des Artistes on Central Park West in 1929. After he suffered a nervous breakdown his marriage ended in divorce, and he returned to New Rochelle.

In 1930 he married Mary Barstow, and moved to Arlington, Vermont. They had three sons, Jarvis, Thomas, and Peter.

During WWII he painted a series of *Saturday Evening Post* covers, "The Four Freedoms," which toured the USA and helped to inspire the public to donate to a war bond drive that raised over $130,000,000.

In 1953 the Rockwell family moved to Stockbridge, Massachusetts, where his second wife died in 1959. In 1961 he married his third wife, Molly Punderson.

In 1963 after painting 321 covers for *The Saturday Evening Post* he was fired. This final collapse of the historic relationship between Rockwell and *The Post* was a milestone event that signalled the end of the classic era of American illustration art. It also signaled the triumph of a mass media that was unabashedly concerned with only the marketing agenda, and without any pretense of serving a secondary and higher purpose of celebrating our nation's finest artists.

He went on to produce many sensational freelance illustrations for *The Boy Scouts of America*, *Look* magazine, and *American Artist* magazine.

In 1977 he received the Presidential Medal of Freedom, our nation's highest civilian honor.

Norman Rockwell died in his Stockbridge home at age 84 on November 8, 1978. He was America's most beloved illustrator. According to the artist, "I paint life as I would like it to be."

© David Saunders 2009

[Editor's Note: Wikipedia says 323 covers; David Saunders says 321. Knowing David's rigor at scholarship, he's probably correct.]

Rockwell's first SEP cover. 1916. Prints of this and many other Rockwell images can be purchased at www.art.com

I *think* it was this pulp that I found while browsing at a pulp convention. Beat up, ragged, it was priced at $1. I set it aside to search for more. Another collector, spotting it, went into a passionate frenzy. He'd been looking for this issue for years. I hadn't bought it yet, but he begged me to let *him* buy it (he even offered me money to do so!). Shucks, I let the guy have it.

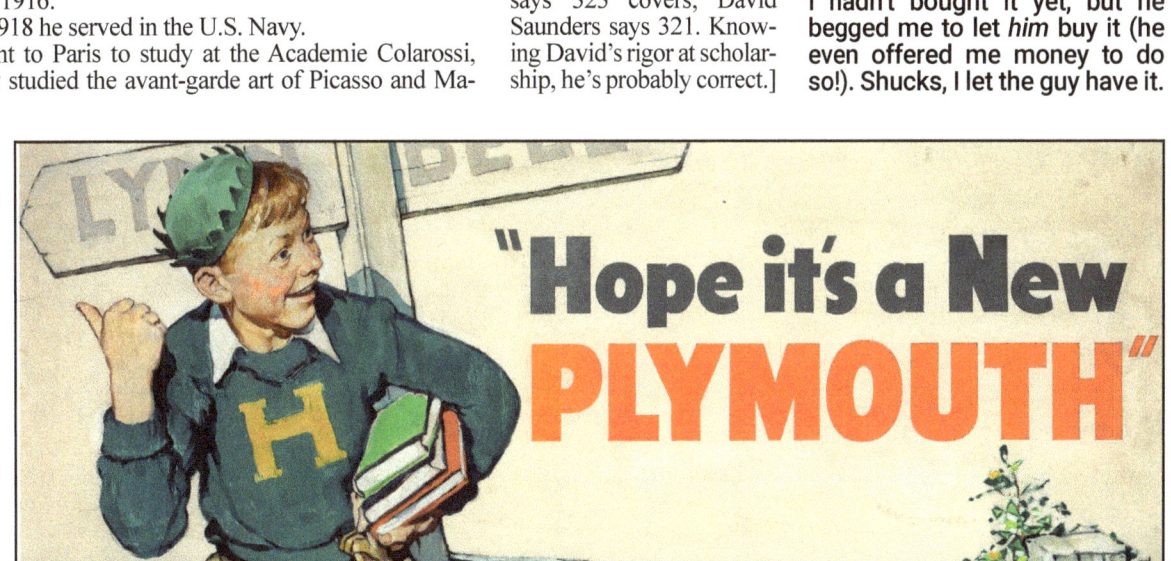

"Norman Rockwell paints Plymouth"? You might have thought that cover blurb was an out-of-season April Fool's joke. But no, here it is. Measuring about 13 x 28 inches, this finished artwork for an ad (perhaps a billboard) was sold by Heritage Auctions for $106,250. What year was this? Long enough ago that the kid felt safe hitchhiking. — HA.com

The Plymouth Review Current

TAKING YOU PLACES WORTH SEEING
Volume 8 • Issue 11 • October 2019

FREE!

The publication that *respects your intelligence!*

German Sausages • German Movies • German Artists
German Ancestry • German Actors • German Pie • German Physicists

October
2019

Cover photo: Albert Einstein as Sculpted by Robert Berks, Washington, DC

Great Movies This Month

A Is A, by Robin Field

SCHRC book reviewed: *The Sausage that Made Sheboygan Famous*

Dreaming of Baking, by Myra Stokdyk Eischen: Coconut-Pecan German Chocolate Pie

Ask a Science Teacher by Larry Scheckel: Why Do Birds and Butterflies Leave for Winter?

PulpArtists by David Saunders: Irene Zimmermann

America's Spunkiest Kid

They Might Not Be Able to Stop You... But Can You Stop Them?

Extortion: How Politicians Extract Your Money, Buy Votes, and Line Their Own Pockets, book review by Michael Dahlen, The Objective Standard

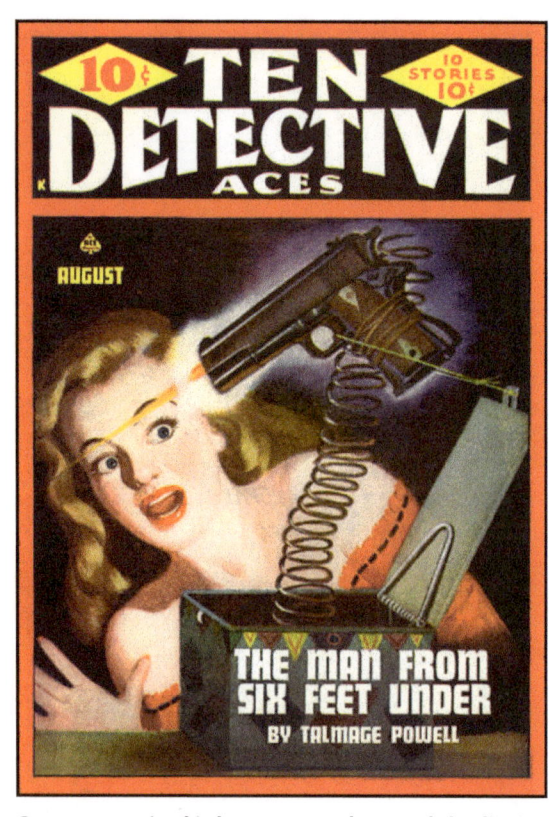

Some practical jokes go way beyond the limits of good taste. Cover painted by Irene Zimmermann.

Bratwurst Phenomenon
in Sheboygan
Born out of Neighborhood Meat Markets

Book review by Beth Dippel
for The Plymouth Review Current

Every summer Sheboygan and most of Wisconsin, for that matter, grills vast numbers of brats in a celebration of sausage and of our collective German heritage. The brat is a social food in this state where Germans first introduced it to the New World. We have brat fries on weekends like folks have BBQs in the south and Chicago has its deep dish pizza. It is part of a deep food tradition.

But, in Sheboygan County, the sausage is something more; it is noble; it is a type of Teutonic soul food. One old-timer described his perfect day, "We would fry some bratwurst and put them on Hirsch's semel and have a few bottles of Schreier's beer. After lunch we would play horseshoes. It was a feast and a day fit for a king."

Nearly 47% of all Sheboygan County residents claim German ancestry. We have the townships of Rhine and Mosel. We have the Gesangverein Concordia German chorus, D'Werdenfelser Schuhplattlers German folk dance group, the Sheboygan Turnverein (Turners) and Mission House (Lakeland) College started by a band of devout Lippe-Detmolders. And we have the bratwurst.

Few things identify one's German heritage more than making sausage. Sausage was a means of survival for our German ancestors during the winter months, as well as a way to use precious meat scraps and pay homage to their porcine good luck charm.

The real story of German sausage in the county lies, not in Bratwurst Day, but in the small neighborhood meat markets where patrons and owners addressed each other as *freund*. In the 1940s and 1950s upwards of fifty meat markets fed county residents with a score of sausage types produced weekly.

Heinecke's Meat Market made baloney on Mondays and Thursdays and wieners on Tuesdays. Wednesdays was for Kesselfleisch, a cooked sausage, liver, tongue, braunschweiger, head sausage and blood sausage. Not until Friday did the butcher make summer sausage and bratwurst.

In reality, summer sausage was Sheboygan County's first "star." The Herziger family, who came from Germany in 1839, opened a tavern on the corner of Calumet and Superior in Sheboygan. They also made and smoked sausage at the rear of the tavern. The Herziger Sausage Company was founded in 1916. By 1952, its output broke the two million pound mark. A family story had Grandpa Hertziger once proclaiming, "Bratvurst, ach, it vas summer sausage, not bratvurst ve first made."

In the days before refrigeration, summer sausage was superior because it was cured and lasted longer. Brats had to be eaten fresh.

Herziger's was also the first sausage maker to produce all-beef brats. Jewish citizens bought them because they didn't use pork.

Schultz Brothers Meat Market, at 11th and Michigan, opened its doors in 1924 selling five pounds of summer sausage for just $1.00. During cold winters, Elmer Schultz used hot coals to keep his feet warm as his horse pulled his delivery wagon through the streets. He also held a kerosene lantern between his knees to light the way. Schultz noted that to alert shoppers of the arrival of vendors, butchers had a bell, fishermen a horn and bakers a whistle.

Germans are acknowledged as the premier sausage makers, but Slovenians also made a very popular Kranski Clobasa. Kranski is derived from the Slovenian village of Kranj at the foot of the Julian Alps where the seasonings originated. Luedtke's Food Market made both fresh and smoked Kranski. They typically sold 500 pounds of it during the holidays and another 500 at the annual St. Cyril and Methodius picnic.

Records of brat production are spotty, but we do know that Michael Gottschalk Sr. of Sheboygan began making pork sausages as early as 1862, sometimes roasting them over

Joseph Spatt's Bratwurst Stand: The Come On In was one of the city's first locally-owned, "fast food" restaurants (also known as "lunch rooms"). It served charcoal grilled bratwurst, hamburgers and steaks on semmel rolls garnished with mustard, onions and pickles. Joseph Spatt and his brother, John, operated the popular metal Quonset hut-style eatery on Michigan Avenue for 15 years in the 1930s and 40s. The site is now a vacant lot. — Photos accompanying this article provided by the Sheboygan County Historical Research Center

In 1863, Michael Gottschalk opened one of the first meat markets in Sheboygan. He got his start on the north side of the eight hundred block of Michigan Avenue in the former Wendt house, built in 1850. Michael, a Bavarian native, was reportedly the original maker of bratwurst in Sheboygan.

charcoal fires for his customers. Because of their popularity, they were soon sold to the general public. But it was years before brat sales surpassed those of summer sausage.

By the 1920s, once ice boxes and later refrigerators were commonplace in homes, bratwurst increased in popularity. From then until the 1960s and 1970s local meat markets flourished and produced tons of bratwurst.

Eateries like Freimund's Brat Stand in Plymouth and Joe Spatt's in Sheboygan popped up in the 1940s and 1950s to sell the grilled wonders.

In 1953, the first brats rolled off the grill at Milwaukee County Stadium, introducing them to the nation. Stadiums across the country soon followed suit, but Miller Park is still the only venue that serves more brats than hot dogs.

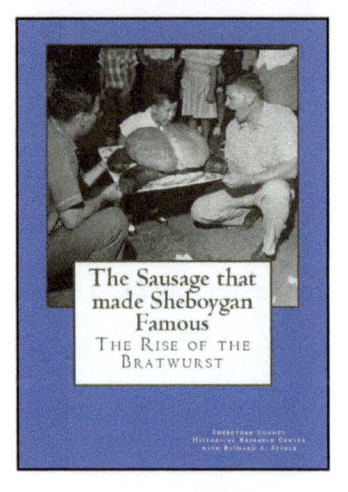

Family-owned meat markets have, for the most part, gone the way of the dinosaur. Government regulations and large supermarkets led to the decline and closure of all but a few. Yet, happily the brat remains.

In this book, *The Sausage that Made Sheboygan Famous,* the history of the brat is documented through the many family-run butcher shops that once graced the county. It is filled with great photos and ends with a discussion of the 1953 celebration of Sheboygan's centennial and the very first Brat Days festival.

You can just smell the brats grilling as you read this fun look at one of our favorite summer pastimes.

An interior shot of Gottschalk's 2nd meat market at 817 Michigan in 1922. Note the sawdust on the floor and the lack of refrigeration.

Freimund Brat Stand. Shown here in 1957, this unprepossessing stand, located in the parking lot behind Kretsch's Tavern (the Brown Bottle today) near the Mullet River, was a favorite of locals and visitors from 1948 to 1982, offering charcoal-grilled Johnsonville bratwurst, steak sandwiches, pork loins and cheese sandwiches. It was owned and operated by Mr. and Mrs. Aaron Kolpin from 1948 to 1952, Waldemar and Millie Jochmann from 1952 to 1955 and, after 1955, by Otto Freimund and later his son Glenweye.

Ask a Science Teacher

By Larry Scheckel

Q: Why Do Birds and Butterflies Leave for Winter?

A: Animals in a Wisconsin winter have three choices; hibernate, adapt, or migrate. Bears hibernate. They eat like mad all summer and get as fat as possible. They sleep a lot in the winter, where all body functions slow down. Frogs, chipmunks, woodchucks, and snakes also hibernate. Lady bugs seek out warm places, like our houses, and hibernate all winter.

Some insects, such as the woolly bear caterpillar, hibernate as larvae. Some moths hibernate as pupae. Still others, like the mourning cloak butterfly, hibernate as adults. Others live up here in the north country as cocoons, eggs, or caterpillars. Come spring, they spread their wings and fly.

Animals can adapt to harsh winter conditions. Owls adapt. Many change color from brown to white. Their soft feathers allow them to be silent flyers. With keen vision and excellent hearing, they pounce down on those field mice and voles.

Rabbit fur changes from brown to white. Rabbits will gnaw on leaves, bark, twigs, and moss and will seek shelter in holes in trees, usually below ground or under brush piles. Deer and squirrels stay active and scrounge for food all winter.

Wolves adapt as their fur grows thicker against the bitter cold. They're excellent hunters, eat well, but leave some of the food behind. The leftovers are for other smaller animals. Eagles, coyotes, and other animals can survive winter because of wolves.

Yes, many birds and butterflies migrate. Monarch butterflies spend the summer in Canada and the Northern U.S. They head for a better climate during the winter migrating as far south as Mexico for the winter. Their annual migration across North America has been called "one of the most spectacular natural phenomena in the world."

Butterflies arrive to overwintering sites in central Mexico around November. They start the return trip in March, arriving around July.

Most migrating insects go much shorter distances. In the western mountains, many animals just go down the mountain to where there is less snow and cold. Migration takes an animal to where the weather will be mild enough to make it easier to find food.

The American Robin is the state bird of Wisconsin, Michigan, and Connecticut. Our Wisconsin robins head for Florida in the winter, same as many Wisconsin retirees. During the spring and summertime there aren't many places in the state that you won't see a group of robins sitting together singing their beautiful song. Don't we all welcome robins as a first sign of spring?

Oddly, every winter a few robins stay in the northern states, surviving blizzards, ice storms, and nights as cold as 20 below. Regardless of how cold it is on the outside of their feathers, their body temperature under the feathers is about 104 degrees. Their thick down feathers hold body heat in. They produce body heat by shivering. And they get the energy to shiver from their food.

There is a consensus that these stay-behind robins are not the brightest birds in their species lineup. They just might be a few bricks short of a full load. The smart ones head south.

November
2019

Cover photo: Your Editor's Side Yard
Great Movies This Month
TOS-Con: A Conference Promoting Philosophy for Freedom and Flourishing
New Off-Broadway Musical Features Plymouth Native
PulpArtists by David Saunders: John Falter
Review of Steven Pinker's New Book "Enlightenment Now," by Marian L. Tupy, HumanProgress.org

SCHRC book reviewed: *Lost Places of Sheboygan County*
Ask a Science Teacher by Larry Scheckel: Who Invented Television?
A Great Book on the Making of 2001
"History of Mystery" Exhibit in Kenosha

Artistic history in the making. We are well-enough along in the present century to start taking note of possible candidates for Greatest Painter of the 21st Century. (The Greatest Painter of the 20th Century is indisputably James Bama.) At the 2019 TOS-Con, Quent Cordair Fine Art set up a mini art gallery. Among the fine works on display were those by Jon Wos (left) and Bryan Larsen, who met here in person for the first time. Behind Larsen, the women in robes are two of his paintings. The globe resting on the open book, and the rose, are paintings by Wos.
— Photo taken by and Copyright © Ari Armstrong, used here with permission

This past August, my wife and I flew in to Salt Lake City, Utah. From there, an hour-long shuttle ride brought us to Park City, a scenic community that had hosted Winter Olympics events. That's where we attended TOS-Con 2019.

Two abbreviations to remember:

TOS — The Objective Standard, a journal that promotes Enlightenment values.

TOS-Con — the convention coordinated by the staff of TOS.

Additional resources

Following lecture descriptions, complete online articles are listed for most speakers. Find them by visiting the TOS website: **theobjectivestandard.com**.

The TOS-Con talks are available online for a small charge as audio-only or video (some presentations have visuals). Website: **tos-con.com**

Disclaimers

I'm giving only a few highlights of each talk.

I am summarizing points as I understand them. If anyone sees an error or misrepresentation of a viewpoint, let me know and I'll print a prominently-displayed correction.

* * *

Speaker: Craig Biddle

Topic: Intellectual Independence: Your Basic Means of Thriving

Biddle is the co-founder and editor of TOS. He, his wife Sarah, and other TOS staff coordinated TOS-Con.

Biddle distinguished between independent thinking and intellectual independence: The first can be done in isolation, turned on or off; the second is a consistently principled approach to thinking and making choices in life.

"Thinking for yourself, being intellectually independent, is a crucial aspect of human life," Biddle said. "Mimicking, following other people's lead, mindlessly, doesn't work. It doesn't work, because it means your mind is not connected to reality. It means that your mind is not in touch with the facts."

Though Biddle doesn't specifically address it, the subject of this talk is a powerful tool in fighting bullying.

Articles online by Craig Biddle:
The above-described talk is available free.
Books by Craig Biddle: Loving Life.

* * *

Speaker: Lisa VanDamme

Topic: Enrich Your Life with Poetry

VanDamme analyzed "On First Looking Into Cahpman's Homer" by John Keats; "The Woodspurge" by Dante Gabriel Rossetti; "Surprised by Joy" by William Wordsworth; and "Hymn to the Sun" by Edmond Rostand.

VanDamme started a private school, The VanDamme Academy. Search online for "Little Candle" and VanDamme's name, and you'll find a documentary about her school and her philosophy of education.

* * *

Speaker: Richard Salsman

Topic: "Democratic Socialism": The Whitewashing of Evil

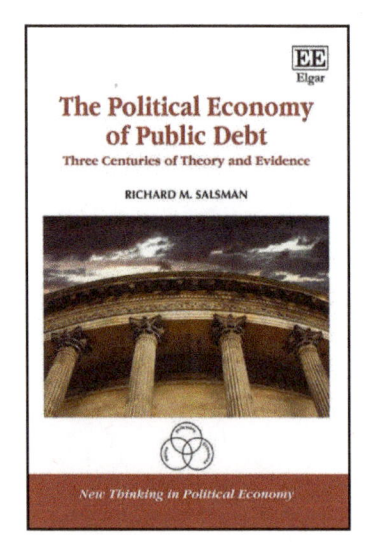

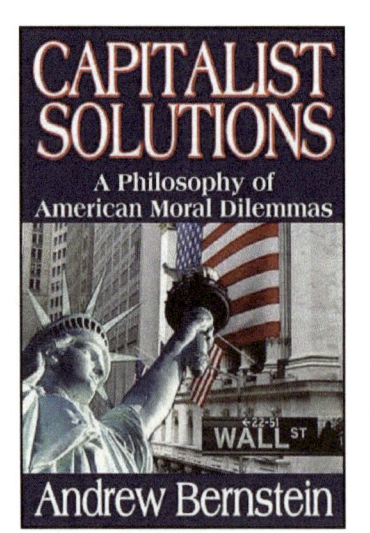

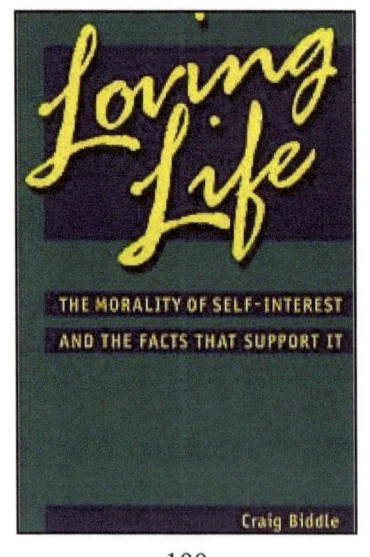

TOS-Con

A conference promoting
Philosophy for Freedom and Flourishing

Salsman reviewed the seeming rising popularity of socialism in this country—mostly among academia and young people coming out of academia. The point of his title's talk: Establishing a social system that perpetrates the initiation of force and violates rights on a massive scale is morally wrong, even if a majority of people vote it in.

Salsman shared results of a Gallup poll, as to what people believe socialism is. About a quarter of those polled held the confused, inaccurate belief that it means "Equality; equal standing for all; equal rights; equality in distribution."

In 1949, roughly a third of those polled identified the correct nature of socialism: "Government ownership or control; government ownership of utilities; everything controlled by the government; state control of business." A year ago, only 17% correctly identified this.

"So there's a real defect in people's understanding of socialism," Salsman said.

Salsman presented a 4-option matrix, reproduced elsewhere with this article, which depicts the four major social systems in an easy-to-understand way.

Articles online by Richard Salsman:
The U.S. Treasury's Unjust Debasement of Alexander Hamilton

Books by Richard Salsman: The Political Economy of Public Debt.

* * *

Speaker: Patrick Reasonover

Topic: Cinema for the Soul

Reasonover discussed movies with positive values. He showed clips from Green Book and Darkest Hour.

Because of the film clips and copyright issues, this talk is not available online.

* * *

Speaker: Andrew Bernstein

Topic: The Trader Principle and the Harmony of Rational Values

The point of this talk, which he's given several times recently throughout Europe, is: A social system where interaction between people is by mutual consent, free from coercion, leads to greater harmony and benevolence.

Examples include working for an employer and receiving an agreed-upon payment; and buying an item in a store for money.

But Bernstein didn't limit his examples to those involving money. He mentioned his teaching experience, where one of his former students became a good friend. The former student did favors for Bernstein, for which Bernstein wanted to pay him. The ex-student repeatedly said, "Andy, with me, you are paid up for life."

The "trader principle" of this talk refers to an exchange of values.

Close relationships such as romantic love, he said, involved "a ceaseless quid pro quo with nobody keeping score."

"A just person wants to repay an act of kindness, wants to make it a trade rather than an act of charity," he said. Sometimes, the only "payback" one needs to return is gratitude—acknowledging and showing appreciation for something positive someone has done for you.

"For one concerned to uphold human

life, the trader principle must be embraced full-mindedly, whole-heartedly, and good-naturedly," he said.

Bernstein said one criticism of capitalism is that it promotes too much materialism. His first response was, "You say that is if it were a bad thing." His second response: "Look at the flourishing of every type of intellectual, spiritual value made possible by the principle of individual rights. The novels written, the symphonies composed, rock music, rap, whatever it is, theories in science, architecture, medicine, every book imaginable in every subject, every field, every point of view."

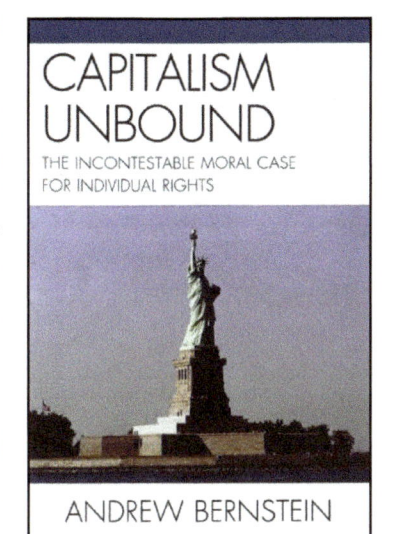

Bernstein began his talk with the news, received just hours before the lecture, that another book he's written has been accepted for publication: Heroes, Legends, and Champions: Why Heroism Matters. "I'm excited," Bernstein told the audience.

Articles online by / about Andrew Bernstein:
His book, Capitalism Unbound, reviewed by Ari Armstrong
His book, Capitalist Solutions, reviewed by Ari Armstrong
Review of the movie, Zero Dark Thirty
Books by Andrew Bernstein: Capitalism Unbound, Capitalist Solutions, Ayn Rand for Beginners, Cliffs Notes for Atlas Shrugged and The Fountainhead.

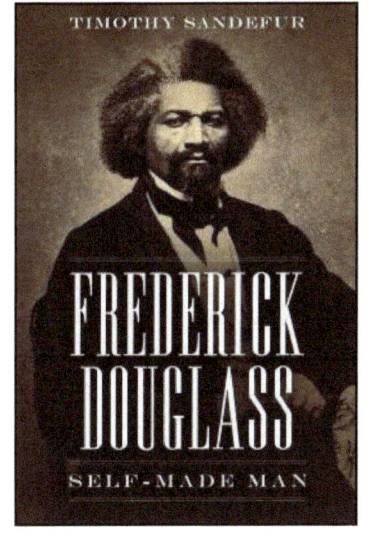

* * *

Speaker: Robin Field
Topic: How Music Conveys Meaning (Lecture & Performance)

This was a different kind of talk. While demonstrating by playing short pieces on a piano, Field related instrumental music to low-level concepts.

Some understanding of the nature of concepts is needed to fully understand this talk. However, if you believe music will play an important role in your life—as a part-time or full-time career, for instance—this important lecture will give you something to really think about; it would be personally worth it for you to pay for all the TOS-Con lectures just to listen to this one. If you don't understand what is said about concepts, you can always pick that up later.

Field said music was part of his early life. He learned to play piano without reading music.

As a child, Field once heard composer Leonard Bernstein claim that instrumental music had no content; that it was about *nothing*.

Field heard this and similar claims throughout his life.

Others believe music directly creates an emotion in a listener's mind. But Field broke this process down:

Percept: A piece of music; for example, The William Tell Overture (also known as The Lone Ranger Theme).
Concept: "Fast and steady."
Evaluation: I *like* fast and steady.
Emotion: Excitement, anticipation.

This four-step process happens so quickly, that some people think there is only the percept (the music) and immediately thereafter, the emotion.

Contrary to the claim that instrumental music is about *nothing*, Field said it is able to convey low-level concepts. "Low-level" here means close to perceptual. "Fast and steady" is close to perception. (In contrast, "justice" is a much higher-level concept.)

Pretty technical stuff? Field's lecture introduced a lot of new ideas to me; I'll be listening to it *more* than once. Again: If you take music seriously in any capacity, this lecture is fascinating and important.

Field ended his presentation with a tribute to George Gershwin's "Rhapsody in Blue." To Gershwin's melody, Field composed lyrics telling the story of how Gershwin wrote the song.

Music online by Robin Field: A wealth of free music downloads are at **robinfield.org**. The Gershwin tribute can be found under the category "Daugherty & Field: Special Material." Also highly recommended is "Reason in Rhyme," a concert Field composed, giving the history and content of philosophy. (We ran "A is A," an excerpt from this, in last month's issue.)

Articles online about Robin Field:
The Most Delightful Performer Ever to Say "A is A," by Craig Biddle
Robin Field on Objectivism and the Performing Arts, interview conducted by Craig Biddle

* * *

Speaker: Isaac Morehouse
Topic: How to Create a Career that Makes You Come Alive

"Isaac Morehouse is, among other things, the founder and CEO of Praxis, an apprenticeship program that trains young adults in the art of value creation and matches them with startups and businesses who need talented, disciplined, creative people to make their ventures thrive."

This introduction is from an interview Craig Biddle conducted with Morehouse, available online (see below).

"What is the point of living, if you're not fully alive?" Morehouse asked his audience. He offered seven tips:

1. Hunt down victimhood, and destroy it. Ruthlessly. Watch out for the phrase, "Because I have to."

2. Don't do things you hate. One of Morehouse's books carries this title.

3. Don't do stuff you suck at. Double down on your strengths; combine them. If you're a pretty-good accountant, and a pretty-good yoga instructor (taking two skill sets at random), "that's interesting. That's unique. You're probably the best in the world accounting-yoga instructor."

4. Do stuff other people value. (This is not the same as, "Do stuff other people praise you for.")

5. Do one thing each day. Whatever it is—blogging, exercising—doing something to add value to your life on a modest scale, yet on a regular basis, will accomplish more for you than setting a lofty goal, such as, "Some day I'm going to write a book," and continually putting off that "some day."

6. Live, work and learn out loud. Let the right people know what you're learning and accomplishing. When someone else needs the kind of skill or expertise you have, they'll know to come to you.

7. Ask yourself some questions. Is what I'm doing fun? Is what I'm doing too easy? After doing what I'm doing now, will I be more valuable to the market six months from now? Have I added to my lists of stuff I hate and suck at? Am I doing anything only for prestige from others? (If so, kill it.)

"Invest in yourself," Morehouse told the audience. "You are your own company. You are your own startup."

Articles online about Isaac Morehouse:

Interview conducted by Craig Biddle: Isaac Morehouse on Praxis, Apprenticeships, and Creating Value. A very interesting look into how this entrepreneur is starting to remake education.

Many articles, blogs, etc. at **isaacmorehouse.com**.

Books by Isaac Morehouse:

At the above website, two books are available as free PDF downloads. Other books are available as Amazon Kindle ebooks at no charge.

* * *

Speaker: Bryan Larsen
Topic: Optimism in Visual Art

Larsen's work appeared in the December 2018 issue of The PRC, along with a detailed interview conducted by Craig Biddle (see below).

Larsen told his audience that optimism is a central theme to his work. "It is my belief that optimism as a basic aspect of a person's world view directly leads to a more satisfying, fulfilling life."

Larsen said, "I generally assume, unless given good reason to think otherwise, that other people are, on balance, good, reasonably intelligent, and will generally behave rationally—or at least, predictably—given the information they have available."

In a slide show, Larsen commented on works by himself and others. The video available online will be of interest to anyone hungry for excellent art.

When Larsen took questions, one person asked about artwork being destroyed, because it offends current political sensitivities. "I don't personally think a piece of art should ever be destroyed," Larsen answered. "It's really popular right now to tear down things that don't fit popular narratives. I think that's a huge mistake. I think that's dismissing things that you don't agree with, rather than addressing them. Some art is made to be confrontational, and often for a good reason."

Artwork online by Bryan Larsen: Cordair Fine Art represents Larsen and several other artists worthy of your attention. Start at **cordair.com** and let your eyes (and mind) wander (and wonder).

Articles online about Bryan Larsen: Painter Bryan Larsen on His Artwork and Ideas, interview conducted by Craig Biddle.

* * *

Speaker: Chad Morris
Topic: Basic Principles and Pitfalls of Fitness Training

Morris said reasons for exercising include muscle strength, ability to resist and help recover from injury, stamina, bone density, joint integrity, balance, insulin sensitivity and glucose disposal, reducing osteoarthritis pain, reducing risk of cardio-vascular disease, and changes in gene expression.

But exercising incorrectly or too much can cause harm. The challenge of exercise is to yield significant net benefits.

Safety and intensity are the main principles in judging the effectiveness of exercise.

* * *

Speaker: Tim Chermak
Topic: The Morality of More: How Advertising Inspires Us to Be More Productive, Make More Money, and Achieve More Happiness

Chermak first acknowledged that many people view advertising negatively. In fact, some people pay for services that skip ads.

"I think advertising is amazing, and it's morally heroic," he told the audience.

He then asked a question that seemed off-topic. "Who would prefer that we adopt a system of arranged marriages, where dating is illegal? Who would trust your parents to marry you off, without your opinion mattering? Is that a good idea?"

I saw no one in the audience raise a hand.

"Stop thinking about advertising as being synonymous with the word 'annoying,'" Chermak challenged the audience, "and start thinking of advertising as anything whose stated purpose is persuasion."

Chermak asked: What is the alternative to persuasion? Coercion. Initiated force. He argued that advertising is "a leading indicator, and a lagging indicator, of how much a culture values free will. Advertising is a celebration of autonomy. No wonder progressives and Marxists hate it."

Advertising, he said, is inherently optimistic. "It's all about how your life could be better. Advertising inspires us to achieve more, to buy more, to invest more. And we're deluding ourselves if we think this is a bad thing."

People who claim they don't like ads, he said, are often responding to bad ads, which he said are out there.

Chermak returned to his question about arranged marriages. Getting rid of dating and the whole "love industry" might strike some as being more efficient, he said. "Unless you actually inherently value the 'game' and the 'dance' of persuasion. That's the magic and whimsy of living in a free society."

* * *

Speaker: Alex Epstein
Topic: The Human-Flourishing Framework: A Powerful Tool for Clear Thinking

Epstein's "human-flourishing framework" is a perspective taking into account both positive and negative factors of an issue, using human flourishing as a standard of measure.

"The value is human flourishing, including a good environment. We don't get a good environment by leaving the environment alone. You get a good environment by intelligently transforming it."

A quote from Epstein from the interview mentioned below: "I often think of my framework as the Earth Enhancer framework and the opposite framework as the Earth Worshipper framework. I think the Earth is imperfect and needs to be continually upgraded to be fit for human flourishing; they think the Earth is perfect and needs to be continually protected from human impact. I want to show how the Earth Enhancer framework can illuminate and guide issues such as GMO, vaccines, development, and, of course, energy. And how the Earth Worshipper framework is making us take a primitive, antihuman approach to all of these areas."

Articles online by / about Alex Epstein:

Alex Epstein on How Fossil Fuels Make the Environment Cleaner and Safer, by Craig Biddle

Alex Epstein on An Inconvenient Sequel and Al Gore's Methods of Deception, interview conducted by Craig Biddle.

Books by Alex Epstein: The Moral Case

for Fossil Fuels

Epstein's Human Flourishing Project has a Facebook page.

Epstein created the Center for Industrial Progress: **industrialprogress.com.** On this website is a link to a very recent debate Epstein had with Robert F. Kennedy, Jr., on the topic, "Should the world radically restrict fossil fuel use to prevent climate change?" Hear both sides of this issue!

* * *

Speaker: Timothy Sandefur
Topic: How to Lead an Enlightenment Life in an Anti-Enlightenment World

At the start of his talk, Sandefur named three women and their books. During his presentation, he kept coming back to them:

Yeonmi Park, In Order to Live: A North Korean Girl's Journey to Freedom, with Maryanne Vollers

Ayaan Hirsi Ali, Infidel: My Life

Deborah Feldman, Unorthodox: The Scandalous Rejection of My Hasidic Roots

"It is only in the past two centuries, that a portion of the human race has risen out of darkness into enlightenment," Sandefur said. While the three women he mentioned give accounts of personal liberation and discovery, "Western civilization as a whole went through something very similar on a culture-wide level, beginning around 1700, in a period we appropriately enough call the Enlightenment." Intellectual leaders emphasized "reason and discovery, rather than power and dogma."

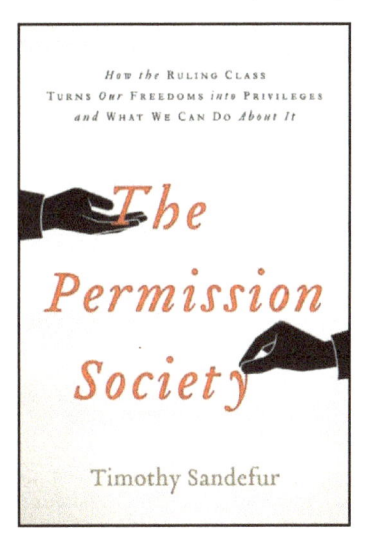

These ideas, Sandefur said, are responsible for improving human life in the past two centuries.

"The word *'improvement'* is hardly adequate. The transformation of the world in the past 200 years is so mind-bogglingly enormous that the English language does not contain powerful enough superlatives to describe it."

Sandefur referred to a book by Steven Pinker—Enlightenment Now: The Case for Reason, Science, Humanism, and Progress. This book (which Sandefur has reviewed; see below) documents the many dramatic improvements made in the past 200, even just in the past 50, years.

"The Enlightenment was an era that prioritized humanity, that sought universal, moral values rooted in human nature rather than tribal background or circumstance, and that pursued answers to scientific and philosophical questions through reason, skepticism, curiosity, experiment and free speech."

Sandefur said Enlightenment ideas and their benefits to human life are not specific to a race or culture; they are universal. That is why the three women he mentioned, each from a different background, can be drawn to these values.

"Only a racist would suggest that these values are off-limits to them, or that they were too deluded to realize that they were white supremacists all along. Only a sexist would imply that these feminist heroes, by consciously embracing the Enlightenment legacy, are somehow male chauvinists."

I recently came across this comment by Rob Tracinski: "There is a whole wing of the left that absolutely reviles [author Steven] Pinker [and his book documenting the Enlightenment] and rejects the idea that there has been any progress against global poverty. The reason is simple: if such progress has occurred, as it undoubtedly has, then it happened under capitalism and not under socialism. It is a rebuke to their whole world view."

Articles online by Timothy Sandefur:
[Book review] Enlightenment Now: The Case for Reason, Science, Humanism, and Progress by Steven Pinker
Bravery That Broke the Berlin Wall
Enter The Twilight Zone This November
Three Masters of Watercolor
Celebrate and Exercise Your Right to Read
Charles Sumner's Principled Attack on Slavery
John Fogerty's Disciplined Focus
[Painter] John Singer Sargent: Master of Elevated Grace

Books by Timothy Sandefur:
Frederick Douglass: Self-Made Man
The Permission Society: How the Ruling Class Turns Our Freedoms into Privileges and What We Can Do About It
The Conscience of the Constitution: The Declaration of Independence and the Right to Liberty
The Right to Earn a Living: Economic Freedom and the Law

Editor's comment: Search **humanprogress.org** for an article, Five Graphs that Will Change Your Mind About Poverty. The article concludes, "The facts are unambiguous: despite public perceptions to the contrary, extreme poverty has declined significantly, to the point where its end may actually be in sight. So next time you hear someone bemoaning a supposed rise in world poverty, encourage them to have a look at the evidence for themselves."

* * *

Speaker: Jon Hersey
Topic: John Locke: The Father of Liberalism

Jon Hersey is the associate editor of TOS. He's written several articles about figures of America's founding.

Hersey told his audience that Thomas Jefferson considered John Locke "one of the three greatest men the world had ever produced," the other two being Isaac Newton and Francis Bacon.

Benjamin Franklin and John Adams were two other Founding Fathers heavily influenced by Locke. Hersey said Locke was the "guy behind the guys. He's the hero behind so many American heroes. He was at the forefront of Enlightenment thinkers that supported a rational, scientific, this-worldly approach to knowledge."

In one word, "the distinctive social and political philosophy of the Enlightenment was liberty." The system of ideas developed to support and defend liberty became known as "liberalism."

Hersey said this word has a quite different meaning today.

"Locke so well encapsulated the Enlightenment, because he passionately pursued any and all knowledge that could be used to enhance human life and happiness."

Locke wrote clearly, and can be easily understood by readers then and now.

Locke believed that, because a person owns his own body, he owns what his body produces. "You can legitimately trade your effort for a paycheck," said Hersey, "but no one can rightfully take the product of your effort, without paying you." Similarly, if you mix your labor with the land, that becomes your property. The root of property rights (and all rights), he thought, was man's right to his own life.

Articles online by Jon Hersey:
The Moral Courage of Rosa Parks
Life-Enhancing Ideas from Alex Epstein's Human Flourishing Project
Obscure Manuscript Further Reveals John

Locke's Intellectual Honesty
   The Man Who Electrified Music [Leo Fender]
   Greta Thunberg *Should* Be Angry—and So Should You
   The Boston Tea Party's Principles and Heroes
   Live Free or Die: The Story of General John Stark
   By John Locke
   An Essay Concerning Human Understanding (full text available several places online for free)

* * *

Speaker: Tal Tsfany
Topic: Turning Philosophy into Technology

Much of Tsfany's lecture was autobiographical, presented with an entertaining slide show, expressive gestures, interesting life experiences and genuine enthusiasm. (As with other lectures, you can get the main ideas from listening to the audio-only version; but watching the video presentation gives you so much more.)

One of several careers in his life took him to Silicon Valley. He described how he loved Silicon Valley and its culture of high-tech expertise.

He explained that physicists study basic science, and engineers take that theoretical science and apply it to make things.

Tsfany compared this translation of the theoretical into the practical in science, to philosophy. When he talked philosophy with people, he found they sometimes had difficulty translating an abstract, theoretical principle into everyday, practical use.

(Editor's Note: Tsfany did not mention this, but this is exactly the challenge the Founders of America faced. They took abstract, moral / political principles from people like John Locke, and assembled the workings of a constitutional republic. It wasn't a simple task.)

"After I sold my company, I really didn't want to do tech anymore," he told the audience. "I wanted to do philosophy, education, and writing." He wanted to make philosophy "acceptable, understandable, and actionable for people."

Tsfany's goal led him to the very basics. To childhood. He wrote a children's book, Sophie. "I wrote this book. It was a family project. I loved it. I enjoyed every minute of doing that."

Tsfany is currently the CEO of the Ayn Rand Institute.
Articles about Tal Tsfany:
Sophie, by Tal Tsfany, Reviewed by Ella Wilson
Tal Tsfany on Sophie, the Book, interview conducted by Craig Biddle
Books by Tal Tsfany: Sophie

* * *

Speaker: Craig Biddle
Topic: Purpose X: Understanding Objectivism and Using It to Thrive

"The reason we chose 'Philosophy for Freedom and Flourishing' as the title of this event, is because as I see it, the most important things in the world are freedom and flourishing," said Biddle.

All topics at the conference, he said, were all aimed at the same thing: human flourishing. "And they're all based on the same fundamental premise, and that is, your mind is capable of knowing this reality, so that you can flourish."

Biddle went on to describe a tool for understanding philosophy that I won't cover here, because I don't think it can be summarized easily.

Biddle received warm and appreciative applause and cheers from the audience as he wrapped up the speaking portion of the conference.

Obviously, attendees enjoyed the experience.

> TOS-Con has been renamed to "LevelUp." If you are a student, and interested in the kind of topics described here, scholarships are available to help you attend these conferences.

> Many TOS-Con lectures can be viewed online. Here are some from 2019. (More are available.) I have verified that these links are still active.

How to Create a Career that Makes You Come Alive, Isaac Morehouse
   https://www.youtube.com/watch?v=Pd9Ad6m3YZs

John Locke: The Father of Liberalism, Jon Hersey
   https://www.youtube.com/watch?v=jvSKdJU5kg8

The Human Flourishing Framework: A Powerful Tool for Clear Thinking, Alex Epstein
   https://www.youtube.com/watch?v=Rngecou_FNM

The Morality of More, Tim Chermak
   https://www.youtube.com/watch?v=VSKNBo-2pvg

How to Lead an Enlightenment Life in an Anti-Enlightenment World, Timothy Sandefur
   https://www.youtube.com/watch?v=36pE8qMUhrs

How Music Conveys Meaning, Robin Field
   https://www.youtube.com/watch?v=hceGAPG-Y0M

Optimism in Visual Art, Bryan Larsen
   https://www.youtube.com/watch?v=7sLl0G44sJA

Turning Philosophy into Technology with Tal Tsfany
   https://www.youtube.com/watch?v=SJCm3CEW4NI

Timothy Sandefur used this image to represent Enlightenment values in his talk. This sculpture, "Lifting the Veil of Ignorance" by Charles Keck, depicts Booker T. Washington removing a veil from a newly-freed slave. The gesture Washington makes with his left hand seems to say, "The world is now yours; it awaits you." – Public domain image from picryl.com

A few months ago, we printed some "infinity cover" examples. Here's another we found recently... a 1925 Western Story Magazine pulp cover.

John Falter, 1938 McCalls magazine. Falter's technique here was to paint the girl in sharper "focus," to bring the viewer's attention to her. Notice the complex interaction of the stairway curves, serving to frame the adults.

This original John Falter painting for a 1948 Saturday Evening Post cover sold at Heritage Auctions for $325,000. — HA.com

The cover of the Saturday Evening Post was a coveted assignment for many artists. John Falter's work made the cover *129 times!* The anxiety in this piece could have been increased a few notches by having the kid standing on top of the water tower.

185

The Plymouth Review Current

Taking you places worth seeing
Volume 9 • Issue 1 • December 2019

Wisconsin Authors • Sports pulps • Seven Keys to...WHERE?? Have Aliens Visited Us? • Lake Michigan Views

December 2019

Cover photo: Dramatic clouds roll out over Lake Michigan after a reported tornado sighting in the Sheboygan area. Photo by Lisa Lehmann; Copyright © Lisa Lehmann. From her book, *Lake Michigan: The Wisconsin Shore.*

Great Movies This Month

No Safe Spaces (book and movie)

Dreaming of Baking, by Myra Stokdyk Eischen: Fruit Twist Bread
U.S. Poverty — What's the Status? by Chris Edwards, Cato.org
Ask a Science Teacher by Larry Scheckel: Did an Advanced Technological Civilization Live Here on Earth or Visit the Earth a Long Time Ago?
PulpArtists by David Saunders: F. A. Carter
Authors in Autumn
Are You a Svengoolie Fan?
WOSS on TOS
SCHRC book reviewed: *The Chordettes of Sheboygan*

The Chordettes

Book review by Beth Dippel
for The Plymouth Review Current

Mr. Sandman, Lollipop, Pink Shoelaces and the list of number one hits goes on for Sheboygan's most famous homegrown musical group, The Chordettes.

Formed in Sheboygan in 1946 as a barbershop quartet, by 1947 they had bookings to sing all across the United States. In 1949, they appeared in a contest on the popular Arthur Godfrey Show and soon after worked as regulars on Godfrey's variety shows for almost four years.

By 1953, they decided to try a different kind of music and the following year, they recorded "Mr. Sandman," a song that would reach number one on the pop charts and sell over two million copies. From 1956 to 1959, the Chordettes had a song on the top 100 chart almost continuously.

A new book, available from the Sheboygan

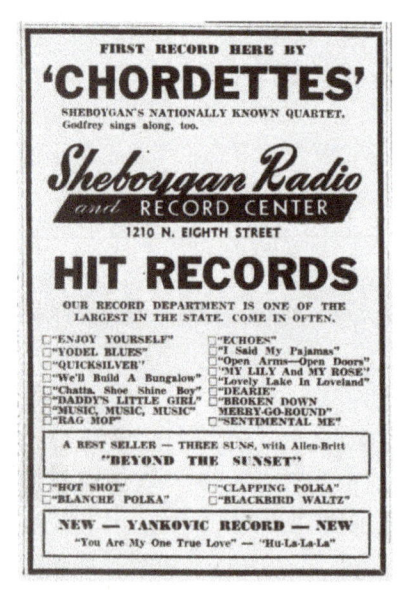

1950 ad. — Courtesy of the SCHRC

County Historical Research Center, tells the story of the Chordettes from their high school days in Sheboygan through 2004 when the Chordettes were honored in their hometown of Sheboygan before a crowd of more than 500 people.

This book also includes information on Cadence Records and its owner, Archie Bleyer. Bleyer married one of the Chordettes and lived his final years in Black River.

Compiled by Scott Lewandoske before his death in 2018, the information was gathered from newspaper articles, scrapbooks, record albums, and interviews with the Chordettes themselves. Scott's book about the Chordettes, written about 2010, is being published in an altered form. Some photos had copyright issues and could not be used, but the rest of the book compiled by Scott still tells a great story; it conveys his encyclopedic knowledge of his favorite musical group.

Thanks to the Sheboygan Press for the

ability to freely use information and photos.

Excerpt from the book

On Sunday, August 18, 1946, four young women gathered around a piano to sing barbershop music at the home of Arthur and Emma Hummitzsch, 1435 Superior Avenue.

The women were Miss Dorothy (Dottie) Hummitzsch, Mrs. Virginia (Jinny) Osborn, Mrs. Janet Ertel, and Mrs. Alice Mae Phelps. The sheet music was supplied by Virginia Osborn, whose father, H.O. (King) Cole, was vice president of the local Kingsbury Brewery and president of the Sheboygan chapter of the Society for the Preservation and Encouragement of Barber Shop Quartet Singing in America, Inc. (S.P.E.B.S.Q.S.A.).

Less than three weeks later, on September 7, 1946, the Sheboygan Barbershoppers, Wisconsin Chapter No. 8, held their first annual parade of quartets in Sheboygan in the auditorium of Sheboygan North High School.

The auditorium was jammed with enthusiasts waiting to hear more than 100 barbershop singers from Sheboygan, Manitowoc, Appleton, Milwaukee, Beaver Dam, Chicago, St. Louis, and Grand Rapids, Michigan.

The Sheboygan Press, in their September 9, 1946 issue, described barbershop singing as "a form of American music produced by four voices unaccompanied, when the lead sings the melody consistently below the tenor, with the baritone and bass rounding out the four parts, when rules of time, expression and word theme are frequently sacrificed to obtain more blending harmony satisfaction. With Barbershoppers, harmony comes first, last, and always."

The Press continued, "Having its origin in the early day barbershop where patrons gathered to swap news, tell stories, sing, and otherwise enjoy the clubby atmosphere, it is not surprising that such establishments lent their name to this distinct type of music."

The Press later added, "The parade of quartets began with the Sheboygan Four singing, 'Sweet Rose' and 'Sailing Away on the Henry Clay.' Sheboygan's other contribution to the program was a quartet of girls, the Chordettes, who do not belong to the society, but worked with it on such programs as that of Saturday evening. They sang, 'Tell Me Why' and 'Beautiful Isle of Make Believe' in the full male quartet range of tenor, lead, baritone and bass."

This was the first public appearance for the Chordettes. For the next seventeen years the Chordettes were one of America's favorites, and at the top of their industry.

But, finally during the first half of 1963, the Chordettes decided to stop accepting additional show dates. They would do shows that were already scheduled. There were a number of reasons for reaching this decision, but more time with family was number one. The second, best expressed in a quote from Lynn in a 2002 interview said, "When Jinny left, we decided that we didn't want to get another tenor to replace her. Once you've worked hard to perfect a sound, it's hard to be satisfied with anything less."

This enjoyable book is available at the Research Center, 518 Water Street, Sheboygan Falls for $15.00. Or it can be ordered online at schrc.org/shop. Please call 920.467.4667 for questions.

The Chordettes are shown here singing at the National Barbershop Convention, held in Milwaukee, Wisconsin, June 13-15, 1947. New Chordette, Carol Hagedorn is shown second from the left. Notice that she had not yet been fitted with costumes to match the other Chordettes. The other Chordettes are, left to right, Janet Ertel, Dorothy (Dottie) Hummitzsch, and Virginia Osborn. Alice Mae also sang with the group in Milwaukee. – Photo courtesy of Dorothy Schwartz

WOS on TOS

Last month, we covered TOS-Con, a philosophy conference held by The Objective Standard (TOS).

Oshkosh artist Jon Wos was commissioned to paint the cover of the forthcoming issue of TOS. The painting depicts three women mentioned by Timothy Sandefur, in his TOS-Con talk, which is printed in this issue of TOS.

Left to right, the three women (and their books) are:

Yeonmi Park, In Order to Live: A North Korean Girl's Journey to Freedom, with Maryanne Vollers

Ayaan Hirsi Ali, Infidel: My Life

Deborah Feldman, Unorthodox: The Scandalous Rejection of My Hasidic Roots

The TOS cover below is Copyright © The Objective Standard. A print or electronic copy can be purchased at:

theobjectivestandard.com

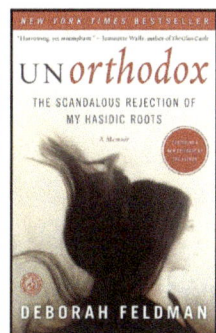

Books written by the women portrayed in Jon Wos' cover painting.

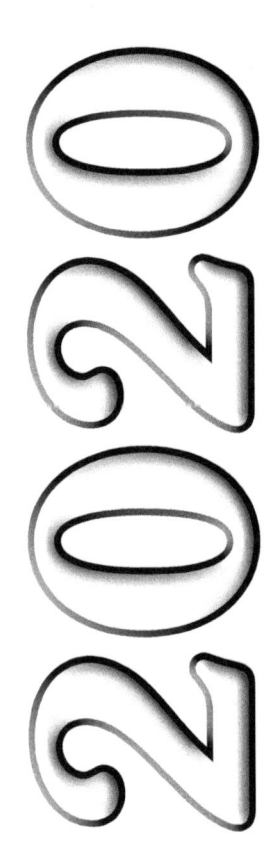

2020

The Plymouth Review Current
TAKING YOU PLACES WORTH SEEING
Volume 9 • Issue 2 • January 2020

FREE!

The Publication that respects your intelligence.

Local Dining • Camp Haven, Sheboygan
Recycling • Fantastic Movies • Dessert

January
2020

Cover photo: Dessert at Alinea
Great Movies This Month
PulpArtists by David Saunders: J. Allen St. John
SCHRC book reviewed: *Camp Haven, Sheboygan County's Anti-Aircraft Training Base*
Ask a Science Teacher by Larry Scheckel: Are There Scientific Achievements that Are Overlooked and Didn't Get a Lot of Attention?
Restaurant of the Month by Melissa Niedfeldt: Turner Hall, Plymouth
The World's Recycling System Is Falling Apart. What's Going On? by Walter Donway, FEE.org
The Alinea Experience
New Year's Eve Dinner at the Blind Horse

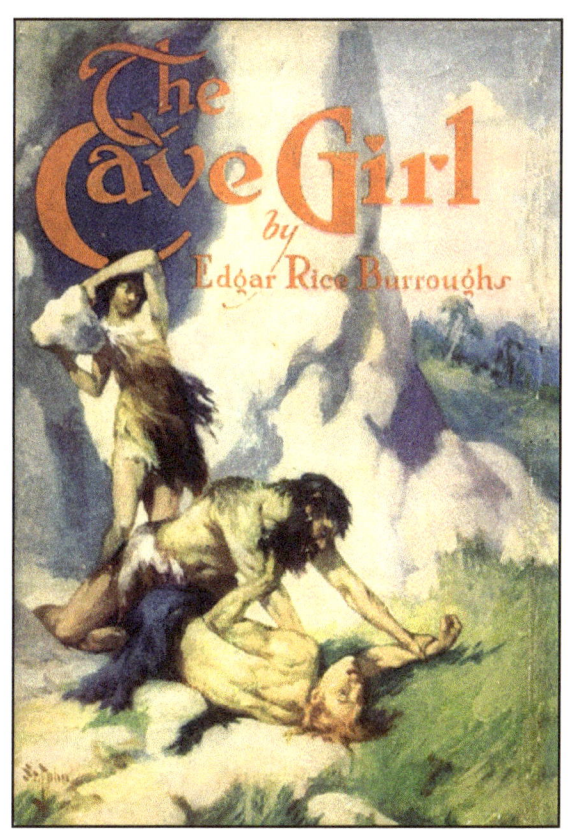

J. Allen St. John did many illustrations for books and stories by Edgar Rice Burroughs (creator of Tarzan).

J. Allen St. John: Burroughs Illustrator

(1872-1957)

James Allen St. John was born October 1, 1872 in Chicago. His friends called him "Jim St. John." His father, Dr. Jospehus Allen St. John, was born 1831 in East Hubbarston, Vermont. The St. John family moved to Janesville, Wisconsin in 1837, where they were among the first settlers in the region. They worked a family farm and eventually sent their son Josephus to college, where he studied Allopathic Medicine and became a physician. The artist's mother, Susan Hely, was born 1834 in Ireland. Her father Hilliard Hely (1800-1858) had been a portrait painter and graduate of Dublin's Trinity College. In 1937 her family moved to America and also settled in Janesville, Wisconsin, where they also worked a family farm. In his spare time Susan Hely's father painted portraits and taught his daughter to paint, but she yearned for academic art training.

In 1859 her older brother, George Hely, married Eliza St. John, the older sister of Josephus St. John. That same year Susan and Josephus also married. By 1870 they had moved to Chicago and lived at 311 22nd Street, where Josephus had a private medical practice and Susan attended the Art Institute of Chicago.

The artist's mother was a free spirit. She loved art school and enjoyed the company of Bohemians. She invited two women artists to board at their home. According to the artist, "My first recollections are of my mother's art studio and the magic way the eyes of her portraits followed me as I walked about the place."

In 1880 his mother left his father and moved to Paris to study at the Ecole des Beaux-Arts. She brought her eight-year-old son. They lived in Europe for three years, where visits to the great museums made him want to become a painter.

In 1883 at the age of eleven he and his mother returned to America. She decided to continue her studies at the National Academy of Design in New York City, so his supportive father closed up shop in Chicago and moved to a Manhattan townhouse at 231 West 69th Street, where he opened a new medical practice and their son attended public school.

By 1877 his mother completed her training and opened her own portrait studio in the family home.

In 1888 James Allen St. John quit school after completing the eight grade. At that time this was the most common practice. Although he was privileged to attend prep school and ivy league college, he preferred to become an artist. He did not want to enter the work force and he rejected his father's offer to finance his own trading company.

In 1888 at the age of sixteen he left NYC and moved to California to live with his wealthy uncle George Hely, Aunt Eliza St. John Hely, and his three cousins, James, Guy, and Levi St. John Hely, on their two-thousand acre grain and livestock ranch in San Joaquin Valley of Southern California. There he painted landscapes and studied with Eugene Torrey (1862-1930), an acquaintance of his mother's from the Ecole des Beaux-Arts, who was based in Los Angeles as a landscape painter.

In 1891 at the age of nineteen he returned to NYC to live with his parents and study with William Merritt Chase (1849-1916) at the Art Students league.

His first published illustrations were for *The New York Herald* in 1898, where he continued to work for several years. This exposure led to illustrating several novels.

In 1901 his parents moved back to Chicago, so he remained in NYC and opened his own art studio at 393 Eighth Avenue, near 30th Street,

A common theme this artist was assigned: Beautiful women in a savage environment.

just two blocks south of Pennsylvania Station.

By 1902 at age thirty he was an established illustrator, landscape painter, and portrait artist in NYC.

In 1903 his father became ill, so he closed his art studio and moved back to Chicago to live with his parents and help his mother care for his father.

On April 19, 1904 his father died in Chicago at the age of seventy-two.

He began to work as a commercial artist for publishers in the Chicago mid-western region. He illustrated books, newspapers and magazines. In 1904 he illustrated *The Face in the Pool* for A. C. McClurg Company of Chicago, which led to his important association with this publisher.

He met Ellen May Munger while learning to type at a secretarial school. She was born July 21, 1884 in Illinois. They married on November 11, 1905.

In 1908 at the age of 36 he returned to Paris, France, with his wife, where he studied for two year at the Academie Julian.

In 1910 he and his wife returned to Chicago and lived with his widowed mother. On October 25, 1913 Susan Hely St. John died at the age of seventy-nine.

In 1913 he and his wife moved to 3 East Ontario Street in Chicago. This remarkable three-story building, known as "The Tree Studio," was designed with living and working areas for resident artists. The St. Johns lived on the ground floor, which also included a picturesque private garden.

In 1915 he illustrated chapter headings for The Return of Tarzan by Edgar Rice Burroughs for McClurg Publishing. The dust-jacket was painted by N. C. Wyeth. In 1916 he drew the story illustrations as well as the dust-jacket cover for *The Beasts of Tarzan*. This was the first of many painted covers for Tarzan books, for which the artist is most renowned.

In 1917 he began to teach Painting and Illustration classes at the Art Institute of Chicago. He continued to teach for the rest of his life.

In 1917 at the age of forty-six he was too old to serve in The Great War. He produced several patriotic posters for recruitment and Liberty Bonds to support the war effort.

In the 1920s he illustrated

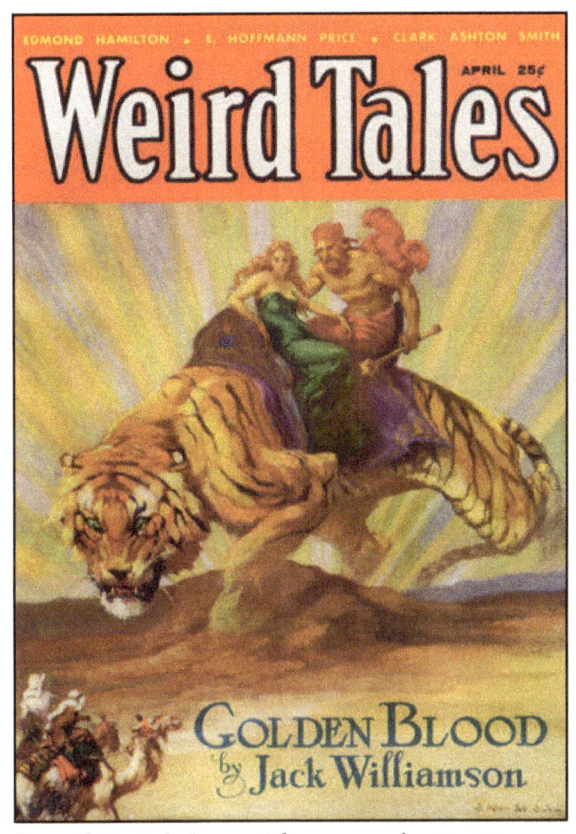

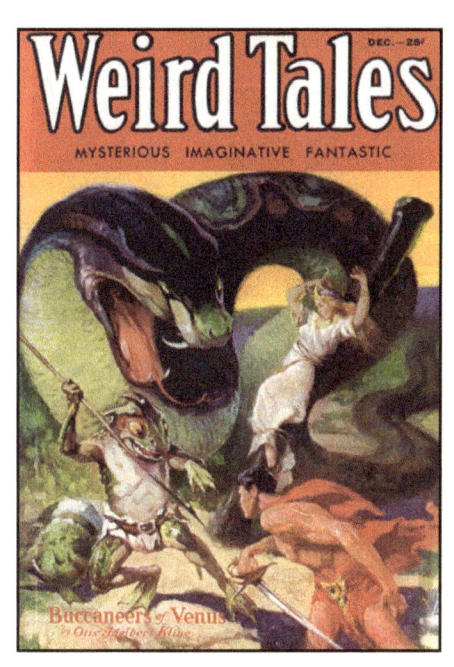

One of St. John's most famous pulp covers.

— HA.com

This 1932 issue features the first published Conan the Barbarian story, written by Robert E. Howard.

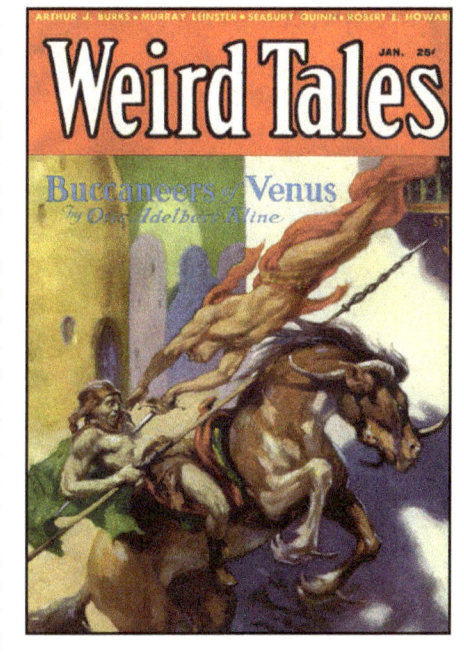

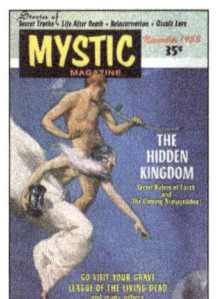

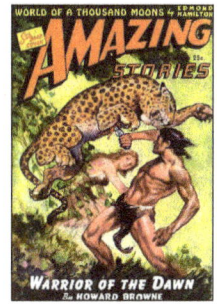

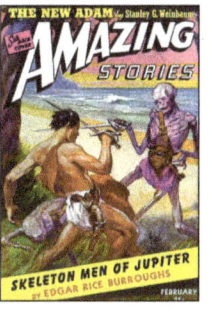

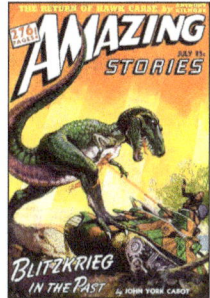

stories for many of the top magazines, such as *Colliers, The Rotarian,* and *Liberty.* He also painted covers for *The Green Book, The Red Book* and *Blue Book.*

In 1928 he taught a painting class at the Businessmen's Art Association in Chicago, which was a private club for professional artists that worked for newspapers and advertising, but wanted to hone their skills, work from nude models, and enjoy weekend outings to paint landscapes and socialize with other professional artists.

During the years of the Great Depression he worked for *Boy's World, Amazing Stories, Fantastic Adventures, Magic Carpet* and *Weird Tales.*

In 1942 at the age of seventy he was too old for draft registration during WWII.

In the 1940s and the 1950s he worked for *Amazing Stories, Fantastic Adventures, Fate, Other Worlds,* and *Mystic Magazine.*

In the 1950s he taught Life Class and Illustration at the American Academy of Art in Chicago.

J. Allen St. John died at age eighty-four in Chicago on May 23, 1957.

© David Saunders 2012

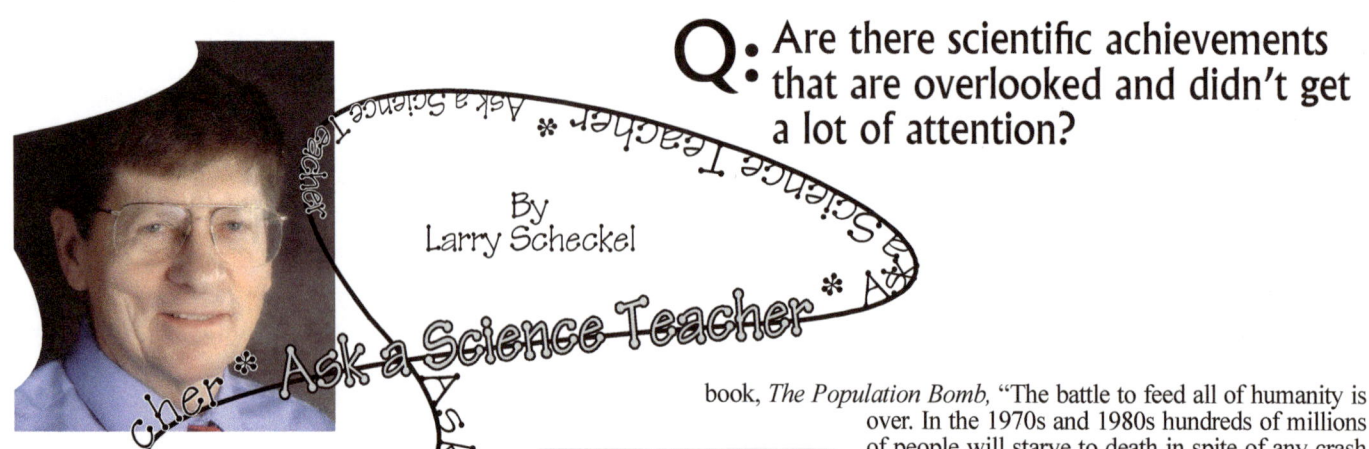

Ask a Science Teacher
By Larry Scheckel

Q: Are there scientific achievements that are overlooked and didn't get a lot of attention?

A: There are men that are responsible for taking lives, and those that are known for saving lives. Hitler, Mussolini, Tojo, Stalin, and Pol Pot are guilty of killing and destroying millions of humans. They are well known, filling the pages of history books.

Some people that save lives get a lot of ink in the history books. Edward Jenner, an English physician and scientist, pioneered the smallpox vaccine, and is called the "father of immunology." Louis Pasteur, building on the work of Jenner, developed a food processing technique, pasteurization, where bacteria are destroyed by heating liquids and allowing them to cool. He was prominent in developing the germ theory that gave us vaccinations for anthrax and rabies. Dr. Jonas Salk developed the polio vaccine. Mother Teresa, Catholic nun, founded the Missionaries of Charity, which has 5,000 sisters active in 133 countries and runs soup kitchens, dispensaries, orphanages, schools, and hospices.

Norman Borlaug's name is perhaps not as well-known as Jenner's or Salk's. But he saved more lives than any other human being, a reportedly one billion people. A plant breeder and biologist, Borlaug was born in 1914 at Cresco, Iowa. He has been called "the Father of the Green Revolution" and solved the problem of world hunger. He spent the majority of his life in developing countries of Mexico, Pakistan, India, China, and regions of Africa.

Borlaug received the Nobel Peace Prize in 1970 in recognition of his work in reversing the chronic food shortages suffered by India and Pakistan in the 1960s. Working in Mexico, Borlaug and his team developed a breed of dwarf wheat that resisted a wide variety of pests and diseases, wheat that produced two to three times more grain than traditional varieties.

In the mid1960s, mass starvation was predicted in India after two successive droughts. Biologist Paul Ehrlich wrote in his best-selling book, *The Population Bomb,* "The battle to feed all of humanity is over. In the 1970s and 1980s hundreds of millions of people will starve to death in spite of any crash programs embarked upon now."

Borlaug bred wheat that had shorter, but thicker stalks or stems that could support larger seed heads. The shorter stalks did not have to compete as much for sunlight, so a farmer could have more plants per acre. Yields increased by two, three, and even four times. In Mexico, the harvest was six times larger in 1963 than it was in 1944 when he arrived. Borlaug's team also developed wheat varieties that were adapted to tropical climates.

Pakistan doubled its wheat production in just five years. By 1974 India was self-sufficient in the production of wheat. Borlaug went on to develop a wide variety of rice plants that produced outstanding yields.

Public Domain photo of Norman Borlaug, taken in 2004 by Ben Zinner, USAID

There may be a lesson here. Paul Ehrlich was just one of many scientists who predicted mass starvation, even extinction, due to over-population. We see the same gloom-and-doom predictions from some scientists and politicians on climate change. Yes, global warming could turn out to be a huge problem, but one never knows exactly what the future holds.

And you never know what can inspire a person to make contributions to mankind. At age 21, Norman Borlaug took a job as leader of a CCC (Civilian Conservation Corps) group. He needed a job to finance his college education. Many of the people working for him were starving. "I saw how food changed them. All of this left scars on me."

Borlaug was not without his critics. Some environmentalists opposed genetic crossbreeding to be unnatural or having negative results. Borlaug dismissed these environmental lobbyists. "They've never experienced the physical sensation of hunger. They do their lobbying from comfortable office suites in Washington or Brussels."

Borlaug met his future wife while waiting on tables at a coffee shop when in college. They had three children, one dying a few days after birth due to spina bifida. His wife died in 2007 following a fall. Borlaug died in 2009 of lymphoma in Dallas at age 95. They were married for 69 years.

An estimated one billion lives saved. That's a quite a legacy.

When editing A Wisconsin Harvest Vol. II, Your Editor included an article about Norman Borlaug, written by Audra Hilse. Paul Ehrlich continues to make ludicrous doomsday predictions totally divorced from reality, which are repeated uncritically and with religious fervor.

The Alinea Experience

by Rodney Schroeter
Editor, The Plymouth Review Current

The Uber driver pulled up to the curb. She couldn't get directly in front of 1723 North Halsted Street, in the Lincoln Park section of Chicago, but assured us it was only a building or two up.

I'd read online comments that it was hard to find where to enter the place. I found a door, reached for the handle, but it opened before I could touch it.

"Alinea?" I asked.

"That's right," came the answer. "Welcome to Alinea."

In a cramped entryway, well-dressed staff members took our coats and our names, confirming our reservation.

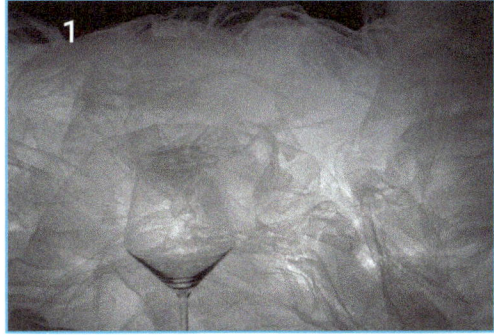

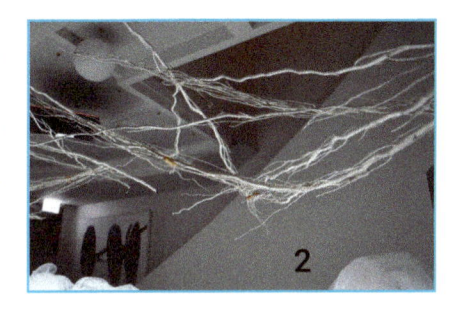

* * *

Months before, Kathryn and I had planned to spend a few days in Chicago. Researching the restaurants, I discovered the only Michelin-rated, 3-star establishment to be Alinea, headed by chef Grant Achatz.

Ah ha! I'd heard that name before. Two chefs I've talked to in Sheboygan County have named him as a great influence on their careers.

Further research revealed Alinea to be on several "best of" lists. In fall of 2006, Gourmet magazine named it the best restaurant in America. Elite Traveler named it number one on its list of Top 100 Restaurants in The World for 2011 through 2016, and again in 2018.

Two things about Alinea are very different from typical restaurants.

First is getting a reservation. Most places, you call up a few days before and make the reservation. Heck, lots of places you just walk into and pretend to apologize for not making a reservation.

Reservations at Alinea could only be made online. For a given month, reservations opened up two months before, on the 15th of the month, at 11 a.m.

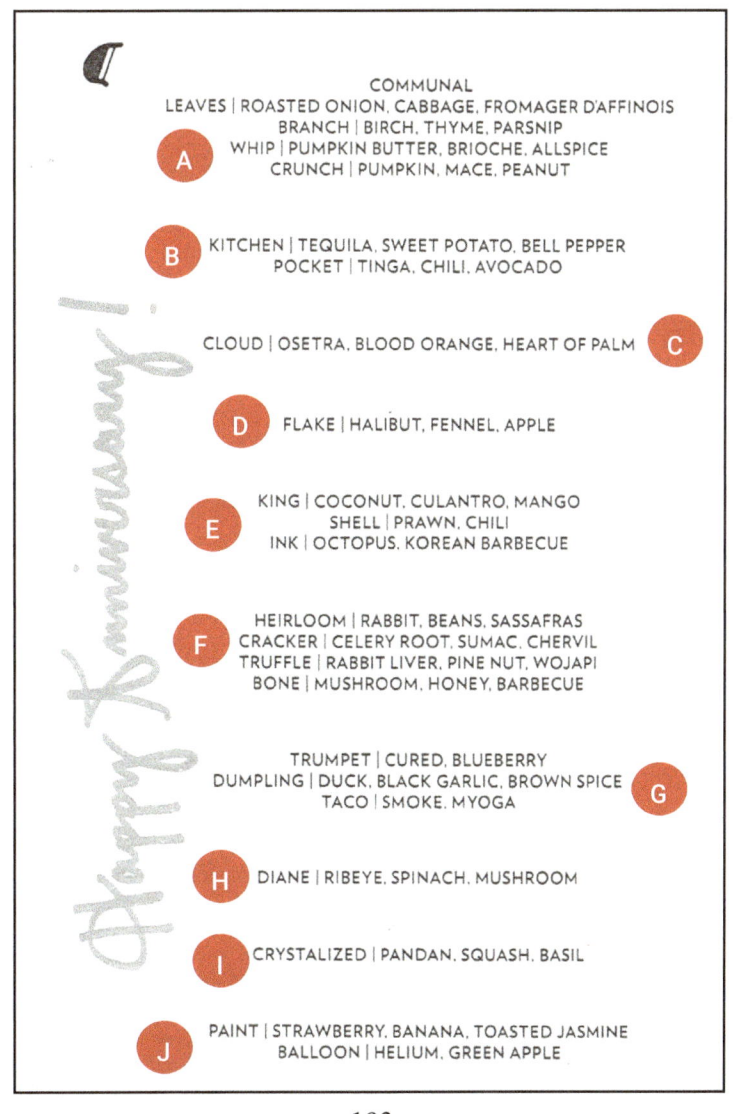

As 11 a.m. approached on September 15, I refreshed my browser every few seconds. When the month of November became active (turning from unclickable gray to clickable black), I quickly made the reservation for Monday, November 25, for myself and Kathryn.

Speed was essential. We'd planned this trip months in advance, so I was able to "practice" on the 15th of June, July, and August. Speed was important, because there is limited seating in the restaurant's section I wanted, and the entire month is booked up for tables of two within minutes of 11 a.m.

The second different thing about Alinea: You don't receive a menu. You don't tell them what you'd like to eat. The kitchen staff decides all of that.

I think that's just great! But Kathryn—well, she's just not as omnivorous as I am. Her agreement to accompany me on this culinary adventure took a lot of courage on her part.

* * *

The Gallery portion of Alinea held 18 people. We were all seated at a very long table. That surprised me (which is good, because Alinea prides itself on the element of surprise). The table was covered with a white tablecloth. In the center, white lace hid people across from us. (1) (Numbers refer to photos.)

A series of interlocked twigs hung above the table. (2) Little motors gave them a slight movement. Two food items were already in

193

place, but we were asked not to eat them, yet. One bite-sized item rested on a stone (3). The other looked like a bowl of dried, paper-thin leaves (4).

Everyone was present for the 5 p.m. meal/experience. (There would be another group at 9 p.m.)

A soft, whispery sound, as of a wintry wind blowing across a snow-covered field, arose behind me. Servers poured warm broth into the bowl with the paper-thin leaves; these dissolved and became a soup.

Diners were directed to add one more item to the assembly before them. Each of us reached up to the moving twigs and picked out a small, dark item. This was a rolled, dried parsnip (plainly visible, once you know to look for them, in photo 2).

Several servers marched into the room. They poured a liquid into tall glass bottles which stood amidst the frilly, white lace. Fog erupted from each bottle (5). The arctic wind sound blew more loudly. Cool fog settled over everything and everyone, with a potent, dizzyingly fragrant aroma of—what? Licorice? Root beer? (Or, perhaps...? Another dish, described in a book about Alinea and its chef, mentioned "vanilla-scented burdock root, sassafras root." Could that have been it?)

This was section (A) on the menu. (We received printed menus at the end of the meal. The letters have been added by Your Editor.)

When we'd finished those items, all 18 diners were then invited into the kitchen for a special drink. We lined up along a metal table. Atop a wooden block rested our next course. (6, 7). We spent five, maybe ten minutes in the kitchen, watching drinks containing sweet potato and red bell pepper being prepared, then sipping them (mine and Kathryn's minus the alcohol) and eating our course composed of tinga, chili, and avocado. I took a good look around the kitchen and saw a tray full of a later course (8).

This was section (B) on the menu.

Diners were asked to return to the dining room, where—

—Surprise! The long cloth-covered communal table was gone—or, more likely, disassembled into the individual tables we were now seated at. Some tables had two diners (those went the quickest when reservations opened); some had four.

Kathryn, who'd worked as an operating room nurse for some years, drew her fingertips along the table's polished metal surface. It reminded her of a sterile surgery table. I'd read how Grant Achatz did not want table cloths on his restaurant's tables.

Next was a dish with osetra caviar, blood orange, and heart of palm (9) (C).

Then halibut, fennel, and apple (10) (D).

Neither of us are big wine drinkers. I know a little something about food, but about wine I'm pretty ignorant. A server asked if we wanted some drinks. I took a ginger beer (non-alcoholic); Kathryn had an iced tea. She liked the tea, but found the bent, stainless-steel straw (11) quite entertaining, and couldn't resist telling the server that it resembled a surgical suction device. The server said they are sterilized and re-used.

Restaurants serving chef-chosen tasting menus like this often serve several courses together, if they represent a theme. We next had three shellfish items (E).

On a glass crab, which servers said had been designed exclusively for Alinea, was a course composed of coconut, culantro (no, not cilantro), and mango (12).

We had octopus, Korean barbecue style (13).

From glass seashells (also designed for Alinea) (14), one sipped a shellfish soup.

The next four courses contained rabbit (F). Alas! The quality of these photos are unworthy of the printed page. (And those with sharp eyes will see that some that are used here, are not so sharp. I did what I could in the subdued light.)

But Kathryn again perked up at a tool placed on our table (15). This, she explained to me, was a bayonet forceps, so-called for obvious reasons. She picked it up and demonstrated the proper technique of holding it.

When a server used the forceps to pick up an item, he fumbled slightly with it.

"That wouldn't have happened, if you'd held the bayonet forceps properly," Kathryn told him, in a tone developed after years as a nursing instructor—a tone carrying gentle yet firm guidance, without a shred of condemnation.

He was all too happy for her to demonstrate the correct procedure, which she explained was how it was done in the operating room, etc., etc., etc., and he gratefully gave every indication that he would hold and operate it that way henceforth.

The next three courses (G) included trumpet mushroom and duck (16, 17). Set in the table's center was an arrangement of smoking oak leaves (18), one more example of a course's taste being complemented, enhanced, by a fragrance.

A small cooking station was brought into the room (19, H), where a chef prepared a ribeye, from which a portion was cut for each diner (20, 21).

Our pre-dessert course (I) contained pandan (a southeast Asian plant), squash, and basil (22).

Two more desserts followed (J). The main attraction was a presentation that can be seen online and on the Netflix program mentioned elsewhere.

A plastic sheet was placed on each table. Accompanied by jazzy music, a server at each table spooned out sauces, dropped powder, and placed cakelets on the plastic, creating a visually dazzling work of abstraction (see cover) which we scraped up with spoons.

Ah, but wait! The meal was not yet complete. One more dessert, something we'd also seen on Netflix. Sugar cooked correctly can be made pliable. Inject helium into this plastic substance, and you can create a balloon, which each diner received (23) (this photo is of a nearby table). We were warned to remove our glasses, and to be careful to hold it away from clothes, etc., when it popped. I saw/heard that a diner at another table possessed the skill required to pierce the balloon and inhale its contents; he squeaked out a few helium-enhanced words.

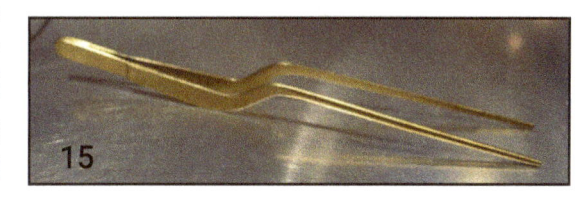

My balloon popped and instantly wrapped around the back of my hand.

Warm, moist wash cloths were distributed at tables and used by many.

Back out in the entrance, getting and donning

our coats, being handed my copy of the Alinea cookbook, Kathryn entering an Uber request on her phone, a server told me, "I hope we'll see you again!"

I don't know why, but his question surprised me.

But the thought shouldn't have surprised me at all. I confidently answered:

"I think you will."

Chef Achatz' Biggest Challenge

If you see any documentaries (I'll recommend Netflix' "Chef's Table") or read any books (a good one is "Life on the Line") about Grant Achatz, the prime creative mover behind Alinea, there's something you'll soon learn about him, so you might as well hear it here first.

In 2007, seeing a doctor about a spot on his tongue that had become increasingly painful, he was told he had stage 4 cancer.

Achatz thought that didn't sound too bad, as he assumed there were ten stages of cancer. However, stage 4 was pretty much the End of the Line, on that One-Way Journey we are all taking.

But Achatz is still with us. Alinea (and his other restaurant, Next, also in Chicago) are doing well.

Books / Videos About Grant Achatz and Alinea

Life, on the Line: A Chef's Story of Chasing Greatness, Facing Death, and Redefining the Way We Eat
by Grant Achatz and Nick Kokonas
2012

Kokonas is the entrepreneur who saw great potential in the talent of Chef Achatz. He put up the money for Achatz to start Alinea. (He also invented a restaurant reservation app, Tock, which is now used by many restaurants, including the Bartolotta restaurants in the Milwaukee area.)

The two authors document Achatz' career; creation of Alinea; and the chef's encounter with cancer.

Grant Achatz: The Remarkable Rise of America's Most Celebrated Young Chef, by the Chicago Tribune Staff

Available only as an e-book: Barnes & Noble Nook and Amazon Kindle, 2012

Newspaper articles document Achatz' career and Alinea's rise to fame.

Alinea, by Grant Achatz, 2008

A cook book. Yes, you, too, can create 3-star cuisine. All the instructions are here. And all the equipment, such as liquid nitrogen. Not for the faint of heart. Most (like myself) will be content to peruse this book as spectators. Superb photography and super-interesting reading.

Spinning Plates
DVD. Director: Joseph Levy

Three very different restaurants, including Alinea, are profiled. The final statement by Achatz serves to exhilaratingly integrate the three diverse restaurants, and is the perfect summary of the entire documentary.

Chef's Table
Netflix series. Season 2, Episode 1. Profiles Achatz and Alinea.

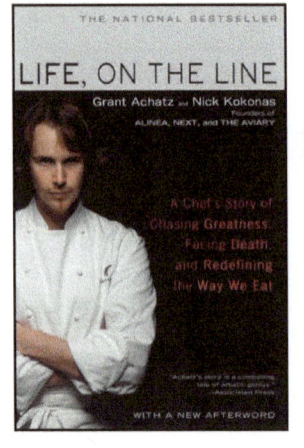

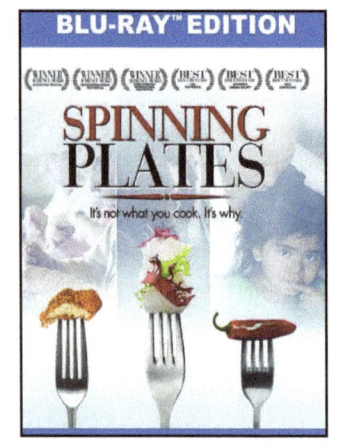

The Current
Plymouth Review
TAKING YOU PLACES WORTH SEEING
Volume 9 • Issue 3 • February 2020

FREE!

The publication that respects your intelligence

Fun Movies • Lippers Mills • Nautical Adventure
Scientific Discoveries • French Bread • Sweet Basil • Twilight

February 2020

Cover photo: Your Editor's Front Yard
Great Movies This Month
PulpArtists by David Saunders: Paul Strayer
SCHRC book reviewed: *Lippers Mills: A History*; Starting life over in a foreign land
Ask a Science Teacher by Larry Scheckel: What Is a Notable Science Discovery that Was Made by Accident?
Restaurant of the Month by Melissa Niedfeldt: Sweet Basil, Plymouth
Dreaming of Baking by Myra Stokdyk Eischen: French Herb Bread
How Cognitive Bias Destroyed the Livelihood of California's Gig Workers, by Barry Brownstein, FEE.org
"Let Them Eat Whole Foods": The Appalling Elitism of Dollar Store Bans, by Laura Williams, FEE.org
The First Pop! at the Blind Horse

Painting by Paul Strayer. — HA.com

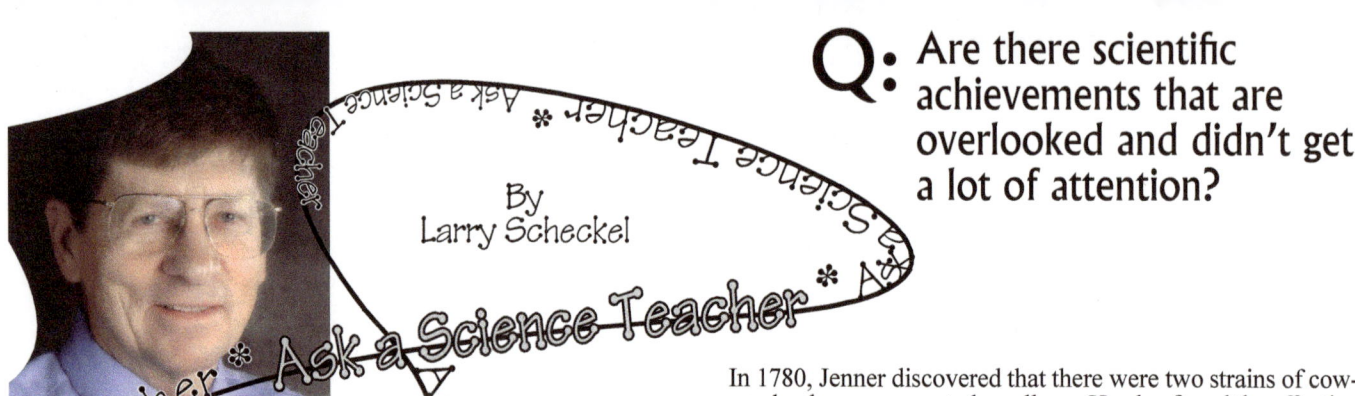

Ask a Science Teacher

By Larry Scheckel

Q: Are there scientific achievements that are overlooked and didn't get a lot of attention?

A: Penicillin, sulfanilamide, and other bacteria-killing drugs have saved millions of lives. More lives have been saved from disease by the preventative action of vaccination. Vaccination was an accidental discovery by Edward Jenner.

One of the great scourges of mankind was smallpox. Only the plague and malaria have killed as many people as smallpox. Plague was eventually controlled in developed counties by sanitation, after the disease was known to be spread by fleas on rats. Malaria was subdued by quinine and insecticides that eliminated mosquitoes.

Edward Jenner is credited with presenting to the world a vaccine that saved millions of people from a horrible death due to smallpox and many more millions from frightful disfigurement.

Edward Jenner was born in Gloucestershire, England in 1749. He was raised by an older brother after his father died when he was six. Jenner liked medical science and studied under two famous doctors. When he was 19 years old, a milkmaid told him that she couldn't get smallpox because she had had cowpox. Milkmaids often caught cowpox through exposure to infected cows.

That idea was generally known at the time. Even when a person helped to care for smallpox victims, somehow, it gave them immunity from smallpox. The idea of inoculating patients with cowpox in order to prevent them from contracting the more deadly smallpox occurred to Jenner.

Smallpox was caused by a virus, with symptoms occurring about 2 weeks after infection. It brought delirium, bleeding, malaise, severe headache, and raised pink rashes that turned into sores. Arthritis, brain swelling, eye infections, blindness, fluid-filled blisters, and death resulted. If a person did survive smallpox, he bore scars and pock marks for life and had to live with many health complications. Smallpox was not pleasant.

In 1780, Jenner discovered that there were two strains of cowpox and only one prevented smallpox. He also found the effective form of cowpox protected only when contacted at a particular stage of the disease.

Smallpox goes way back to the Pharaohs of Egypt. By Jenner's time, smallpox was killing 400,000 people per year in Europe. Half of all people who got smallpox died, but the death rate among children was about 80 percent. Europeans brought smallpox with them to the New World. Tribes of Native Americans were severely reduced in number, even wiped out, as they had no natural immunity to the disease.

Cowpox is in the same family of viruses as smallpox, but much less virulent. In May 1797, Jenner drew the contents of a blister on a milkmaid's hand, and injected it into 8 year old James Phipps. In the following July, Jenner carefully injected smallpox into the boy. He did not develop the disease. Jenner went on to inoculate 23 people, none of whom came down with smallpox.

In 2002, Jenner was named in BBC's list of the 100 Greatest Britons. He is often called the father of immunology, and his work is said to have "saved more lives than the work of any other human."

Inoculation or vaccination just might have saved the American Revolution. George Washington watched many of his soldiers die during the 1777-1778 winter at Valley Forge, Pennsylvania. Of his 11,000 troops, 2,500 died of disease and exposure. Then he remembered his wife describing what she had heard about inoculation.

He ordered his medics to cut a small wound in a healthy soldier's arm, and then smear or rub some of the contents from the sores of the pox developed by an infected soldier. It was a crude method, but it worked. From then on, only one in fifty died of smallpox. What Jenner proved was that a deadened or weakened virus placed into a healthy human could give protection against a virus.

Today, a long list of diseases is controlled by vaccination; polio, anthrax, hepatitis, measles, mumps, rubella, tetanus, tuberculosis, diphtheria, yellow fever, rabies, typhoid, and rubella (German Measles).

As a former farm boy, I must give credit to the cow. The word "vaccination" comes from "vaca," the Latin work for "cow."

David Saunders'
pulpartists.com

PAUL STRAYER:
OUTDOOR ADVENTURE ARTIST

(1886-1981)

Paul Strayer was born on January 30, 1886 in Park Ridge, Illinois. His father, Thomas Allison Strayer, was born in 1859 in Ohio. His mother, Grace Louisa Cone, was born in 1862 in Chicago. His parents married in 1883 and had two children, Bessie Strayer (b. 1884) and Paul Strayer (b. 1886). The father was the Business Manager of *The Chicago Times* newspaper. His mother was from a prominent American family.

In 1888, when the artist was age two, his father died at the age of twenty-nine. After this tragic death, the mother raised her two infant children.

In June of 1902, Paul Strayer completed the tenth grade of high school at the age of sixteen, after which he entered the work force as a staff artist at his father's newspaper, *The Chicago Times*. In the evening he attended the Art Institute of Chicago, where he studied with John H. Vanderpoel. While a student at the school he met Harvey Dunn and Howard Pyle (1853-1911). Strayer noted in his journal that Pyle had advised him to "keep your values close, and don't break up the masses with needless details."

On September 21, 1910 Paul Strayer visited and photographed the art studio of Howard Pyle in Wilmington, Delaware, where the artist was at work on the last of three murals, painted on canvas, six feet high by sixteen feet wide, for the Hudson County Court Hose in Jersey City, New Jersey. Howard Pyle was assisted by two of his students, Stanley Arthurs (1877-1950) and Frank Schoonover.

On November 11, 1911 Paul Strayer married Dollie Bernice Murray. She was born in 1881 in Chicago of Scottish English ancestry. The bride was age thirty and the groom was age twenty-five. She was a trained pianist. The newlyweds moved to 253 Ashland Avenue in the River Forest section of Chicago.

By 1917 Paul Strayer became a staff artist at the *Fort Dearborn Historical Magazine.*

On September 12, 1918 Paul Strayer registered with his local draft board, at which time he was recorded to be of medium height, slender build, with blue eyes and light brown hair. As a married man at the age of thirty-two, he was not selected for military service.

By 1919 Paul Strayer began to paint covers for pulp magazines, such as *Adventure* and *Sea Stories.*

On July 9, 1921 *The Green Bay Wisconsin Press-Gazette* reported that Paul Strayer and his wife had visited the Kellogg Public Library to inspect the historic murals by Howard Pyle, as research for designing his own historic scenes for the Chicago Industrial Pageant, as well as for the Green Bay Homecoming Celebration and Indian Pageant of 1921.

On December 18, 1922 *The Chicago Daily Tribune* reported the public was invited to attend a display of "Christmas Cheer for the Fort" by Paul Strayer at the Chicago Historical Society.

During the 1920s Paul Strayer painted pulp cover art for *Triple-X, West, Blue Book, Short Stories,* and *The Frontier.*

He also worked for slick magazines, such as *Woman's World, The American Boy,* and *Country Gentleman.*

Paul Strayer also illustrated adventure novels for book publishers, such as Houghton Mifflin, Rand McNally, and A. C. McClurg.

In 1928 the artist and his wife moved to a larger home they bought at 530 Ashland Avenue in the River Forest section of Chicago, where one large room became the art studio. The couple lived in this house for the rest of their lives.

In 1930 the artist's mother, Grace Louisa (Cone) Strayer, died at the age of sixty-eight.

In 1935 he illustrated "Tales Of India" by Rudyard Kipling for the Rand McNally publishing Company.

During WWII Paul Strayer was age fifty-seven, and too old for military service. According to *The Chicago Tribune* of October 18, 1942, Paul Strayer designed a signal card to be placed in the windows of homes that have tin cans awaiting collection by the Chicago Women's Volunteer Corps.

In the 1940s he illustrated advertising, calendars, and men's adventure magazines such as *Outdoorsman* and *Hunting & Fishing Magazine.*

In the 1950s Paul Strayer returned to his creative roots, and became

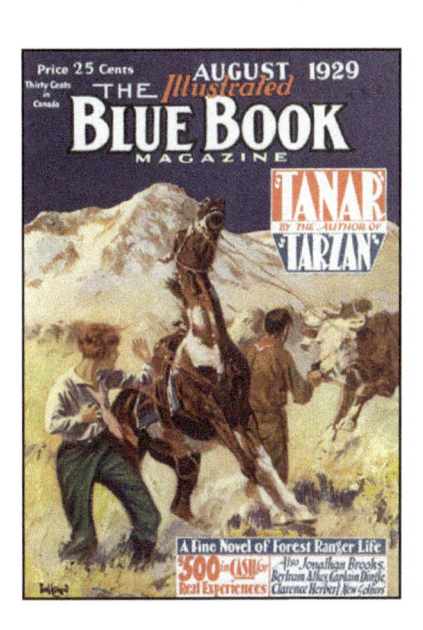

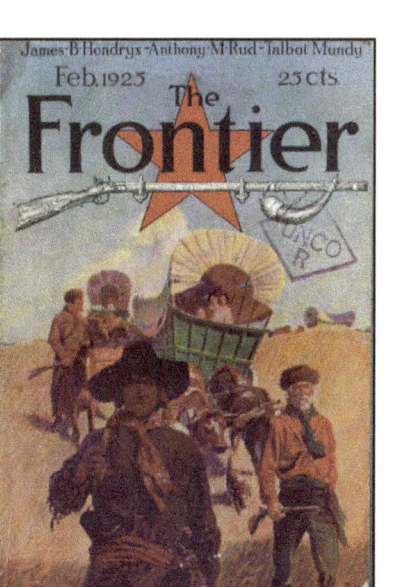

Sometimes, Your Editor is asked, "Why are pulps so interesting?" Instead of a long, verbal answer, this pulp cover says it all. Published in 1923, it was painted by Paul Strayer (the subject of this month's PulpArtists). For nearly a decade, Sea Stories carried superbly painted, story-telling covers like this one. All of Sea Stories' covers (and thousands of other pulp covers) can be found at philsp.com (where you'll find this issue's entire contents—stories, heading illustrations, poetry, sea facts, and ads). So... what story *does* this cover tell?

a top illustrator for *The Chicago Tribune Sunday Supplement Magazine*.

In 1958 the artist's wife, Dollie Bernice (Murray) Strayer, died at the age of seventy-seven at home in River Forest, IL. They had no children.

Paul Strayer died at the age of ninety-five at home in River Forest, IL, on February 1981.

© David Saunders 2018

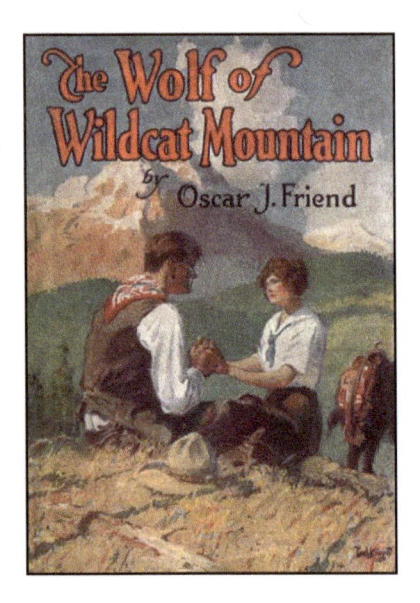

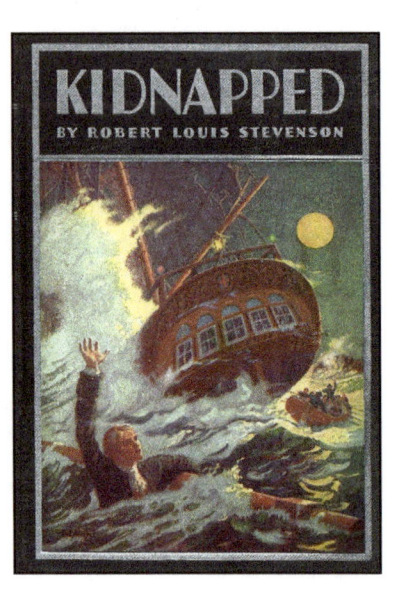

In many publishing firms, one or more art directors were responsible for setting the tone and standards for the covers of its publications. Art directors needed to find artists who could meet strict deadlines and handle the publication's themes. An art director might sometimes "typecast" an artist, thinking narrowly, "This one's good at creating dramatic ships at sea." Looking at the four corners of the globe (erh, that is, the four corners of this *page*), one might think Paul Strayer had been "typecast" as a nautical (but nice!) artist. But the other examples on this page demonstrate otherwise.

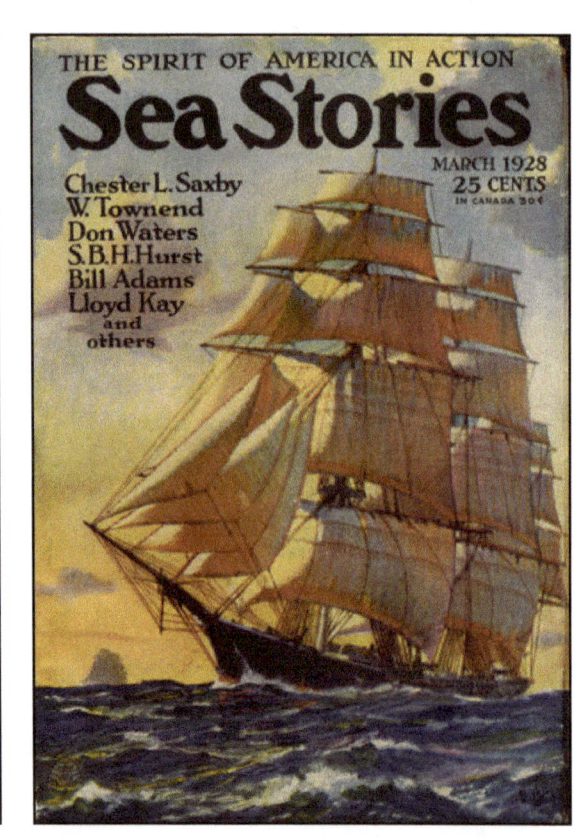

The Plymouth Review Current

Taking You Places Worth Seeing
Volume 9 • Issue 4 • March 2020

FREE!

The publication that respects your intelligence

Baseball Curves
Joe E. Brown
Sudoku
Miss Virginia
Akira Kurosawa
Crossword
Silent Movies in Sheboygan
Edd Cartier
Restaurant Review
Celtic Song
Heliocentrism

March 2020

Cover photo: Copernicus Statue, outside the Adler Planeterium in Chicago
Great Movies This Month
PulpArtists by David Saunders: Edd Cartier
Ask a Science Teacher by Larry Scheckel: How Can a Pitcher's Arm Be Injured by Throwing Curveballs and Sliders?
Restaurant of the Month by Melissa Niedfeldt: Seeboth Delicatessen
Dreaming of Baking by Myra Stokdyk Eischen: French Herb Bread
As They Were Meant to Be Seen
Miss Virginia Discusses Miss Virginia, by Virginia Walden Ford
Virginia Walden Ford, by Charlotte Hays
Miss Virginia and the Political Realities of Public-School Reform, by Samuel R. Staley

Copernicus sculptures at (left) Chicago (photo by Another Believer, used here under terms of Creative Commons) and (right) Warsaw, Poland (photo by Marek and Ewa Wojciechowscy, from their site, tripsoverpoland.pl).

David Saunders'
pulpartists.com

EDD CARTIER: UNKNOWN SHADOWS, ASTOUNDING SF

(1914-2008)

Edward Daniel Cartier was born August 1, 1914 in North Bergen, New Jersey. His father was Joseph Cartier, born 1883 in New York of French and German ancestry. His mother was Frances Cartier, born 1887 in New Jersey. They were married in 1907. They had four sons. The eldest, Joseph, was born in 1910, then Alfred was born in 1912, and Edward in 1914, and Vincent in 1919. His family of six lived at 104 Grand Avenue, along with his Uncle's family of four.

His father worked as a skilled toolmaker at a machine shop.

During prohibition, Joseph Cartier opened a lucrative speakeasy, which included decorative murals by his son. By the time Edward had graduated high school in 1933, Prohibition was repealed and his father had opened the legitimate *Cartier Saloon*.

Edward was fascinated by the art of Frederic Remington and Charlie Russell, so he decided to become an illustrator. He studied at Brooklyn's Pratt Institute, which at that time was a technical school that only offered a certificate of course completion. He took courses in drawing and commercial illustration. His painting teacher was Harold Winfield Scott. Cartier later recalled, "Harold Scott taught pictorial illustration, and through him I feel privileged to trace an unbroken

A collection of Cartier's work, published in 1977. The images in this book were clear and sharp, because they were reproduced from original pieces in the collection of publisher/collector Gerry de la Ree. de la Ree also published several books of work by Virgil Finlay; each image in those books were also reproduced from original art in his collection. – HA.com

Filling an awkward space and trying to be funny at the same time department:

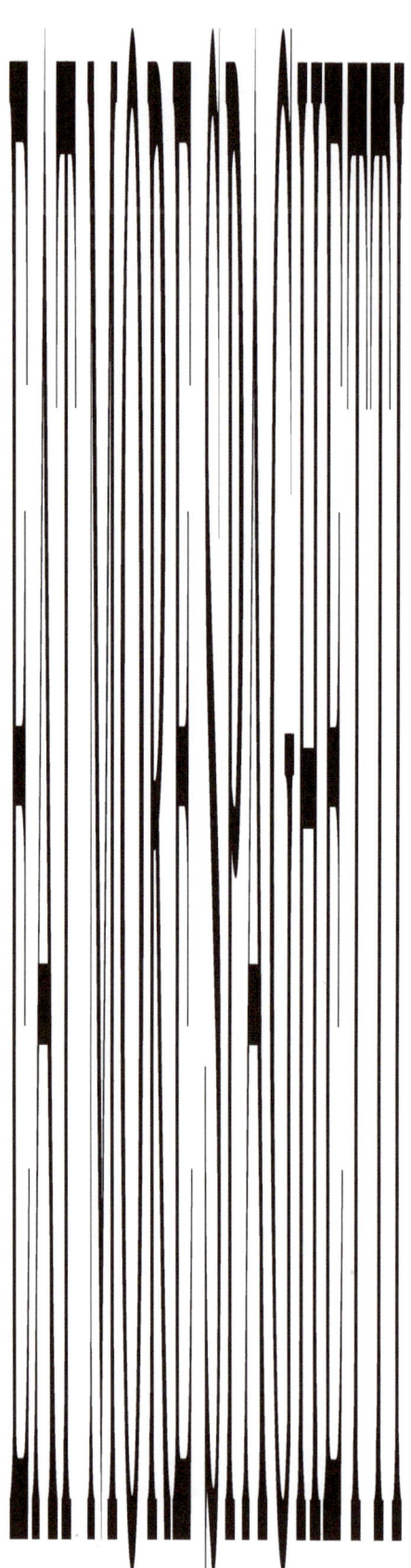

The above is a Public Service announcement

chain of art instruction back to Howard Pyle, the father of American illustration. Scott became my mentor and advisor." Another of his teachers was William James, a Street & Smith art director who gave Cartier his first professional assignments while he was still a student at Pratt.

In 1936 Cartier opened an art studio on the Upper West Side, which he shared with a fellow graduate of Pratt, Earl Mayan. His first published illustration appeared on his twenty-first birthday in the August 1st issue of *The Shadow* for Street & Smith. Cartier went on to draw over eight hundred illustrations for *The Shadow* magazine. "I began by doing a single illustration per week for Street & Smith pulps like *Wild West Weekly, The Wizard, The Whisperer, Movie Action,* and *Detective Story Magazine.* I was paid eight dollars for each drawing."

Besides interior story illustrations, Cartier also painted pulp covers for *Unknown, Astounding Science Fiction,* and *Unknown Fantasy Fiction.*

He married his wife Georgina in 1943 before reporting for Army duty. During WWII, Cartier fought in France and Germany. He was seriously wounded in the Battle of the Bulge.

After the war, he returned to illustrating, while also attending college courses at Pratt on the G. I. Bill. He received a BFA college degree in 1953.

During the 1950s Cartier became a prolific illustrator for science fiction pulps, such as *Planet Stories,* and *Astounding*, as well as for sci-fi digests, and paperbacks in the 1950s. He illustrated stories by Isaac Asimov, L. Ron Hubbard, John W. Campbell, and Robert A. Hienlein. Cartier was the main artist working for the publishers Fantasy Press and Gnome Press.

According to the artist, "I put a bit of humor into what I drew. I was even told at times that I put too much humor into drawing science fiction. It's a serious thing. When I started out doing science fiction, it was all kind of a weird thing."

Cartier eventually moved to Ramsey, New Jersey. In his later years, he suffered from Parkinson's disease.

Edd Cartier died at the age of ninety-four on December 25, 2008.

© David Saunders 2009

1946 Shadow pulp illustration. — HA.com

"Er, ah... [gosh, but you're a tall one] pardon me, but I think I took a wrong turn at that last fork... about 200 miles back... heh heh... and I kinda think I'm a little lost... I mean, I don't quite rightly know where I am... so do you think... can you tell me how to get back on the Interstate? Ah... OK... if you don't know, that's, that's fine... thanks anyway, just the same... This is a real nice place you have here, yeah, a *real* nice place. Well, thanks for... for *everything*, and... have a nice day!" — HA.com

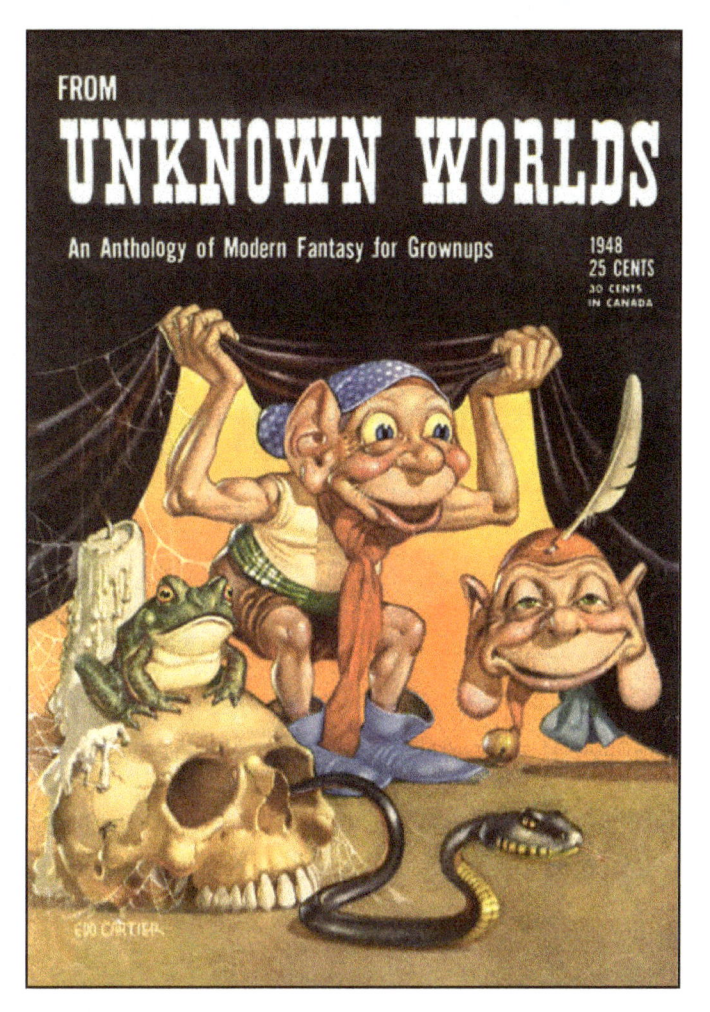

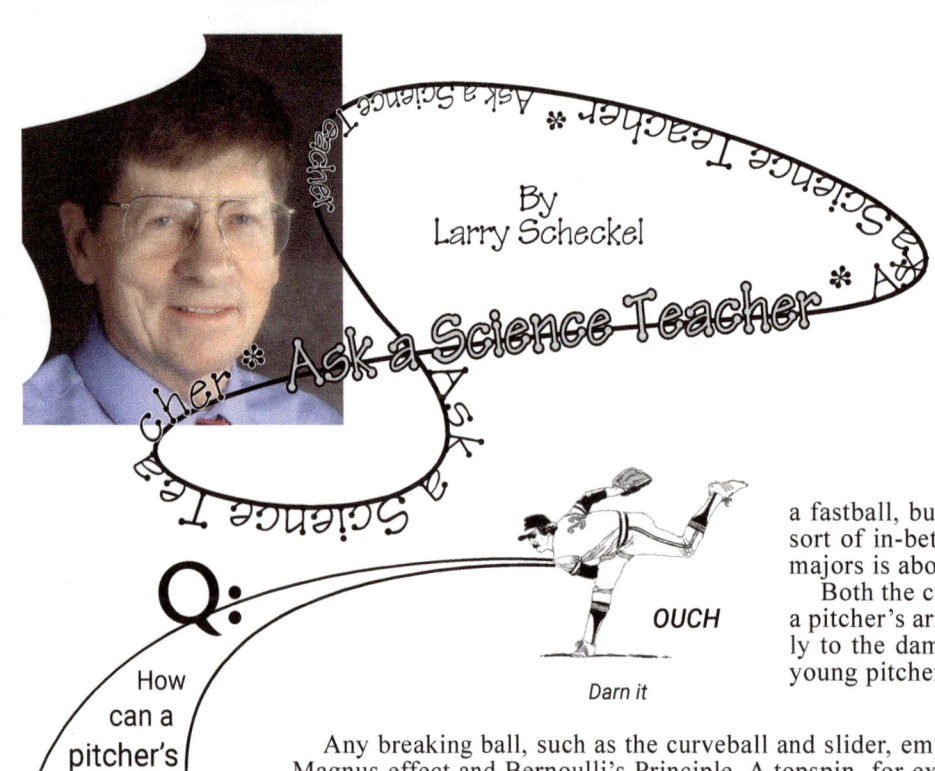

Ask a Science Teacher

By Larry Scheckel

Q: How can a pitcher's arm be injured by throwing curveballs and sliders?

A: A curveball is thrown with "top-spin." At the top of the throwing arc, a pitcher will snap the arm and wrist in a downward motion. The degree of break on the ball depends on how hard the pitcher can snap the throw and how much forward spin can be imparted on the ball. The harder the snap, the more the pitch will break downward. A typical curveball in the major leagues averages to about 77 mph.

A slider is a breaking fast ball that tails sideways and down as it moves through the batter's strike zone. The slider is thrown will less speed than a fastball, but with a greater speed than a curveball, sort of in-between speeds. The average slider in the majors is about 84 mph.

Both the curveball and the slider can take a toll on a pitcher's arm. Much attention has been paid recently to the damage that these two pitches can take on young pitchers' arms and shoulders.

Any breaking ball, such as the curveball and slider, employ the straight forward physics of the Magnus effect and Bernoulli's Principle. A topspin, for example, creates a higher pressure on the top of the ball which deflects it downward.

The ligaments, elbow, biceps, and forearm muscles take a beating. Throwing a curveball requires the pitcher to twist the wrist. It's like turning a doorknob hard while throwing. It puts a lot of torque on the elbow.

Throwing a slider is much like throwing a straight fastball. But the pitcher flicks his wrist inward just before the ball is released. The mechanics needed to throw a slider are more stringent than those necessary to execute a curveball. It requires a more violent arm motion. The ball is made to move to the side just as the batter is about to hit it. It's a wicked pitch that keeps batters awake at night.

A higher speed of air (or fluid) flow results in reduced pressure. The spinning of the baseball, toward the direction it's traveling, would deflect it downward. Similarly, the curve of an airplane's wing causes the air above it to move faster, creating lift. (The wing in this diagram would be moving from right to left.) — Image at left: Public domain image from Wikipedia. Right: from aviation.stackexchange.com. For more information, see "Bernoulli's Principle."

Overuse is the foremost cause of arm injuries to young baseball pitchers, whose muscles, ligaments, and bone are still developing. But throwing curveballs at any early age increases the risk, according to a huge study by the University of North Carolina.

Pitchers with a previous history of injury are five times at greater risks of elbow and shoulder injuries. The increase in risk is due to not getting enough rest, no medical treatment, such as icing, and a lack of recovery time.

In the old days, some 25 years ago, the number of innings a pitcher could pitch was discussed. These days, the conversation and rules center around the pitch count. Much criticism is reserved for the elite teams, the traveling, or all-star teams. These pitchers might be playing on one or two regular teams, but they go on the road on weekends. These teams often have different coaches from their regular teams. Most of the time the coaches are parents of one or two kids. And the kids want to play, of course, and they are not always up front about how many innings or pitches they threw during the week. Twenty percent of pitchers throwing for traveling teams report arm pain, the study revealed.

On the positive side, most parents and coaches realize the dangers of arm misuse and overuse. Many won't allow a Little League pitcher to throw breaking stuff. Many leagues put in a pitch count limit.

It even happens at the major league level. In early April, 2016 Dodger pitcher Ross Stripling had a no-hitter going into the eighth inning when Dodger manager Dave Roberts pulled him from the mound and put in a relief pitcher. Roberts received a lot of criticism, but Stripling's pitch count had reached 100; he'd never thrown more than 78 pitches in spring training; it was his first time ever pitching in the majors; and he missed the whole 2014 season undergoing elbow ligament repair through the Tommy Johns surgery.

Just imagine, he was the first pitcher since 1892 on his way to throwing a no-hitter in his major league debut. But out of the dugout comes "the hook." Manager Roberts had no apologies for taking Stripling out of the game, and most baseball people seemed to agree it was the prudent and right thing to do.

Manager Dave Roberts met the parents of pitcher Ross Stripling at their hotel earlier that day and left 21 tickets for friends and family. A few minutes after taking Stripling out of the game, Manager Roberts was thrown out of the game for arguing balls and strikes with the umpire. San Francisco went on to beat the Dodgers 3-2 in ten innings.

From Fan to Publisher

First Spider-Man Comic Leads to Book Projects

I've enjoyed reading comic books most of my life. I still do.

And it all started in Random Lake, the area where I grew up and went to grade school and high school.

The first comic book I remembers having was purchased by my mom at the Burmesch-Leider Variety Store (referred to simply, as I grew up, as "The Drug Store"). It was The Amazing Spider-Man #4. The year was 1963. I was 8 years old.

In that comic, Spider-Man fought The Sandman, a villain who could turn into sand. (He could, because he'd been on a sandy beach when a nuclear blast went off nearby. As long-time Marvel readers know, radiation and atomic bombs are like magic: Spider-Man gained his powers when bitten by a radioactive spider; Bruce Banner became The Hulk when bombarded by gamma rays; The Cobra took on characteristics of the radioactive snake that bit him; etc., etc., and more.)

Like most kids, I suppose, I read a comic book the same way I watched a TV show or movie—with no awareness of the people who put the story together. No thought of writers for comics or dramas; no concern for artists who drew comics; no interest in the names of actors bringing dramatic scripts to life.

Eventually, one realizes the work that one responds positively resulted from someone's efforts.

Some comics companies would not give their artists and writers credit. Carl Barks wrote and drew the Disney duck stories, including that of Donald, his three nephews, and his Uncle Scrooge McDuck, for well over twenty years, never once having his name attached to his published work. (But one fan did the research; discovered the writer/artist's identity; and a new career was launched for Barks, who went on to create oil paintings of the duck characters he drew for decades.)

Marvel, on the other hand, listed the creative team that produced each of their comics. Those early Spider-Man comics, for instance, were written by Stan Lee and drawn by Steve Ditko.

But it wasn't quite that simple. Over the years, the "Marvel method" of creating a comic story was revealed: The writer (usually Stan Lee) and artist would confer, coming up with a basic storyline for an issue. The artist would then break down the story into the allotted number of pages; and further break down each page into several panels. The artist would draw the story in pencil, and make notes as to what was going on. Those penciled pages would be given to the writer, who would write the dialogue. The dialogue was given to a letterer, who hand-lettered the dialogue on the page. (That method became obsolete when it became possible to combine computerized lettering with the image.)

The penciled and lettered pages would then be given to an inker, who would go over the penciled lines with pen and/or brush and ink. This step was needed because a solidly black line was needed for clear, sharp reproduction.

(Marvel once skipped the inking step in an early 1970s issue of Conan the Barbarian, because of time constraints. It wasn't a pretty sight.)

Sometimes, an inker could be the same person who drew the original pencils. Sometimes, it was another artist. This would make for some interesting artistic combinations and variations.

In later years, Ditko wrote about this "Marvel method" and made the point that listing Lee as writer and Ditko as artist was not accurate, especially when Ditko started creating new characters and deciding on his own what direction story events would take. Instead of merely "Drawn by," the credits soon read "Plotted and drawn by Steve Ditko."

But all of this was beyond my awareness in the 1960s. In fact, astounding as it seems to me now, I didn't even notice (at first) when Ditko stopped (plotting and) drawing Spider-Man. It took a few months before I got a sense of, "Hey, this just doesn't look the same."

What happened to Steve Ditko? There was no Internet to answer that. I wasn't connected to any fan news sources. An announcement in Marvel comics at the time simply said he'd decided "for personal reasons" to leave Marvel.

I soon discovered his work in comics of other publishers. In a 1967 issue of T.H.U.N.D.E.R. Agents, I discovered a story that seemed... the artwork looked like...

At this point, at age 12, I learned enough to distinguish between artistic styles, enough to identify the artist on this T.H.U.N.D.E.R. Agents story as Ditko.

I also discovered Ditko's work in several ghost-story comic titles.

Two years after I first read Atlas Shrugged, I learned that Ditko, like me, was interested in the philosophy of Ayn Rand. Some of his work, which he did on his own terms and copyrighted, dealt with sophisticated philosophical themes.

I continued to follow Ditko's career. One editor and writer Ditko worked with was Robin Snyder, who worked for several publishers. I started corresponding with Snyder over 30 years ago. In one of his letter columns, he mentioned a "fanzine" (fan magazine), Ditkomania. I

And here's the cover of the comic that started it all. The Amazing Spider-Man #4, from the summer of 1963. (It says "Sept." on the cover, but comics were post-dated by several months.) Cover art by Steve Ditko. Picturing the main character in the cover's upper left corner was Ditko's idea, and implemented on all Marvel comics. — Copyright © Marvel Entertainment subscribed, and contributed a few articles.

In the late 1980s, I wrote a longer article on why I considered Ditko's work so interesting. I sent a copy to Robin Snyder. The article was published in Amazing Heroes #111 (easily available on eBay for well under $10).

Robin had sent the manuscript to Ditko. I found this out when Ditko sent me a 13-page letter, commenting on the article.

It's gratifying to write to a person you respect, and then get a response.

It's on quite a higher level when that same person initiates contact with you.

I exchanged letters with Ditko from then on.

In 1991, I had an opportunity to travel with my wife to New York City. I asked Ditko if we could visit him in his Manhattan studio, and he agreed. I've heard that many fans had asked this, over the years, but few had been invited. Some had even appeared unannounced at his studio (his phone number and studio address were in the Manhattan phone directory); Ditko would talk to these people through a partly-opened door, but that's as far as they were allowed.

When my wife and I visited, there were not enough chairs to seat three people in his studio, so we all stood for about three hours. Steve Ditko smiled continuously as we talked about one thing after another.

My correspondence lasted nearly up to Ditko's death in 2018. The last letters I received from him were favorable comments on many features in The Plymouth Review Current.

Ditko remained a dynamic idea generator all during his career. In the last decade of his life, he and Robin Snyder published a series of 27 comics, where he introduced a multitude of creative characters, showing he'd not lost his creative vision and imagination.

Some stories in this series evoke the eeriness of the old Twilight Zone TV show. For example, there is a series called "Personality Masks," where people visit a mysterious shop, find a mask giving them some character strength they need. The recipient of the mask then proves worthy—or not—of the characteristic they desired.

Ditko passed the copyrights to his independent work to Snyder. In late 2018, I contacted Snyder and proposed reprinting these 27 comics, some of which are now out of print, in book form. Snyder agreed, and the result is a 5-volume set, "The 32 Series by Ditko," which assembles over 800 pages of art Ditko created for this final major project of his life.

I used Ingram-Spark to make the "32 Series by Ditko" books available online from Barnes and Noble, Amazon, and other online booksellers. This "print on demand" method of publishing avoids the need to pay a printer for hundreds or thousands of copies, and then seeing them stockpiled in a garage or basement (something I *have* done at points in my life).

I've donated a set of the five books to the Lakeview Community Library in Random Lake. If you have access to the Monarch Library System, check them out.

I went from a kid reading Spider-Man (a character co-created by Stan Lee and Steve Ditko) in 1963, to co-publishing books by Steve Ditko in 2019. Designing those five books and working with Robin to refine them, was a milestone for me.

Robin and I are happy with those five books, and we're planning more projects that will make Steve Ditko's work more accessible.

Promotional leaflet for the five books in The 32 Series by Ditko.

Steve Ditko's
The Outline

The Outline was one of numerous characters Steve Ditko created for the "32 Series."

No "origin story" or explanation of his special abilities was ever given. He is invisible and intangible. He seems able to read thoughts. When he whispers to someone, his "voice" isn't heard by human ears. Rather, his words fall upon a person's mind as if they were thoughts occurring to that person.

This short but effective story, from *Opening Acts,* Volume II of The 32 Series by Ditko, ends with Ditko's typical life-affirming benevolence.

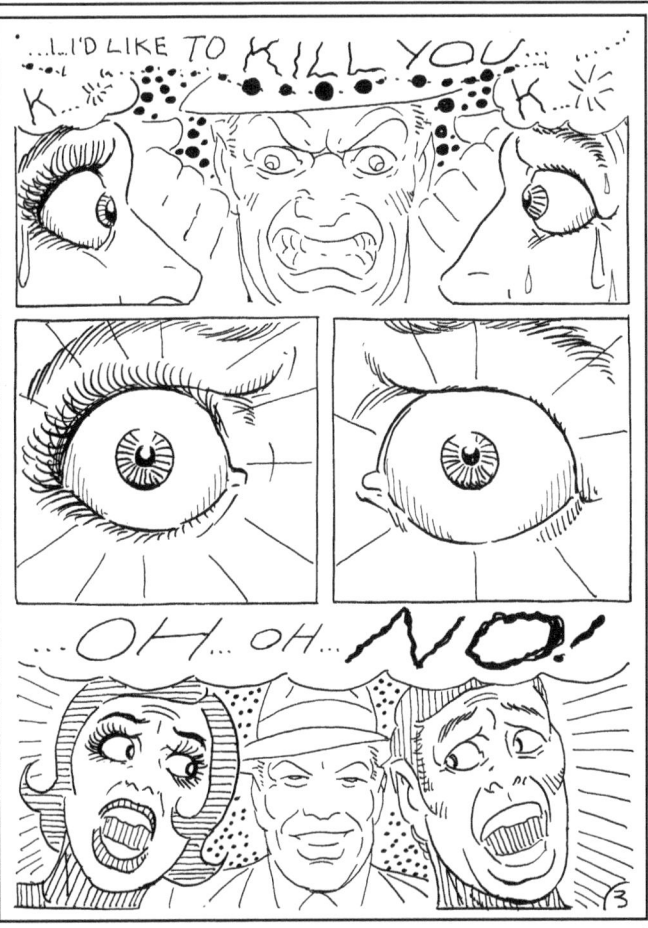

More by Edd Cartier

Imagine writing a story for this illustration. That's not how it usually worked, of course; the story would typically be given to an artist, whose job it was to come up with a clever visualization. — All Cartier art here: HA.com

Andrew Burmesch behind the counter at the Burmesch-Leider Variety Store, where Your Editor purchased *many* comic books in the 60s and 70s. John Burmesch estimates the photo was taken about 1960. — Photo provided by Becky Rivett. Thanks to her and to other members of the Facebook group, "You Know You Grew Up Around Random Lake When..."

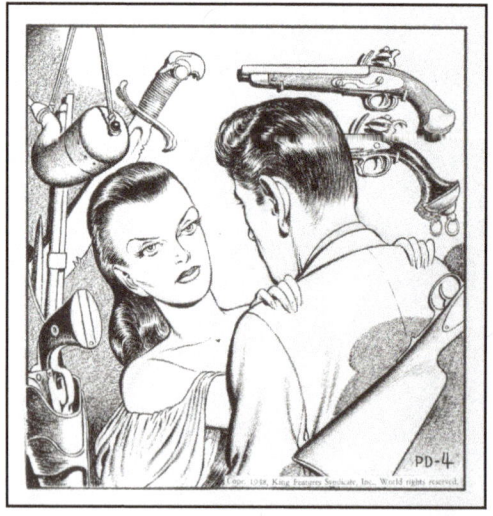

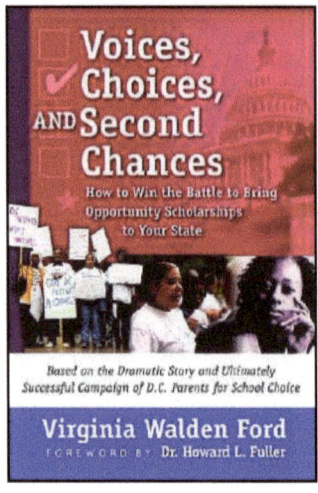

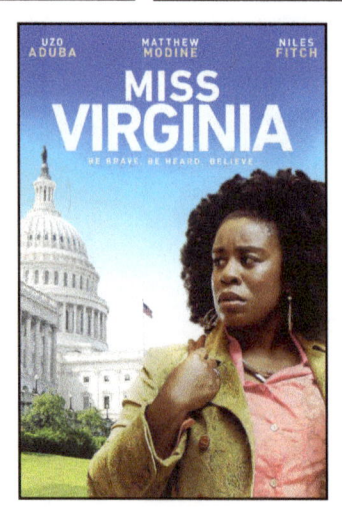

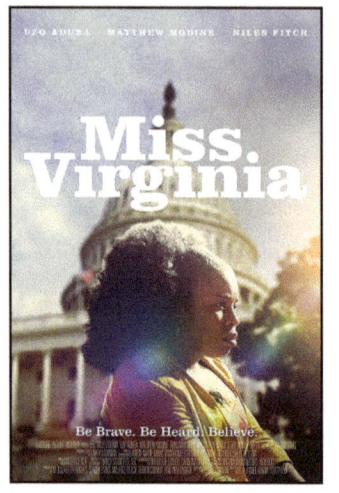

For this book, we didn't include any of the articles we ran about Virginia Walden Ford, the courageous woman who crusaded for better schools in Washington, DC. But here is a book she wrote (left; from Barnes & Noble, BN.com), and three versions of movie posters based on the highly recommended movie based on her efforts (from IMDB.com).

208

The Current
Plymouth Review
TAKING YOU PLACES WORTH SEEING
Volume 9 • Issue 5 • April 2020

FREE!

The publication that respects your intelligence

Bond... James Bond

Bad news, collectors! This issue is *scarce!* We haven't seen a *single one* on eBay! With the "pandemic," it was decided not to distribute copies to gas stations, restaurants, etc. Only Review subscribers received this, and a few subsequent, issues.

SPECIAL ISSUE! See page 2 for why you should SAVE THIS!

April 2020

Books by the Silver Creek Press

Specializing in making available previously-uncollected works by Albert Payson Terhune

The Tête-Bêche Series
Read one novel, turn the book upside-down, and you have another novel!

- Albert Payson Terhune — *Forty Ali Babas and a Thief* — A Silver Creek Press Tête-Bêche Book, Volume I
- Albert Payson Terhune — *Their Last Hope* — A Silver Creek Press Tête-Bêche Book, Volume II

The Albert Payson Terhune Reader Series
Dozens of stories, from 1900 to the 1920s, anthologized for the first time

- An Albert Payson Terhune Reader, Volume I
- An Albert Payson Terhune Reader, Volume II
- An Albert Payson Terhune Reader, Volume III

The Flood Fighters by Albert Payson Terhune — Two boys on a runaway table, assisted by a canine saint. From 1920

In Treason's Track by Albert Payson Terhune — General Washington perseveres, despite his greatest betrayal. From 1911

These and other titles are available online from Barnes & Noble and other booksellers

Previous page: When I learned that no advertisers wanted the front-page space, I stepped up and placed an ad for some of the books I published. These books *and more* are still available!

The Plymouth Review Current
TAKING YOU PLACES WORTH SEEING (AT HOME)
Volume 9 • Issue 5 • April 2020

~~REJECTED~~

In this issue:
- Coronavirus
- Coronavirus
- Coronavirus
- Coronavirus
- Coronavirus
- Coronavirus

Plus: • More on the Coronavirus

Another view of the Aston Martin DB5. We were *thinking* about using this approach for our cover... but we didn't have to think *very* long.

This car is on display at the International Spy Museum in Washington, DC. According to the museum's website (www.spymuseum.org): "The Aston Martin DB5 first appeared in the 1964 James Bond thriller Goldfinger. The ultimate spy car came fully loaded with machine guns, tire slashers, bulletproof shield, oil jets, dashboard radar screen, rotating license plate, and ejector seat. The Bond car not only captured the public's imagination, but inspired intelligence agencies to incorporate similar features into high security vehicles used in dangerous areas." *YEAH?* Ejector seats and everything?? **Cool!**

This autographed photo of Roscoe Arbuckle, sold by Heritage Auctions, is signed, "Dear Sam/The car is insured/how about the dog?/Yours truly/Roscoe." That's some big car! — HA.com

• **The coronavirus!** Yes, even in the peerless pages of The PRC, you cannot escape mention of this onerous organism. We've found several articles that, in true PRC style, might challenge "conventional wisdom."

• **...which leads us** to an important announcement about this issue, and hopefully, *only* this issue. Copies are being inserted with the month's first Friday edition of The Review (in this case, April 3), as usual. ***But none will be distributed*** to the usual gas stations, restaurants, and other high-end businesses classy enough to regularly carry The PRC. We've told our readers in the past that The PRC is a publication worth keeping, because of its timeless articles on arts, entertainment, dining, sciences, practical philosophy, and other topics relevant to a happy, successful life. Now, I'm not *saying* this issue will become a sought-after collector's issue. But I might—just *might,* that is—be *thinking* it!

Cover photo: James Bond's Car, International Spy Museum, Washington, DC
Great Movies This Month
PulpArtists by David Saunders: George Avison
SCHRC book reviewed: *Ploughs Among the Eskers*
Ask a Science Teacher by Larry Scheckel: Why Do Roosters Crow?
A Government Monopoly Led to Botched COVID-19 Test Kits, but Private Labs Are Now Saving the Day, by Ben Johnson, FEE.org
How Price Gouging Helped My Family during a Storm, by Mark Steckbeck, FEE.org
A Few *FREE* Ideas for Home Activities
Is This Hate Speech?

Ploughs Among the Eskers

Book review by Beth Dippel
for The Plymouth Review Current

The western part of Sheboygan County, today known as the Kettle Moraine, is graced with lakes, hickory groves and cedar swamps. Long considered to be the least productive region of the counties in which it is located, it also happens to be the most beautiful. More than a century and a half ago, arriving settlers named this unique area the Kettles, the name suggested by the resemblance of its rounded hills and hollows to that indispensable utensil of the frontier.

Designated as a state forest of almost thirty thousand acres in the 1930s, the Kettles are situated within the boundaries of three southeastern Wisconsin counties. From its northern-most point in western Sheboygan County, the forest follows the flow of its glacial ridges to the southwest, straddling the Sheboygan-Fond du Lac County line and ending in the northern townships of Washington County. Officially titled the Northern Purchase Unit of the Kettle Moraine Forest, it has been known simply the Kettle Moraine since the first 6,000 acres were purchased in Sheboygan and Fond du Lac counties.

The farm of Bernard Michaels' parents lay on the eastern edge of the forest and at the time of his youth, countless reminders of the settlement period remained in the neighborhood. Split-rail fences zig-zagged along dirt roads, water-powered mills leisurely ground farmers' grain into meal, and log farmhouses, despite their disguise of asphalt siding, dotted the countryside. Most importantly, old men and women lived whose memories could still envision the epidemics, the blizzards, and the great flights of wild pigeons and gloried in telling of them to all who would listen. And Bernard listened and remembered.

As a boy, young Bernard Michaels enjoyed walking and playing among the glacial hills adjoining his family farm. Slopes which once bore crops of timothy and wheat yielded to the spread of sumac and thorn apple. Still-visible outlines of furrows brought to one's mind images of strong-armed men fighting the buffeting handles of ox-drawn plows, while scattered piles of limestone and granite produced visions of sun-bonneted women wearily collecting stones from the plowing in the folds of their muslin aprons.

From today's enlightened perspective, it's probably quite true that the clearing and cultivation of the Kettles should never have occurred. This fact, however, should in no way detract from the intention and ambition of those who accomplished the feat. To the Yankee farmer, lately of the sand hills of western New York or rock-strewn New England, as well as the land-starved immigrant of Ireland and Germany, the rolling landscape doubtlessly appeared as a Garden of Eden. They arrived on this isolated frontier with the common goal of enjoying a new and better way of life. As a group, they worked hard, endured much and too often gained little in return. Then during the first half of the present century, their descendants, tired of farming the rugged terrain, began to leave the family farmsteads for more rewarding livelihoods.

An unnamed small moulin kame located just east of Dundee on Highway F.

A bird's-eye view of Dundee with Dundee Hill in the background. Trinity Lutheran Church is at left and old Sacred Heart Catholic church is at far right. This image was taken prior to 1923 when the Catholic church was razed. It was a mission of Our Lady of Angels in Armstrong. Dundee is located in the town of Osceola, Fond du Lac County, just over the county line from Sheboygan County. — Images accompanying this article: SCHRC

Since its establishment, some ninety years ago, much has been written of the geological and topographical origins of the Kettle Moraine. In this book Michaels combines history and culture with geology and geography to create a fascinating perspective of the area.

Included are chapters on early residents of the Kettle Moraine, the fur trade, the surveyor, the coming of the settler, mills and villages including Dundee, New Prospect and New Fane, the Civil War, threshing machines and cheese factories, the three Rs, social welfare, trails and turnpikes and effects of the 20th Century.

Ploughs Among the Eskers is available for sale at the Sheboygan County Historical Research Center, 518 Water Street, Sheboygan Falls or online at schrc.org/shop.

Parnell Esker near Butler Lake.

A view of Butler Lake found on Butler Lake Road in the town of Mitchell. The Michael and Ellen Brown Butler family settled in section 19 across the road from today's entrance to Butler Lake.

A few *FREE* ideas for home activities

The need to stay at home more can be challenging. Here are a few random ideas, suggestions for resources to make things more interesting.

Put things in perspective

Listening to officials drone on hour after hour about what precautions to take can be helpful. But you can better understand the present situation (as you can better understand so many things) by finding something that is both similar and different.

I therefore recommend reading about the flu pandemic of 100 years ago.

This is certainly not the only site; it might not be the best (so I need The PRC's readers, who have sharp eyes and even sharper minds, to let me know if I'm promulgating an unreliable site), but I found Vox's article to be an excellent overview.

"5 lessons on social distancing from the 1918 Spanish flu pandemic"

https://www.vox.com/policy-and-politics/2020/3/24/21188121/coronavirus-covid-19-social-distancing-1918-spanish-flu

(All links given in this article can be found on The PRC's Facebook page.)

Free movies

For the past few years, writing about movies has been one of the most time-consuming aspects of creating the typical issue of The PRC. It has also been one of Your Editor's greatest pleasures.

You might think Your Editor exaggerates when describing The General, Buster Keaton's film scheduled for Turner Classic Movies on May 16. What's that? You don't *get* TCM? Well, see *the whole movie* for FREE at www.youtube.com/watch?v=iHlBMKtgPOA. — HA.com

You'll find the usual items and images in this issue. But here's a little more.

I've often said that some silent films are available online. Free. They're in the public domain. Allow me to prove that. The following are not excerpts, but the entire films!

Fatty and Mabel Adrift (1916).
www.youtube.com/watch?v=f1wJrXD7mvM
One Week, with Buster Keaton (1920).
www.youtube.com/watch?v=hHo1cvbDlpA
Safety Last (1923), with Harold Lloyd. The title note says "excellent quality," but I've seen better, so if you keep looking, you might find better.
www.youtube.com/watch?v=V-XZWZVVhvQ
Charlie Chaplin, The Rink (1916). Watch how he spells "spaghetti." Excellent quality and a dozen laughs a minute.
www.youtube.com/watch?v=0i5zlnZBD1A
The Butcher Boy (1917). A Roscoe Arbuckle film, with Buster Keaton's first job in the movies.

Image generated by Amberlight, a graphics program that is not free, but is reasonably priced. See www.escapemotions.com — Created by Your Editor with Amberlight

www.youtube.com/watch?v=O0AD8___Aq4

Arbuckle and Keaton in Back Stage. Watch for the "eccentric dancer" at 3.5 minutes. This man was the father of an actor who starred in a popular 1960s TV monster comedy.

www.youtube.com/watch?v=IT8mP5umswg

Something a little different: Sunrise, a 1.5-hour drama. One of the finest films ever made. Check out how many people have viewed this one.

www.youtube.com/watch?v=6NayFytQeBE

Free books

Project Gutenberg has tens of thousands of public domain books, in a variety of formats, including e-books. A few of Your Editor's author recommendations:

Robert E. Howard. The pulp writer who created Conan the Barbarian.

Albert Payson Terhune. Famous for his dog stories. (Have we heard that name elsewhere in this issue? I wonder where...)

Victor Hugo. Author of The Man Who Laughs, Les Miserables, Notre-Dame de Paris (also called The Hunchback of Notre Dame) and more.

Their main webpage:

www.gutenberg.org/wiki/Main_Page

Free audiobooks

Left to Right: Albert Payson Terhune; Closette from the first edition of *Les Miserables*; Robert E. Howard. — Public domain images

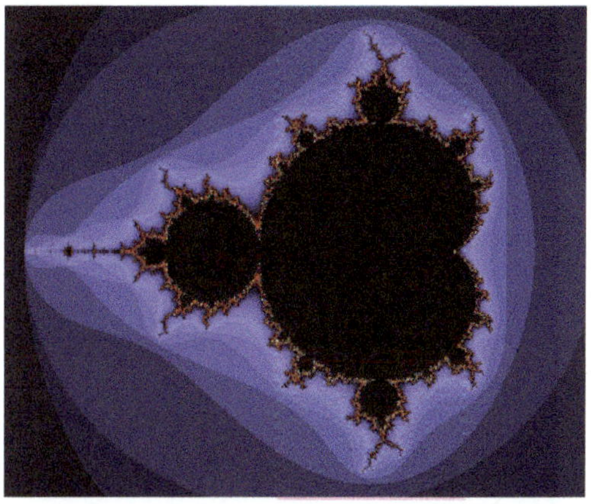

Fractals generated by a download-for-free fractal program. This common fractal design, called a Mandelbrot, is named after mathemetician Benoit Mandelbrot, who did work in fractal mathematics. The difference between the two images comes from tweaking one of the mathematical parameters used to generate the images.
— Created in moments by Your Editor

LibriVox. librivox.org

From their website: "LibriVox audiobooks are free for anyone to listen to, on their computers, iPods or other mobile device, or to burn onto a CD."

Want to practice reading aloud? Their webiste also says: "LibriVox audiobooks are read by volunteers from all over the world. Perhaps you would like to join us?"

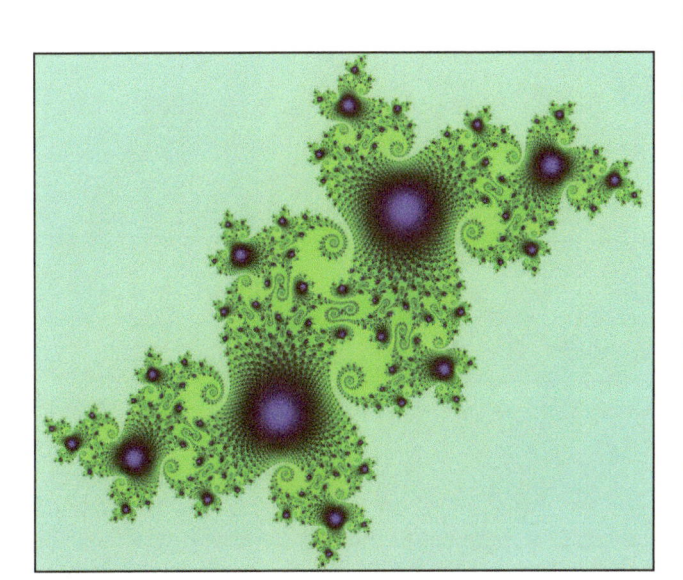

An image generated by one of the samples that comes with the free POV-Ray program. — Created by Your Editor with the POV-Ray samples

Creating computer graphics

I'd like to write an article about this, someday. Not sure how wide the appeal would be. But:

Fractals.

Search the Internet on "free fractal software." You'll find several! Fractals are designs generated by mathematical formulae. You don't need to understand the math to be able to create fantastic designs, for your own pleasure, or for graphic arts projects. Many books and online

A Julia Set fractal. — Public domain image from Wikipedia

articles can be found on the subject.

POV-Ray.

POV stands for "Persistence of Vision," a graphics program has been around a long time. It's a ray-tracing program that... well, let's skip all that for now.

It's available for free download. Some programming skills are required, but the basics (which is where anyone would start) are easy to learn. I had generated many images with this software, but after a computer crash last year, cannot seem to find them.

Here's an example (of which I have no visual to show). With POV-Ray, I can easily generate a sphere with the texture of granite. But suppose one sphere isn't enough. I want to create a circle of 72 spheres, equally spaced.

To do this, I used another program to write BASIC instructions, using geometric equations to calculate the location of each sphere, 5 degrees apart from the next sphere.

Sound complicated? Well... kind of. Perhaps not as difficult as you might think.

Interested in learning more about creating POV-Ray images? If enough people e-mail me, I'll write more about this, and give you all my secrets.

In the meantime, you can find an overwhelming amount of samples, images, and techniques online.

Another fractal. One fun thing about fractals is that you can zoom in on one area, and find new details and patterns. — Created easily by Your Editor

POV-Ray is explored further in the next month's issue.

GEORGE AVISON: TELLING STORIES WITH ART

(1885-1970)

George Alfred Avison was born on May 6, 1885 in Norwalk, Connecticut. His father, Alfred Avison, was born 1859 in Connecticut of English ancestry. His mother, Ardella A. Daniels, was born 1861 in New York City. His parents married in 1883. There were two children in the family. His younger sister Leila was born in 1892. They lived at 158 Main Street in Norwalk, CT. His father was a businessman and local politician.

He attended school and developed a natural talent for drawing.

In June 1903 he graduated from Norwalk High School, and started to work as a staff artist at an engraving house in Boston.

In September 1903 he moved to New York City to study at the New York School of Art. His instructors included Robert Henri (1865-1929) and Edward

David Saunders'
pulpartists.com

Penfield (1866-1925).

By 1908 he began to work as a professional freelance artist. His illustrations appeared in *St. Nicholas Magazine, Youth's Companion, Boys' Life, American Girl, The Century,* and *Scribner's Magazine.*

In 1909 he married Edith Dalton and raised three children, George Marshall (b. 1909), Mildred (b. 1911), and Alfred (b. 1920), who grew up to become a renowned Golden Age comic book artist. The Avison family moved to an artist's colony founded by the sculptor Solon Borglum (1868-1922) in Silvermine, CT. This same group later evolved into the Silvermine College of Art.

By 1916 they lived at 43 Perry Avenue, Norwalk, CT.

He had a steady job as a staff artist at the Van Derveer Publishing Company, on the corner of 23rd Street and Broadway

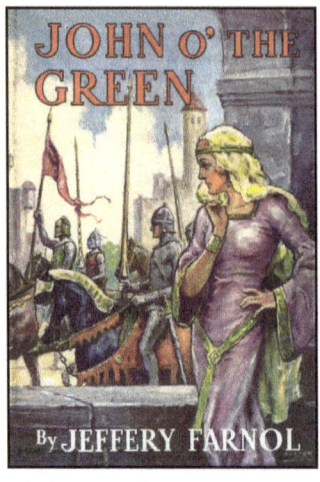

From left to right: 1932 Blue book interior illustration; 1935 book cover; 1940 pulp cover (ruining another man's morning cup of coffee is an especially egregious affront on the frontier); 1934 mural done under the Works Progress Administration, an attempt to alleviate a government-created depression by spending more money (something we're smart enough to avoid today, right?) (wink).

in New York City.

On September 12, 1918 he registered with the draft in the Great War, at which time he was recorded to be thirty-three, medium height, medium build, with brown eyes and brown hair. He did not serve in the military.

During the 1920s he painted covers and illustrated stories for pulp magazines, such as *Short Stories, Blue Book,* and *West.*

During the 1930s he worked as a muralist for the WPA Federal Art Project, an enlightened government program that provided relief income for artists during the Great Depression. Pulp artists Delos Palmer, Elton Fax, Lee Browne Coye, and Remington Schuyler also worked on mural projects for this same government program.

In 1939 he was commissioned by the Edison Electric Company to create a mural for their pavilion at the New York World's Fair.

He moved to 1069 Main Street in Stamford, CT, where he lived and worked.

During WWII he illustrated three books for MacMillan, *Uncle Sam's Army, Uncle Sam's Navy,* and *Uncle Sam's Marines.*

After the war he moved to New Canaan, CT, where he painted watercolor landscapes for fine art galleries.

George Avison died in Norwalk, CT, at the age of eighty-five on May 30, 1970.

© David Saunders 2011

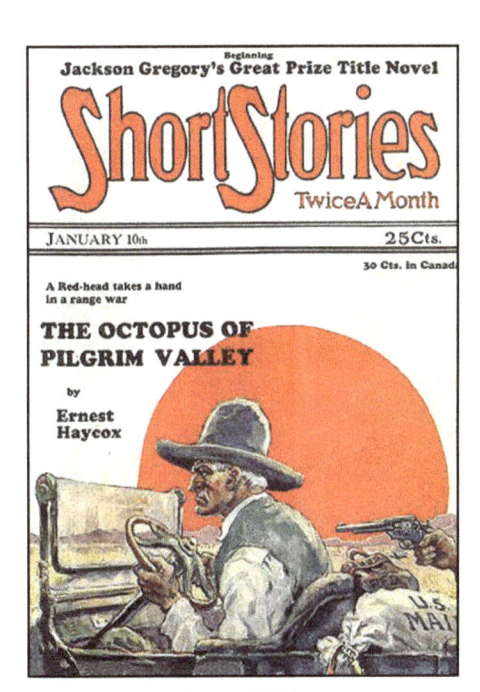

From 1928.

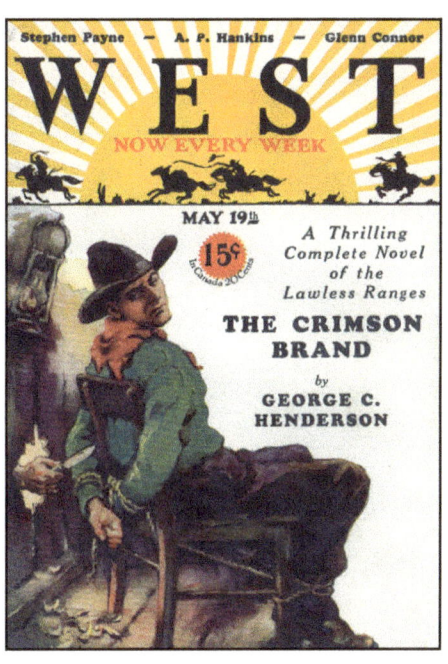

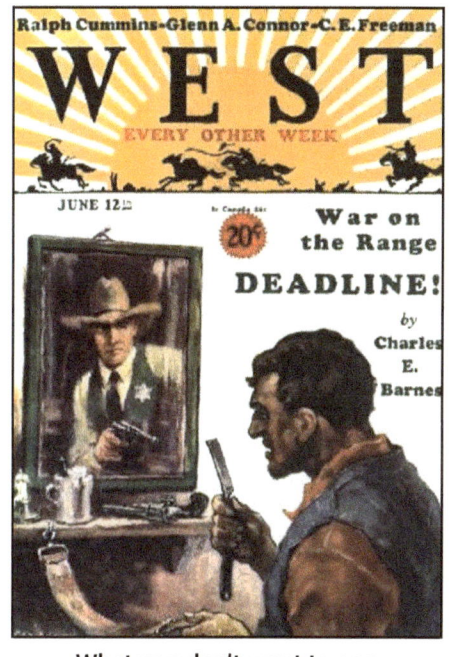

Help sometimes comes from unexpected sources.

What you don't want to see when you need a steady hand.

An illustrator for the pulps had to capture the attention of a prospective reader. Cover artists had to convince a person browsing the newsstand to pick out one magazine, from all of his or her choices. If the potential buyer was not convinced by the cover alone, the magazine relied on interior, black and white illustrations, like the ones above, to promise the kind of stories that would interest a reader, thumbing through the magazine. LEFT: from *St. Nicholas Magazine,* 1913. This magazine was aimed at younger readers. In its history, it carried work by Louisa May Alcott and Mark Twain. Scans of entire issues of this magazine can be found online. CENTER: From *The Century Magazine,* 1919. Scans of this title are also online. RIGHT: We jump a couple of decades ahead, to a 1935 *Blue Book* illustration. – From PulpArtists.com

The Plymouth Review Current

TAKING YOU PLACES WORTH SEEING
Volume 9 • Issue 6 • May 2020

FREE!

Create crazy designs like this one at home with free software!

The publication that respects your intelligence • Intellectual Stimulation • Art • Movies

May 2020

This issue also had very limited distribution. Another collector's item!

Cover image: Generated with POV-Ray
Great Movies This Month
PulpArtists by David Saunders: Frank X. Leyendecker
Restaurant of the Month by Melissa Niedfeldt: Kim's 5 Corners Tavern & Eatery, Sheboygan Falls
Ask a Science Teacher by Larry Scheckel: How Did Anesthesia Come About?
Harvard Magazine Calls for a 'Presumptive Ban' on Homeschooling: Here Are 5 Things It Got Wrong, by Kerry McDonald, FEE.org
An Over-the-Top Fun Mini-Session with Your Child(ren)
A Leyendecker Influence
Dean Cornwell Speaks His Piece
POV-Ray • Just BASIC

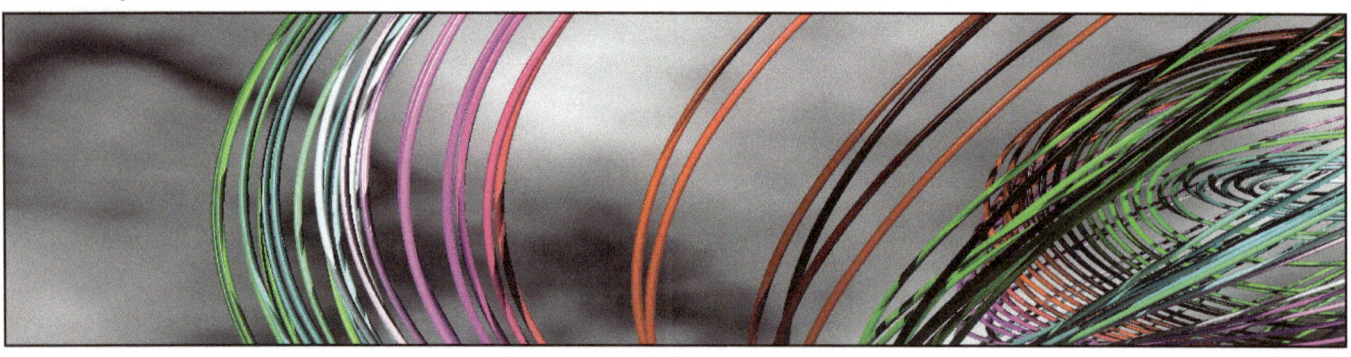

An over-the-top Fun Mini-Session with your child(ren)

by Rodney Schroeter
Editor, The Plymouth Review Current

Background
I've made the claim, for decades, that parents (or grandparents) can have loads of fun with their children (or grandchildren) watching silent movies together. Allow me to prove that to you.

Length of this session
Approximately 15 minutes.

Suggested age range
4 and up. With older children, less prep will be needed.

Required
The 1928 feature-length, silent film, **Steamboat Bill, Jr.**, starring **Buster Keaton.**

It is widely available on home video. If you don't have it on home video, the entire film can be found **FREE** on YouTube. (Or record it from TCM, May 10.) But trust me—if you don't have your own copy now, you'll *want* one, by the end of this mini-session.

Preparation
Initially, you will view only a small part of this film for this session. (Trust me—you

— HA.com

and your child will, ultimately, *want* to see the whole film. *Passionately.*)

You don't have to watch any portion of this film to prepare.

Tell your child, "You need to go to another room and close the door. I'm going to get something ready, and we're going to have some fun." (Feel free to improvise with this and other quotes, of course.) (And make this step as mysterious as possible, to stoke the curiosity to combustible level.)

Fast-forward the film to approximately the 55-minute mark, where the frame says, **"WEATHER CONDITIONS, Storm Clouds in the Offing."**

Pause the movie.
Call your child in. Sitting with him, tell him the story so far:

Buster tried to get his dad out of jail. ("Why was his dad in jail?" your child asks. "Because he lost his temper with someone he doesn't like; threw a rock; and broke a window. That's how people get in trouble.")

Buster was hit over the head. He was badly hurt, and had to go to the hospital. (Getting hit over the head is not funny, etc. etc.)

Buster is in the hospital. But he won't be for long, because the hospital is going to fly away. ("Have you ever seen a hospital fly away?")

Read the title card where you paused the movie. Verify that your child understands: *Windy weather is coming!*

Explain: This is an old movie. Old movies do not have color. *Very* old movies do not have *talking!* "But I'll read what they're saying."

Un-pause the movie.
Techniques for watching this movie with your child:

Read the dialogue cards out loud, channeling your most melodramatic inner thespian.

Keep your finger on the pause button. Pause any time you need to explain something (or your child needs to explain to *you*).

Don't explain *everything*. Ask your child *what is happening*. "Why are they running? What are they scared of?" The answers you get will be some of the most rewarding aspects of this session. (The squeals of sheer delight—your child's and your own—will be another.)

If you haven't watched the whole movie, and your child asks a question you can't answer, admit it. "I don't know! We'll have to watch the whole movie, sometime." (Trust me—you'll *want* to.)

When you see the Hospital, say, "Buster's inside there, but he isn't running out!"

When the hospital flies away, identify Buster and keep using his name.

When you see Buster's dad: "Do you remember, I told you, Buster's dad is in jail?"

By this point, you as a parent will know what to do.

Future fun with this movie
While watching the movie from the start, keep his interest by asking questions. Have your child explain what's going on.

For example: Pause the movie at certain close-ups. Ask, "Can you tell what he's thinking, by the look on his face?" (Silent movie stars had to be *experts* at this!)

No need to watch the whole thing at one sitting. Break it up as needed.

Further research
More information about Buster Keaton and his other works, and which ones are considered as good as (or even *better than*) Steamboat Bill, Jr. is available online.

You'll want that information.

You'll use it.

Trust me.

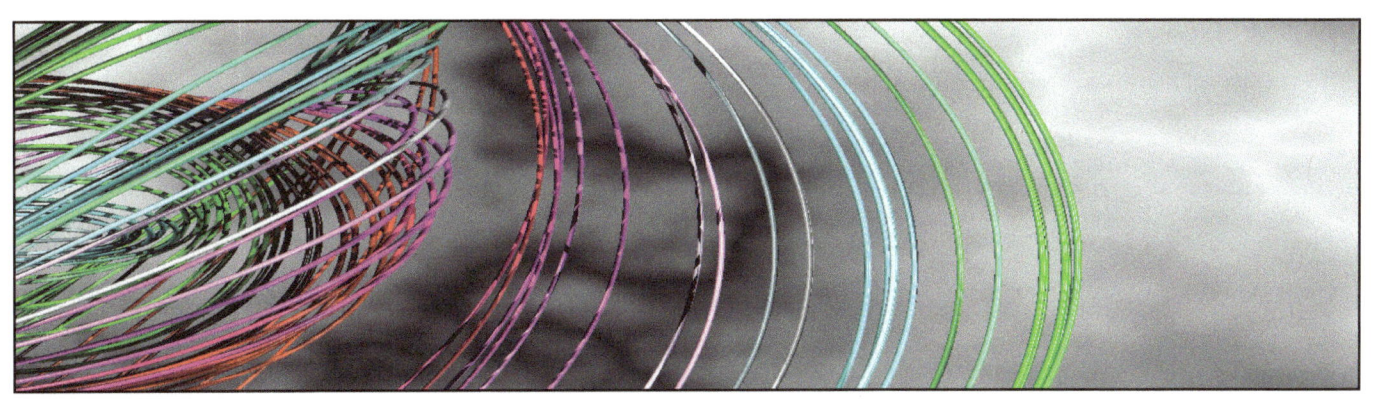

Walter Baumhofer, artist, was the subject of a past PulpArtists column. Your Editor likes his artwork, and likes George Washington; so here this 1967 image is. — HA.com

This painting was up for auction on Heritage, and I bid on it, but it went a little higher than I wanted to go.

POV-Ray • Just BASIC

Long, long ago, when I started editing The PRC (2014), I wrote several columns in a series, The Science in Science Fiction.

I created a heading I thought was as eye-catching as its subject matter was mind-catching. I used two computer programs to do this (and to generate the image on this issue's cover).

In the six years I've edited The PRC, I thought about writing an article like this. I asked myself if this would be of general interest. I thought, maybe not. But sometimes, you have to do something that will appeal to that small portion of readers—in this case, those who like to experiment with programming languages.

The first program was POV-Ray, which I started puttering with twenty years before, when I bought the book, Ray Tracing Creations, Second Edition, by Chris Young and Drew Wells.

POV stands for Persistence of Vision; the "Ray" part means it's a ray-tracing program, which calculates light rays...

Rather than try explaining that, I refer you to POV-Ray's website, where you'll find complete background on POV-Ray; images formed by incredibly advanced users; and a free download of the program.

POV-Ray is a programming language where you define objects, light, and how they interact.

One nice thing about a programming language: Many reserved words will do a lot for you. For example, there are many pre-defined "textures" you can apply to objects. Apply stone textures to make it look like different types of stone. The plane is formed of Pink Alabaster and Jade (not very visible in the example). The sphere has a texture of Blood Marble (well visible on the top of the sphere).

The sphere is highly reflective, so the tiles of the plane beneath it are mirrored in the bottom.

Why is the sky so dark? Because we didn't define any.

Suppose I'm not satisfied with one sephere. I want a ring of spheres. I want a sphere every 5 degrees, which means I'd have to calculate the locations of 72 spheres.

But I'm not going to do that.

Remember, I said I used *two* programs to generate these images, once they became complex. The second program is Just BASIC, another program that can be downloaded for free.

I used Just BASIC to write the file that would run in POV-Ray. Why? Because once I had the formula to calculate the location of a sphere, I just had to write a repetitive loop, running the formula 72 times, placing a sphere every 5 degrees. The results: **A.**

You'd think a ring of 72 spheres would satisfy me. I mean, what an accomplishment! But nooooo—

I created three rings, at different heights. Using Just BASIC, it was a snap! I did exactly what I'd done for the single ring, but three times, with different heights. The result is shown in **B.** (Notice I have a sky. I used my own photo of some clouds.)

As I became more comfortable with POV-Ray, I experimented with textures and colors. For example, many stone textures are pre-defined; I used a different stone texture for each sphere in the image below.

Colors are light (not pigment) and thus defined by combinations of red, green, and blue. I changed the amount of red incrementally; then of green; then blue — to get the gradient effect you see in the pillars below.

Three rings of spheres is fine; what about a spiral, where each sphere is on a longer radius than the previous one; and each sphere is a little higher than the one before? (That's part of what's going on in **C.**)

And when I grew weary of spheres, I played around with tubes (or toruses). I combined that with patterns of spheres. That led to the image on this issue's cover.

Some POV-Ray programmers develop a more focused, disciplined approach. They replicate actual things in the real world: animals, furniture, water, robots (well, robots are real, aren't they?), and scenery. **D is** one example, called Balcony, generated by Christoph Hormann. The POV-Ray code is one of many examples that are included when you download the program. For this and others, you simply open the code in POV-Ray; run it; and an image is generated. It only took a few seconds to create this image.

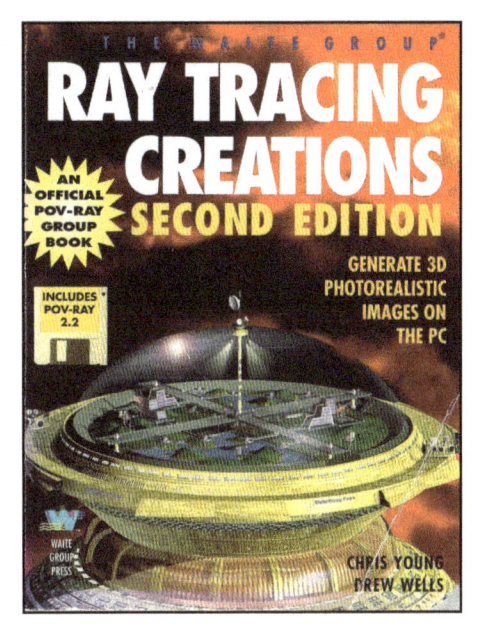

This 1994 book got Your Editor started in the wacky world of POV-Ray programming. Do you really need a book like this? Perhaps not. Just about everything within can be found online.

This 2019 book goes above and beyond POV-Ray, using the same technique (ray tracing) to generate images. This, too, is available free online (search on the title). Search also on Real-Time Rendering.

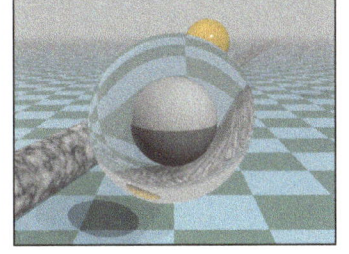

These three images were generated with sample programs that come with the POV-Ray program. For each file, you open the POV-Ray code; run POV-Ray; and the image is created. Each one takes seconds to create (more, if you want higher resolution). You can compare what's in the image to the POV-Ray code, and discover, "Ah! So THAT's how it was done!" You can then use isolated parts of the code (for example, the checkered or textured plane) in your own POV-Ray programs.

Your Editor, off in a little world of his own making, created with POV-Ray. From an earlier issue of The PRC.

Using Just-BASIC and POV-Ray Together

The tutorial on these two pages is new to this book, and might appear in a future issue of The PRC.

Step 1
With Notepad (or any other plain text editor), create the file **01_one_ball.bas**

Step 2
Use Just-BASIC to run **01_one_ball.bas**
This will create file **01_one_ball.pov**

Step 3
Use POV-Ray to run **01_one_ball.pov**
This will create file **01_one_ball.jpg,** with one sphere in the middle of a vast checkered plane.

Step 4
Hey, hold on a minute! Why would you go through all the rig-a-ma-role of writing **01_one_ball.bas,** when you could simply write **01_one_ball.pov** in the first place?!?
You wouldn't.
If this is the most complicated image you intend to make.
It's *not*.

Step 5
Make a copy (or "save as") of **01_one_ball.bas;** call it **02_many_balls.bas**
Here's what you're going to do differently:
• Change the file names in the first few lines.
• Use variables for the x and z coordinates (see POV-Ray documentation; that indicates the position of the sphere).
Set x and z to zero to start.
• Create a loop. The start of the loop is:
For i = 1 To 20 (The part after the apostrophe is a comment)
The end of the loop is:
next i
The code lines between the start of the loop, and the end, will be repeated 20 times.
• Use the variables instead of hard-coded values for each sphere's position.
Hard-coded in **01_one_ball.bas:**
print #myfile, "sphere { <0, 7, 0>, 3"
With the variables in **02_many_balls.bas:**
print #myfile, "sphere { <"; x; ", 7, "; z; ">, 3"
Yes, the syntax takes some understanding and getting used to.

Step 6
Use Just-BASIC to run **02_many_balls.bas**
This will create file **02_many_balls.pov**

Step 7
Oh, ho!! Do you see how much time you saved by using Just-BASIC? Suppose you wanted to create 100 spheres, instead of 20? Suppose...

Step 8
Suppose...
If you are the typical reader of The PRC, your mind has already jumped ahead to several higher layers of speculation as to what can now be done. As stated elsewhere, what you've read

---

01_one_ball.bas

```
open "I:\Archives\Current\Content_2020\2020_05\POV\b_sky_plane_OneRing\01_one_ball.pov" for output as #myfile

' This is JustBasic program         01_one_ball.bas"
print #myfile, "// This is POV-Ray file 01_one_ball.pov"

print #myfile, "#include " ; Chr$(34) ; "colors.inc" ; Chr$(34)
print #myfile, "#include " ; Chr$(34) ; "textures.inc" ; Chr$(34)
print #myfile, "#include " ; Chr$(34) ; "shapes.inc" ; Chr$(34)
print #myfile, "#include " ; Chr$(34) ; "stones.inc" ; Chr$(34)

print #myfile, "camera {location <0, 20, -30> look_at <0,3,0>}"
print #myfile, "light_source { <10, 30, 0> }"
print #myfile, "plane { <0, 1, 0>, 0  texture"
print #myfile, "   { tiles { texture {PinkAlabaster}"
print #myfile, "      tile2 texture { pigment {Jade scale .4}"
print #myfile, "    finish { reflection .1 } } scale 3 } }"
print #myfile, "sphere { <0, 7, 0>, 3"
print #myfile, "   texture {Blood_Marble} finish { reflection .3 }}"

close #myfile
end
```

01_one_ball.pov

```
// This is POV-Ray file 01_one_ball.pov
#include "colors.inc"
#include "textures.inc"
#include "shapes.inc"
#include "stones.inc"
camera {location <0, 20, -30> look_at <0,3,0>}
light_source { <10, 30, 0> }
plane { <0, 1, 0>, 0  texture
   { tiles { texture {PinkAlabaster}
      tile2 texture { pigment {Jade scale .4}
    finish { reflection .1 } } scale 3 } }
sphere { <0, 7, 0>, 3
   texture {Blood_Marble} finish { reflection .3 }}
```

01_one_ball.jpg

02_many_balls.bas

```basic
open "I:\Archives\Current\Content_2020\2020_05\POV\b_sky_plane_OneRing\02_many_balls.pov" for output as #myfile

' This is JustBasic program          02_many_balls.bas"
print #myfile, "// This is POV-Ray file 02_many_balls.pov"

' #version 3.7;
print #myfile,  "#include " ; Chr$(34) ; "colors.inc" ; Chr$(34)
print #myfile,  "#include " ; Chr$(34) ; "textures.inc" ; Chr$(34)
print #myfile,  "#include " ; Chr$(34) ; "shapes.inc" ; Chr$(34)
print #myfile,  "#include " ; Chr$(34) ; "stones.inc" ; Chr$(34)

x = 0
z = 0

print #myfile, "camera {location <0, 20, -30> look_at <0,3,0>}"
print #myfile, "light_source { <10, 30, 0> }"
print #myfile, "plane { <0, 1, 0>, 0 texture"
print #myfile, "   { tiles { texture {PinkAlabaster}"
print #myfile, "    tile2 texture { pigment {Jade scale .4}"
print #myfile, "   finish { reflection .1 } } } scale 3 } }"

For i = 1 To 20 '-- Create 20 spheres --

print #myfile, "sphere { <"; x; ", 7, "; z; ">, 3"
print #myfile, "   texture {Blood_Marble} finish { reflection .3 }}"

x = x + 5
z = z + 9

next i

close #myfile
end
```

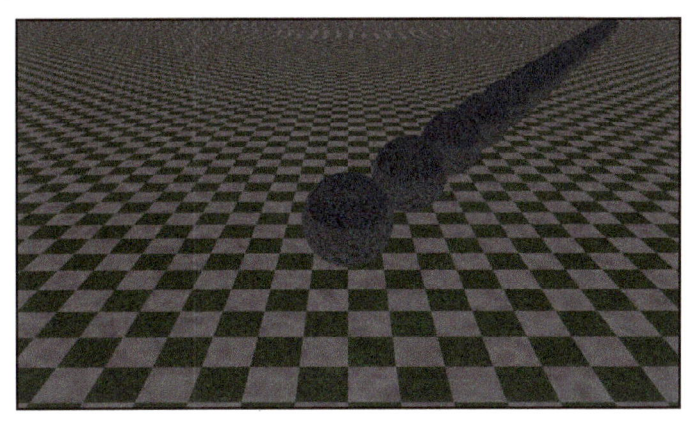

02_many_balls.pov

```
// This is POV-Ray file 02_many_balls.pov
#include "colors.inc"
#include "textures.inc"
#include "shapes.inc"
#include "stones.inc"
camera {location <0, 20, -30> look_at <0,3,0>}
light_source { <10, 30, 0> }
plane { <0, 1, 0>, 0 texture
   { tiles { texture {PinkAlabaster}
    tile2 texture { pigment {Jade scale .4}
   finish { reflection .1 } } } scale 3 } }
sphere { <0, 7, 0>, 3
   texture {Blood_Marble} finish { reflection .3 }}
sphere { <5, 7, 9>, 3
   texture {Blood_Marble} finish { reflection .3 }}
sphere { <10, 7, 18>, 3
   texture {Blood_Marble} finish { reflection .3 }}
sphere { <15, 7, 27>, 3
   texture {Blood_Marble} finish { reflection .3 }}
sphere { <20, 7, 36>, 3
   texture {Blood_Marble} finish { reflection .3 }}
sphere { <25, 7, 45>, 3
   texture {Blood_Marble} finish { reflection .3 }}
sphere { <30, 7, 54>, 3
   texture {Blood_Marble} finish { reflection .3 }}
sphere { <35, 7, 63>, 3
   texture {Blood_Marble} finish { reflection .3 }}
sphere { <40, 7, 72>, 3
   texture {Blood_Marble} finish { reflection .3 }}
sphere { <45, 7, 81>, 3
   texture {Blood_Marble} finish { reflection .3 }}
sphere { <50, 7, 90>, 3
   texture {Blood_Marble} finish { reflection .3 }}
sphere { <55, 7, 99>, 3
   texture {Blood_Marble} finish { reflection .3 }}
sphere { <60, 7, 108>, 3
   texture {Blood_Marble} finish { reflection .3 }}
sphere { <65, 7, 117>, 3
   texture {Blood_Marble} finish { reflection .3 }}
sphere { <70, 7, 126>, 3
   texture {Blood_Marble} finish { reflection .3 }}
sphere { <75, 7, 135>, 3
   texture {Blood_Marble} finish { reflection .3 }}
sphere { <80, 7, 144>, 3
   texture {Blood_Marble} finish { reflection .3 }}
sphere { <85, 7, 153>, 3
   texture {Blood_Marble} finish { reflection .3 }}
sphere { <90, 7, 162>, 3
   texture {Blood_Marble} finish { reflection .3 }}
sphere { <95, 7, 171>, 3
   texture {Blood_Marble} finish { reflection .3 }}
```

02_many_balls.jpg

in these pages is the briefest introduction to this fun programming language.

For this issue's cover, I used Just-BASIC to generate a series of loops (or toruses), each at a different angle; different size; different color. The differences were all calculated again and again, within a programming loop.

I also generated several circles composed of spheres. Few of us remember from our school days how to calculate points on a circle (and as I understand, few are now *ever* taught it), but how to do that kind of calculation is easy to find online, so I was able to place a sphere every so-many degrees on a circle. And I wasn't content to generate the same color/texture sphere; I varied that with each sphere. (Notice that the spheres on this page have the same texture: Blood_Marble.)

While I have spent many hours working with POV-Ray, and saving many more hours using Just-BASIC to generate POV-Ray files, I myself have only scratched the surface of this rich programming language.

Working with POV-Ray helps to exercise the mind's spatial imagination, and to apply mathematics. ***It's fun!***

David Saunders' pulpartists.com

FRANK X. LEYENDECKER: BEAUTY AND TRAGEDY

(1877-1924)

Franz Xavier Leyendecker was born January 19, 1877 in Mountabaur, Germany. His parents were Peter and Elizabeth Leyendecker. He was the youngest of their four children. His brother Adolph was the oldest, then came his sister, Augusta, and then Joseph Christian Leyendecker, who became the most celebrated illustrator of his generation. The family immigrated to America in 1882. They lived at 5334 East Lake Avenue, Chicago, Illinois. The father worked as a brewer at the McAvoy Brewery.

In 1897 Adolph moved to Kansas City to start his own business and family. Frank and Joe went to Paris to study at the Academie Julian for one year, where they were both profoundly influenced by the work of Alphonse Mucha, the founder of the Art Nouveau movement. Frank returned to Chicago with an addiction to morphine. The two brothers set up a shared art studio in the Fine Arts Building at 410 South Michigan Avenue, where they experienced early success in advertising.

In the fall of 1900 the parents and their daughter and two youngest sons all moved together to New York City, where they lived in an Eastside townhouse.

Frank's first assignments were book illustrations and book cover designs.

On May 10, 1905, his mother, Elizabeth, died at age 60.

In 1909 he illustrated Rudyard Kipling's futuristic science fiction story entitled, *With The Night Mail,* for Doubleday.

In 1910 the Leyendecker family moved together to 114 Pelham Road in New Rochelle, NY.

He made advertisements for many clients, including Luxite Hosiery, Remington Arms, Palmolive Soap, and Willy's Motors.

He sold freelance interiors and covers to slick magazines, such as *Colliers, Leslie's, Life, McClure's, The Saturday Evening Post, Vanity Fair,* and *Vogue.*

In 1914 he moved into a private wing of his family's newly built mansion at 40 Mount Tom Road, New Rochelle, NY.

On November 16, 1916 his father, Peter, died suddenly at midnight at age 79.

Painted for a 1910 advertisement. What do you think they were advertising? — HA.com

In 1918 Frank Leyendecker was too old to serve in the World War, although he painted several popular recruitment posters.

He also painted covers for Street & Smith pulp magazines, such as *People's Favorite Magazine* and *The Popular Magazine,* as well as for Fawcett's pulp magazine *Battle Stories.* His painting for *Battle Stories* was originally created as a WWI recruitment poster that Fawcett Publications posthumously reprinted as a pulp magazine cover in 1931.

Frank's profligate lifestyle had undermined his health, his happiness, and his professional career. He reached a tragic turning point when he fought with his brother and left the mansion in 1923. One of Frank's last published illustrations appeared on *Life,* October 4, 1923. It shows a charmingly seductive "Modern Witch" riding on an electric vacuum cleaner. That same month J. C. Leyendecker created his own Halloween cover for *The Saturday Evening Post,* as a parody of Frank's cover. Instead of a sexy young witch, he shows a silly old witch desperately clutching a knobby broomstick between her shrimpy legs. Her toothless grinning features are a clever caricature of Frank's own prematurely aged appearance, and a private joke about his brother's fragile vanity in a very public setting.

Frank moved into Norman Rockwell's unfinished garage apartment. Rockwell later said, "Frank had the furniture from his bedroom in the mansion moved in. A magnificent four-poster Baroque Italian bed, set against the west wall, occupied half the floor space. He also moved in hand-carved chairs from the same period and a large oriental rug that he never bothered to unroll. With his failing health and a career that was all but over, Frank Leyendecker passed away on Good Friday, 1924."

Frank Leyendecker was depressed and in ill health from his ongoing drug addiction, when he most likely committed suicide by morphine overdose on April 18, 1924. Although he was only 47 the police report listed his apparent age as "60."

© David Saunders 2009

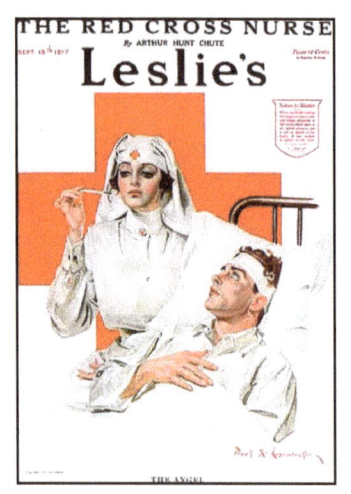

An influence for LEYENDECKER

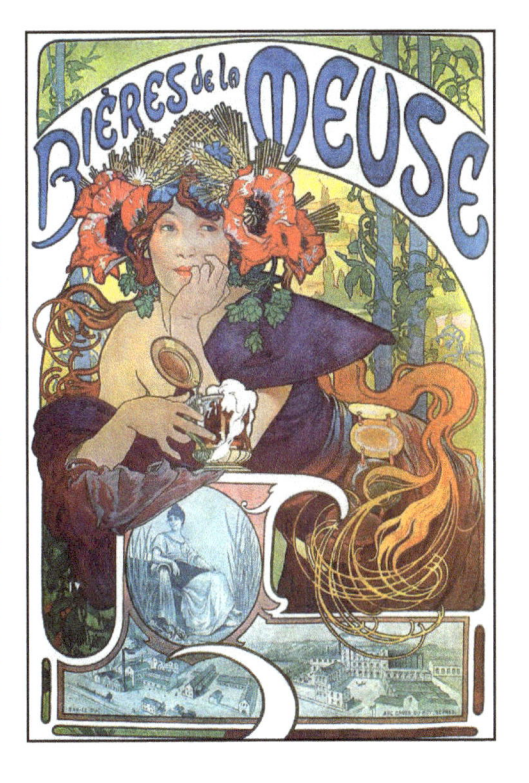

The PulpArtists article mentions Alphonse Mucha as one of Leyendecker's influences.
Left/Above: An advertisement created by Mucha in 1897. – Public domain image
Right/Below: Among Plymouth's many excellent Walldog murals is this tribute to Mucha. – Review file photo, reversed to allow better comparison

Dean Cornwell speaks his piece

Your Editor recently purchased this superb fine-art book of illustrator Dean Cornwell's work. The book was published by The Illustrated Press, and written by Dan Zimmer, editor of Illustration Magazine.

You can view the ***entire book,*** at low resolution, at Illustrated Press' website.

The following quote from Dean Cornwell is taken from this book.

"I'm a reactionary and proud of it. The long hairs don't like me because my pictures can be understood by everybody and because, when I paint people, they look like people.

"I don't read art magazines. Why should I? The critics don't like me. They say I'm too accurate. They want artists to be stumble-bums with their hearts pent up with emotion. But the real reason the critics don't like those who paint rational art is because the public can understand our paintings without an interpreter. In other words, we eliminate the middle man.

"There is a distinct dividing line between decoration and illustration. Certain decorative quality in an illustration is of great value. It must not, however, at any time be carried to the point where it ceases to be an illustration. One is a cold, formal theme of pattern and ornamentation and is most successful when devoid of character and human warmth, while the intimate and emotional quality must be always foremost in a good illustration. Romance and adventure should always be predominant.

"The decorator resorts to arbitrary forms and shapes, while the illustrator seizes upon the decorative value of any natural contours without resorting to these liberties. When one is inclined toward the decorative in illustration he must be very careful that in this he does not lose too much of the sense of reality.

"The reason we have few competent artists today is because the apprentice system has been eliminated. Everybody wants to be an individual overnight. No one fully learns his craft. In other words, you're condemned for being a good workman."

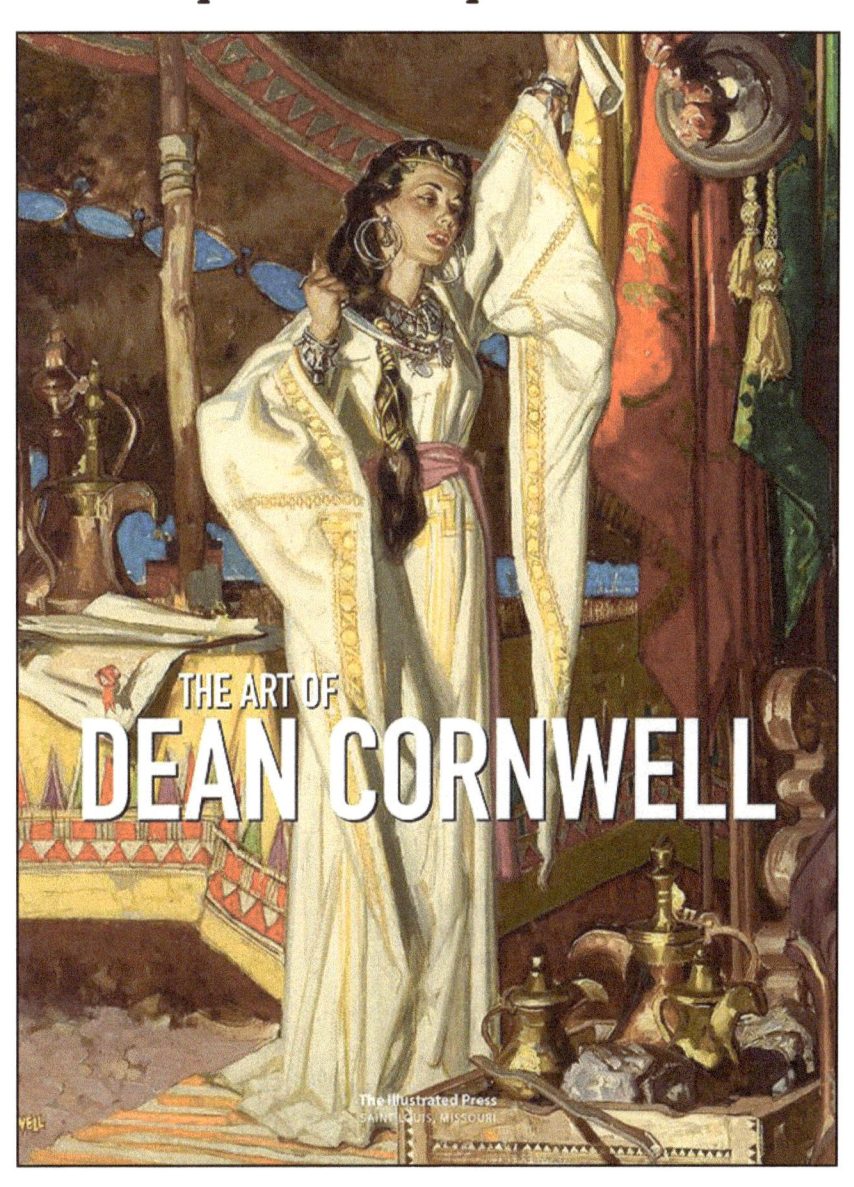

223

June 2020

Cover image: Silver Creek Pottery & Forge
Great Movies This Month
PulpArtists by David Saunders: Arnold Kohn
Ask a Science Teacher by Larry Scheckel:
  What is an idiot savant?
The Institute for Justice's Project on Immunity and Accountability, IJ.org
A Letter from Nanek

A Letter from Nanek

I saw the letter from Nanek, and I bought it.

The letter itself is... interesting enough:

• It has a stylistic, though perhaps somewhat amateurishly drawn, dragon at the top.

• It's addressed to a famous pulp illustrator.

• The return address is Crandon, Wisconsin.

But was that enough for me to buy it from the dealer at the Windy City pulp show?

No. I bought it because I knew who Nanek was.

In 1978, readers of a publication called *Xenophile* learned all about Nanek, the girl from the northern Wisconsin town of Crandon.

But first, a bit about the word "Xenophile." Interesting title! "Xeno" can mean alien; strange; guest. "Phile" is one who loves, or is attracted to.

"Xenophile" is to be contrasted with "xenophobe," one who fears people or things that are unknown or different; this often takes the form of an irrational or unjustified antipathy toward "foreigners."

Xenophile was edited and published by Nils Hardin. It carried articles and advertisements related to pulps, fantasy fiction, science fiction, and much more. Collectors would buy and sell (at prices we now consider painfully low!) to each other, and form friendships. It was a pre-Internet network.

Xenophile #40, July 1978, carried a photo on its front cover of a young woman holding a gun. The signature "Nanek" appeared at the lower right.

Hardin's introductory comments to this 120-page issue informed readers they were about to read of a "woman who grew up in a small town during the Depression and who later captivated hearts with her spirit, and with her words.

"This is also a story about editors, writers and artists of the pulps," Hardin continued. "You'll discover that, in the late 1930s and early 1940s, the people associated with the

1940s photo of Virginia Combs, from the cover of *Xenophile* #40.

April 16, 1942
Box 62
Crandon, Wisconsin U.S.A.

Hannes Bok
527 West 121st Street,
New York, N. Y.

Dear Hannes:

It seems absurd to call any one I so much admire by a more formal title............ and Bok seems silly, since I'm addressing you personally, so I'll just call you Hannes. Well, anyway, I've admired your work so long that when a friend sent me what they thought was your address I just had to use it to tell you how much I admired your work.

I couldn't begin to say any one drawing of yours I've seen was better than the others. I just like em all. And the news that you were striking out from Fantasy illustrating was a blow, for half the beauty of many a story has been the exquisite droll beauty of your illustration. The great yen of my life is to own , one, a Bok, second, a Finlay. I'd ask you for one, bold as brass, only I've heard you're generous that way and I can't take advantage of such a delightful weakness, preferring to get mine the hard way than to insinuate myself upon you. (that sounds silly but it's what I mean and I hope you see it as I think it, for it just won't go down any other way.) But it is the great passion of my life to acquire one, and I feel about your drawings as a friend of mine once said of Finlay......"I shall own one if I have to live to be the last person on Earth and so inherit them all."

Many and many the argument have we had over who is the greater artist, you or Finlay, my friend in favor of Finlay, I of you.......now I had to admit that Finlay drew the prettiest, but Petty does alright with an air brush too........but for sheer whimsy and imagination........heck, I just swammed all over my friend and told him off about there. The argument always ends with each of us as firmly convinced as ever that he alone is right.

So I just thought I'd write and tell you how sorry I am you aren't going to do anymore fantasy illustrating, and how much I like your work......you see, I draw a little too, and no one appreciates the character of your work more than I, who am so woefull weak in the imagination.

your sincere admirer
Nanek
Virginia "Nanek" Combs

224

pulps really cared about their readers... The kind treatment of 'Nanek' by Rogers Terrill of Popular Publications bears this out, as you will discover.

"This article gives a glimpse of what fandom was like at one time, a fandom that probably no longer exists as such."

The "article" Hardin mentions consists of:

• Letters between pulp historian William Papalia, and Virginia Anderson, then (1978) living in Milwaukee.

• Memories of Virginia Anderson, whose maiden name was Combs.

• Letters from editors and authors who worked for the pulps.

From the late 1930s to the early 1940s, when Combs was in her late teens and early twenties, she wrote many letters to pulp fiction publishers. And she received many replies.

One (printed on page 13), from Rogers Terrill, Associate Publisher at Popular Publications. It is obviously a reply to a letter from Virginia, who had written praise for one of Popular's best-selling titles, The Spider.

In over 100 novel-length stories, The Spider fought insane, sadistic criminals. It was incredibly violent. But The Spider (whose secret identity was Richard "Dick" Wentworth) was motivated to take these monsters down by a passionate sense of morality, a moral fervor that is rarely seen in other crime-fighting heroes.

The hand-written PS to this letter needs a comment. The adventures of The Spider were written by Grant Stockbridge.

Actually, they were not.

Publishers of continuing characters (The Shadow, Doc Savage, The Phantom Detective, The Black Bat, The Spider) used a "house name" for authorship. This practice (in my own opinion not an honest one) gave the illusion that one person was responsible for all adventures featuring that particular character.

In 1940, when Virginia received this reply, author Norvell Page was writing most of the Spider stories. It was Page who made Dick Wentworth the passionate moral crusader that appealed to Virginia, and to so many other readers.

Virginia Combs continued to write fan letters, praising the writer of the Spider stories. They were passed on to "Mr. Stockbridge," actually Norvell Page, and certainly impressed Page, because he started writing to Combs. Not only did Page reveal his true name to Combs; he composed a 7-page typed manuscript, a short story featuring The Spider! (Can you imagine a popular writer doing that?)

Page even wrote a character into one story, Jinnie, who was based on Combs.

(Your Editor proudly admits to enjoying the original Spider stories, especially those written by Norvell Page. So much so, that he purchased a Norvell Page autograph. But that wasn't enough. See the photo elsewhere of Your Editor's home office door.)

Virginia Combs gave herself the nickname "Nanek." Such self-christened aliases are common among fandom.

Forty years after publication of the special "Nanek" issue of *Xenophile,* I saw the letter you see reproduced here. It was written in April, 1942, to artist Hannes Bok, living in New York City.

Amidst the praise for his work, the letter shyly asks if Bok would send her one of his illustrations.

This was at a time when there was no market for original illustrations. A drawing was drawn; a painting was painted; it was published; the artist was paid; there was no further (perceived) value to the original drawing or painting. Many of them were destroyed by the publisher. Some artists requested and received their original work back.

But it was common to send an original drawing to someone who asked for one.

So I purchased this letter from "Nanek" of Crandon, Wisconsin.

Why did this letter still exist?

Papers and drawings from the estate of artist Hannes Bok have been on the collector's marketplace for some years. This letter was apparently among them. But it is the only vintage letter written *by* Nanek that I've seen. (Perhaps many of them still exist, in the papers of Popular Publications, which were purchased by a collector some years ago.)

On the other hand, there are many letters written *to* Nanek, reprinted in that 1978 Xenophile. Among them are a couple from Hannes Bok... including the answer to the letter I purchased!

So here, for the first time ever (that I know of) the two letters are published together: Nanek's letter to Bok; Bok's reply to her.

It doesn't appear Bok granted her request for a published drawing. But at least he included a little sketch on his reply!

Virginia Combs in the 1940s.

116 West 109 Street
New York N. Y.
May 5

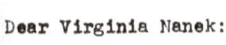

Dear Virginia Nanek:

Thanks a lot for your good letter and the highly decorative critter. I am in no habit of showing my mail around, but I am blessed with snoop-nosed friends who, unearthing your letter, raved at length on your drawing. Do you do much of it?

Perhaps some day I can dig up a drawing for you, though it will be a job: I have so very few on hand. I wonder what becomes of my drawings? Is there a gooblesnitch wandering around threatening editors, and they feed him my pix to pacify him?

Glad you prefer me to Finlay. Finlay I think is one of the greatest pen and ink technicians alive, but he's pretty poor on composition, and I lost all respect for him when I discovered he wasn't above copying photographs and even other artist's work and signing his name to them. You may be sure that, however unnatural my anatomy may be, it's entirely mine. Too bad about Finlay, because I believe that he had the makings of a really great artist at one time. My favorite s. f. artists are Dolgov and R. E. Lawlor. Remember Lawlor's stuff in the old Amazings of 1930? He wasn't a cheap photographer: he was a maker of moods.

I appreciate your encouragement very much. I haven't terribly much faith in myself. One nice thing about not drawing for pulps though is that I can concentrate on some big splashes of color: I have a lunar landscape in mind about three by four feet that I'm eager to start upon.

David Saunders' pulpartists.com

ARNOLD KOHN: SF'S THINKING ARTIST

(1920-1984)

Arnold Lupo Kohn was born on December 26, 1920 in Chicago, Illinois. His father, David Lupo Kohn, was born 1886 in Roumania. His mother, Jennie R. Kohn, was born 1894 in Russia. His Jewish parents emigrated to America and met in Chicago, where they married in 1918. They had two children. His younger sister Cecil Lupo Kohn was born in 1925. They lived at 6953 South Halstead Street. His father was a salesman at an auto parts store.

Arnold Kohn attended public school in Chicago and developed an interest in art. He was unusually small, intelligent and opinionated. These traits earned him the childhood nickname "Napoleon."

On December 19, 1937 he was awarded honorable mention in the 3rd Annual Chicago Commerce Association student art show. The art jurists were the celebrated illustrators Andrew Loomis and Haddon Sundblom.

In June 1938 Arnold Kohn graduated from Francis Wayland Parker High School, where he had been the Art Editor of the school year book, which he profusely illustrated. He was a member of the school's Honor Society and the Debating Squad.

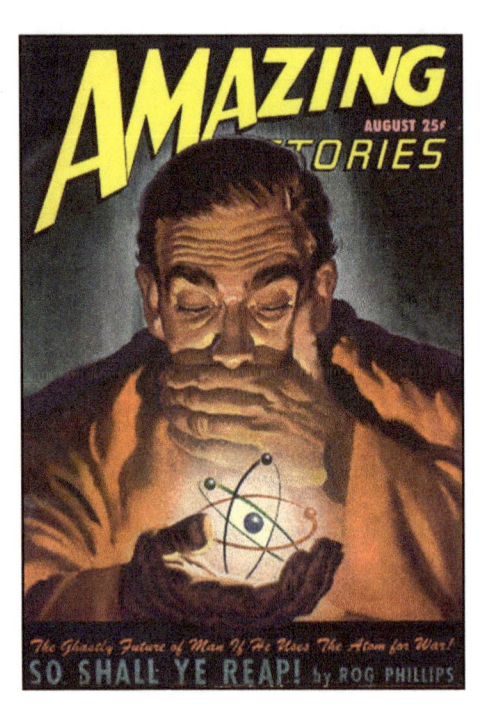

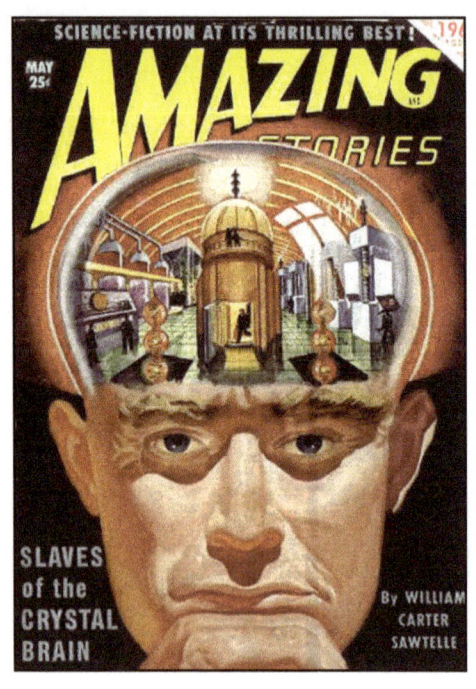

After graduation he worked as a salesman and clerk at his father's newly-opened bicycle repair shop. He also attended weekend classes at a Chicago art school.

Although he wanted to serve in the armed forces during WWII he was rejected because of poor eyesight, which required him to wear powerful prescriptive glasses throughout his life.

In 1944 his first pulp magazine illustrations appeared in the May 1944 issue of *Mammoth Detective*. He went on to sell freelance interior story illustrations and cover paintings to *Amazing Stories, Fantastic Adventures, Mammoth Adventure, Mammoth Detective, Mammoth Mystery,* and *Mammoth Western,* which were all produced in Chicago.

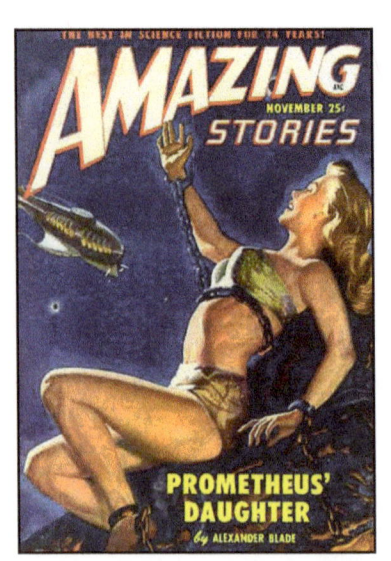

In the 1950s he painted pin-up art for men's adventure magazines and calendars. He was an early contributor to *Playboy* magazine, which was also produced in Chicago.

In 1956 he married Shirlee Jean Rice, a famous night club singer, who performed with Big Bands at the Millionaires Club under the stage-name Carol Lane. She also hosted a popular radio show "A Serenade at Night" that was broadcast coast to coast on WBBM. She was born in Chicago on August 8, 1927. Her father was the stage manager of the Ambassador Theater, so she grew up in an artistic family.

The newlyweds moved to a Chicago apartment on Chappel Avenue and later moved to an apartment on Ogelsby Avenue, where they raised two children. Their son David was born in 1960 and daughter Mari in 1963.

During the 1960s he illustrated children's books for Childrens Press, Cook Publishing, Southwestern Company, and Whitman Western Publishing Co.

According to the artist's son, "My sister and I were often pressed into service as models for projects. Dad posed us in outfits appropriate to the subject, while he snapped a Polaroid for reference. I have vivid memories of one such session in a summer when he was illustrating a Patty Duke Mystery novel for Whitman Publishing, which was some sort of North Pole adventure. In mid-July temperatures, I stood in the backyard wearing a full-length winter parka and brandished a hockey stick to represent an ice-scythe or something. It probably lasted only fifteen minutes, but it seemed to me like an eternity! I remember yelling, 'Dad, could you please hurry up and take the photos so I can get out of this god-damned parka!'"

In 1965 the Kohn family moved to 55 Shenandoah Road in Deerfield, Illinois, where their children could attend Deerfield High School.

In 1975 he illustrated a popular series of Doc Savage novels, which were abridged and revised for juvenile readers by Golden Press.

In his later years he was an art director of textbooks and encyclopedias at United Educators Inc., of Lake Bluff, IL.

Arnold Kohn died in Chicago at the age of sixty-three on February 4, 1984.

© David Saunders
2012

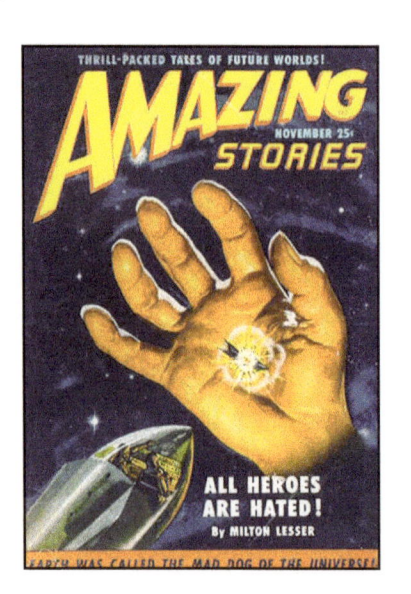

Ask a Science Teacher

By Larry Scheckel

Q: What is an idiot savant?

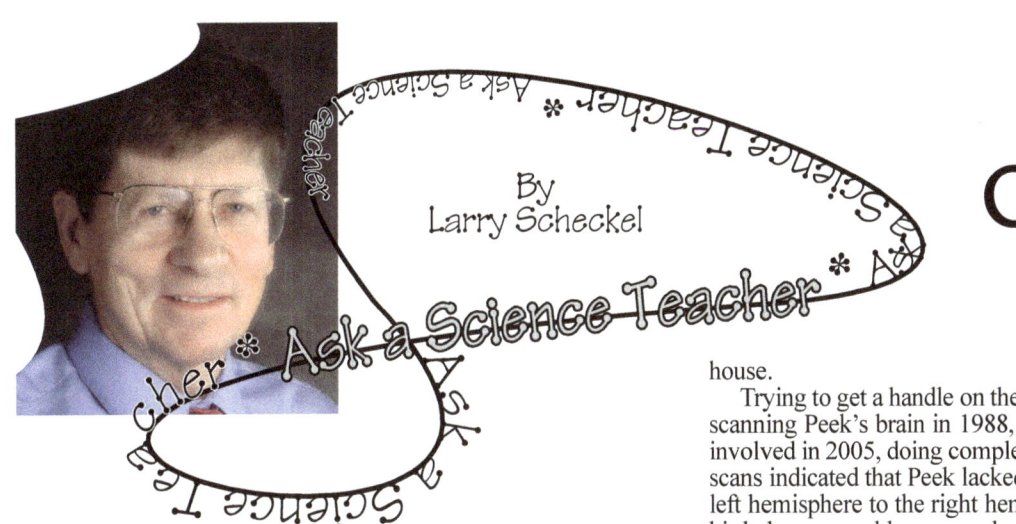

A: A dictionary definition, "A mentally defective person with an exceptional skill or talent in a special field, as a highly developed ability to play music or to solve complex mathematical problems mentally at great speed."

Today's polite society tries to downgrade the word "idiot." Savant is rare, about one in one million births, and megasavant, even rarer. The 1988 movie, *Rain Man*, is based on the real life megasavant, Kim Peek (1951- 2009).

Peek had enviable and unbelievable knowledge in 14 different categories, including geography, American history, Shakespeare, classical music, sports, dates, and the Bible. He had total recall of over 9,000 books he memorized, starting at age 18 months. Yet, he could not walk until age four. He read by scanning the left page with his left eye, then the right page with his right eye. Peek could speed read through an entire book in an hour. When finished with a book, he placed it back on the shelf with the spine upside down to indicate he read that one.

Peek spent many hours in the Salt Lake Public Library. He knew the entire United States zip code and every detail of Mormon theology. His father took him around to public school to demonstrate his vast encyclopedic knowledge.

For all his vast mental abilities, Peek lacked many fine motor skills such as tying his shoes or buttoning up his shirt. He walked in a sideways manner. He couldn't find the silverware in his own house.

Trying to get a handle on the phenomena, doctors in Utah began scanning Peek's brain in 1988, when Peek was age 37. NASA got involved in 2005, doing complete MRI and tomography scans. The scans indicated that Peek lacked the tissue that connects the brain's left hemisphere to the right hemisphere. Peek's father recalled that his baby son could move each eye independently of the other, most likely because of the discontent between the right and left side of his brain.

Despite his Google-like recall, Peek couldn't grasp common proverbs. Told by his father to lower his voice in a restaurant, Peek slid down in his chair bringing his mouth closer to the floor. He could not make sense of puns.

Doctors also knew that Kim Peek had a rare genetic disorder, FG syndrome, in which a single malfunctioning gene on the X chromosome causes a stretch of DNA damage in the left hemisphere. That causes the right side of the brain to overdevelop and it is the right side of brain that savants use to exhibit extraordinary mental feats. FG syndrome also causes large heads and low muscle tone.

Actor Dustin Hoffman plays the savant, Raymond Babbitt, in the 1988 movie, *Rain Man*. Tom Cruise stars as Charlie Babbitt, Raymond's money-grubbing brother. Dustin Hoffman met Peek and other savants to get an understanding of their nature and character, how they moved, talked, and carried themselves.

The screenwriter for the movie, Barry Morrow, gave his Oscar statuette for Peek to carry around with him. For over 20 years, Peek appeared on dozens of talk shows and fulfilled personal appearance requests. He travelled with his father, who cared for him, and carried out motor tasks for his son. They flew over 3 million air miles and Kim was the focus of thousands of print articles and 22 TV documentaries. Kim Peek died of a heart attack on December 19, 2009, at age 58.

July
2020

Cover image: Old Mackinac Point Lighthouse, St. Ignace, Michigan
Great Movies This Month
PulpArtists by David Saunders: John A. Coughlin
Ask a Science Teacher by Larry Scheckel: When was paper money first used?
Dreaming of Baking by Myra Stokdyk Eischen: Baby Elephant Ears
How Hollywood Stereotypes the Rich, by Dr Rainer Zitelmann, FEE.org
The Crisis Has Exposed the Damage Done by Government Regulations, by José Niño, Mises.org

(1885-1943)

John Albert Coughlin was born January 23, 1885 in Chicago, Illinois. His father, James Joseph Coughlin, was an Irish-American grocer born 1854 in Illinois. His mother, Mary McClarney, was born 1856 in Ireland. She immigrated to America in 1871. They married in Chicago in 1884. He was their first born. His younger sister Theresa was born in 1889. They lived at 248 North State Street.

In 1900 he took a two-year course at the University of Notre Dame, which is 80 miles east of Chicago. The school was serviced by eight different railroad lines from Chicago. Along with regular business training, he also took classes in drawing and painting from Jobson Emilien Paradis, who had studied in Paris with Gerome. In 1902 he was awarded a commercial diploma.

In 1903 he began to study at the Art Institute of Chicago, from which he graduated in 1906. After he completed his training he worked in advertising, which appeared in Chicago publications.

In 1912 he moved to New York City, where he opened an art studio at 880 West 181st Street in the Washington Heights section of Upper Manhattan. His apartment building was on the corner with Riverside Drive, so his studio had a spectacular view of the Hudson River. This was decades before construction began on the George Washington Bridge, so his art studio was filled with unobstructed sunlight.

In 1913 he painted his first pulp cover assignment for Street & Smith's *The Popular Magazine*. That same year he also painted covers for *Harper's Weekly*.

In 1914 he illustrated *The Brown Mouse* by Herbert Quick, editor of *Farm and Fireside* Magazine. He also painted several covers for *People's Magazine*.

He painted the April 24, 1915 cover of *The Saturday Evening Post*. In October

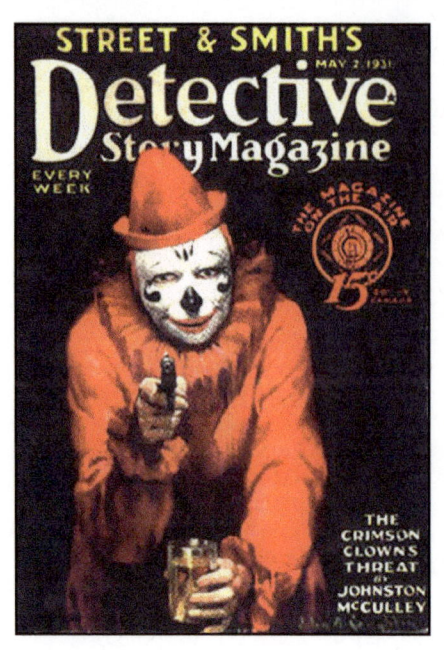

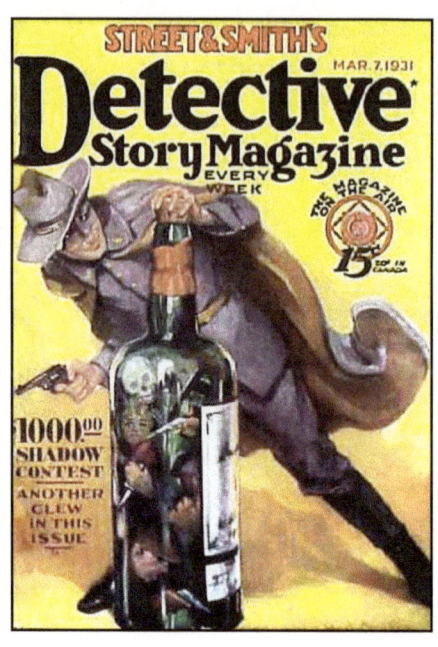

Left: The Crimson Clown was a crime-fighter created by Johnston McCulley. Right: Before The Shadow actually had his own pulp magazine, readers were given ten clues (or "clews," as it was then spelled) about what The Shadow looked like. This cover (mentioned in the article) depicts The Shadow for the first time. Artist John Coughlin did many covers for this title. Both of these are from 1931.

David Saunders'
pulpartists.com
ARNOLD KOHN:
SF's THINKING ARTIST

of that same year he created the pulp cover for the first issue of Street & Smith's *Detective Story Magazine*. He went on to create almost all of the covers for this same title over the next twenty years.

On September 14, 1916 he married Walletta M. Yeakle in NYC. She was born 1892 in Illinois. On September 21, 1917 their first son John Albert Coughlin Jr. was born. He was known as Albert.

In 1917 he painted a popular recruitment poster for the U.S. Marine Corps.

On September 12, 1918 he reported for draft registration. He was thirty-three years old and was not selected for military service. Records list him as tall, medium build, with grey-blue eyes and black hair.

Around 1922 his son Albert died of spinal meningitis at about the age of six.

After this tragic loss he and his wife moved five blocks south to a new apartment at 370 Fort Washington Avenue, near 176th Street.

In 1924 his second son James Joseph Coughlin was born.

On December 22, 1930 his third child, Robert Tuliss Coughlin was born.

Besides painting covers for *The Popular* and *Detective Story*, he did pulp covers for *Argosy, Complete Stories, Detective Fiction Weekly, Detective Tales, Real Western, Short Stories, Top-Notch,* and *Wild West Weekly*.

His cover for the March 7, 1931 issue of *Detective Story Magazine* is the first painted appearance of The Shadow on a pulp magazine.

In 1934 he opened an art studio in College Point, Queens, where his next-door neighbor was the renowned sculptor Hermon MacNeil.

He did not serve in WWII. In 1942 he was fifty-seven years old.

John A. Coughlin died in College Point, Queens, NY, at the age of fifty-eight on April 3, 1943.

© David Saunders 2011

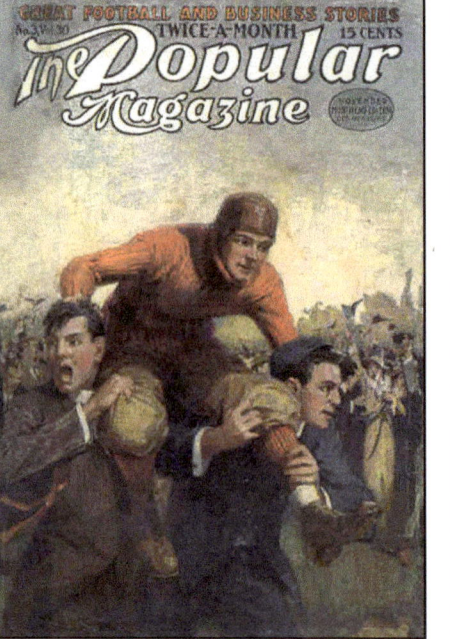

228

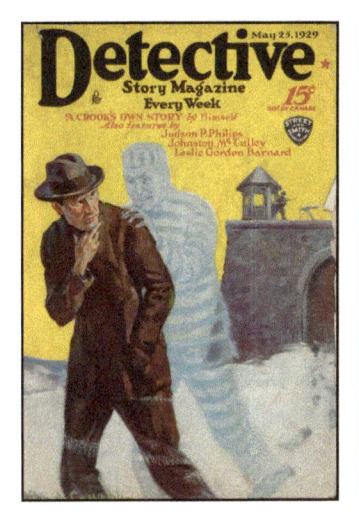

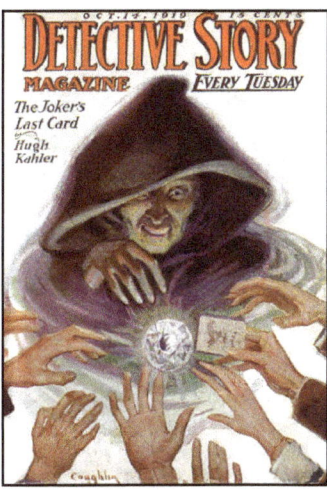

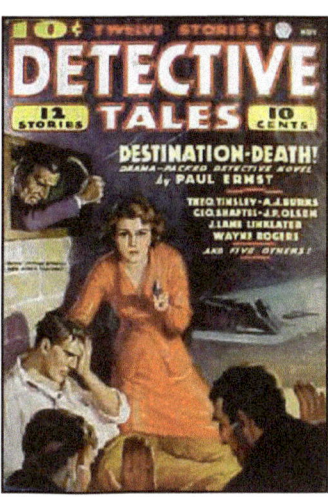

More by John Coughlin.

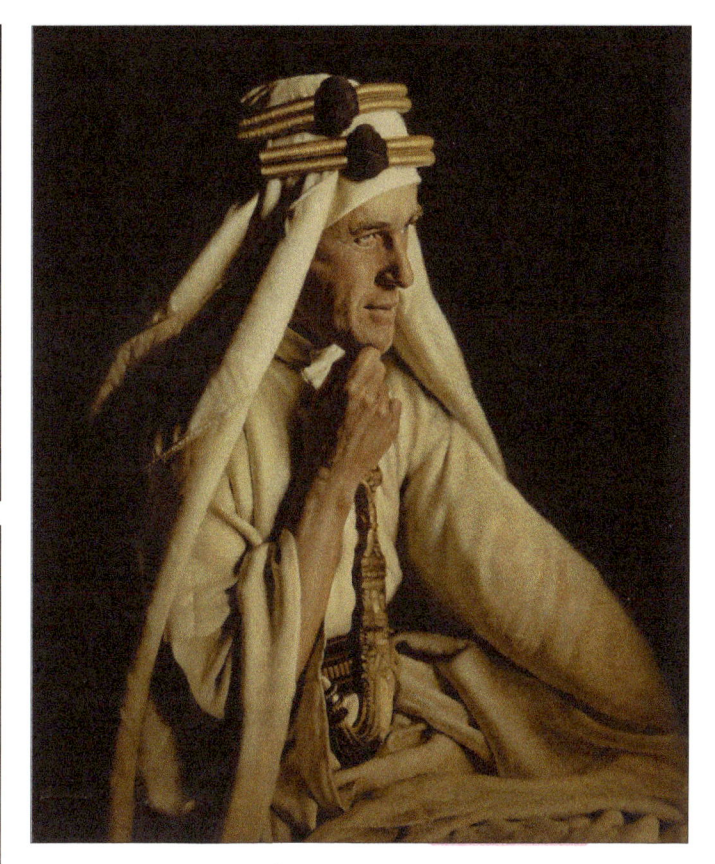

Lawrence

T. E. Lawrence, the subject of the film Lawrence of Arabia, is depicted in this painting, created for a paperback cover by James Bama (the greatest painter of the 20th Century). The original painting sold at auction for just under $22K.
— HA.com

Q: When was paper money first used?

By Larry Scheckel
Ask a Science Teacher

A: Coins go way back to 600 BC when the Lydians, a kingdom in what is now Turkey, made coins of a natural gold and silver alloy called electrum. The coin featured the head of a lion. It didn't take long for counterfeiters to make coins of lead, tin, or iron coated with gold.

Over there in Merry Olde England, Isaac Newton wanted a plush government job, with a steady income, after he formulated the Laws of Motion and co-invented calculus. He was appointed Master of the Royal Mint in 1699, a post he held until his death in 1727.

Bad people, termed coiners, were filing off the edges of silver coins, melting the scraps, and making new coins. Newton came down hard on those miscreants. Counterfeiting was considered high treason. William Chaloner, a repeat offender with friends in high places, was hanged, drawn, and quartered on March 23, 1699, in public. That could be considered a deterrent!

Mongol emperor, Kublai Khan, in China, introduced paper money in the 1200s. He executed anyone who didn't use it. The Bank of England came to paper currency late, issuing notes in 1694. It was obvious by that time that metal coinage had serious limitations. The ores for making coins were expensive and hard to come by. Coins were cumbersome and the value depended on which country had the mineral resources. In those days, counterfeiting coins was easier than counterfeiting paper money; today, it's just the opposite.

There was a reason at one time for the U.S. Mint to make coins with a special edge, called a reeded edge, and often referred to a ridged or grooved edge. It was introduced to prevent coin clipping and filing. Indeed, our dimes and quarters have a reeded edge today.

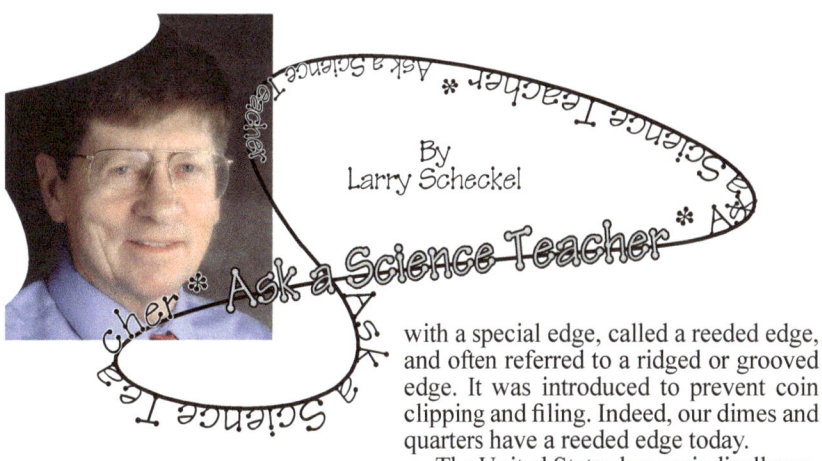

The United States has periodically updated the currency to stay ahead of counterfeiters. A watermark is the most difficult part of a bill to forge. Watermarks show a shadow of a president when you hold it up to the light. Security threads are built into the paper. A woven thread runs from the top to the bottom of the bill. Those threads are not printed on the surface of the paper, but rather are designed into the underlying paper. The threads are hard for counterfeiters to duplicate. Color shifting ink was added after 2006. Check the lower right-hand corner of a bill at the printed numbers, tilt the bill back and forth and you will see the numbers shift color from a gray to a green-gold and back again.

Normal paper that we use on a daily basis is made from trees. Our currency paper is made from cotton and linen, basically the same stuff as blue jeans. It's often referred to as rag paper. It doesn't disintegrate when you and I accidently run it through the washing machine. Currency paper is squeezed with thousands of pounds of pressure during the printing process. It makes the bill thin and gives the new bill a special crispness.

The euro (European) bank notes are said to be one of the more difficult currencies to copy. There's a dark security stripe across the note. There is a hologram whose image changes from the value number to a window or door system. The number on the back changes from purple to a greenish color depending on the angle of viewing.

Those clever Europeans are using one of the rarest of rare-earth elements called europium, number 63 on the Periodic Table of Elements. Europium became highly prized, big-time, in the mid-1950s, when color television sets came on the market. Red, blue, and green phosphors were needed on the inside of the picture tube, and red was the weak one. Adding a little europium to the red phosphors improved the intensity of the red.

Those European bank note printers add europium to their inks. It's an additional anti-counterfeiting tool. Under ordinary light, the ink appears dull, but shoved under a laser light, the banknote paper goes black, but randomly oriented fibers pop out, a sketch of Europe glows green and other parts of the bill show yellow, red, or blue. Oh, *that's* a hard one to copy!

Editor's note: For an interesting essay on the role money serves in a free society, search the 'net for "Francisco's money speech" or "meaning of money Francisco." After you read this, consider whether you think of money differently from the way you did before.

August 2020

Cover image: Tiki Mailbox, Sheboygan County
Comics: Pure Escapism that Has Nothing to Do with Real Life
Great Movies This Month
If It's Monday, This Must Be Murder
PulpArtists by David Saunders: Alfred N. Simpkin
Ask a Science Teacher by Larry Scheckel: What Happened to Einstein's brain?
Dreaming of Baking by Myra Stokdyk Eischen: Triple Chocolate Nutella Cupcakes
What Do You Need (And Who Should Decide)?
5 Charts That Will Shift Your Perspective on Poverty (excerpt) by Chelsea Follett, FEE.org

What do you *need*?
(And who should decide?)

Logic in your Life

Have you ever heard this expression?

"From each according to his ability,
To each according to his needs."

This was made popular in the 1800s by Karl Marx. It is one of the principles of communism. (I'll refer to it hence as the "From/To.")

In this article, I will totally discredit that phrase. Prove it to be wrong; a contradiction; impossible. I'm going to demolish this phrase so thoroughly that, by article's end, you'll be able to hear the ghost of Karl Marx squealing like a whipped hyena.

It's like an unbalanced equation, as false as saying: $2 + 2 = 100$.

I hasten to say: It is not enough to prove something "unworkable." Some light-weight, so-called defenders of freedom will prove (very convincingly, with every fact supporting them) that, for example, socialism is "unworkable" and "impractical," but then say nothing about the immorality of socialism, or the morality of a free society (capitalism).

I will not address at length the moral issues. Author/philosopher Ayn Rand spends a good portion of her novel, Atlas Shrugged, telling of an auto manufacturer (by coincidence, located in Wisconsin) that operated by the "From/To" code of morality, and effectively refutes it.

Consider this example. Suppose one man's ability allows him to gather 50 sticks; the Master Planners conclude that he doesn't *need* any sticks (he has too many at his home, already); the Master Planners confiscate the 50 sticks and give them to another man, whom they decide *really needs* them. If that example leaves you asking, "Well, what's wrong with that?", please go read something else.

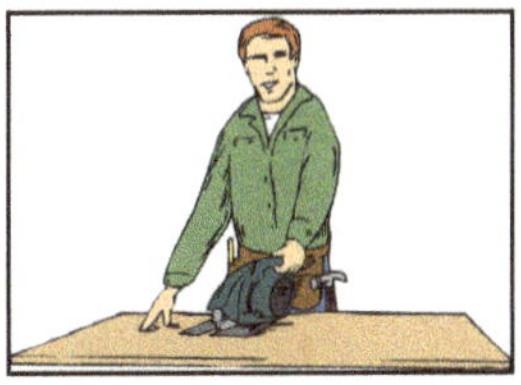

Three examples

Thanks for continuing to read. Here are three more examples I'll use throughout this article. Please keep them in mind.

Mr. Homebody and his family have a nice home, which he designed and built. He is continually improving the appearance of his property. He would like to buy more land, and is seriously thinking about building an addition onto his house.

Ms. Jazz has a fine collection of 78 rpm records, and takes great pleasure in listening to them. She's very knowledgeable about the musicians represented by her collection. She is constantly going to record shows, and browsing eBay, and continues to acquire more records for her collection.

Mr. Cash has a lot of money saved up. He is always looking for ways to make more money.

Where's the "from" from?

To prove the "From/To" false, we need to fill in some missing elements.

"From each according to his ability."

How does something come *from* somebody?

The 50 sticks "came from" the man because he went out, searched for them, and picked them up. The man had to choose to go out, take some action, and gather them.

To state the first line of the "From/To" more completely: "A Master Planner can take whatever a person produces.

Ah ha! The "From/To!" didn't say anything about producing or creating anything. (That's likely deliberate.)

Ah ha!—again! The "From/To" didn't say anything about a Master Planner! Again, that's probably deliberate. But it's implied. There has to be *someone* to "take *from*" the person who has produced the item or service, to "give *to*" the person in needs.

Mr. Homebody, Ms. Jazz, and Mr. Cash have something now. Each already has a good life, and has a plentiful supply of what they value.

But each *wants more*.

Is it *good* to want more?

Most rational (reality-oriented) people have no problem with wanting to achieve a certain level of comfort and security (home, reliable income), and then, wanting more. Sustaining and furthering one's life is inherent in life itself. I won't address this further—other than to suggest you look up the symptoms of "flat affect."

How does one get more?

How did our example people acquire what they have? How does each intend to *get more?* These are very important questions.

Mr. Homebody has worked in landscaping and home construction and repair for years. He used income and knowledge from his work to build his fine home and environs.

Ms. Jazz has worked for years in a manufacturing firm, working her way up to planner and supervisor. She uses her income to provide a comfortable life, and to support her interest in 78 rpm records.

Mr. Cash makes his money from investments. He works with markets not as a gambler, but as an informed risk-taker.

Each person has used skills, knowledge, physical work or some combination thereof to produce a value. The production of that value is a creation of wealth; the amount of wealth in the area increases. The creator of that value/wealth can then offer it for sale (if a free market exists).

In contrast, each person could have decided to get what he/she wants through theft. By stealing goods and money, a home can be improved; more records can be purchased; one's cash is increased—as long as one can get away with it.

With theft, no wealth is created. In fact, if theft is widespread, the people creating it will shrug and say, "If it's going to be stolen, why create it in the first place?" The wealth in the area actually decreases.

Why should a person choose to produce, create wealth, and trade on a free market (that is, why should a person choose to be a *capitalist?),* instead of stealing and looting? For a detailed answer, I again refer you to Atlas Shrugged.

Creating wealth—stunning implications

There are people who consider all of life a zero-sum game. Obviously, this is not true.

By applying skills, knowledge, physical work or some combination thereof, something new is created that had not before existed. If what is produced it of value, to the producer or to others, then wealth has been created.

See the Foundation for Economic Education's graph, on page 7.

Read a brief history of India, whose massive population suffered terribly for most of the 20th Century under socialism and communism, but then started experiencing greater prosperity when it took some tentative, imperfect steps toward freedom (capitalism).

Contrary to the zero-sum advocates, more people, producing (in a free market) more, creates more wealth.

In fact, with the Earth's continued population growth, it is conceivable that extreme poverty can be ended (if mankind does not turn its back on capitalism, which is a pretty big "if" in view of current self-destructive trends).

There's another *very* important implication. Allowing more immigrants into this country will increase the wealth of the country—for every immigrant willing to be a producer.

The typical immigrant wants a better life. Maybe he/she was doing all right back home; but he/she *wants more*. Each wants a nice place to live. Nice things for the family. A comfortable home. Good furniture. Recreation. Entertainment and art. Good food.

OK, as any xenophobe will point out, the immigrant might take someone's specific job away, because he is willing to work for less. But by *wanting more* and operating through free-market prnciples, working hard and smart enough to be able to buy what he wants, the immigrant's *wanting more* has created a *greater demand* for goods and services, which means *more opportunities* for that guy who lost his job. (If that guy thinks the job he lost is his only opportunity in life, that's his mistake.)

So if you ask yourself, "Am I in favor of allowing more immigrants into the country?" you should also ask: "Do I want to live in a wealthier country, with more opportunities, with more people trying to think of innovative ways to improve my life?"

Well, *do* you?

(Of course, immigration should not be a free-for-all. For example, there is no reason to allow entry to known terrorists.)

The "From" is limited

It's good to know one's limitations.

And good to push them, sometimes.

There are a limited number of days in the week, and years in one's lifetime.

By building upon past knowledge, people can become more productive, allowing more values to be created. A person with a bulldozer can move more earth in an hour, than a person with a shovel.

But the amount of goods and services that any one person can produce, at any level, the "from" in the "From/To" equation, will be finite. That's important to understand, before moving on to...

The "Need" is limitless

What a person *needs* or *wants* is potentially limitless.

What, after all, does a person truly need?

Bare sustenance? Enough rice and water to keep a person alive?

A few blankets to keep warm on cold days?

A small apartment, or a section of a communal shelter?

A car to get to work?

Internet? Broadband?

What a person needs or wants in life has the potential to grow, expand—limitlessly. It is limited only to one's imagination.

This is why the "From/To" equation is unbalanced. One side is finite; the other infinite. An impossible contradiction.

No, wait, we have to ask something else here...

Who decides?

Suppose Mr. Smith looks at Ms. Jazz's record collection and says, "What foolishness! She doesn't *need* that junk."

The proper response to Mr. Smith is: "Butt out, buddy!"

The same applies to the *degree* of how much more a person wants. Some people achieve a certain level, and are happy with what they have. If someone with bigger dreams comes along and sneers, "You ain't ambitious enough, you bum!", the same "Butt out, buddy!" response is appropriate.

Likewise, when satisfied people look at an ambitious go-getter and say, "Why does she have to chase after more?", the same response applies: "Butt out, buddies!"

If you support individual rights (that is, a free society (that is, capitalism)), you are comfortable with each person setting his/her own life goals, and expect your own life goals to be your exclusive domain (adjusting them to be compatible with significant others in your life).

In a free society, there's no need for contempt for someone less ambitious than you, and you're not envious of someone with greater ambition—just as there's no reason to hold in contempt someone motivated by a different *kind* of ambition.

(You might privately wonder if someone with *no* ambition can be happy. You can also realize the tragedy of someone wanting *more* of something objectively harmful—like drugs or alcohol.)

But in a non-free society, one or more Master Planners decide what each person needs. Non-free societies come in a disgustingly plentiful variety: socialism, semi-socialism, democratic socialism, communism, fascism... and more.

In a society with Master Planners in charge, need must becomes finite.

"You *want* or *need* an addition to your home, comrade Homebody? How dare you ask such a selfish thing! Be happy with what you have, and be grateful if we Master Planners don't take your home and give it to someone with greater need!"

"You *want more* records, comrade Jazz? Are you kidding? We're glad you brought this to our attention. You don't *need* those records, comrade. We have just sent a squad to confiscate them. They will be converted to cash, and the money given to those *truly in need.*"

"You want *more* cash, comrade Money-Grubber? GUARDS!"

We're better off

...when wants or needs are left to each individual, and when they are potentially infinite.

Because that means there is potentially an infinite amount of work that can be done.

After making all the plans, Mr. Homebody could provide income to an army of carpenters and landscapers by hiring them to enlarge his home and improve his grounds.

Ms. Jazz could hire dozens of search services to scour rummage sales and roam antique malls for the records she wants.

Mr. Cash could create a chain of financial offices that make more money for him, by making more money for his clients.

But let's face it. "Infinity" is only a *potential*, beyond any person's or society's *actual* reach.

There are limited numbers of landscapers and carpenters. Mr. Homebody's funds, however rich he is, are limited. And Mr. Homebody couldn't (and wouldn't) live in a house that is infinitely large.

The number of 78 rpm records that Ms. Jazz actually wants are limited. Even if she were able to magically snap her fingers and have every such record ever created, she might spend the rest of her life listening to each one, but the thrill of finding a rare label would be denied her.

And Mr. Cash? Like any of our examples, so long as he respects the individual rights of every other individual (that is, so long as he is a capitalist), the only way he can make more money is to create more values, wealth, innovations, and improvements for everyone else. Let no limit be placed upon him! (Or the others.)

With all the people who want more, and act to produce more to get what they want, overall wealth is increased; innovations improve our lives; and more opportunities are created.

With Master Planners in charge, society not only screeches to a halt, but starts sliding backwards. History shows this.

Restating the formula

"From each according to his ability,

To each according to his needs."

I think we can now clarify this vile equation.

"Master Planners will confiscate finite wealth from those who create it, and give it away to fill an infinite need."

This is, obviously, incompatible with individual rights.

What kind of sentiment would be compatible with individual rights? This is definitely not the only way this could be stated, but it might be something like:

"Each person owns his/her own life, and has a right to life, liberty, and the pursuit of happiness. Each person retains those rights unless he/she violates those rights in another. Each person owns whatever he creates with his own mind and body, and is free to trade those goods or services, or give them away, at the producer's sole discretion."

As this book is being assembled, members of the World Economic Forum are calling for increased totalitarianism (to allegedly ward off mythical climate scares), the end of agriculture, and human death on a massive scale (from depopulationism, which disvalues human life as detrimental to the Earth). The immigrant situation? The worst of them take advantage of not being prosecuted for crimes, while the best of them struggle to make an honest living and thereby improve all our lives.

Ask a Science Teacher

By Larry Scheckel

Q: What happened to Einstein's brain?

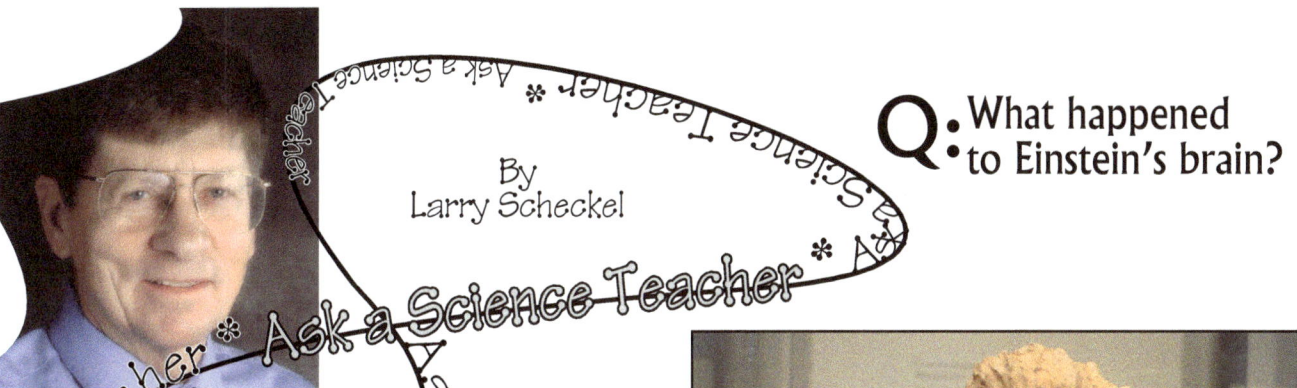

A: It's not a pretty picture, gruesome, to be sure. Einstein visited the United States in February 1933. Hitler took over in Germany at about that time and the Jewish Einstein knew he could not reside permanently in his homeland. He visited Cal Tech for two months, then returned to Europe (Antwerp, Belgium) in March 1933. Einstein received information that he might be arrested if he returned to Germany, so he renounced German citizenship. His Berlin cottage was raided and turned into a Hitler Youth Camp. His beloved sailboat became property of the Third Reich.

Einstein and wife, Elsa, stayed in England for a few months, and then was offered a job at the Institute for Advanced Studies at Princeton University. He went back and forth between the United States and England for two years but decided to stay in the United States permanently starting in 1935 and become a U.S. citizen. Einstein lived and taught at the Princeton, New Jersey campus for some 20 years until his death at 1:15 am on April 18, 1955. Five days earlier, Einstein had suffered an aortic aneurysm.

Einstein's body was taken to a local hospital for a routine autopsy. Now, over the body stands 43-year old pathologist, Dr. Thomas Harvey, knife in hand, facing a stark decision. Who wouldn't want to know what made Einstein tick? He, the greatest scientist of the 20th century.

Without the family's permission and against Einstein's written wish for cremation, Dr. Harvey "liberated" the brain and released the body to the family, minus the brain. Weighing is one of the first things a pathologist does with a brain. It came in at 43 ounces which was just a tad below average.

It didn't take long for word of the purloined brain to leak out, especially when Harvey's son blurted out in school, "My Dad's got his brain!" The next day, newspapers across the United States revealed Harvey's plan, to which the peeved Einstein family eventually gave their OK.

After measuring the size with a caliper and photographing it, Harvey sawed the brain into 240 Hershey Kiss-sized chunks and embedded each one in celloidin, a material used to preserve tissue. Many of those pieces were sliced into slivers and mounted on slides and stained, a typical lab procedure for specimens. He mailed off many specimens to neurologists for study with the provision they be returned. Over a period of 40 years, scientists found nothing out of the ordinary. Einstein's ashes were scattered, but the family refused to say where.

Dr. Harvey kept all 240 lumps, each wrapped in cheesecloth, in two wide-mouthed cookie jars filled with formaldehyde. There they sat for 32 years in a cardboard box labeled "Costa Cider" in his office, under a sink, right behind a beer cooler.

Dr. Harvey retired in 1988 and motored to Lawrence, Kansas, the two brain-filled jars riding along strapped in the front seat. In the 1990s, Dr. Harvey shared pieces of Einstein's brain with researchers. They did find that the prefrontal cortex was thinner, which gave him a greater density of neurons. Such density may help the brain process information more quickly, thus helping to solve multistep problems. In 1998, the remaining uncut portions were delivered to the University Medical Center at Princeton.

On the fiftieth anniversary of Einstein's death, 2005, pathologist Dr. Thomas Harvey finally gave interviews regarding the history of Einstein's brain. He died two years later in 2007, at age 94.

This bust of Albert Einstein, sculpted by Jo Davidson in 1933, resides at the National Portrait Gallery - Smithsonian Institution in Washington, DC.

David Saunders'
pulpartists.com
ALFRED N. SIMPKIN: CLERK AT 16, ARTIST AT 26

(1898-1983)
Alfred Nelson Simpkin was born October 28, 1898 in Brooklyn, NYC. His father, George Fredrick Simpkin, was born in 1874 in England and came to America in 1877. His mother, Beatrice V. Darby, was born in 1874 in New York City of English ancestry. His parents married in Brooklyn in 1895, and had two children, Mae Manon Simpkin (b.1896), and Alfred Nelson Simpkin (b.1898). They lived at 86 Fourth Avenue in Brooklyn. The father worked as an expert marble cutter and polisher.

On October 12, 1903 a third child was born, George Fredrick Simpkin, Jr.

On July 6, 1904 the younger brother, George Fredrick Simpkin, died at the age of nine months in NYC.

In 1907 the mother, Beatrice Simpkin, died at the age of thirty-three in NYC.

After these two tragic deaths the father abandoned his children and moved to Montreal, Canada, where he continued to work as a marble polisher. Alfred N. Simpkin was age nine, and his older sister was age eleven.

New York City Social Services sent the two children to live at foster homes.

Alfred N. Simpkin lived on a farm that was owned by Mr. & Mrs. Willett Vanderwater in East Meadow, NY, where he worked as a farm laborer.

In 1914, at the age of sixteen, Alfred N. Simpkin moved to New York City, where he lived with his Aunt Alice Beggs, at 196 Lexington Street in Brooklyn. To earn his keep, he worked as a clerk at the New York Telephone Company Building at Walker Street and Sixth Avenue.

On September 12, 1918 during the Great War, Alfred N. Simpkin reported for draft registration. He was recorded at the time to be age nineteen, tall, medium build, with gray eyes and brown hair. He served overseas as a private in the U.S. Army.

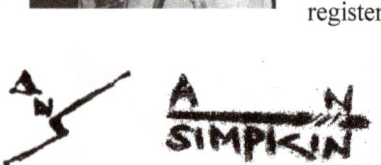

After his honorable discharge in 1919 he returned to NYC and studied at art school for three years.

In 1920 his older sister, Mae Manon Simpkin, married John W. Lowe, a farmer in Walton, NY. They had one child, Beatrice Ruth Lowe, who was born on May 29, 1921.

In 1924 he began to draw pen-and-ink interior story illustrations for pulp magazines.

In 1925 Alfred N. Simpkin painted a cover for the pulp magazine Adventure. [Seen on this page, bottom left.]

By 1927 the artist's estranged father had left Canada and returned to Brooklyn, where he married a second wife, Jacqueline A. Borner, and continued to work as a marble finisher.

In 1930 Alfred N. Simpkin painted dust jackets for hardcover novels produced by the Doubleday Doran Company.

On August 26, 1931 the artist's father, George Fredrick Simpkin, died at the age of fifty-seven in Brooklyn.

During the 1930s Alfred N. Simpkin drew pen-and-ink story illustrations for Blue Book Magazine.

In 1940 he was listed as the occupant of an art studio in the Broadway Arcade Building at 1947 Broadway, between 65th and 66th Streets. Many professional illustrators lived and worked in this building, such as Richard Lillis, George Gross and Rafael M. DeSoto.

In 1943 during WWII Alfred N. Simpkin again registered with his draft board as required by law, but at the age of forty-five, he was not selected for military service.

On February 25, 1946 The Detroit Free Press reported that Alfred N. Simpkin had joined the art staff of New Center Studios, a Detroit advertising art agency. He produced story illustrations for syndicated newspapers.

On July 30, 1951 Alfred N. Simpkin married Dorothy Ernestine Workman. She was born on April 24, 1904 in Detroit, Michigan, where she worked as a public school teacher. The bride was age forty-seven and the groom was age fifty-three. They had no children.

By 1961 the artist had retired from commercial art. The married couple left Detroit and moved to Palm Beach, Florida, where they lived on North O Street.

On August 27, 1965 the artist's older sister, Mae Manon Simpkin Lowe, died at the age of seventy-one in Walton, NY.

Alfred N. Simpkin died at the age of eighty-four in Palm Beach, Florida, on August 15, 1983.

© David Saunders 2017

This original pulp-cover painting sold at Heritage Auctions for $3,883.75 in 2011. Note how the artist conveys chaotic movement through the angles of the chair, candle, and drapery; but the rock-solid, deadly calmness of the gunman. — HA.com

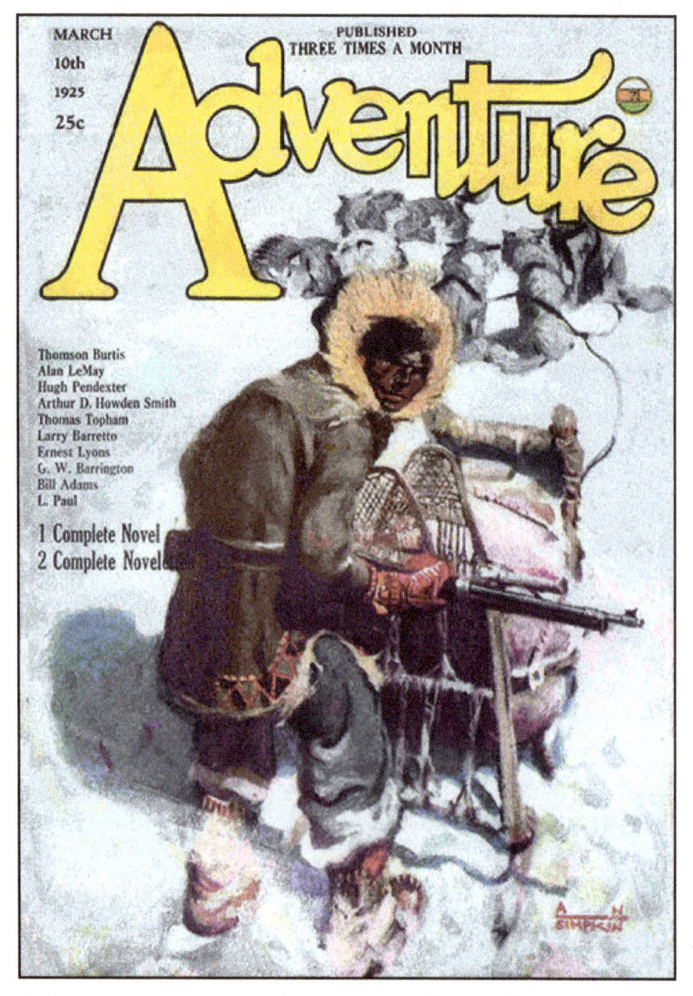

Adventure magazine featured stories and cover art of outstanding quality. This thick magazine came out three times per month. In 1925, when this was published, the country was enjoying prosperity, and the general populace was very literate.

September
2020

Cover image: Cirque du Soleil, KA, MGM Grand, Las Vegas
Great Movies This Month
PulpArtists by David Saunders: Kelly Freas
Ask a Science Teacher by Larry Scheckel: How did tin pest doom the Scott expedition to the South Pole?
Dreaming of Baking by Myra Stokdyk Eischen: Pistachio Cream Cheese Bars
Yes, America's Birthday Deserves to Be Celebrated by Lawrence W. Reed, FEE.org
An important book: Apocalypse Never by Michael Shellenberger
The Woman on Blue Book
Give Me Some of That Good HARD Science Fiction

The woman on Blue Book

Browsing eBay, I found the 1918 Blue Book pulp shown here. Good thing it wasn't an issue I wanted, as it finally sold at auction for $311.

But I received permission from the seller, grapefruitmoongallery (website grapefruitmoongallery.com), to print their image here.

The contents of pulp fiction magazines cannot be described with generalities. There were plenty of women characters who were totally inept, helpless, and had to be rescued constantly by the masculine heroes.

But that sure does *not* apply to this image!

Strong, confident, taking what life gives her with a good-natured smile... there were many such images and characters in the pulps. Of both sexes.

One reason the bidding went so high on this item: "Complete novel by the author of 'TARZAN'." That would be Edgar Rice Burroughs.

Burroughs' story in this issue does not feature Tarzan. His novel-length piece is called Out of Time's Abyss.

What's that? Never heard of it? Well, it was a sequel to two others by Burroughs: The Land That Time Forgot and The People That Time Forgot.

Oh, you've heard of *those*?

I couldn't read the artist's signature at bottom right, so I consulted one pulp source (philsp.com) and found it was painted by M. S. Musselman. I then consulted pulpartists.com, hoping Musselman was one of the hundreds of artists David Saunders has on his website.

He isn't.

I couldn't find any biographical info on M. S. Musselman elsewhere. There's an M. *E.* Musselman, who did similar work (beautiful women) around the same time... any relation?

This is an example of the strange paths that collectors sometimes find themselves traveling.

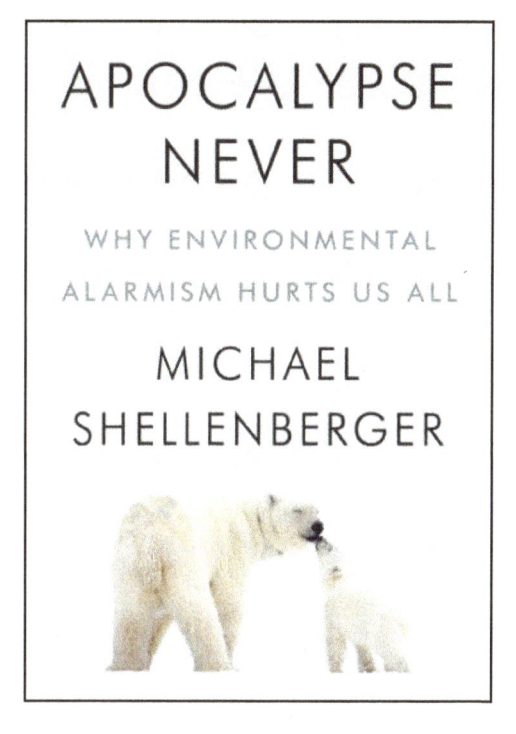

Give me some of that Good, HARD Science Fiction

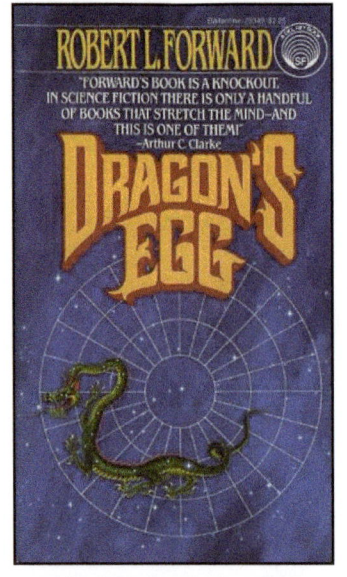

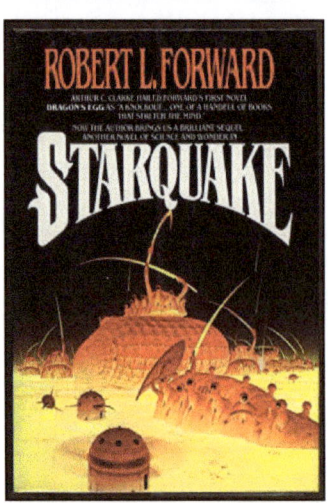

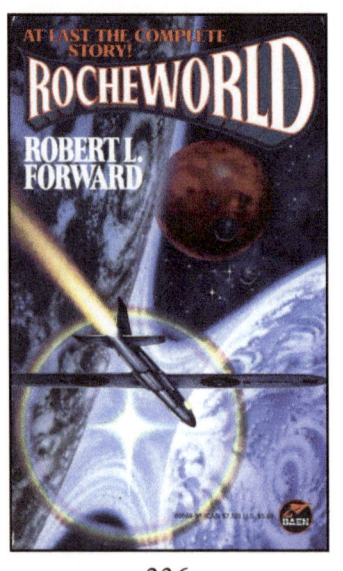

Certain "science fiction" entertainment fails to interest me.

There are series, or movies, or books, consisting mostly of sword fights, with characters in medieval clothing spouting such witticisms as "Take that, thou knave!" This goes on and on. So where's the "science fiction"? Well, a dragon comes along, and burns the whole village. Or a witch casts a spell on everyone.

To me, that's not science fiction at all. It's fantasy.

(And yes, it is possible to tell the difference between the two. And it's simple.)

The best, the very best science fiction for my personal preferences, is called "hard science fiction" (or "hard SF").

My understanding of the term "hard SF" is that the author understands, has researched, and works with the limits of actual scientific principles.

Which means, as just one example, explosions in the vacuum of space do not make sounds.

Does a reader need greater familiarity with science, to read hard SF? That depends on the work. I think it helps. Just as it helps to have background knowledge about the Civil War, to read and better comprehend a novel set in that time.

But don't let that discourage you. A good author leads the reader by the hand, somewhat, and explains things along the way. Some books I'm about to describe have maps, diagrams, even a technical appendix, which explains all the science.

Let's dive right in for a few examples. If you're interested in any, do a 'net search. Some are still available new; some are available as audiobooks; others can be found easily on eBay at very reasonable prices.

Dragon's Egg
by Robert L. Forward

I don't know how, but I once found myself at a Halloween party, with several young couples. I asked one fellow the usual, "So what do you do?" He replied he was an astrophysicist.

He was not a reader of SF, so I described the premise of Dragon's Egg:

A neutron star is discovered passing near our solar system. It's the remains of a star that went supernova, half a million years before. It is about 10 miles in diameter; it spins 5 times per second; and is made of dense, neutron material (a cubic inch would weigh as much as a mountain).

People on Earth plan a manned expedition to the neutron star (NS). They execute an elaborate method of getting the ship close to the NS, while avoiding its gravity waves, which would tear apart the very atoms of the ship and everything in it. (Just this sub-plot takes a lot of explanation.)

The Earth people don't realize that life has evolved on the NS. It lives, moves, and thinks much faster than people. So as the humans photograph and map the surface of the NS, there suddenly appears an artefact. A structure. Signs of intelligent life.

How do they communicate, when it takes a NS inhabitant's lifetime, for a human to say one sentence?

The word "awesome" is so blitheringly overused that it has lost its meaning. But see if the following event from the novel doesn't inspire awe:

The NS inhabitants tell the humans: We did some exploring of your sun, and found some tiny black holes rotating at its core, causing instabilities—ice ages every tens of thousands of years. We went in there and removed the black holes, so it should be working better now.

At that party I mentioned, the astrophysicist was smiling, his eyes sparkling. Others at the table were looking at each other, saying, "Huh? Wha? Are we in the right place?"

Like Forward's other work, this novel's tone is *benevolent*. The protagonists are rational and respect each other.

The book has a technical appendix to explain neutron stars and other science concepts used in the book.

Forward died in 2002 at age 70. I recommend *anything* he's done.

Starquake
by Robert L. Forward

The only sequel to Dragon's Egg. Neutron stars are known by astrophysicists to have quakes—cracks forming in their crusts. An earth-quake, which we living on Earth are familiar with, are bad enough (some of them), but a star-quake... well, in this book:

A quake is so severe that the NS civilization is destroyed. Its inhabitants descend into savagery. A few NS scientists salvage what knowledge they can, and restore some semblance of order.

This all happens in 24 Earth hours!

Rocheworld
by Robert L. Forward

All right, one more by this author. The main idea: Send a shipload of people to a planet orbiting Barnard's Star, which is six light-years away. The trip will take 40 years. The method of getting there uses known, established science. The ship would accelerate by having a laser aimed at a solar sail. But the laser was powered by a ring of lenses, orbiting the planet Mercury (right up front and close, where the sun's rays were powerful), and focused into one intense beam.

(I attended a conference where Dr. Forward, a research physicist who specialized in gravity, gave a talk on "Novel Propulsion Methods" for getting around in the solar system. He described this solar sail system, and told the audience he planned to use it in a novel. He did!)

The ship reaches its destination and discovers a double planet. Two planets, only some miles apart, which are rotating around a common center of gravity so quickly, that they stay those miles apart.

The author enjoyed the concepts created for this novel (and readers responded with enough enthusiasm) that several sequels were written.

Ringworld
by Larry Niven

Imagine a star, as hot, bright, and large as our sun.

Imagine a ring around it.

The distance from the star to any point on the ring is the distance from our sun to the Earth.

The ring has walls. It rotates around the sun. Centrifugal force keeps an atmosphere inside it. The surface area of the entire ring is three million times that of the Earth's surface. That's a *lot* of area to explore!

There are people (and other beings) living on it. But no one there knows where it came from, or who built it.

On Earth, the horizon curves downward, and away from our visibility. On Ringworld, the horizon curves *upward*. You'd see it rise and fade away with distance.

One novel, even a thick one, couldn't contain all the concepts and story of Ringworld. Would you believe *nine* hard SF novels tell that story? There are five Ringworld novels:

Ringworld
The Ringworld Engineers
The Ringworld Throne
Ringworld's Children
Fate of Worlds

A related series, the Fleet of Worlds, also has five novels. You've heard of a fleet of ships? The "fleet of worlds" consists of many planets moving through space. Novels in that series are:

Fleet of Worlds
Juggler of Worlds
Destroyer of Worlds
Betrayer of Worlds
Fate of Worlds

Notice that the two series share the final book. That's when everything comes together, and... and...

Describing the Ringworld seems like one of the simplest concepts. Maybe that's plenty.

Larry Niven has written books on his own, and he's collaborated with other authors, such as Jerry Pournelle, Steven Barnes, and Edward M. Lerner.

Tau Zero
by Poul Anderson

What is there in outer space? I had a friend who believed there was *nothing* in space. Total, absolute nothing.

Wrong!

There are all kinds of molecules and particles. It's just not thick enough to breathe (or friendly enough, if we *could* breathe it).

If you could scoop up enough of those particles, you could burn them in a nuclear reactor, generate energy, and you'd be able to power your ship. You wouldn't have to carry a fuel tank. The fuel would be whatever you could scoop up in front of you. And as long as you scooped up particles and burned them, you could keep accelerating. Go faster and faster.

Several people are aboard a ship like this. They're continuing to go faster.

Then they find the brakes don't work.

Now, that's probably a vast oversimplification, scientifically speaking. But that's the essence of it.

Anderson died in 2001, age 74.

Mission of Gravity
by Hal Clement

Imagine a very dense world (not a neutron star) where the gravity would be 1500 times heavier than Earth's.

Not only would you find it hard to walk (multiply your current weight by 1500), you'd find it impossible to keep your body from immediately being smashed into compressed liquid.

However! This planet rotates quickly (not as quickly as a neutron star). Once every 15 minutes. Therefore, at the equator, the gravity is only *(only!)* three times that of Earth's. Still not comfortable for humans. The farther away from the equator one would travel, the less centrifugal force, and the higher the gravity.

And yet, a ship of men lands on this planet. And their ship has problems.

Fortunately, they learn to communicate with the millipede-like inhabitants of this world. The inhabitants can withstand gravity much more easily, and can live farther away from the equator.

Author Hal Clement is delightfully imaginative when it comes to describing his alien worlds. He shows just as much creativity in describing the mindsets of his alien beings. In the psychology of this world's beings, gravity is a *big* factor. They are completely terrified of two things: falling, and having something fall on them. (Both actions could be fatal.)

So what happens when one of the humans picks up one of the little natives? (They *never* leave the ground, for *any* reason!)

What happens when a group of natives floats down a river, into a cave, where millions of tons of rock are above them? (They *never* crawl under *anything!*)

As with Robert L. Forward, Clement's work is very benevolent. The "enemy" in many of his stories are the forces of nature on alien planets, with humans and aliens assisting each other. Further trouble ensues when there is a misunderstanding (like violating a taboo, and picking up a native).

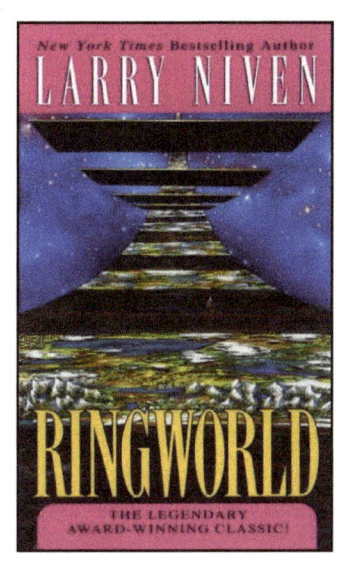

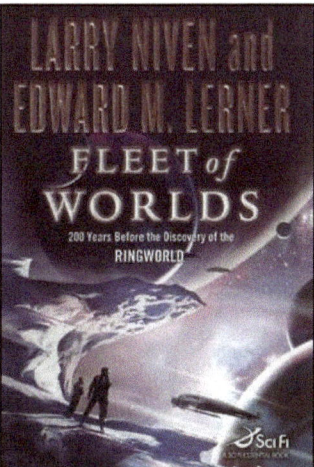

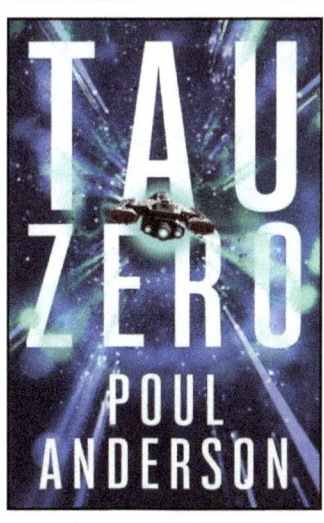

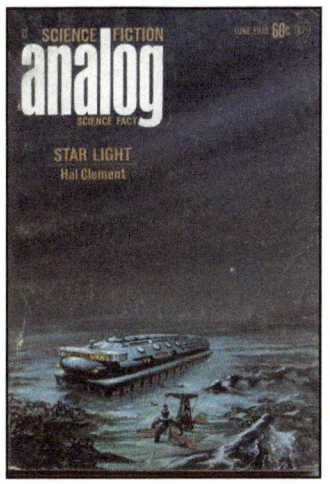

David Saunders' pulpartists.com

Kelly Freas: Carnival Life to Mad & SF

(1922-2005)

Frank Kelly Freas was born Francis Sylvester Kelly on August 27, 1922 in Hornell, New York. His father, Francis Kelly, was born 1901 in New York of Irish ancestry. His mother, Miriam Sylvester, was born 1902 in New York. They married in 1922. He was their only child.

He lived with his mother, a twenty-year-old grocery cashier, and her parents, Walter and Harriet "Hattie" Sylvester, at 70 East Washington Street. His father lived eight blocks away with his widowed mother, Ellen R. Kelly, and two sisters at 34 Franklin Street. His father was a twenty-one year-old unemployed unskilled laborer with a grammar school education.

In 1930 Walter Sylvester died. Widowed Hattie Sylvester decided to move to Canada with her daughter and grandson. They settled in Crystal Beach, a resort town near Fort Erie, in the Niagara region of Ontario, Canada.

Crystal Beach is about twenty miles west of Buffalo, NY. After the 1901 World's Columbian Exposition in Buffalo, the Crystal Beach area had become a popular tourist destination with amusement park, boardwalk, and resort hotels. By 1930 the area attracted around 20,000 daily visitors throughout the summer months. Most people traveled from Buffalo on the *S.S. Canadianna* or the *S.S. Americanna,* historic pleasure craft that disembarked at the splendid Crystal Beach Pier. Each ship carried 3,000 passengers, each of which paid 30 cents for the three-hour boat ride.

Advertisements for Crystal Beach boasted of 100 midway sideshows. One of these was a novelty photography shop operated by James Conoley, born 1882 in Montreal. Hattie Sylvester, who was also born in 1882, married him. Her daughter worked as a cashier, while her grandson spent his formative years absorbing the carnival atmosphere and crowd-pleasing antics of the garish midway.

He soon discovered his natural drawing talent and interest in a career as a commercial artist.

In 1939 his mother married Keith L. Freas (pronounced "Freeze"), a visitor from Buffalo, NY. He was thirty years old and lived at home with his parents, and worked as a machinist at the Curtis Aeroplane factory in Buffalo.

Until that time Francis had attended public school in Ridgeway, Ontario, where he was a high school senior. In December 1939 he lived in Buffalo with Keith's married sister, Gwendolyn LaFlamme, at 153 Massachusetts Avenue. This is only four blocks from the Peace bridge, which straddles the USA/Canada border, as well as the Niagara River. That address is also fifteen blocks from Lafayette High School, which entitled Francis to attend Lafayette as a local resident from January until June of 1940. That was the second semester of the 1939-40 school year. While at Lafayette High School he joined the sketch club and studied with the renowned art teacher, Elizabeth Weiffenbach, several of whose former students pursued careers in art, such as newspaper cartoonist Bruce Shanks and architect Gordon Bunshaft.

Francis Freas returned to Lafayette High School in the fall semester of the 1940-41 school year, but he did not return after December 1940. He did not graduate from the school but his enrollment in the 1941 senior class entitled him to appear in the yearbook.

After high school he worked with his step-father at the Curtis-Wright Aircraft Company. He applied for a job in the art department and was hired to work at their factory in Columbus, Ohio.

On October 27, 1942 he joined the U.S. Army Air Corps under the name Francis Sylvester Kelly. He served two years at the Aviation Mechanics School at Keesler Army Airfield in Biloxi, Mississippi. In his spare time he amused fellow servicemen by painting a mural in the club for enlisted men. In late 1944 he was reassigned to the South Pacific as a reconnaissance flight photographer, where he served until his discharge as Staff Sergeant in early 1946.

After WWII he returned to live with his mother and step-father at 3197 Roosevelt Drive in Massillon, Ohio, where they had moved in 1944 after his grandmother Hattie Conoley was committed to the Massillon State Hospital for the Insane. Miriam and Keith Freas worked at the hospital in the psychotherapy department, where Keith ran a shop class and Miriam was the choir-master as well as the librarian.

After struggling to find work as a commercial artist in Ohio he decided to attend college on the G.I. Bill at the Art Institute of Pittsburgh.

In 1950, while still an art student, he won first prize in a design contest sponsored by the Lane Bryant Store of Pittsburgh. It is noteworthy that he signed this work "Frank Freas" instead of "Frank Sylvester Kelly."

That same year he sent unsolicited cover illustrations to the pulp magazine *Weird Tales,* where his work was accepted for publication.

In June 1951 he graduated from the Art Institute of Pittsburgh. He soon sold cover illustrations to other pulp magazines, such as *Astounding Science Fiction, Planet Stories, Science*

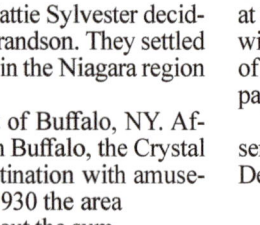

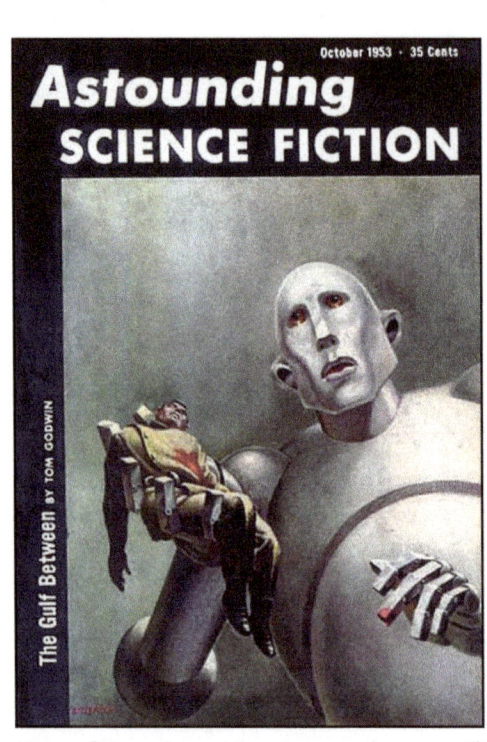

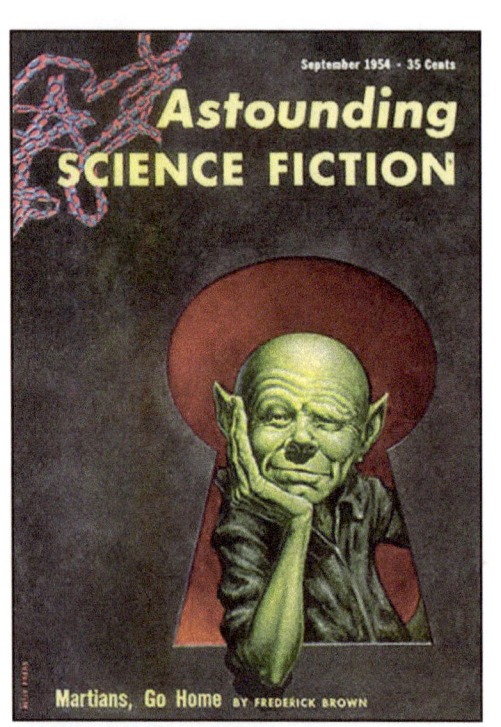

Two of Freas' most iconic cover images. If the one at left seems familiar, and you are not a pulp collector, see the article for where else this image was used. Fredric Brown (his name is spelled wrong on the cover, right) lived in Wisconsin for part of his life.

238

Fiction Quarterly, and *Super Science Stories.* These works were often signed "Kelly Freas."

His illustrations also appeared in digest magazines, such as *Analog, Fact,* and *Ellery Queen's Mystery Magazine.*

In 1952 he married Pauline "Polly" Brussard. They moved to Yonkers, NY, where they raised two children, Jeremy and Jacqueline.

On May 13, 1953 his step-father Keith L. Freas died at the age of forty-four.

In 1957 he painted his first cover illustration for *Mad Magazine* featuring Alfred E. Newman. He went on to paint many subsequent covers for *Mad Magazine.*

He also painted covers for paperback books published by Signet, Ballantine, Avon, and Ace Books.

In 1960 he moved to 4216 Blackwater Road in Virginia Beach, Virginia.

On August 16, 1961 his grandmother Hattie Conoley died at the age of seventy-eight in Massillon State Hospital for the Insane. Her body was buried in Ridgeway, Onatario, beside her second husband James Conoley.

In 1968 his thrice-widowed mother, Miriam Sylvester Kelly Freas Alkire, retired from the psychotherapy department of Massillon State Hospital for the Insane and moved to Richmond, Virginia, to be near her son.

In 1973 he was commissioned to create the insignia design for the NASA Skylab program.

In 1977 he was commissioned by rock band Queen to paint their album cover for the *News Of The World,* for which he recreated an altered version of his earlier cover painting for Astounding.

In January 1987 his wife Pauline died of cancer.

In 1989 he married his second wife, Dr. Laura Brodian.

On September 8, 1991 his mother died in Virginia at the age of eighty-nine.

In 1996 he moved to the West Hills section of suburban Los Angeles, where his wife worked as a radio host of a classical music station.

In 2004 he painted the portrait of a werewolf that appeared in the third Harry Potter movie.

Frank Kelly Freas died at the age of eighty-two at his home in suburban Los Angeles, CA, on January 2, 2005.

© David Saunders 2011

Q: How did tin pest doom the Scott expedition to the South Pole?

By Larry Scheckel

Ask a Science Teacher

A: The race to be the first to reach the South Pole is a familiar story to school children and adults alike. What is not well known is the role that chemistry played in the deaths of Englishman Robert Falcon Scott and his four companions.

The Scott caravan set off from their base on the edge of the Antarctic continent for the South Pole in November 1911. Most of the 50-man group were support team members, dropping off caches of food and fuel on the way so that a smaller team of five men would make a final dash for 90 degrees south and could retrieve those supplies on the way back.

The five reached the South Pole on January 17, 1912 only to find the Norwegian team of Roald Amundsen had been there five weeks earlier. They found the Norwegian flag flying over a brown pup tent and a letter to Scott. The deflated party began the 860-mile return journey.

In the best conditions, it would have been an arduous trek. However, the Antarctic gave them some of the worst weather possible. The team was marooned for weeks in snowstorms, facing starvation, scurvy, dehydration, hypothermia and gangrene.

Most devasting was the lack of heating fuel. Kerosene, in cans, was used to cook food and melt snow for drinking water. Pemmican is a highly condensed form of food made from dried ground meat and fat, heavy on protein. A small amount provides a ton of calories.

Robert Falcon Scott had traveled in the Arctic a few years before and noticed the leather seals on the kerosene cans leaked half of the contents. He decided to go with tin-enriched cans with pure tin solder as seals. It turned out to be bad idea. The returning bedraggled party of four (one had died earlier) found many of the tin kerosene cans empty. Worse, the fuel leaked into the cache of food.

Without kerosene for their stove, they could not cook food or melt snow for drinking water. One went insane and wandered off. The last three pushed on, making their final camp on March 19, 1912, only 11 miles from One-Ton depot, which was loaded with food, fuel, and shelter. A fierce blizzard kept the threesome holed up in their tent, which became their tomb.

What about that tin pest? Whenever pure tin gets extremely cold, a whitish rust creeps over it, much like frost on a window. The white tin breaks into boils and pimples, weakening and corroding the tin until it crumbles and erodes away. In short, it disintegrates. Tin pest has also been called tin disease, tin blight, and tin leprosy.

In extreme cold, pure tin transforms from a silvery, ductile metal, called beta-form white tin to a brittle, nonmetallic, alpha-form gray tin, basically a powder. A phase change is occurring. Once the decomposition starts, it speeds up so that the presence of tin pest leads to more tin pest.

Tin pest raises its ugly head in electronic equipment. Tin whiskers occur in electrical equipment where pure tin solder is used. Small metal hairs, or tendrils, grow between metal solder pads causing short circuits. Traditionally, lead was added to solder to prevent or slow down the hair growths. Since lead is not environmentally friendly, small amounts of antimony or bismuth are added.

Robert Falcon Scott and his two companions perished in the last days of March 1912. A search party found their frozen bodies on November 12, 1912. All their records and logs were recovered. Each had left letters of farewell to their loved ones. Next to their bodies was found 35 pounds of Glossopteris tree fossils, proving that Antarctic has once been warm and connected to other continents. The search party lowered the tent roof over the bodies and a high cairn of snow was erected over it, topped with a cross fashioned from skis. Scott became a national hero in England.

Editor's note: See "Comparison of the Amundsen and Scott expeditions" on Wikipedia.

October
2020

Cover image: The Smithsonian National Portrait Gallery in Washington, DC
Great Movies This Month
PulpArtists by David Saunders: Charles LaSalle
Ask a Science Teacher by Larry Scheckel: Who discovered oxygen, and when?
Property Is People by Robert Tracinski
The search for Harriet Tubman
Expertise in Action
Give Me Some Good, Wisconsin-Style Science Fiction

The search for Harriet Tubman
(Spoiler: We didn't find her)

Way back in March, prior to the world going full pandemicmonium mode, we took a trip to Washington, DC. Prior to eating at Minibar (yeah, I'll have to tell you about *that*, sometime, too), we went to the Smithsonian Institution's National Portrait Gallery.

From online research, it sounded like a highly interesting place in general. But the one, single piece in the collection that I wanted to see was a portrait of Harriet Tubman, painted by Robert Savon Pious.

Pious is one of the PulpArtists that David Saunders has done a biography for. I featured Pious' work in a past issue of The PRC, and even received permission from the Portrait Gallery to run Harriet Tubman's portrait.

So as we entered the Portrait Gallery, my mind was zoomed in on that Harriet Tubman portrait.

I asked at the front desk about the portrait. They look it up on their system and tell you what wing it's located in. A good system. Well...

I also wanted to give the people at the front desk a few copies of The PRC with the R. S. Pious article, including the Harriet Tubman portrait. No, they couldn't accept anything from the general public, but I could try giving them to one of the security guards, that is, if he'd take them.

Well, when I showed the guard the article, the Tubman portrait, the caption explaining how I secured permission from the Portrait Gallery, he was all eagerness, and showed genuine interest in The PRC. Yes, I could tell he was *our* kind of reader.

We went to the wing that allegedly held the Tubman portrait, in no rush at all as we examined hundreds of fine pieces of work along the way.

But we did not find Harriet Tubman.

We asked another guard. She thought it was off somewhere in that direction (which we were going, anyway).

More wonderful works. To my complete surprise, a painting *(a painting!)* of Frederick Douglass!!

The grandeur that is the National Portrait Gallery.

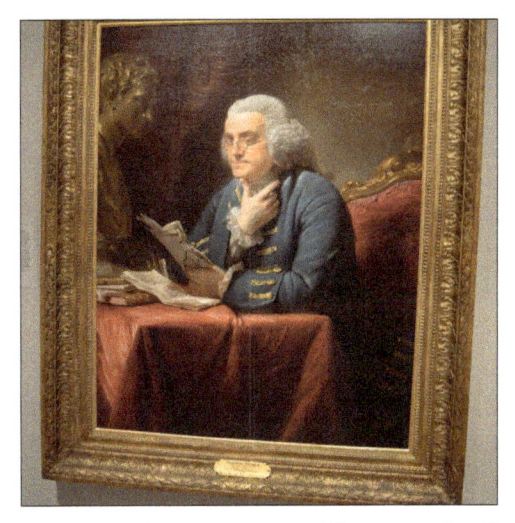

A contemplative Ben Franklin. I wonder if JoAnn's would have a frame like that.

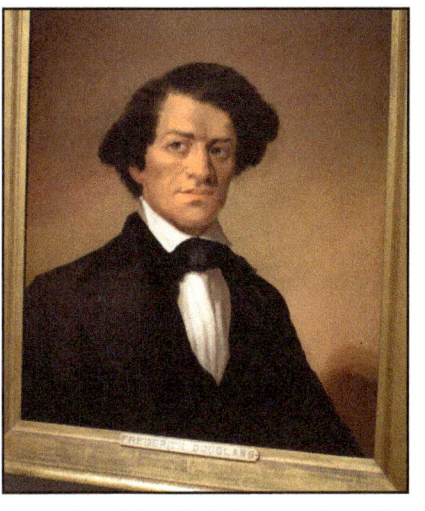

Portrait of Frederick Douglass, by Artist Unknown.

George Washington Carver.

This, ladies and gentlemen, *this* is a portrait. Of whom or what, I don't know. I wasn't curious enough to read the plaque next to it. *This* is why I often (though not exclusively) need to turn to the past to find artwork I consider interesting and worthwhile enough to include in The PRC.

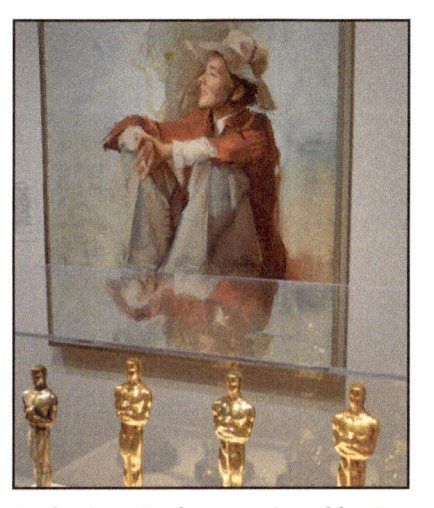

Katharine Hepburn, painted by Everett Raymond Kinstler, with the Oscar awards she won in her lifetime.

Ronald Reagan, also painted by Everett Raymond Kinstler

Ayn Rand, *also* done by Everett Raymond Kinstler. Charcoal, 1959. See article for the story on this one.

Now, why is that such a big shock? Because Douglass *rarely* sat for a painted portrait. He preferred the photograph. He is one of the most-photographed individuals of his time.

I was also pleased to see several portraits painted by Everett Raymond Kinstler. Long-time PRC readers will recall an article run on Kinstler, with his cooperation while he was still living (he died a little over a year ago). (Want to see an original painting by Kinstler? Visit the Kohler Design Center, where you'll see Kinstler's portrait of Herbert Kohler.)

But no Harriet Tubman.

So I went back to the info desk and asked for another piece that I knew *(knew)* to be in the Gallery's collection: A drawing of Ayn Rand by Everett Raymond Kinstler. (If you're wondering why you're hearing his name so often, do a 'net search on "everett raymond kinstler portraits.")

The woman at the info desk checked her computer. Ayn Rand? No such item.

Oh, it's there, all right. Given the decline of our culture, I wouldn't be surprised to learn that her inability to find that portrait in their system was politically motivated. So if you're ever at the Portrait Gallery, and want to irritate the person on duty at the information desk, ask for the charcoal sketch of Ayn Rand, executed by Kinstler, **Object Number NPG.97.56.** (And then go over to the security guard and enjoy a pleasant chat with him/her.)

Aside from all that nonsense, the National Portrait Gallery is a wonderful place to visit. We'd recommend it, as long as it seems Washington, DC is safe to travel to.

Oh... right... we *never found* the Tubman portrait. Maybe next time.

Harriet Tubman, MIA. Painted by Robert Savon Pious. — From PulpArtists.com

Give Me Some Good, Wisconsin-Style Science Fiction

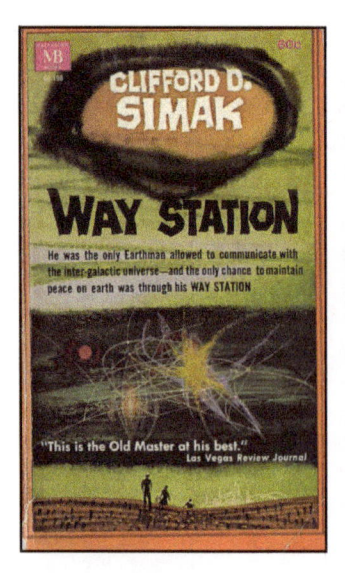

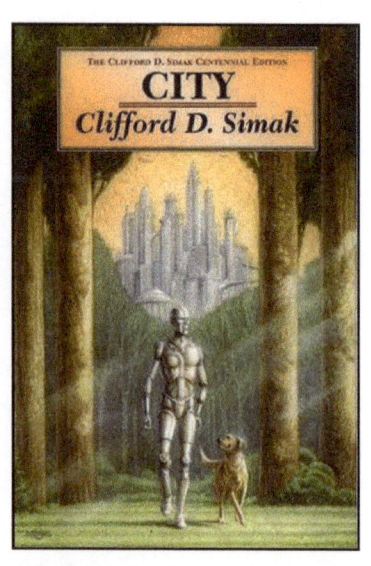

LEFT: Cover art for this paperback edition is by Richard Powers. CENTER: Cemetery World was first serialized in three issues of Analog. RIGHT: The stunning artwork for this edition of City was created by Douglas Klauba. For more superb artwork by Klauba, see douglasklauba.com.

Enoch's life has been extended, and he's been put in charge of a "way station" that operates within his farmhouse. Beings traveling through the galaxy stop there to rest, just as travelers from Sheboygan to Fond du Lac once stopped to rest at the Wade House. And they're just as interested in visiting with Enoch, sharing big news from different parts of the galaxy. (I say "galaxy," and limit it to that area of real estate, rather than saying "universe," because that would make this story sound a little far-fetched.)

Simak's many stories and novels are filled with kooky but benevolent aliens who don't want to destroy Earth; they just want to have a good talk. One alien, Ulysses, visits Enoch often, and enjoys his favorite drink: coffee.

Many visiting aliens enjoy Enoch's hospitality so well, they leave him gifts. *Alien* gifts.

"Wisconsin-style science fiction?"

Is there such a thing?

Well, yes.

Clifford D. Simak lived much of his life in the midwest, including an area in southwestern Wisconsin.

Authors don't necessarily use the settings of their actual lives as settings for the stories they write. But Simak did so.

Besides "Wisconsin-Style," I would characterize Simak's work as being science fiction for people who would doubt they could ever enjoy science fiction.

When you read Simak's description of the countryside, you can feel his affection for the outdoors.

Way Station
by Clifford D. Simak

This novel's main character is Enoch, a soldier who returned to his family farm in southwestern Wisconsin after he fought in the Civil War.

The novel takes place in the 1960s. So those who know Enoch wonder—though they are considerate and sensible enough to mind their own business—they wonder, why he is still alive.

The guy has to be over 100, but he looks like he's in his 20s.

Way Station was serialized in Galaxy magazine in 1963. To my complete delight, I discovered that one of my favorite artists, Wallace Wood, did the illustrations. You'll see some here.

Cemetery World
by Clifford D. Simak

OK, maybe this doesn't take place in Wisconsin (yeah? Prove it *doesn't!*), but you'll find many elements that readers have come to enjoy in his work, including loving descriptions of scenery and the outdoors.

It's 10,000 years in the future. Mankind has spread throughout the galaxy. But people have a strong desire to be buried back on the home planet, Earth. So widespread is this desire, that Earth has become (mostly) one big cemetery.

A man, a woman, and a robot explore the Earth, going off the beaten path and finding it is more than a cemetery. Earth still has some interesting, highly mysterious, and potentially dangerous inhabitants.

Two drawings by Wallace Wood, for Way Station. FAR LEFT: Enoch, out for one of his walks through the Wisconsin countryside, sees the mysterious deaf-mute neighbor girl pick up a butterfly whose wings had been broken, then release it, healed and whole. LEFT: Enoch thinks Ulysses, the alien he's been dealing with for the past century, is essentially human-looking, but discovers the truth when Ulysses has trouble with his disguise. Notice the old-style water pump. — From Galaxy magazine, 1963

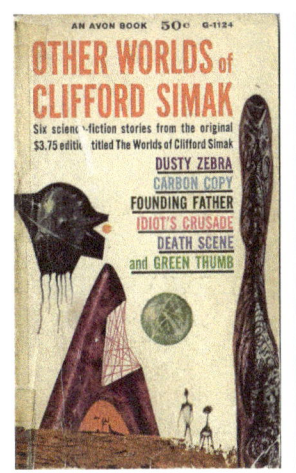

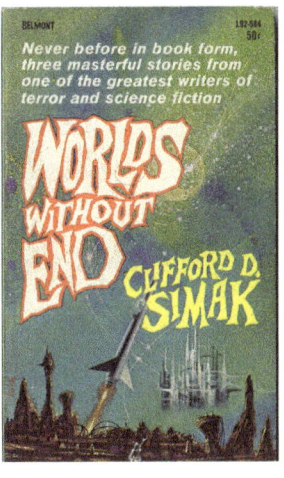

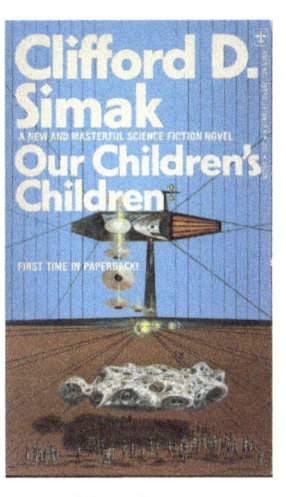

Three Clifford Simak paperbacks (stories not discussed here). Cover art on each by Richard Powers (remember that name!). — From Your Editor's collection

The robot's comments as he surveys the countryside, and sees a red-wing blackbird, are priceless.

City
by Clifford D. Simak

Dogs talk. Robots have the intelligence of people (as in many Simak stories). Eccentric, reclusive geniuses roam the countryside.

The basic question asked in this story is: If transportation is easily available, what is the point of living close to where I work? Why live in a city?

(In real life, today, we are now asking: If I can do my work remotely in this pandemic, why can't I *continue* to do so, thus removing the need for living close to where I work, or constantly traveling back and forth?)

As with many Simak science fiction works, this one is full of wonder and challenge.

Expertise in action

A few years ago, I purchased the illustration at left. The only clue to the artist's identity is the initials "ABS" in the corner.

Two years ago, at a collector's convention, I asked illustration historian and dealer Fred Taraba if he could identify the artist. He examined it and said, "This might be the work of Alice Barber Stephens."

Taraba looked at the back of the artwork, where the artist's name and address are sometimes printed. No such luck here. But there was a strip of paper adhered to the top, which Taraba said was the practice of a certain book publisher he knew used Stephens' work.

Taraba told me his guess that it was Alice Barber Stephens was only that—a guess—but as he shared his thought processes out loud, I knew that it was a very, very *educated* guess.

I was wide-eyed and thrilled to hear such expertise in action.

At right is a color piece, with Alice Barber Stephens' full name at the bottom.

Both are from HA.com.

November
2020

Cover image: Firewood
Great Movies This Month
PulpArtists by David Saunders: Frederick Blakeslee
Ask a Science Teacher by Larry Scheckel: What Is the Most Dangerous Poison Used to Kill Someone?
SCHRC book reviewed: *Among the Badgers,* Rediscovering Sites Associated with Abraham and Mary Lincoln in Wisconsin, by Steven K. Rogstad

Restaurant of the Month by Melissa Niedfeldt: Knosh Eatery and Taverne, Plymouth
Donna Hahn: 20 Years at the Plymouth Arts Center
'Mr. Jones' — The Horrors of Evading the Truth, by Jen Maffessanti, FEE.org
Far-off Fine Dining (Minibar, Washington, DC)
Local Fine Dining (The Blind Horse, Kohler)
Give Me Some of That Good HARD Science Fiction

'Mr. Jones' — the horrors of evading the truth
When the New York Times covered up one of communism's worst atrocities.

by Jen Maffessanti

One of the great, universal truths is that everybody lies. From tiny white lies to great big whoppers, everyone does it, even babies. Don't believe me?

"Sorry I'm late, traffic was terrible."

"It's so great to see you!"

"Doing well, thanks for asking!"

"I have read and agree to the above terms and conditions."

These are just a handful of the easy, casual lies that we all offer up on an everyday basis. And much of the time, these kinds of lies are fairly harmless. These tiny deceptions are baked into most of our social interactions and, in many ways, grease the wheels of polite society. After all, how awkward and uncomfortable would our conversations be if we actually told the truth every time someone asked how we're doing?

These are the lies we expect to be told and are expected to tell. And while I would personally like to see more honesty in everyone's day-to-day interactions, I understand the purpose of these kinds of deceptions.

That said, the truth always matters. We may expect some level of insincerity in certain situations, but in others, honesty is more than simply suggested—it's required.

When it comes to reporting news, telling the truth is vitally important.

The term "fake news" has been abused to the point of uselessness, but false reporting does exist and has for a long time. The information we receive through various media outlets and platforms is frequently critical for how we plan our days and how we plan our lives. When that information is false, intentionally or not, it can cause us very real problems.

Sometimes, the consequences are as simple and relatively

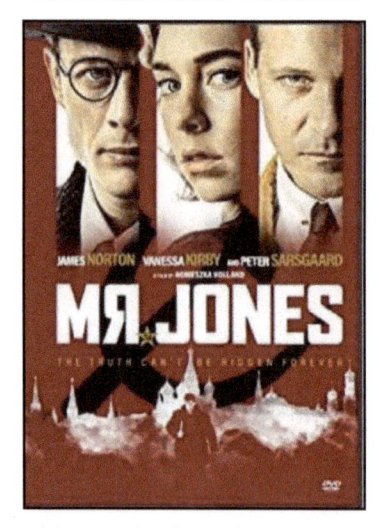

This movie, based on actual events, dramatizes an honest journalist's dedication to the truth. — From Barnes & Noble, BN.com

benign as getting caught in the rain without an umbrella. Sometimes, though—and especially with intentionally misleading or false information—the results can be devastating to livelihoods and lives.

One of the most egregious examples of this was the coordinated cover-up of the Holodomor—a famine in the Ukraine deliberately created by the Soviet Union in 1932 and '33.

In the span of a year, decreased output due to the forced collectivization of farms and the confiscation of foodstuffs by the Soviet army led to the deaths of between seven and ten million people, mostly ethnic Ukrainians. It was, in short, a genocide by means of starvation.

Freelance reporter Gareth Jones broke the story. He did what he was supposed to do as a journalist. He told the truth.

Unfortunately, Jones's reporting shined an incredibly unflattering light on the fact that the news reports coming out of Moscow regarding the impressive successes of Soviet agriculture were false. Walter Duranty, the Moscow Bureau Chief for the New York Times, and the rest of the foreign press corps in Moscow promptly launched a coordinated campaign to discredit Jones's reporting, despite the fact they all knew Jones was telling the truth.

Eugene Lyons, who was the Moscow correspondent for United Press at the time, even wrote in his 1937 book Assignment in Utopia:

> Throwing down Jones was as unpleasant a chore as fell to any of us in years of juggling facts to please dictatorial regimes—but throw him down we did, unanimously and in almost identical formulations of equivocation. Poor Gareth Jones must have been the most surprised human being alive when

the facts he so painstakingly garnered from our mouths were snowed under by our denials. … There was much bargaining in a spirit of gentlemanly give-and-take, under the effulgence of [Foreign Press Corps Soviet Official Konstantin] Umansky's gilded smile, before a formal denial was worked out. We admitted enough to soothe our consciences, but in roundabout phrases that damned Jones as a liar. The filthy business having been disposed of, someone ordered vodka and zakuski.

It should be noted that both Duranty and Lyons were true believers in the communist cause and didn't hesitate to use their positions as arbiters of truth to deceive the western world regarding the actual situation in the Soviet Union. As a result, around ten million people were starved to death during the Holodomor, and yet the Soviet Union continued to be propped up by Western governments and their investments. Furthermore, in total, approximately 100 million people have been killed by communist states since the Bolshevik Revolution which was allowed, in part, by the deceptions of professional "truth-tellers."

This is not to say that bias, in and of itself, is to blame. Another great, universal truth is that everyone has some kind of bias. No matter how hard we try to be objective and relate only the facts, at least a little bit of that bias is going to show through. But there isn't anything inherently wrong with having a bias, especially when it's acknowledged.

The problems come when the bias in people we rely on to report the actual facts internally absolves them of telling outright lies to further their ideological goals.

This is not a problem of the past, either. Whether it's an incident of claiming to have COVID-19 when they don't or building an entire career out of fabricated "news" articles, the long and sordid story of falsified reports continues to this day.

This kind of "reporting" isn't limited to simply lying, either. Blithely passing along uninvestigated press releases or unconfirmed allegations as fact also damages our trust in news media. Given how common such reporting is, it's no wonder trust in news media in the US is only about 29 percent.

And then we wonder why so few people comply with suggestions and warnings given by the news media.

A commonly-offered solution to this problem with news media trust is fact-checking by a small handful of officially approved arbiters. However, the reason that Duranty and the New York Times, Lyons and the United Press, and the other members of the foreign press corps in Moscow were able to cover up the horrors of the Holodomor is precisely because only a handful of media outlets were considered legitimate.

Policies, regardless of who institute them, that centralize the distribution and judgment of truth would end up doing the opposite of what they intend. We would be right back to the bad old days of journalism where media monopolies could spread misinformation largely unchallenged.

It's not hard to find some pretty spectacular fact-checking failures, and this is beside the fact that people tend to reject fact-checks that contradict their core beliefs regardless.

We in the US enjoy fairly robust legal protections for free speech and a free press, which, to be clear, is a good thing. But what can we do when reporters don't do their jobs correctly?

The solution is not to curb or restrict speech that doesn't meet certain criteria. And it's certainly not to limit the sources of various kinds of information. The only way to improve speech is to encourage more speech. We need an actual marketplace of ideas where consumers of information are able to judge for themselves what sources of that information meet their quality requirements and which do not.

The solution isn't a single, official voice of truth. It's billions of voices. It's the competition of different ideas and their purveyors. It's individuals thinking for themselves and accepting the responsibility that comes with that.

The reason the true believers of the Moscow foreign press corps faked their stories was that they feared the truth would hinder the cause they'd placed their faith in. But if a cause can be crushed by the simple telling of truth, it's not much of a cause at all.

The truth matters and the truth will out, even in our world of "fake news" and clickbait.

But only if we let it and only if we demand it.

Jen Maffessanti was a Senior Writer at FEE and mother of two. She is now Director of Communications of the Libertas Institute. When she's not advocating for liberty or chasing kids, she can usually be found cooking or maybe racing cars. Check out her website:

jenmaffessanti.com

This article was originally published on FEE.org and is reprinted here under the terms of Creative Commons Attribution 4.0 International License.

(The online article contains links that serve as footnotes and sources for further information.)

"FEE" stands for Foundation for Economic Education.

Editor's comments on the movie:

Any time you see a movie that says "Based on true events," you should relax, watch the movie, and enjoy it (or not, as the case might be).

Only later should you ask, if it inspired you to wonder, "How accurately did that film portray actual events?"

Even a filmmaker with the highest, most passionate devotion to the truth can find it impossible to fit that truth into the limitations of a movie.

So it is fortunate when we have "fact checkers" for films like Mr. Jones.

The website **garethjones.org** is devoted to the real-life Gareth Jones. There is a tremendous amount of interesting material here.

On the main website at the upper left is a link, **Stop Press.** Click this and find the February 5th 2020 entry. Follow that, and you'll find a long article thoroughly comparing and contrasting events portrayed in the film, with the actual events the film is based on. It's written by Philip Colley, Gareth Jones' great nephew.

The movie itself is not rated, but if it were, it would likely be rated R. There is some nudity at a party thrown by one of the villains in this story, and there is some drug use at the same party. (In my opinion, the film does not glamorize drug use.)

The production values on this film are superb. Watching this, you can tell that a lot of time, work, and craftsmanship went into it. (I don't think you need to be a professional filmmaker to tell when a film is made cheaply, or sloppily.)

Great acting, fantastic photography and lighting that make you feel you're really there. You might have to put on a sweater after some of the winter scenes.

This is an important movie that helps uncover a shockingly outrageous cover-up.

Go to **FEE.org**. Search on "mr. jones". You'll find this article. At the bottom of the article is a link to a video which contains a trailer for the movie, and much more info. After watching this, you'll know for sure if you want to see the film.

Journalist Gareth Jones (played by James Norton) is horrified by what he photographs... but the horrors will only be added to, when other "journalists" with an agenda seek to discredit him. — From FEE.org

The Lincolns Visit the Badger State

Millhouse Press, an imprint of the Sheboygan County Historical Research Center, announces a new and exciting book, **Among the Badgers: Rediscovering Sites Associated with Abraham and Mary Lincoln in Wisconsin,** by Steven K. Rogstad.

This study represents the first scholarly treatment of the visits Abraham and Mary Lincoln made to the Badger State. Although they visited Wisconsin five times between the two of them, they did so at different times, and never together. Abraham Lincoln entered the state's borders for the first time in 1832 during his military service in the Black Hawk War, returning in 1859 to make speeches in Milwaukee, Beloit, and Janesville. Mary toured northern Wisconsin and Racine in 1867, returning five years later to take advantage of the healing waters of Waukesha.

Aside from the visits, Wisconsin has numerous monuments, memorials, and markers which honor the Lincolns. Most of them are concentrated in southern Wisconsin, although some unusual tributes can be found in the Northwoods region. The book describes how each monument has its own unique and sometimes unusual history: donors who died prematurely; a sculptor who demolished his statue with an axe; a statue with a plaque that misidentifies its creator; and a will that was contested all the way to the Wisconsin Supreme Court to prevent funds from being used to create a Lincoln monument.

Now, don't be put off by the term "scholarly." This is a fun and interesting book with amazing trivia. And, it's not really so much about Abraham and Mary Lincoln, as it is about the people who knew them, or whose lives were affected in some special way by being associated with events commemorating the lives or deaths of the Lincolns.

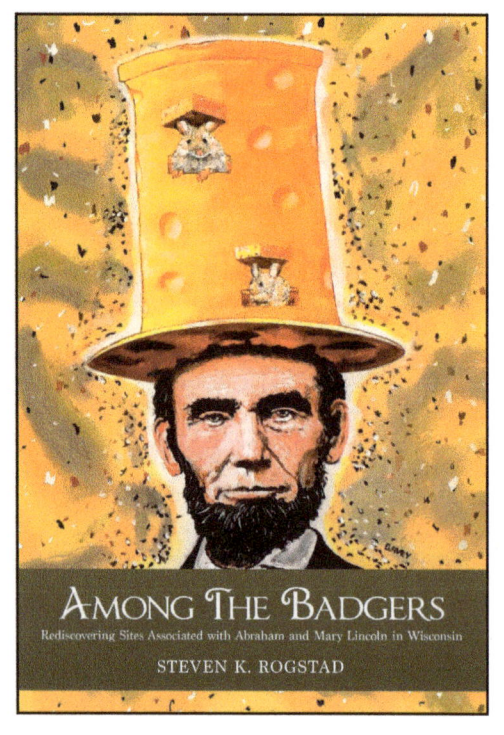

Book review by Beth Dippel for The Plymouth Review Current

Whenever the Lincolns visited Wisconsin, they encountered friendly people who were respectful, courteous, and affectionate. In return, the Lincolns were always gracious and thoughtful towards their hosts. The Wisconsinites who met them never forgot them. However brief, their encounters with the future president and former first lady became cherished memories and important parcels of family history. The numerous Lincoln-related monuments in our state continue to intrigue us, and offer a bond between the Lincolns and Wisconsinites that endures even after so many years.

We walk through the Tallman home with wonderment and awe simply because Lincoln once spent the night there. We stop and gaze up to the top windows of Hanchett Hall because we know Lincoln once spoke there, and strain to listen if Lincoln's voice can somehow yet be heard. We stroll the grounds of Racine College and enjoy the beauty inside St. John's Chapel because Mary Lincoln once listened to a choir rehearse in its sanctuary. The buildings, monuments, and markers are public expressions of our ongoing respect and affection, which keep the Lincolns forever among the Badgers.

Our sixteenth president first traveled north of the Illinois border as a twenty-three year-old Illinois volunteer soldier during the Black Hawk War of 1832. After serving eighty days and marching throughout northern Illinois and southern Wisconsin in a vain search for Black Hawk and his warriors, he was mustered out of service near Whitewater. The young volunteer returned to his home village of New Salem by a combination of horse, canoe, and foot after his horse was stolen the night before his departure and his return to Illinois.

A disputed visit is said to have been made by a youthful Lincoln to the communities of Port Washington and Sheboygan in 1835, but the contention has never been sustained by solid, or even convincing, circumstantial evidence. In 1859, Lincoln made his second visit when he was invited by the Wisconsin Agricultural Society to speak at the Wisconsin State Fair in Milwaukee on September 30th of that year. An aspiring Republican candidate who received national acclaim a year earlier for his senatorial debates against Democrat Stephen A. Douglas, Lincoln delivered his only address on the subject of agriculture at a spot near what is today the heart of the Marquette University campus. He took advantage of two additional opportunities to address large Republican groups in Janesville and Beloit the following day before returning to Springfield. He resumed his law practice and was elected to the presidency slightly more than a year later, never to enter Wisconsin's boundaries again.

Mary Lincoln's three trips to the Badger State were made during the early years of her widowhood. She spent fifty days in Racine during the summer of 1867, where she toured a local school in contemplation of enrolling her fourteen-year old son Thomas "Tad" Lincoln, but also attempted to improve her health by taking exercise and enjoying the cool Lake Michigan climate. Her extended stay was also due to a bad fall down a flight of stairs at her hotel, which kept her bedridden for an extended period of time. Shortly after returning to Chicago in early August, she and Tad embarked on a two-week leisurely boat cruise that took them sight-seeing along the shores of Lake Michigan and Lake Superior on their way to Bayfield and Madeline Island, at the very northern tip of Wisconsin.

It would be another five years before Mary returned to the state, but when she did it was to restore her health by drinking the Bethesda Mineral Waters in Waukesha that had achieved national recognition as a restorative. Living quietly in a boardinghouse west of the downtown, she frequently paid visits to the local spas, but also made time to tour Baraboo, Devils Lake, and supposedly the Madison area. Since becoming a widow, her public campaigns to raise money in an effort to live in a style appropriate with being the widow of Abraham Lincoln made her a controversial and not always agreeable celebrity in the eyes of many Americans, including the press. She became a newsworthy item in two newspapers during her time in Waukesha, when—courtesy of an embryotic form of a paparazzi—she visited spiritualistic mediums in Milwaukee to receive communications from her dead husband and sons. She would leave the community restored to better physical health, but anxious and mentally fatigued over having been followed and spied upon. It would be Mary's final visit to Wisconsin before her death ten years later.

The idea for this book germinated in Mr. Rogstad's mind

over many years, as he spent over fifty years collected anything related to the Wisconsin-Abraham Lincoln connection. He organized and condensed it into this volume. It is the first time accounts about the Lincolns in Wisconsin, and the histories of their monuments, have ever been collected in a single volume. It contains many illustrations, photos, and maps.

The book will appeal to a wide range of readers: historians and scholars, people who travel, individuals and families who enjoy exploring historic sites, persons interested in Wisconsin history, and that larger and broader audience that to this day remains fascinated with every aspect and facet of Abraham Lincoln.

About the Author

Steven K. Rogstad is a Racine, Wisconsin, native, who is known nationally for his scholarship in Lincoln studies. He has served as Secretary and Editor for the Lincoln Fellowship of Wisconsin, and Review Editor for the Lincoln Herald (Lincoln Memorial University, Harrogate, TN). In 2008, he was appointed Secretary of the Wisconsin Lincoln Bicentennial Commission by Governor Jim Doyle, and served on the commission's Markers & Memorials Committee. He has edited and introduced several volumes, authored numerous articles and reviews, coordinated restoration projects for Lincoln statuary in Wisconsin, and delivered dedicatory addresses for Lincoln monuments in Racine and Burlington. He is the former board chair for Racine Heritage Museum, and current board president for Preservation Racine.

Among the Badgers: Rediscovering Sites Associated with Abraham and Mary Lincoln in Wisconsin by Steven K. Rogstad is available at the Sheboygan County Historical Research Center, 518 Water Street, Sheboygan Falls, WI or online at schrc.org/shop. Or you can call 920.467.4667 or order copies. Cost per book is $30.00. For more information on the book go to schrc.org.

Back Cover Blurbs

"So you thought Abraham Lincoln had close ties only to Kentucky, Indiana, and Illinois? As this handsome, exhaustively researched book demonstrates, he worked, orated, visited, and owed much to Wisconsin, too—as did his family. Lincoln may not have lived there, but certainly lives on in the Badger State. Part travelogue, part landmark survey, part art book, part Lincoln family history, Steven Rogstad's authoritative and engaging volume shines with his love for both Lincoln and his home state, and he and his publisher have spared nothing in producing a major keepsake. A must-have for every Lincoln collector, no matter how near or far from Wisconsin they may dwell."

—Harold Holzer, Jonathan F. Fantgon Director, Roosevelt House Public Policy Institute at Hunter College

"There are facets of Abraham Lincoln's life that still need research in primary sources. Steven Rogstad has just filled one of them. This very talented historian has devoted his entire adulthood to photographing and writing about the Lincolns in the Badger State. The Sixteenth President—and his family members—had more connections and spent more time in Wisconsin than is commonly known. If you enjoy new and important Lincolniana that is superbly told and well-illustrated, do not miss this wonderful work by a dedicated and thorough explorer, who uncovers new facts in hidden sources."
—Dr. Wayne C. Temple, Former Deputy Director of Illinois State Archives

"This handsome, lavishly illustrated, encyclopedic omnium gatherum about Lincoln-related people, places, buildings, sculptures, and monuments is a feast for the eye as well as a treasure trove of fresh information about Lincoln, his wife, his admirers, his contemporaries and numerous Wisconsin sites related to them. The artwork ranges from the sublime to the kitschy, and the large cast of characters from the profound to the eccentric. No one knows more about the subject than Steven Rogstad, whose lifetime of diligent research and collecting has enabled him to create this delightful, entertaining, and enlightening cornucopia." —Dr. Michael Burlingame, Naomi B. Lynn Distinguished Chair of Lincoln Studies at University of Illinois, Springfield

"Lincoln Among the Badgers is a delightfully unusual book full of stories and images which are amusing, disturbing, informative, and sometimes downright weird. All reveal things few of us ever knew or could hardly have imagined about the Lincolns and Wisconsin and their impacts on one another. Steven Rogstad, a life-long student of all things Lincolnesque, has given us a very well-written book, full of fascinating details and well-kept secrets, which altogether make for an exceptionally good read and deepen understanding about the Lincolns and our state." —Dr. Kerry A. Trask, author of *Fire Within: A Civil War Narrative from Wisconsin.*

"Wisconsin then and now may lay claim to more Lincoln sites, artworks, associates, scholars, and fans than any state where the Emancipator did not live. Rogstad leaves no hole unfilled in this brick of a tasty, nourishing, and sustaining book, particularly with new information about Mary Lincoln, who did briefly live there. The illustrations alone are worth the price; the text is even better."
—James Cornelius, Editor of the Journal of the Abraham Lincoln Association.

The James Tellen Woodland Sculpture Garden in Sheboygan features this sculpture of Lincoln. — Image from the book

The grave of William Henry Noble in Manitowoc. Noble was part of the group that guarded Lincoln's body during its cross-country funeral pageant. — Image from the book

December
2020

Cover image: Lake Michigan from within the Milwaukee Art Museum
Great Movies This Month
PulpArtists by David Saunders: Jon Arfstrom
SCHRC book reviewed: H.C. Prange, A Sheboygan Institution
Dreaming of Baking by Myra Stokdyk Eischen: Gingerbread Toffee Cheesecake
A Little SF Christmas Cheer
The Stairway of L&H Fanaticism
L&H: Ultimate Book by Randy Skretvedt
L&H Home Video: Stan & Ollie Solo
L&H Home video: The Definitive Restorations
L&H home video: The Essential Collection
Three articles in the Heroes of Progress series, from HumanProgress.org, all written by Alexander C. R. Hammond:
— James Madison: Father of the U. S. Constitution
— Louis Pasteur: Father of Microbiology
— Norman Borlaug: Father of the Green Revolution

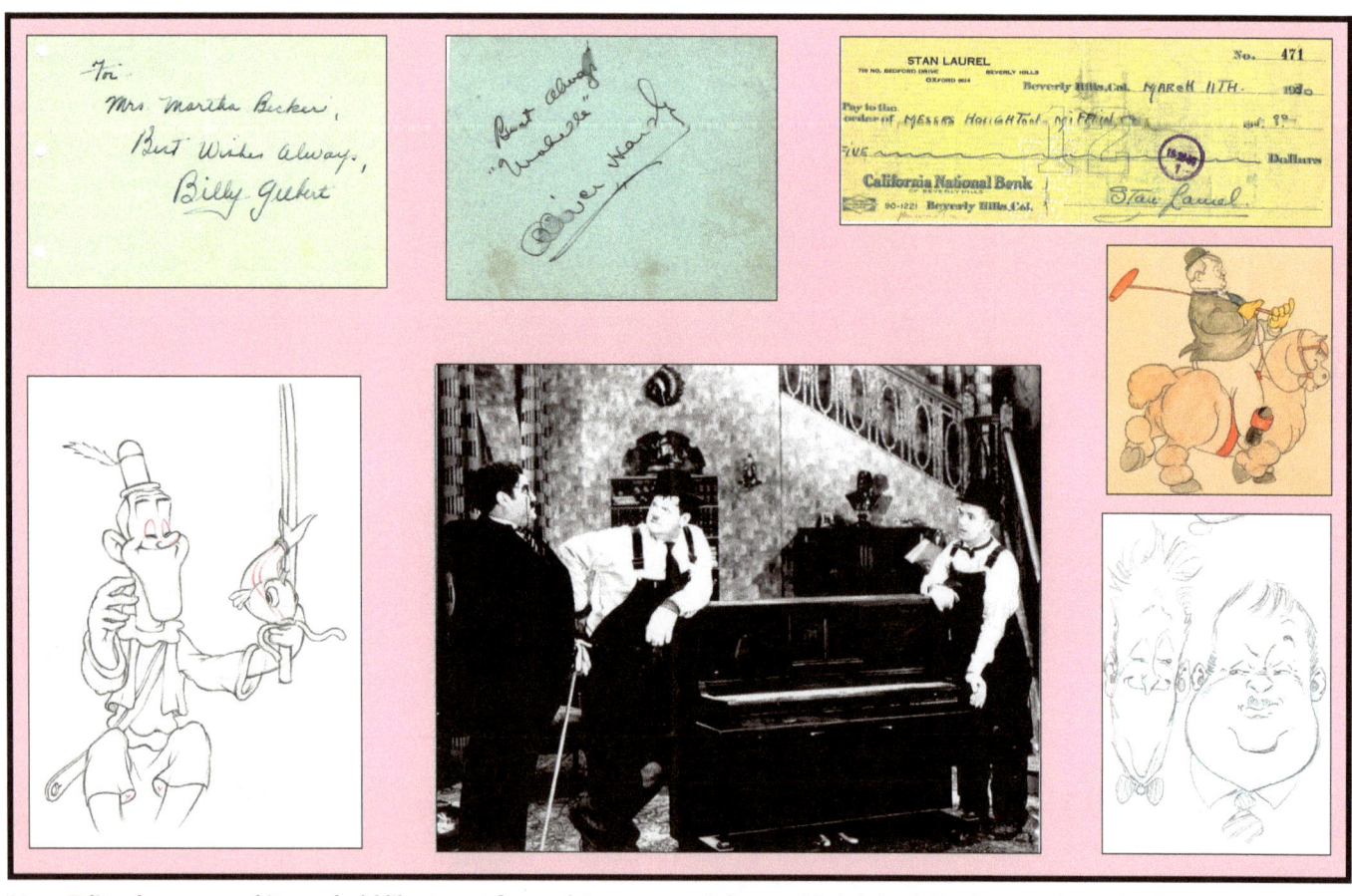

Your Editor has several items he'd like to get framed. I composed them with Adobe InDesign, to show the framing specialist what I want. Alas, pandemicmonium closed down the framing service I'd trust with these items. Maybe it will open again. The three items along the top are autographed by (from left) Billy Gilbert, Oliver Hardy, and Stan Laurel. All three are in the photo (and in that order) from The Music Box (where they carried the piano up the long stairway). I settled for autographs that were less expensive. A single photo that is signed by both L&H could cost (at least) hundreds more than two separate signatures. The smudge in the Hardy signature made it even less expensive. I purchased the animation drawing of Stan with a fishing pole from Heritage Auctions. The picture of Ollie riding a horse is a copy of an item sold by Heritage. The drawing of the two faces is by Michigan comic artist/creator William Messner-Loebs. — Composed by Rodney Schroeter

It's Not Yours 'Til You Like It

Mention the name Prange's and no matter your age from 40 to 90 you probably have personal memories of the legendary Sheboygan department store. Whether those memories are of the annual animated Christmas window displays and caramel corn, the use of due bills, charge-a-plates, layaways, will-call, the x-ray machine in the shoe department or the escalators, they are shared by many and are part of the cherished collective history of the H.C. Prange Company.

This publication is by no means a comprehensive history of the H.C. Prange Company. It is more a trip down memory lane, filled with images, stories and recipes submitted by former employees and loyal shoppers. The story is further enhanced by clips from Prange Company publications, old newspaper articles and images, along with just enough original text to connect the pieces and tell a good story. There are so many stories it's impossible to tell them all so we have chosen to document some of the happenings of the company from its beginning in 1887 to the old store's demise in 1983. Prange's continued on for a number of years after 1983 before it was sold to Younkers, but in a different building and in a different way. The era of the giant "H.C. Prange family" and the big city store in a small town was over. But what a life and influence it had! Enjoy the memories.

The Prange story in America began in 1848 when William Prange, born in Hanover, Germany in 1817, immigrated to Sheboygan County. He married Miss Eleanor Ackermann on March 8, 1849. Mrs. Prange was also a native of Germany, although from Schaumburg. The couple purchased their 160-acre farm located one mile west of the Green Bay Road (now Highway 32) in the town of Sheboygan Falls. They had seven children, the youngest of whom was Henry Carl (H.C.).

When William Prange died in 1865, his wife was left to support and raise seven children. Henry was a frail child who according to his parents wasn't up to the rigors of farm life, and as he approached his twenty-first birthday Eleanor Prange suggested young Henry go to Sheboygan to find a job better suited to his health. And so began Henry Prange's life in retail.

Few would have been able to foresee when partners H. C. Prange, his sister Eliza Prange and brother-in-law, J.H. Bitter opened the original H.C. Prange store on Tuesday, October 4, 1887 that it would turn into a Sheboygan landmark and icon. That first store, located on the southeast corner of Eighth Street and Wisconsin Avenue in Sheboygan, occupied a space of just 30 feet x 110 feet. It was a small two-story building with offices and living quarters upstairs. Louise Rosenthal

Book review by Beth Dippel
for The Plymouth Review Current

and John Bertschy were the first and only employees for the first eighteen months when Otto J. Kohl joined the staff.

It was a true family business from the start. For many years Mr. Prange and his sister bought the dry goods, while Mr. Bitter bought the groceries and had charge of the books. Mr. Otto Kohl, who at first devoted his energies to the Grocery Department, in 1891 took over the Ladies' Ready-to-Wear and Men's Apparel sections, which he successfully handled until his death on July 1st, 1920.

After leaving home at age twenty, Henry Prange found employment in John Plath's general store where he spent the next 11 years coloring butter, packing eggs, delivering groceries and learning the business. Hours were long, 7 a.m. to 8 p.m. and even later on Saturdays, 9 p.m.

After working with Plath, the Wieboldt brothers and several other businesses, Henry Prange began his own business in 1887 always keeping in mind the shopper and the need for superior customer satisfaction. This philosophy helped make his business a success from the beginning. Personally greeting everyone who entered the store by name, he would inquire about their families. Those close relationships with customers made Prange's the place to shop. Those relationships were the key to his business success.

Henry married Miss Augusta Bodenstein on December 29, 1891. The couple originally lived on Michigan Avenue, but later built a home at 617 Erie Avenue where they raised their six children. The family attended Trinity Lutheran Church in Sheboygan. Henry and his sister Eliza were generous donors to their church. Gifts from the Prange family paid for the eighth grade addition to the Trinity School. Prange was always interested in civic organizations and was a great philanthropist.

One of Henry Prange's favorite places was his summer home at Elkhart Lake, which he acquired about 1907 after spending many years staying at summer hotels there. The lake property was the scene of many family reunions and company parties.

The Pranges enjoyed traveling especially in their later years when they spent a number of months each year in Florida escaping Wisconsin's harsh winters.

Henry C. Prange died of pneumonia in St. Augustine, Florida on January 25, 1928. He was 69 years old. His son H. Carl Prange took over the store upon his father's death. Under H. Carl's leadership, the business grew from a single store in Sheboygan to a company with twenty-six stores in three states. But, the emphasis on customer service remained; "It's not

1910-1911 H.C. Prange catalog.

H.C. Prange Department Store, Eighth and Wisconsin, Sheboygan. 1930s image. — Images accompanying this article courtesy of the SCHRC

yours 'til you like it" endured.

First Customers

On Saturday, October 1st, 1887, before the store was officially open, while the shades were drawn and the store filled with lumber, shavings and dry-goods boxes, and the carpenters still busy putting on the final touches, there came a rap at the door. Imagine the surprise of H.C. Prange, J.H. Bitter and Miss Eliza Prange who were busy unpacking goods at the time, when they were met by Mr. William and Mrs. Otillie Fiebelkorn, who inquired in German, "Kann man schon was kriegen?" meaning "Are you ready for business?" Of course, they were ready. The Fieblekorns bought a generous bill of goods — the first ever sold by what is now the H.C. Prange Company.

The Fiebelkorns owned a large farm west of Cascade and traveled nearly 25 miles to shop, quite a distance in 1887. Something caused them to come back time and time again. Odds are that service and quality caused them to become lifelong customers. The Fiebelkorns' loyalty helped the store grow steadily year after year, until it became the largest store in this part of Wisconsin.

Customer Service

In the days before World War I, German was heard in the store nearly as often as English. The German colloquial expression, "Down by Prange's" came to signify the high regard of the community for Prange's as the downtown center of the city.

Henry Prange was credited with the large patronage among the people of the city and county. He spent a great deal of time in the grocery entry greeting customers, many of whom he learned to know by name, visiting with them in German.

At Prange's in Sheboygan it has always been the customer who is central, ergo the mantra, "the customer is always right." The slogan, "It's not yours 'til you like it," was another hard and fast rule, created by H.C. Prange and put into action by Prange employees. Customer service was one foundation of the Prange business. This was seen and put into action through the constant changes that kept the store fresh and attractive to customers.

The backbone of Prange's business was the farmer. Farmers brought their produce (i.e. apples, potatoes, eggs, milk, berries) to the store and were given "due bills" in exchange.

These due bills or certificates (booklet seen at left) could be used only at Prange's and were spent like cash. This exchange system was a way for people for whom cash was scarce to buy items they needed (shoes, clothing, cooking utensils, and a few fineries). For some farmers it was a weekly stop; for others it was a highly anticipated special event. Prange's treatment of the farmer created an intense loyalty which benefitted both shopper and store.

Prange's always had a policy to pay two cents more per dozen for eggs than any other competition would pay. Once, during an egg pricing war in the 1930s, the store bought 400 cases of eggs, thirty dozen eggs in a case (That's 144,000 eggs). The company had to ship an entire freight car load to Boston just to get rid of them.

During the national bank holiday of 1933, Prange's accepted checks from customers and issued due bills, many of which were used to pay dental or doctor bills or buy groceries. People had no money. The checks weren't cashed until the moratorium was over.

The summer of 1937 witnessed the opening of Prange's new escalator . . . The only moving stairway, as it was called at the time, in Wisconsin. Prange's escalator preceded those in Milwaukee by five years. The escalator took shoppers from the first floor to the second floor, but not back down.

The escalator was electrically driven, running continuously and silently, and was capable of carrying as many as 6,000 people per hour. Situated at the rear of the store the escalator ran from the first to second floors and could accommodate as many as 42 people at one time.

The escalators were upgraded in 1947 when shoppers could go from the second to the third floor and also take the escalators down, as well. The originals only went up.

Among other improvements made in 1937 was the installation of an up-to-date soda fountain and luncheon service. This new department on the main floor offered the latest in comfort and convenience for customers. Tables were Formica-topped steel tables and had comfortable genuine red leather and chrome chairs. The table tops were advertised as scorch and scratch-proof. The tables also had purse and package rails for the comfort of the customers. Ninety people could be seated at one time.

Improvements were constantly being made at Prange's as the need for them arose. As a result the store enjoyed the reputation of being one of the finest and most complete stores in Wisconsin. Prange's placed customer confidence first among all its assets.

This book takes you through the growth of the landmark and then the demise of the great store in 1983, all because of a leaky pipe. You can find recipes for treasured lunch specialties including the sour cream donuts. You will take a trip back in time through newspaper ads and article, images, recipes and much more. This is a fun read.

This book can be found at the Sheboygan County Historical Research Center, 518 Water Street, Sheboygan Falls. Check out schrc.org/shop to order online. Call 920.467.4667 for curbside pickup.

1926 photo of Hadji Ali, demonstrating his ability to (ugh) regurgitate water he has swallowed. Ali's appearance in the Spanish-language version of one of L&H's films made it unforgettable. — Public domain image from Wikipedia; this also appears in the Randy Skretvedt book

Left: A stairway in the Los Angeles area as it appeared in 1932, when The Music Box was made by Laurel & Hardy (see December 13). From the L&H film, The Music Box. Right: That same stairway in modern times, when Your Editor made a pilgrimage to it in April of 2016.

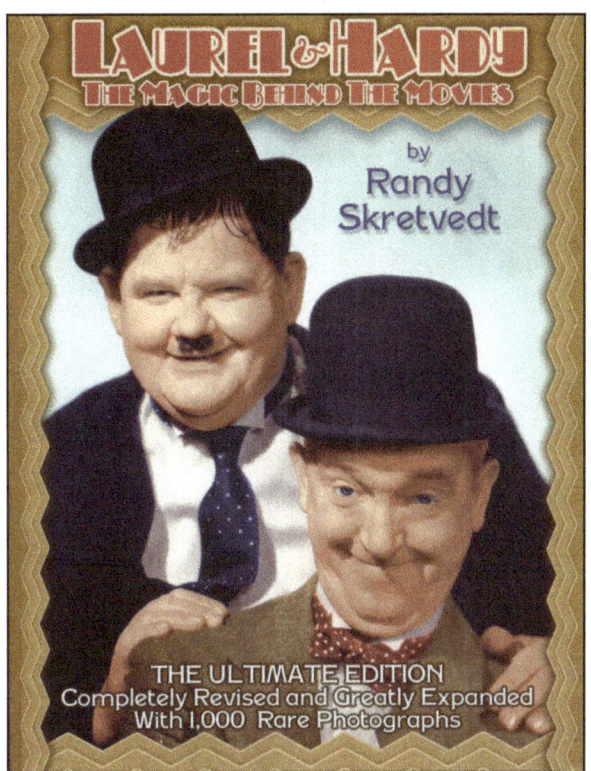

ULTIMATE

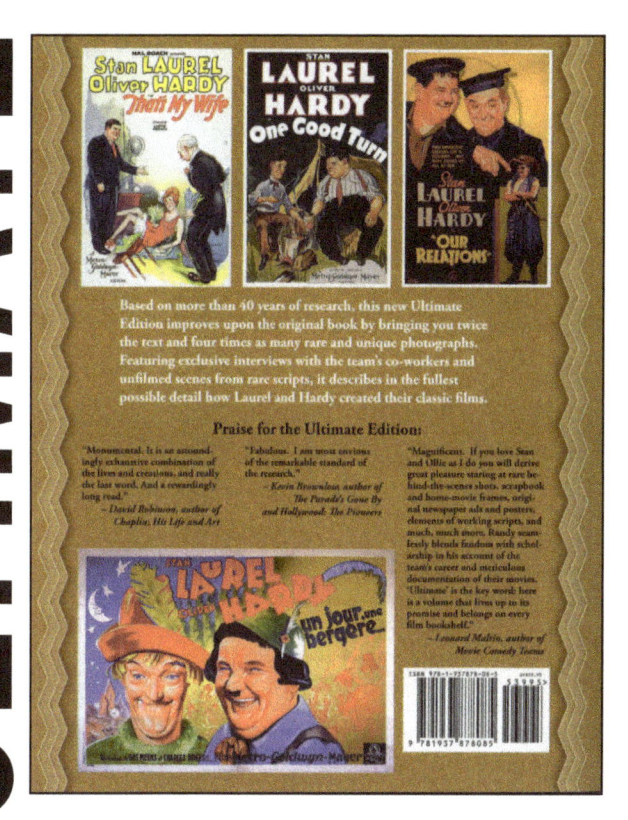

"Ultimate" is the word, all right!

You can't always trust front-cover blurbs on books. How many paperbacks, for instance, have "The Ultimate Horror!" bursts? They can't all be "ultimate."

Well, when it comes to L&H, this book's blurb, "The Ultimate Edition," has to be accurate.

This mammoth, 8x10-inch, 630-page, nearly 3-pound book has information on every L&H film: Dates of production; complete Hal Roach studio credits; a synopsys; film photos and posters; behind-the-scenes photos; background on the film; background on secondary stars.

I doubt you can get any more ulimater than that.

Remember what I said about "levels" of L&H fanaticism? Sure, you can watch their films, and be satisfied with that. That's one level. Nothing wrong with that.

But then, you can take it to another level and listen to commentaries on the "Essentials" or the "Definitive Restorations" sets.

And you can crank it up to another level with this book.

Somewhere in Limbo, by Jon Arfstrom, painted in 1982. — HA.com

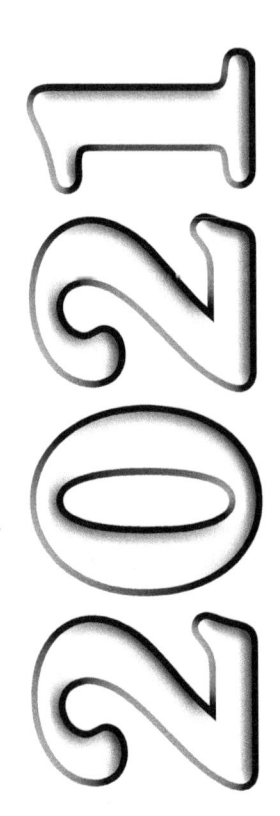

2021

The Plymouth Review Current

TAKING YOU PLACES WORTH SEEING
Volume 10 • Issue 2 • January 2021

FREE!

On Track at Kohler Co.
Pulp Artists ◆ Crossword ◆ Waiting for winter

• The publication that respects your intelligence •
• Intellectual stimulation • Movies • Art •

January
2021

Cover photo: Waiting for Winter
Great Movies This Month
PulpArtists by David Saunders: John Newton Howitt
SCHRC book reviewed: *On Track at Kohler Co.*, by Peter J. Fetterer
"A Couple's Winter Blast" to Open in Gallery 110 North
Ask a Science Teacher by Larry Scheckel: Is There a Plus Side to Having a Genetic Disorder?
What Are People Saying about The PRC?
Now That's a Big Book!
Restaurant of the Month by Melissa Niedfeldt: Stone Dagger Pizzeria, Kiel
From Your Editor's collection

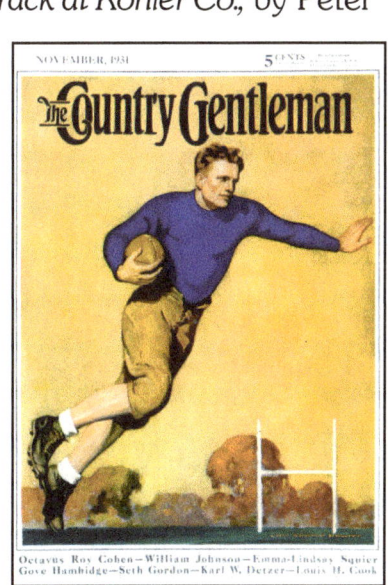

From 1931. This magazine was published from 1852 to 1955.

1909 advertising art by John Newton Howitt. What a treasure!

253

John Newton Howitt: From Slicks to Pulps and Back Again

(1885-1958)

John Newton Howitt was born May 7, 1885 in White Plains, New York. His parents were John and Addie Howitt. His brother Louis was five years younger. They lived at 21 Lake Street. His father manufactured ladies' clothing.

At age four John Newton Howitt contracted polio. During his convalescence, his father interested him in drawing. After his recovery he wore a metal brace on his right leg. In 1901 he graduated White Plains High School at age sixteen.

In 1902 Howitt studied in New York City at the Art Students League with George Bridgman and Walter Clark.

Howitt was a devoted landscape painter. He was a lifelong member of both the Westchester Arts & Crafts Guild as well as the Hudson Valley Art Association. He exhibited in their annual shows, won awards, gave demonstrations, headed committees, and served as president. His friend and neighbor, the pulp artist Sidney Riesenberg was also a member.

Howitt's landscapes were sold at fine art galleries in New York City, such as the Art Center Gallery, The City Club of New York, and Ainslie Galleries.

In 1905 he began to sell freelance illustrations to *The New York Herald Tribune, This Week, The American Sunday Monthly Magazine, The Hampton Magazine,* and *Broadway Magazine.*

In 1908 he opened an art studio in New York City at 147 West 23rd Street, which he continued to rent for the rest of his life. He joined the New York City Artists Society and the Salmagundi Club.

Howitt then worked for *Red Book, Woman's Home Companion, The Household, Maclean's,* and *Scribner's.* He also painted advertisements for Crisco Shortening, Devoe Paints, Jello Foods, and Post Bran Flakes.

In 1918, at age thirty-three, Howitt reported for his WWI draft registration and was described as medium height, slender build, with gray eyes, brown hair, and "crippled right leg."

In the decade after the war, Howitt worked for *Country Gentleman, Farm Life, Liberty,* and *The Saturday Evening Post.*

By 1930 Howitt's elderly father had died. Although Howitt was forty-five and his brother, Louis, was forty, they both still lived in their childhood home with their mother, who was seventy-two.

When commerce collapsed during the Great Depression, slick magazines suffered from lost advertising. Howitt began to work for pulp magazines instead. The pulps were funded by newsstand sales and were growing extremely profitable as idle workers began to read more. Howitt was an excellent pulp cover artist. He signed his covers for Western pulps and romance pulps with his regular professional signature, "JOHN NEWTON HOWITT," but he also painted many ghastly and shocking pulp covers, and these were all signed with only his initial "H." Most pulp artists who wanted to disown the covers would conventionally leave them unsigned and uncredited. Howitt's "H" is only a modest deception, which seems to imply some ambivalent pride in even his most outrageous pulp covers.

He sold freelance pulp covers to *Adventure, Dime Detective, Dime Mystery, Horror Stories, Love Story, Operator 5, The Spider, Terror Tales, Top-Notch, The Whisperer,* and *Western Story.*

In 1936 Howitt started a legal battle with Street & Smith when he was charged $28.20 city sales tax on $410 paid for sixteen paintings. The case grew through appeals court to historic proportions and embroiled the entire illustration industry. The tax was finally voided when the State Supreme Court ruled that the publishing houses should be taxed and not the individual artists.

By 1939 the economy had recovered to the point that Howitt once again received ample assignments from slick magazines, such as *Liberty* and *The Saturday Evening Post,* so he stopped working for the pulps.

Another factor was his recent marriage to Bertha Howitt, who disapproved of scandalous pulp magazines. Howitt finally left home and moved seventy miles west to live near Bertha's family in Port Jervis, New York. They were both in their mid-fifties. They had no children.

During WW2 Howitt was too old to serve, but he did contribute several important propaganda posters to the war effort.

After the war he continued to work for slick magazines and advertisements. He also continued to paint landscapes. In the 1950 Annual Exhibition of the Hudson Valley Art Association his painting "The Blue Hills" won an award for the best landscape.

According to the artist, "Too much emphasis is put on art fashions of the moment and there is not enough recognition of good painting. We who are not 'modernists' have found that we get no recognition today in art circles unless our work is clothed in the style that is considered fashionable. It does not matter how well or how forcibly we express it; we get no attention from critics or museums or even the large exhibitions. Museum collections of American paintings will never be important as long as they only follow the latest fad in art. Painting should have a more solid basis than fashion. As long as it is not possible for an artist to paint for mass production and do good work, many painters today are quite willing to adapt their prices to the buyer's pocketbook. We artists are ready to meet the private buyer half-way. We believe that no painting stacked against the wall is fulfilling its function. We must sell to continue painting and unless we can continue, art will die, because painting is not a part-time job."

John Newton Howitt died at age 72 on January 25, 1958.

© David Saunders 2009

February 2021

Cover photo: Truffles and Squab, Lake Park Bistro

Great Movies This Month

PulpArtists by David Saunders: John Newton Howitt

The Crook in the Corn Shredder

SCHRC book reviewed: *Sheboygan County's Native American Past*

Black Truffle Dinner at the Lake Park Bistro

The Sketches and Art of Saul Tepper

Book Review: America's Revolutionary Mind: A Moral History of the American Revolution and the Declaration That Defined It, by C. Bradley Thompson, reviewed by Jon Hersey, The Objective Standard

Ask a Science Teacher by Larry Scheckel: What is Meant by a Gold Rush?

The Plymouth Review
Current
Taking you places worth seeing
Volume 10 · Issue 3 · February 2021

FREE!

Dick Tracy & Farm Machinery
Saul Tepper ◇ Crossword ◇ Black Truffle Dinner

From preliminary pencil sketch to finished piece. The final ad is from the book, The Art of Saul Tepper, by Daniel Zimmer.

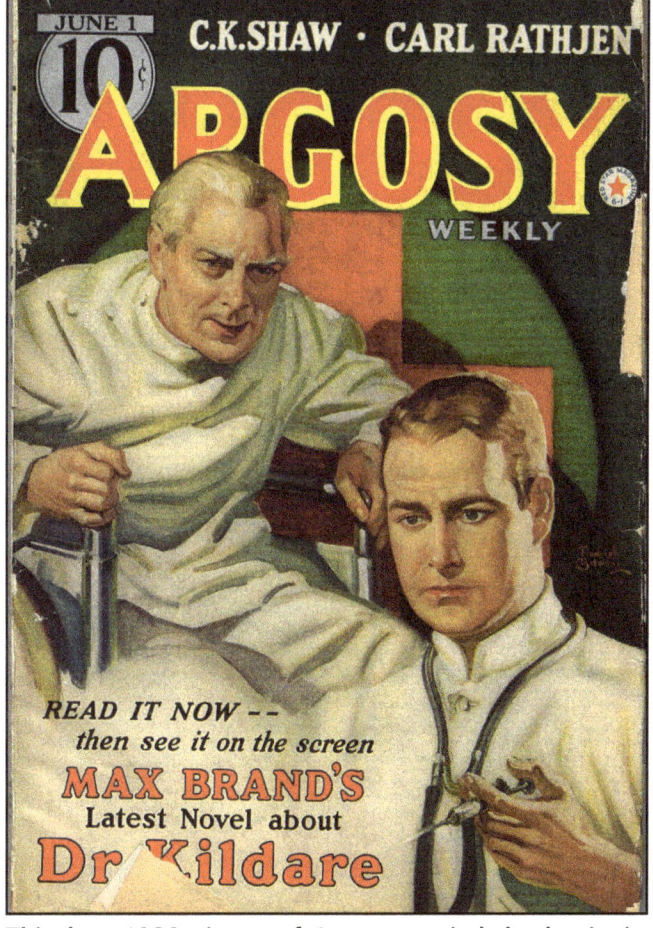

The letter that fathered a million-dollar phrase

This late 1930s issue of Argosy carried the beginning chapters of a Dr. Kildare serial. "Read it now... then see it on the screen" the cover urged. There are at least three Dr. Kildare movies on TCM this time around. Did you *know* the original Dr. Kildare stories were written by Frederick Schiller Faust? (Did you *know* that was Max Brand's *real* name?) — From Your Editor's collection

255

The Crook in the Corn Shredder

Or... What goes around comes around   *Or...* Connections bring coincidences

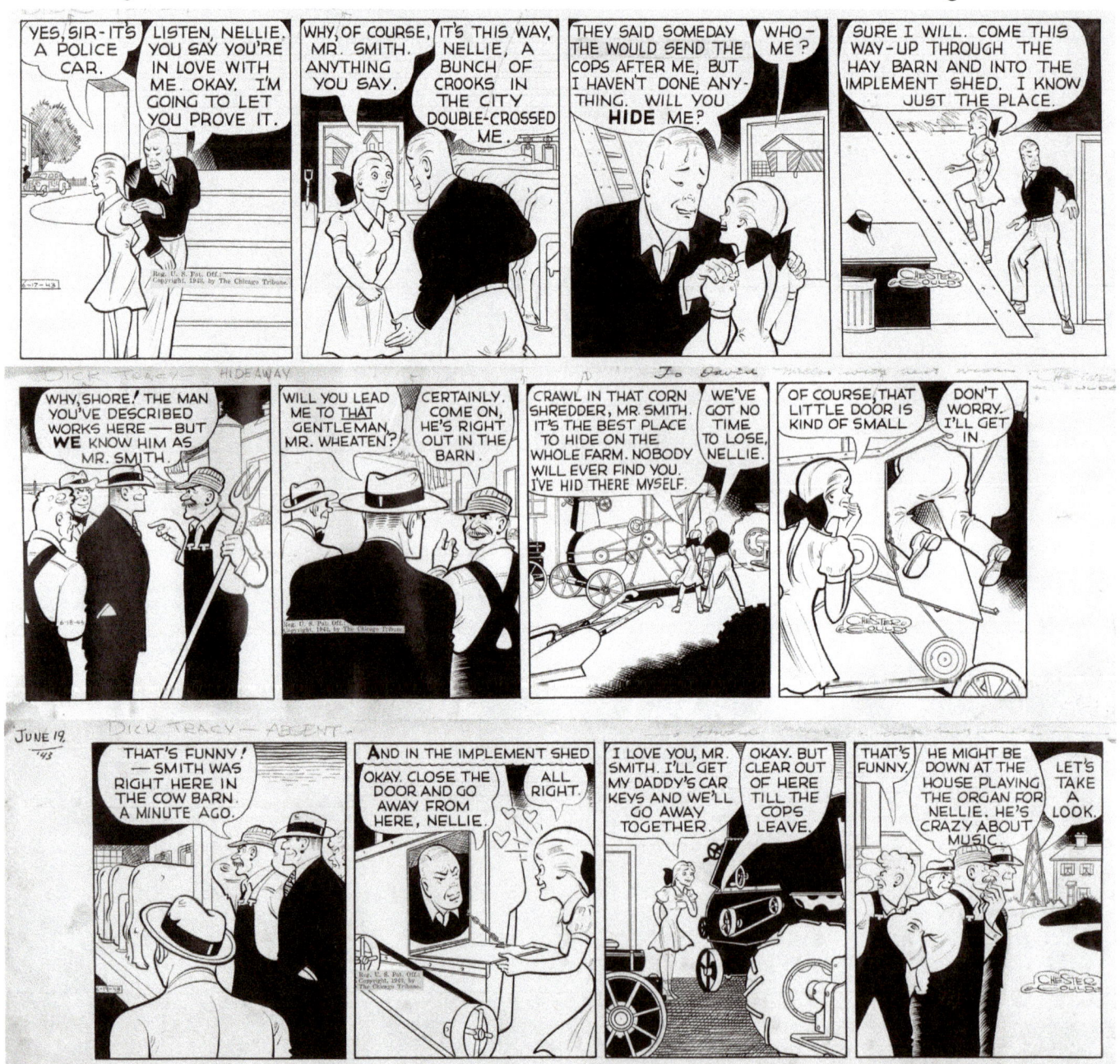

Three consecutive original daily Dick Tracy strips: June 17, 18, and 19, 1943. Villain 88 Keys is hiding on a dairy farm to escape the law. Nellie is infatuated with him, unaware he's a murderer.
    Look closely at 6-17, panel 3: A correction had been made and rubber-cemented over the 2nd line. It fell off over the years, leaving a discolored area. — All three strips, HA.com

    I bought my first Dick Tracy original at the 1978 Chicago Comicon. Since then, I've purchased a few others. But recently, I purchased the oldest, and what I consider the nicest, of all my Tracy originals.
    The strip I recently bought is a daily, dated June 19, 1943.
    (A little background, if needed: Dick Tracy was a "continuity" strip, continued from day to day in the newspapers that carried it. From Monday through Saturday, readers saw one of these "daily" strips; on Sunday, the strip was in color and had more panels. Sadly, the continuity strip is now nearly extinct. Newspaper comics fans have various theories on why that is so. When I say "original," I'm talking

The Rosenthal steel 40 corn husker/shredder. Could it be similar to the machine 88 Keys, above, crawled into to hide? — Courtesy of *Farm Collector* magazine, www.farmcollector.com

about the actual drawing the artist created; you can often see pencil lines, corrective white-out, and—as on two strips here—an inscription to someone Gould gave the drawing to, likely a gift.)

What makes the 6-19 original attractive for the collector?

• It features Tracy in two panels (1 and 4). Tracy appears nowhere in the 6-17 strip.

• Many collectors consider the 1940s to be artist/writer Chester Gould's best years on Tracy.

• It features a villain in one panel. This is 88 Keys, so named because he's a pianist. The law is after him because he's a murderer. He's hiding out on a farm, pretending to be an experienced farm hand (but the farm owner is highly suspicious of his soft hands, and ignorance about dairy cattle). 88 Keys was not an *iconic* Tracy villain, like Flattop or Pruneface. Originals with such iconic villains bring much higher prices.

What makes it attractive for *me, personally?*

• As established in an earlier strip, the dairy cows shown are Brown Swiss, which my dad milked on the farm I grew up on.

• This is one of my favorite Tracy continuities. I used it as an example when writing an article, Dick Tracy: Morality in Black and White. I described Nellie as an example of a good person who gets mixed up with evil (because of her youthful naivete). In the history of the Tracy strip, such characters were sometimes harmed or killed. Nellie realizes her error in time to extricate herself.

• It features interesting farm machinery.

Looking at the 6-19 strip, I thought maybe the machine was a threshing machine. My dad once had one of those, and I'd seen it in operation several times.

But in the 6-18 strip, Nellie identifies it as a "corn shredder." That wasn't something I was familiar with.

I had to know more. Searching the 'net, I found photos of a corn husker/shredder on **Farm Collector** magazine's site. Could this be similar to the machine 88 Keys crawls into in the 6-18 strip?

My thirst for knowledge not quite sated, I continued searching, and found another photo, this one also from **Farm Collector.** I contacted the editor, who graciously granted The PRC permission to run the photos.

On finding the second corn husker/shredder photo, I knew I wanted to run it. By coincidence, I'd stumbled onto a photo by Larry Scheckel, whose name will be familiar to long-time PRC readers.

Less than two months after drawing the 88 Keys strip I purchased, Chester Gould was in the midst of one of his most famous and creepiest story lines: Mrs. Pruneface. Of course, there *was* a *Mr.* Pruneface; he was a Nazi spy (remember, this was 1943). *Mrs.* Pruneface captured Tracy and was going to get revenge...

Here, I'd normally tell you: Pick up a copy of The Complete Dick Tracy, Volume 8, for *all* of these stories...

Alas, this book seems to be out of print. One book service has copies starting at $140. An eBay search comes up with a couple of copies, both at that price or higher.

What a shame!

The sketches and art of Saul Tepper

At a Windy City Pulp and Paper Show a few years ago, illustration art dealer and expert Fred Taraba had at his table many sketches by Saul Tepper for sale. I bought a few dozen—many selling for $2 or $5. — Sketches from Your Editor's collection; finished paintings from the Illustrated Press book, Saul Tepper (now out of print)

Tepper was probably given the main idea for what the advertising client wanted. He then worked up these three variations (maybe even more). The "best" one was selected by Tepper's art director (or maybe Tepper himself), and the artist created a full-size, finished painting. The preliminary sketches are reproduced here full size; the finished paintings would be much larger.

Right: Preliminary and published piece. Below: It was priced at $2; what the heck—BUY it!

Bottom row: Not shown at actual size.

258

The Plymouth Review Current

TAKING YOU PLACES WORTH SEEING
Volume 10 • Issue 4 • March 2021

FREE!

The publication that respects your intelligence • Intellectual Stimulation • Movies • Art

Brainstorm ◆ 5000 Fingers ◆ Girl Shy
Sheboygan History ◆ Crossword ◆ Hiking the back 40

March 2021

Cover photo: Hiking the Back 40 (or Maybe Only 25)
Great Movies This Month
SCHRC book reviewed: *Sheboygan, A City Defined by Water*
PulpArtists by David Saunders: H. W. Kiemle
Finding St. John, by Doug Ellis
Eyes of The Shadow, by Doug Ellis
Ask a Science Teacher by Larry Scheckel: How was life in Europe in the Middle Ages?
Personal Transformation, by Aruna Krishnan

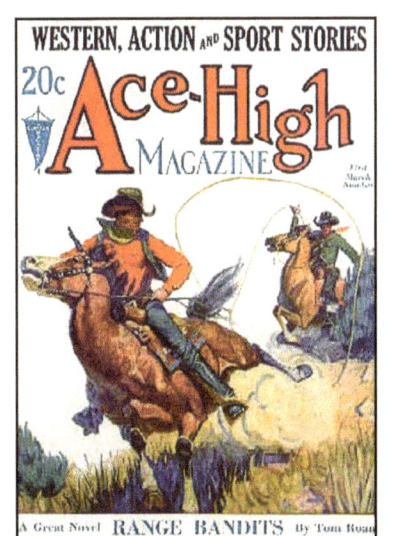

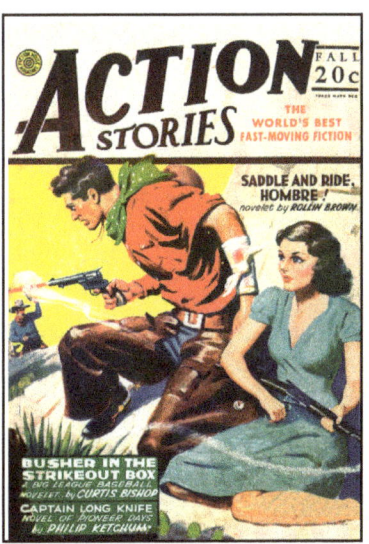

Examples of H. W. Kiemle's cover art for the pulps.

David Saunders' **pulpartists.com**

H. W. KIEMLE: BLAZING WEST ARTIST

(1908-1969)

Henry William Kiemle, Jr. was born June 27, 1908 in New York City. His father was also named Henry William Kiemle. His father was the only son of German immigrants from Stuttgart. His mother was Elizabeth A. Sandgraff Kiemle. They lived at 2163 Clinton Avenue in the Bronx. His father was employed by the Fire Department as a fireman with Ladder Company 38. His younger brother Wallace Kiemle was born July 22, 1910.

By 1917 his father had left the Fire Department and moved the family to a farm on Adams Pass in Putnam County, NY. His grandmother, Katherine "Katie" Dreascher Kiemle, also lived with them.

In 1923 his father began to work as a machinist at a local factory. They leased the farm to renters, sold the team of work-horses, and moved to 123 Arnold Road in Poughkeepsie, in Dutchess County, NY.

In June of 1924 he graduated "with extra credit" from Poughkeepsie High School. His yearbook inscription reads, "Henry, you remind us of a cool, deep pool over which sunbeams play. You are always so quiet and pensive." In fact, he was socially out-shined in most ways by his younger brother, who was popular, outgoing, and athletic.

He was a faithful bird watcher and he painted detailed renderings of birds that were inspired by John James Audubon. In 1925 he joined The American Ornithologists Union as an associate member. That same year his grandmother died at age seventy-six.

In 1926, at the age of eighteen, he moved to Brooklyn. He lived as a lodger in a boarding house at 270 Ryerson Street, while he attended art classes at Pratt Institute, where he studied with H. Winfield Scott. While still a student he began to make his living as a freelance commercial artist. He graduated Pratt in 1928. His yearbook entry says, "Henry W. Kiemle of Salty Point N.Y. is one of the most conscientious workers in the class, and he is Salty Point's all-around animal painter, who is out after Charles Livingston Bull's honors!" His illustrations soon appeared on the covers of the pulp magazine *Wild West Stories* and *Complete Novel Magazine*.

Over the next ten years, his covers and interior story illustrations regularly appeared in such pulp magazines as *Ace-High Magazine, Action Stories, Clues Detective, Short Stories, Western Story, Western Trails,* and *Wild West Weekly.*

In 1935, as the Great Depression lingered on, he found it difficult to make ends meet from his occasional low-paying assignments in the pulp magazine industry, so he returned to live with his parents and younger brother in his family home in Poughkeepsie, NY.

In 1940 he joined the Dutchess County Art Association, where he regularly showed his landscape paintings for many years in their Annual Art Week and Christmas Art Exhibitions.

His draft notice arrive on April 17, 1941 but he was classified as 4F and did not serve in the military during World War II.

After the war, instead of working as a cover artist, he primarily worked as an interior story illustrator. He created many black and white line drawings for pulp magazines, such as *Double Action Western, Exciting Western, Famous Western, Fighting Western, Giant Western, G-8 & His Battle Aces, Leading Western, Masked Rider Western, Popular Western, Range Riders, Real Western Romances, Rio Kid Western, Six-Gun Western, Super Detective, Texas Rangers, Thrilling Western, Western Action,* and *Wings*. His last published pen & ink drawing for an interior story illustration appeared in 1956.

Very few pulp artists were also credited as published authors. A few pulp artists, such as Gerard Delano, Norman Saunders, Frederick Blakeslee, and Hannes Bok, also wrote short pieces, such as articles, essays, and poetry. But H. W. Kiemle wrote a published pulp novel, entitled "No Place For Any Man," which appeared in the April 1955 issue of Western Action Magazine, and he also wrote several short stories and essays that also appeared in pulp magazines. In this respect his contribution to pulp magazine history is unique.

He never married and he had no children. He lived with his father, who died in 1952 at the age of eighty. Afterwards he lived alone and spent his retirement years painting the local landscape.

In 1965 he moved to live with his widowed younger brother, Wallace, and his nephew at their home in Locust Valley on Long Island, NY. He painted landscapes of Long Island and exhibited at the Annual Locust Valley Art Show.

H. W. Kiemle died on Long Island at the age of sixty-one on December 29, 1969.

© David Saunders 2009

April 2021

Cover photo: Clocks for Sale
Great Movies This Month
Plymouth Arts Center: An Evening of the Classics
Water's Edge Artists
Ask a Science Teacher by Larry Scheckel: What is Psychic Surgery?
Winsor McCay
PulpArtists by David Saunders: Frank Schoonover

How Free Speech Drives Economic Progress, by David Chapek, FEE.org
Your Editor Toots His Horn
Dreaming of Baking by Myra Stokdyk Eischen: Cappuccino Hazelnut Scones
SCHRC book reviewed: *The Cheese Factories of Sheboygan County*

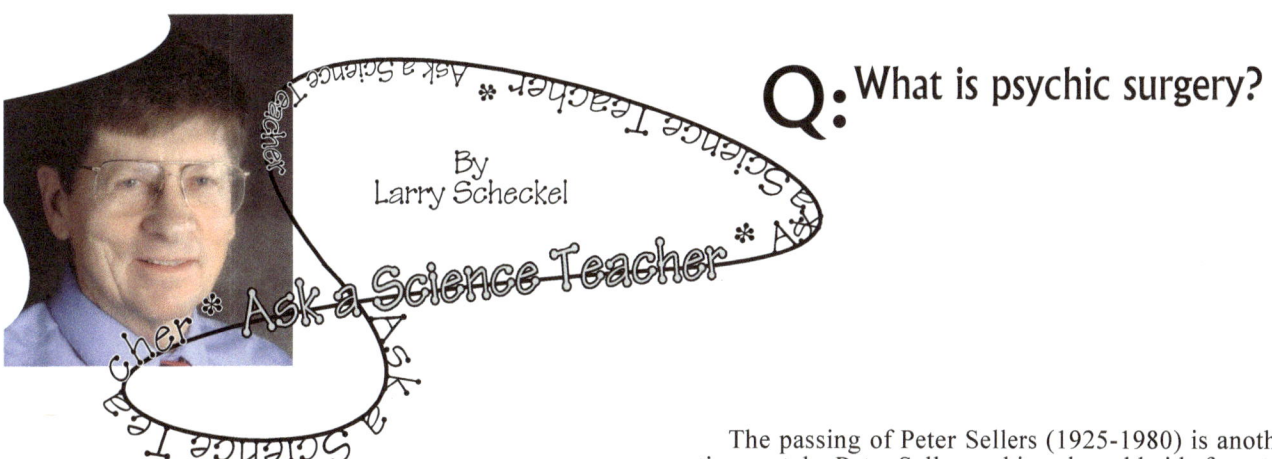

Q: What is psychic surgery?

Ask a Science Teacher By Larry Scheckel

A: Psychic surgery is a cautionary tale of faith misplaced in the paranormal and occult. From a website, "Psychic surgery is a pseudoscientific medical fraud in which practitioners create the illusion of performing surgery with their bare hands and use trickery, fake blood, and animal parts to convince the patient that diseased lesions have been removed and that the incision has spontaneously healed."

The Philippines remain the hotbed of "bloodless surgery", in which a psychic surgeon pulls out what appears to be tumors and organs. The skin is left untouched, which the psychic surgeon attributes to miraculous and speedy healing.

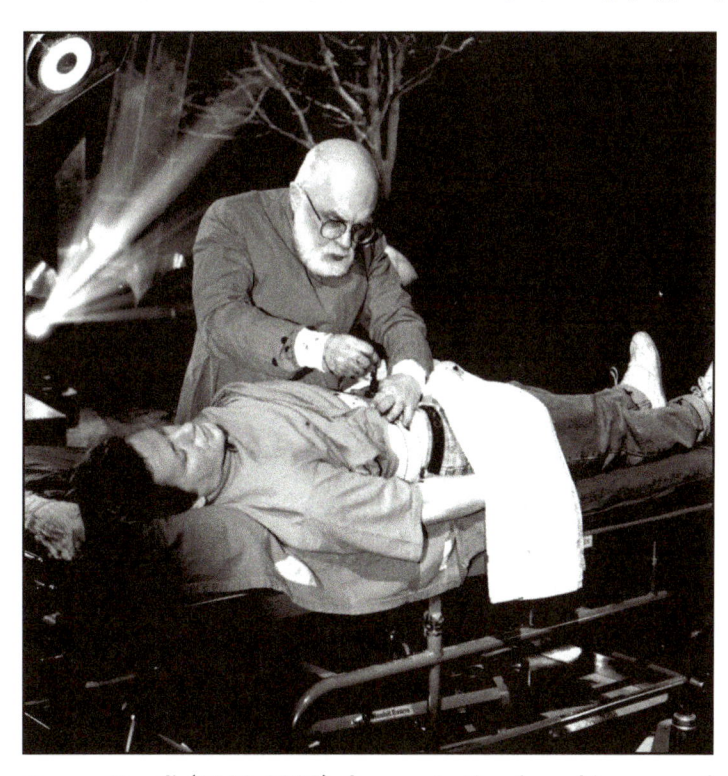

Andy Kaufman was a comic genius. He opened a Saturday Night Live show and appeared on the Letterman show, and starred in the movie, Man on the Moon. At a November 1983 Long Island Thanksgiving dinner, friends noticed his persistent coughing. He went to a doctor who told him nothing was wrong. He visited a quack clinic in a Hollywood strip mall and the holistic doctor treated his left arm with radiation.

In November 1983, Kaufman checked himself into Cedars-Sinai Medical Center in Los Angeles for a series of medical tests. He was diagnosed with large cell carcinoma lung cancer, an aggressive cancer with a high mortality rate.

Kaufman's final public appearance was at the premiere of My Breakfast With Blassie in March 1984, where he appeared thin and emaciated. The following day, he and girlfriend, Lynne Margulies, flew to the Philippines for a six-week course of psychic surgery. That trip made U.S. tabloid headlines. Kaufman died at Cedars-Sinai Medical Center in Los Angeles on May 16, 1984, at the age of 35.

James Randi (1928-2020) demonstrating 'psychic surgery' on the ITV series James Randi, Psychic Investigator, made by Open Media in 1991. Fortunately, this photo is not in color. – Courtesy, Open Media

The passing of Peter Sellers (1925-1980) is another cautionary tale. Peter Sellers achieved worldwide fame as Chief Inspector Clouseau in the Pink Panther series of films. He played three different characters in the Dr. Strangelove movie. He was a movie legend.

In 1964, at age 38, Sellers suffered a series of heart attacks that caused major damage to his heart. Four unsuccessful marriages, using popper pills, marijuana, and cocaine did not do his failing heart any good. Refusing to have open heart surgery, which could have saved his life, Sellers turned to psychics, whom he visited twice a year.

On July 22, 1980, Sellers flew in from Switzerland to stay at his favorite suite in the Dorchester Hotel in London. He visited the ashes of his overbearing mother, whose funeral he had refused to attend. Sellers had a lot of demons in his life, real and imagined. Preparing to meet some old friends for dinner that evening, he fell out of his chair, turned blue, was rushed to Middlesex Hospital, and never regained consciousness.

The medical profession will generally agree that there is a role for holistic healing. But turning to the paranormal or the occult while ignoring proven tradition medical practices is not on the positive side of the ledger. In the case of Andy Kaufman, the odds seemed stacked against him, given his diagnosis. It appears that Peter Sellers, on the other hand, made some really bad choices.

Speaking of bad choices, right before his death, Sellers was about to divorce his fourth wife, actress Lynne Frederick. However, she got his $7 million estate and Seller's own three children each got a measly $1,000. Lynne Frederick married twice more and later succumbed to drugs and alcohol. The bulk of the money went to Lynne Frederick's daughter, Cassie, fathered by Frederick's third and last husband.

Pulp covers by Frank Schoonover. — HA.com

By Winsor McCay. Boy, was I ever tempted to use this image on this issue's cover! But, nope... it just wouldn't work. — Public domain image

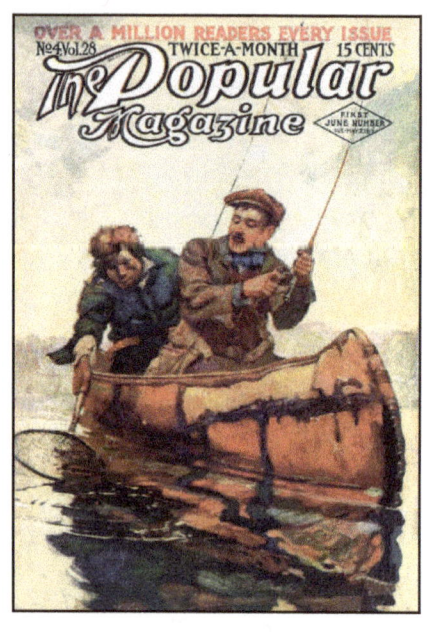

Schoonover cover from 1913. — HA.com

May
2021

Cover photo: 1975 New Idea 705 Uni-System with a John Deere Planter, Photo by John Schomburg, Courtesy of *Farm Collector* Magazine
Great Movies This Month
Historic Figures Who Recognized that Speech Is Freedom's First Line of Defense, by Lawrence W. Reed, FEE.org
Alive in the Arts
Ask a Science Teacher by Larry Scheckel:

262

Why Does Toast Land Jelly Side Down?
My Dad, the Uni Collector, by Danielle Lorenz, from *Farm Collector* Magazine
PulpArtists by David Saunders: P. V. E. Ivory
Follow-Up: Winsor McCay
SCHRC book reviewed: *The Ultimate Sacrifice*
Outbid Again!
Spring Art Tour

Outbid again!

Your editor bid on this watercolored pen and ink piece by cartoonist R. F. Outcault (probably done in the 1910s).

But I told myself, "This beautiful piece will go for much, much more than my feeble bid."

I sure called *that* one right! It went for $4,920. (I'm not revealing *my* bid.)

It's unusual for the artist to portray the two main characters with their backs to the viewer.

It's a meaningful scene: This boy, wearing an idealized version of a sailor's outfit, stands respectfully in the midst of real seamen. What wonderful stories are they telling the boy? (And what new words are they teaching him?)

Oh... by the way... who *are* the two main characters shown here? I posted this on The PRC's Facebook page, and soon had correct responses on their identities.

The only clue I'll give here: At one time, kids liked to step on their faces. But if that's not enough, look for the answer elsewhere in this issue!

If you're a collector of old postcards, you've likely come across cards with these characters. And they're usually signed, as this piece is. Maybe this image was used on a postcard; it has the right proportions.

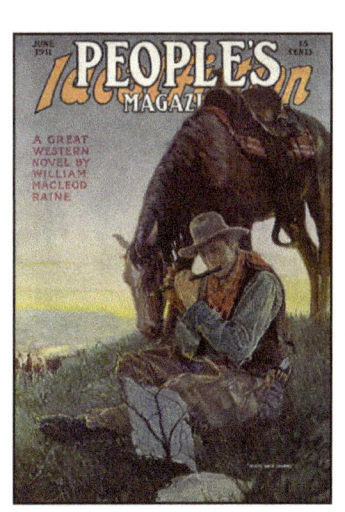

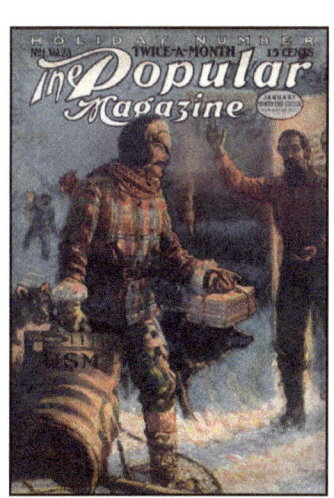

Pulp covers by P. V. E. Ivory

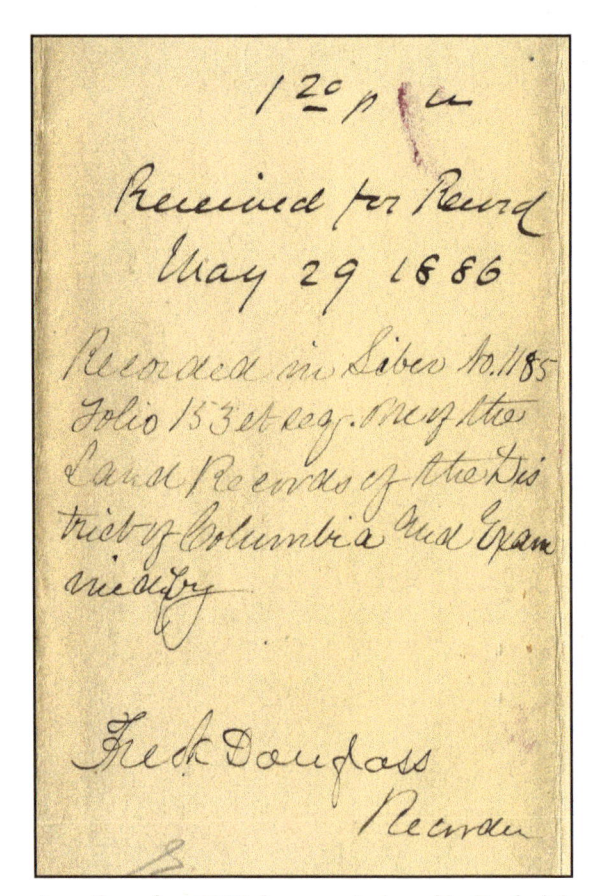

A portion of an 1886 document, signed by Frederick Douglass in his role as Recorder of Deeds for the District of Columbia. Douglass was the greatest, most powerful advocates for freedom of speech in the history of America. — From the collection of Your Editor

A book illustration by P. V. E. Ivory from the 1910s.

The Plymouth Review Current
TAKING YOU PLACES WORTH SEEING
Volume 10 • Issue 7 • June 2021

FREE!

Hingham • Two Days of Hitchcock
Systemic Non-Racism • Scrapyard Thunder-Lizards

The publication that respects your intelligence • Intellectual Stimulation • Movies • Art

264

June 2021

Cover photo: Scrapyard Thunder-Lizard, Fillmore

Great Movies This Month
PulpArtists by David Saunders: Milton Luros
Kids From Wisconsin Summer Art Camps
Ask a Science Teacher by Larry Scheckel: How can we see color without pigment?
Mill Street Live 2021
Spring Art Tour
SCHRC book reviewed: *The History of Hingham*
Marvel Comics' Non-Racism
I Believe in *Yesterday*
Resources Are More Abundant than Ever, and People Are the Reason, by Marian L. Tupy & Gale Pooley, HumanProgress.org

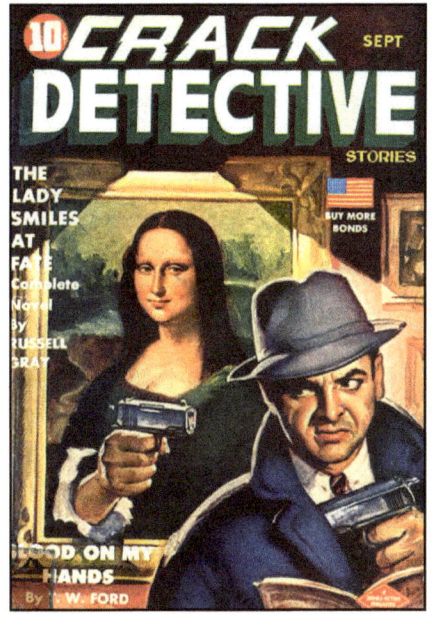

Two covers by Milton Luros. Criminals have no sense of decency whatever! You can tell from the expression on the cop's face that he's in a moral quandary. If he fires, he'll damage this masterpiece even more. Too bad it's not a painting by Jackson Pollock, or Pablo Picasso—he could shoot with a clear conscience, knowing he's doing the world a favor (besides taking out a crook).

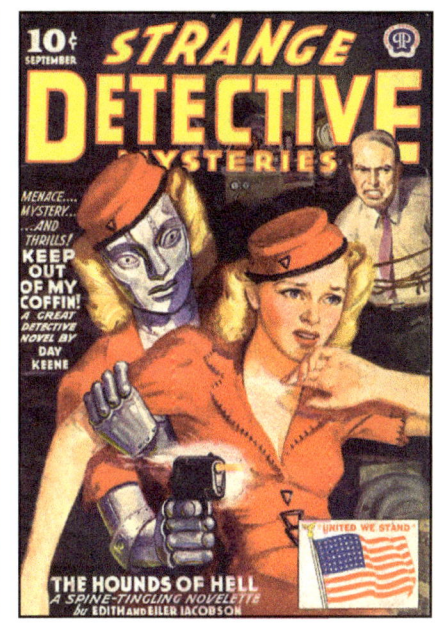

I don't know... a gun-toting robot? I wouldn't consider *that* to be so "strange." But a gun-toting robot with *blond hair*? Now THAT's strange! From late 1942. While America struggled to free itself from the darkness of WWII, by *fighting* the forces of darkness, publishers often proudly carried patriotic messages on their magazine covers, such as this one.

I believe in Yesterday
A recent movie worthy of your attention

It's wonderful when a movie offers you genuine surprises. While Yesterday does offer several delightfully unexpected developments (which I will *not* spoil), its core surprise is given away before you ever see it—in the case of the home video package, right across the front cover:

Everyone in the world has forgotten The Beatles. Everyone except Jack...

In the instant that Jack suffers a serious trauma, the world changes. How? Why? That's not important. It happens.

Now what?

This was directed by Danny Boyle, a British film/TV producer/director who's done several movies I really liked. (One is Slumdog Millionaire. I saw that one a few hours after I'd been "downsized" after a 22-year IT career; the movie was such a pick-me-up, that it helped prepare me to eagerly step into the next phase of my life.)

In Yesterday, Jack soars to stardom as he plays the brilliant musical gems of The Beatles, which nobody has heard before.

Jack finds that the brand of stardom thrust upon him threatens to transform him into a heavily processed product. Worse, it threatens to cheapen and trivialize the greatness of the music itself.

I'm listening to Philip Glass' memoir, Words Without Music. He mentions being told that the music world, and the music business, are two different things.

Perhaps that's so. Jack discovers this in Yesterday. His challenge is to decide whether to compromise his artistic integrity for that fame and fortune.

(This is not to say that artistic integrity and commercial success are always at odds with each other. Sometimes, artistic integrity is *necessary* to reach commercial success.)

Two words about the ethnicity of the main character: *It's irrelevant.* As it should be! Another refreshing aspect of the film.

My wife had to point out that one supporting character is a popular, real-life singer in England. (Heck, how would *I* know that?)

And Himesh Patel, who plays Jack, is a British actor who lovingly and more than competently sings the Beatles songs. In the video's extra features, he sings three Beatles songs at the Abbey Road Studios.

Speaking of extras... there are many: an alternate ending; about 20 deleted scenes; and the three above-mentioned performances at Abbey Road Studios.

Need I say it? **Highly recommended!**

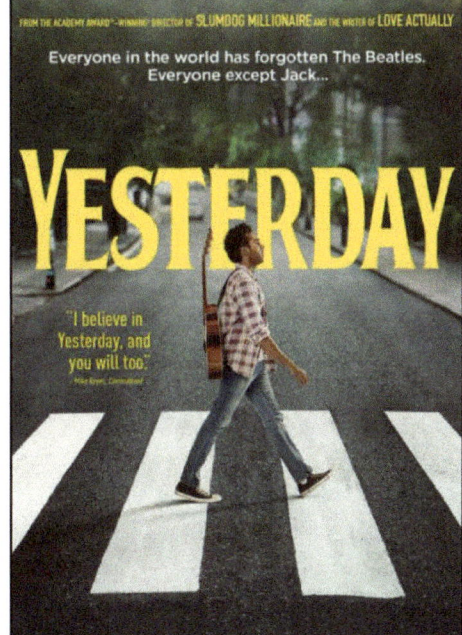

The Plymouth Review Current

Taking You Places Worth Seeing
Volume 10 • Issue 8 • July 2021

FREE!

A Soldier's WWII Story ◇ Cool Events for Hot Days in Plymouth
Fitzcarraldo ◇ James Bama

July
2021

Cover photo: Chuck Wagon in Snow / Circle M Ranch / Cody, Wyoming, 1972 painting by James Bama, imaged by HA.com
Great Movies This Month
Mill Street Live Summer Musical Series
Ask a Science Teacher by Larry Scheckel: Why Does Wisconsin Not Have the Death Penalty?
The Art of James Bama
The Books of James Bama
Buster Brown Abroad
Wow! What a Movie! (Fitzcarraldo)
Kids from Wisconsin Coming to Plymouth

Dee Smith with Saddlebag. 1973. Included in The Western Art of James Bama. *Would you believe:* I once took the son of the artist, and the son of the man portrayed in this painting, to see Who Framed Roger Rabbit? — HA.com

---

Jim Bama
is a regular reader of
The Plymouth Review Current!
He comments that it seems The PRC
is edited especially for him!
(And in some respects, *he's right!*)
This one's for you, Jim! *Thanks, Pal!!*

Q: Why does Wisconsin not have the death penalty?

By Larry Scheckel

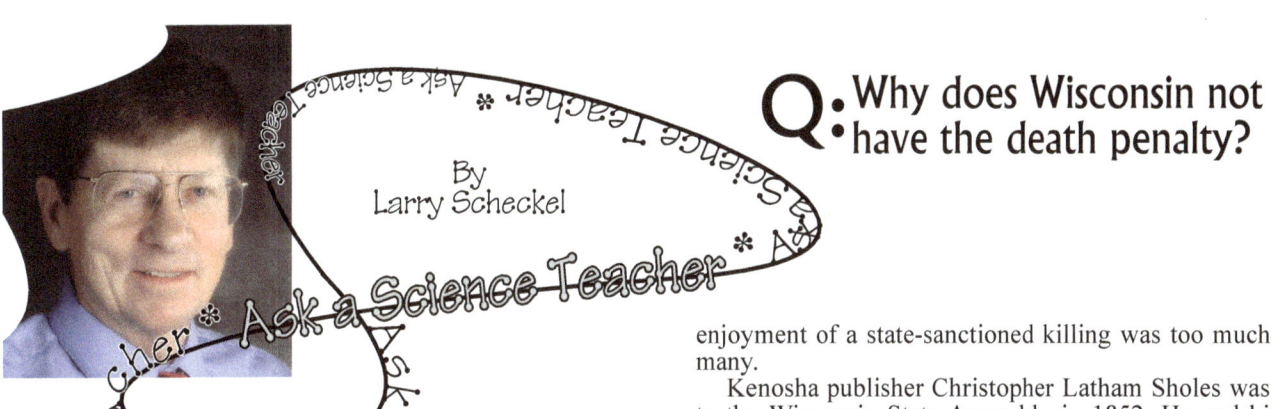

A: John McCaffary was an immigrant from Ireland who settled in the Kenosha, Wisconsin area. McCaffary was a domestic abuser with a violent temper. On July 23, 1850, McCaffary had a noisy argument with his wife, Bridget. He held Bridget's head down in a backyard rain barrel full of water until she stopped moving. Neighbors had heard Bridget's shrieks but arrived too late.

McCaffary was duly arrested, and his trial began on May 6, 1851. Less than three weeks later, the jury convicted him of first degree murder. The judge sentenced McCaffary to death by hanging. The death warrant was signed by Governor Dewey Nelson.

The death sentence was carried out on August 21, 1851. McCaffary was taken out of prison and strung up from a tree before an estimated crowd of from 2,000 to 3,000 citizens. About a third were women. Families brought picnic lunches.

The hanging did not go as planned. McCaffary remained alive, struggling and kicking on the end of the rope for over 20 minutes, slowly being strangled to death. McCaffary, with his elongated neck, was buried in an unmarked grave in Kenosha's Green Ridge Cemetery.

The gruesome spectacle was too much for the several thousand onlookers. Add to the fact that Wisconsin, newly admitted to the Union, prided itself as a "reform" state. In a few years, the anti-slavery Republican Party would be founded in Ripon, Wisconsin. The display of public enjoyment of a state-sanctioned killing was too much for too many.

Kenosha publisher Christopher Latham Sholes was elected to the Wisconsin State Assembly in 1852. He and his newspaper, The Kenosha Telegraph, took up the cause of abolishing the death penalty. Sholes denounced the execution in his newspaper, writing, "The crowd has been indulged in its insane passion for the sight of a judicially murdered man. We hope this will be the last execution that shall ever disgrace the mercy-expecting citizens of the State of Wisconsin."

On July 12, 1853, Wisconsin followed the example of its neighbor, Michigan, and abolished the death penalty full stop. Wisconsin Governor Leonard J. Farwell signed a law that abolished the death penalty in Wisconsin and replaced it with a penalty of life imprisonment.

There had been a few executions in Wisconsin before McCaffary's, but his was the first one after Wisconsin attained statehood in 1848. Thus, John McCaffary was the only person ever to be executed by the State of Wisconsin. Newspaperman Christopher Latham Sholes' claim to fame is the invention of the first commercially successful typewriter with the QWERTY keyboard that became standard.

There are 31 states in the US where the death penalty is legally upheld. Also known as capital punishment, the death penalty is a legal punishment also exercised by the federal government. The U.S. is the only Western nation that currently uses capital punishment, and it is one of the 57 countries in the world that has the death penalty.

The last public hanging in the United States was on August 14, 1936 at Owensboro, Kentucky, before a crowd estimated at 10,000 to 20,000. Rainey Bethea, aged 22, was convicted of the murder of a 70-year-old woman. Race made this public execution controversial.

From Wikipedia, which says: "Wisconsin Historical Marker identifying the site in which Christopher Latham Sholes invented the first practical typewriter, at a machine shop located in Milwaukee, Wisconsin." — Copyright © 2005 Sulfur; file used and licensed under the Creative Commons Attribution-Share Alike 3.0 Unported license.

Christopher Latham Sholes, newspaper publisher, politician, and developer of the typewriter. Per Wikipedia: "Sholes died on February 17, 1890, after battling tuberculosis for nine years. He is buried at Forest Home Cemetery in Milwaukee." — Public Domain image from Wikipedia

Editor's comment
The case for capital punishment for the worst crimes (for example, murder) might be made plausibly... *if* human knowledge and action were free of, and immune from, **error**. However, the number of people convicted, sentenced to death, and later found to be innocent, is appalling. Do a 'net search on the topic. For that reason, this publication stands with Christopher Latham Sholes and those like him who oppose the death penalty.

Comment, 2024
Your Editor continues to hold this view, even as basically rational people, outraged (justifiably) by horrific crimes against children, call for automatic death penalties for such crimes.

Buster Brown Abroad

I recently acquired Buster Brown Abroad, a 1904 book written and illustrated by R. F. Outcault, creator of Buster Brown.

I thought I'd share a couple of passages from the book, written in the voice of Buster Brown, describing his trip to Europe with his dog Tige (that's short for "Tiger"). Now remember, in the following—Tige *is* a dog.

From Chapter VIII—Basle—A Predicament

TIGE stayed in all next day, writing in his diary and reading about William Tell and the Alps. We were going to see the Alps in a few days, and he wanted to know all about them. He said he wan't afraid to go up on an Alp because he was still on the ground, but he was afraid to look out of our window in the "Three Kings" hotel because it went down for several stories straight into that rushing, roaring river Rhine.

THE funniest thing that happened to us during all our trip was when we left Basle. Pa and Uncle Jack decided on Monday night to leave for Lucerne the next morning, so, after they were all ready for bed, they set about packing the trunks.

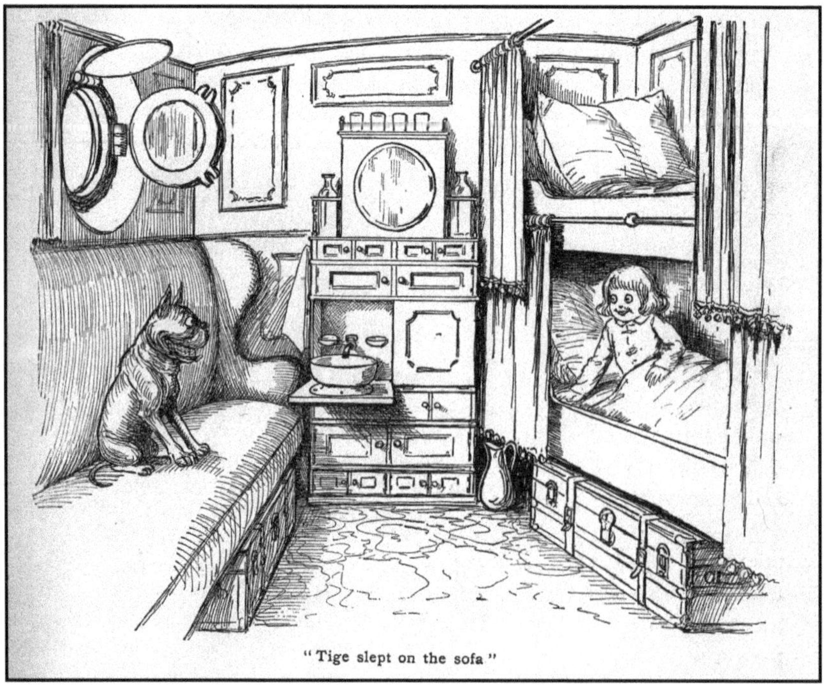

MA had told Pa, before he left, that he must be very careful, in packing, to see that he didn't forget anything. She had told him to look in closets, under beds, in all the drawers, and all around the floor, to see that he hadn't overlooked anything.

SO Pa and Uncle Jack crept all around on the floor, on their hands and knees, looking under beds and chairs. They got up on tables and looked on top of the wardrobe, and at last, when they were convinced that everything was packed, they locked their trunks and big bags, and called the porter.

"PORTER," said Uncle Jack, "take these trunks to the station and ship them to Lucerne."

SO the porter did as he was told. After the baggage had gone I was put to bed, and Pa and Uncle Jack sat down to smoke and congratulate themselves on their good packing. They were still sitting there, looking out at the river and laughing, when I went to sleep; but next morning, when I awoke, there was an awful row going on. They had just discovered that in their effort to pack everything they had packed all their own clothes except the pajamas they had on, and that all the baggage was now in Lucerne.

THINK of two men doing such a thing and then screaming with laughter over it. It was a mighty lucky thing for them that Pa had his money and watch under his pillow. Well, we had our breakfast in our rooms, and while we were eating they were talking over the best thing to do. Tige offered to lend Pa his pants, but Pa spurned his offer.

AT last they decided to send me out for some clothes. It was my first experience at buying anything. I strolled up the street until I came to a store. I got Pa a suit which was not a very stylish fit, and a hat and a pair of shoes. They were still laughing at each other when I got back. Their idea was that when Pa had got these clothes he could go out and buy clothes for Uncle Jack; but when I got back to the hotel, Uncle Jack had bought a suit from the head porter. It had gold braid and a velvet collar and cuffs, the "sassiest" suit you ever saw. When Pa got his clothes on we were exactly like a traveling minstrel company.

WELL, we got on the train and went to Lucerne, which is only about two hours away. As we went along we saw, in several different places, men digging square lumps of earth. It was very black earth. They were piling it up like bricks,—big black bricks. When we asked the conductor he told us it was for fuel. He said that when it was dry it burned just like coal.

PA said that he hoped he wouldn't meet any one he knew until he got those dreadful looking clothes off or he would be disgraced for ever. But his hope that he hoped didn't come out; for as we got off the train we bumped right into a General Somebody with his wife and three daughters. That old General nearly laughed himself to death. But he and his family decided not to go away that day, but to return to the hotel with us and stop a day or two longer. So they went with us to the Hotel Nationale, and all stood in front of Pa and Uncle Jack until they got to their rooms, to keep any one from seeing them. Every time Tige looked at Pa he would burst into another fit of laughter, and I thought he would surely have hysterics.

From Chapter XIV—London—The King and Queen—Seeing the City—A Trick

WHEN Pa and Uncle Jack arrived in London the fun commenced. They had been to Ostend, and had been bathing until they were all sunburned and tanned, but they were still laughing. I never saw any two people who could find so much to laugh at. They never complain about anything, or kick, because it is too much trouble, and they say that it never makes any difference except to make folks dislike you.

"Tige slept on the sofa"

"We rode on top of penny 'busses"

A "John Darms"

One Soldier's Story
The WWII Memoirs of a Sheboygan County Man
a book by Arthur G. Kroos, Jr.

Book review by Beth Dippel
for The Plymouth Review Current

As Americans, we are the products of a great many factors; our family and our ancestry, our friends, our community and the time in which we live.

This was true of the men and women who were just reaching maturity in 1940. They were children of the Great Depression, which meant they knew how to do with very little. They understood the value of hard work. Many were descendants of recent immigrants who valued the things in life that mattered most—family and freedom.

We were fortunate in 1941 to have a citizenry ready and able to meet the demands put upon it in the face of war. Adolph Hitler and his cronies changed the face of civilization. These young Americans, along with their Allied counterparts, changed it back.

Millions of men and women from across this country worked for more than five years to protect those freedoms we've had since 1776. Sheboygan County alone lost 227 young people as casualties of WWII. But upwards of 3000 other Sheboyganites fought and then came home to a world much changed from their lives before serving.

The story told in the book *One Soldier's Story* is that of one such man, Arthur G. Kroos, Jr., a descendant of German immigrants who fought the Nazis and was imprisoned near his familial homeland. Other soldiers had similar experiences during their tenure in the military, but Art's experiences are special because they were so thoroughly documented as they took place. Patty Raab Kroos, wife of Arthur, kept remarkable records which tell this tale like nothing else could.

This is certainly not an all-inclusive history of WWII or Mr. Kroos's experiences. It is an overview designed to give a feel for what he and many others endured. This story is told through original documents, newspaper clippings, journal entries and diary notations. These primary source documents tell the story most accurately. Little commentary by others is required or given.

Follow "One Soldier's Story" from enlistment in 1940 to liberation in 1945. Read about his time in France, in Italy, as prisoner of war in Luft Stalag One, and about the Dutch citizens who risked their lives to help four young Americans. It's a great adventure.

Following are three excerpts from *One Soldier's Story*.

• • •

June 5, 1943

Arthur Kroos, Jr. and his dog, Mathias, at their Kohler home circa 1922, aged six. — Photos accompanying this article courtesy of the SCHRC

Arthur G. Kroos, Jr. promoted to 2nd Lieutenant, March 1942 at Fort Benning, Georgia.

Started parachute school. Tough!

So then, we started to move to North Africa from Morocco. We got out there between the middle to the end of May. It came down the line that anyone who wanted to go to parachute school and become a jumper, could do so.

The most important thing was that you would get an extra one-hundred dollars a month if you were a jumper. I'm married with a kid, and I could transfer my entire First Lieutenant's pay home each month. Jump pay could not be transferred because if you did not maintain so many jumps in a period of time, you could lose it. So I went to Jump School. There were only ten fellows out of the entire 82nd Division that volunteered to go to Jump School in North Africa.

Believe you me, the month of June in North Africa is HOT! The training of the remainder of our entire Division was stopped between noon and three o'clock in the afternoon. All men were instructed to get out of the sun until after three o'clock. Then training would start again.

Parachute School was damn tough because they did not put us into a pup tent between twelve and three. Hell no! We were out running or doing push-ups or practicing packing chutes. It was not as well organized as Ft. Benning.

I got my jump wings after six jumps, the last being a night jump, and the next day, the 82nd moved to Kairovan (Tunisia). Shortly after, the Allies invaded Sicily and the 82nd Airborne made its first combat airborne jump.

Arthur G. Kroos, Jr., 2001 D-Day Interview with Elmer Koppelmann

• • •

Ireland, Aide de Camp and D-Day

Kroos's 80th Airborne Battalion shipped out on November 20th leaving the warm climes of Sicily and Italy, headed for Northern Ireland. The Battalion was at sea from November 20th to December 10th, 1943.

From there we headed to Ireland, arriving in Belfast on December 10th. When we arrived, the 82nd Airborne Division was scattered all over Northern Ireland. As we were getting off the boat, mail was passed out. We hadn't received any mail for damn near two months. There were letters from my wife almost every day. I remember that the first letter I opened in January 1944 said, "I want you to know how happy we are that our son Patrick has recovered nicely from his operation." I didn't even know he was born! Of course, I got to read all the other letters to get to know what had happened, but that first letter was an eye-opener. Patrick was born December 14, 1943.

Arthur G. Kroos, Jr., 2001 D-Day Interview with Elmer Koppelmann

• • •

September 22, 1944
Captured by the Germans

For the seven months that Art Kroos was held prisoner by the German military machine, he thought frequently of his beloved wife, Patty, and sons at home in Sheboygan. In December of 1944 he was given a post which gave him access to paper and pen. From that time on he kept a diary and was allowed to write three letters home per month to stay in touch with Pat and let her know something about his experiences. The diary tells the poignant story of a man far from home, dealing with shortages of water, clothes, and food. It also tells the story of ingenuity and the eternal hope for rescue by the Allies.

Kroos later writes:

The story of my capture will be written after I leave Germany—it would not be fitting for prying eyes to pick up my simple story so easily. I was shot down September 18th and captured on the 21st. An honorable end, to an honorable army career—I think there is nothing in the last chapter of my active army life that I would hesitate to proudly tell. My capture was unfortunate, but nothing could have been done to prevent it—we were confronted by the enemy in numbers and expounded all our ammunition. The manner in which they finally delivered us to this camp and the experiences enroute are a story in a whole; The interrogations in a small village near Rotterdam; The manner in which the Germans took over the homes they needed; The way a German Sergeant kicked and beat an old Dutch civilian before our eyes; The flea ridden transit camp at Amersfoort. The American P-51 which knocked out the engine on the train taking us into Germany; the derailing of our train the next day by Dutch Partisans; the dreaded Dulag Luft at Frankfort, where the real interrogations took place. And all the P.O.W.s are held in solitary confinement. Many rare tales have come out of that stay there.

Captain Kroos at his release from Luft Stalag One, seventy pounds lighter.

• • •

This is a book everyone will enjoy. Every page is full of adventure and history. More than 150 pages in length, it can be purchased at the Sheboygan County Historical Research Center, 518 Water Street, Sheboygan Falls, Tuesday through Friday from 9-4 or at schrc.org/shop. Or you can order by phone, 920.467.4667.

Countdown for Cindy, an early space-race novel. James Bama used his wife as a model for the main character (something he did often). In 2010, the painting was up for auction, and Bama asked me to bid on it on his behalf. It went over his limit (I even bid higher than his limit) (sorry, Jim, I don't think I ever told you that), so... that one got away. Inset shows the published paperback cover; look how much was truncated. – HA.com

The Plymouth Review Current

TAKING YOU PLACES WORTH SEEING
Volume 10 • Issue 9 • August 2021

FREE!

• The publication that respects your intelligence •
• Intellectual stimulation • Movies • Art •

Systemic Non-Racism ◆ Arts Near and Far
Summer Under the Stars ◆ Burls for Bowls

August
2021

Cover photo: Bowl Dog Woodturning, Batavia
Great Movies This Month
Jason Hill Vindicates the American Dream against Ta-Nehisi Coates's Delusional Race Rhetoric, book review by Timothy Sandefur, from The Objective Standard
Cheese Capital Jazz & Blues Crawl for the Arts

Ask a Science Teacher by Larry Scheckel: Why Are Manhole Covers Round?
SCHRC book reviewed: *A Tour of Black River, Gem of Sheboygan County*
Summer Freshet: Artful Abundance
PulpArtists by David Saunders: Charles Dye

The book by Jason Hill, reviewed by Timothy Sandefur.

Oshkosh artist Jon Wos, giving a talk on how a rational philosophy and his interest in art made his life meaningful at the recent TOS-Con.

CHARLES DYE

Cover of Outdoor Life magazine. — HA.com

Fifteen Western Tales pulp cover from 1950. — HA.com

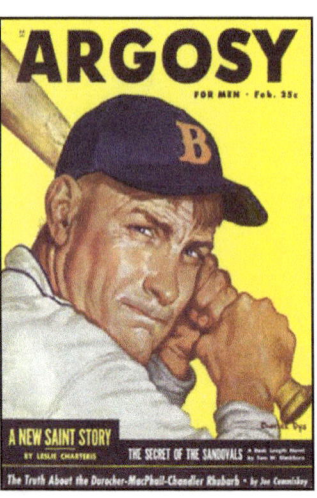

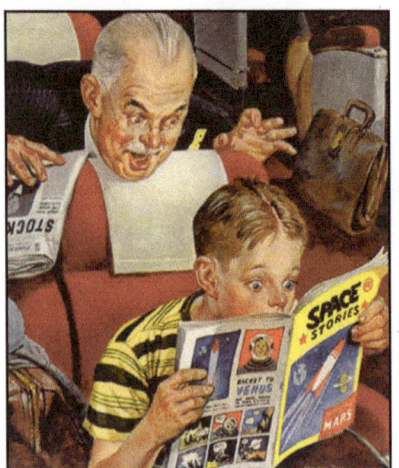

It *could be* the older fellow still has a youthful exuberance for adventure and imagination; or he *could be* about to take action after listening to the kid's toneless whistling for the past 700 miles.

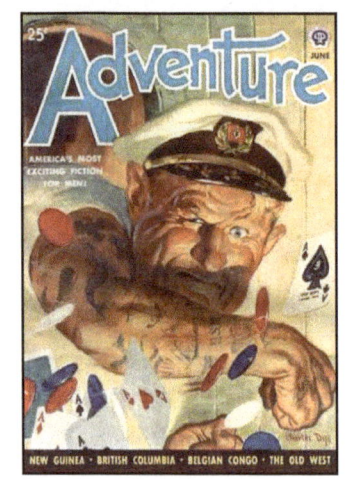

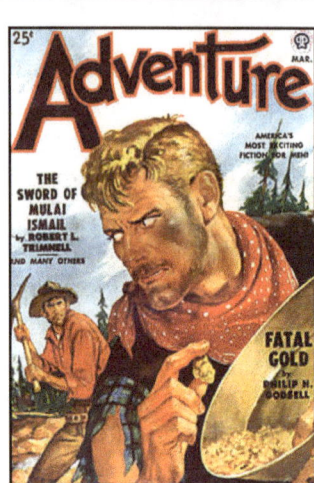

272

Woodturning

Creations of Bowl Dog Woodturning, LLC, Batavia. Dick Bemis, artisan.

The Plymouth Review Current

Taking you places worth seeing
Volume 10 • Issue 10 • September 2021

FREE!

Great Movies ◆ Brandywine Artists
Flash Gordon ◆ Lake Michigan's Stonehenge?

September 2021

Cover photo: Lake Michigan's Stonehenge? Great Movies This Month

Ask a Science Teacher by Larry Scheckel: I Am in Sixth Grade. My Teacher Says I Could Win the Nobel Prize. How Many Girls Have Won the Nobel Prize?

SCHRC book reviewed: *Dissolving Myths and Legends*

We Just Got Proof That Uber Has Saved Thousands of Lives, by Brad Polumbo, FEE.org
PulpArtists by David Saunders: Stan Drake
Connections
More about Alex Raymond and Stan Drake
The Strange Death of Alex Raymond, by Dave Sim & Carson Grubaugh
Remember These things? (Fun, Inc. Joke Novelties)
A Brandywine Style Movie? (Treasure Planet)
Examples of Brandywine School Artists

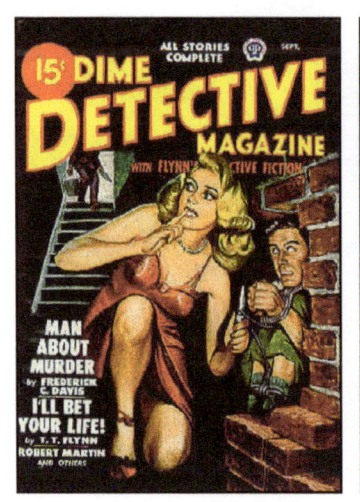

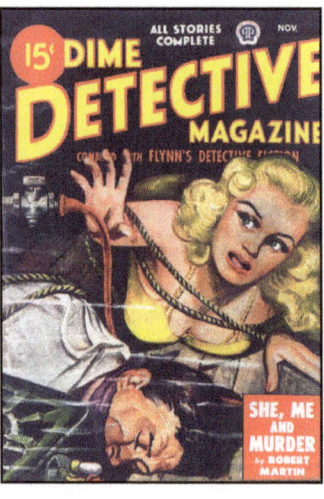

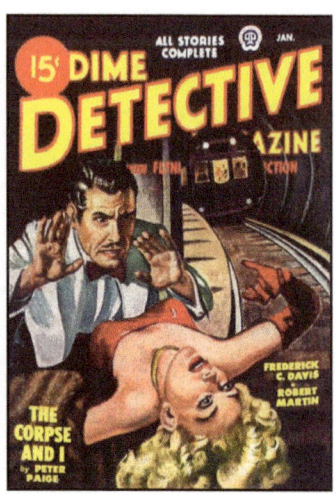

Pulp covers by Stan Drake, who mostly made his name in newspaper strips. From 1948 to 1951. Dime Detective typically featured compelling, story-telling covers. Looks like Drake used the same model for these.

Dissolving Myths and Legends

Book review by Beth Dippel and Steven Rogstad
for The Plymouth Review Current

Dissolving Myths and Legends: Rivalries, Allies, Histories & Cultures that Shaped the Black Hawk War is a new publication available at the Sheboygan County Historical Research Center. Published after SCHRC's 2019 Black Hawk War Symposium, the information in this volume is new, important and amazing.

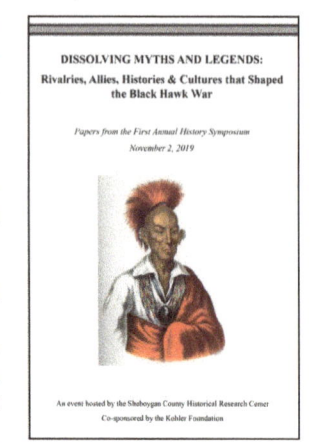

In the introduction written by Steven K. Rogstad we are reintroduced to Black Hawk and the dreadful events of the day, and the background needed to put the writing into context.

Without wanting to admit it, white settlers in the late 1700s envied the Sauk nation, which occupied large areas of land in the lower Rock River Valley near the Mississippi River in northern Illinois. The tribe's economic prosperity was owed to the corn planted on hundreds of acres of rich black soil that was abundant in the northwest section of the state. This land was viewed as central to the Sauk and Winnebago's spiritual and economic lives. Inevitably, the westward migration of white men onto the tribe's sacred ground resulted in violent interactions that led the Sauk to be banished to the west side of the Mississippi River in 1831 by the United States government. Removed from their ancestral land with their economy decimated and their traditions eroding, Black Hawk realized that something decisive must be done to save the Sauk way of life from ruin.

In an effort to reclaim their homeland and recapture cultural norms that were quickly vanishing within Sauk society, Black Hawk and nearly a thousand of his followers crossed the Mississippi River from Iowa in the spring of 1832 to resettle in Illinois. The very presence of Indians once more east of the Mississippi River caused immediate suspicion and alarm among white settlers, who now considered land that was once occupied by the Sauk their own personal property to do with as they pleased. To bolster Sauk power and might, Black Hawk endeavored to establish an alliance with the Fox and numerous other tribes to make an impressive stand against the authority of the United States. He also anticipated receiving assistance from his British "fathers" in Canada. The ensuing conflict, commonly known as the Black Hawk War, was in some ways a "battle for the heart of America," both geographically and in terms of value systems. In the end, it would drastically decimate the Sauk population and mark the end of Indian warfare against the United States east of the Mississippi River.

Yet, there is far more to the story of Black Hawk and his war against American expansion than what appears on the surface. Beneath the outward show of a unified Indian front against the states of Illinois and Wisconsin, there were disturbing and powerful forces at work that adversely affected the resistance. The pan-Indian alliance Black Hawk hoped would sustain military superiority was undermined by intertribal rivalries and conflicting interests that only hampered his efforts. Also, the anticipated support from the British never came. Three months after it began, the war ended through the massacre of the Sauk band at the mouth of the Bad Axe River. Sauk culture was reduced to almost an erasure in the history of the United States. Black Hawk, however, became a captured celebrity in the white man's civilized world.

The Black Hawk War has often been the subject for historians, who have often simplified its origins and outcomes. Recent scholarship has shown, however, that a proper understanding of the conflict requires an understanding of racial consciousness, military incompetence, intertribal dynamics, and cultural practices of the Sauk and other tribes of the Upper Mississippi region. The new information that has been gleaned from previously untapped oral histories, original sources, and revisionist interpretations has allowed present-day scholars and biographers alike to take a fresh and enriched examination of the last Indian war that was fought in Illinois and Wisconsin, and provide needed insight to both sides of the struggle.

The papers contained in this volume were delivered on Saturday, November 2, 2019, as part of a Black Hawk War Symposium entitled, "Dissolving Myths and Legends: Rivalries, Allies, Histories, and Cultures that Shaped the Black Hawk War," hosted by the Sheboygan County Historical Research Center. Each paper offers information that enhances our understanding of why the conflict occurred and how it was militarily conducted:

• In *The Path to Glory is Rough: The Causes and Course of the Black Hawk War, 1804-1832,* Dr. Patrick J. Jung positions the Indian uprising within a century of American Indian Anti-Colonial Resistance and provides a detailed and comprehensive discussion of several causes, a revealing profile of Black Hawk, and the intertribal complexities associated with the conflict.

• The role of the Rock River Ho-Chunk band during the 1832 crisis is the subject of *Protectors of the Corn Moon: How the Rock River Ho-Chunks His 1,200 Fugitive Indians and Mired U.S. Troops During the 1832 Black Hawk War,* by Dr. Libby Tronnes. She maintains that the Ho-Chunks attempted to thwart violence by playing both sides in the conflict by guiding both United States troops and Sauk Indians.

• Dr. Kerry A. Trask discusses the importance of Sauk culture, ideologies, and economics in his paper, *The Centre Cannot Hold: The Collapse of Sauk Society and the Black Hawk War.* Showing how rapid improvements in hunting technology replaced a vital government-run trading system between Indians and American settlers, Trask makes the argument that the fall of the Sauk economy led to a downward spiral that nearly eradicated Sauk culture and traditions even before the war.

These essays reflect the latest scholarship on the Black Hawk War, a subject that has captured the attention of historians and the general public alike for generations. While often seen as a small and sometimes insignificant conflict in the larger study of Native Americans, the Black Hawk War remains a prominent piece of Wisconsin history that is reflected in numerous monuments and markers throughout the southern portion of the state. What is equally fascinating in presenting these papers is the fact that Dr. Jung, Dr. Tronnes, and Dr. Trask are all Wisconsinites, who have devoted decades of study to the Black Hawk War and continue to bring forward new insights and conclusions that illuminate and enhance our understanding of this important regional topic in our state history.

In conclusion:

Dissolving Myths and Legends: Rivalries, Allies, Histories & Cultures that Shaped the Black Hawk War is filled with maps, drawings and the most amazing original and new research. It is a great addition to a valuable and elusive part of Wisconsin's history.

You can find *Dissolving Myths and Legends* at the Sheboygan County Historical Research Center, 518 Water Street, Sheboygan Falls. Business hours are Tuesday through Friday from 9-4. Or check out schrc.org/shop to order online. Call 920.467.4667 for curbside pickup.

Ask a Science Teacher

By Larry Scheckel

Q: I am in sixth grade. My teacher says I could win the Nobel Prize. How many girls have won the Nobel Prize?

A: Four women have earned the Nobel Prize in Chemistry. The best know is Maria Curie, in 1911, for the separation of pure radium. Her daughter won the Chemistry Prize in 1935 for the discovery of artificial radioactivity.

Two women won the Nobel Prize in Physics. One, Maria Curie in 1903 for the discovery of radioactivity; the other, Maria Goeppert Mayer in 1963 for the discoveries of how atoms are put together.

Ten women earned the Nobel Prize in the field of Physiology and Medicine. Best-known are Rosalyn Yalow (1977) for work in radioisotope tracing and Barbara McClintock (1983) for her efforts in genetics.

Pearl Buck is one of twelve women awarded the Nobel Prize in Literature. Her 1938 Nobel Prize cited her "rich and truly epic description of peasant life in China." Her best-known book is *The Good Earth,* which also won the Pulitzer Prize.

The first and only woman to win the Nobel Prize in Economic Sciences is Elinor Ostrom (2009) "for her analysis of how common property could be managed by groups using it."

Fifteen women have won the Nobel Peace Prize. The most recognized is Jane Addams (1931), founder of Hull House in Chicago, and Mother Teresa (1979), a native Albanian nun who founded missions in India, starting in Calcutta.

The Nobel Prizes in Chemistry, Physics, Physiology/Medicine, Literature, and Economic Science are awarded annually in Stockholm by the Royal Swedish Academy of Science. The more famous Nobel Peace Prize is awarded annually in Oslo, Norway on December 10, the anniversary of Nobel's death. The King and Queen of Norway attend.

There is one woman that history now recognizes got cheated out of a Nobel Prize. That would be Lise Meitner. Born in Austria in 1878, Meitner worked with Otto Hahn at the Kaiser Wilhelm Institute in Berlin, Germany.

When Hitler came to power in 1933, Lise Meitner, born of Jewish parents, was protected by her Austrian citizenship. But after the Anschluss, the annexation of Austria into the Third Reich in March 1938, her situation became desperate. She made a daring undercover escape to the Netherlands, then traveled to neutral Sweden.

Lise Meitner corresponded with Otto Hahn and the two met in Copenhagen in November 1938. They planned to carry out a new round of experiments on the fission of uranium, but Meitner could not go back to Nazi Germany, so the experiment was done by Otto Hahn and Fritz Strassmann.

Maria (or Marie) Curie, about 1920.
– Public Domain image from Wikipedia

Lise Meitner in 1946.
– Public Domain image from Wikipedia

It was Lise Meitner and her nephew Otto Frisch, who correctly interpreted the results of the experiment that detected the element barium after bombarding uranium with neutrons. Now the whole world knew that the uranium atom could be split, with a tremendous release of power, and that several neutrons were also released. A chain reaction and the atomic bomb were now possible.

Otto Hahn was awarded the Nobel Prize in 1944. Missing from the ceremony was Lise Meitner. In 1964, The "Physics Today" magazine concluded that "personal negative opinions led to the exclusion of a deserving scientist" from the Nobel Prize. Element 109, "Meitnerium," is named in her honor.

Rosalyn Yalow in 1977. — Public Domain image from Wikipedia

from the Brandywine School

William James Aylward. Imagine this large painting hanging in your home, and visitors standing transfixed, studying it. WOW! — HA.com

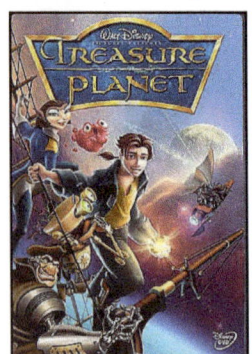

Jessie Willcox Smith, 1915. — HA.com

Treasure Planet, Disney's "Brandywine movie." — BN.com

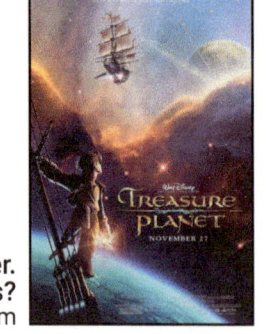

Treasure Planet movie poster. Brandywine School style colors? — HA.com

Harvey Dunn, 1916. — HA.com

October
2021

Cover photo:
Dealer's Table at the Windy City Pulp and Paper Convention. Photo by Paul Herman

Great Movies This Month

PulpArtists by David Saunders: Remington Schuyler

Ask a Science Teacher by Larry Scheckel: My Mom Makes Me Cut up Onions.

Why Do They Make Me Cry?
A Few Finlays
SCHRC book reviewed: *The Kneevers Hotel, A Sheboygan Landmark*
An Encounter with F. Paul Wilson
An Exclusive Interview with F. Paul Wilson
An Evening of the Classics
With Economic Freedom Comes Female Empowerment, by Chelsea Follett, HumanProgress.org
In Theaters Now (Cry Macho)
A Jaw-Dropping Film (1917)
Plymouth Arts Center Accepting Applications for Holiday Membership
Windy City: Expertise in Action

A Few Finlays

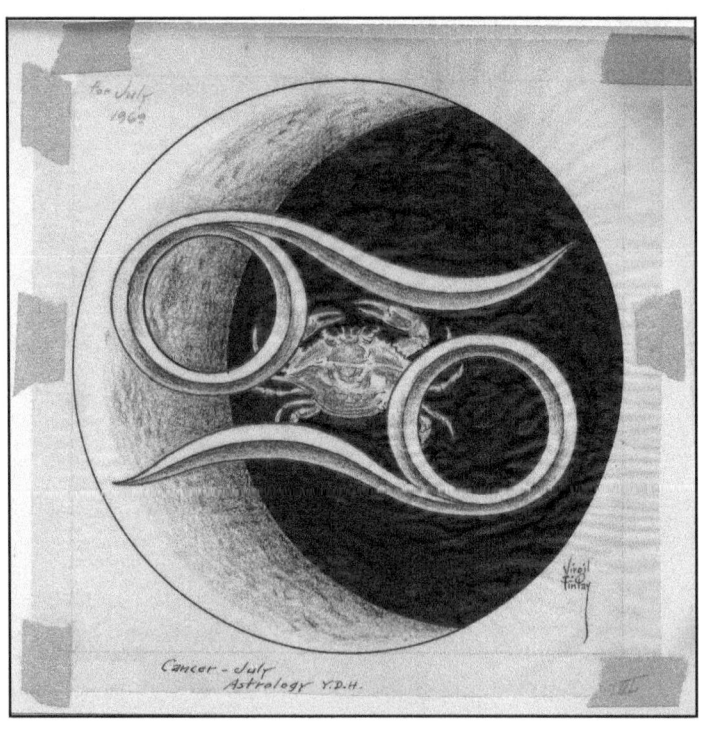

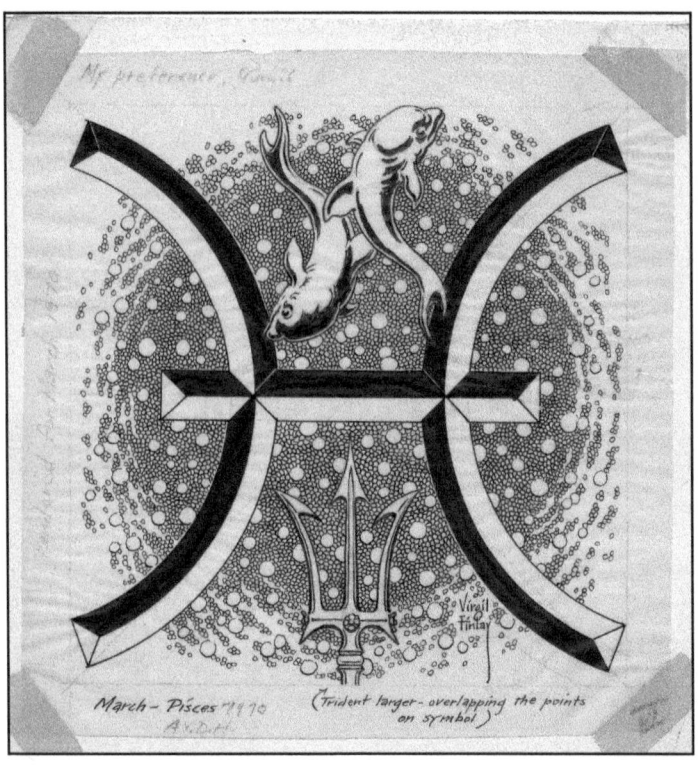

Three pieces of art by Virgil Finlay which I bought at the Windy City show. The astrology pieces are preliminaries.

F. Paul Wilson
An Encounter With

Those cosmic, common coincidences. They're all over the place! Opportunities waiting to be plucked, if you're alert and willing to take advantage of them.

Take, for example, my recent attendance at the Windy City Pulp and Paper Convention (WCPPC). At the show three years ago, author F. Paul Wilson was the convention's guest of honor. After meeting him, I decided to try some of his books. I liked what I read, and I read more.

(You might have seen a 1983 movie, The Keep, which is based on one of Wilson's books.)

When we checked in to our hotel for WCPPC, I was part-way through an F. Paul Wilson novel, Deep as the Marrow.

That book's premise: The President of the United States announces a personal crusade: He will do whatever it takes to legalize drugs for adults.

Cocaine. Heroin. Everything.

I won't tell you any more about this thrilling suspense story. But I will ask you to consider this:

What type of person, or group, or organization, *would be most opposed to this kind of change?*

If you think that over, you might be able to guess one small aspect of the book's plot. But even if you are that insightful, it will spoil nothing for you, as surprise after surprise motivates you to turn page after page.

So I sit in my hotel room, read a few pages of this novel, and then it's time to visit the dealer's room at WCPPC. I walk around, and see—

F. Paul Wilson.

The author of the book I'm reading.

He tells me he's just attending the show because he enjoys it. I tell him I'm reading—and I misremember the title. "Deep to the Marrow," I tell him. He corrects me. (You know how **embarrassing** that is?)

All right. Day one of WCPPC. Coincidence one.

Day two. I'm thinking, "I should ask Wilson a few questions for The PRC." I look for him all day and don't see him.

Day three. I still didn't find him. I sit in the front row for the show's auction. And F. Paul Wilson comes walking in and sits two chairs from me. Coincidence number two.

Sometimes, I think quickly enough to take advantage of such opportunities. In this case, Wilson kindly agreed to a brief (the five minutes the auctioneer took for a break) interview.

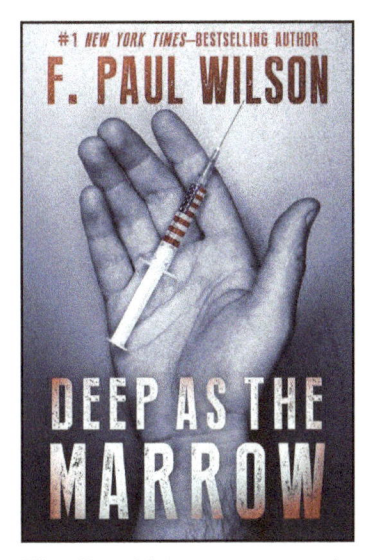

The President wants to do WHAT??!! — From Barnes & Noble, BN.com

F. Paul Wilson
An Exclusive Interview With

The PRC: Dr. Wilson, you told me you're here at this show as a visitor. What attracts you to this show?

F. Paul Wilson: Well I just love the people that are here. We all have something in common. We all have a common frame of reference that seems to be dying out. I like the camaraderie and love the ambiance of all the books, because a lot of science fiction conventions now, their book room has no books. So this place is unique, for me.

PRC: I hope Tom Roberts will forgive me for asking a question he asked when interviewing you at this show three years ago. Are you still a practicing physician? If so, are your patients aware of your books?

FPW: No, I retired in January of 2019, just before the pandemic. But, yeah, a lot of my patients were my readers. But others, I'm sure, certain ones read my stuff and decided not to come to me anymore. So it goes both ways.

PRC: Your book, Deep as the Marrow, started with a premise of legalizing all drugs for adults. Does that reflect your own view?

FPW: I believe that, if you don't own anything else in this world, you own your body. And you have a right to pollute it any way you please. So I just don't think there should be any restrictions on what you can put in your bloodstream. I think that's one of the foundations of freedom—owning yourself, and being responsible for yourself.

That [book] was dear to my heart. There was a Hollywood production company that wanted to make a movie out of it. But they wanted to change the McGuffin, and they wanted to change it to something other than legalizing drugs, because that was too controversial. And I said, No. No, you can't do it. Either you do it like it was in the book, or we don't do it. And so we didn't do it.

PRC: What can you tell us about your recent book, Double Threat, without any spoilers?

FPW: It's actually a rewrite of my first novel, Healer. I contemporized it, because of a movie version. Chris Morgan said he loved the book, he'd love to make a movie of it someday. And I said, Well everything takes place in Duad's head. And he said, No, I would make Pard visible, to Duad only, and then he would have someone he could interact with. And I said, Well, that's brilliant. And so I said, I have to rewrite it. And so I dedicated the [new] book to him, and I totally re-imagined it, and then I changed Duad to a female, and the dynamics between the two changed so dramatically, it was like a new book.

PRC: The springboard for your novel, Healer, and now the rewrite, Double Threat, was the short story, Pard, correct?

FPW: Yes, that was the [December 1972] Analog story.

PRC: Thank you.

F. Paul Wilson signs a book at the 2018 WCPPC.

Editor's Note: Information on F. Paul Wilson and his books can be found at **repairmanjack.com** (a reference to one of Wilson's popular series characters, Repairman Jack, who... *fixes* things... when you can't get them... *fixed*... through conventional means.

Oh... you're wondering what a *"McGuffin"* is? It's a term used by Alfred Hitchcock to describe a catalyst that sets off events in his movies. In one film, it was a roll of microfilm.

Windy City: Expertise in Action

Some months ago, I wrote about an experience I had at a past Windy City Pulp and Paper Convention (WCPPC).

I had an old black and white painting of William Penn negotiating with some Native Americans. The only indication of the artist's identity were the initials "A. B. S."

I showed the painting to Fred Taraba, who owns Taraba Illustration Art LLC. (Check out his website at **tarabaillustrationart.com**.) My jaw dropped as he started thinking out loud, putting the evidence together to give me an educated guess as to who "A. B. S." likely was.

That situation took a complete reversal at the recent WCPPC. I wasn't even in the dealer's room when I ran into Fred. He told me someone in the dealer's room wanted *my* expertise.

That stunned me. An expert like Fred had been consulted by a dealer, and now the two wanted *my* expert opinion? **Beyond belief!**

But the question concerned James Bama.

Ah! You see, I call myself (only half-jokingly) a "world authority on the art of James Bama." (Er... maybe only 25% jokingly.) I don't claim to be the *most* knowledgeable person about Bama's career in the world, but... I know enough to be helpful. A few years ago, when Fred was working for an auction house, I was able to identify for him which paperback a piece of art had appeared on. I was able to identify another piece used in Argosy magazine as a preliminary; the auction house selling it thought it was the finished, published version. (It wasn't.)

So I trekked to the far back of the dealer's room, and the man behind the table knew I was coming and was ready for me. (It was kind of eerie.) He showed me the painting in the accompanying photo and wanted to know, Is this a work by James Bama?

It is. (In my opinion.)

I recognized the image as being from one of the 300-some paperbacks I've scanned for my "Bama project" I've worked for years on. Yes, this was painted by Bama.

I couldn't recall the paperback's title, but I knew it was published by Dell.

I also told its owner something that might be completely useless: The male model looked like the model Bama used on another paperback cover: The Detective. The painting's owner looked up that cover on his phone. He agreed.

(Looking closely at The Detective, I now think... Uh, maybe—and then again, maybe not. Take a look for yourself, below.)

I also thought (but did not verbalize): The woman looked like Bama's wife. (Why did I not say this out loud? Maybe there was too much other verbiage flying around.)

I checked out this art several times that day. My wife looked at it. "Oh! That woman is Bama's wife!" she said. I nodded in agreement. Bama often used his wife as a model. I have two original paperback paintings by Bama; his wife's features appear in both.

Bama usually signed his paintings. Why no signature on this piece? A possible answer came when we finally found the book it was used on. The art director reversed the image for publication. Why? Your guess is as good as mine. This set us to looking on the art for signs of a signature that was painted out (they don't usually print signatures backwards). We found no such thing.

This is just a small part of the enjoyment of WCPPC.

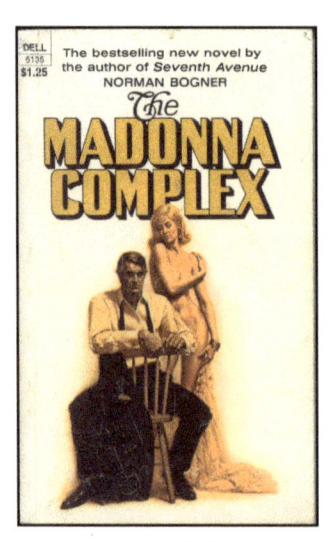

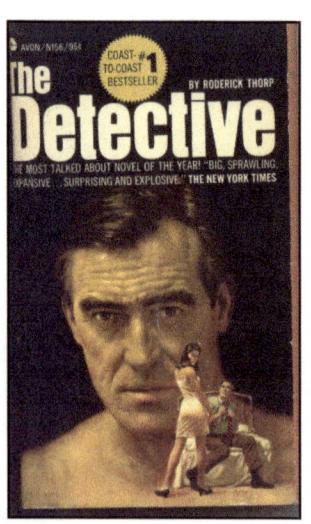

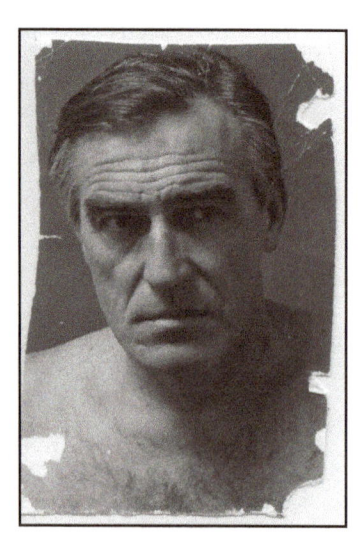

Is this painting by James Bama? I say YES.

Left to right: 1) The paperback on which the mystery painting was used. A closeup of the man in the above painting. 2) Enlargement of the man's face in the mystery painting. 3) Another paperback which Bama painted. Is this the same man as in #2? 4) You won't see this anywhere else! A scan of the reference photo James Bama used to paint the cover for The Detective. And maybe for The Madonna Complex? Borrowed during one of my visits, scanned, and returned to Bama's files. Definitely a PRC exclusive!

George Washington, surveyor, by Remington Schuyler. — HA.com

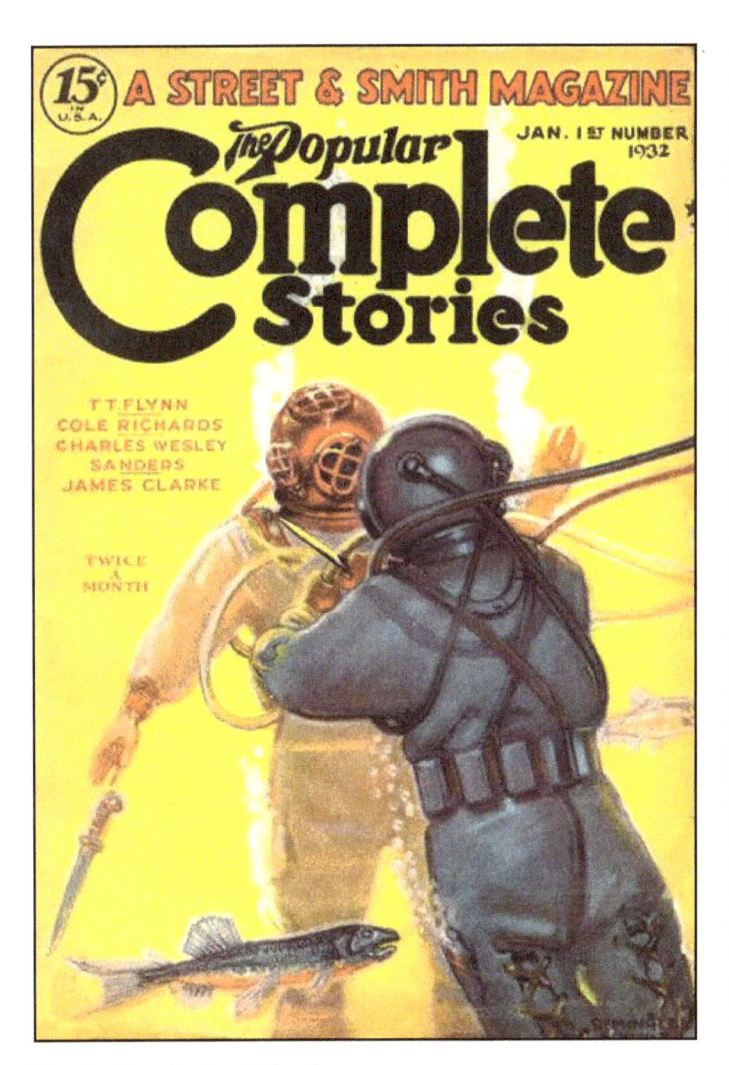

Two by Remington Schuyler.
Left: From 1932. Looks like they're playing for keeps. — From PulpArtists.com
Right: This superbly-composed image was likely used on a magazine cover. A good example of why collectors seek illustration paintings to hang in their homes. Remington Schuyler. — HA.com

The Current

Plymouth Review

TAKING YOU PLACES WORTH SEEING
Volume 10 • Issue 12 • November 2021

The publication that respects your intelligence

What-Not • Film • Art • History • Books

Dazzling Art • Founding Thoughts • Entertaining Movies
Leather • Farming a Century Ago • Mustard

FREE!

November 2021

Cover photo: The National Mustard Museum, Middleton

Great Movies This Month

Farming as it Was a Century Past (The Guardians)

The National Mustard Museum

PulpArtists by David Saunders: Mel Crair

Ask a Science Teacher by Larry Scheckel: My Car Has a Display that Shows the Air Pressure in each Tire. How Does it Do That?

How to Think Like the Founders: A Review of "America's Revolutionary Mind," by C. Bradley Thompson, by Robert Tracinski

Colors of Christmas, Celtic Christmas presented by Arts Center

SCHRC book reviewed: *Leather Ties, Leather Producers in the Sheboygan Area*

Alexander Botts Books

Farm Collector Magazine

Book: The Art of Pulp Fiction

"I'm Charles Foster Kane!"

Would you pay $27,000 for this typewriter, simply because it appeared in Citizen Kane (see Dec. 6)? Well... somebody did. Per Heritage Auctions: "Used in the memorable sequence when 'Charles Foster Kane' (Orson Welles) finds 'Jedediah Leland' (Joseph Cotten) passed out drunk over his typewriter while writing a very negative review of Kane's wife's operatic performance... Acquired at the 1970 MGM Auction with other RKO assets, this typewriter was among Debbie Reynolds' most revered pieces and was prominently displayed at her Las Vegas museum alongside the fur coat worn by Welles in the same scene that sold for $120,000 in Profiles in History's Debbie Reynolds: The Auction Finale."
— HA.com

LES FILMS DU WORSO PRESENTS
NATHALIE BAYE   LAURA SMET   IRIS BRY

The GUARDIANS

A FILM BY XAVIER BEAUVOIS

France 1915.
Men on the battlefield.
Women on the homefront.

The Plymouth Review Current

Taking You Places Worth Seeing

Volume 11 • Issue 1 • December 2021

FREE!

- Life-Affirming Art
- Truth & Justice
- Great Movies
- Outbid Again!
- Black-Market Butter
- Bottled Light

The publication that respects your intelligence • Thought Triggers • Whimsies & Witticisms • Oddities

December
2021

Cover photo: Creations of Northern Lights Bottle Company LLC

Great Movies This Month

Outbid Again!

Lipidleggin' by F. Paul Wilson

Ask a Science Teacher by Larry Scheckel: What U.S. Presidents Were Also Scientists?

SCHRC book reviewed: *To the Hills and Lakes, The Story of Streetcar and Interurban Lines in Sheboygan County*

Outbid Again!

Small-Plate Pleasures, Trattoria Stefano, Sheboygan

Outbid Again!

Small Town Dreams Turn Into Nightmares, IJ.org

Sartori Big Cheese Drop Rings in the New Year at the Plymouth Arts Center

Something to Think About

Outbid Again!

PulpArtists by David Saunders: J. Clark Work

Outbid Again—No! *No!* I **Got** It!

When Love Story Magazine was published by Street & Smith, it became so popular that it was published weekly. Cover by J. Clark Work.

Outbid Again!

Some day, I hope to acquire an original piece of art by Richard F. Outcault, featuring two of his creations—Buster Brown and Tige. This 1906 ink and watercolor piece, intended for a calendar, would go nicely on my wall. Alas, final bidding went well over $5,000, leaving Your Editor tumbling and coughing in the dust. — HA.com

Outbid Again!

"OK," I thought, "this 1906 piece, without color, shouldn't go that high." But again, I am utterly defeated by a bid of $1,200, which far surpassed my own bid. Seems there are plenty of *other* Buster Brown fans out there! — HA.com

Outbid Again!

So. Again I adjust my goal in acquiring a Buster Brown original, to a more modest level (compared to the masterpiece at top of this page). The lot shown here consisted of three pieces, each cut and incomplete. Attractively colored, but—(gasp)—no Tige! That might be too much of a compromise. Should I bid? Yeah, sure. The price on these shouldn't soar so insanely high, right? **Wrong.** Ownership of these three pieces slipped like quicksilver through my fingers. When the dust had settled and bidding for this lot was closed, it had brought over $800. And I wonder—yes, I wonder—will I *ever* own an Outcault Buster Brown original drawing (with Tige)? — HA.com

Outbid Again!

All right, now my expectations are *really* getting modest. But at least Tige is in here. This piece, obviously incomplete, measures 9.25 x 2.5 inches. From the way the lettering is crossed out, I suspect it was never used for publication. Bidding shouldn't go high on this one.

Wouldn't you think? Hm. Yeah, right. It went for over $700. No Buster Brown original for me, for now, I guess. — HA.com

~~Outbid Again!~~
No! *No!* I *got* it!

I was top bidder on the painting at right, with a bid of—ah... *that's* confidential. No, it's *not* Buster Brown and Tige. But it features one of my favorite fictional characters: **The Shadow.** This is not the actual painting used for the August 1934 Shadow pulp magazine cover (if that painting still exists, it would be worth a small fortune). It's a re-creation. (Not *rec-reation.*) The original was done by George Rozen (see PulpArtists, July 2018), and is shown below left. George's twin brother, *Jerome* Rozen (PulpArtists, Sept. 2018), did the re-creation (right) in the 1980s (pretty close, aren't they?). The signature at bottom left reads, "Jerome Rozen after George Rozen." By an interesting coincidence (the kind of cosmic coincidence that happens all over the place), Gypsy Vengeance is the next Shadow novel I'll be reading (I'm reading all 325 Shadow novels in order of publication). So I'll probably be reading it when the painting arrives! That's a little weird, ***but it's also pretty darn cool!!*** — HA.com

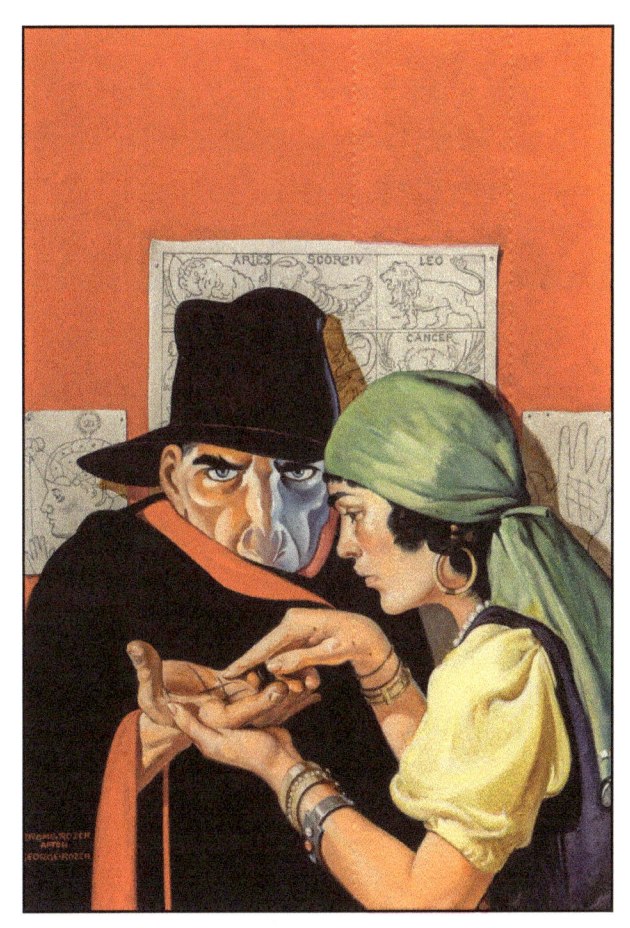

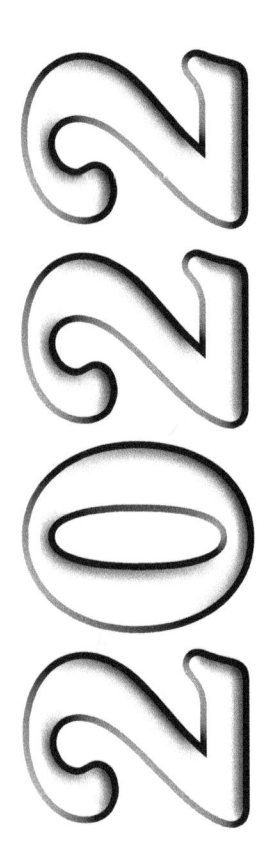

2022

The Current
Plymouth Review
TAKING YOU PLACES WORTH SEEING
Volume 11 • Issue 2 • January 2022

FREE!

Alexander Botts, Salesman ♦ Riding a Pig
Landverhuizers ♦ Great Movies ♦ The Latest Comics

Thought Triggers • Whimsies & Witticisms • Oddities

January
2022

Cover photo: The Bugle Comics & Collictibles, Sheboygan
Great Movies This Month
Saddle-Riding a Pig
Ask a Science Teacher, by Larry Scheckel: What Is This Quantum Physics or Quantum Mechanics I Hear About?
I'm a Hard-Boiled Bozo, by William Hazlett Upson
SCHRC book reviewed: *Landverhuizers: Dutch Immigrants Come to Sheboygan County*
NYE Dinner at the Blind Horse
New Art Show Opens in Gallery 110 North
PulpArtists by David Saunders: Fred Craft
Casting Call for Alexander Botts
The Two Artists...

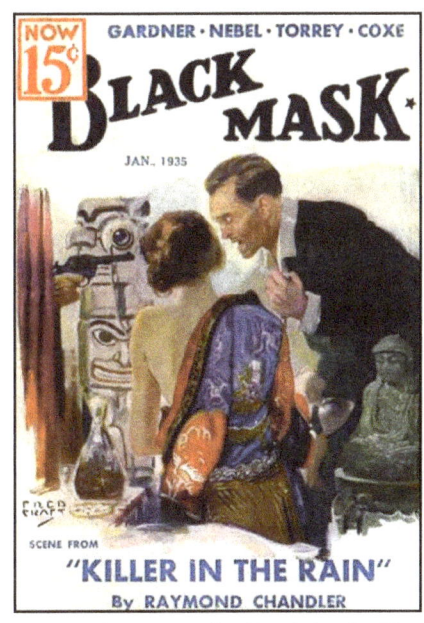

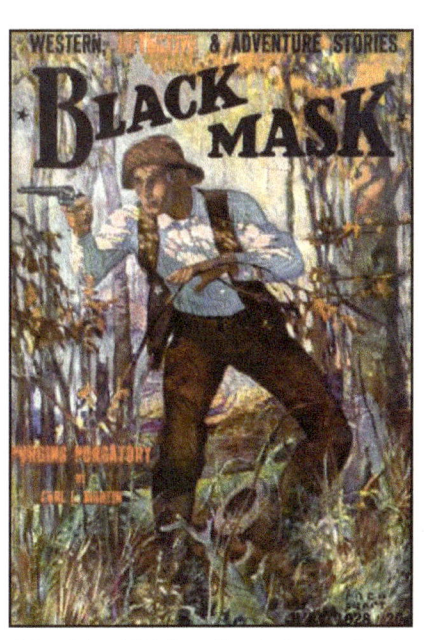

Two pulp covers by Fred Craft. Black Mask had high editorial standards for its art and fiction.

Saddle-Riding a Pig
A Cautionary Tale from Buster Brown (and Tige)

Last issue, Your Editor regaled the Dear Readers of The PRC with his unsuccessful attempts in bidding on several original Buster Brown and Tige drawings.

Unsuccessful with my bids for original art, I settled for some books by Outcault. These were nowhere near as expensive as going prices for original art; on the other hand, you won't find them at the dollar stores.

- *"Tige," His Story,* 1905 by R. F. Outcault (but allegedly written by Tige himself); and
- *My Resolutions,* 1906 (by Outcault / Buster Brown).

Resolutions? Yes, at the end of each Buster Brown Sunday comic disaster, Buster would make a resolution, wherein he swore he'd learned a lesson, and pledged to aspire to higher moral standards and better behavior.

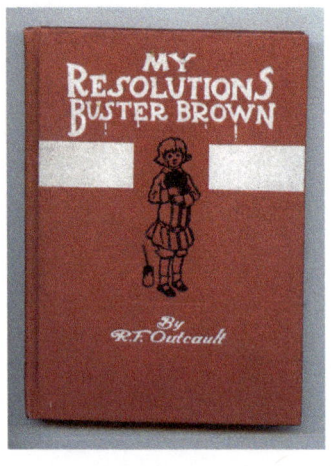

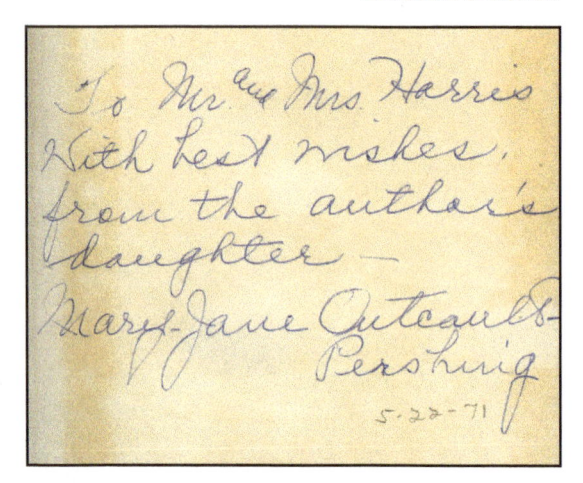

On opening My Resolutions, by Buster Brown—surprise! An inscription from Outcault's daughter, who gave the book as a gift! That reminds me: A photo of Mary Jane Outcault, with a loving father's drawings of Buster and Tige in the margins, was auctioned off about a year ago. And (sigh), yes, I bid on it... but... *Outbid Again!* Its $1,560 final price left Your Editor feeling he was running after a jet plane, trying catch it. — Photo of Mary Jane Outcault, HA.com

Buster resolves, "I'll never try to ride a pig again." For details, let's see what Tige himself wrote. Yes, he wrote the following. See—there he is, at his writing desk.

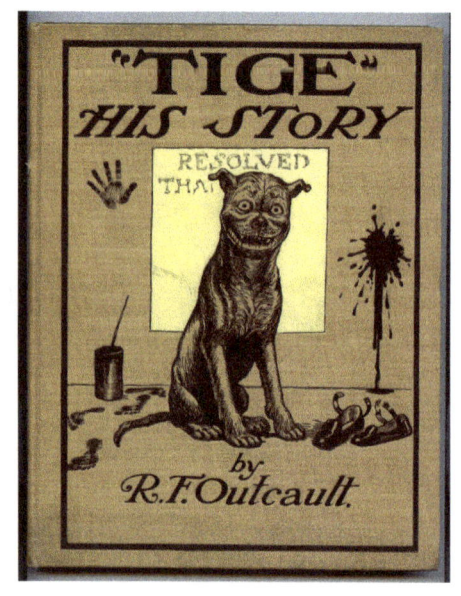

From "Tige," His Story

THE next day [Buster] came out of the stable with a saddle. He did n't see me, so I just followed him. At last he came to an old sedate-looking hog that was blinking in the sun. Yes! that's what he did, put the saddle on the pig and got aboard!

THE pig decided to go away, and when he did, he went away fast, *awfully fast!* Down the hill he went, and headed directly for a hedge. I could see the finish of that ride, I thought. But I was mistaken, for when the pig dashed out on the other side Buster was still on his back. Piggy kept on running and snorting, and attracted the attention of a lot of other pigs, who joined the race. I suppose they thought it was a race.

NOW in all my life I never saw such a funny sight. Buster Brown on piggy-back at the head of a whole herd of snorting swine. The more I ran, the more excuse they had to get excited and believe they were being chased. The bees from the three or four hives that they had tipped over now joined in, and gave the pigs more reason to increase their speed. It was a race fit for the Coliseum at Rome. Buster hung on; he could n't well do anything else now with all those pigs at his heels.

DOWN in the barnyard, where the pigs live, there is a puddle of the dirtiest water I ever saw, where the pigs wallow. That's where that herd was headed for, and that's where the race wound up. Oh, *dear me,* what a sight for sore eyes was my dear little comrade when he crawled out of that hog-hole! I would love to have an instantaneous photograph of what Uncle Jack said when he saw his nice new saddle. Buster's aunt thought some serious things when she had to put him under the pump. He wanted to save his money and buy that pig! What do you think of that? I laughed until I got hysterical and Uncle Jack had to throw a pail of cold water in my face. I was afraid there was more coming, and so I made tracks!

"The pig decided to go away!"

FALL IS COMING. ... Besides Buster Brown and Tige, R. F. Outcault (1863-1928) created the Yellow Kid, who first appeared in newspapers in 1984. (Buster and Tige first appeared in 1902.) This original sold at auction in 2021 for $10,0800. — HA.com

You Get A Square Deal at the Best Store And this one sold in 2017 for $16,730.00.

The two artists...

...who had the greatest impact on Your Editor's life are represented here: Steve Ditko (left) and James Bama (right). I was introduced to the work of each artist at age eight, in 1963.

These two pieces of original art went up for auction at Heritage Auctions. — HA.com

My first Amazing Spider-Man comic, #4 (which introduced The Sandman), was drawn by Ditko.

Ditko created Spider-Man with Stan Lee in 1962, and eventually plotted the stories. (Note the credit—"Plotted and drawn by.")

In this opening page from Amazing Spider-Man #37, 1966, Ditko did something interesting. He emphasized Peter Parker; the Spider-Man mask hangs in the background—limp, less important. Showing Parker, contemplating the events and characters of the story (as if in retrospect), Ditko emphasized the importance of the characters. When Ditko plotted the stories he drew (in contrast to working with a full script from a writer), his stories were driven by the characters: their differences in viewpoint, misunderstandings, and conflicting values.

Ditko conveyed expressions not only through his faces, but through his hands. Note the tapping finger. It adds thoughtfulness to the contemplative expression, with Parker's raised eyebrow and wry smile.

In 1966, even as the popularity of Spider-Man and Dr. Strange (another character Ditko helped to develop) grew, Ditko left Marvel to work for other companies. From that time until his death in 2018, he worked for a variety of comics companies, applying his imagination by creating many, many characters and stories.

Ditko returned to work at Marvel in 1979, but refused to again draw Spider-Man or Dr. Strange.

Your Editor has had the pleasure of working with Robin Snyder to design and co-publish several books collecting Ditko's work, including *Avenging World, A Touch of Genius, The Complete Four-Page Series, Overture, Opening Acts, Character Twists, Postshadowing,* and *Curtain.*

(This original sold for $336,000.) (Yes. It did.)

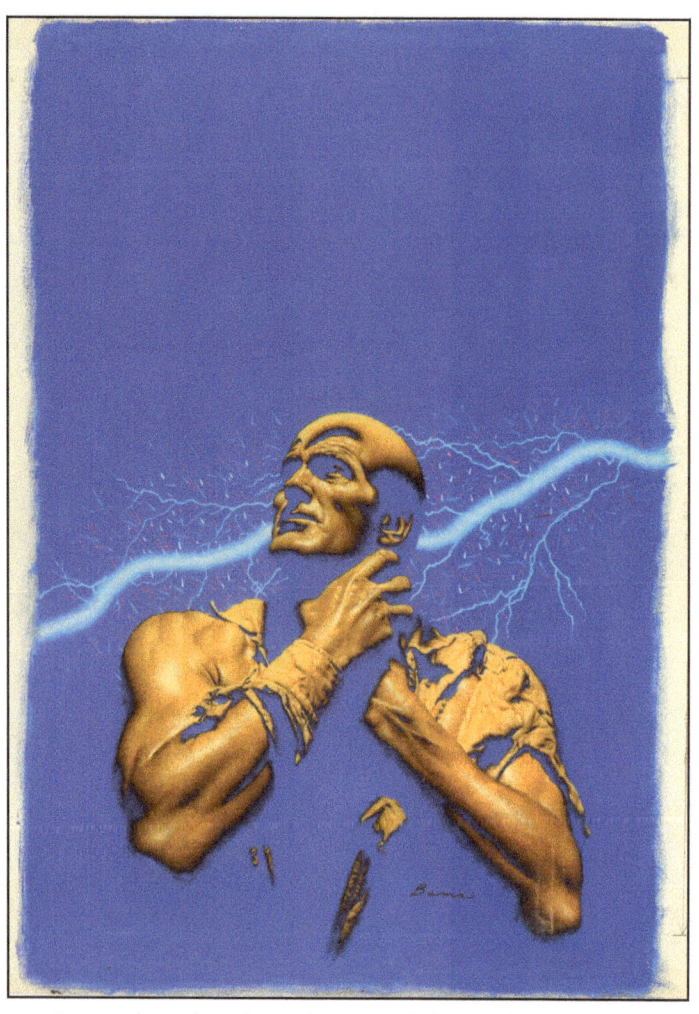

I was introduced to the art of James Bama (though I would not know his name until a few years later) through my first Aurora Universal Monster model kit, Dracula. (Bama did about 20 box-cover paintings for this series, including Frankenstein, the Wolf Man, the Mummy, Dr. Jekyll and Mr. Hyde, King Kong, Godzilla, and The Munsters).

Bama painted several hundred paperback covers, including over 50 for the Doc Savage series. The Doc Savage cover shown here, for Merchants of Disaster, symbolizes the story's menace: an invention that destroys oxygen. The electrical chiaroscuro glare and the bolt of lightning makes me want to squint, as from a welder's torch, I can almost smell the ozone and feel the suffocation as Doc clutches his throat.

Bama grew up in New York City but made a radical change to his life when he and his wife moved to Wyoming in the late 1960s. He started painting interesting people he met in his new home; found he could sell those paintings at ten times what he was making on paperbacks; and began a career as a fine artist, earning him recognition as the Greatest Painter of the 20th Century. (Recognized as such, that is, by Your Editor, and perhaps a few others.)

Will I bid on either of these originals? Just thinking about it raises my body temperature a couple of degrees (Celsius), but only until I consider realistically what I think they will bring... at which point I answer: *Nah, I don't think so!* (Talk about a dash of cold water (the kind Tige was doused with (see two pages ago)).)

This original painting sold for $50,400.

Casting call for Alexander Botts

Readers like to play a "Casting Game" for favorite books that have yet to be made into movies. What actor would be right for this or that character, when/if a movie is made?

Since it's fantasy in the first place, players don't always feel limited to living actors. And that premise will be used here.

First: A movie *was* made of Alexander Botts' exploits. The character had appeared in the Saturday Evening Post for close to ten years, when Earthworm Tractors was released in 1936, featuring the popular Joe E. Brown as Botts.

Brown was **perfect** for the role. He was always good at playing characters full of braggadocio, who made up excuses as one calamity happened after another.

But still. Supposing Brown had never done that role?

I think I have another perfect fantasy casting for Botts: Charley Chase.

The specific character type I'm thinking of for Charley Chase can be seen in the Laurel and Hardy film, Sons of the Desert, where Chase plays a crazed representative from Texas, having way too much fun at a convention.

I won't be able to read another Botts story without visualizing him as Charley Chase. I don't know yet, if that is a blessing or a curse.

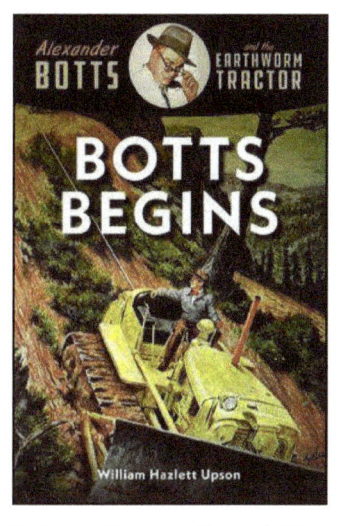

Charley Chase. The face of "a natural-born salesman"? — Public domain image from Wikipedia

Octane Press allowed The PRC to reprint an entire story from this book in the January issue. Available from Barnes & Noble, BN.com; or Octane Press, octanepress.com.

February 2022

Cover photo: Out Standing in its Field

Great Movies This Month

Ask a Science Teacher, by Larry Scheckel: What Are Some of the Famous Science Hoaxes in History?

A Good Hard Science Fiction Novel (Hail Mary, by Andy Weir)

SCHRC book reviewed: *Welcome to Sheboygan Falls!*
Straight Talk About Modern Farms and Rural "Decline" by Robert Paarlberg, HumanProgress.org
The Short Films of Charley Chase
"A Wee Bit Irish" Concert
And Currently at the PAC...

Release the dove! This Dec. 28, 1918 Saturday Evening Post cover by J. C. Lyendecker (note the stylish signature) has several levels of symbolism. The world was relieved by the end of the world-wide war, which at that time was considered so horrifying, that mankind had learned its lesson and would never fight another war. Hopes ran high that the birth of 1919 would bring better times. — HA.com

The short films of Charley Chase, 1930 to 1936, are available on these sets. There is excellent commentary on each short film.

Two disks; 17 short films; nearly 7 hours total.

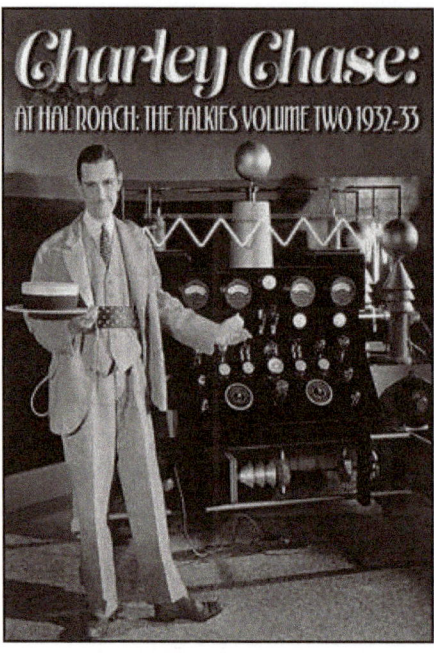

Two disks; 15 short films; 5 hours 40 minutes.

Three disks; 22 short films; 7 hours 20 minutes.

Q: What Are Some of the Famous Science Hoaxes in History?

By Larry Scheckel

A: The Cottingley Fairies has to be near the top of the list. In July 1917, two young girls, ages 9 and 16, in Cottingley, England, took a series of photos of fairies. They were widely published and in December 1920, Sir Arthur Conan Doyle, scientist and creator of Sherlock Holmes, authenticated the photos as real and clear proof of the existence of fairies. Some 66 years later, in 1983, the two girls admitted they faked the photos by using cardboard cutouts.

Ranking right up there with the fairies is Piltdown Man. The human-like skull, discovered by Charles Dawson in 1912 in Pleistocene gravel beds near Piltdown, in England, was said to be the missing link between apes and humans. It was celebrated as one of the most important archaeological discoveries in history. Noted archeologists and anthropologists hypothesized it was from a human ancestor some 500,000 years ago.

Piltdown Man was exposed as a forgery in 1953. Dawson had taken a 300-year-old human skull, a 500-year-old lower jaw from an orangutan, and teeth from a chimpanzee, and fused them together in a convincing specimen of the missing link. Charles Dawson (1864-1916) was later found to have committed numerous archeology forgeries.

Proof positive that fairies exist! Ten-year-old Frances Griffiths gazes in wonder in this 1917 photo taken by her friend, Elsie Wright. "Photographs don't lie" was a phrase commonly accepted—by some people. That belief, and a belief that nice little girls simply wouldn't lie, convinced the creator of Sherlock Holmes that these fairies were really real. — Public Domain image from Wikipedia

The Cardiff Giant, oh that's a good one. A 10-foot tall "petrified man" was uncovered in 1869 by workers digging a well behind a barn in Cardiff, New York. William Newell, cousin of the perpetrator, George Hull, set up a tent over the giant and charged 25 cents, equivalent to $4.80 today, for people who wanted to see it. Hull later sold his interest to investors for $465,000 in today's money. P.T. Barnum made a replica when Hull refused to sell.

Clever George Hull hired men to quarry a 10.5-foot-long block of gypsum in Fort Dodge, Iowa, had it shipped to Chicago, and hired a German immigrant stonecutter to carve it into a likeness of a man. Hull swore the stonecutter to secrecy. Stains, acids and needles were used to make the giant appear to be old and weathered. The "man" was shipped by rail to his cousin's farm near Cardiff, where he was entombed behind the barn, just waiting to be discovered.

The Loch Ness monster is another good one. The image most often seen is known as the "Surgeon's Photograph," taken in 1933 by a London gynecologist, Robert Wilson. Loch Ness is in the highlands of Scotland. For 60 years the photo was considered evidence of the monster's existence. Marmaduke Wetherell, his father-in law, Christian Spurling, and several co-conspirators, bought a toy submarine from F. W. Woolworths, and fashioned a wooden head and neck. Photographer Wilson later admitted his photo was a hoax.

Crop circles grabbed the public's attention big-time in 1985 in the Wiltshire, England area. Many claimed that only extraterrestrial beings could possibly make such perfect geometric figures. That is until 1991, when Doug Bower and Dave Chorley admitted that they, two bored young men, created the circles with a plank pulled by ropes. To prove their claim, the pair make a circle in front of journalists. Many copiers followed.

Interested readers can look into: perpetual motion machines, Clever Hans, the Mechanical Horse, Uri Geller, Sidd Finch, the "Spaghetti Tree" April Fools caper, the Unbeatable Mechanical Chess player, the "Paul McCartney is dead" prank, Beringer's Lying Stones fraud, and the Lady Who Gave Birth to Rabbits.

For Educators

This instructor's guide to the Cottingley Fairies is available free through the James Randi Educational Foundation. Download it at web.randi.org; select Education / Education Modules.
— From web.randi.org

From *The Case of the Cottingley Fairies,* published by the James Randi Edicational Foundation:

[Edward] Gardner [a leader in London's Theosophical Society, a philosophical organization with an interest in the occult] and [Arthur] Conan Doyle both believed in the existence of fairies until their deaths, and neither stopped defending the authenticity of the Cottingley photos—even after the public almost universally accepted the incident as a hoax.

The case was closed for good in 1988, when Elsie Wright [one of the girls involved in the hoax], shortly before her death, confided in Crawley, "The whole affair had been a practical joke that had fallen flat on its face. The laugh was on us." The story briefly reemerged into popular culture in 1997 with the release of a movie version of the events, called *Fairytale: A True Story.*

Closing remarks by James Randi, from *The Case of the Cottingley Fairies:*

I had frequent communication with Elsie for several years before she passed away. She always joked with me but never actually admitted that the fairies were just a game she and Francis played with the rest of the world. Today, people know much more about photography, but 95 years ago most people were mystified by it. Sir Arthur Conan Doyle certainly should have been smart enough to solve the hoax, but he wanted to believe in ghosts, spirits, and rather silly things of that sort, so he decided that two little girls couldn't have dared to deceive him.

Unfortunately, many people in this day also have such delusions, and the James Randi Educational Foundation is doing everything possible to educate the public (that's you!) about these matters.

I hope this lesson has taught you that being skeptical is a healthy, useful attitude. And there will be more...

March
2022

Cover photo: The Kitchen at the Blind Horse, Kohler
Great Movies This Month
John Deere Evolution: The Design and Engineering of an American Icon, book by Lee Klancher
Totalitarian Surveillance
Ask a Science Teacher, by Larry Scheckel: My Sister Has a Birthmark. What Caused It?
Movie Posters
Student Art Show

SCHRC book reviewed: *Time in Hell, The Battle for Buna*
"A Wee Bit Irish" Concert
PulpArtists by David Saunders: Charles Wrenn
Wisconsin Artists Invited to Apply For
Gallery 110 North's 27th Annual Juried Art Exhibit
Valentine's Dinner at the Blind Horse
10 Terrifying Facts about the East German Secret Police, by Dr. Laura Williams, FEE.org
More about The Lives of Others

Totalitarian Surveillance

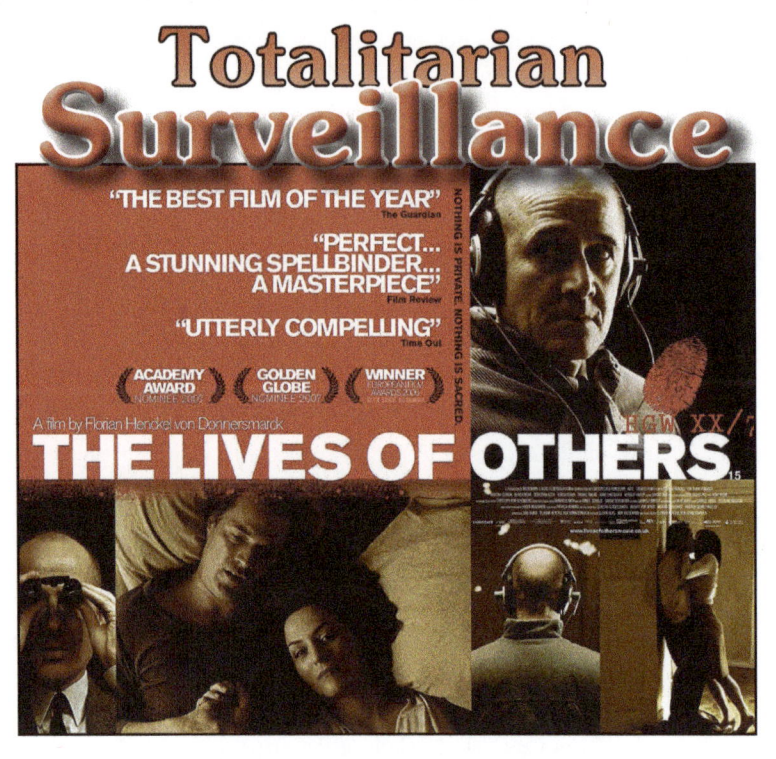

The Lives of Others:
A movie written and directed by Florian Henckel von Donnersmarck

This 2006 German-language film immediately sets its story's historical context:

"1984, East Berlin. Glasnost is nowhere in sight. The population of the GDR [East Germany, or the German Democratic Republic] is kept under strict control by the Stasi, the East German Secret Police.

"Its force of 100,000 employees and 200,000 informers safeguards the Dictatorship of the Proletariat. Its declared goal: 'To know everything.'"

The film first intercuts between two scenes: A prisoner being relentlessly interrogated, finally breaking down; and a classroom where Stasi students learn the techniques of effective interrogation from Wiesler (played by Ulrich Mühe). This establishes the total control over human life wielded by the "Shield and Sword" of the omnipotent State.

Wiesler and his superior attend a play written by Dreyman (played by Sebastian Koch). There is no reason to believe that Dreyman is other than a good, loyal, obedient socialist. But the order comes down the chain of command, for Wiesler to put Dreyman under surveillance. This means Weisler and another agent must listen round-the-clock to what happens in Dreyman's apartment, and make complete notes. Reporting to his superior, Wiesler describes Dreyman as "an arrogant type, the kind I warn my students about."

Suspecting he's being bugged, Dreyman and some friends discuss some false information that the Stasi would act on. No action is taken (the Stasi suspect it's only bait and don't act on it), and Dreyman and his friends falsely assume that he is not under surveillance.

Wiesler betrays no emotion as he monitors every aspect of Dreyman's life. You know, in a strongly authoritarian situation like this, there are obvious oppressors (the government), and the victims (those being oppressed). Remember, socialism is public ownership of the means of production, and that "means of production" is human lives and minds. You can't get any more "totalitarian" than ownership of a person's life and mind. (It is, essentially, a form of slavery.)

So the life-damaging effects of a dictatorship on someone like Dreyman are easy to see, and a decent person would have sympathy for this victim.

But here's something interesting to think about. In his book, *The Ominous Parallels,* Leonard Peikoff describes not only the mind- and life-deadening effects of totalitarianism on the oppressed; he claims the same effects rebound onto the oppressors.

That's a complicated idea that can't be explored here; but I couldn't help thinking about it as I watched Wiesler during this movie. In a free society, a person finds a productive purpose and feels pride over his achievement. But can a Stasi agent feel a sense of achievement, or pride, on discovering little details about another person's life, which can be used to destroy that person? Or would the agent repress any such thoughts, thinking, "I'm only doing my duty"?

Something really interesting starts happening behind Wiesler's stone face. This is a key part of the story.

At one point, Dreyman's apartment is searched by a squad of Stasi goons. They throw books and other items on the floor as they search. They slash the sofa's cushions. They find nothing. The head goon, handing Dreyman a form, says, "In the unlikely event that damage has occurred, you may claim compensation." (You can probably guess what would happen if he *did* claim compensation!)

You know how I review movies. I give very little away. I'm skipping over dozens of plot details, including Dreyman's actress lady-friend. But here are a few items:

It's four years later. The Berlin Wall has fallen.

Two more years pass. Dreyman discovers for the first time that he had been under full surveillance. He requests the records the Stasi made on him. He makes a startling discovery.

Two more years pass.

This film has one of the most satisfying endings I've ever seen in a movie. No, there is no bloodbath where the ex-Stasi agents are reduced to the garbage they already were.

I'll tell you exactly how it ends! (And this will spoil ***nothing!***)

Wiesler enters a bookstore and buys a book.

All right, all right... I'm not telling the ***whole*** story here.

Now, if you watch this movie, consider the following odious fact: There are people today who openly, unashamedly, unapologetically advocate the kind of society depicted under the Stasi.

Of course, few such people are honest enough to admit there would be a need for a Stasi-like government entity to ensure that each person is a "good citizen" in any society where human life needs to be "regulated."

But poison sprinkled with a little sugar is still poison.

I first watched The Lives of Others (Das Leben der Anderen) some months ago. I watched all the extras, including a short but interesting interview with the film's writer/director. I watched it again, to prepare for this article. Next? I'm doing what I seldom do with my home videos: I'll be watching it again, with the writer/director's commentary.

The movie makes an interesting side point. Alcoholism and suicide are rampant in dictatorships, resulting from the physical helplessness of being unfree, and the need to hide what one is thinking, both from the ever-vigilant authorities, and from oneself. The character Jerska is a director (Volkmar Kleinert) who has displeased the Stasi (somehow), and is now blacklisted and unable to work. It's not that he can't *find* work; people would appreciate his talents in a free society. He is *forbidden* by the State to work. Several characters in the film are like this: Not prisoners in a jail, but wearing invisible chains and straight-jackets; walking, not-quite-alive because they've been deprived of their life's goals. What can one do? Drink and not think too much.

This movie is rated R, for "some sexuality/nudity."
It was issued on DVD and Blu-Ray.
Barnes and Noble does not seem to carry it.
New and used copies are available on Amazon.
Many, many copies are listed on eBay.

"Those who declare, today, that force is the only way to deal with men (with the unstated footnote that they, the speakers, would be safe in the position of rulers), ought to take a careful look at the history of absolute monarchies—and of modern dictatorships as well. Under the rule of force, it is the rulers who are in greatest danger, who live—and die—in permanent terror. The court intrigues, the plots and counterplots, the coups d'état, the known executions and secret assassinations are a matter of record. So are the purges of Party leaders and their cliques, in Nazi Germany and Soviet Russia." — Ayn Rand, "A Nation's Unity." You'll see this point in the film, as each Stasi bureaucrat is terrified by what the whims of the next-level bureaucrat will bring.

More about
The Lives of Others

I wrote that I planned to watch The Lives of Others for a third time, with the commentary by screenwriter / director Florian Henckel von Donnersmarck. Well, since I set those words down, I *did* watch the commentary. (Yes! Developments are developing, even as this issue of The PRC is in development!)

You can view a movie on many levels. Take it for what it is; what you see is what you get; that's it. A totally legitimate approach to a movie.

In this case, however, the historical and political background got me thinking, and wanting to learn more. It led me to do some online research, some of which led to two other articles in this issue.

Directing my research in another direction led to viewing the writer / director commentary. I wanted to know his thoughts on his own film. Here are a few points I gained from that commentary:

• This was a difficult, long-range project. Research and writing took a long time. (Hey, that should come as no surprise to me, or certain others reading this.)

• von Donnersmarck selected the actors carefully, even if they had very small roles. He remarked on the importance of one actor with a very short role and said nothing, who had just the right expression of evil menace as he stood in the background. He commented that several actors had prominent careers on the East German stage (something few of us watching this in the States would be expected to know). Several actors (in real life) were persecuted by, even imprisoned by, the Stasi. von Donnersmarck many times expresses his high regard for the quality of acting, commenting on an especially well-done expression or gesture. He brought my attention to several subtleties I had not picked up on, watching the film twice previously.

• The film was made 20 years after the fall of the Berlin Wall, and German re-unification began. von Donnersmarck remarks on the difficulty of finding suitable locations. Something else interesting: A person making a phone booth call from the West German side is shown for a few seconds. The writer / director points out several visual background cues that indicate it was on the Western side, which are possibly lost on non-German audiences.

• There are several comments on the detrimental effects a dictatorship has on human life. Some very perceptive thoughts. It reminded me that I'd like to do an article, someday, on "Why Do Some People Hate Freedom So Much?"

• I've elsewhere remarked on how much I liked the film's ending. von Donnersmarck's comments enhanced my enjoyment even further.

I re-watched other special features on the DVD: deleted scenes; the half-hour interview with Florian Henckel von Donnersmarck; the "making of" documentary.

I certainly got more than my money's worth when I purchased this DVD. I hope you get much of value from it, if you decide to seek out The Lives of Others.

10 "Subversive" Jokes
That Could've Landed You in an East German Prison

Here are 10 more jokes that were popular in East Germany,
but were almost certainly too hot (or just too honest) fAor the Stasi.

Making fun of politicians is an American tradition. Some jokes cross lines of good taste; some are unfair or unfunny. Good taste and humor aside, Americans take it for granted that we can poke fun at politicians and our leaders.

What's the difference between Obama and God? God doesn't think he is Obama.
What does the Trump administration use instead of emails? Alternative fax.

Mocking political leaders seems to be a bipartisan pastime, accepted by the right and the left. And for good reason. A good joke has psychological, social, and spiritual benefits, research shows. Humans use jokes to lift the spirits of others, reduce stress, and to mock absurdity and dogmas.

Because of their potency, historically many have seen such jokes as less than funny. As we near the 30-year anniversary of the

by Jon Miltimore
FEE.org

fall of the Berlin Wall, it's worth noting that East Germans faced the threat of prison for mocking the state.

Bodo Müller, an author of East German jokes, says the Stasi (official name ***Ministerium für Staatsicherheit,*** or Ministry for State Security) viewed jokes as subversive propaganda. ***The Lives of Others,*** perhaps the best film of the 21st century (one guy's opinion), revealed the terror an ill-timed joke could trigger.

Telling these jokes invited investigation by the Stasi, Müller says. They'd show up at a joker's home and interrogate friends and neighbors. Of the 100 people identified in Müller's research, 64 were convicted. Convicted joke-tellers served between one and three years. At least one man served four (he must have told a real knee-slapper, like the one about *General Secretary Honecker kissing Brezhnev). The accused were of course never convicted of telling jokes. Rather, they were found guilty of "state-endangering propaganda and hate speech"; the jokes themselves were never read publicly.

This joke about two East German communist leaders, Wilhelm Reinhold Pieck and Otto Grotewohl, for example, landed a man before a judge in 1956.

> Pieck and Grotewohl are visiting Stalin in Moscow.
> Stalin gives them a car. But when they want to leave, they realize the car doesn't have a motor.
> Stalin says: "You don't need a motor if you're already going downhill."

Image Credit: Wiedemann & Berg Filmproduktion

Here are 10 more jokes that were popular in East Germany, but were almost certainly too hot (or just too honest) for the Stasi, including several about the Trabant, the worst car in history.

1. Why do Stasi officers make such good taxi drivers? — You get in the car and they already know your name and where you live.
2. What's the best feature of a Trabant? — There's a heater at the back to keep your hands warm when you're pushing it.
3. Capitalism is the exploitation of man by man. Under socialism, it is exactly the other way around.
4. What would happen if the desert became a socialist country? — Nothing for a while… then the sand becomes scarce.
5. Why do the Stasi work together in groups of three? — You need one who can read, one who can write, and a third to keep an eye on the two intellectuals.
6. The Stasi held a competition for the best political joke. First prize? Fifteen to twenty years.
7. How can you use a banana as a compass? — Place a banana on the Berlin Wall. The bitten end would point east. (Bananas were scarce and deeply desired in East Germany, in contrast to West Germany, where they were ubiquitous.)
8. A man-on-the-street poll was taken in three countries: "What is your opinion of the recently announced shortage of meat?" In the US, they asked, "What shortage?" In Poland, they asked, "What is meat?" And in East Germany, they asked, "What is an opinion?"
9. How do you catch a Trabi? — Just stick chewing gum on the highway. (An allusion to the Trabant's weak motor.)
10. Why did Erich Honecker get a divorce? — Because Brezhnev kisses better than his wife. (This joke is a reference to the socialist fraternal kiss, also known as the Triple Brezhnev.)

Jonathan Miltimore is the Managing Editor of FEE.org. His writing/reporting has been the subject of articles in TIME magazine, The Wall Street Journal, CNN, Forbes, Fox News, and the Star Tribune. Bylines: Newsweek, The Washington Times, MSN.com, The Washington Examiner, The Daily Caller, The Federalist, the Epoch Times.

This work is licensed under a Creative Commons Attribution 4.0 International License. It was published on the Foundation for Economic Education's website, FEE.org, on November 7, 2019.

The photo heading this article is from The Lives of Others. How the photo relates to the article would require elaborate explanation (see the movie, and you'll know). Apparently, Your Editor is not the only one who holds this film in high regard.

The "10 more" in the subtitle implies there was a previous article on this topic. Your Editor failed to find it.

April 2022

Cover photo: Valentine's Day, Disneyworld, Orlando
Great Movies This Month
The Joy of International Movies
SCHRC book reviewed:
  The Random Local History Reader
Ask a Science Teacher, by Larry Scheckel: Are Microchips Put in Covid Vaccines?
Musical Potpourri
PulpArtists by David Saunders: Malvin Singer
2 Ways We're Still Superstitious about Natural Disasters, by Michael Munger, FEE.org

Malvin Singer: Love-Letter Romance

(1911-1974)

Malvin "Mal" Singer was born November 25, 1911 in Brooklyn, NYC. His father, Meyer Singer, was born in 1878 in Krasnopolye, Russia, of Jewish ancestry and came to America in 1902. His mother, Bessie Cohen, was born in 1882 in Russia of Jewish ancestry, and came to America in 1896. His parents married in NYC on April 4, 1904, and had three children, James (b. 1905), Isaac (b. 1909), and Malvin (b. 1911). They lived at 852 Sutter Avenue in Brooklyn. His father was a lithographer at a print shop.

Malvin Singer attended public school in Brooklyn. In 1925 he began to attend Thomas Jefferson High School at 400 Pennsylvania Avenue in the East New York section of Brooklyn.

By 1927 Malvin Singer had become interested in a career as a commercial artist. In his Junior year at high school he won Honorable Mention in a school poster contest.

On June 26, 1928 he graduated from Thomas Jefferson High School. His year book inscription says, "Malvin Singer: He's Tom Mix's rival — he's quick on the draw!" His was only the second graduating class in the brand new school, which surpassed DeWitt Clinton in having the largest enrollment of any high school in America with over seven thousand students. The art department was run by Bernard I. Green (1887-1951), a talented artist who had studied at the National Academy of Design in NYC. Green worked hard to promote a greater interest in the school's Art League and he also submitted his students' work to a variety of art competitions to generate scholarships for further study at art schools and colleges. The artist Morr Kusnet also attended Thomas Jefferson and graduated in the school's first graduating class.

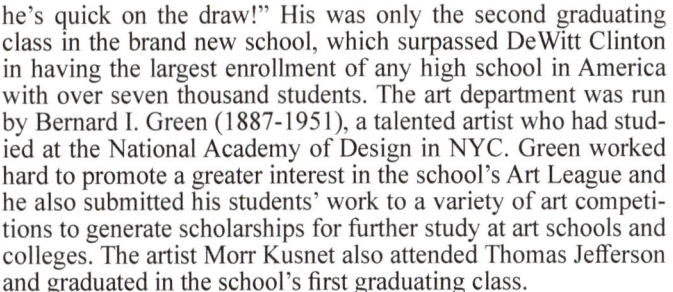

In September of 1929 he began to attend Brooklyn College, but by 1930 he had left the school without enough credits to graduate, and instead began to study art at the National Academy of Design, where in 1934 he was awarded Honorable Mention for his outstanding work in the Etching Class.

In 1936 Malvin Singer was age twenty-five. He lived at home with his parents in Brooklyn, but he also rented an art studio at 54 West 74th Street on the Upper West Side of Manhattan, where he began to paint freelance covers for pulp magazines. His work appeared on Ace G-Man Stories, Ace-High Detective, Adventure, Argosy, Captain Satan, Dime Mystery, and Dime Sports.

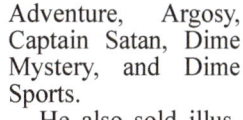

He also sold illustrations to slick magazines, such as Redbook, Cosmopolitan, Liberty, and McCalls.

The 1940 U.S. Census listed Malvin Singer as twenty-eight, with three years of college, living with his parents at home in Brooklyn, while also renting his art studio in Manhattan.

During World War II Malvin reported for induction on June 28, 1943. He did his basic training at Fort Dix in New Jersey, and was stationed with the Signal Corps in the United Kingdom. After D-Day he served in the communications unit of General Patton's 7th Army, and saw active duty in Europe.

While serving overseas a Jewish community group organized morale events for young women to write letters to Jewish servicemen, including Private Malvin Singer, who was grateful for the mail. He kept up the correspondence with his pen Pal, Anne Fleischer, and after the war, he looked her up and persuaded her to date him.

In 1946 Malvin Singer married Anne Fleischer. She was born on July 18, 1921 in New York City. The married couple left NYC and moved to Long Island, where they lived in a suburban home on Elmwood Avenue in the town of Roosevelt, NY.

In 1955 Mr. & Mrs. Malvin Singer had a daughter, Jane Bess Singer.

After the war the artist illustrated paperback book covers, such as Pocket Book #506 "The Pursuit of Love" by Nancy Mitford, also #574 "Unmarried Couple" by Maysie Greig, and #599 "Secret Marriage" by Kathleen Norris.

In 1948 Malvin Singer began to teach a painting class in the techniques of illustration at The Brooklyn Museum Art School, where he continued to teach until 1951.

Duirng the 1950s he worked for men's adventure magazines, such as Stag and True War.

In 1958, Malvin Singer left NYC and moved to Atlanta, Georgia, where he was hired as a staff artist at the Lockheed Corporation, an aerospace company, with offices in Marietta, GA.

Malvin Singer died in Atlanta, GA, at the age of sixty-three on December 8, 1974.

© David Saunders 2016

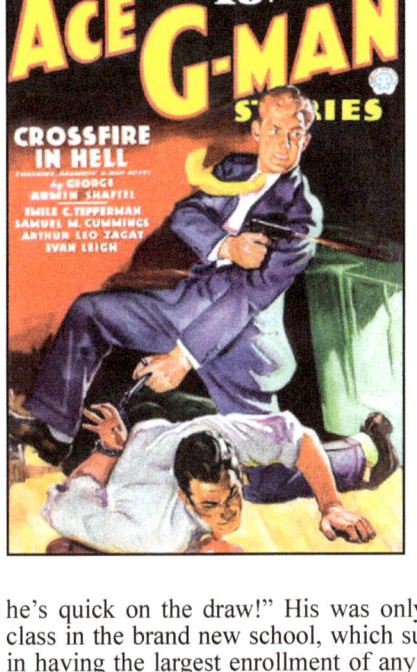

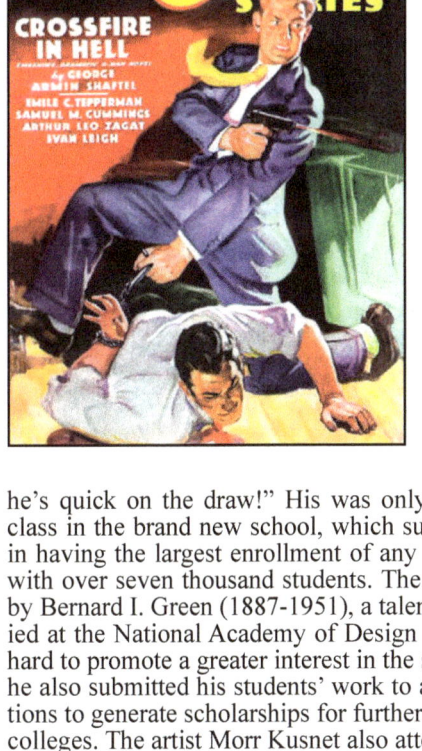

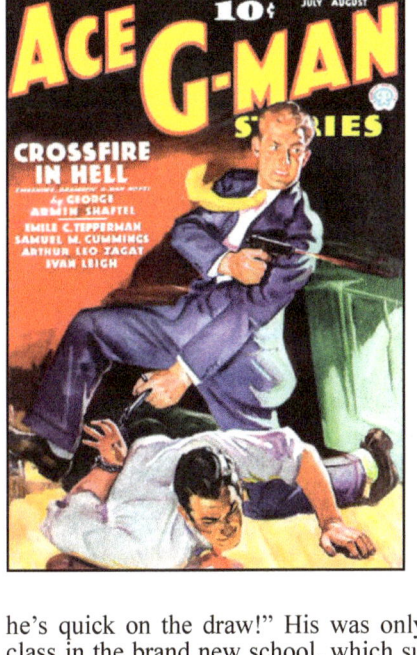

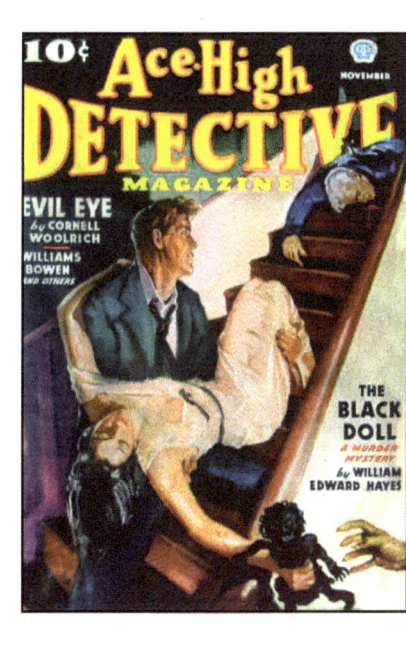

May

2022

Cover photo: Peas All Around, Restaurant Guy Savoy, Las Vegas
Great Movies This Month
What Can I Say about James Bama that I Haven't Said 100 Times Already?
Popular Arts Event Returns in June
PAC Hosts 'Alive in the Arts'
How Free Are We?

I Waited 15 Years for This
PAC Offers Free Birchbark Workshop with Pat Kruse
Clint Eastwood Calls James Bama
The How and Why of James Bama
SCHRC book reviewed: *I End With My Pen, But Not With My Heart*
Ask a Science Teacher, by Larry Scheckel: My Parents Rented a Car in Britain and Drove on the Left Side of the Road. Why the Left Side?

What can I say about James Bama that I haven't said 100 times already?

Images on this page are Copyright © the James Bama estate
Some were imaged by HA.com

Ladies and gentlemen:

I believe our culture is in a state of decline. That it has been for decades.

I won't try to justify that statement, or give details of how, or why I believe it's happening. I will only say that I don't consider that decline to be inevitable or irreversible. And I will identify the culture I have in mind. It is often called Western Civilization, but I prefer the term Enlightenment Culture.

What has all that to do with James Bama? Well, you see, I believe the work of James Bama has slowed that decline.

I have no idea how I could prove that, or even what I could use as evidence. I wouldn't even dignify the statement as an opinion; let's call it an impression, even a suspicion.

I'll tell you what values I have found in James Bama's work for nearly sixty years of my life. That might help you see why I harbor that suspicion.

I am speaking of Bama's *fine art*—that is, work he did for himself, which he started creating after he moved to Wyoming.

I certainly don't denigrate his commercial art. It has the same technical mastery of painting as his fine art. That's why it's worth collecting. I own two of his paperback cover paintings. They are gems, proudly displayed in our home.

But whereas his commercial work was done to illustrate another person's vision, his fine art was done strictly for his own satisfaction; to his own artistic standards; embodying purely his own vision and view of life.

And what is that view of life? What values can we find in the work of James Bama?

One of the first things I hear people say when introduced to his work is, "Why, it looks just like a photograph!"

That's not technically true. If you are intimately familiar with the esthetics of both photography and painting, you'd realize it. If you had the opportunity to compare a reference photo Bama used, and the resultant painting he did from it, you'd realize it.

But the essence behind the initial, "It's just like a photo!" remark is valid. Bama's paintings *are* realistic (he called himself an "American realist").

The ***style*** of a painting relates to ***epistemology***—that branch of philosophy dealing with the functioning of the mind, a proper methodology of thinking, and the validation of knowledge.

What epistemological principles can we glean from the style of a James Bama painting? One obvious thing is a sense of clarity. Just as a sharp, clear photo is in focus, so, too, are Bama's paintings in focus. Bama chose to paint with clarity. His style tells a viewer, "Choose clarity of thought. Observe and think with precision. Keep your mind focused."

What, then, can we learn from the subject matter of Bama's work? A painting's ***content*** relates to ***metaphysics***—that branch of philosophy concerned with what exists, and the nature of what exists.

Bama's chosen content, like his style, is oriented to reality.

Many of Bama's paintings are of one person. Sometimes there is a background; often, there is not. (Bama once told me, or I saw it quoted somewhere, that adding a background never improved a single one of his paintings.)

What does an artist say about reality, by creating painting after painting of individuals (background or not)? He is saying, "The individual exists."

If that seems ridiculously obvious, I congratulate you for holding that element of Enlightenment Culture. In contrast, there are entire schools of philosophy that denigrate or even deny the existence of individuals—something those who have inherited Enlightenment Culture by default just can't fathom. However, have you ever seen paintings with numerous people in them, each person anonymous and indistinguishable from all the others? An artist who depicts people that way, in work after work, is denying the importance—or perhaps even the existence—of the individual.

Building on the epistemology of clarity, and the metaphysics of reality, we now touch on the evaluative branch of philosophy, ***ethics,*** which is concerned with the ***choices*** an individual makes.

How has James Bama ***chosen*** to portray individuals in his paintings? Several terms come to my mind. Proud. Dignified. Seriously reflective and contemplative. Self-respecting. Joyous (despite Bama telling me once he preferred not to paint a person smiling; there are exceptions). Most importantly: efficacious.

All of these qualities of personality are acquired through choice. In other words, the individual has free will.

These are the epistemological, metaphysical, and ethical principles, and the view of the individual person, that I believe are present in James Bama's work. These are the principles valued by people who respond strongly and fall in love with

Bama's work—even if they are unable to articulate those principles. Many people (including the artists themselves) hold values (Enlightenment or otherwise) implicitly, and are unable to explicitly identify them. Some people claim to have no philosophy; yet lacking philosophy would leave a person helpless, unable to act for one's short-range survival or long-range flourishing and happiness. Some say they know nothing about art; yet they respond positively to the work of James Bama (clearly showing they know **something** about art).

Choose reality.

Choose to be in focus and keep a clear mind.

Choose to recognize the existence and importance of each individual.

Choose to understand and accept that each individual is capable of achieving (by a series of choices) pride and dignity in his/her own life.

You're only able to choose these things because you have free will. That's your nature. That's the kind of consciousness you have.

These values are inherent in the work of James Bama.

They are also the foundation of Enlightenment Culture.

As I said, I believe Enlightenment Culture is in decline. If that subject interests you, I refer you to work by Ayn Rand (the most effective defender of Enlightenment Culture in my lifetime) and Leonard Peikoff (who wrote three important books on how philosophy shapes history). These two people will help you to reverse that decline (if it is indeed happening). Artists like James Bama can slow the process, but will not stop it. While art has all the elements of philosophy, art is not a substitute for philosophy.

The work of James Bama is more than just pretty pictures that "look just like photographs." Each one shows a viewer what kind of thinking and living is possible. Every person who responds positively to a Bama painting, stops to admire it, identifies with it, buys a print of it, introduces other people to it, has helped slow the decline of Enlightenment Culture.

If you find Bama's work speaking to you; if you find yourself passionately responding to it—you can make your own personal contribution to Enlightenment Culture. First, monitor and understand your own thought processes as you evaluate his paintings. Define your own reasons for those evaluations. Then, learn a little about philosophy and history. No PhD degrees necessary; just enough to understand how we have inherited Enlightenment Culture, whether it's truly in a state of decline, and what **you** can do about it.

James Bama died on April 24, 2022, four days short of his 96th birthday.

For reasons I have given here, I consider James Bama the greatest painter of the 20th Century.

Of course, he was not the only painter to express Enlightenment values. There were many before him; many contemporaries; and those who came after.

And now? The 21st Century eagerly awaits his equal.

Clint Eastwood Calls James Bama

This is the story, as I remember Jim telling it to me.

Jim was working away at home (as he did so many hours each day) when he received a call. The woman identified herself as Clint Eastwood's secretary.

She told Jim that Clint Eastwood really wanted Bama to paint him for a movie poster (supposedly Pale Rider, which was released in 1985).

Jim did not want to do it, but he told the secretary, if Eastwood really was interested, Jim wanted Eastwood to call and talk to him.

Some amount of time goes by.

Jim gets another call, and it is indeed Clint Eastwood. After some discussion, Bama set the terms under which he would paint Eastwood:

• Eastwood would have to come to Wyoming and pose for Jim.

• This would not be commercial work (for a movie poster). Bama said he would paint Eastwood as a fine art piece, like other work he was doing at this time.

Eastwood seemed to find those conditions acceptable.

Did it ever happen? Sadly, no.

Two similar incidents took place. The Greenwich Workshop, which published Jim's limited-edition prints, convinced him to paint Paul Newman As Butch Cassidy. He did, in 1990 (see the bottom of pages 16-17).

Bama was also asked to paint Wes Studi as Magua, from Last of the Mohicans. He did.

Both works were released as prints by the Greenwich Workshop.

The How and Why of James Bama

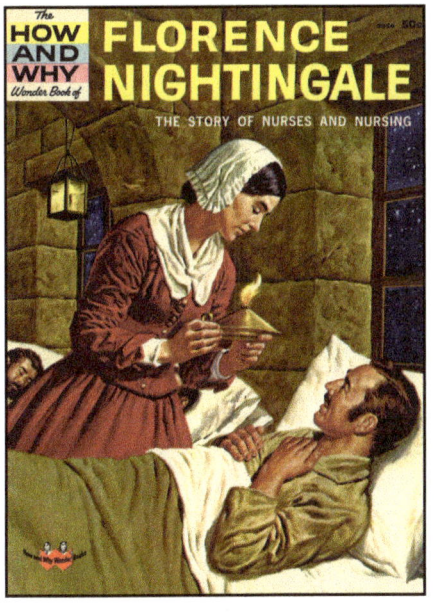

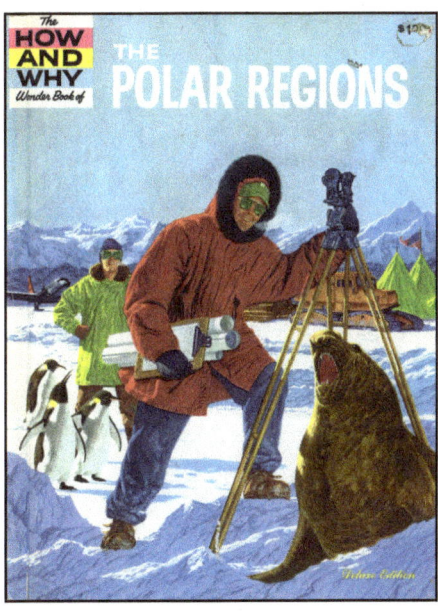

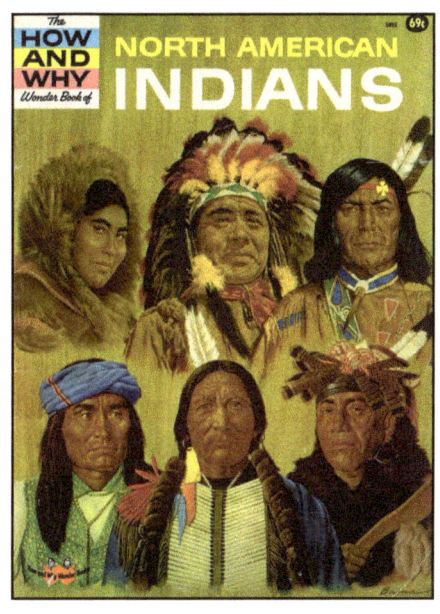

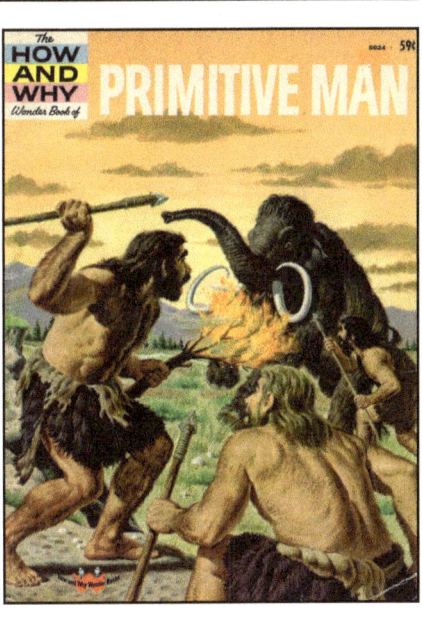

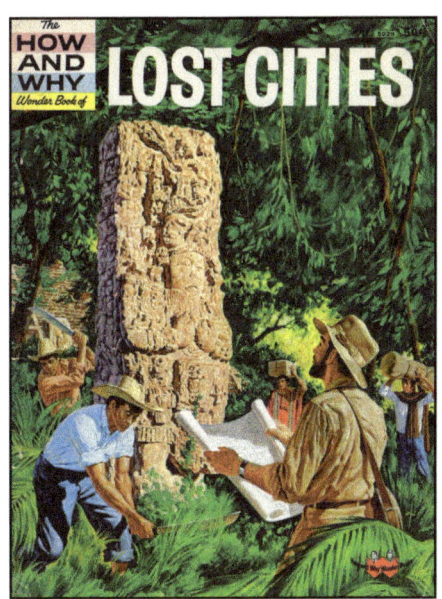

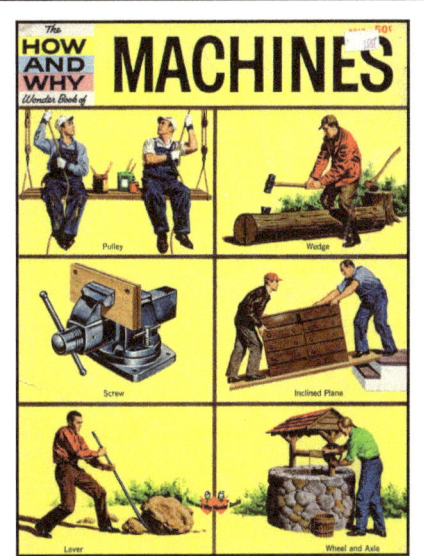

Who out there remembers these educational booklets, published from about 1960 to 1965?

Fun, weren't they?

There were dozens of titles, but the few you see here had cover art by James Bama.

You'd think the publisher would state on the title page, "Cover art by James Bama." But no. That would make the job of an obsessive Bama collector like Your Editor too easy. (Only one of these has his signature on the cover art, at the bottom right corner; can you spot it?)

I first learned Bama had done some of these in 1987 or 1988, when I stayed with him and his family, going through his files and making lots of notes. I discovered a few he did not have copies of, recognizing his style and verifying them with him.

The inside pages were not illustrated by Bama. Of course, *those artists* were identified.

One more achievement of Bama's career as an illustrator.

Preliminaries

Generally, this was James Bama's working procedure:

• He would take many photos. This could be arranged with the subject, at a specific time and place; wearing certain clothing; including a certain item (wagon, saddle, rifle, etc.). Or it could be what Jim called "grab shots," taken where and when it happened—at a pow wow, rodeo, or other special event.

• Jim would develop the photos. Most would be black and white, because he preferred to compose a painting with his own color scheme. The exception wold be clothing where the colors had historical or cultural significance.

• Selecting the photo with the best composition, Jim would make a preliminary pencil sketch on tissue paper.

• Jim would then create a very small, preliminary color painting, establishing the color scheme for the final work.

• With the photo and the two preliminaries at the upper corner of his painting board for reference, Bama would create the finished painting.

Preliminaries can be interesting, because they often give insight into the artist's creative process.

Bama's prelims are as good as (or better than) the finished work of many artists. In fact, some auction houses have listed prelims by Bama, not even knowing they were not the finished work.

So the availability of a book devoted to preliminary pencil and paint pieces by Bama offers an excellent opportunity to enjoy these pieces.

James Bama Sketchbook is one of three excellent books published by Flesk Publications featuring Bama's work. Sadly, none are currently available from the publisher. But they can be found on the secondary market (eBay, for example).

In 1986, I went to Cody, Wyoming, where the Big Horn Gallery had an exhibition of Jim Bama's work. I also had (at Bama's invitation) a very agreeable visit of several hours at his home (which was about 18 miles from Cody). The finished paintings at the Gallery were priced at $10,000, $20,000, $30,000... *and up*, which was out of my reach. I settled, instead, for the purchase of this color preliminary, which is reproduced here full size.

Bama's neighbor, Dee Smith. — From the Flesk Publications book, James Bama Sketchbook

Wes Studi, a Native American actor who appeared in Dances With Wolves, posed several times for Bama. Bama completed several paintings of Studi, including one in Studi's role as Magua, from Last of the Mohicans. — From the Flesk Publications book, James Bama Sketchbook

The Sketchbook features Bama's comments on each piece. For the one at left, he wrote, "This is an adorable little Indian boy. I've always wanted to paint this but never did. This was at Crow Fair. There were a lot of great-looking kids, all dressed up in powwow finery." The man at right was a personal friend of Jim's. — From the Flesk Publications book, James Bama Sketchbook

June
2022

Cover photo: Marvelocity Exhibit, Sheboygan
Great Movies This Month
Jazz & Blues Crawl for the Arts
Crawler Tractors Conquer Snowy Mountain Passes in New Book
How One of the Most Renowned Architects in History (Accidentally) Exposed the Problems of Central Planning, by Joseph Kast, FEE.org
Marvelocity
PulpArtists by David Saunders: C. R. Schaare
Kids from Wisconsin Tour
Why Did I Buy This?
Ask a Science Teacher, by Larry Scheckel: I Bought a Laser-Cut Wood Toy Trebuchet for Our Son. It Got Me Wondering: How Do Lasers Cut Things?
An Interview with David Saunders

An interview with David Saunders

The following interview took place at the Windy City Pulp and Paper Convention, held May 6-8, 2022, at Lombard, Illinois. It has been edited to avoid repetition and to keep related ideas together. [Bracketed numbers] refer to Editor's Notes, found after the interview.

Alahznee Lewis-Schroeter: So... Why are you here?

David Saunders: I love pulp magazines.

I'm 68 years old now, but when I was a little kid, I didn't even know what pulps were. But my father had been an illustrator, and he'd always said, "I worked for the pulps, I worked for the pulps." And I was like—I don't know what that even means!

I knew what paperbacks looked like. And I knew what books looked like. And newspapers. I knew what comic books looked like. But I didn't know what a pulp was. It was maybe when I was 20 years old or so, that I first even saw a pulp in a used bookstore. I brought it home and I said, "Dad, is this the thing you're always saying you worked for?"

I'm mostly interested in the art in them. Some of the other people that would come over to my house would be old friends of my father's. They were also illustrators. So I got to meet this friendly crowd of older men and women that were illustrators that had worked for the publishing industry.

But this Windy City show is one convention where people buy and sell pulps, trade them, or just talk about them. It turned out there was this hobby group of people collecting pulps. And it was just fun to go meet people, buy more, and eventually find out more and more about all the different artists that worked for them. So it's a hobby that I've just been interested in.

AL: I heard you contributed to one of these conventions in 2005, and you made it a huge success. Do you remember what you did?

DS: (Laughs) No. What was that? [1] Unless you mean— I forget what year it was, maybe it was 2005— One pulp convention did this award ceremony. They had an old photograph of a famous magazine, which they blew up, framed, and gave to a person as a trophy, for being the most wonderful person in the pulp community that year. Like a little Oscar award. They had run out of these enlarged photographs, and wanted something different.

And I said, "I'm an artist. I can make something for you." So I made a kind of a funny painting. We printed enough copies to last for the next 20 years or so, because this award was given every year. The painting has these two skeleton hands, typing on a typewriter, and the paper, as they're typing it, is catching on fire. It's in a dark room. The flames burst up in the air, and they create the silhouette of the character, The Shadow, which is one of the more famous pulp characters. It's meant to be kind of funny and creepy at the same time. [2]

It always surprises me that you can really be interested in pulp magazines, but only in the stories, the fiction. Other people are interested in their illustrations.

David Saunders holds a Walt Kelly drawing he purchased at the recent Windy City Pulp and Paper Convention. — Photo by Alahznee Lewis Schroeter

Interview conducted by Alahznee Lewis-Schroeter

For people who love comic books and say, "Oh, I love the Hulk," I never know if they mean that they love the drawings of the Hulk, and how cool those drawings are, or if they love the stories in the Hulk, or the character of the Hulk. Because in comics, it's really tightly mixed together. But in pulp magazines, there's a sharper separation between text and image. Most pages inside a pulp don't have pictures. It's mostly just fiction. What got you interested in pulps?

AL: Me? My uncle introduced me. And I agree with you. I like the art, rather than the story.

DS: Well, it's interesting that you like art a lot, but do you also read fantasy stuff?

AL: Yes, I do.

DS: Because you said you like dragons. Is that [indicating her shirt] like a magic mushroom or something?

AL: Yes, it's a cat.

DS: Oh, from Totoro? Or Spirited Away?

AL: Could be. So, do you watch a lot of anime films?

DS: Well, I have two kids that are grown up, now. One's 30, and one's 34. And they really love Japanese animator Hayao Miyazaki. They love his work, and I love it, too.

As an artist, I would get a job, or do a show, in Korea, or Japan. And while I was there, I really fell in love with all those incredible films and books and stuff. I'd bring them back for my kids when they were tiny. At first, they'd say, "I'd rather just have Donald Duck, or some American thing they were already familiar with. But then, they really fell in love with the anime and manga. Because they really are beautiful things.

AL: They are.

DS: Yeah. So they grew up with it, and it became normal for all kids in America, now.

AL: Yeah, it's more of a diverse thing, now.

DS: You know, I think when they teach art—I don't know this, for a fact, but I suspect—that they teach kids how to draw anime-style things, because so many young art students, when they show me their portfolio, it's really influenced by the anime look.

AL: I find that, instead of being taught it, it's what the students tend to enjoy more.

DS: OK, so they just gravitate towards it.

AL: Pretty much. It's weird how a different thing from a different country comes here and it catches on.

DS: But it's the stories, right, that captivate you?

AL: The stories and the art. A combination.

DS: Did you learn how to draw people with gigantic eyes, when you were a little kid?

AL: (Laughter) Ah, a funny thing. I actually started with horses. And then I moved into dragons.

DS: Well, ponies have huge eyes, so maybe you got it— (mutual laughter)

Did you know, it's a weird thing, that children have to be protected, because they will actually toddle and fall down, and anything can happen to them. They're incredible. They're very flexible. But they're also little nincompoops. So they'll totally

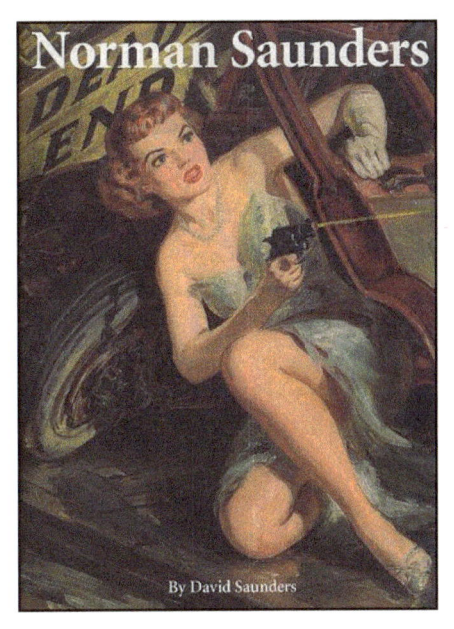

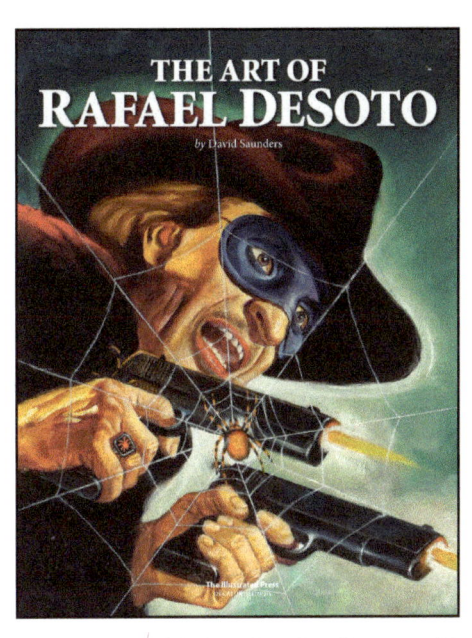

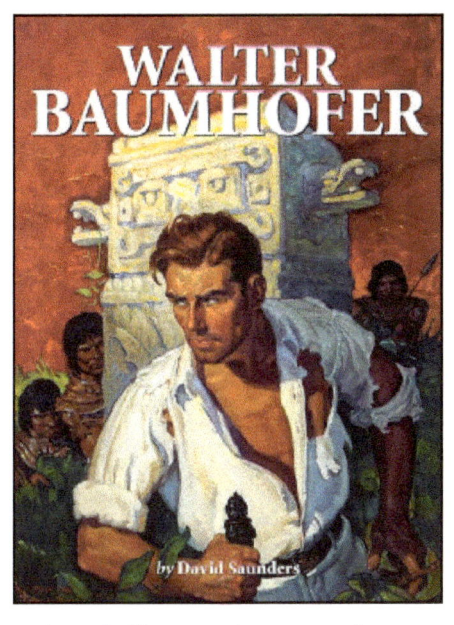

Some books authored by David Saunders, all published by The Illustrated Press (see theillustratedpress.com).

walk right out the window if you don't hold onto them.

But there are these two little qualities they have. Children's voices, when they scream, it's really loud and piercing. It sounds like a twelve o'clock siren or a fire truck or something. Nature made it that way, because you can hear them a block away when they scream. They have to be protected. So the parents will never lose sight of them. The other thing is, when we see children, the eyes can't really be miniaturized that much, and so when children are first born, their eyes are almost adult-size. From the time you're a baby until you're an adult, your eyes don't grow that much. They can't be miniaturized in nature. Isn't that strange?

AL: It is.

DS: We have such complex eyes, that when children are born, their heads are this big (gesturing), their eyes are that big, and later, they're almost the same size. So when you draw children, or even small puppies and stuff, their eyes are much, much larger in proportion to their face. And when an animal, like a lion, is eating sheep or something like that, and it sees a baby sheep, with big, big eyes, it says, "Aww, I can't eat that." It's a funny design of nature to protect children. So you have huge eyes.

Anyway, anime characters all have these beautiful cute, big eyes.

AL: You said you're an artist. What have you done?

DS: Well, when I first got out of art school, I would go to my favorite artists and say, "Do you need any help?" So I would go work with other artists. That was a real fun kind of extra training for me.

I spent five or ten years working with other artists in their studios, just learning the business. And little by little, I was able to get exhibitions of my own work. Then I had shows all over. I could make art, and make a living doing it.

AL: Who did you work for?

DS: Well, you work for yourself when you're an artist, so you eventually get a dealer. They get a percentage. It's their job to show it and sell it. My work was shown in galleries in New York City. It was fun.

AL: So it seems like you traveled a lot. Where have you been?

DS: Oh boy. Yeah, I think I've had shows all over the world. And all over America.

AL: Did it affect your art style, or what you draw?

DS: Well, yeah. One of the great things about art—and maybe it's true of other fields, also, I don't know—but in any big metropolitan city you go to will have a great museum. Those museums typically have masterpieces by all types of people. You don't know who it's going to be. Sometimes they'll have wonderful pieces from all over the world. You feel like you're a part of a separate kind of tradition. You become influenced by other artists. So one of the fun things that artists can do, that other people don't do, is that when we get together, we can speak almost a different language, and say, "There's a little Rubens in my work, and a little Caravaggio, but I have a little Baldessari in me, too. Non-artists don't know what we're talking about, but we do. We're just talking about how different artists affect our styles. How each of them emphasizes something cool in their art. Because every different artist is completely unique. But it's fun that, at the same time, we're part of a tradition.

AL: Do you have a favorite artist?

DS: Yeah... I guess one of my favorites is Joseph Cornell. He was an American. A surrealist. He took the simplest objects and assembled them in a collage. It's similar to using Photoshop, to put all types of odd things together. But he would do it physically, and assemble these really cool collages of things. I just thought he's the greatest. I still love his work. It's almost like a poetry of objects, rather than story-telling. You can't tell what he's referring to. It's evocative, like poetry. It's not specific. For example, he'll put a postage stamp, and a little gold ring, and a window with some snow falling outside, and they're all together in a little room. And—like—what is that? It's beautiful. He's a weird kind of artist.

Among the classic people, I also love Rubens, a lot. He was a great Flemish painter, unbelievably good. He's my hero, because I'm a painter.

AL: What do you normally paint with?

DS: Oil paints. On canvas. It's a really great medium. My father, the pulp artist, taught it to me. That was his medium, also.

Some people say that the piano, in music, is one of the most versatile instruments: You can use it as almost a drum. You can use it as a piccolo, as a violin, or a tuba. It's actually a strange instrument, because it covers all the different instruments in the symphony. In a way, oil paint is similar. It's just so versatile. You could make watercolors, or pencil sketching, or what would look like CGI illusionism, all with oil paint. There's no other medium that has such a wide range of versatility. It's by far the most difficult one to learn, and it's the most incredible.

AL: My dad does oil paints.

DS: Oh, really? Cool.

AL: Yeah, he does portraits.

DS: That's really hard. You know, there's a quote, something like, "The difference between a painting and a portrait, is that a portrait always has something wrong with the mouth."

AL: (Laughter) Always?

DS: Always. It's kind of a joke, but— You can paint, paint, paint, paint, paint, and make hundreds and hundreds of great paintings, which no one will criticize. But if you do a portrait, they look at it and say, "There's something wrong with the mouth," you know? So it's really hard to do portraits.

AL: Have you bought anything here [at the convention] yet?

DS: (With great enthusiasm) Yeah! (Shows large drawing) This is a drawing by one of my heroes, Walt Kelly. He drew a newspaper comic strip called Pogo. When I was a little kid, maybe three or four, and couldn't read, I was just in love with these drawings. I would keep looking at them, pretending I was reading them. I thought they were the coolest drawings. Something in his mind made it seem like they were alive to me, the way he drew. So I was able to read Walt Kelly before I could read English. I've never owned any of his work until now. I finally got one. It's a really good drawing for me, I love it, because it's got his drawing style, and he's really my hero.

How did you learn to do interviews? It's really hard. I had to do an interview once. The first time, I couldn't think of any questions to ask. And you're really good.

AL: Oh, really?

DS: Have you done it before? You're great.

AL: I've been in interviews and I've watched interviews. I haven't done one.

DS: One of the funny things I've found out in doing interviews is, there's stuff you want to know, but you also have to see what the person wants to talk about. So there's this weird thing where you try to steer them, but they go somewhere else, you know. It's not easy. It's a skill.

AL: So, you were talking about the pulp community. How has it changed you—if it has?

DS: It has changed me. So many people here will go home, and I know we'll see each other within a year or two, somewhere again. But I know that in the interim, they'll be lying in bed, reading some pulp or other book. In a sense, they'll be visiting the same world of fantasy that I visit when I go home. I mainly read after dinner, and before I go to sleep. I read until I'm exhausted. It's a wonderful thing to become a reader, and to enjoy living other lives.

That's what it feels like. We would probably have a much more confined experience of life without literature. When you read, you get to meet other people, more intimately than you can in normal life, because writers put a lot of effort into describing those characters.

It's a nice community. They say COVID is not that bad if you're healthy and strong. But many in this community are older, and a number of us have passed away in the past couple of years. But the pulp community is really neat. It's like a family.

AL: So what do you like reading?

DS: Well, I like reading silly, escapist things.

One of my favorites is Doc Savage. If you've never read one, you'd think from his name he was a brutal witch doctor named Doc Savage. But he's actually really, really smart, the highest educated person on Earth, supposedly. Doc Savage is just a guy, and he solves crimes for free. He speaks every language in the world, he knows every science in the world, and he's one of the greatest athletes in the world, and he's able to invent all these crazy contraptions, like the cell phone—he actually had something like that.

They were written almost a hundred years ago (in the 1930s and 40s), and they're just silly adventure stories. He and his gang of friends go and solve problems, all over the world. It's just escapism. But I love it. [3]

AL: Do you have any recommendations?

DS: It's unfair, because the greatest books are not pulps. I don't say that pulps are terrible, or anything, but I really love a lot of the escapist type of pulps. That would be Operator 5, Secret Agent X, The Shadow, The Spider, and Doc Savage. They're all fun, fun, fun books to read. [4]

Some really good authors that worked in the pulps are Dashiell Hammett, F. Scott Fitzgerald, Ernest Hemingway, and Raymond Chandler. That's about it. Most pulps aren't really written like great literature. They're written more like TV shows, which are not really great literature. But great literature? There are all types of good things you could read. First off, there's William Shakespeare, Don Quixote by Cervantes, The Iliad and the Odyssey by Homer. There are so many great, great, great books. Faust. They're so superior. There is a lot of great literature.

AL: [Indicating book on Saunders' table] Did you work on this book?

DS: This is a book on Rafael DeSoto [5]. He was born in Puerto Rico, and studied with other artists, and then got his start in the 1920s. He became really famous for drawing [indicating book cover] The Spider. This character has a little ring with a spider on it. He always went masked, and carried two 45-calibre automatics. I wrote the book. He's an artist of my father's generation, so I knew him growing up. And I could research and write a biography of his life's story. He was the sweetest man on Earth. His work fits in with the escapist kind of thing. He was kind, very spiritual, and just a sweet guy. He loved making paintings, and he loved working.

But I've always noticed there's a kind of brutality in the way DeSoto painted. He was of Spanish ancestry. I found it interesting, that the training he received in Puerto Rico as a child was geared to an art career where he'd become someone who would paint icons for the Catholic church. He'd paint gruesome sort of crucifixions, and paintings of saints being martyred. Almost all the saints in some way or another were brutally murdered. So there's this Catholic tradition, in Spanish art, which has a lot of fire, and a lot of pointy things, and this sensitive portrait of a saint. So in a weird way, DeSoto actually continued that tradition, even though his work appeared in escapist publications.

It's neat stuff, though. One of the greatest museums in the world is the Prado, in Madrid. During the last two years, during COVID, there were two exhibitions of pulp art in Spain. One in Barcelona, and one in Madrid. They very much love the look of American pulp art.

AL: I see. You said your dad did work for pulps. What kind of work did he do?

DS: Typically, a pulp artist had two options. He could do a cover painting in full color, or draw a black and white illustration for the inside. Here's a pulp. The cover painting is by an artist named Schaare.

[Opens up the pulp] On the inside it would just be fiction, and two or three little pen and ink drawings. And that's all pulp art was.

They had no color printing inside the pulp, so it would be like drawing with a Sharpie or something now. But they drew them with a pen or brush dipped in an inkwell. And they would draw beautiful, beautiful drawings.

You see, inside, most pages are two columns of text. In this pulp, there's one illustration at the top of the story. It's called a "header." This one's by a woman artist named Lauren Stout. I recognize it because of her signature. And there's no other illustration for the rest of the story, but another illustration, or "header," at the top of the next story. It's not like a graphic novel or a comic book.

I like to document these artists, find out who they were. That's not always easy, because look—this one only has the initials "H. S." It's an OK drawing.

AL: I like the shading, and how it shows the person in back.

DS: I don't know quite how they did that, but it's definitely just pen and ink. But they drew millions of little dots or something.

AL: We did that for an art project once. We had to do drawings of our shoes. We had to color it in fully with dots, and do the line art fully with dots.

DS: Even the lines were done with dots.

AL: Yep.

DS: [Referring to the pulp] At the beginning, they have a Table of Contents. Sometimes, they'll say the cover painting is by so-and-so, and the interior illustrations are by so-and-so. In this issue, they don't give credit.

Artists would be paid about $50 for a cover painting. And if you did one of the interior pen and ink drawings, you'd be paid about $5. And that's all they would get, so it was low-paying work. But luckily, rent at the time was about $30 a month. If you had one cover accepted, you had your rent and some money left over. So artists didn't become even middle-class doing that kind of work. It was sort of a low-class job, because it was hard to live on that kind of money.

AL: I imagine so!

*David Saunders is a writer, artist, and the creator of the **PulpArtists.com** project. With his permission, The PRC has run his pulp artist biographies from this website for the past several years.*

Alahznee Lewis-Schroeter is a student living in the Milwaukee area and is somehow related to Your Editor.

Editor's Notes on points of the interview:

1. In the early 2000s, Saunders was trying to identify an artist who did several hundred uncredited pulp covers. He discovered it was Ernest Chiriacka, born in 1913. Saunders interviewed Chiriacka in Illustration Magazine, and arranged for Chiriacka to attend the 2005 Windy City show as Guest of Honor, at age 92. The interviewer was given this question, a practice that carries both potential benefits and hazards; the hazards coming when the interviewee does not know what is being referred to. Both interviewer and interviewee, however, handled this situation with aplomb.

2. The award Saunders describes is the Lamont Award, named after Lamont Cranston (one of The Shadow's identities), initiated at Pulpcon on 1977; this award then transitioned to the Munsey Award (from the name of a pioneer pulp publisher), as Pulpcon was discontinued and Pulpfest was initiated. It's complicated.

3. 180 Doc Savage adventures were published in pulps, from 1933 to 1949. In 1964, Bantam Books started reprinting Doc Savage stories in paperback form, and eventually reprinted all the original pulp novels. Over 50 of these paperbacks featured cover paintings by James Bama (you've heard of *him*, right?).

4. If you're curious enough to want to read adventures of any of these characters mentioned by Saunders, you do not have to buy expensive, original pulps from the 1930s. Many reprint editions have been published. eBay is only one easy source for these.

5. Saunders is the author of several books on artists, including one about his father, Norman Saunders.

The image David Saunders created for the Lamont/Munsey award.

The Best Photo I Ever Took of James Bama

When I visited Jim Bama at his Wyoming home, he would carry on a conversation as he worked. And this photo, taken in the late 1980s, shows very well *how* he worked to create a painting:

On his board are two photos he took, seemingly in different contrasts.

At the upper left is the pencil sketch he did from the photos.
The actual oil painting is partly covered by one photo.

The stick (antenna?) in Bama's left hand is to rest his right wrist, as he works on the painting, so as not to smudge it.

You may well ask (if you can make out the subject), "How many elderly Chinese men with pot-bellied pigs are there in Wyoming?"

Most likely, very few.

Bama was asked in 1987 to join a group that toured China. Bama took over 1000 photos on that trip.

The Greenwich Workshop, which published Bama's signed and numbered prints, released several China-themed prints, and planned to release the old man and pig.

But then came the Tiananmen Square massacre, which even some of the staunchest apologists for dictatorships could not ignore, and demand for All Things China diminished. This was never published as a print.

A few art pieces Your Editor purchased at the Windy City pulp show. Top: Captain America and Nick Fury (Copyright © Marvel Characters, Inc.), drawn by Jim Steranko. Above: Preliminary and unfinished piece by Virgil Finlay. To the right: Detail of flowers, showing fine pen and ink work.

The Current
Plymouth Review
TAKING YOU PLACES WORTH SEEING
Volume 11 • Issue 8 • July 2022

FREE!

Repurposing ◆ Jazz Crawl
Mysterious Island ◆ Patent Medicines

July
2022

Cover photo: Medical History at the Sheboygan County Historical Society Museum
Great Movies This Month
Crawl for the Arts
Repurposed: Church Converted into Residence, Belgium
Total Film Five Star Collection
Deviled Egg of the Day
Ask a Science Teacher, by Larry Scheckel: My Wife Bought Me a Quartz Watch for My Birthday. Just How Does a Quartz Watch Work?
How Estonia—Yes, Estonia—Became One of the Wealthiest Countries in Eastern Europe, by Luis Pablo de la Horra, FEE.org
Mill Street Live
PAC Has New Education Coordinator
Would This Guy Give Long-Underwear Heroes a Bad Reputation? (The Crimson Clown, by Johnston McCulley)
PulpArtists by David Saunders: Colcord Heurlin

From 1929. This is not your typical movie poster! This is a "24-sheet," assembled from 12 separate sheets of paper. The total image is 8.5 feet high and over 19 feet long. It's incredible to think that any such posters still exist. They were pasted onto long fences, the sides of buildings, or onto billboards, and did not survive removal intact. — HA.com

David Saunders' pulpartists.com

COLCORD HEURLIN: ARTIST OF THE ARCTIC

(1895-1986)

Magnus Colcord "Rusty" Heurlin was born July 5, 1895 in Kristanstad, Sweden. His father, Berndt Felix Heurlin, was born in 1859 in Sweden. His mother, Sofie Annette Bjorklund, was born 1864 in Sweden. His parents married in 1892 and had two children, Anna L. Heurlin (b. 1893), and Magnus Colcord Heurlin (b. 1895). In 1896 the family moved to America and settled in Wakefield, Massachusetts, where they lived at 2 Nichols Street. The father worked as Clerk at a Cold Storage Company.

In 1898 his parents had their third child, Ingrid M. Heurlin.

In 1903 his parents had their fourth child, Greta Heurlin.

In 1914 Colcord Heurlin attended the Fenway School of Illustration in Boston, MA, where his art teacher was Harold Mathews Brett (1880-1955), who was also Director of the newly-opened school.

In 1916 Colcord Heurlin traveled to Seattle, Washington, by steam ship and then visited Valdez, Alaska.

On June 15, 1917 during the Great War Colcord Heurlin registered with his draft board. He was recorded at the time to be of medium height, medium build with light blue eyes and light red hair. He joined the Navy and served in the Naval Railroad Batteries in France as an orderly to Admiral Plunkett, and was honorably discharged on March 21, 1919.

After his return to America he resumed his art training in New York City at the Grand Central School of Art, where he studied with Harvey Dunn and Howard Smith (1877-1954). N.C. Wyeth visited the school to conduct a seminar class in advanced painting.

In 1921 he began to illustrate adventure stories for *Boy's Life, The Open Road, Everybody's,* and *Outdoor Stories.*

In 1922 he again visited Alaska, where he explored hunting and whaling traditions among the Inupiat Indians around Barrow Point. When he returned to his parent's home in Massachusetts he entertained a benefit party at the local church with

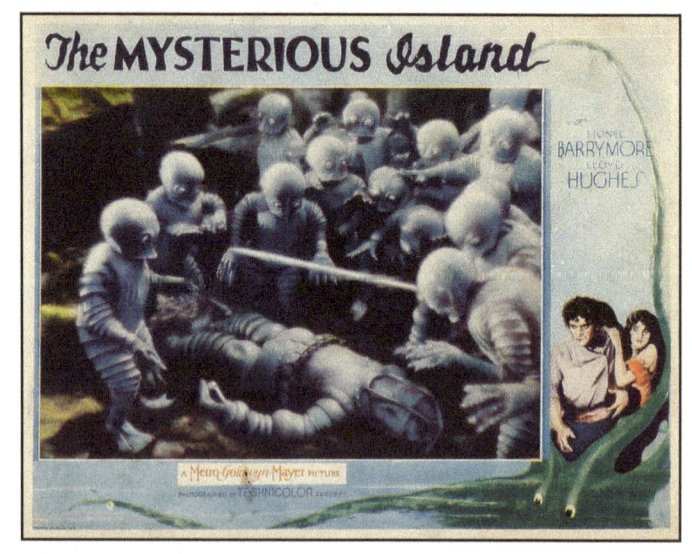

Whoa! Looks like they found more than fish and crustaceans at the sea floor. While the film was black and white, lobby cards like this were often colored. Dishonest? Well... — HA.com

guitar playing and rope tricks he learned out west.

From 1923 to 1933 Colcord Heurlin painted covers for pulp magazines. His work appeared on *Adventure, Aces, Flying Aces, Complete Stories, Everybody's Combined with Romance, North-West Stories, The Popular, Short Stories, Sky Birds, Sea Stories, Top-Notch, War Stories,* and *Western Story.*

In 1933 Colcord Heurlin moved to Westport, Connecticut, which was a community popular with artists. His neighbors at that time included Remington Schuyler, Charles LaSalle, Leland Gustavson, Ralph Nelson and McClelland Barlcay (1891-1943).

On February 8, 1935 The *Norwalk Hour* newspaper of Connecticut reported "WPA artist Colcord Heurlin is working on an oil painting that will depict a panorama of arctic life."

He returned to Alaska in 1936 and lived outside of Fairbanks in the gold mining village of Ester. He worked at Independence Mine for the Fairbanks Exploration Company. He lived and worked in a tiny art studio in the hills of Ester, which is near Fairbanks, Alaska. His only address was P.O. Box 822 in Anchorage, Alaska. According to the artist, "I lived in many parts of the Alaskan Territory where I worked as a fisherman, miner and hunter both to earn a living and to learn about the people. I also spent four seasons whaling along the Arctic coast from which I drew subjects for some pictures."

On May 20, 1942 during WWII Colcord Heurlin registered with the selective service as required by law for all male citizens between the ages of 18 and 65. He was forty-six. He was recorded at the time to be a freelance artist working of his own accord. He was six-foot-one, 190 pounds, with blue eyes, red hair and a ruddy complexion. He served as a Captain in the Alaska Territorial Guard. He was a rifle instructor and helped to organize the supply of guns, uniforms and training to Eskimos along the Northwestern coast for protection against Japanese invasion. He also painted several patriotic posters for recruitment and sales of War Bonds.

In 1945 Colcord Heurlin taught art classes in a public high school at the Eskimo colony in Point Barrow, Alaska. According to the artist, "There are many promising artists among these students. I've never seen such appreciation of color."

In 1951 the Eskimo Indian colony of Point Barrow Alaska was stricken by a devastating epidemic of influenza and pneumonia. According to the Office of Indian Affairs "Colcord Heurlin administered sulfa pills to the sick natives and saved probably hundreds of lives."

In 1951 Colcord Heurlin was the judge of a high school student art contest.

On February 24, 1952 Colcord Heurlin married Anne Downer Severin at the University Community Presbyterian Church in Fairbanks, Alaska. She was born in Davenport, Iowa on September 9, 1909. She was forty-four at the time of the marriage, while the groom was fifty-seven.

She worked in the Alaska Territorial Employment Service. Her nineteen-year-old son from a previous marriage, John Severin, lived in San Francisco with his wife and son, Jimmy Severin, who spent his summer months with his grandparents in Ester, Alaska.

In 1955 Colcord Heurlin taught introductory drawing to students at the University of Alaska in Fairbanks. He was the school's first art teacher. According to the artist, "Art is a simple method of telling a story. It is no different from music, writing, or any of the other arts. Robert Henri, whose teaching resembles Howard Pyle's, expressed this fact very well in his book *'The Art Spirit.'* Anyone can draw if they possess the interest. Talent is nothing other than the results of applied interest."

On May 14, 1958 The Fairbanks News-Miner reported on a popular exhibition of student work from his drawing class.

In 1967 Alaska celebrated the 100th anniversary of its founding. The Governor commissioned Colcord Heurlin to paint fifteen panoramic scenes from the era of the Gold Rush. His historic mural remains on permanent display at Alaskaland.

In 1970 he painted an impressive mural for the University Library of the historic discovery of Alaska by world explorers.

On May 12, 1971 Colcord Heurlin received an Honorary Doctoral Degree in Fine Arts from the University of Alaska.

On September 15, 1971 Colcord Heurlin's wife, Anne Dower Heurlin died in San Francisco at the the age of sixty-three.

In 1973 Colcord Heurlin was commissioned to paint a mural of the progress of Eskimos from the stone Age to the present for the University of Alaska.

Colcord "Rusty" Heurlin died at the age of ninety in Ester, Alaska, on March 10, 1986.

© David Saunders 2015

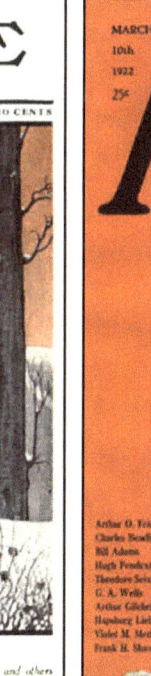

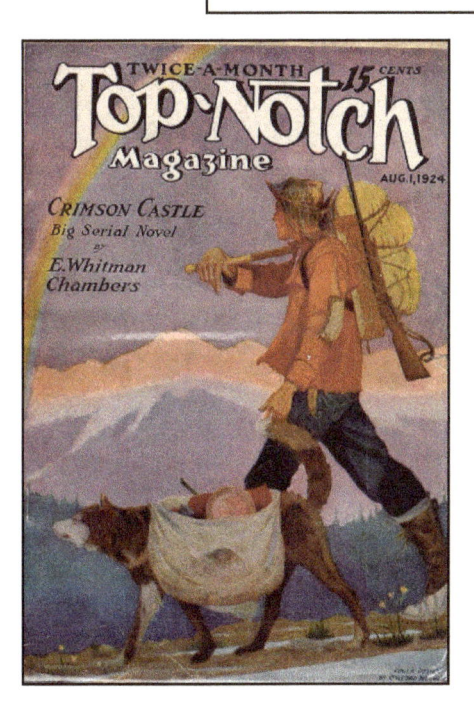

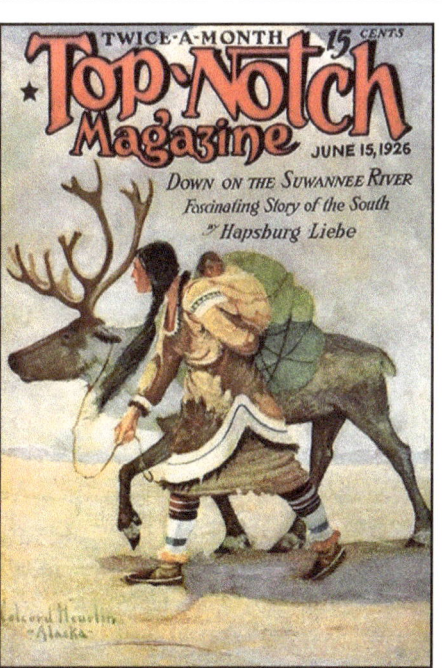

August

2022

Cover photo: Jon Wos and Yeonmi Park. Photo by Ryan P. Murphy. Courtesy of the photographer, and The Objective Standard Institute.

Great Movies This Month

The Simon Abundance Index 2022, by Gale Pooley and Marian L. Tupy, HumanProgress.org

The Beautiful Legacy of Silent Movie Posters

Crawl for the Arts

Now I Own Myself!

New Edition of John Deere's Company Offers Incomparable Insight into Tractor History

The Teacher

Take a Walk on the Wild Side

PulpArtists by David Saunders: Lawrence Sterne Stevens

I Want *You* to Flourish!

Crawl for the Arts

Ask a Science Teacher, by Larry Scheckel: My Uncle Went to California and Had His Car's Catalytic Converter Cut Off and Stolen. Why Did Thieves Steal It?

LEFT: Yeonmi Park's book, published in 2015. RIGHT: A new book by Park, scheduled for January 2023 release.

TOS-Con Report

Last June, we attended TOS-Con near Denver. That's where this month's cover photo, by Ryan P. Murphy, was taken.

I could write much about this content-rich conference, but I'll concentrate *mainly* on the woman in the cover photo.

There have been four TOS-Cons. I have attended three.

At TOS-Con 2019, I saw and heard Timothy Sandefur deliver a lecture, How to Lead an Enlightenment Life in an Anti-Enlightenment World. In this talk, Sandefur told of three women who had escaped repressive countries or lifestyles to find freedom.

When plans were made to publish Sandefur's talk in The Objective Standard (the *TOS* in *TOS*-Con), its publisher arranged with Oshkosh artist Jon Wos to paint the three women for the journal's cover.

In the months preceding TOS-Con 2022, speakers announced included Jon Wos (whose subject was Realizing Romanticism); Ayaan Hirsi Ali (the woman at center in Jon's cover painting); and Yeonmi Park (the woman at left in the painting, and sitting with Jon on this issue's cover).

Every speaker at this convention of 500 attendees was surrounded, after his/her talk, by people who wanted to know more.

Every speaker, that is, except two. Both Ayaan Hirsi Ali and Yeonmi Park were well-protected by heavy security, because each has received serious death threats. The communists hate these women and want to see them dead; and those are just the communists in *this* country.

This paragraph on Barnes & Noble's page for an upcoming book gives us a clue as to why, in Park's case:

"After defecting from North Korea, Yeonmi Park found liberty and freedom in America. But she also found a chilling crackdown on self-expression and thought that reminded her of the brutal regime she risked her life to escape. When she spoke out about the mass political indoctrination she saw around her in the United States, Park faced censorship and even death threats."

Jon's meeting with Park at his table, where he had on display several of his paintings, and Murphy's cover photo, resulted from the fortuitous timing, quick communication, and unhesitating action.

I also benefitted from good fortune.

I selected a front-row seat well before Park's talk. I had a copy of The Objective Standard I hoped to get signed. But when I heard conference coordinators say, "We'll bring her in, she'll give her talk, and she'll have to leave right away," I knew it would be nearly impossible to approach her. So much for getting an autograph!

But she came in and, as preparations and introductions were made, she sat *three seats* away from me.

I passed her the journal and a felt-tip pen.

She signed the cover. (See upper left.)

In Korean! (An extra special treat.)

A good friend, sitting on my other side, witnessing my triumphant acquisition, high-fived me.

Park's talk was powerful and emotional. She told of her life in totalitarian North Korea, where the word "I" was almost unknown; where people were forbidden to take actions needed to simply sustain themselves; where people informed on their neighbors and "friends" to the authorities for any suspected subversive thought, word, or action; and how she escaped. (This is detailed in her book, In Order to Live.)

During the Q&A session following her talk, more people lined up to ask questions than she had time to answer. More than once, she was asked how young people in the civilized world who advocate socialism or communism could be convinced they are pursuing an anti-life ideology.

"They need to spend some time in North Korea," was her reply.

Yeonmi Park is on Facebook and X (formerly Twitter).

The Winter 2019-20 issue of The Objective Standard. Pictured in this pastel painting by Jon Wos, from left to right: Yeonmi Park, Ayaan Hirsi Ali, and Deborah Feldman. As recounted in the article, Yeonmi Park signed this cover in Korean. — Courtesy of the Objective Standard Institute

The Teacher

"But you can't have a free society without brave people who have the courage to take a stand against injustice. This was just as true back then as it is today."

Petr Jarchovsky, Screenwriter, The Teacher

The Teacher, released in 2016, takes place in Czechoslovakia in 1983. At that time, the country was controlled by the Soviet Union.

On the first day of class, the teacher asks each student to stand, give his or her name, and tell what his or her parents do for a living. The teacher takes careful notes.

The students and their parents soon receive "friendly requests" from the teacher to assist her. She has kids cleaning her apartment; parents with mechanical ability fixing her appliances.

Now, wait. Why would they submit to such "requests"? Why wouldn't they tell her she's out of line?

Because she is a high-ranking official in the communist party.

And of course, comrades in a worker's paradise are treated equally, right? Or, maybe, some people are more equal than others... sometimes?

The parents gather to discuss what they can do about the teacher. There are those who completely support the teacher; their kids are getting good grades (though learning nothing). Other parents, who receive demands to do illegal things, and whose children are suffering humiliation from the teacher, believe this injustice ought to be confronted.

The children are also carefully considering what can be done. In fact, one student's action is very satisfying.

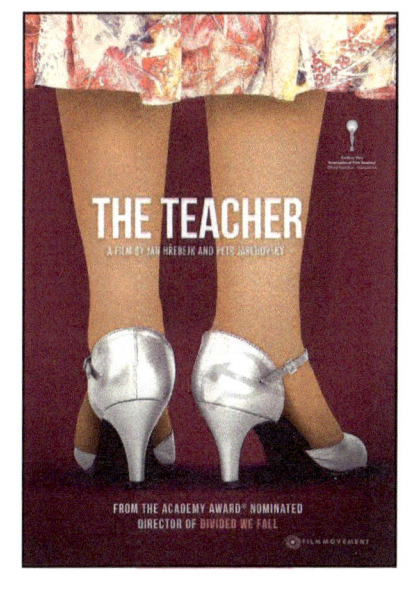

Many home video sets have plenty of extras: making-of documentaries or interviews with actors. After viewing the film, I wanted to know more, and would have gladly listened to a director's commentary for further insight. There is none. So I found several interviews online with people who made the film. I learned that the story had a basis in actual events.

IMDB.com has three trailers for this film.

Production values are excellent. Acting, sets, dialogue, story, are all of the highest quality.

And the theme? It is pricelessly, universally relevant.

"When I think of The Teacher, I see it as a carefully organised and engrossing analysis of how a society can slowly grow numb and browbeaten to the point of losing hope of effecting any change at all. It is a film about how collective lethargy can lead to tragedy. And a film about the hope contained in refusing to stand idly by, about overcoming one's own fears. This is something that I find extraordinarily topical, and if it is well filmed, it always will be!"

Jan Hřebejk, Director, The Teacher

The Beautiful Legacy of Silent Movie Posters

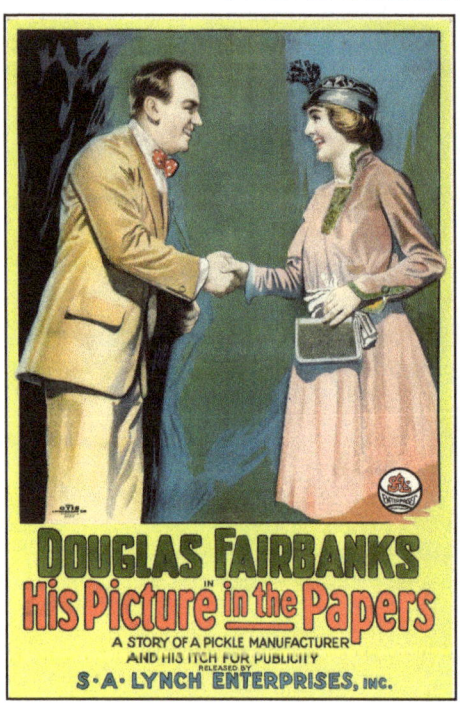

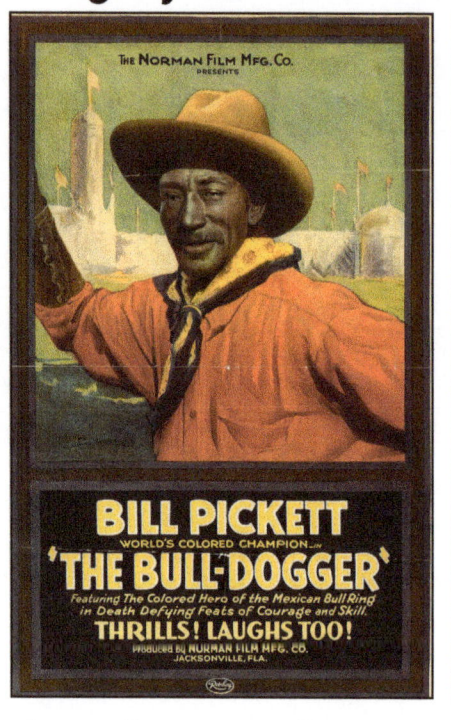

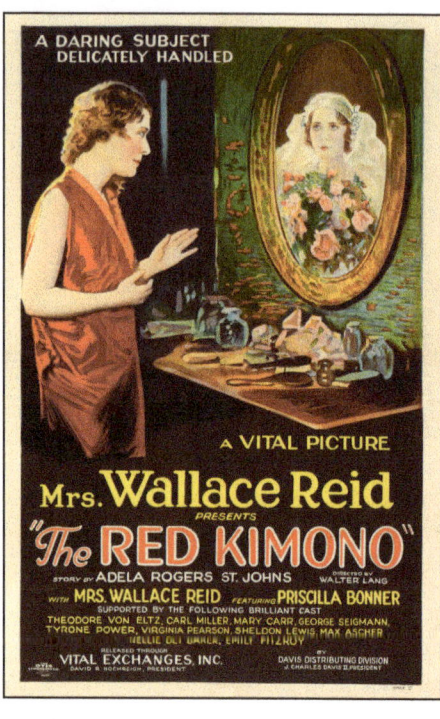

Left: Before Douglas Fairbanks made swashbuckler movies like The Mark of Zorro (1920), The Three Musketeers (1921), and The Thief of Bagdad (1924), he was already wildly popular, making contemporary comedies that satirized modern life. In His Picture in the Papers (1916), "A story of a pickle manufacturer and his itch for publicity," Fairbanks tries to pull a stunt that will get... you guessed it: his picture in the papers. Center: Bill Pickett, a real-life African-American/Caucasian/Cherokee rodeo star. His trademark event was bull-dogging, which is grabbing a steer by the horns and wrestling it to the ground. (Pickett used an unusually different technique.) Your Editor recalls reading a biography of this man, who was 51 when this 1921 film was released.

Right: A 1925 film about human trafficking. When Wallace Reid died of drug addiction, his wife devoted her life to making "socially-conscious" movies.

The Simon Abundance Index 2022

The Earth was 448.5 percent more abundant in 2021 than it was in 1980

by Gale Pooley and Marian L. Tupy
HumanProgress.org

Does population growth lead to greater resource scarcity, as argued by the English scholar Thomas Malthus and, more recently, by the Stanford University biologist Paul Ehrlich? Or does population growth coincide with, and perhaps even contribute to resource abundance, as the University of Maryland economist Julian Simon has argued? The Simon Abundance Index (SAI) measures the relationship between population growth and the abundance of 50 basic commodities, including food, energy, materials, minerals, and metals.

Main Findings

Global resource abundance fell by 22.6 percent in 2021, according to the fifth annual Simon Abundance Index. The base year of the index is 1980, and the base value of the index is 100. In 2021, the index stood at 548.5. In other words, the index rose by 448.5 percent over the last 41 years, implying a compound annual growth rate in global resource abundance of 4.24 percent and a doubling of global resource abundance every 16.7 years.

Analysis

The SAI is measured in time prices. To calculate a commodity's time price, the nominal price of a commodity is divided by the global average nominal hourly wage. Over the last 41 years, the average nominal price of the 50 commodities rose by 103.9 percent, and the global average nominal hourly wage rose by 413.6 percent. So, the overall time price of the 50 commodities fell by 67.9 percent.

The personal resource abundance multiplier is calculated by dividing the average time price of the 50 commodities in 1980 by the average time price of the 50 commodities in 2021. The multiplier tells us how much more of a resource a person can get for the same hours of work between two points in time. The same number of hours of work that bought one unit in the basket of 50 commodities in 1980 bought 3.088

units in the same basket in 2021.

The resource abundance for the average inhabitant of the planet rose by 208.8 percent. The compound annual growth rate in personal resource abundance amounted to 2.79 percent, implying that personal resource abundance doubled every 25.2 years.

Over the last 41 years, the overall time price of the 50 commodities fell by 67.9 percent. Meanwhile, the world's population increased by 77.6 percent. So, for every 1 percent increase in the world's population, the average time price of the 50 commodities decreased by 0.88 percent (67.9 percent ÷ 77.6 percent = -0.88).

Note that the personal resource abundance analysis looks at resource abundance from the perspective of an individual human being. The question that we aim to answer is: "How much more abundant have resources become for the average inhabitant of the planet?"

Population resource abundance analysis, in contrast, allows us to quantify the relationship between global resource abundance and global population growth. You can think of the difference between the two levels of analysis by using a pizza analogy. Personal resource abundance measures the size of a slice of pizza per person. Population resource abundance measures the size of the entire pizza pie.

The population resource abundance multiplier is calculated by multiplying the change in personal resource abundance by the change in global population (3.088 x 1.776). The multiplier of 5.485 corresponds to the 548.5 value in the SAI 2022. It indicates an increase in the global resource abundance of 448.5 percent and a compound annual growth rate of 4.24 percent. Using these values, we can estimate that global resource abundance doubles every 16.7 years or so.

Finally, let us say a few words about the resource abundance elasticity of population. In economics, elasticity measures one variable's sensitivity to a change in another variable. If variable X changes by 10 percent, while variable Y, as a result of the change in X, changes by 5 percent, then the elasticity coefficient of X relative to Y is 2.0 (10 ÷ 5). A coefficient of 2.0 can be interpreted as a 2 percent change in X corresponding to a 1 percent change in Y.

We found that every 1 percent increase in population corresponded to an increase in personal resource abundance (the size of the slice of pizza) of 2.69 percent (208.8 ÷ 77.6). We also found that every 1 percent increase in population corresponded to an increase in population resource abundance (the size of the pizza pie) of 5.8 percent (448.5 ÷ 77.6).

Changes between 2020 and 2021

Over the last 12 months, the SAI declined from 708.4 to 548.5 (22.6 percent). This was the largest one-year drop recorded by the index. The largest previous one-year drop amounted to 11.3 percent in 2010. On average, the index increased by 4.69 percent a year between 1980 and 2021.

What accounts for the SAI decline between 2020 and 2021? First, although the long-term trend in resource abundance is a positive one, prices can and do move up as well as down. Julian Simon noted as much when he wrote in his 1996 book The Ultimate Resource 2,

There is no physical or economic reason why human resourcefulness and enterprise cannot forever continue to respond to impending shortages and existing problems with new expedients that, after an adjustment period, leave us better off than before the problem arose. . . . Adding more people will cause [short-run] problems, but at the same time there will be more people to solve these problems and leave us with the bonus of lower costs and less scarcity in the long run. . . . The ultimate resource is people—skilled, spirited, and hopeful people who will exert their wills and imaginations for their own benefit, and so, inevitably, for the benefit of us all.

Second, prices and wages can be adversely affected by government policy. The COVID-19 pandemic–related restrictions on economic activity, for example, resulted in a supply shock from which many an industry is yet to fully recover. The supply shock was exacerbated by fiscal and monetary stimuli, which kept some workers from reentering the job market once the restrictions were lifted. These stimuli also resulted in a demand shock, with money flowing into real estate, the stock market, and commodities as savers attempted to protect themselves from rising inflation. Additional regulations on new resource exploration and production may have helped to reduce output, particularly in the energy sector. Finally, the spike in resource prices was greatly enhanced by the Russian invasion of Ukraine (although the conflict is not reflected in this year's SAI).

Third, humanity has experienced similar shocks and accompanying reductions in resource abundance before. Mercifully, history suggests that growth in the abundance of resources can be restored. The index, for example, grew by 28.4 percent, 20.0 percent, and 19.3 percent in 1986, 1985, and 2009, respectively. When government policies and proper monetary management encourage entrepreneurship, the discovery of new knowledge and creation of new wealth can return and flourish.

Conclusion

In spite of the recent decline in SAI, resource abundance is still increasing at a faster rate than the population is growing. We call that relationship superabundance. We explore this topic in a new book coming out on August 31, titled Superabundance: The Story of Population Growth, Innovation, and Human Flourishing on an Infinitely Bountiful Planet.

Professor Gale L. Pooley teaches economics at Brigham Young University, Hawaii. He is a Senior Fellow at the Discovery Institute and a board member of HumanProgress.org

Marian L. Tupy is a senior fellow in the Cato Institute's Center for Global Liberty and Prosperity and editor of HumanProgress.org.

This article appeared on HumanProgress.org, which is a project of the Cato Institute with major support from the John Templeton Foundation and the Searle Freedom Trust, as well as additional funding from the Brinson Foundation and the Dian Graves Owen Foundation. The website requires no registration or membership. All of its content and features can be used free, but acknowledgment is always appreciated.

The reader is directed to the following site, where this article appeared. It contains graphs and figures that have not been reprinted here.

https://www.humanprogress.org/the-simon-abundance-index-2022/

"The Story of Population Growth, Innovation, and Human Flourishing on an Infinitely Bountiful Planet." This book, by the authors of this article, was just published.

The Ultimate Resource II: People, Materials, and Environment
by Julian L. Simon
is available *online, free:*
http://www.juliansimon.com/writings/Ultimate_Resource/

I Want You to Flourish!

They Live, the 1988 film directed by John Carpenter, ran recently on Turner Classic Movies. I watched it again. (The 3rd time. At least.)

I thoroughly enjoy the movie's soundtrack and storytelling. But its underlying premise is ridiculously absurd. Unbelievable!

Its main idea: An elite group of humans colludes with aliens, to keep the general populace in a cattle-like state, consuming, producing, and reproducing. The purpose: to allow the elite humans and aliens to live off the efforts of the suppressed general populace.

To keep the rabble in their place, subliminal messages are everywhere, including:

OBEY
NO INDEPENDENT THOUGHT
CONFORM
STAY ASLEEP
SUBMIT
NO IMAGINATION
DO NOT QUESTION AUTHORITY

Isn't that a ridiculous premise?

No, no, **no!** I don't mean the existence of aliens. I mean the part that is *so* foolishly unrealistic, that alien conspiracies are *easy* to believe by comparison.

It's a false belief, though I realize many people hold it. And I know why they hold it; it's based on yet another false belief (which is also widespread).

Elsewhere in this issue is an article, The Simon Abundance Index 2022, written by Gale Pooley and Marian L. Tupy, originally published by HumanProgress.org. Please read this, if you haven't already. Don't let all the numbers intimidate you. Get what you can from it.

The egregiously (I wish there were a word even **stronger** than "egregiously") false belief in They Live is the idea that someone can suppress people, "keep them down," and then benefit from their efforts.

What is that false belief based on? The false belief that resources are finite, limited.

We're bombarded constantly with the message that resources are limited. Well, isn't that just obvious, common sense?

But the data of the past couple of centuries (or even decades) in human history, with interpretive assistance from Julian L. Simon, has shown otherwise. Something once considered useless is now a resource; new supplies of scarce resources have been discovered or gained access to; methods to extend the use of certain resources have been developed. And therefore, more resources are available, despite an increased population.

And Ayn Rand's philosophical analysis of human nature makes the case that two things, not mentioned in the HumanProgress article, are needed for this increasing abundance: freedom, and rationality.

Now **because** I reject the idea that resources are finite and limited...

...**therefore**, I reject the idea that there is a fixed amount of wealth, and that your gain is my loss; or that my gain is your loss.

Therefore...

I have absolutely no interest in enslaving you, suppressing you, "keeping you down," "keeping you in your place," or any of those paranoid phrases. I could not possibly gain from that.

It's a happy coincidence that I recently attended a conference where seventeen different talks emphasized some aspect of "human flourishing."

Flourish:

"To grow well or luxuriantly; thrive."

"To do or fare well; prosper."

"To be in a period of highest productivity, excellence, or influence."

(The American Heritage® Dictionary of the English Language, 5th Edition.)

I want to flourish.

I also want *you*—every person reading this, every person alive, anywhere on Earth—to be free, to be rational, and to *flourish.*

It's obvious why a person would want this for himself. Buy why would I want everyone else, including *you,* to flourish?

Because if you're free and rational, you'll seek, to whatever level of ability and ambition you aspire to, to produce more, in order to provide more for yourself, your family, and anyone else you value.

By applying what Julian L. Simon calls the "ultimate resource" (the human mind), and utilizing the energy and technology developed by previous generations, you'll be able to create more wealth than you can consume. And you'll trade that surplus, making it available to me.

I'll have more opportunities to improve my life with the new inventions, new products, new works of art, or new services you have created or helped to create. I can't even imagine all the not-yet-invented benefits millions or billions of people can offer me.

If *you* flourish, *I* do, too.

That is... *if* we both live in a free society. For that reason, I will do everything possible to me to preserve and protect your freedom; your individual rights. I understand fully that, supporting *your* rights, I also support *my own* rights.

A violation of your rights is a limitation on your opportunities (and a potential threat to mine). A minimum wage law that stops you from getting an entry-level job is a violation of your rights, and a limitation of your opportunities. If the service you offer is hair braiding, and a law mandates you spend $20,000 you don't have on classes to learn something you already know (a real-life situation), your rights are violated and your opportunities smashed, by government force.

I want you to have as much freedom of opportunity as possible.

This is my view if you, who read this, live in the Plymouth area; in Sheboygan County; in Wisconsin; in the United States; in any part of the world. Rights and freedom are a natural expression of human nature, and applies to every functional person, anywhere.

This is my view if you live in the developed, empowered world, where you enjoy the benefits of advanced technology and have access to abundant energy.

It is also my view if you live in a poorer, less developed country.

Check the numbers of people who live in extreme poverty in the world. Those numbers have shown a stunning **decrease** in the past few decades, thanks to those discovering freedom and rationality. While some people in the richest, most developed countries are fighting every value that has led to wealth and development, more people are discovering that freedom leads to a better life. If you are one of those people, I am a hundred per cent behind you, and I hope you and your country prosper; the sooner, the better. (We ran an article in last month's issue about Estonia's successful growth.)

To the extent that anti-freedom, anti-opportunity, and the anti-rational are forced upon a populace, we see tragic poverty and human suffering. The less free people are, the less they can produce, to the point where they cannot even sustain their own lives. (See the article about Yeonmi Park, elsewhere in this issue.)

To the extent that people in the film They Live are kept down and taught to suppress independent thought, to that extent the production of wealth would stagnate and collapse.

Two famous novels take completely opposite approaches on this idea. The first is 1984 by George Orwell; the second is Anthem by Ayn Rand. Both have totalitarian dictatorships as settings.

In 1984, the government uses advanced technology to suppress its citizens.

In Anthem, society has collapsed to a pre-technological level. Rand held that initiated force (total government control) rendered human thought useless; that technology would decline and disappear under a dictatorship. (History corroborates that view. Ever seen one of those photos of both North and South Korea at nighttime? How many lights sparkle in the northern section?)

Look. Tell me there are aliens flying around in the universe, and I'll consider that a distinct possibility.

But tell me those aliens, who are technologically advanced enough to invent super-luminal transportation, are also stupendously dumb enough to think they could possibly benefit by keeping the majority of Earth inhabitants living and working at the level of unthinking slaves...?

I wouldn't believe that for a second!

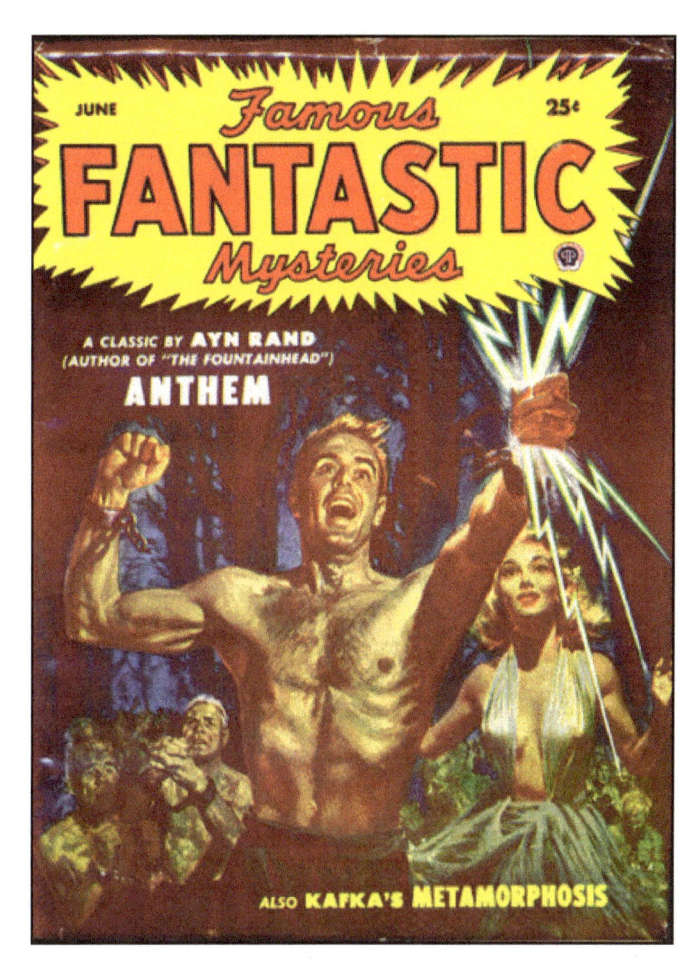

Two of Your Editor's favorite Lawrence covers. Left: This 1948 issue reprinted Nordenholt's Million, a 1923 novel of a scientist assembling the top million brains on the planet to stop a plague. The allegorical cover shows that the plague will be *halted*. Right: This 1953 issue (the last published for this title) carried the short novel Anthem, Ayn Rand's 1930s story of one individual who broke free from the chains of selfless collectivism, and escaped a world where the word "I" was unknown. – Both from philsp.com

September
2022

Cover photo: Chihuly Glass Sculptures

Great Movies This Month

Ask a Science Teacher, by Larry Scheckel: My Teacher Said Presidents Lincoln and Kennedy Had Some Diseases. Is That True?

TOS / TOS-Con Follow-Up

Book Series Portrays Hot-Rod Culture

Letters to Gary Owens

Big Rise in Interracial Marriage Since "I Have a Dream" Speech, by David M. Simon, @HumanProgress

PulpArtists by David Saunders: Sam Cherry

Here's a Great Movie! (Everything Everywhere All At Once)

And Here's Another One! (Searching)

SCHRC book reviewed: *Meet Me on the Midway*

Gloria Stoll Karn: 1923 - 2022
You're the Only One There Is
Sri Lanka's Food Crisis Reveals the Dangers of Environmental Planning, by Zilvinas Silenas, FEE.org
Tractors Are the New Dinosaurs!

Q: My Teacher Said Presidents Lincoln and Kennedy Had Some Diseases. Is That True?

Ask a Science Teacher By Larry Scheckel

A: Yes, your teacher is correct. President Abraham Lincoln suffered from Marfan's disease and President John F. Kennedy had Addison's disease.

Marfan's syndrome is a rare inherited degenerative disease of the connective tissue. Marfan syndrome is named after Antoine Marfan, a French pediatrician who described the condition in 1896.

Marfan sufferers can have deformed chests and curvature of the spine (scoliosis). The bones grow abnormally long, so people with Marfan syndrome tend to be unusually tall. Sometimes these people will have heart murmurs because of defects of the aorta and heart valves. The lungs may be affected. The dural sac around the spiral cord may be challenged. Marfan syndrome people tend to be very nearsighted.

Scientists discovered the gene that is responsible for the Marfan syndrome in 1989. They found that the syndrome is inherited by a dominant trait, carried by the FBN1 gene on chromosome 15. Being a dominant gene, a person with Marfan syndrome can inherit the gene from either parent.

Marfan syndrome is diagnosed by a series of tests, including echocardiogram, electrocardiogram, and a slit lamp eye test. The slit lamp eye test helps the doctor determine if the lenses in the eye are dislocated or out of place. A CT scan or MRI of the lower back can also help in the diagnosis. Marfan suffers might have lung capacity issues.

President Kennedy had a long history of illnesses. He missed two-thirds of kindergarten due to sickness. When he reached adulthood, he had hormonal pellets injected in the thigh every two months, the prevalent treatment in those years for Addison's disease. He collapsed regularly and received the last rites twice. Big shot politicians and the press in Washington D.C. knew he was ailing during the 1960 campaign, but Kennedy's handlers misled the public through cleverly worded statements.

Addison's disease ruins the adrenal glands and depletes the body of cortisol. There are two adrenal glands, one sitting atop each kidney. They produce more than a half dozen hormones, the important ones being cortisol and aldosterone. Cortisol ensures that the bloodstream has enough glucose, a sugar essential to brain function. One of the most common symptoms of Addison's disease is fatigue.

A common side effect of Addison's disease is a bronze skin, which supplied Kennedy with his vivacious and telegenic tan which went over well on television. Kennedy was treated for Addison's disease when he had back surgery in 1954.

Doctors discovered in the 1800s that Addison's disease is a side effect of tuberculosis. Treatment these days consists of daily replacement with adrenal hormones, or prednisone. Today, people with Addison's disease can expect to lead healthy, normal lives.

Sources: WebMD, Mayo Clinic.

You're the Only One There Is
There **never was** another You. Never **will be.**

I recently thumbed through a 1960s magazine and paused at one article.

The author told how two parents, strangers to each other, were watching their kids frolic on the beach. One parent said, "Wow, your kids sure have a nice tan for this time of year."

It turned out the "tanned" kids were biracial.

The article's author then went on to address the "problem" of biracial children. I didn't read the whole article, but one said "problem" in the author's mind was: To which world does a biracial child belong? The mother's world? Or the father's?

My Philosophical Detection buzzer went off (rather loudly; my ears are still ringing), tagging what I was reading as **BOGUS**.

For decades, the philosophy I've studied and put into practice has been one of individualism, in contrast to collectivism. Decades. Yet now and then, I still gain some insight; find a fresh way of looking at something I've known to be true for all these years; strengthen my understanding; express an old thought with a new combination of words. And I came up with:

You're the only one there is.

A cute little saying. Something you'd see on a bumper sticker, or a motivational poster.

But if you really understand that phrase, to the point where you feel you're living it, you'll understand how **BOGUS** the magazine article's perspective is.

You are unique.

The word "unique" is misused a lot. You've probably heard how something is "kind of unique," or "very unique." Both are completely wrong usages. "Unique" is an absolute, either-or term. It either is, or it isn't. No middle ground.

OK, so what is it that makes you unique?

Choices.

Every time you make a choice, which is every waking moment of each day, you are differentiating yourself from every other person.

The human mind is so constructed to allow these choices. Contrast a person's mind with that of a spider. Does a spider say, "What kind of web should I spin today?" Not at all. A spider is programmed, just like a computer, to spin a web. There is no choice.

Your choices aren't limited to deciding to take an action or not. You choose the content of your mind, and ultimately you choose the content of your character.

Just a few important choices you face:

• Will you choose to be rational, and make decisions based on evidence and knowledge you've validated? Or will you choose to buy something, or enter a career, or marry someone because "you feel like it"?

• Will you choose to be honest with yourself and with others? Or will you lie when (you think) you can get away with it? Will you deceive yourself and evade important knowledge because it makes you uncomfortable? (That can wreck your life.)

• Will you think for yourself, or let others think for you? Will you buy clothes because you like them, or because your friends will like them? Will you override your better judgment and do something harmful or dangerous because "everybody else" is doing it?

• Will you support yourself and your family on your own terms, doing the kind of work you like, or do you think the rest of the world owes you a living?

• Do you choose to respect the rights of other individuals, and refrain from initiating force against them? Or are you contemptuous of their rights, and choose to perpetrate force and fraud against them?

You're making choices constantly. Some affect your life a little: What TV show should I watch tonight? Some affect you life significantly: Should I be honest, independent, and respect the rights of others?

Some things in life you can't choose. Your ancestors. Your ethnic heritage. Where and when you were born. Your physiological identity. Those things might or might not be important, to varying degrees, depending on your values. But here's the important thing:

Your identity as a person is the result of all things you have choice over. That which you have no choice over, does not define you as a person.

But what about your DNA? Your ethnic heritage? The physical body you're born with? Isn't that a part of one's identity?

While all of that is an important part of you, you chose none of it, and therefore *it contributes nothing to your true uniqueness as a person.*

OK, you might have an interesting family heritage. You might or might not like your relatives. None of that determines your choices, or you as a person.

OK, maybe your ethnic heritage offers some spectacular cuisine. Maybe you like it so much, you become a chef and promote that cuisine. And sure, what you eat affects your physical health. But food does not determine the content of your character.

OK, perhaps your ancestors had their own style of dancing and clothing. You could be indifferent to that, or you could meticulously design your costume and dance passionately in a powwow. If you win awards for such performances, your pride for that specific achievement is well-earned. But if you try using that as a substitute for your overall efficacy as a person—or even balancing a checkbook—you'll be very disappointed in the long run.

OK, you're a descendant of kings and queens; or you're the offspring of rapscallions, jacks, knaves and court jesters. Would you puff out your chest at thought of the first, or hang your head in shame at the second? That would be a serious mistake. It's not your predecessors' choices that matter in *your* life; it is *your* choices.

OK, you have an unusually flexible body, and you're able to do a contortionist / acrobatics act for Cirque du Soleil. You deserve every accolade your audience gives you. But those abilities won't help you form healthy relationships with others.

OK, your skin pigmentation is light or dark, depending on your race. Neither will guarantee that your choices will be right or wrong (that is, if they further your life, or harm it).

I believe many social trends of the past decades have been for the worse. But one trend is described in an article, elsewhere in this issue of The PRC: Please see Big Rise in Interracial Marriage Since "I Have a Dream" Speech. This documents a trend for the better.

If you agree that it is choices that make up the composition of a person's uniqueness, then you'll understand how ridiculous it is for that magazine to agonize over which "world" the biracial children "belong to." The right answer is: The children (while they are children) belong to the world of their parents. If their parents do their job as parents, they will train their children to each create his or her own "world," or personhood. (That happens, regardless, but it happens best with good guidance.)

If you agree that *you* are the only one there is, you will understand when I say: *I* am the only one there is.

In that respect, you and I (whoever you are) are on equal terms with one another.

And then, look at each person you meet or see walking by, and understand: *That person* is the only one there is.

When you start thinking of people this way, you will be thinking as an individualist. You will be untainted by a specific, **BOGUS** (and thus destructive) belief: *racism*; and a more general, **BOGUS** *(very* destructive) belief: *collectivism*.

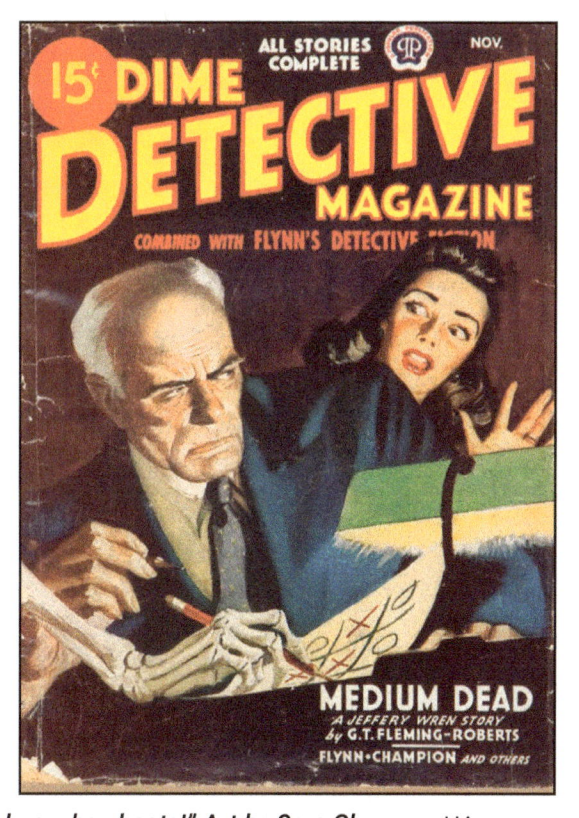

ABOVE: "No, Dad! *Don't* play tic-tac-toe with *Death! You* know he cheats!" Art by Sam Cherry. — HA.com

Gloria Stoll Karn: 1923 - 2022

This month's PulpArtists biography on Sam Cherry mentions three other artists who worked for the pulps: Rafael DeSoto, Ernest Chiriacka, and Gloria Stoll.

We have featured work by all three artists in past issues of The PRC. One is worth special mention this month.

Six years ago, in the September 2016 issue of The PRC, Gloria Stoll Karn was the featured PulpArtist. At the time, Your Editor discovered she was still living (a rarity, considering how long ago the pulps were published).

This led to me contacting Gloria, talking a little about her career, letting her know some of her cover paintings would be used in The PRC, and promising she'd receive a few copies.

A couple of paragraphs from Saunders' biography on Gloria demonstrate how choices can affect a life:

One fateful day in April of 1941 she impulsively threw away all of her student artwork. The janitor rescued her portfolio from the incinerator room and showed it to another tenant in the building who happened to be the pulp artist, Rafael DeSoto. DeSoto asked to meet the discouraged seventeen-year-old art student, and inspired her to become a commercial illustrator.

With DeSoto's introduction she sold her first freelance story illustration to a Popular Publication pulp magazine. From 1941 to 1949 she sold story illustrations and cover paintings to *All-Story Love, Detective Tales, Dime Mystery, Love Novels, Love Short Stories, New Love, Rangeland Romances,* and *Romance Western.*

I recently received a call from Gloria's daughter. Gloria passed away this past July 23.

On this page are some examples of her work.

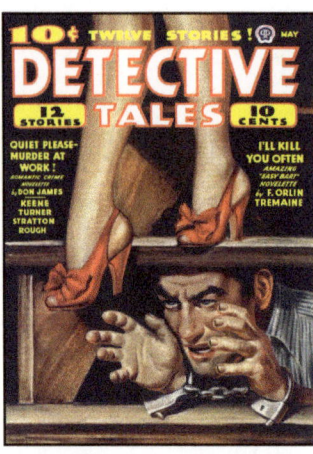

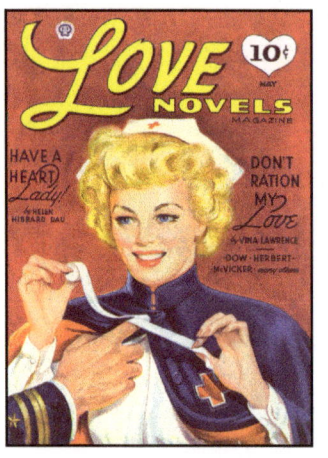

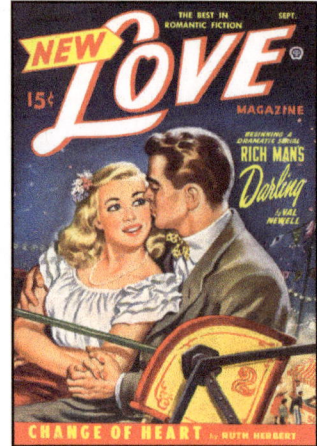

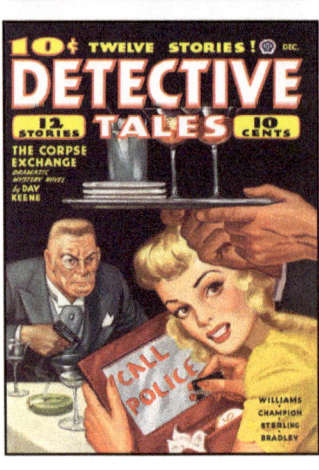

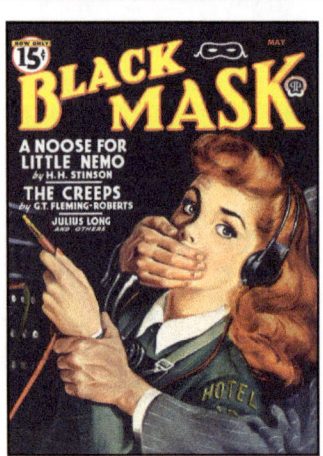

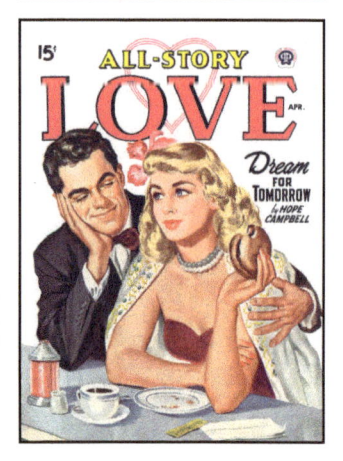

"Why Did I Even Bother?" Dept.: Jim Bama painted the formidable military officer at left. He likely hired a model; had to find the right uniform; and worked long hours to create this very effective piece. So what does the art director at Bantam Books do? Shrinks it down to near-illegibility for this paperback cover. Why? *Why??* — Thanks again to Tom Roberts for identifying the paperback this image was used on. I found a transparency of this painting among Jim's files; was not familiar with it; ran ads asking if anyone knew where/if it had been used; finally heard from Tom.

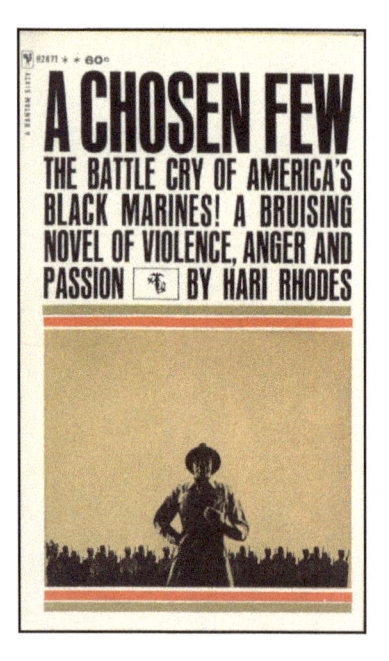

The Plymouth Review Current

TAKING YOU PLACES WORTH SEEING
Volume 11 • Issue 11 • October 2022

FREE!

The Shadow Solves a Clue
Still River ◆ Floral Tigers

October 2022

Cover photo: Bellagio, Las Vegas
Great Movies This Month
Remembering artist James Bama, by Vicki Stavig, Editor, *Art of the West* Magazine
The True Identity of "Our Writer"
Fame Is a Funny Thing
Ask a Science Teacher, by Larry Scheckel: I Have a Device with a Lipo Battery. I Heard Those Batteries Can Catch on Fire. How Likely Is That?
The Shadow Solves a Code
Public Invited to 'Paint the Towns' Reception
Call to Artists
Say "Thanks!" to a Vet With a Ticket
PulpArtists by David Saunders: Robert Gibson Jones
The Ultimate Field Trip

Yeah, I'd say that qualifies as being pretty "fantastic."
Art by Robert Gibson Jones. From 1951.

Fame is a Funny Thing

Some people want fame. Badly. And that can be an innocent thing, if it's not a matter of wanting to be liked by others, to cover up a serious lack of self-esteem. (Because there is no substitute for regarding oneself positively.)

Some people regard fame with indifference, yet that fame affects their lives in some not-so-positive ways.

James Bama is an example. I can't imagine a person more indifferent to the fame that descended upon him. But it still had some annoying consequences.

I wrote to Jim in 1980, asking if I could visit him if ever I were out in his part of Wyoming. (Had he said yes, I would "just happen" to make a special trip to be in that part of the world.)

He was good enough to reply, but explained that he discouraged visitors. After his Western Art of James Bama book was released by Bantam in 1975, he wrote me, he had over 200 visitors during the summer, mostly strangers who just dropped in.

As Jim told me in later years, he'd explain to people that he couldn't get any work done that way. What if he were to stop in unannounced where these people worked, he would ask, and want to visit for a couple of hours?

I can understand the widespread enthusiasm for Jim's fine art ("western") work. For decades, so-called artists threw away everything fine about fine art: rules of perspective, artistic technique, coherence, until "art" was just a bunch of paint thrown on paper. Along comes James Bama, using actual artistic techniques and portraying dignified human beings. The honest majority of people responded like starved refugees being presented with a royal banquet.

But Jim is not famous only for his fine art. He has many admirers for his Doc Savage covers. I count myself as one; I purchased many Doc paperbacks in Plymouth or Sheboygan in the late 1960s and early 70s.

I can understand admiration for the Doc Savage covers. But there are those who love the Doc covers, but don't care for Jim's later fine art.

So when fans contacted Jim about his Doc Savage covers, he was flattered that people still remembered and liked that work he did decades before, but he considered it in the past; of little relevance to his present life; "yesterday's news," as he'd put it.

Many asked him if he'd do a re-creation of a Doc Savage cover for them. Some older artists welcome that; it can be lucrative, and might be their only source of income. But Jim was not interested.

I was 13 years old when I saw my first Doc Savage paperbacks with cover art by Jim Bama. But his influence on my life, and on many others, began even earlier.

In the 1960s, Aurora issued plastic assembly kits of famous Universal monsters: Frankenstein, The Mummy, Wolf Man, Dracula (my first, at age 8), The Creature from the Black Lagoon, King Kong, The Phantom of the Opera, The Hunchback of Notre Dame, Dr. Jekyll as Mr. Hyde, The Addams Family House, The Munsters...

Jim did about 20 paintings for Aurora.

Just as with Doc Savage, there are fans who focus on Jim's art for Aurora... and have no interest in his other work. (Which I find incredible.)

Jim told me, and said in interviews, that he grew to dislike doing these monster paintings so much, that the art director would drop off an assignment for one while Jim was out for lunch. (At that stage of his illustration career, he was working for an illustration studio in New York City, where he grew up.)

Fame is a funny thing? That's right. And sometimes people are fortunate enough to be famous for what they are most proud of.

But here's something ironic (and maybe incomprehensible). Above are three paintings that have been sold (or is selling) by Heritage Auctions.

The Aurora Munsters box cover painting (1965) sold a year ago for $81,250.

The Doc Savage painting for Cold Death (1968) sold for $68,750.

The fine art painting, Dee Smith with Saddlebag (1973), sold last year for $21,250.

Sometimes, a person learning that I knew Jim would ask me, to ask him, to do this or that, related to Doc Savage or the Aurora kits. Rather than pass that request on, I'd explain as best I could that Jim had the freedom and passion to paint what he wanted. While he acknowledged the skill, effort, and time that went into his commercial work, he was proud of it, but not interested in revisiting it. No matter what level of fame was attached to it.

Instead, from 1971 on, he concentrated on the work he considered important.

And I'm glad.

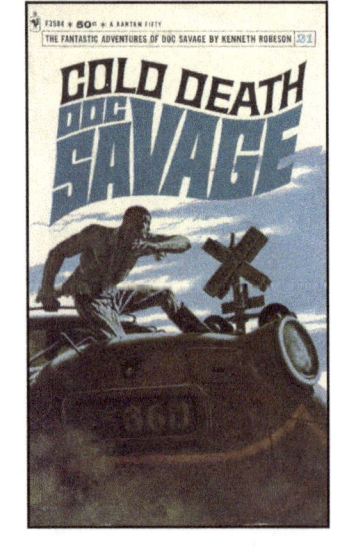

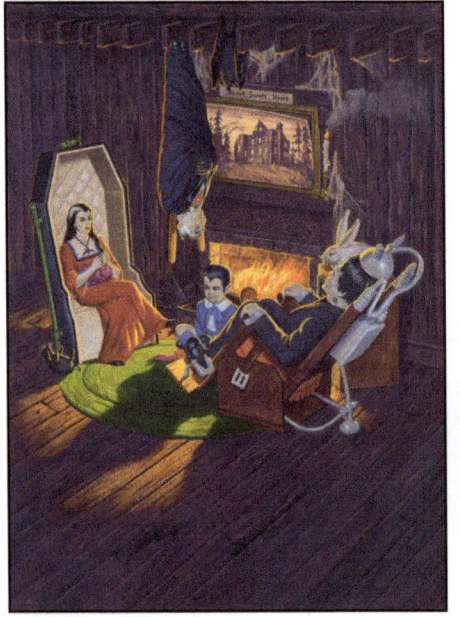

A tale of three original paintings, all auctioned off through Heritage Auctions. From left to right: Box cover for The Munsters, an Aurora plastic assembly kit from about 1965; cover for Cold Death, a Doc Savage adventure (1968); Dee Smith with Saddlebag (1973). Which of these would you most like to hang on your wall? Which one do you think brought the highest price? (See article for that.) — HA.com

The Ultimate Field Trip
Or: You think *you* have problems?

Has this ever happened to you? (It's sure happened to me.)

You need some kind of help over the phone. You wait on hold for two hours (you know I'm not exaggerating, right?), listening to terrible music (no exaggeration there, either), and you gasp with relief when you hear a voice start to speak.

A living, human being! you think, in desperate joy.

That joy is short-lived. The person on the phone is speaking with an accent that makes it nearly impossible for you to understand what is being said.

I had a hearing check not long ago. It checked out reasonably well. But I can't decipher the mumblings and mutterings of many modern actors. And while attending the highly-regarded musical Hamilton, less than 20% of the words spoken were intelligible to me. (The lyrics to the songs? I had to ask my wife if they were singing in English.)

But... let's imagine, for a moment...

(Yes, that's one thing good science fiction (SF) does.)

...imagine that most language barriers are removed.

...that a translation program converts any other language (or dialect) into clear words you can easily understand.

Would there still be communication problems? Misunderstandings? Words that don't translate?

That is one interesting point to an SF novel by Hal Clement: Still River.

I attended an SF convention in Oconomowoc in 1986, where Hal Clement (then 64) was Guest of Honor. Still River had just been released. He read a passage, and discussed the story.

(And, dang if he didn't give away the biggest discovery of the book! Something which *I* will *not* do!)

The basic story: Five completely different intelligent species (including one human woman) are given the educational task of going to a Planet, Enigma, to determine why it has an atmosphere.

Why *wouldn't* it have an atmosphere? It's too small. Like the Earth's moon, it wouldn't have enough gravity to *keep* an atmosphere, if there ever *were* one.

The five characters each come from very different worlds, with different climates. Each has his/her own protective suit.

When one being speaks, that language is translated into four other languages. The translation program is very effective. For all practical purposes, language is not an issue between the five beings.

Despite being biologically and chemically different (while the human's body is water-based, another team member's body fluid is ammonia), the five are able to examine planet Enigma, gather data, and agree on what they observe. Each knows what the other is talking about when temperatures, wind speeds, atmospheric composition and pressure are discussed. That's because, no matter what part of the galaxy each being comes from, the laws of matter *are the same.* Chemistry and physics *are the same.*

This has some very interesting implications, which I'll touch on later.

The five-student team does *not* know why Enigma has an atmosphere, but two *guesses* are made: Enigma is very young and hasn't lost its atmosphere so soon after forming; there is life on Enigma which generates gases.

These are *guesses,* not even hypotheses and certainly not theories, because (in the beginning) they have no clue how old Enigma is; nor whether life is present.

Hal Clement likes to emphasize (in this book, and in others) the dangers of assuming something, when there is no basis for the assumptions. The term "of course" used in conversations and chapter titles offers painful reminders of this.

Another thing Still River has in common with Clement's other work: This is a problem-solving story. The conflict comes with the struggle to overcome one's assumptions and to discover the facts.

There is no hideous, monstrous menace that the five-student team has to battle. Planet Enigma offers plenty of danger. One being, from a world where there is no air, makes the mistake of stepping out of the ship, into the moving air (which we call "wind"), and immediately blows away. Two others, descending into a cave (as all five puzzle over the seemingly complete lack of geological forces on Enigma which could *create* caves), backtrack, hoping to return to the surface—only to find the "ground" they previously covered has changed by some unknown process, and is now unrecognizable.

This is a wonderful story of discovery. But be warned: You will need some basic understanding of chemistry and physics to follow the conversations between these five highly intelligent yet assumption-ridden students. One of my favorite snippets comes when the being who comes from an airless planet is told that the effect of moving air would cool an object down faster than stationary air of the same temperature. He asks, "Why would motion of the air be a factor—" He thinks for a moment, then says, "Oh, of course." (Could *you* figure that out?)

Now for those "interesting implications."

Without the barrier of different languages, these five beings, completely alien from each other, are able to study planet Enigma and reach conclusions that all five understand and agree upon.

As I said: The laws of chemistry and physics are the same, no matter what part of the universe you're from. All other elements of the universe follow the same laws. In other words, *metaphysical laws are universal.*

All five students in the story have sense organs, nervous systems, and brains that are physiologically different. However, each has a consciousness capable of forming concepts. That's what makes it possible for the five different species to come together, form a team, and communicate intelligibly. If this is a feasible scenario (and it's SF, after all; we haven't yet observed five different conceptual species coming together in real life), the implication is that *epistemological laws are universal for conceptual consciousnesses.*

That is, logic, reason, and any other rule or technique for successfully understanding reality would be the same, for any mind that uses concepts as its building blocks of knowledge.

Now, sure, some of you might say, "Wow, man, you're way too far out there, up in the clouds! That has nothing to do with reality."

Oh, yeah?

I have the unpleasant task of informing you that certain debased intellectuals consider logic and reason (rationality) to be *racist.*

Go ahead. Research that thought on your own, if you wish. But I warn you, as you do so, you'll feel like you're poking among decaying corpses, looking for the smelliest, rottenest corpse of them all.

The truth is, as Still River demonstrates to its readers, that rationality (the epistemological prerequisite to the scientific method) makes acquisition of knowledge and communication possible. It brings conceptual beings together, in common cause, and is the necessary condition to *prevent* racism.

When you consider the communication challenges between the five students in this story, it makes the communications problems we commonly face—trying to understand someone through an accent—a piece of cake in comparison.

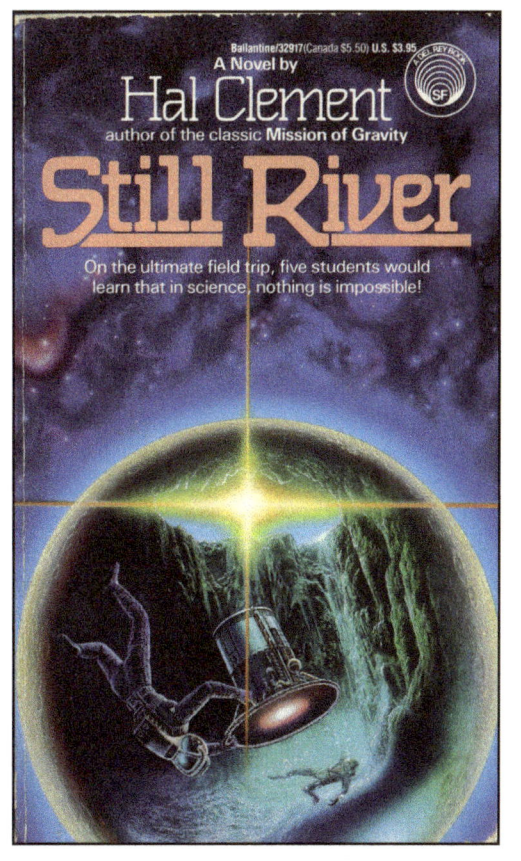

November 2022

Cover photo: Jack Bishop, Kohler Food & Wine Experience
Great Movies This Month
Ask a Science Teacher, by Larry Scheckel: Is Tupperware Still Around?
Musical Tribute Honors US Veterans and Active Military Personnel
PulpArtists by David Saunders: Rafael Valdivia
Local Authors to Meet Readers, Sign Books at Manitowoc Book Show
SCHRC book reviewed: Two New Booklets on Sheboygan County History
Meeting Jack Bishop
Celebrate a Celtic Christmas
New Discovery About an Old Favorite!
A Nutty Movie for Three Stooges Fans
The Time Price of Watching Baseball Has Fallen to Seconds, by Gale Pooley, HumanProgress.org
Ideas Are Not Like a Jar Of Jellybeans. We'll Never Reach the Bottom and Go Hungry, by Marian L. Tupy, HumanProgress.org
Musical Abundance, by Gale Pooley, HumanProgress.org

Portraits by Rafael Valdivia. Charles Lindbergh.

Artist self-portrait.

Never heard of Thomas Thursday? A humor writer.

By Larry Scheckel — Ask a Science Teacher

Q: Is Tupperware Still Around?

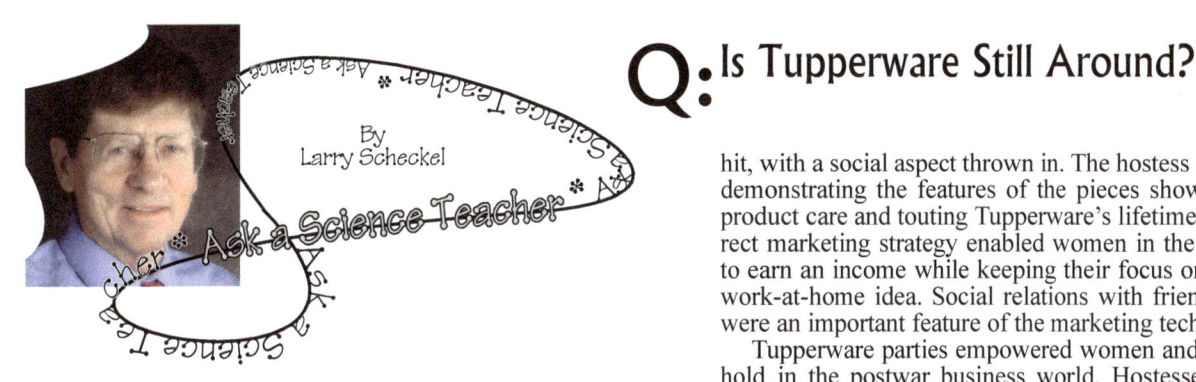

A: Yes, Tupperware is alive and well, with sales of $2.26 billion per year in over 100 countries. They sell on the Internet and the familiar Tupperware parties. They have 13,500 employees and 2.6 million Tupperware ladies and are headquartered in Orlando, Florida.

Until Earl Tupper (1907-1983), in Leominster, Massachusetts, came along, most housewares were made of glass, ceramics, wood, or metal, proven materials at the time. By the mid-1940s, plastics, made from crude oil, were being incorporated into consumer products. In 1945, Tupper tried to market his containers in retail stores. His first product was a simple bowl. Tupper's products bombed. Women shoppers feared that plastic material would be too flimsy and didn't understand that Tupper's airtight seal would keep foods fresh. Tupper had patented a "burping seal."

Tupper was persuaded that demonstrating his products would cause sales to mushroom, a "sale through presentation." In 1951, his products were removed from store shelves and Tupperware Home Parties started.

Tupperware parties proved to be a big hit, with a social aspect thrown in. The hostess acted as a teacher, demonstrating the features of the pieces shown and discussing product care and touting Tupperware's lifetime warranty. The direct marketing strategy enabled women in the 1950s and 1960s to earn an income while keeping their focus on family, sort of a work-at-home idea. Social relations with friends and neighbors were an important feature of the marketing technique.

Tupperware parties empowered women and gave them a toehold in the postwar business world. Hostesses were rewarded with free products based on the level of sales. Top-selling and top-organizing women were treated to rallies held in cities across America.

Tupperware came up with a brilliant idea to rouse interest in Tupperware parties. A technique called "carrot calling" helped promote the parties. A Tupperware rep would go door to door in a neighborhood and ask the lady of the house to "run an experiment" in which carrots would be placed in a Tupperware container and compared with "anything that you would ordinarily leave them in." The ploy would often result in the scheduling of a Tupperware party.

Tupperware has been going strong for 75 years and their top market is now Indonesia, followed by Germany. In recent years, Tupperware has developed a new business model, moving to an emphasis on direct marketing. Tupperware is being sold by Target stores and on Amazon.com. Rubbermaid is a formidable competitor.

These days, Tupperware has become a generic name for any plastic or glass container with snap-close lids. The market is now flooded with plastic container and household items, many from overseas.

Recent Tupperware items. — Photo by Melissa Highton, Creative Commons Attribution-Share Alike 4.0 International license

Musical Abundance

For the time it took our grandparents to earn the money to buy one song in 1955, we get 19,750 songs today.

Thomas Edison developed the original phonograph record in 1877. The first playable records were made from paper pressed between two pieces of tin foil.

On March 15, 1949, RCA Victor became the first label to roll out 45 rpm vinyl records. They were smaller and held less music than the popular 78s and were printed in different colors. *Rolling Stone* notes, "Teenagers of the Fifties took to the portable, less-expensive format; one ad at the time priced the records at 65 cents each. One of rock's most cataclysmic early hits, Bill Haley and the Comets' 'Rock Around the Clock,' sold 3 million singles in 1955."

Unskilled workers in 1955 were earning around 97 cents an hour. This puts the time price of a song at 40 minutes of work.

Apple launched the iTunes Store on April 28, 2003, and sold songs for 99 cents. By this time, unskilled wages had increased to $9.25 an hour. The time price of a song had dropped 84 percent to 6.42 minutes of work. Listeners in 2003 got six songs for the price of one in 1955.

Apple Music launched on June 30, 2015. Today a student can get access to 90 million songs for $5.99 a month. Unskilled workers are earning around $14.53 an hour, so the time price is around 25 minutes of work. Users stream as well as download albums and tracks to devices for offline playback. If a typical song runs three to four minutes, you can play 12,342 songs per month. The time price per song is around one-eighth of a second of work.

For the time it took our grandparents to earn the money to buy one song in 1955, we get 19,750 songs today. Since 1955, personal music abundance has been growing around 15.9 percent a year, doubling in abundance every 4.5 years.

All of the products we enjoy today are the culmination of billions and billions of little bits of knowledge that humans discover and then share with the rest of us in free markets. Create a song and share it with the planet. We can lift ourselves up and make life better for one another.

Do we still have problems? Of course we do. And we will always face challenges. But look at what we have accomplished in the last 200 years. This is what happens when people are free to solve one another's problems.

You can learn more about these economic facts and ideas in our new book, *Superabundance*, available on Amazon or Barnes & Noble.

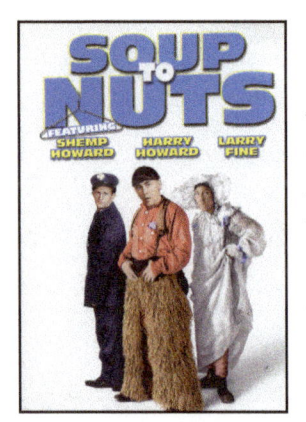

A nutty movie for Three Stooges fans

I recently re-watched Soup to Nuts, a wacky 1930 film with several things to recommend it:

• It was scripted by Rube Goldberg, a cartoonist whose name has become synonymous with crazy inventions. If you're familiar with the game Mousetrap, then you know what I mean. You can learn all about Goldberg at **www.rubegoldberg.org**, the site of the Rube Goldberg Institute for Innovation & Creativity.

• It features an early appearance of the Three Stooges. At this point in the Stooges' career, they were managed by Ted Healy, who played the dominant role in the acts in this film. And while the names Shemp Howard and Larry Fine are familiar to Stooge fans, the name Harry Howard might not be. "Harry" would soon after call himself Moe.

• Several comedic actors from the silent films, or Vaudeville, or both, are present, though uncredited. See **imdb.com** for a detailed cast list.

A home video does not seem to be in print, but DVDs can be found on eBay or Amazon for $10 or less.

December 2022

Cover photo: Your Editor's Back Side Yard
Great Movies This Month
Making Spirits Bright
Sushi Dinner at the Blind Horse, Kohler
Ask a Science Teacher, by Larry Scheckel: What Are the Top Ten Engineering Feats in the Last 100 Years?
Wow! What a Fan-tas-tic Book!!
PulpArtists by David Saunders: H. L. Parkhurst

The Most Dangerous Man in the World (John Locke), by Dan Sanchez, FEE.org
SCHRC books: Holiday Gift Ideas for Your Favorite Readers

Q: What Are the Top Ten Engineering Feats in the Last 100 Years?

By Larry Scheckel

A: At a recent meeting of the National Academy of Engineers, 1500 members were polled on what they thought were the top 10 engineering feats in the last 100 years. On almost everyone's list was the Apollo landing and Neil Armstrong's walk on the moon in 1969. These engineers rated our going to the moon right up there with the building of the Panama Canal or the Egyptian Pyramids. The array of scientific information, basic research and development, and product spin-off from the Apollo program had given an estimated 10 to 1 return on our investment. Here is the entire list of the top ten:

1. Apollo landing 1969
2. Laser 1960
3. Optical fibers 1965
4. Microprocessor 1971
5. Genetic engineering 1973
6. CAT Scanner 1971
7. Jumbo Jet 1969
8. Satellites 1957
9. Channel Tunnel (Chunnel) 1993
10. Large Hadron Collider 2008

The Channel Tunnel is a 31.4 mile railway tunnel that connects England with France beneath the English Channel at the Strait of Dover. You don't actually drive through the Channel Tunnel. You sit comfortably in your own car while you are carried through the tunnel on a special train, the Car Transport.

The Large Hadron Collider is the world's largest and highest energy particle collider (atom smasher). It was built by the European Organization for Nuclear Research (CERN) between 1998 and 2008 in collaboration with over 10,000 scientists and hundreds of universities and laboratories, as well as more than 100 countries. It lies in a tunnel 17 miles in circumference and as deep as 574 feet beneath the France–Switzerland border near Geneva.

The top ten list is not unanimous. Others include: The Three Gorges Dam in China, Palm Islands, the London Underground, the Burj Khalifa Skyscraper in Dubai, and the Millau Viaduct Bridge in France.

The 7,661-foot-long Three Gorges Dam spans the Yangtze River and is the largest hydroelectric power station in the world with 34 enormous generators. The man-made reservoir covers over 400 square miles. It costs $30 billion and is designed to withstand a large earthquake.

Palm Islands in Dubai are three manmade islands made by dredging the seabed connected to the mainland by a 6-lane underseas tunnel hosting the Middle East's first monorail. Palm Island is home to about 10,000 Emirati.

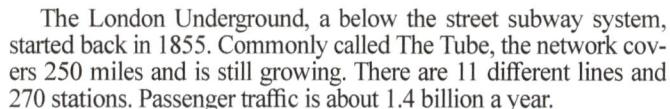

The London Underground, a below the street subway system, started back in 1855. Commonly called The Tube, the network covers 250 miles and is still growing. There are 11 different lines and 270 stations. Passenger traffic is about 1.4 billion a year.

Originally dubbed the Dubai Tower, it's now called the Burj Khalifa Skyscraper in honor of the president of the United Arab Emirates. It is the tallest skyscraper in the world at 2,722 feet, boasting 163 floors above ground level, 58 elevators, 900 apartments, 304 rooms, and parking spaces for over 2,900 cars.

The Millau Viaduct in the south of France is a cable-stay 4-lane 8,070-foot-long bridge. It was built to relieve congestion from France to Spain. The bridge opened for traffic in December 2004. Tolls are collected to pay for it.

In this year of 2022, it's hard to imagine life without many of those top ten inventions or engineering achievements. They touch every facet of our life. Just look what microprocessors (computer) and satellites have done for business, industry, and communication via the Internet. Genetic engineering, the laser, and CAT scanner have revolutionized medicine. Some, such as fiber optics, are often hidden from direct view, but show up in our ability to communicate and receive information. Hard to imagine what the next 100 years will bring!

The Queen of Something-or-Other. Original painting by H. L. Parkhurst. — HA.com

Wow!

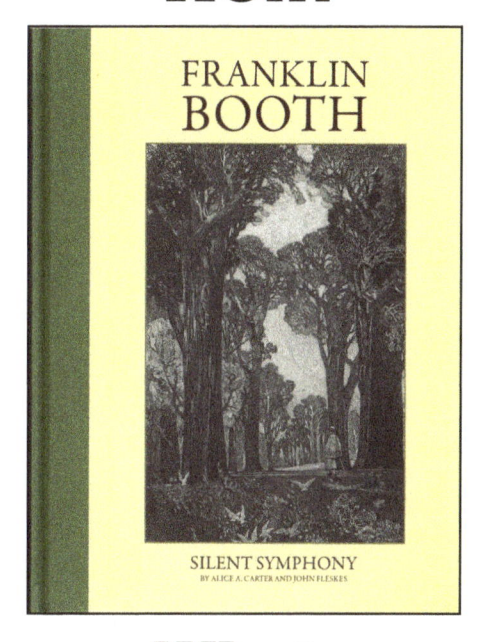

What a Fan-tas-tic Book!!

Check out the Flesk Publications for this and other fine art books:

fleskpublications.com

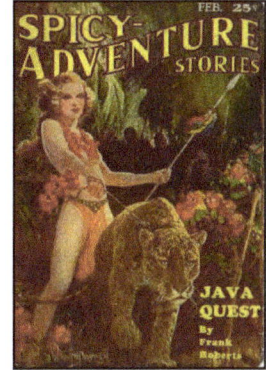

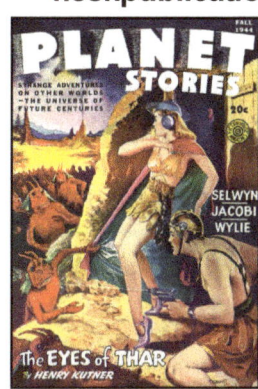

SILENT SYMPHONY BY FRANKLIN BOOTH

From the book shown on the previous page.

"And I'm not foolin', big boy. If you think I am, just try me." Original painting by Parkhurst. — HA.com

This 8.5 x 6 inch portrait of Marion Davies, painted by Frank Leyendecker, sold for $10K. — HA.com

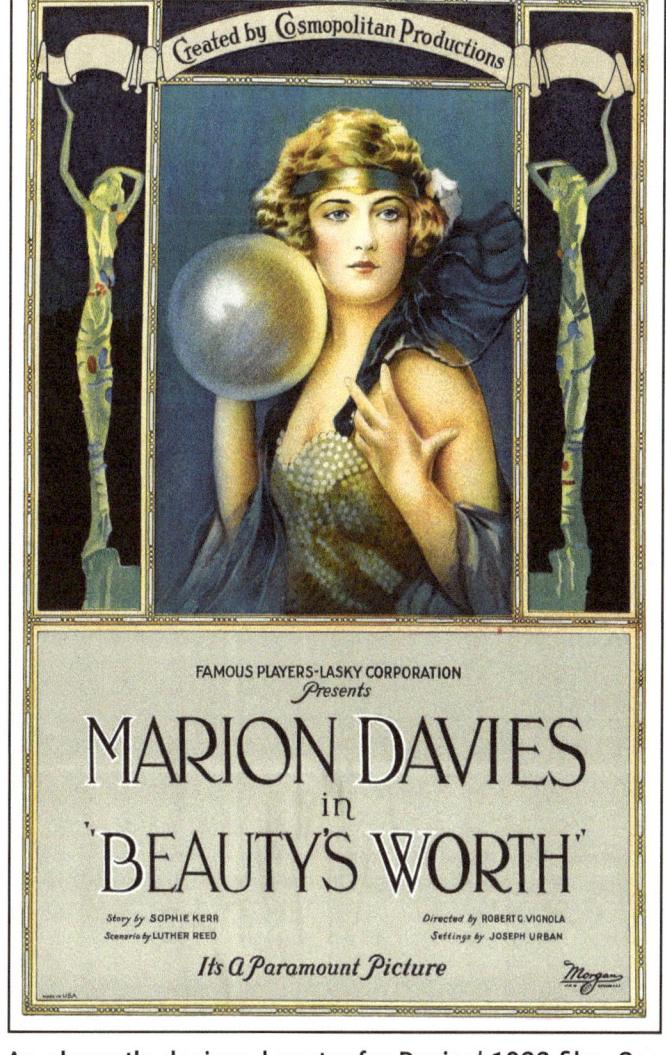

An elegantly-designed poster for Davies' 1922 film. See Jan. 3. — HA.com

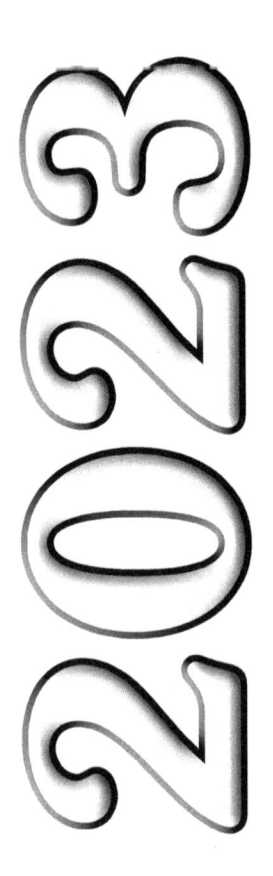

2023

The Plymouth Review Current
TAKING YOU PLACES WORTH SEEING
Volume 12 • Issue 2 • January 2023

FREE!

Illustrator Howard Pyle in Green Bay
Students of Howard Pyle

• The publication that respects your intelligence •
• Allegories • Aphorisms • Idioms • Colloquialisms •

January
2023

Cover image: 1922 Illustration by Gayle Porter Hoskins

Great Movies This Month

Ask a Science Teacher, by Larry Scheckel: What Is the Relation Between Heart Rate and Breathing Rate?

Howard Pyle in Green Bay

Students of Howard Pyle

See You at the Sock Hop

Meanwhile, Elsewhere in the Art World...

Flame Ignition

New Year's Eve at the Blind Horse

Kohler Foundation Announces 78th Season of Distinguished Guest Series

PulpArtists by David Saunders: Gayle Porter Hoskins

You think *you've* had a rough day?? Both pieces by Gayle Porter Hoskins. — HA.com

331

Students of Howard Pyle

Spread across the bottom of pages 12-13 are seven paintings by artists who at some point studied under Howard Pyle.

The following information on each piece and each artist was assembled from the Heritage Auction descriptions (where the "Sold on" numbers are from), from Wikipedia, and other Internet sources.

1. Jessie Willcox Smith, 1863-1935. From *A Child's Garden of Verses,* written by Robert Louis Stevenson and illustrated by Smith. Originally published in 1905, it had many printings since, and is easily and cheaply available (I just bought a copy for $4.50, including postage!).

Sold in 2010 for $310,700.00

2. N. C. Wyeth, 1882-1945. From the 1917 book, *The Boy's King Arthur: Sir Thomas Malory's History of King Arthur and His Knights of the Round Table.* Per Wikipedia: "Wyeth created more than 3,000 paintings and illustrated 112 books—25 of them for Scribner's, the Scribner Classics, which is the body of work for which he is best known. The first of these, *Treasure Island,* was one of his masterpieces and the proceeds paid for his studio."

Sold in 2019 for $615,000.00

3. Frank Earle Schoonover, 1877-1972. From The Outing Magazine, 1907. The PRC ran David Saunders' PulpArtists biography of Schoonover in 2021. He worked in Wilmington, Delaware—the city Howard Pyle grew up in, and the location of the Delaware Art Museum, which holds over a thousand paintings by Pyle.

Sold in 2019 for $68,750.00

4. William Harnden Foster, 1886-1941. Done in 1925 for *National Sportsman* magazine. Foster did some work for *Scribner's Magazine,* which assigned Foster to cover the building of the Panama Canal. (A link on our Facebook page leads to a long and *very* interesting article on this artist.)

Sold in 2009 for $8,962.50

5. Harvey T. Dunn, 1884-1952. 1932 Ticonderoga pencil advertisement. Colonial soldiers move towards a victorious surprise attack on Fort Ticonderoga.

Sold in 2020 for $60,000.00

6. Alice Barber Stephens, 1858-1932. Illustration for a poem, 1896.
Sold in 2017 for $2,750.00

7. Gayle Porter Hoskins, 1887-1962. See this month's PulpArtists column for more about this artist.
Sold in 2011 for $1,912.00

GAYLE PORTER HOSKINS

By Gayle Porter Hoskins. — HA.com

We had to crop this image by Gayle Porter Hoskins for our cover, so here is the entire piece. — HA.com

Howard Pyle, Washington Before the Trenches at Yorktown. From the book, *Howard Pyle in Wisconsin.* — Courtesy of, and part of the collection of, the Neville Public Museum

333

The Plymouth Review Current

TAKING YOU PLACES WORTH SEEING
Volume 12 • Issue 3 • February 2023

FREE!

Black Innovators and Entrepreneurs in History
Movies • Art • A Plethora of Truffles

February
2023

Cover image: A Treasure Trove of Truffle Dishes

Great Movies This Month

Black Innovators and Entrepreneurs Under Capitalism, by Andrew Bernstein, FEE.org

Ask a Science Teacher, by Larry Scheckel: How Does a Microwave Oven Cook Food Without Flame or Hot Coil?

A Plethora of Truffles

With a Little (Lotta) Help From His Friends

Sheboygan Student Awarded Evans Scholar Scholarship

PulpArtists by David Saunders: Ehler Dahl

Peter Thiel's Pessimism Is (Largely) Mistaken, by Marian L. Tupy & Gale Pooley, HumanProgress.org

Blacksmithing

Willis O'Brien worked on the 1933 King Kong movie. In 1949, he brought life to Mighty Joe Young (see March 2), which landed O'Brien an Academy Award for Best Visual Effects. This is a pre-production painting by O'Brien, showing cowboys capturing Joe. It doesn't surprise me a bit that this piece of cinematic history sold in 2021 for $32,500 — HA.com

March

2023

Cover image: Cereal Killerz, Miracle Mile Shops, Las Vegas
Great Movies This Month
PulpArtists by David Saunders: Walter DeMaris
Ask a Science Teacher, by Larry Scheckel: Is There Any Science Behind Superstitions?
Is This Cause for Concern?
'Aspect Ratio?' What's That?
Enjoy "Musical Potpourri"
The Eternal Wall, by Raymond Z. Gallun
PAC Hosts Artist Retrospective
What I Have in Common with Ernst Lubitsch
Wisconsin Artists Invited to Apply for Art Show
PAC Presents: A Night at the Opera
Tractor Wars
Botts Goes to War

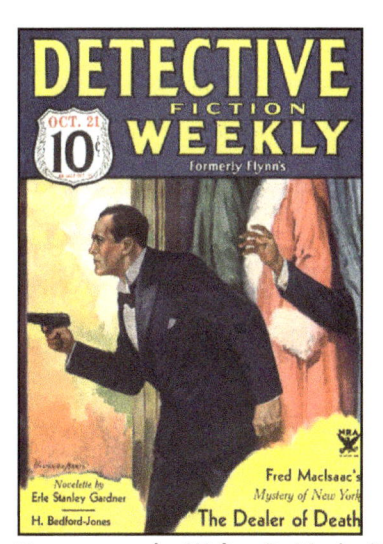

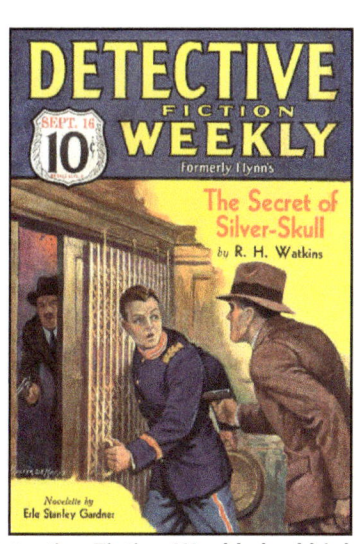

Two covers by Walter DeMaris. Detective Fiction Weekly had high editorial standards for fiction. For that reason, much of what appeared in this pulp would later be reprinted in hardcover books and/or paperbacks. The above carried stories by Erle Stanley Gardner, creator of Perry Mason. Movie studios would also monitor this title's contents for possible screenplay adaptations. — From PulpArtists.com and philsp.com

Is this cause for concern?

...or... How to think critically while reading

I have started using Twitter only recently.

I'd never seen much value to it. But with all the news of Elon Musk purchasing Twitter, and subsequent discoveries that government agencies have brought pressure on Twitter (and other social media platforms) to suppress and silence certain viewpoints, I was curious. I downloaded the app on my phone a few weeks ago.

(Everything I say about Twitter—and it won't be much—is from the perspective of the most basic beginner. If you're curious, I don't believe you have to create any kind of account; just go to **twitter.com** on your computer or phone, and you'll see an endless stream of comments, of varying levels of relevance and intelligence. You can search, as I did, for a subject—for example, "Roald Dahl.")

Here is one great benefit I see in Twitter (and, to a degree, in Facebook). If something important is going on in the world, you'll hear of it, if you're tapped into (following; liking) sources you trust.

I was once told that Facebook (and, presumably, Twitter) are the worst possible places to get news stories from.

I disagree.

First, when there are dozens of tweets on Twitter, posts on Facebook, reports on TV, articles in newspapers, referring to an event, you're fully justified to *tentatively* conclude, "This really happened."

But the next step is up to you.

Are you reading or listening (1) uncritically, accepting every claim (because it's from a certain source, or a certain writer)? Or do you think with (2) an active and *critical* mind, pausing now and then to ask questions?

(Brief note: "critical" in this context is not the same as "skeptical.")

If (1), you'll be easily swayed by the slickest-talking writer or speaker who comes along, and you'll quite possibly end up following some *movement*-of-the-moment. You'll be trained that the worst crime is to question the *movement.* You'll be absorbed as a selfless unit into that *movement.* (Or "assimilated," as into the Borg, in the Star Trek stories.)

If (2), you're making it possible to live and operate as an independent thinker. An individual. And you'll be able to accept or reject ideas, trends, or movements on the basis of their validity or unsoundness, not on blind faith as in (1).

So here's what set this thing off for me.

I browsed Twitter on my phone the morning of Feb. 19 and discovered claims that works by the late Welsh-born author Roald Dahl's were being edited by the author's publisher. Dahl was the author of ***James and the Giant Peach, Charlie and the Chocolate Factory, Matilda, The Witches, Fantastic Mr Fox, The BFG, The Twits, George's Marvellous Medicine*** and ***Danny, the Champion of the World.***

Allegations of fact (that the changes were being made; examples of the changes) were mixed with evaluations (some disapproving, some approving).

Here's what *links* are for on the Internet: You don't have to be satisfied with "Someone said something happened." Many tweets telling of the edits to Dahl's work linked directly to news sources where this information originated. I found enough references to safely assume it was actually happening.

Read the following. I'll then break it down. It was written by Tom Slater on 2-19-2023 at spiked-online.com:

"When the *Telegraph* revealed yesterday that Puffin, Dahl's publisher, has made 'hundreds of changes' to his beloved children's books, in line with suggestions from so-called sensitivity readers, the response was one of horror and disbelief. An author beloved by generations of children for his magical, spiky and sometimes sinister work has had his literary edges sanded off. All new copies will feature the newly cleansed text. Dahl's words and stories will be changed forever, no longer truly his own, all because some weirdo with a red pen thinks they know better. The philistinism, the cultural vandalism, is stunning."

Let's take that a piece at a time.

When the *Telegraph* revealed yesterday that Puffin, Dahl's publisher, has made 'hundreds of changes' to his beloved children's books,

A pretty-much straightforward statement, asserting something to be fact. One can accept this claim as factual with some degree of confidence, since the same thing has been stated by numerous sources—but be careful; a hoax can spread a plausible-sounding falsehood far and wide, before being uncovered as a hoax.

in line with suggestions from so-called sensitivity readers,

Note the "so-called." Realize the author is saying, "I don't really consider them 'sensitivity readers,'" or else he considers the term itself questionable.

the response was one of horror and disbelief.

The author is summarizing. It's his impression. It's not accurate to say *"the* response," as there were many; and he's likely not

Roald Dahl. – Public domain photo from Wikipedia

Changes to **James and the Giant Peach**	
2001 edition	**2022 edition**
queer ramshackle house	strange ramshackle house
Aunt Sponge was enormously fat and very short	Aunt Sponge was quite large and very short
One of those white flabby faces that looked exactly as though it had been boiled	A face that looked like a great soggy overboiled cabbage
She had a screeching voice	She had an annoying voice
those two ghastly hags	those two ghastly aunts
Aunt Sponge, fat and pulpy as a jellyfish	Aunt Sponge, pulpy as a jellyfish
Waving her fat arms and starting to dance around in circles	Waving her arms and starting to dance around in circles
In another minute, this mammoth fruit was as round and large and fat as Ant Sponge herself, and probably just as heavy	[removed]
They were like a couple of hunters who had just shot an elephant	They were like a couple of hunters who had just shot their prey

seen *every* response. I myself saw some responses that were lukewarm; others were approving. It's a judgment call to have said **"many** responses were"; it would not be accurate to say **"most** responses were" unless there were a reliable tally of "responses," and there was a reliable breakdown of how many expressed "horror and disbelief." It's perfectly legit to say, "Most of the responses I've seen were negative, some of them expressing horror and disbelief."

An author beloved by generations of children for his magical, spiky and sometimes sinister work

Another generalization, but if the author is knowledgable about Dahl's work and its popularity, he can make that generalization, and should be ready to defend it if he believes a specific challenge warrants that defense.

has had his literary edges sanded off.
Again, evaluation.

All new copies will feature the newly cleansed text. Dahl's words and stories will be changed forever, no longer truly his own,
Straight-forward statement.

all because some weirdo with a red pen thinks they know better. The philistinism, the cultural vandalism, is stunning.
Full-blown, unrestrained evaluation, to which the author is completely entitled.

Now, mind you, I'm not saying Tom Slater's paragraph was wrong, evil, an abomination, slipshod, or any of that. He's free to express his personal views, just as I am (I do it all the time; have you ever noticed?). It's just that you, as a reader, need to understand what is going on, for reasons explained above.

Once you get a smattering of *facts* and *opinions* when reading something like this (and in the process, distinguishing between the two), it's time to come up with your own questions. Here are a few of my own:
• Some people defended the publisher's changes by comparing it to editing, which most authors experience. But when an author is alive, he/she can respond to such edits, and agree to accept them or not.

| Changes to **Charlie and the Chocolate Factory** ||
2001 edition	2022 edition
Like all extremely old people, he was delicate and weak.	Like most extremely old people, he was delicate and weak.
"Tell Charlie about that crazy Indian Prince," said Grandma Josephine.	"Tell Charlie about that ridiculously rich Indian Prince," said Grandma Josephine.
"You mean Prince Pondicherry?" said Grandpa Joe, and he began chuckling with laughter. Completely dotty," said Grandpa George. "But very rich," said Grandma Georgina.	"You mean Prince Pudcherry?" said Grandpa Joe, and he began chuckling with laughter.
"Prince Pondicherry wrote a letter to Mr Willy Wonka."	"Prince Pudcherry wrote a letter to Mr Willy Wonka."
"The crazy prince"	"The prince"
A nine-year-old boy who was so enormously fat he looked as though he had been blown up with a powerful pump	A nine-year-old boy who was so enormous he looked as though he had been blown up with a powerful pump
Great flabby folds of fat bulged out from every part of his body, and his face was like a monstrous ball of dough.	Great folds bulged out from every part of his body, and his face was like a ball of dough.

If an author does not like the editing standards of a publisher, the author can take his work elsewhere, or self-publish. In this case, the deceased author cannot defend his work. More questions arise from this.
• Some people call this "censorship." My own understanding of the term is that only a government entity can perform censorship. What this publisher is doing might not be properly called censorship. (In contrast, when a government agency "suggests" or "requests" a privately-owned platform like Twitter or Facebook suppress certain viewpoints, which documentation has shown has happened, that is a fascist-style form of censorship; "fascist" in the sense of government dictating what a privately-owned company must do. —The American Heritage Dictionary of the English Language, 5th Edition.)
• Just what changes have been made? Examples accompany this article. I found these on many, many Internet sites. I believe they originated from **The Telegraph,** a daily United Kingdom newspaper. Some of these changes seem "innocent" enough, but... *is that really the point?* Or is the main point that they *are being made at all?*
• These changes were discovered for one deceased author. *Can we safely assume this is happening to other authors who are no longer able to defend their work?*
• (As the title asks) Is this cause for concern? (I do hope that question, by this point, is rhetorical.)

Several Twitter users, commenting on this topic, have quoted George Orwell's novel, *1984:*

"Every record has been destroyed or falsified, every book rewritten, every picture has been repainted, every statue and street building has been renamed, every date has been altered. And the process is continuing day by day and minute by minute. History has stopped. Nothing exists except an endless present in which the Party is always right."

(I've seen t-shirts saying "Make 1984 fiction again." Maybe it's time to actually buy one, and wear it proudly.)

I've handled hundreds of Bantam paperbacks published from the 1950s through the 70s (many of them with James Bama cover artwork), and was always impressed by a statement proudly made on their Copyright page. When indicating the paperback was a reprint of an earlier hardcover, a separate line in italics read: *"Not one word has been omitted."*

Perhaps publish-

| Changes to **Esio Trot** ||
2001 edition	2022 edition
Tortoises used to be brought into England by the thousand, packed in crates, and they came mostly from North Africa.	Tortoises used to be brought into England by the thousand. They came from lots of different countries, packed in crates.
But not many years ago a law was passed that made it illegal to bring any tortoises into the country.	But not many years ago a law was passed that made it illegal to bring any tortoises into the UK.
This balcony belonged to an attractive middle-aged lady called Mrs Silver.	This balcony belonged to a kind middle-aged lady called Mrs Silver.
...like saving her life or rescuing her from a gang of armed thugs...	...like saving her life or rescuing her from a gang of armed robbers...
Try to think how miserable it must make him feel to be so titchy! Everyone wants to grow up.	Try to think how miserable it must make him feel! Everyone wants to grow up.
"That's where all these tortoises in England come from, and a bedouin tribesman told me the secret."	"That's where some of these tortoises in England come from, and a local person told me the secret."

ers of integrity could express this sentiment (one by which I guide my own publishing efforts, when collecting public-domain fiction): *"This is the text as originally published."*

As far as offending delicate sensibilities, that can easily be taken care of. On the Copyright page of a book that I published is the following subtle note:

"These stories were published at a time when political correctness had not yet caused serious cultural and moral decay. Certain ideas, terms and social conventions found herein are no longer considered acceptable (some for rational reasons, others not). A mentally healthy reader (the kind for whom this book was lovingly compiled) will understand that, and not give the matter further thought."

A few other comments I found on Twitter and elsewhere:

Salman Rushdie: "Roald Dahl was no angel but this is absurd censorship. Puffin Books and the Dahl estate should be ashamed."

The Washington Post, in a 2-19-2023 online article:
"The changes in Dahl's children's books were done in partnership with Inclusive Minds, a collective for people who are passionate about inclusion, diversity and accessibility in children's literature, the Roald Dahl Story Company said."

From Inclusive Minds' website:
"Founded in January 2013, Inclusive Minds is a collective for people who are passionate about inclusion, diversity, equality and accessibility in children's literature, and are committed to changing the face of children's books."

Suzanne Nossel, chief executive of Pen America, tweeted: "At Pen America, we are alarmed at news of 'hundreds of changes' to venerated works by Roald Dahl in a purported effort to scrub the books of that which might offend someone.

"Those who might cheer specific edits to Dahl's work should consider how the power to rewrite books might be used in the hands of those who do not share their values and sensibilities."

mir_and_a on Twitter:
"I just bought 16 used Roald Dahl books so my future kids can read them as they were written without the input of an 'inclusivity' team. @penguinrandom Rewriting classics is an erasure of literary history, and morally reprehensible."

@RogerHelmerMEP on Twitter:
"Thomas Bowdler, who expurgated Shakespeare in the days when Victorians covered table legs for modesty reasons, is now rightly an object of ridicule. It can only be a matter of time before today's woke warriors, who have sanitised Roald Dahl, suffer the same fate."

[**Editor's note:** "bowdlerize" — "To remove material that is considered offensive or objectionable from (a book, for example); expurgate; To expurgate, as a book, by omitting or modifying the parts considered offensive; to remove morally objectionable parts; — said of literary texts." — The American Heritage Dictionary of the English Language, 5th Edition.]

Brendan O'Neill, The Spectator ("Britain's best weekly"), 2-19 at www.spectator.co.uk:

"What right do blue-pencil-wielding sensitivity readers have to drive the juggernaut of correct thought through Dahl's imaginary landscape?

"Every fashionable political belief of the 2020s is being crowbarred into Dahl's fictional universe. So Matilda no longer reads Rudyard Kipling – that imperial old brute! – but Jane Austen. One of Dahl's witches who posed as 'a cashier in a supermarket' is now a 'top scientist'. We wouldn't want any young witch to feel that the STEM subjects aren't for her. Words like 'crazy' and 'mad' have been excised, lest they appear to make light of mental-health problems. Even such everyday words as black and white are out. Characters no longer turn 'white with fear' and the Big Friendly Giant no longer wears a 'black cloak'. Why? In case a black kid feels offended when he reads that fantastic tale? The patrician urge of the sensitivity police to protect ethnic-minority children from certain words is infinitely more insulting to them than Dahl's tales could ever be.

"Let us be frank about what is going on here. This is a cultural purging. These arrogant alterations represent a profoundly censorious attack on one of Britain's best-loved writers. They can doll it up in the language of 'sensitivity' and 'inclusion' as much as they like, but to the rest of us it still smacks of a Stalinist correction of wrongspeak.

"Puffin's vandalising of Dahl's work was carried out in conjunction with an organisation called Inclusive Minds, a collective of sensitivity readers who are 'passionate about inclusion and accessibility in children's literature'. I find the modern use of that word 'inclusion' grimly fascinating. It so often means its opposite. When people say they are devoted to 'inclusion' it usually means they're devoted to excluding problematic people and difficult ideas. And so it is with the haughty overhaul of Dahl's world of make-believe: under the banner of 'inclusion' all sorts of words and characters and jokes are being excluded, bowdlerised [**Editor's Note:** There's that word again, with British spelling], blacked-out. (Sorry, I know you shouldn't say 'black' anymore.)"

Timothy Sandefur on Twitter:
BUY HARDCOPY BOOKS. OLD EDITIONS.

Changes to **George's Marvellous Medicine**	
2001 edition	**2022 edition**
	[Dedication added] This book is for doctors everywhere
He didn't have a brother or a sister.	He didn't have any siblings.
His father was a farmer	His parents were farmers
She had pale brown teeth and a small puckered-up mouth like a dog's bottom.	She had rotting teeth and a small puckered-up mouth like a dog's bottom, from years of frowning.
She certainly was a very tiny person.	She certainly was very small.
Her legs were so short she had to have a footstool.	It was as if she was shrinking, as she had to have a footstool.
Daddy says it's fine for a man to be tall.	Daddy says it's fine for people to be tall.
Owch	Ugh
Mummy washes them down the sink.	Mummy and Daddy wash them down the sink.
Mummy's as stupid as you are.	Mummy and Daddy are as stupid as you are.

Flash!

As this issue is literally being put together, we hear from our "London contact" (thanks, Matthew) that, according to The Evening Standard:

"Publishers Puffin UK has announced the release of the Roald Dahl classic collection 'to keep the author's classic texts in print', following criticism of recent editing of his work to remove potentially offensive language.

"The 17 titles will be available later this year and will include archive material relevant to each of the stories by the much-loved but controversial children's author.

"The classic collection will sit alongside the newly-released Roald Dahl books for young readers, which have been rewritten to cater for the sensitivities of modern audiences."

Reassuring, but... is this *still* cause for concern?

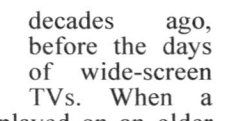

'Aspect ratio?' What's that?
And why should anyone care?

Images from The Wildcat, released by Kino

The aspect ratio is simply the shape of the screen image at your movie theater or on your TV.

Most viewers are not aware of it. Why should they be? It almost always remains constant. Not a factor.

It was an occasional issue, a couple of decades ago, before the days of wide-screen TVs. When a wide-screen movie was played on an older (narrower) TV, broadcasters had two choices: First, cut off the sides of the picture and move the viewing area back and forth to fit the TV screen—a technique called "pan and scan." I've seen interesting examples of what is lost when wide-screen movies, for example Lawrence of Arabia, are pan-scanned for TV. So much is lost, that the viewer sometimes wonders what's going on.

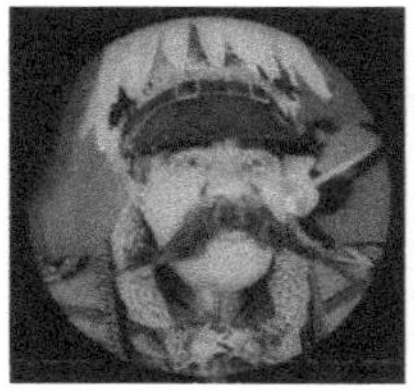

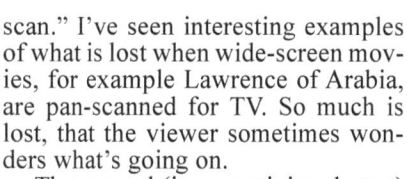

The second (in my opinion, better) choice is to shrink the entire image so it fits on the TV screen horizontally. That leaves black bars at the top and bottom of the TV screen—and yeah, I know, some people don't like that, but at least you're seeing the whole movie.

Other than that, the aspect ratio is of no concern to the viewer.

Unless the filmmaker tinkers with it! *Heh heh heh!*

I recently saw a dazzling example of that tinkering in The Wildcat, a 1921 German film. That's right—a movie over a century old features some creative, over-the-top aspect ratio manipulations. See examples below.

There are other reasons to seek out this film:

• It's pure wackiness. A soldier who is loved by hundreds of women (and called "Papa" by hundreds of children) meets a wild woman, a member of a gang of robbers living in the mountains. An unlikely romance? You bet!

• It's co-written and directed by Ernst Lubitsch, who created a body of great film work in his native Germany, then another body of masterpieces when he came to America: Ninotchka (1939 with Greta Garbo); The Shop Around the Corner (1940 with Jimmy Stewart; this story was remade with Tom Hanks and Meg Ryan as You've Got Mail); To Be or Not To Be (1942, with Jack Benny, Carole Lombard, and Robert Stack (hey, is that movie mentioned elsewhere, this issue?)); and more. The stylistic fingerprint of his films is called "The Lubitsch Touch," about which, more, anon.

• The "wildcat" is played by Pola Negri, born in Poland. She made movies in 1910s and 1920s Germany; came to America to make silent and later talking films; returned to Germany in the 1930s; fled Germany when the Nazis started their toxic goose-stepping; made her last film appearance in the Disney film The Moonspinners. Negri was a beautiful and talented actress.

• The sets look like they were designed by Dr. Seuss. A few examples are shown here. I kept pausing the DVD to get a good look at this architectural craziness.

My DVD of The Wildcat is part of a set, Lubitsch in Berlin. Several films in this set feature Negri. It's a few years old, and seems no longer available. But Kino Lorber is about to release a new version of The Wildcat on Blu-Ray. See **kinolorber.com** for details.

For other films with Pola Negri, see **grapevinevideo.com**.

The Plymouth Review Current

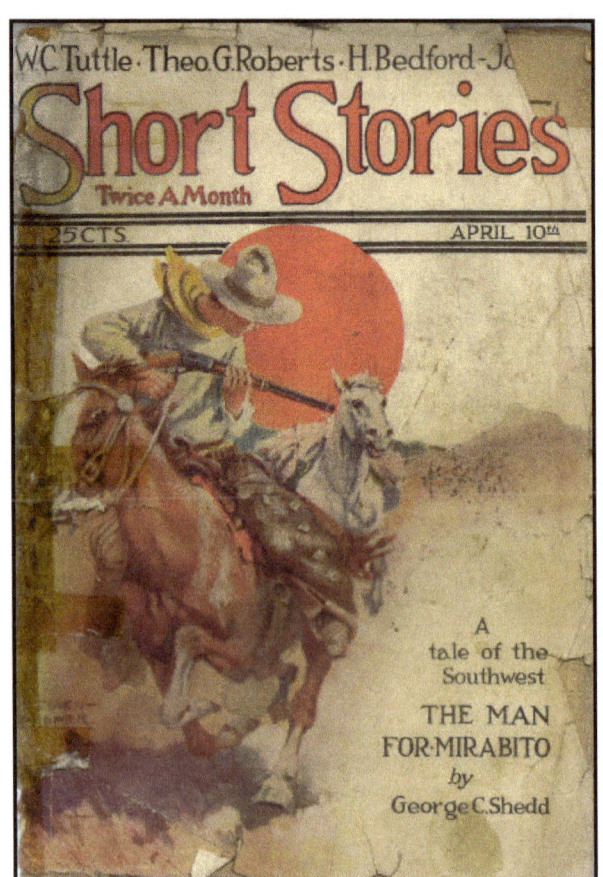

Taking you places worth seeing
Volume 12 • Issue 5 • April 2023

FREE!

Warner Brothers Celebrates Centennial
Saving the Work of WML

Nick Eggenhofer cover from 1922. — From philsp.com

April
2023

Cover image: Life on the Frontier, by William Messner-Loebs

Great Movies This Month

Mission of Benevolent Greed

PulpArtists by David Saunders: Nick Eggenhofer

Ask a Science Teacher, by Larry Scheckel: When I Buy a Candy Bar, How Does a Vending Machine Know that a Dollar Bill Is Real Instead of a Same-Size Sheet of Paper?

49 and a Half Shades of Collaboration, by William Messner-Loebs (excerpt)

IJ Helps WI, by Suranjan Sen, IJ.org

Get $2.35 Billion Worth of Books for Free, by Gale Pooley, FEE.org

Plymouth Arts Center Plans Two Events

Two Books Celebrate Farmall Tractor Centennial

Mission of Benevolent Greed

I am not usually aware of my skeletal system. And I don't consider the stretch of Hwy. 144 from my home to Random Lake to be especially bumpy. But just a few miles into my trip of March 1, 2013, the truck hit a section of road that sent corrugated waves through my bones. The resulting clacking of upper and lower teeth made me glad I wasn't in the habit of sticking my tongue out often.

This was only the first few miles of the trip! And how far did I have before me?

Six hundred miles? One way?? Twelve hundred miles of having my skeleton rattled around in that truck?

I looked in the rear-view mirror. Oh, right. There wasn't one. Two side mirrors. It was dark. The only thing I could see in those mirrors were headlights behind me. And you know how well you can estimate the location and distance of a car, relative to you, based only on headlights in the dark?

You *can't*.

And it started to rain.

Why was I making this trip?

Roberto Benigni's film, *The Tiger and the Snow*, was released in 2005. Amazingly, I first saw it when my wife gave me a copy for Christmas in 2012. Had I known of it earlier, I would have purchased and watched it immediately.

I commented thus on the the film at Barnes & Noble's site:

How did I miss this one??? After *Life is Beautiful*, I became a complete Roberto Benigni fan. This movie came out a few years ago, and I just saw it tonight. HIGHLY RECOMMENDED. Without giving a thing away, this is about a virtuously, nobly selfish man who WILL NOT GIVE UP. Not your typical Hollywood anti-hero. The greatest of civilizations, my friends, are made up of people like the main character in this movie.

It has to be a coincidence, right, that if you drop the last letter of Benigni's name, it spells...

Or maybe it's not.

The title, *The Tiger and the Snow*, describes a sign, an omen in the movie's story. "You will know [something], when you see a tiger in the snow." Esthetic crafting in books and movies sometimes requires that kind of coincidental sign. But real life doesn't offer up such tidy symbolism, does it?

Or maybe it does.

Why was I making this trip?

My ultimate destination was Brighton, Michigan, home of Bill Messner-Loebs.

Bill and I first got to know each other in early 2006. From then until 2012, we slowly worked on a comic book which I wrote and he drew: Human Interest Stuff, adapted from a story by Albert Payson Terhune.

Bill and his wife had suffered financial hardships for over a decade. They'd lost their home. All they owned was in storage lockers. They were living in a motel when I first contacted Bill in 2006.

To help them out, I sold original comic art pages from his series, *Journey*, on eBay. Sales were good. The market had never seen *Journey* originals before. The first few pages brought over $300 each, and went to places like Austria, West Wales, Canada, France, and many places within the US. Some of these buyers became more than customers, but friends, as I dealt more and more with them. After that initial frenzy, pages would go for $100 to $200 each.

This helped, but it wasn't enough. In early 2013, amidst continued financial difficulties, a new development rose to sink their spirits: They'd missed too many payments on their storage lockers. The contents were to be auctioned off on Feb. 19, Bill's 64th birthday.

Bill had posted this dismal fact on Facebook on Feb. 12. I did not see it until a few days later.

What could I do? Why hadn't he told me about this? I emailed him, expressing concern.

Bill replied: "What a pal you are! I'm sorry you had to find out about all this through Facebook, but I'm trying not to talk about it in front of Nadine, who was hit really hard by all this. We've had all this stuff in storage since the foreclosure and it was 6 massive one-car garages full of stuff. I tried various schemes to get them emptied, but trying to get folks organized and able to sort through things, especially when it wasn't killing heat, or killing cold or pouring rain—on a weekend when most people could do things was very hard. As you know, dreams die hard. I spoke to the storage people and it turns out they have to return everything obviously personal or legal. I mentioned the missing *Journey* artwork—looks like 1-12—and explained that it would have no real value to anyone but me. They promised to keep an eye out [for personal photos and papers]. I have not even the slightest clue where in all the bins [the art] might be. So, who knows what may happen? I'm depressed a bit, but not as depressed as I could be."

The original art for *Journey* 1 through 12? Wow!

What else would there be in lockers owned by a comic artist and writer? Correspondence with other creators? Drawings? Sketches? Scripts?

I didn't have the money to help out. No way. Very little savings. Part of my problem was the credit card debt I already had, the monthly fees of which ate into my finances viciously enough. I was happy with recent progress I'd made on one card, not charging anything on it and steadily lowering the balance farther from the card's limit.

How much (just for the sake of curiosity (I mean, nothing I could do about it, mind you)) did the storage company need, I asked Bill.

I was at work when he replied by email on Feb. 18: "So the actual deadline is tomorrow at 11 am. And they need [$x], which is half of what I owe, to stop the auction. This is the reason I never mentioned it to you. It just seemed impossible." He gave me the storage company's contact info, as I'd requested.

Oh. [$x]? A considerable sum. And that, only half.

What could be done? Have someone attend the auction in Michigan, and buy the good stuff? Who? Me? Then what?

> **Editor's / Author's Note:**
> This article is an abridged version of the title essay from the book, *Mission of Benevolent Greed*. Artwork accompanying this piece are from the book, and are Copyright © William Messner-Loebs

341

Empty the bins? Then what? Take it where?

Now what?

I did have enough available on that one credit card.

Wow. Now, wait just one moment. I'd better think about that. Cautiously.

I started walking. Walking, to be alone. To think with a clear mind. Contemplate this situation real well. Look at every angle. I walked until there were no people. No buildings. Just a flat, glaring-white, featureless plane on which the clicks of my footsteps faded off into the infinite. I stared ahead, but heard ominous, obscenely garbled laughter behind me. I pivoted on my heel and looked up. Three credit cards towered over me. I recoiled, but they leaned closer, over me, laughing. Things darkened.

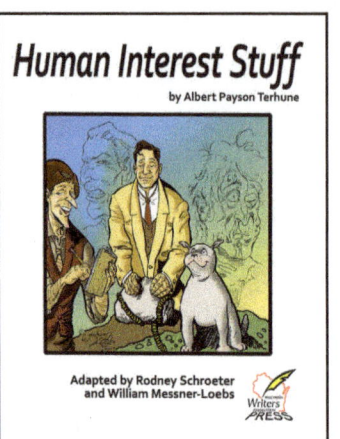

I heard a soft noise from behind. Spinning back 180 degrees, I stared over the totally calm, blue surface of Lake Michigan. Through the mist drifting over the water, on the other side of the lake, I could see something glowing. Something shiny, and very inviting.

The three gigantic credit cards loomed behind me, whispering their odious discouragement. But I heard another voice.

My own.

I blinked and stared at my computer screen. I willfully made myself aware of the florescent lights above, the conversations and other sounds in the large open office area. Down the aisle, a young man held a heavy coat tightly wrapped around himself. A woman walking to her desk wore a sweater that seemed to be about the fifth layer of clothing on her.

I wiped the sweat from my forehead.

I reviewed the numbers again. Wrote them down. Stared at them. [$x].

I called the storage place. Answering machine. I left a message.

Was it too late in the day? About 4:30 in Michigan. Closed?

I called. Answering machine. Message.

I called several more times.

I powered down my computer, left work (it wasn't really quitting time, but I was an independent contractor at that point, and came and went as I pleased), and started driving home.

I'd just have to call the storage place in the morning, though that was cutting it pretty close.

My phone rang.

It was the storage company. I verified the amount, and said I was prepared to pay the amount to stop the auction. But I could not dig out my credit card and read the number to her while driving. Heck, it's hard enough for me to even conduct a coherent conversation while concentrating on dodging the psychotics of the highway. I needed to find a place to park. Verifying that she would be in the office for awhile, I thumbed off.

I exited, drove around for several maddening minutes, and parked.

My phone rang.

My wife. I told her I was very glad she called, whatever the reason. This matter would have been better discussed with her face-to-face, but I had to act. Now.

What I told her was likely pretty non-linear, so I had to back up a bit before she understood what in the world I was talking about. I said I could make several times the [$x] I'd have to pay, by selling art (if I found it) and splitting the income with Bill.

She was supportive.

Go for it.

I called the storage company. She was as nice as Bill had said she was. She took my credit card number, and the auction was halted.

How many lockers were there?

Five.

Of varying sizes.

I thanked her, adding, "I hope I haven't ruined any plans for you to have a TV crew there, like on *Storage Wars.*" She laughed and said they'd planned no such thing.

But someone else had had plans. This manager later told me she'd received a call *that night,* asking, "So! Those lockers owned by William Messner-Loebs. Those are going on auction tomorrow morning, right?" When she'd informed the caller the auction had been halted, he'd responded, "Dang! *click*"

I made one more call. I told Bill what I'd done. He was quite happy, even going so far as saying this was the best birthday he'd ever had. When I asked if that weren't a bit hyperbolic, he said that sometimes, just the absence of pain was the greatest of rewards (or some such). I told him I hoped he wouldn't feel too much like Dr. Faustus in the weeks ahead.

All right. Now what?

The gears in my brain spun faster than usual, the next couple of days. Plans and alternatives zipped through my mind like a greyhound chasing a mechanical rabbit round and round and round the track.

Well, what *would* I do?

I'd store it all in the upstairs of my dad's barn. Yeah. That's the ticket.

I did some research on the 'net, trying to find what that would cost. Impossible. You couldn't estimate anything without talking to someone, and I didn't have enough specifics, anyway. Were we talking a semi-truck full? More?

At that point on my lifeline, my main "job" was part-time, hourly. My typical lackadaisical schedule consisted of a stop at the Random Lake Post Office at 8:30 or after, driving out to Hwy. 57, and heading south from there to Milwaukee. On such mornings, I passed Mueller's Sales and Service.

Driving past Mueller's south driveway the morning of Wednesday, Feb. 20, I saw a bright yellow truck parked with the rest of their used vehicles. In the truck's window was a big sign:

RENT ME

"When you see a tiger in the snow..."

No, no, no, it wasn't the same thing. Totally different. Apples and oranges.

Let's get one thing straight. My view of metaphysics doesn't entertain the idea of signs or omens. All right, I'll admit to liking M. Night Shyamalan's *Signs,* as a movie. But as I understand the relationship between reality and the human mind, there is an abundance of opportunities. I consider reality as tightly packed with opportunities, just as the physical world is tightly packed with resources. There are so many opportunities waiting for a receptive mind to recognize them that some of them seem too fortuitous, too providential, to be a coincidence.

It was a yellow, former Penske rental truck with the lettering painted over. It had an automatic shift. That was important.

The mental clockwork smoked furiously, the rest of that day. I stopped at Mueller's that night. "Oh, we'll give you a good deal on that truck, Rodney," I was told. "When do you need it?"

Friday, March 1, 2013. I'd wanted to start out with the truck that day, but we had an appointment that lasted and lasted. I would not get to Mueller's before they closed. I called them. They said I could just get in the truck and drive off with it.

Darn. I'd have liked some expert orientation on truck operation. I finally figured out how to open the latch at the back and gazed into its cavernous maw. My wife suggested I'd need a lock if I put anything valuable inside.

I dropped her off at home and got on my way.

I stayed that night in Green Bay, wasting many miles trying to find a hotel at an exit sign. The next morning, after scraping ice off the windshield with a credit card, I wasted many miles asking my phone's GPS to take me back to Hwy. 41, and twice being sent south instead of north.

Now, why would I drive over the top of Lake Michigan? Through the U.P.? Wasn't that a lot farther than driving through Chicago?

Well, yes, but not that much farther.

According to Mapquest, from Random Lake WI to Brighton MI via the U.P. was 597 miles, a trip of 10.5 hrs.

The route via Chicago would be 389 miles, and 6.5 hours.

I mean, look, an additional 200 miles, that's not so much farther. Not much... really. And an additional... well, four hours more of driving. That's not so much longer, considering the whole trip. It... it really wasn't that much of a difference in the grand scheme of things, was it?

All right, I'll admit it. I just didn't want to drive through Chicago. Sheer terror. Avoid that heckhole at any cost.

So I progressed up Hwy. 41, then 35, along the Lake Michigan coast. Very scenic.

I called my brother and asked if he would arrange to have the driveway leading to the barn plowed out. With the snow drifts as high as they were, I wouldn't have even been able to get the truck off the road before getting stuck.

At Escanaba, I drove onto Hwy. 2. I connected with I-75 at St. Ignace, heading south down to Flint, then onto 23.

My GPS's ETA for Brighton continually said I'd arrive a little after the 5:00 closing time for the storage office. I called the manager. She'd be there later than 5:00. Great.

It started to snow.

The Brighton exit at last. I found the place, parked, and staggered into the office.

"Guess who I am," I said.

She guessed. She gave me a map of the lockers and marked Bill's. I spied a vast selection of locks on the wall, and purchased a stout one. She gave me the keys and the secret code that would raise the gate.

Bill and Nadine had other plans they couldn't back out of that evening, so I was on my own. I maneuvered the truck in front of one locker and opened it.

A gigantic refrigerator, an old chair, bags and bags and bags. And a great deal of unidentified miscellanea.

I started to dig. I found several long boxes of comic books. More long boxes. Some of them falling apart, the comics spilling out. Those blasted long boxes, designed for comics collectors and dealers who were younger. I put these in the truck.

Some of these comics were copies Bill had picked up over the years; others were complimentary copies he received while working for certain companies; some (in multiple copies) contained his art or writing.

I put several mystery bags and boxes on the truck, just to get them out of the way. Things were piled nearly to the top of the bin, and my vision couldn't penetrate the Stygian blackness toward the back.

A long, cardboard portfolio. My pulse quickened. I brought it into the truck, switched on the electric lantern. Inside were about 100 signed and numbered prints by Bill, from 1982, of a mutated role-playing gamer. Heartbreakingly, every one was water-stained.

Two more portfolios. These were even better. They included *Journey* pages!

Sketchbooks of various sizes, some of them full of drawings. Excellent. A beautiful watercolor drawing of kids at play.

Smaller boxes from a publisher. I opened a few. Hundreds of copies of *Journey* comics. On the truck these all went.

I reached a point where I had to contort my body, twisting a leg this way, an arm another, to get into the bin, past the giant chair, behind the refrigerator, to get what I wanted. I was very much aware of things leaning toward me, wary of a deadly junkalanche.

Finally having had enough of this fun, I closed and locked the bin and snapped my new lock on the back of the truck. Finding a wonderful hotel, I carried several sketchbooks and portfolios to my room for further examination. I called my wife and assured her that, already, the trip had proven worthwhile.

Sunday, March 3, 2013. I entered the compound and went to work on the same locker. After awhile, I went to each of the other lockers, just to peek within. Mostly furniture in one. Unidentified boxes in another. I was doing well with the first locker, so I didn't move the truck.

As expected, Bill came along about noon. He got out of his car and studied me. I had no illusions about him remembering me from when I last saw him in-person—at the 1990 Chicago Comicon. At that time, I was just one of the hundreds of thousands, perhaps even millions of fans clamoring for his attention. At that convention, I'd arranged for him to draw his character Wolverine in a peaceful situation with an Indian. He said he'd do the drawing during the convention. So I looked for him, for two days, not finding him at his table. His presence must have been in great demand elsewhere. I told my wife I felt like Richard Kimball in *The Fugitive*. But I finally found him; he had my drawing; it was worth the pittance he charged for it.

We visited the other lockers together. In one, we found his early 1980s portfolio. He'd carried this to conventions, trying to convince comics publishers that he had talent. We are all fortunate that he succeeded in that quest. We couldn't open it; the zipper was green and rusted shut.

With the truck loaded to maybe 15% of capacity, I decided I'd reached my own physical capacity. Bill and Nadine treated me to dinner at a great Asian buffet.

I decided to drive back home via Chicago. With four hours less driving, I could possibly arrive back home at a reasonable time, instead of the middle of the night.

That trip through Chicago wasn't so bad, overall. I was in the express lanes a couple of times, zipping through Chicago, only then noticing the signs, "No trucks in Express Lanes." Every lane change was a risk with those side mirrors. And I dropped a few quarters on the pavement at the automatized toll stops, as I tried pushing them into slots with icy hands.

I got home around 9:30 p.m. and pulled up to the barn. There was no danger of getting stuck in the snow; my brother had seen that the driveway was plowed perfectly.

Monday, March 4, 2013. I took off from work and spent the day unloading the truck. I lugged everything into the bottom area of the barn, stacking long boxes of comics where once stood cows. I stacked the smaller boxes of *Journey* comics in another section, and built other miscellaneous stacks.

Within a few days, I had *Journey* pages and other items from the trip on eBay. I made arrangements with Bill to split the income, in a way that made us both happy.

Now, why would I do all this? Many hearing this tale would assume I'd done it altruistically and say, "Gee, you're a great guy for helping Bill out like that."

I wrote this account partly to dispel any false belief that I'd acted "unselfishly." I consider altruism, properly defined, to be a destroyer of values, happiness, and even life. If this trip, and my other efforts to help Bill, were altruistic, it would mean I didn't value him any more than I would a stranger. It would mean I'd be giving up values for lesser values, or non-values; that I'd have taken a loss.

Previously, when I sold *Journey* pages for Bill and absorbed the eBay / PayPal costs, yes, I was helping Bill out, but it was help I could easily afford. While I lost small amounts of money with each sale, it still wasn't altruism.

The [$x] I paid to stop the locker auction was large enough that, had there been no chance of financial gain for me, I would not have considered it. The money I hoped to make selling things from Bill's lockers was an important factor in putting up the [$x], but only one factor.

I value Bill because he helped me create *Human Interest Stuff*, a milestone in my life. For that alone, he'll have my support above and beyond what any stranger could ever expect from me.

Further, I consider his work, which I myself have enjoyed for many years, to be worth preserving and promoting. I can stand behind what Bill has achieved in his career. It would be very different if I'd purchased an abandoned locker and found it full of Jackson Pollack paintings. I'd violate my integrity and honesty by trying to convince people they were worth paying anything for.

It's in my self-interest to remember that Bill created (or otherwise legitimately acquired) the work (or goods) that I later sold for our mutual benefit. That's the virtue of justice. Does a rational person want to neglect or harm the source (whether some thing, or some one) of that which benefits him? Certainly not. A rational person would want to nurture and promote that beneficial source.

For these reasons, I am uncompromising when it comes to my ethical treatment of Bill. ("Ethical" in the context of Objectivism, the philosophy I've studied and lived by since 1971. Search the 'net for "Objectivist virtues" for more details; see Ayn Rand's work for even more details.)

The situation with me and Bill is an example of greed that promotes human life.

In our corrupt culture, it is necessary to distinguish between greed for the unearned, and greed for the earned. The first is destructive to human life, while the second advances human life and flourishing. But many do not make that distinction, and carelessly, or through innocent ignorance, or through dishonesty, simply say, "Greed is evil and destructive."

"Greed" is simply *wanting more.*

I wanted more money. But I was willing to work for it. I was willing to offer value for value, dealing with people honestly and fairly.

I also wanted more of Bill's work. I wanted to preserve his artwork, hold it in my hands, and enjoy it, even if I knew I would not keep most of it.

This *wanting more* led to my own benefit. But by acquiring the *more* through ethical means, all those I dealt with gained *more,* as well. Bill gained personal items he thought would be lost to him; he also gained money from my sales. Those who purchased from me gained art they valued. I heard from some of my customers how much they valued having original art from *Journey* comics they read and loved in the early 1980s. Among the intangibles Bill gained was my telling him there are still many people, world-wide, who highly value him and his work.

Now, OK, *wanting more* can become a destructive mania. Things have to be put into perspective in one's life—like washing one's hands, or spending money on hobbies, or exercising, or collecting something. Isolated, fixated upon, and divorced from reality, any one of those things can turn against one, or feed a neurosis, or be used as an excuse to avoid important aspects of one's life.

As an Objectivist, I consider it in my long-range, selfish interest to earn what I want, ethically. In the context of interacting with people who are free to deal with me or not, the only way I can acquire more money (or substantial non-monetary values) is to offer value for value. I could not (and would not want to) advance otherwise. Each sale of Bill's work was a win-win-win situation. I benefitted financially; Bill benefitted financially; the buyer received a piece he valued.

A movie character famously said, "Greed is good." This quote has been repeatedly held as morally contemptible. *As I understand* the quote (I've never seen the movie), I'd agree with that assessment, though perhaps not for the same reasons. It implies it's OK to want and get more through any means, a view expressed in the phrase, "It's just business." But business requires the same virtues that are required by a commitment to one's own life, friendship, romantic relationships, or any rational endeavor—virtues including honesty, justice, and integrity. Only when those virtues are applied to one's business relationships can one deservedly, proudly call oneself a businessperson, or a capitalist.

Rational self-interest and rational greed are creators of values and wealth. *Wanting* more in a free society leads to *creating* more, offering more values available for trade or sale. A society becomes wealthier, in proportion to the freedom and ambition of its individuals.

In the months following this and other trips, I would sell *Journey* pages, sketchbook drawings, graphic novels, and comics from Bill's long boxes. Among the items I would find:

• Various comics signed by their creators to Bill. This included four early issues of the *Teenage Mutant Ninja Turtles.*

• A comic with four covers. I've seen double covers several times in my collecting career. I've even seen a triple cover (maybe twice). But never before this, a quadruple cover.

• Early drawings by Bill.

• Bill's birth certificate.

• Three spiral sketchbooks almost filled with finished drawings, doodlings, and studies for faces.

• A Mattel Junior Detective ID, with a small photo of an 11-year-old Bill. I told Bill about this before I sent it to him. He recalled that it also came with a pair of handcuffs, a gun, and a shoulder holster for the gun. "I never was much good with shoulder holsters," he told me wryly, "so I'd stick the gun in my belt."

• The original art from several issues of *Journey.* Some of this I sold through Heritage Auctions instead of on eBay.

• Hundreds if not thousands of clipped articles, recipes, and store coupons. Most of these last were expired by years, of course, but I did find one that made me shout with glee: a 15-cent coupon for a package of wieners, with No Expiration. When I put that one to the test, the grocery store clerk passed it under the scanner several times before looking at it perplexedly. But it was good!

• A money order made out to Bill for $14.00. Though nearly 20 years old, he was able to cash it.

• Tons of fan mail (some from other comics pros).

There was a big value at risk here. Bill's storage lockers. But there was also Bill and Nadine. When you've lived at the edge for so long, it sometimes happens that you get too close to that edge. You start teetering, but all it takes is for someone to recognize the situation, to reach out, grab an arm (or even an empty sleeve), stop you from falling into the abyss, pull you back from that precipice, and stabilize you once again.

* * *

As the years went by, I continued selling Bill's work on eBay. But with me in Sheboygan County, and he being in central Michigan, working together was difficult.

Fortunately, Bill found a new Patron of the Arts in Mike Jones, who lived near Bill. Jones asked to purchase what I still had in my possession from Bill's lockers. So I loaded up the car (and it was a *full* load!), took the ferry across Lake Michigan, and handed everything off to Jones. Bill joined us. Once

Jones paid me in cash, I counted out half of that cash and handed it to Bill. It was our last financial transaction.

But not our last personal transaction.

* * *

To learn more about Bill Messner-Loebs:
- Join the Facebook group, Fans of William Messner-Loebs. Mike Jones is the admin.
- Go to YouTube.com and search on "Messner-Loebs." You'll find many interviews.
- Buy a copy of *Mission of Benevolent Greed* from Barnes & Noble or another bookstore. The publisher's share of the book price will go to Bill Messner-Loebs.

The Plymouth Review Current
TAKING YOU PLACES WORTH SEEING
Volume 12 • Issue 5 • May 2023

FREE!

Movies ♦ Art ♦ Events ♦ Things ♦ Eudaimonia
Jon Wos: Realizing Romanticism

The publication that respects your intelligence

Allegories • Aphorisms • Idioms • Colloquialisms

May
2023

Cover image: Jon Wos, Assembling a Raven
Great Movies This Month
Realizing Romanticism, by Jon Wos
Ask a Science Teacher, by Larry Scheckel: Can Lead Be Turned Into Gold?
'Alive in the Arts' Entries Now On Exhibit
PulpArtists by David Saunders: R. Farrington Elwell
A Celebration of Story-Telling
Popular Arts Tour Returns

All four panels, installed in a northern Wisconsin home.

One of the four stained glass panels, ready for transport.

Realizing Romanticism

by Jon Wos

Editor's Notes:

In 2021, Jon Wos invited several people (Your Editor among them) to his Oshkosh home, where he gave a practice run of a talk and slide show he prepared.

Jon then gave this talk to a small group at TOS-Con in Boston, 2021. It was so successful and popular that TOS-Con organizers asked Jon to give the same talk to all attendees at the following year's conference, in Denver. (Your Editor was present at both conferences.)

The Objective Standard then published Jon's talk in its Fall 2022 issue, accompanied by 46 photos and artworks. That issue can be purchased at theobjectivestandard.com/issues/

With Jon Wos' permission The PRC here reprints the talk he delivered at TOS-Con.

For reasons of space, we could not reproduce all images used by The Objective Standard. Original numbers of the images have been retained. That is why, as you read the article, there are gaps.

A few images are not in numerical order.

In May 1981, my parents were looking forward to their first child. My arrival, however, was *not* what they anticipated.

It was immediately evident that something was wrong. My body appeared to be broken. And X-rays showed that I had thirteen broken bones. Most of these were from the process of being born, but I also had fractures sustained in the womb, plus evidence of others that had healed before birth. Twenty-four hours after I was born, I was diagnosed with osteogenesis imperfecta—OI for short.

OI is a group of genetic disorders that prevent the proper formation of the connective tissue collagen. The primary manifestations of the disorder are fragile bones and short stature, but it can also include weak joints, fragile teeth, hearing loss, and even lung, heart, and neurological problems. Here (fig. 1) you can see my baby teeth capped in silver to prevent them from chipping or breaking off.

My parents had to deal with the risk of breaking my legs when they changed my diaper or breaking my ribs and arms when they picked me up. My early childhood was rife with fractures, casts, hospitals, and surgeries. By the time I was ten, I'd fractured my right forearm *alone* about ten times, and the forearm bones had fused together. The first time I remember breaking my right arm was when I fell out of my wheelchair in the parking lot before going to see Santa with my grandmother. It wasn't all bad, though. I insisted on seeing Santa before we went to the hospital, broken arm or not.

But broken femurs were the worst. They were the most painful and took the longest to heal. I had several surgeries in an attempt to straighten my femurs and thereby reduce fractures. But they continued. Most of these fractures required a spica cast, which went from chest to toes and was kept on for an average of three months. They kept me immobile and were uncomfortable, hot, and itchy.

My fractures were unpredictable. One day I could fall off a chair and not break anything, but the next I could break my arm while drying my hair with a towel. My life could be stopped and my physical freedom taken from me at any random time. This looming uncertainty caused a lot of anxiety at an early age.

But this is not to suggest that it was always fractures and casts. Although I was born with unfortunate genetics, I was also born with an amazing family, who brought immense joy to my life. Living on a dairy farm until I was about ten made finding things for me to do challenging, as most of the activities of farm life are pretty physical. But I insisted on keeping up with my peers, fractures or not. I did everything from making straw bale tunnels to racing my brother on the four-wheeler with my wheelchair. Unavoidably, though, there were times when my condition kept me from physical activity, and I often turned to art.

I loved to create and considered myself an artist before I could even say the word, proudly telling everyone I was an "arsonist" as I peddled my drawings to family at holidays. This (fig. 3) is one of my grandmother's favorites, being the comedian she was, for if you can read my writing, you will see I could draw a horse before I could spell it. The form of creation didn't matter: drawing, blocks, Legos, painting. I could always undertake *something* creative, even when I had a fracture. It gave me both physical and mental stimulation when I needed it most. I started out aiming very high with my creative endeavors. I wanted to build Lego cathedrals and mansions out of Lincoln Logs. My dad likes to talk about how I would get so frustrated with him because he couldn't help me build a three-story, five-bedroom mansion out of Lincoln Logs.

(1) Me as a child, showing my capped teeth

(3) *Hores and Buggy*, **1991**

(7) *Imperfect Bone Origin*, **2005, glass and ceramic**

In middle school, I began experimenting with oil paint, inspired by my virtually religious commitment to watching Bob Ross on TV. By the time I started high school, I was well versed in the Rossian technique. I focused on drawing and painting, but I actively sought to try as many different media as I could. My middle- and high-school teachers, Mrs. Voight and Mr. Dickson, were excellent. They let me spread my creative wings in all media and helped me develop some of my artistic foundations. I tried everything, from metalwork, to ceramics, to stained glass. I was particularly drawn to glasswork. I began creating stained glass at home on my own and, by the end of high school, I was doing commissions for teachers and family friends.

Amid all the experimenting with different media, I continued to draw and paint. I often didn't have much concern for or even understanding of the subjects I chose. That was partly because I focused simply on learning how to master the techniques in the different media—but also because I didn't understand myself psychologically, or what drew me to certain subjects.

By this point, my fracture rate was declining due to increased bone and muscle mass, as well as a better understanding of how to mitigate the risks. However, even with the lower frequency of fractures, I was still dealing with the psychological consequences of my condition: anxiety and depression (fig. 4). Art was one of the few things that melted these away—except when I was assigned self-portraits. I hated doing them because they brought my anxiety and depression to the fore, effectively advertising things I tried to hide as best I could (fig. 5).

I made it through high school and started college at the University of Wisconsin, Oshkosh, in 1999, pursuing a bachelor's in fine art. Early on, I focused on studying drawing, but I couldn't give up my love of glass. I sought to expand what I had learned creating stained glass. At the end of high school, I had taken a workshop on glass bead making, in which I learned to use a small table torch to melt glass rods into beads. This form of glass sculpting is called lampworking. I was in love with it and wanted to delve deeper, but there were no glass programs or classes available at my university. So, my amazing sculpture professor, T. C. Farley, set me up with a small glass station in the sculpture studio so I could study lampworking independently. The new space he supplied enabled me to create new things, including marbles and large pendants.

Soon, I became interested in using glass to make more complex things. I started a series of glass sculptures drawing on the analogy between the material and my own body. I focused, though, not on my fragility, but on *overcoming* it. The theme was: Even with bones of glass, I can still accomplish what I want in life.

This (fig. 7) became my final project for sculpture class—a skeleton about half my size, sitting on a ceramic rock. Essentially, it is a self-portrait symbolizing my precarious life and my perseverance.

Then I met Li Hu, a drawing and painting professor at the university (fig. 8). I was blown away by his skill and passion. I was also enthralled by his life story. He was an adolescent during the so-called Cultural Revolution, launched by Mao Tse-tung in China. His father was sent to a labor camp, and Li was sent to work in the rice fields, not even allowed to attend high school. However, he overcame these barriers. He got into Shanghai University Fine Arts College in 1984 and learned the ways of traditional masters. Four years later, he was teaching there, and he came to America a few years after that.

Li's work is monumental in scale—his largest painting, *Birds of Nu Woh,* is sixteen feet by forty-two feet—and he was prolific. I took every class I could from him, studying portraiture and the human figure, primarily by drawing live models. He taught me the foundational skills to re-create any subject I chose, whether in charcoal, pastel, watercolor, or oil paint. Much to my dismay, one of his favorite assignments to improve our drawing skills was self-portraiture. Some semesters, Li assigned one or two dozen self-portraits. Self-portraits are one of the most convenient ways to learn portraiture. After all, you always have a model right there in front of you. But there was more to Li's preference than mere convenience.

This (fig. 10) was one of the first assignments where he asked us to do more than just a straight-up portrait from a mirror; he asked for a self-portrait that showed something beyond our physical likeness. I reflected on what I had dealt with and how far I had come—from fractures, to surgeries, to psychological struggles. This piece ended up being a major professional boost for me—in part because it won the top award of $10,000 in a national show for artists with disabilities. But more important, this painting started me on a path of introspection. I reluctantly began working with more self-portraiture, driven by a higher confidence from winning the award, Li's direction, and the goal of understanding my own psychology. My work was becoming my diary, each painting like a page in a growing book.

(10) *Self-Introspection,* 2003

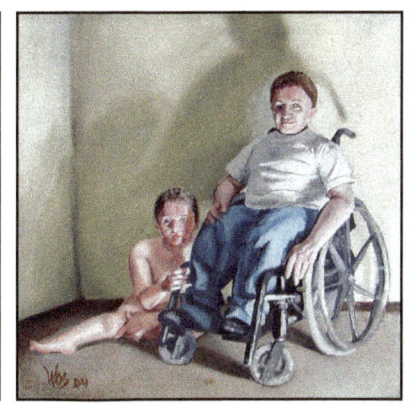

(12) *Gemini,* 2004

I began using my work to come to terms with my experiences and identity. Dealing with OI will always be part of my life, and I need to put in the effort to make doing so as easy as possible. Although having OI is out of my control, I can control how I deal with it. Being honest and vulnerable through my work was a challenge, but Li's assignments helped push me forward.

One of these was to paint a double self-portrait (fig. 12). One version had to show how I saw myself, and the other had to show how I thought others saw me. Li got us to ask an important question of ourselves and, in answering this question, I was more honest with myself about my own psychology than I had been before. Others would often tell me how brave and strong I was and how happy I seemed, but this was not how I saw myself. I saw myself as weak and fearful, and I would often hide behind the persona others created for me.

I had a major surgery coming up the following semester, to remove the plate from one of my femurs and replace it with a rod down the center. I was dreading it. I was also overwhelmed by my new freedom and the responsibility of living on my own, overwhelmed with college, overwhelmed with loneliness. I was overwhelmed by life and didn't have the self-esteem to combat my sense of futility.

Jon Wos is represented by Quent Cordair Fine Art. To view many of his works, and for information on purchasing art prints and original works, please visit **Cordair.com**

I had struggled with depression and suicidal thoughts throughout high school. In college, on snowy days, I had an unusually hard time getting to class and back in my wheelchair. On one occasion, I reached a tipping point, my mind broke, and I tried to take my own life. Afterward, this was something I had to come to terms with and find a way to heal. Creating self-portraits, it turns out, was one such method. This painting (fig. 13) is painful, but it is something I should never forget. It is important to me in that it represents my rebirth—in the sense that my suicide attempt showed me that there is something hard I must face.

I have always felt a dualism within myself. I could swing dramatically from being very optimistic to being deeply cynical, even nihilistic. Creating art was one area of my life where I could escape this feeling. Being an artist was more than just a professional aspiration for me, but I couldn't really explain why.

So, it was serendipitous that, around this period, I read *The Fountainhead* by Ayn Rand, at the suggestion of a good friend. *The Fountainhead* sparked something in me like nothing before had. It moved me intellectually, aesthetically, and spiritually. I wanted to create art that motivated me like *The Fountainhead* did. There were so many important things in it that made me think deeply, so many things I got from it. Primarily, though, was that Rand showed me, through her character Howard Roark, what I needed to gain: a *self.* Roark asks the question; "And isn't that the root of every despicable action? Not selfishness, but precisely the absence of a self?" This question started me down a whole new road.

I graduated from UWO in 2005 with a bachelor of fine art, with an emphasis in drawing, painting, and sculpture. While my senior show was still hanging, the gallery curator of a local college, Ripon College, saw it and asked if I would create a larger collection of self-portraits for a solo show there.

This pushed me to introspect even deeper. It would be my first solo show, and I had a year to create enough work to fill the gallery. Delving further into self-portraiture while devouring everything I could by Rand, my perspective began to change. This new self-portrait series would again start with my past. I realized that I could not ignore my past struggle or its importance to understanding myself. But, more than ever, I would stress the value in overcoming adversity.

I started with a series of twelve small paintings that hang like a filmstrip, each symbolizing a week in a spica cast, twelve weeks being the average to heal a femur. The series included the roller coaster of emotion that accompanies a major fracture: from the pain and fogginess (fig. 14) to the unavoidable boredom (fig. 15), even the small joys and pleasures that helped me forget about the state I was in (fig. 16), ending in the longing to be free (fig. 17) and the inevitable, indescribable, feeling of being free from the cast (fig. 18). These experiences are important to me as a simple reminder of how much I love my freedom and of the fact that I can overcome fractures—a reminder to take full advantage of every moment of freedom that I can.

This is *Pity Party* (fig. 19), which expresses the view that life is only struggle, only about escaping pain, that it is futile to try for anything beyond that. It is about hopelessness, apathy, and nihilism—about playing the victim. *And* it's about the fact that this leads to more depression and anxiety, a self-fulfilling cycle—the most futile of all. This is the view that I needed to purge. Rand's work caused me to question the value of pity. I could now admit how much I disliked being pitied, but also that I sat in self-pity far too often, wasting the time during which I was free of the cast. Having been completely helpless at many times in my life, and having little to no self-esteem, I implicitly held that pity was the only currency I could rely on. Self-pity gave me excuses to give up and not even try. Dwelling on the negative earned me pity from others and fooled me into feeling justified for giving in to resignation.

(8) *Li Hu*, 2017

This painting (fig. 20) is about my shift away from *Pity Party*, to looking ahead rather than only backward. Through art and Rand's philosophy, called Objectivism, I was beginning to understand myself, which resulted in a shift of perspective. I started to heal my soul, to get out of my head and enjoy life, to focus on and act on positive thoughts. I realized that I have free will and am not doomed to dwell on the negative. Life is not about avoiding death but about achieving happiness.

These elements—free will and a focus on achieving values or overcoming obstacles—is the province of Romantic art. Such art, as Ayn Rand put it, is about what might and ought to be. It is a source of optimism because it is about choices and values and what can be changed for the better. And it stands in contrast to Naturalism, the school of art that denies free will and focuses on life allegedly as it is and can only be.

A quote from Rand's *The Romantic Manifesto* really struck me in this regard. She wrote:

Consider the significance of the fact that the Naturalists call Romantic art an "escape." Ask yourself what sort of metaphysics—what view of life—that designation confesses. An escape—from what? If the projection of value goals—the projection of an improvement on the given, the known, the immediately available—is an "escape," then medicine is an "escape" from disease, agriculture is an "escape" from hunger, knowledge is an "escape" from ignorance, ambition is an "escape" from sloth, and life is an "escape" from death. If so, then a hard-core realist is a vermin-eaten brute who sits motionless in a mud puddle, contemplates a pigsty and whines that "such is life." If that is realism, then I am an escapist. So was Aristotle. So was Christopher Columbus.[1]

I was fine being labeled an "escapist" as well, because I was escaping that which *should* be escaped: pain, depression, and anxiety. My life would never be what I wanted it to be if I just settled

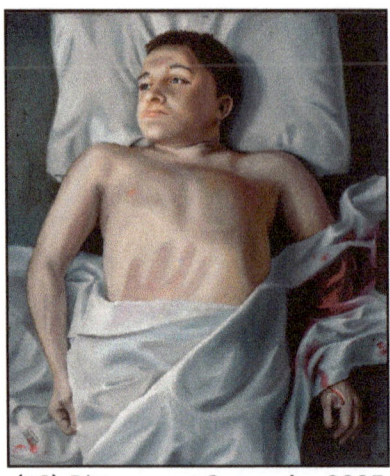

(13) *Bittersweet Surrender*, 2005

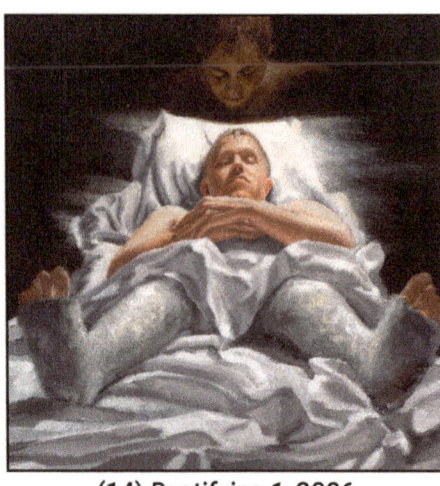

(14) *Rectifying 1*, 2006

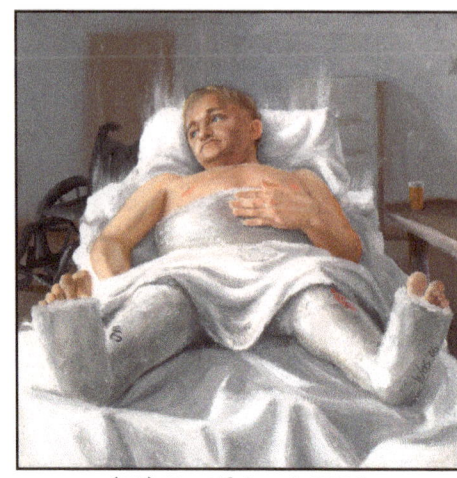

(15) *Rectifying 4*, 2006

for the given.

I was re-creating my relationship with myself, eliminating my self-pity so I could push myself to greater heights. My self-confidence was growing. After I graduated college, I took a trip to the Grand Canyon with some friends, which was the first time I had traveled that far without family or my usual safety net (fig. 21). This was something I had to do in spite of my anxiety about it. The dreaded surgery to rod my other femur was successful, and I was now able to walk short distances without aid for the first time in my life. I was even able to climb around on the edge of the Grand Canyon.

I could now see the view I wanted to have of myself and of existence. By coming to terms with my past, accepting my identity, and clarifying my values, I could finally look to the horizon and set realistically challenging goals.

This painting (fig. 22) symbolizes the opposite of *Pity Party*. My life should be celebrated, not pitied. It is a reminder to always work to improve my self-image, that it is a never-ending process, that giving life meaning and setting goals and standards isn't really possible without self-esteem.

Valuing one's self is the first and primary value. Anything I gained from self-reliance was tenfold more fulfilling than all I could gain from the pity of others. It is impossible to accept the love of others when you don't love yourself. I had been habitually skeptical of others' sincerity, feeling that the praise and friendship ultimately were out of pity. Not until I could objectively agree with them, by my own standards and judgment, did I even begin to accept some truth in what others say.

I wanted to see myself more clearly and objectively (fig. 23). Only then could I see the world more clearly and work better within it. I realized that an inaccurate view of myself inevitably leads me to set unrealistic standards. Just as we need standards for measuring the world, we also need standards for measuring our values. This need became all the more real to me after grasping Rand's point in *The Romantic Manifesto* that art is fundamentally a concretization of one's values, an essential psychological need.

Romantic art is particularly important because it highlights the fact that we have free will and focuses on how things ought to be. As such, it can sharpen how we evaluate our choices and values. This focus on values can prompt deep introspection, which is vital for a healthy, growth-oriented mind-set.

My feelings began to catch up with my new perspective. I was the most confident I had ever been (fig. 24). I started doing talks like this, which would have been unthinkable just a few years before. I also started driving my artwork all over the country. Both of these gave me anxiety, but I pushed myself to do them anyway.

Comparing these self-portraits with those

(19) *Pity Party*, 2006

(20) *Leaving the Pity Party*, 2009

(21) *Gemini United*, 2006

(16) *Rectifying 8*, 2006

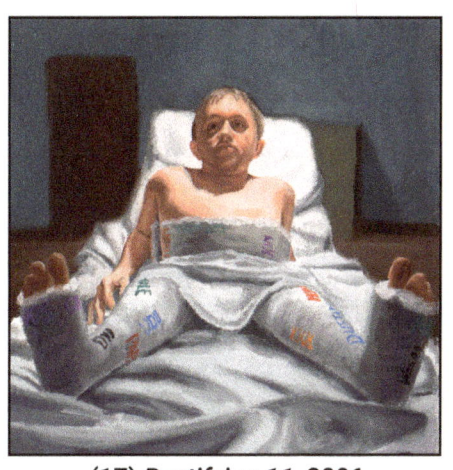

(17) *Rectifying 11*, 2006

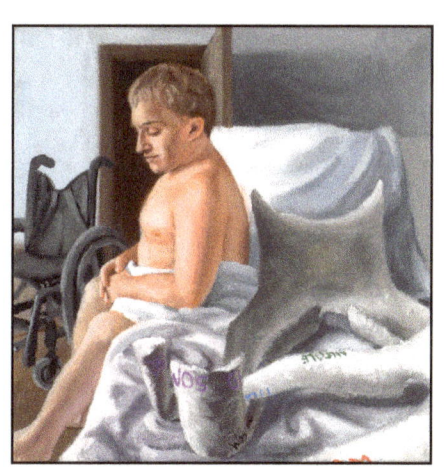

(18) *Rectifying 12*, 2006

Before...   ...and After—

(25) *Leaving a Bad Philosophy*, 2009

(26) *Building a New Philosophy*, 2009

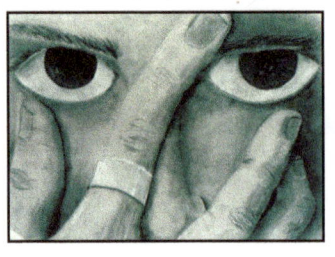

(4) Self portrait, 1997

(5) Self portrait, 1996

Early in life, the philosophy Jon held was a non-systematic, piecemeal collection of ideas that were ready to collapse at any moment (image at top). The result: The self-images above.

(32) *Atlas Rests on Reason*, 2014

(24) *Self Made*, 2008

Jon discovered the plans for a better philosophy. But those plans needed to be made real, in a form he chose for his own life. He built on a solid foundation, constructing each level on what he'd carefully built before. The result is stable, sturdy, and elegant (image at top). The practical result of that philosophy: The satisfaction of his self-recreation, above.

Jon's talk is on YouTube!
https://www.youtube.com/watch?v=0x9AuX7xSgo

(22) *Commemoration*, 2006

(23) *Clarifying Self*, 2010

I did in high school (fig. 5), it is obvious how my perspective of myself has changed. I'm now able to grasp the significance of details I included in my early self-portraits even more clearly than when I created them: the cracked mirror, looking away from myself, the colorless reflection. I now felt a sense of harmony as I continued to introspect and see that I was ultimately responsible for my *self*. I realized that much of my anxiety came from my reliance on others, and it was dissipating as I learned to rely on myself.

This is not to suggest that I do not get help from my awesome family and friends sometimes, but I am speaking about self-reliance in a psychological, even spiritual, sense. Rand said we are beings of "self-made soul," and I now understood what this means. You are the only one with direct access to your soul. You are the only one who can truly feel it. You can show aspects of your soul to others, but they can never perceive it directly the way you can. It is a universe within a universe that only you can sense directly—and *shape*. The choices you make and the development of your character can only be done by you. Others can certainly help through guidance and example, but ultimately the work is yours. In that sense, psychologically speaking, we are all islands and, therefore, are self-made.

I could now clearly see the power of philosophy. This is how other philosophies made me feel (fig. 25). Each brick is an idea piled on the others, trying to reach for something. But it is a disintegrated mess doomed to topple, stifling your potential rather than improving your life. I needed to see, concretized, the attitude I should have about life. This is how life should feel (fig. 26); a proper philosophy gives you a deliberately integrated foundation of wisdom, enabling you to achieve soaring heights. These two paintings are meant to hang together, in contrast, as a reminder that philosophy should not be confusing and disconnected from reality but should instead be a tool for furthering one's own life and purpose. I now fully accept that life is knowable, happiness is possible, and that it is mine to achieve.

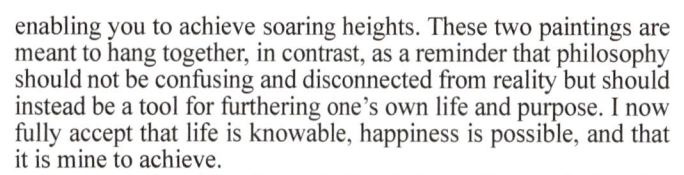

Each painting led to the next, all pointing to the conclusion that I was becoming a Romantic artist.

My love of stained glass never diminished, and I continued to create it between paintings. This is my dining room window, my most extensive glass project, which I created completely for myself (fig. 27). It contains 2,293 pieces of glass and is a little less than three feet by four feet. It is the tree of knowledge, specifically the knowledge that life is all about continual growth, progressing in small steps, piece by piece. It reminds me that I am better than I was yesterday and that tomorrow can be even better than today. This knowledge helps me enjoy the now.

While I created this piece for myself, I was simultaneously building a small art business, doing commission work, and selling pieces in galleries, some of which were glass. I also did a few residencies in schools, where I taught and painted murals with the students.

But commissions filled most of my professional time. I did everything from mosaics to pets (fig. 29), but portraits became my biggest request. I did dozens and dozens of them.

A few years ago, having done so many of them, I needed a break. For a period, I turned my attention to still life. I was curious about how to make the simplest things more interesting (fig. 32). I have come to deeply enjoy creating still lifes. They are like little meditative moments. I can spend days

(27) *The Tree of Knowledge*, 2008

or weeks selecting the objects, the arrangements, and the lighting. From the start, my goal hasn't changed: Make everyday life more dramatic, even exciting. In essence, we all design our lives with the objects we surround ourselves with, and we need to be reminded of our values as often as possible, to stay focused on them, because it is easy to get overwhelmed. We need the important things to be pointed out, emphasized, and integrated with day-to-day life.

As an analogy, I often think back on how, most fundamentally, my mentor Li Hu helped me become a better artist. Ultimately, he taught me to pay closer attention to what I perceive. He helped reveal things that were right in front of me but that I could not fully see, in part because I was overwhelmed by the magnitude of perceptual data coming in. He would walk around the class as we were drawing a model, coming up to each of us and pointing out what we were not seeing.

He would say simple things, such as, "pay more attention to this area," or "there is a reflection on that object that is missing." From then on, I would see instances of such reflections everywhere, even on relatively nonreflective surfaces. They were now glaringly evident, like when you learn a new word and it seems to pop up everywhere all of a sudden.

Still life works this way, too. It shows us what to look for to make every moment special, so that, like hearing a newly learned word everywhere, we can spot these special moments in our day-to-day lives and make life that much more interesting.

But little makes life more interesting and worthwhile than the people we surround ourselves with (fig. 34). Unlike a still life, or even a landscape, the subjects are always one of a kind. The objects in a still life can be replaced, a beautiful scene can be revisited, but the people in your life and the moments you share with them are irreplaceable (fig. 35). Other people can be the source of our greatest joys, and given that we are all inherently finite and irreplaceable, portraits can move us the most. Portrait painting is about more than just capturing a likeness. It is also about capturing emotion, or a shared moment, or the love between two people, or the reverence one feels for someone.

Li had become more than just my professor. He became my mentor and my friend. And shortly before he passed away, I was able to do this portrait of him (fig. 38). Li's love of creation and passion for his work were profound. He told us: "When I am working here, when I am staying in my house, every day I want to go down, even if I don't paint. I just look at my paintings, just like the way you look at your baby, you know you enjoy it, that's your kids!"

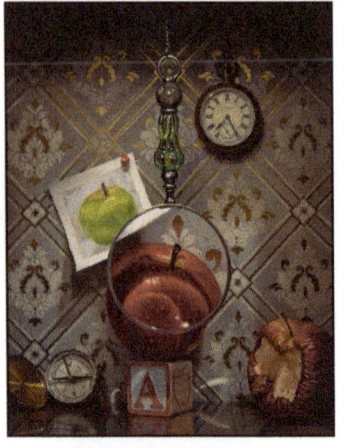

Li would often tell us that passion is more important than talent (fig. 39). What I think he meant was not that passion is a better guide than reason but, rather, that in a certain context, passion has primacy over skill. Your passion for something must be more powerful than disappointment. In other words, my desire to create art was always stronger than the desire to avoid the inevitable stumbling and disappointments involved in learning how to create it. My passion or love of creation is the source of my skill,

(29) *Tilly,* **2009**

(34) *Enlightenment Women,* **2019**
This was used as the cover art for the Winter 2019 issue of
The Objective Standard.

(40) *Life in Focus,*
2022, oil on linen panel

as it is what drove me to develop and improve my skill. My passion came first, and the skill followed. When my passion fades, my skills go unused.

And I realize now that this is applicable to my whole life, beyond just the creation of my work. Passion for my whole life should be stronger than the impulse to avoid the pain it involves. Li Hu and Ayn Rand showed me their passion for life through their work, and they fueled my fire within like no one ever had before. That I was so fueled simply by seeing their example was proof to me of the power of a vision, a vision of the ideal, the essence of Romanticism.

This is best summed up by a quote from The Fountainhead: "Don't work for my happiness, my brothers—show me yours—show me that it is possible—show me your achievement—and the knowledge will give me courage for mine."[2]

I want, and implicitly always have wanted, to show a reverent view of reality. But I have learned that holding a reverent view of life is not automatic. Our minds can focus on only so many things at a time. And what you focus on, you will see everywhere. If you are always focused on the negative, then that is what you will look for and find as a matter of habit. If you can make it a habit to direct your focus to the good, the positive, then there will be less room in your lens for the negative (fig. 40). Whatever you set your gaze upon gets magnified; what you shine your light onto becomes clearer. So it is vital to set your gaze on a vision that helps you flourish. This vision can help you cultivate a sense of serenity that washes away your anxiety and fuels your passion.

Rand's unique conception of Romanticism, "Romantic Realism," hit home with me, and I now identify as a Romantic Realist myself. Romanticism holds that art should be focused on showing life as it could and ought to be. Realism signifies that this ideal can be portrayed realistically, that artists need not rely on unrealistic or supernatural standards to convey the ideal. This is perfectly concretized in a quote from Rand's play Ideal, which touched me on a profoundly personal and artistic level. She wrote:

I want to see real, living, and in the hours of my own days, that glory I create as an illusion! I want it real! I want to know that there is someone, somewhere, who wants it, too! Or else what is the use of seeing it, and working, and burning oneself for an impossible vision? A spirit, too, needs fuel. It can run dry.[3]

I am a Romantic because I seek a better version of life, an improvement on the given. I am a realist because I want this better version to be real and achievable.

Romantic Realism is inherently optimistic. But it is wider than just optimism. It shows that values are possible within this life but also that they must be freely chosen and then earned (fig. 42). Even psychological values must be earned by developing the right attitude. Romantic Realism helps me do that work, cultivating an attitude captured by the first part of the serenity prayer, which reads, "God grant me the serenity to accept the things I cannot change, courage to change the things I can, and wisdom to know the difference." Realism represents the things I cannot change, and Romanticism represents those I can.

I need the realism with the romantic. It was more than mere positive thinking that got me through my struggles and helped me become who I am today. I needed to understand and accept those facts that were outside my control. And I needed the romantic with the realism. Beyond recognizing the immutable facts of my situation, I needed a vision of what could be and the courage to pursue it. Both are necessary elements of objectivity. The dualism I once felt was caused by swinging wildly between them. Now I could understand how each improved my life; I could integrate them and thereby achieve the serenity, courage, and wisdom necessary to fully and deeply love my life.

This ignited my passion, a fire that needs to be fed and protected (fig. 43). One of my favorite quotes is from Rand's Atlas Shrugged:

Do not let your fire go out, spark by irreplaceable spark, in the hopeless swamps of the approximate, the not-quite, the not-yet, the not-at-all. Do not let the hero in your soul perish, in lonely frustration for the life you deserved, but have never been able to reach. Check your road and the nature of your battle. The world you desired can be won, it exists, it is real, it is possible, it's yours.[4]

Everyone has a tipping point; it is only a matter of degree within the context of each individual's life. The struggles of hard times, of loss and disappointment, can swamp one's passion for living, and the darkness of nihilism can begin to encroach. To combat this darkness, we need Romantic art to keep us looking ahead at what is possible, to show the joy life has to offer, and to remind us that overcoming the struggle is worth it. These moments of joy, of experiencing one's values here and now, protect your inner fire from being blown out by the winds of struggle. I created this stained-glass lantern to represent that needed protection (fig. 44). Each piece of glass is like an experience of joy—joy now in the moment, joy remembered from the past, and joy that is possible in the future.

(38) *Who Is Li Hu*, 2016

(39) *Symphonies of Li Hu*, 2017

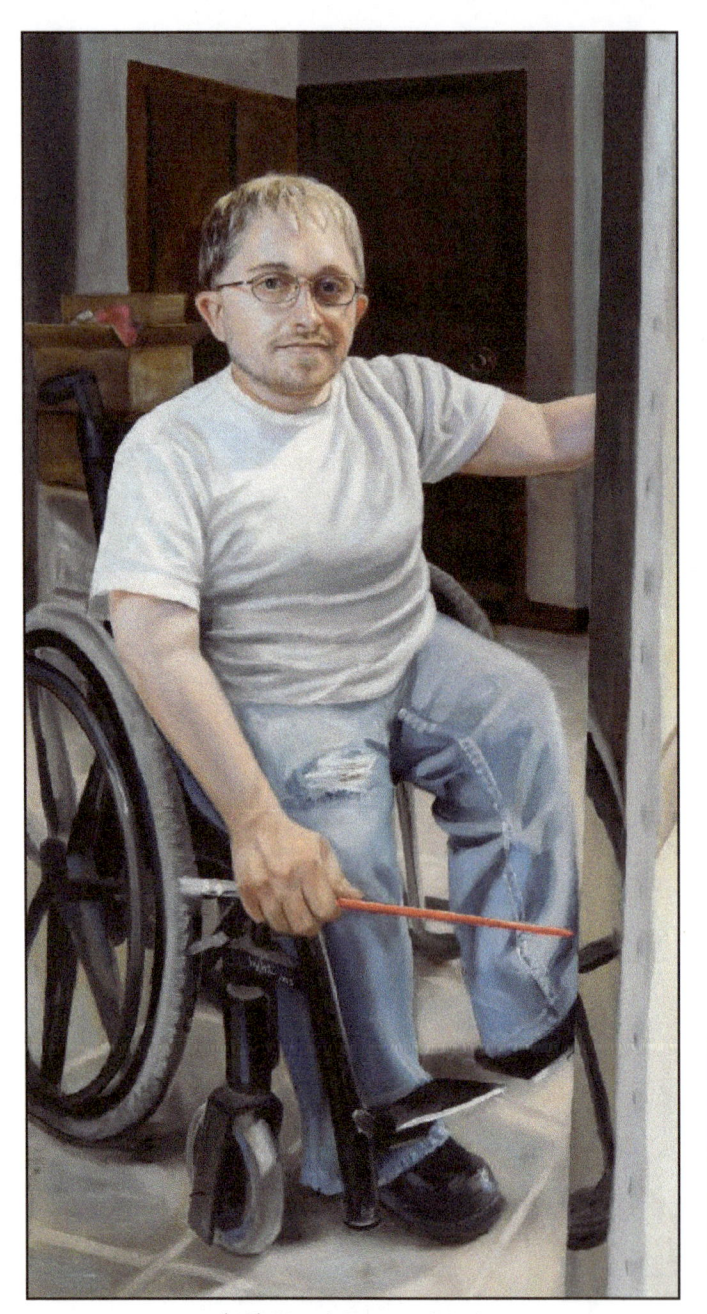

(42) Head Strong, 2010

(43) *The Fire Within*, 2011

(45) *Lighting the Darkness*, 2017

(35) *Understated Elegance*, 2018

(46) *Foraging for Midnight Oil*

Art is like a lantern that we use to illuminate and clarify, spotlighting what's important in life (fig. 45). Romantic Realism is a particular way of using that light, to see both what is and what could be. I now realize it is far more than just a theory of art—it is a whole approach to life. Romantic Realism keeps you focused on where you're going; it keeps your eye on the prize, so to speak. I now choose to focus my light on the reverent moments, the moments that make all the struggle worth it and lead to a passion for that irreplaceable value that is my life.

Your fire, your passion—only you can sense and care for it. It needs to be tended at all times. It is up to you to discover what fuels your fire. Just as you consume the physical values to nourish your body, you must also consume the spiritual values that nourish your soul and keep your passion burning. Passion for your life is the source of curiosity, ambitiousness, benevolence, and, ultimately, success. Like an inoculation against nihilism, Romanticism provides a defense of your passion. It is the vitamin of the soul, of which you need a regular dose.

I now see this as my purpose, to create that regular dose of Romanticism we all need (fig. 46). For some may be able to survive without life's burning passion, but they certainly cannot truly live without it.

Many will tell you that life is not important because it is random, and we are just cells and chemicals, and everything you do is meaningless. Others will tell you life is important because an unknowable higher power created it, that everything you do should be for the glory of God. But, as Ayn Rand made clear, life is important because it is the source of all values. Everything you do should be for the glory of that irreplaceable value that is your life.

So, I will leave you with a question: Do you look down and merely accept things as they are, waiting for the challenge that is life to be over—or do you look ahead and seek something better, taking a step and accepting this great challenge to make your life the best it can be?

(44) *The Source,* 2016 (photo)

Endnotes
1. Ayn Rand, "The Goal of My Writing," The Romantic Manifesto (New York: New American Library, 1971), 167–68.
2. Ayn Rand, The Fountainhead (New York: Penguin, 1943), 528.
3. Ayn Rand, Ideal: The Novel and the Play (New York: New American Library, 2015), 232.
4. Ayn Rand, Atlas Shrugged (New York: New American Library, 1957), 1069.

The *Plymouth Review* Current

TAKING YOU PLACES WORTH SEEING
Volume 12 • Issue 7 • June 2023

FREE!

Movies • Captain Dingle • Art • Windy City
Dessert at Alinea

• The publication that respects your intelligence •
• Human Flourishing • Whimsies • Witticisms • Oddities •

June 2023

Cover image: Return to Alinea
Great Movies This Month
The Hurricane's Rival, by Capt. A. E. Dingle, from the book, Old Sails
Ask a Science Teacher, by Larry Scheckel: How Old Is Mankind?
PulpArtists by David Saunders: Henry Clive

Breezes from the Windy City
Captain A.E. Dingle — Sailor, Yacht Racer, Pulp Writer, by Sai Shankar, pulpflakes.com/blog
Once More at Alinea
Belinda Carlisle at the Weill Center
Something Worth Viewing (Love, Charlie)
Cato's Human Freedom Index 2022

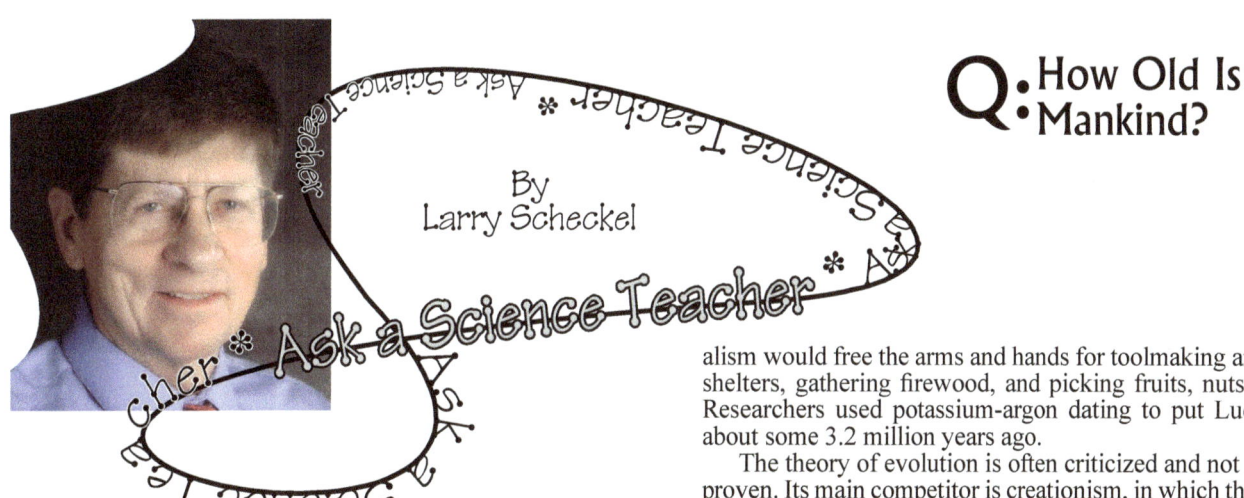

Q: How Old Is Mankind?

Ask a Science Teacher

By Larry Scheckel

A: That's a tough one, fraught with controversy with a myriad of different answers from archeologists, paleontologists, and various religions. A definitive answer is not possible to this day.

In 1976, a team headed by famed paleontologist, Dr. Mary Leaky, uncovered footprints at a Laetoli archaeological site in northern Tanzania, Africa. The footprints of the oldest hominins were well preserved in the moist ash from a volcanic eruption and dated to 3.5 million years ago. It boggles the mind. Two short people and a child walked upright, in what scientists call bipedal, traveling North across an expanse of damp volcanic ash and disappeared into history. Based on the size of the footprints and distance between them, the tallest was pegged at a height of 5 feet and the shortest at 4.2 feet. The footprints indicated these ancient humans walked in a modern manner, heel first, then toe.

The ash was wet when the hominins (fancy name is Australopithecines) walked, giving scientists much information about the soft tissue and gait, something not obtainable from skeletal remains. There were animal prints from elephants, giraffes, rhinoceroses, and a wide variety of extinct mammals. In all, there are 16 sites in that area, the largest of which has 18,000 footprints from 17 different families of animals.

If we look at Homo Sapiens, meaning "intelligent humans," we would be looking at a rather young human species. From all accounts, about 200,000 years ago. This was the result of studies on mitochondrial DNA and skulls from Ethiopia. Every human living today possesses that same set of genes.

The oldest age-proven skeleton was a skull discovered in 1960 in the Olduvai Gorge in Tanzania. It was determined that the remains belonged to a young man who lived 2.5 million years ago. His brain was more massive than a typical hominin and the pelvis allowed a freer use of two legs, and the legs were adapted for an upright movement. Further excavations showed that he built his own tools and used fire.

On November 24, 1974, anthropologist Donald Johanson, leading a team in Ethiopia, uncovered bones of an early human. On the first night after the initial discovery, the tape machine in their camp played the Beatles' hit song Lucy in the Sky with Diamonds. They named the skeletal remains Lucy. A total of 47 bone fragments were recovered, making Lucy 40 percent complete. Tooth-wear puts Lucy at 20 years old at the time of her death. She was three feet seven inches tall and weighed 70 pounds. The angle of the knee-joint showed that Lucy walked upright. Bipedalism would free the arms and hands for toolmaking and building shelters, gathering firewood, and picking fruits, nuts, and eggs. Researchers used potassium-argon dating to put Lucy walking about some 3.2 million years ago.

The theory of evolution is often criticized and not completely proven. Its main competitor is creationism, in which the Earth and every living thing was created by a High Intelligence, Creator, or God. There are young-Earth Creationists that holds to a literal interpretation of the Bible and that God created the whole world in a matter of 6 days, some 7,500 years ago.

The scientific evidence seems overwhelming that early man was alive and well several million years ago. Even so, 3.5 million years is a tiny slice (.0008) of the 4.5 billion years that the Earth and solar system has been around. You and I are newcomers to Planet Earth.

Sources: nationalgeographic.com, discover.com, www.worldatlas.com

Something Worth Viewing

This 96-minute documentary tells how Charlie Trotter rose in popularity, gaining the world's attention with his culinary craftsmanship. His restaurant in Chicago was considered world-class.

In fall of 2011, Trotter gave a presentation at the Kohler Food and Wine Event. I was there; got a book signed.

A year later, my wife and I planned a trip to Chicago. Charlie Trotter's was my first choice for a special meal. But when I called, I was told his restaurant was closing.

In November 2013, he passed away, age 54.

The documentary tells of Chef Trotter's pursuit of excellence through people who knew him: his former wives, and chefs who worked with him and for him—Emeril Lagasse, Wolfgang Puck, and Grant Achatz (who is now Executive Chef and co-owner of Alinea; see page 12).

There's a popular old adage, "Hard work never killed anyone." The early death of Chef Trotter might make one want to add, somewhere in that aphorism, "along with occasional rest and relaxation." Another lesson we could learn from his story is, "See the doctor when you need to." (Trotter hated doing so, as the film explains.)

This is a fascinating, well-made tribute to a fine chef.

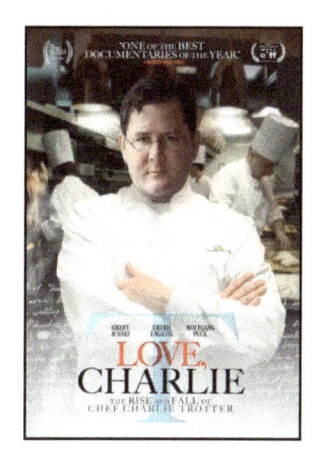

Just a few of the many items from the Alinea tasting menu, Chicago, the day before the Windy City pulp show started. Each course had a special *Name*.

Nacre. Osetra caviar. Diners experienced similar textures simultaneously: The bowl's texture through the hand; the caviar's texture in the mouth. Also with champaign jelly and lychee tapioca pudding. The bowl's multi-colored opalescence matched that of the mother of pearl spoon used to eat caviar.

Plume. Smoked Atlantic black sea bass (note the smoking fish on the plate) (and note the notes above right of the plate), potato crisps, onion/garlic dip with onion ash. The smoking flavor had an intentional, slight cigar flavor to it, and the dip bowl resembled an old-fashioned ashtray. A bit of odd though pleasant nostalgia. The table tops are polished stainless steel.

At your typical comic book convention, Jim Steranko would be listed as a Guest of Honor. At the Windy City pulp show, he was a regular, unannounced attendee, walking around, talking with people, and buying pulps for his own collection. He had with him a portfolio of drawings for sale. Your Editor scored this one. It is obvious what Steranko thinks of Captain America and what he stands for. — Artwork Copyright © Jim Steranko; character ™ Marvel Characters, Inc.

On display but not for sale in the Windy City show's art room: The cover painting for the very last Shadow pulp, from 1949. Your Editor's favorite Shadow cover of All time.

Henry Clive: Magician, Actor, Painter

(1881-1960)

Henry Clive O'Hara was born October 3, 1881 in Melbourne, Australia. His father, Dr. Henry Michael O'Hara, was born in 1850 in Ireland. His mother, Ernestine Klingender, was born in 1857 in England. The parents married in 1876 in Australia and had two children, Eileen Louise O'Hara (b.1877) and Henry Clive O'Hara (b.1881). The father was a doctor at "Cromwell House" in Melbourne, and "Avonlea" in St. Kilda.

On October 7, 1883 a third child was born, Lawrence Edward O'Hara, but it was a complicated birth, and after one day he died. After one week of recuperation, the mother also died.

In 1885 the father married a second wife and had seven more children, Osborne (b.1886), Jay (b.1887), Nina (b.1889), Myles (b.1890), Sylvia (b.1894), George (b.1899), and Peter (b.1903).

On December 15, 1898 *The Melbourne Punch* reported on an evening's entertainment for the Consul-General of Belgium, at which "Master Clive O'Hara, son of the popular Medico, delighted the audience with some very clever sleight-of-hand tricks."

On December 17, 1898 Henry Clive O'Hara, age seventeen, graduated from St. Francis Xavier's High School in Melbourne.

In 1899 he joined the theatrical circuit with the Canary Concert & Variety Company, "delighting the audience with some exceedingly clever conjuring and sleight-of-hand tricks," according to *The Prahran Telegraph*.

On October 11, 1900 *The Melbourne Punch* reported, "Clive O'Hara, a son of Dr. O'Hara, of Collins Street, has taken to the vaudeville stage as a conjurer and illusionist under the stage name Clive. He makes his appearance at Rickard's Adelaide Tivoli. As an amateur young O'Hara has paralyzed audiences around Melbourne by the dexterity of his card tricks and the weirdness of his experiments. His palming is wonderful. He is following in the footsteps of the late Dante, the conjurer, of whom he was a pupil. Possessed of youth, a good appearance and a breezy manner in addition to his talent, the new mystifier should be a hit, and will undoubtedly rank as the best man in his own particular line Australia has to date turned out."

In February of 1903 Henry Clive O'Hara traveled with a touring group to England, where his magic act was filmed by the British Biograph Company.

In August of 1903 Henry Clive O'Hara traveled with a group of actors on the steam ship *Sierra* and arrived in San Francisco on August 17th.

On July 18, 1904 *The Bendigo Independent* of Victoria, Australia, reprinted a letter from Henry Clive O'Hara, "Just a line to let you know I am doing well. I have been in America since August 1903 and have been playing vaudeville dates all the time. I am now in Chicago, where I open at the Chicago Opera House, thence go to New York. I am doing a comedy act, introducing a little legerdemain."

In New York City his theatrical circle included popular illustrators of glamorous show girls, such as Harrison Fisher (1877-1934) and Charles Dana Gibson (1867-1944). Henry Clive O'Hara was inspired by their example and began to study drawing and painting.

On May 9, 1908 Henry Clive O'Hara, age twenty-eight, married Mary Sturgis Walker in NYC. She was born in 1888 in Chicago and worked as an actress. They lived in NYC at 321 West 55th Street.

On October 10, 1909 Henry Clive performed at the Oakland Orpheum in California.

In August of 1911 he and his wife sailed on the steam ship *Lusitania* to perform as an actor for two months in London.

In August of 1912 he and his wife again sailed to England, where he performed at the Hammerstein Theatre in London.

On September 6, 1916 *The Melbourne Winner* reported, "Henry Clive recently toured Australia with his wife, the chic comedienne

Above: from 1939. — All images here HA.com

from America. After their tour ended she continued to tour, and headed one of Schlesinger's comedy companies, and right well she was able to show what a top liner is supposed to put over."

In 1916 he divorced his wife. They had no children.

He worked for Fox Films at West 46th Street in NYC. He appeared in Fighting Odds (1917), Her Silent Sacrifice (1917), On The Jump (1918), We Should Worry (1918), I Want To Forget (1918), and As A Man Thinks (1919).

On December 31, 1917 he married his second wife, Doré Plowden. She was born in 1894 in London and worked as an actress. After the marriage she became known as "the girl on the magazine cover."

On September 12, 1918, during the Great War, Henry Clive O'Hara registered with the selective service and was recorded to be thirty-six, six-two, medium build, blue eyes and brown hair.

In 1919 his illustrations of glamorous women began to appear in periodicals. On June 20, 1919 *The Warwick Daily News* of Queensland, Australia, reported, "Henry Clive has just been commissioned by the New York American to create twelve color front covers. In New York such an order is regarded as a blue ribbon prize among artists, but young O'Hara has for a long time made good both as a painter and designer, as well as an actor, in which role Melbourne knew him best. In each branch he has got to the front."

In 1920 he painted the cover of *People's Favorite Magazine.*

In 1921 he appeared in "The Oath" starring Miriam Cooper.

On April 7, 1921 his father, Dr. Henry Michael O'Hara died at the age of seventy-one in Australia.

On December 17, 1921 *The Chicago Daily Tribune* reported Henry Clive O'Hara had sued his wife for divorce on charges of desertion. She had pursued an acting career on the London stage, where after two years of separation they divorced.

On January 27, 1922 Henry Clive O'Hara married his third wife, Helen S. Cunningham. She was born in 1900 in Kentucky, and was a chorus girl in Florenz Ziegfeld's Follies. They had one daughter, Helen May O'Hara, born November 8, 1922.

On February 8, 1922 nationwide newspapers reported "He Married The Girl He Crowned Queen Of Beauty — The rapid fire romance of Henry Clive, painter of lovely girls. He looked once at a blond vision, and presto! Two divorces and one marriage."

In 1925 Henry Clive became a top artist for *The American Weekly* at 235 East 45th Street in NYC, a Sunday magazine supplement of the Hearst newspaper syndicate. Henry Clive remained a prominent contributor to this publication for the rest of his life.

In 1925 the Australian Film Company produced "Glimpses Into The Studio Life of Clive O'Hara" for national distribution as a "short film" shown between feature films.

In 1927 he and his wife and child moved to Los Angeles. They lived at 1434 Crescent Heights Boulevard.

On April 26 1928 nationwide newspapers carried advertisements for Houbigant, the Parisian parfumer, endorsed by Henry Clive, the "famous painter of gorgeous women," who used their products to enhance the beauty of his models.

The December 1929 issues of Hollywood fan magazines published a publicity photo of Joan Crawford posing for Henry Clive.

On November 7, 1933 nationwide newspapers published a photo of the most beautiful artist model and Henry Clive, a judge in a beauty contest at the Seven Arts Masked Ball in Los Angeles.

In 1933 he appeared in "Obey The Law" starring Leo Carrillo and Ward Bond.

In 1934 he divorced his third wife, Helen (Cunningham) O'Hara.

On August 16, 1935 he married his fourth wife, Sonia Karlov. She was a New York City actress and show girl working under the stage name "Jeanne Williams."

In 1939 he appeared in his ninth and final motion picture, "Frontier Marshal" starring Randolph Scott.

During the 1939 World's Fair in San Francisco Henry Clive ran a concession stand to paint portraits of women, but according to his wife, "After sinking a lot of his money, my money, and my mother's money, into the concession, he paid it very little attention, He would go out drinking instead. The last time he was gone for three days. He finally came back, but then he just left town."

The 1940 U.S. Census listed Henry Clive O'Hara, age fifty-eight, at 8250 Fountain Street in Los Angeles. He shared the apartment with Glenn Pope, age twenty-seven, a variety show performer born in Arkansas.

On March 19, 1940 nationwide newspapers reported that Henry Clive's wife, Sonia O'Hara, had been granted a divorce by the New York Supreme Court. She claimed she "lost him to a bottle, and that life was one long, well-oiled party for hubby, and her efforts to reform him were futile." They had no children.

On April 27, 1942, during WWII, Henry Clive O'Hara registered with his draft board. He was recorded at the time to be sixty-one, six-two, 215 pounds, with blue eyes, brown hair, a light complexion, and "scars on his left hand." He listed his home address as 1979 Grace Avenue in Los Angeles.

On June 8, 1944 nationwide newspapers reported "Henry Clive Turns Out A Masterpiece." The artist's daughter, Miss Helen O'Hara, "is MGM's number one glamazon. She stands six feet one inch in her stocking feet and is being groomed for stardom. She's the daughter of the well-known artist, Henry Clive, who has created no end of magazine covers."

On March 23, 1951 Henry Clive O'Hara, age sixty-nine, married his fifth wife, Burnu Acquanetta, age twenty-nine. She was born July 17, 1921 in Wyoming, an Arapaho native American. She became an orphan at age two and was raised as Mildred Davenport in Norristown, Pennsylvania by adoptive parents William and Julia Davenport, who were African American. She became an actress and in 1944 starred in "Jungle Woman." She was promoted as "Hollywood's Jungle Girl." She and Henry Clive O'Hara remained married for the rest of his life. They had no children.

Henry Clive O'Hara died at age seventy-nine in Los Angeles on December 12, 1960.

© David Saunders 2017

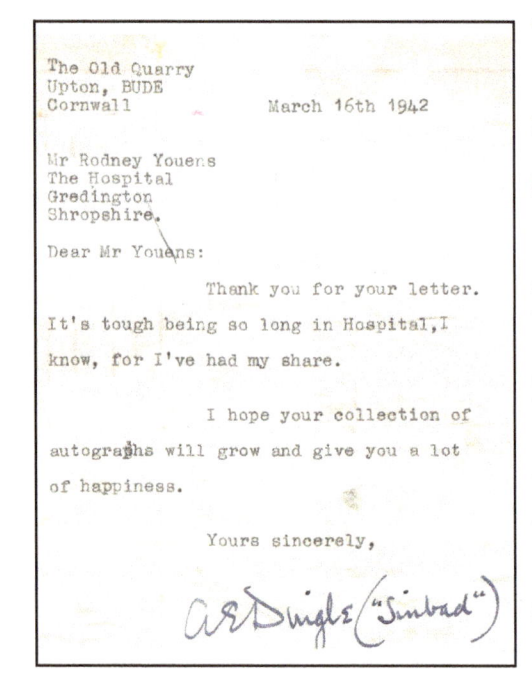

The Plymouth Review CURRENT
TAKING YOU PLACES WORTH SEEING
Volume 12 • Issue 8 • July 2023

July 2023

Movies • Captain Dingle (Again?!) • Art

$C_{12}H_{22}O_{11}$

Cover image: Sucrose Overload at Gessert's, Elkhart Lake
Great Movies This Month
Ask a Science Teacher, by Larry Scheckel: Can You Name a Really Big Science Hoax?
Kids From Wisconsin 55th Anniversary Tour
Mill Street Live 2023
Farmers Will Relate to this Sea Adventure from a Century Ago

PulpArtists by David Saunders: Jes Schlaikjer
An Evening with Adam
Magazines about Movies

Farmers Will Relate
to this Sea Adventure from a Century Ago

In the June issue of The PRC, we featured here an excerpt from the book Old Sails, the cover of which is shown here.

The excerpt we printed was the author's true account of how he navigated his modest ship in the midst of a hurricane, with his faithful dog as his only companion.

But most of the book is made up of a dozen fictional short stories, for which the author drew upon his actual experiences and knowledge of the sea.

One of these, "Old Sails" (also the title of the book), tells the story of two older sailors on a ship, Sails and Chips, who have an ongoing rivalry.

In these stories, many technical terms used to describe the workings of a ship are lost on me. But I can still follow the gist of things.

In this story, the omniscient narrator explains that some bales of jute were part of the cargo, down below in the hold.

And the jute was damp.

Jute is a fiber. One online source says it's also called "burlap." As in a burlap bag. Or gunnysack. (I also read that jute is the 2nd-most commonly grown plant-based fiber; cotton being first.)

The captain of the ship hears from two frantic crew members.

One says the sounding rod he dropped into the hold came back dry, but hot on the end.

As best as I understand, the "sounding rod" was extended into the hold to see if the ship was taking on water. The fact that it came back dry is good, but why would it be hot?

The captain ponders this, not liking the implications, when a second crew member anxiously reports that the barometer had fallen three-tenths in an hour.

The captain asks the mate to tell him how the cargo is stored. Specifically, where in the hold the jute is. And all this is known, because cargo cannot be thrown down into the hold any whichway they feel like; it has to be accounted for, and placed in such a way to maintain the ship's balance.

As the skies become more restless and the wind turns more threatening, the sounding rod is again sent into the hold. It comes back hot, from the location of the jute.

And near the jute is stored a load of coal.

That's not good.

As the ship is tossed on increasingly unstable waters, Old Sails is tasked with crawling down into the hold, dragging the end of a water hose with him.

No electric lights in the hold. To prevent water from sloshing into the hold as waves assault the ship, the hatch must be kept (mostly) closed once Sails descends.

"Blast th' smoke!" [Sails] growled. He was in darkness; suffocating, warm, Sygian darkness. Even the double tot of rum had failed to put the courage of the volunteer into the foremost hands. A man was wanted to creep in under the hatch, which could not be left off, and try to locate the smouldering peril. Even Chips had hung back, grumbling something about being an old man. Sails had gone, while Chips held up a corner of the hatch cover. Now he was crawling over the jute bales, trying to determine with his hands which appeared to feel hottest, and the sweat blinded him as he worked his way between bales and dockhead at the furthest corner of the hatch square from where he had entered.

This story—no, the entire book—is a fine example of edge-of-the-seat reading.

Oh... what's that? "So what's this story have to do with farmers? And where'd the fire come from?"

For that answer, you only need ask any farmer in this area who has ever baled hay (or chopped it loose, for that matter).

(What happens to hay when it's not thoroughly dried before storing it in the barn?)

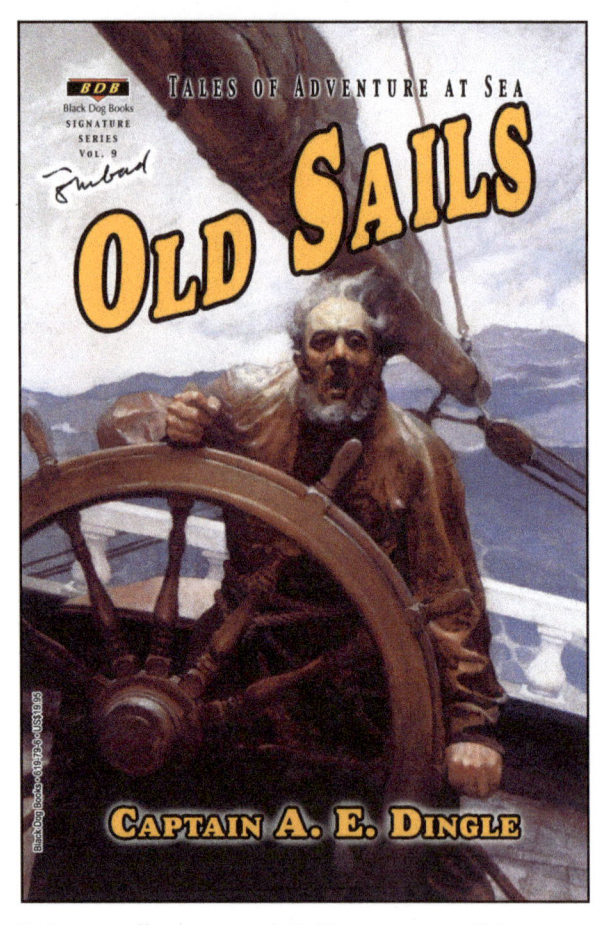

Deja vu all over again? Yes, we ran this cover image last month. But what possible relevance could one short story in this book have to farmers? (See previous page for answer!) The book is available as a paperback or ebook from Amazon (**amazon.com**); and as an ebook from Barnes & Noble (**bn.com**). The cover artwork is by N. C. Wyeth. — Courtesy of Black Dog Books

Art for a Red Cross poster, late 1940s, by Jes Schlaikjer.

August 2023

Cover image: A Load of Crocks at the Red Wing Pottery Museum

Great Movies This Month

The Red Wing Pottery Museum

One Author's Search for the Authentic West, by Frank Gruber

PulpArtists by David Saunders: Remington Schuyler (oops, again)

Jazz Crawl
Ask a Science Teacher, by Larry Scheckel: Is it True what I Heard that Some Criminals Wear a Stun Vest During a Court Trial or Sentencing?
Coalition of Photographic Arts
Short Shrifts
Farming in Kenya, by Jusper Machogu

Farming in Kenya

by Jusper Machogu

> **Editor's Note**
> This is printed, with permission, from Jusper Machogu's Substack blog. It has been lightly edited. The still photos here are from videos that accompany Jusper's article. To see the full videos, visit
> **juspermachogu.substack.com**

2 Apr 2023

Good morning from Kisii Kenya.

What is it like to live here without fossil fuels?

Some refer to it as 'Sustainable', I agree, only if its definition changes to 'break your back if you want to eat even though you'll be poor forever'

I am weeding our maize.

We had a drought this January, as usual. This one went for a bit longer—over 1½ months, it is the longest we go without rain.

Our beans died. Most farmers didn't get what they planted as seeds back—zero harvest. Maize died and we had to do gapping when it started raining.

But most farmers did replant afresh. That is costly and most skipped buying fertilizer (DAP) for the second time and planted maize without. We don't top dress our maize over here. No wonder you see 20-30 Kgs of fertilizer per ha [hectare; 10,000 square meters, about 2.47 acres] compared to 360 China, 250 India, 120 US, 150 EU

We don't plough our lands, we dig using hoes (jembes). This is my bestie digging. The owner planted ⅛ ha of sugarcane but he couldn't sell. 5 years later, realized losses and decided to uproot it.

My bestie is earning $1.50 working from 8 - 1 p.m.

Labor costs
5 men dug for 5 days

My village gets water from a spring 1 km away and when that dries up, we do another one about 2 km away. In various regions in Kenya, people walk for half a day for water.

This is my small bro @GetangeIan fetching water.

Nowadays we have motorbikes, a few people can afford them for fetching water. Five 20-litre cans (100 litres of water) for $1. A cow drinks 20 litres per day during the drought seasons on average. A family of 6 uses about 100 litres per day during the drought seasons.

Our village spring

365

Women carry water by placing a 20-litre plastic can on their heads. Men usually use their fingers to hold the handles on the cans.

Fetching water for our cattle using a wheelbarrow from a water pan gathering runoff water from our road about a km away. It dried before week 2 ended!

We prefer to walk our cattle to the river because it doesn't cost us money. Plus they will drink to their satisfaction. We can also have a bath and wash our clothes before going home.

We have kids fetching water in the morning before or in the evening after school. Depending on water discharge, they can wait for 3 hours before they can fetch water which means they go back home at 9 p.m.!

Oh, walking in the dark!

Our cattle drinking water.

Sustainable living/farming/development as used today is a scam. It is tied to climate change which means:
• Living in grass thatched roofs is sustainable but living in a mansion is.
• Eating vegetables is sustainable but eating meat or drinking milk are not.
• Farming in a tiny garden is sustainable but farming 100 hectares is not.

It is all tied down to climate change. The UN promotes its SDGs [Sustainable Development Goals] in our countries without acknowledging the fact that they literally don't want us to develop. If everyone lived as Americans, the world wouldn't be as is. That's their biggest fear.

Fossil Fuels have really transformed civilization. In the US a ha was producing 2T of maize in early 1800s. Today, farmers in the US produce 11T per ha. And I learnt the other day there is a farmer who has managed 33T per ha! In Kenya we produce 2T per ha. Some farmers do 4T per ha but we have the potential to produce 10-12T per ha. Too bad Americans produce all of that grain and use about 40% for biofuels! A waste of energy in most cases but the term 'Green'—which loosely translates to 'It doesn't matter as long as we are doing it for the environment'—sells it.

Fossil Fuels for Africa.

Harvesting Tea

July 14, 2023

Tea is Kenya's main cash crop. And in Kisii we grow tea. We usually sell it to nearby factories.

As a farmer, I just pluck tea, carry it on my head or shoulders to the buying centre a few metres away, sometimes up to a kilometer or two depending with how far the farm is from the buying centre. Then at a given time usually afternoon, unless it is on Friday, the tea factory sends its staff to pick the tea up.

This is what the tea buying centre looks like. We have the beds and partitions. Farmers place their tea up or on the verandah as they wait for the factory buyers to come. It comes anytime after 12 in the afternoon other than on Friday. They honk once they arrive.

They pick up the tea from tea buying centres by vehicles. But first, they measure the tea to determine how many kilos you sold them. Then wait for your payment at the end of the month. And a bonus at the end of the year.

We usually pluck two leaves and the bud. And we produce CTC black tea. CTC is crush, tear and cut—I will spoon-feed you, don't worry [wink].

We only use fertilizers on our tea—no pesticides, no insecticides, no fungicides. Remember, no fertilizer application, no tea! Urea works very well with tea because urea is all about healthy lively leaves and that is what your kitchen garden with vegetables requires. P and K, phosphorus and Potassium—still spoon-feeding you [smile], are for flowering and fruiting or rooting for tubers.

I thought I should also include this. This is tea pruning. Tea branches need to be pruned to reduce the height of the tea and also increase the number of tea branches—a wider table. You see how a bush grows? If you cut the bush tree near the ground, you'll probably have a single stump left. Cut it up a little bit, you'll have the stem branch into two or three. Up a bit, 4-10, and on and on. Pruning is done once in 2 years.

We usually pluck tea from 7-8 a.m. to 1-2 in the afternoon. A person usually plucks 10-20 kilos a day. Others do 30-50 depending on the location. If you're working in someone's farm, you'll be paid 7 cents (USD) per kilo. The owner is paid 20 shillings a kilo by the factory and a bonus of 5-20 per kilo, yearly.

We pluck tea twice a month. A single tree produces 2 kilos of green tea in a year. If you don't apply your fertilizer properly, you'll get up to 1 kilo, or less. Weeding is also done regularly. But tea forms a canopy that weeds barely grow underneath.

Tea is a perennial crop. We have tree bushes as old as 80 years and still doing well. Kenya is the top tea producer in the world after India and China. Some reports say it is the largest tea producer in the World!

It is Friday night, I am just chilling in bed. I hope you enjoy it.

September
2023

Cover image: Paint the Towns in Fall Colors, photo submitted by Plymouth Arts Center

Great Movies This Month

$1,500 Sandwich Illustrates How Exchange Raises Living Standards, by Chelsea Follett, HumanProgress.org

From Poverty to Progress, by Chelsea Follett, HumanProgress.org

Call to Artists

Ask a Science Teacher, by Larry Scheckel: Why Did My Grandma Have to Take Goiter Pills When She Was a Little Girl?

Blue Peter, by Captain A. E. Dingle

PulpArtists by David Saunders: E. Franklin Wittmack

Musical Memories

Arts at the Waelderhaus

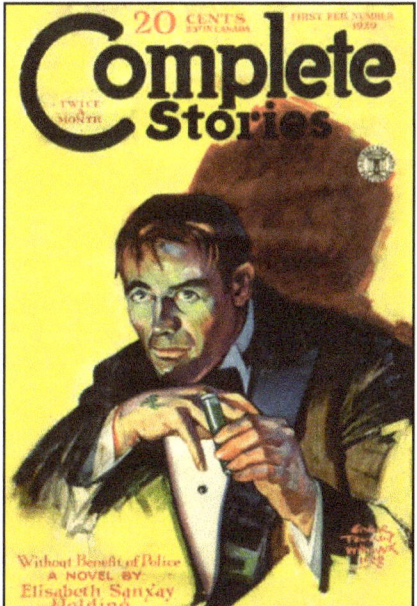

Two effective pulp covers by E. Franklin Wittmack

E. Franklin Wittmack: Pigs to Pulps

David Saunders' pulpartists.com

Edgar Franklin Wittmack was born on July 10, 1894 in New York City. His father, Charles A. Wittmack, was born in 1860 in NYC to German immigrants. His mother, Emma Balthazar, was born in 1865 in NYC, and was also the child of German immigrants. His parents married in 1887 and they had three children, Karl (b.1888), Edgar (b.1894), and Beatrice (b.1896). They lived at 107 West 82nd Street, between Columbus and Amsterdam Avenues. The father was a chemist.

After graduating from high school in 1913, Edgar Franklin Wittmack spend the summer with a friend working as a farmhand on the E. C. Potter pig farm of Clearwater, Montana. He enjoyed it enough to return to the same farm for the next three summers in 1915, 1916, and 1917.

On June 5, 1917 during the Great War, he reported for draft registration, as required by law. At that time his nearest draft board was in Missoula Montana. Although his record stated that his only prior military experience was "reject from artillery," he served in the Army and was stationed overseas in France.

By 1920 he had returned to NYC, where he studied at The Art Students League, and worked as a commercial illustrator from a rented room in an apartment house at 420 West 116th Street.

By 1924 he had moved to 58 West 57th Street, where his monthly rent was $15. This building was near the Art Students League, so it had many artist studios. His neighbors included such notable artists as Abe Hirschfield (1903-2003), Alexandre Archipenko (1887-1964), and Franklin Booth (1874-1948). He introduced his sister Beatrice (aged 21) to Franklin Booth (age 50). They fell in love and married. Booth was renowned for his illustrations in nationwide magazines, such as *Scribner's*, *Collier's,* and *Harper's.* Booth was also one of the founders of the Phoenix Art Institute in NYC, where pulp artist Laurence Herndon taught and where pulp artist Walter Popp took art classes.

— HA.com

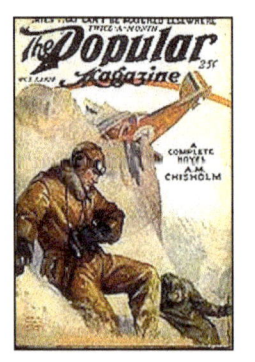

In 1925 Edgar Franklin Wittmack worked as a secretary at the Arthur Balthazar Industrial Appliances Company at One Madison Avenue and 23rd Street. Balthazar was his mother's Uncle. In July of that year he quit his job and sailed to France on the Steam Ship Rochambeau. While in Paris he studied at L'Academie de la Grande Chaumiere. He returned to NYC on November 12, 1925.

His illustrations were published in *American Boy, Collier's Magazine, Everybody's Magazine, Liberty, Outdoor Life, The Saturday Evening Post,* and *Scientific American.* He became the main cover artist for *Popular Science.*

He also painted covers for pulp magazines, such as *Adventure, Clues, Complete Stories, Frontier Stories, Short Stories, The Popular, West,* and *Western Story.*

On April 27, 1942 during WWII, he reported for draft registration, even though at age forty-seven, he was too old to even volunteer for military service. At the time he was recorded to be five-nine-and-a-half, 168 pounds, with blue eyes, brown hair, a light complexion and mustache.

In 1946 he married Maude A. Burris, who was born in NYC on July 23, 1896. They lived at 15 West 67th Street, where he also kept his art studio. They had no children.

After the war he had a regular assignment creating commemorative paintings of newly-built oil tankers. These paintings were a regular feature in *Cities Service Magazine.* He painted a mural of the oil tanker World Glory for the New York City office of the Greek shipping magnate Stavros Niarchros. His last assignments were posters for the National Drive to Employ the Handicapped, which were published posthumously.

Edgar Franklin Wittmack died of a heart ailment in his art studio at the age of sixty-one on April 25, 1956.

© David Saunders 2009

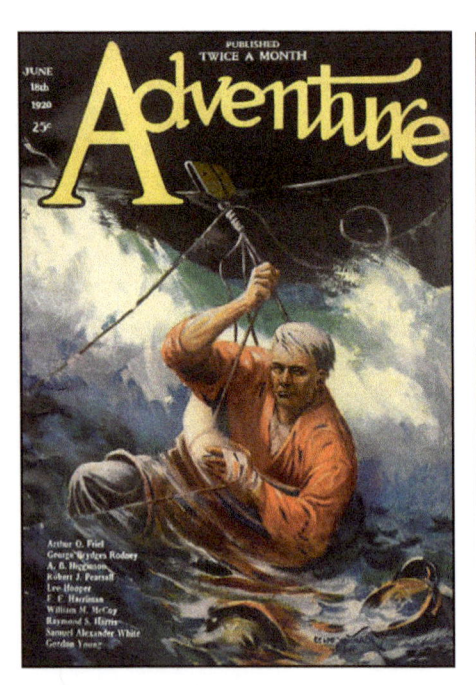

The Plymouth Review Current

TAKING YOU PLACES WORTH SEEING
Volume 12 • Issue 11 • October 2023

FREE!

Book Show/Author Signing Event in Manitowoc
Movies • Art • Tangerine Dream

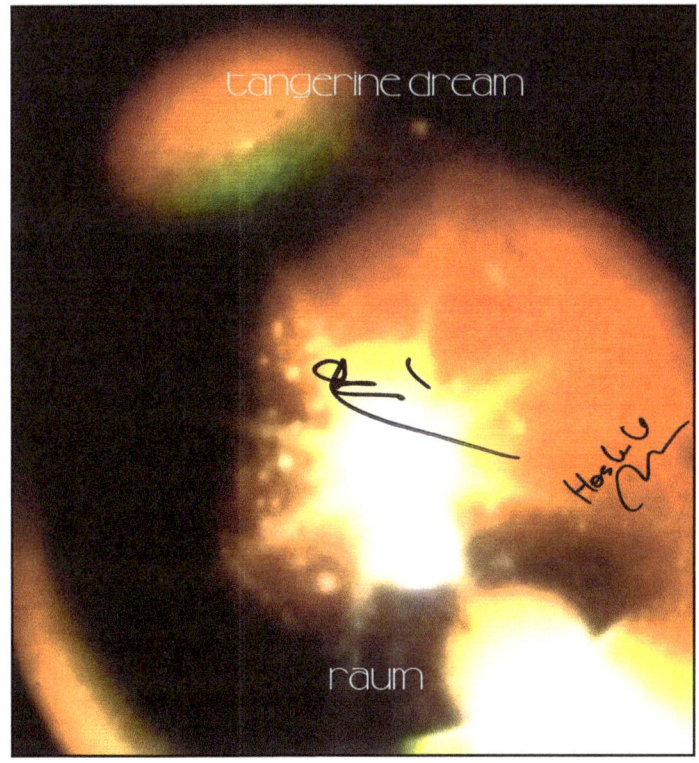

Two members of Tangerine Dream signed this vinyl album, Raum, for Your Editor. Thorsten Quaeschning signed it at center (quite—how shall I put it?—*stylized)*, and Hoshiko Yamane signed at right. This album includes the song, You're Always On Time, which can be heard on YouTube (our Facebook page has a link thereto).

October
2023

Cover image: Tangerine Dream, Atlanta, September 12, 2023, Photo by David McDaniel
Great Movies This Month
Tangerine Dream
Ask a Science Teacher, by Larry Scheckel: What Does "Survival Of The Fittest" Really Mean?
A Class Act(or)
Good News for Laurel & Hardy Fans
Lakeshore Book Show and Author Signing
PulpArtists by David Saunders: Mat Kauten
Artists Reception for Paint the Towns in Fall Color
Outbid Again!
Musical Memories Concert

TANGERINE DREAM

I first became aware of Tangerine Dream's music with the 1977 film, Sorcerer. Sorcerer was directed by William Friedkin, who just a few years before had directed The Exorcist. With a title like Sorcerer, it's understandable that some would ask, "Sorcerer? Is that 'Exorcist II'?"

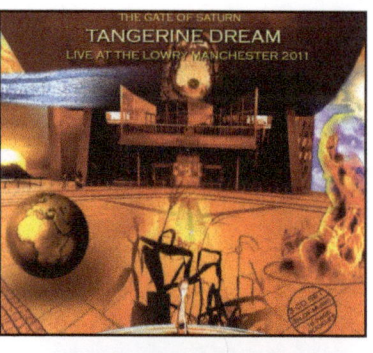

(I don't care for The Exorcist. University classmates at the time of its release told me how much I'd like it; how scary it was. I attended it with a friend. We both reacted with contemptuous laughter. I only mention it here because I've read that, had William Friedkin heard Tangerine Dream music a few years earlier, he would have asked TD to do the soundtrack for The Exorcist. Instead, Tubular Bells by Mike Oldfield became the Exorcist "theme." Anyone alive at that time heard it constantly on the radio.) (I do like Tubular Bells.)

Sorcerer was a ***great*** movie. (If you don't believe ***me,*** ask Quentin Tarantino, the next time you see him.) Nothing supernatural about it; four desperate men drive two truckloads of highly unstable nitroglycerine through 200 miles of jungle "roads."

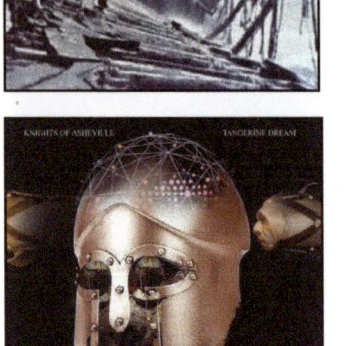

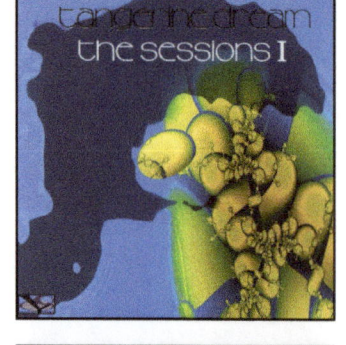

Tangerine Dream was based in Germany. Edgar Froese founded the band in 1967. He was the core of the group as members came and left over the years, until his death in 2015.

Early on, TD used electronic synthesizers to create their mostly wordless music. Their earlier albums were ethereal and sometimes non-melodic. Later, more substantial melodies emerged.

I had heard several TD albums by 1981, when I settled into a theater seat for Thief, a film starring James Caan, Tuesday Weld, James Belushi, and Willie Nelson. As the movie began, with the opening strains of music, I thought, "This sounds like—"
—when the credits

**Music Composed and Performed by
Tangerine Dream**

—faded onto the screen.

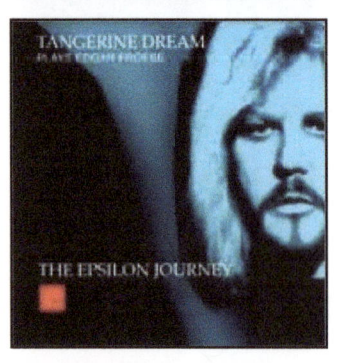

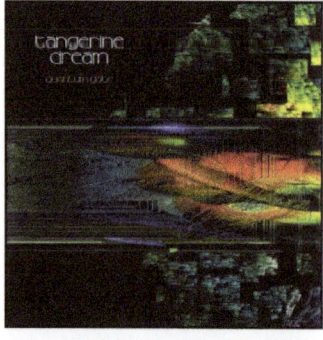

You can bet I purchased that soundtrack.

I missed the next major film released in the US featuring TD music. In 1983, while living in North Dakota (teaching Middle School Science), I called a theater that was only 50 miles away and asked what was playing. I thought the guy said "The Cape," but he'd actually said "The Keep." Perplexed, I asked what it was about. "I think it's some kind of evil movie," the theater owner explained.

I didn't go.

(The Keep has a ***great*** soundtrack.)

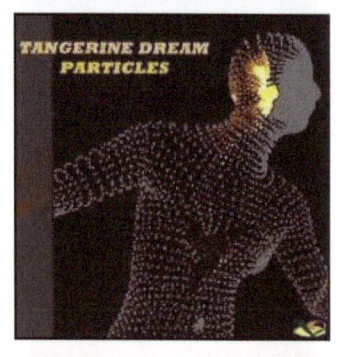

By 1986, I'd left behind the wonderful world of teaching, returned to my native land, and saw that Tangerine Dream would perform in Milwaukee at the Oriental Theater. I saw them then, and again in 1988, at the Riverside in Milwaukee.

I liked TD's music more and more. In 2015, when Edgar Froese passed away, the decision was made to continue the group. Two of the musicians in the current lineup had worked with Froese for several years: Thorsten Quaeschning and Hoshiko Yamane. The band's third member now is Paul Frick.

TD recently toured North America. This past September 12, we attended their concert in Atlanta, Georgia. After two hours of music, band members greeted fans at the merchandise station.

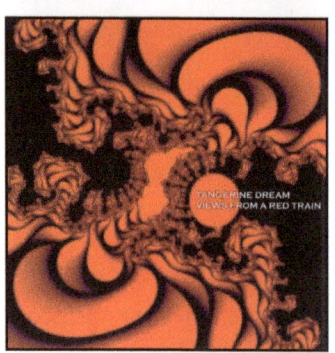

As much as I enjoy music (and not exclusively TD), I rarely write about it. I mean, really, how does one ***describe*** music? I've picked up magazines about music, read all kinds of descriptions, articles, and reviews; but never have found a satisfying answer to that question.

So while I have given you two objective facts about TD (they use electronics; their music is mostly wordless), I find it impossible to describe their music in any way that would help you answer the basic question: "Would I enjoy Tangerine Dream's music?"

You could just get one or more CDs and try them out. But that's such a random, hit-or-miss process (it's not even a "process"), that

TD albums from Barnes & Noble, BN.com

only someone with money to throw away would likely try it.

Fortunately, two methods allow you to easily and cheaply investigate their music: movies; and the Internet.

I. Film music

Since TD did many film soundtracks in the past 40+ years (in addition to their many studio albums), chances are good you've already heard their music.

Most of the following have a trailer on **imdb.com.** Most feature snippets of music. (Incredibly, the trailer for Firestarter features music from Sorcerer!!)

Here is a partial list of movies scored by TD:

Sorcerer (1977). One of the best. It made me a life-long fan of actor Roy Scheider. Certain music from this film is often played at TD concerts. (Other such music is indicated below by "Concert favorite.")

Thief (1981). Concert favorite.

The Keep (1983). Based on a novel by F. Paul Wilson, and part of a double series that included his character, Repairman Jack. Wilson was Guest of Honor at the 2018 Windy City Pulp & Paper Convention, where he commented on the movie as it was screened. Featuring Scott Glenn, Ian McKellen, and Jürgen Prochnow. TD scored at least three films with Prochnow, a German actor who played the captain of a Nazi submarine in Das Boot (The Boat). This film, and Thief, were co-written and directed by Michael Mann. Concert favorite; in fact, there was some trouble in releasing an official soundtrack album, so at one of TD's concerts, they played just about all the music from this film, and released it as the album Logos.

Risky Business (1983). Tom Cruise dances in his shorts! Concert favorite.

Wavelength (1983). With Keenan Wynn and Robert Carradine. A good one for UFO/captured alien theorists. Superb soundtrack.

Firestarter (1984). With a young Drew Barrymore. One of the best soundtracks.

Flashpoint (1984). With Kris Kristofferson and Treat Williams. Concert favorite.

Heartbreakers (1984). My personal favorite soundtrack.

Legend (1985). Tom Cruise once more! Concert favorite.

Red Heat (1985). Speaking of (ugh) The Exorcist... this is a women's prison film starring Linda Blair.

Vision Quest (1985). High school wrestling film with Matthew Modine ("Joker" in Kubrick's Full Metal Jacket). The official soundtrack contains several pop tunes, but *no music* that TD composed for the film.

Near Dark (1987). Directed by Kathryn Bigelow, this film occasionally shows up on TCM. Cowboys and vampires!

Shy People (1987). With Jill Clayburgh and Barbara Hershey. One of the best soundtracks, but scarce.

Dead Solid Perfect (1988). Golfing movie with Randy Quaid.

Miracle Mile (1988). With Anthony Edwards, who played a doctor on the ER TV series.

The Man Inside (1990). As I prepared this article, I was top bidder on a copy of this rare soundtrack. I bought it through eBay from someone in Ireland! Jürgen Prochnow plays Günter Wallraf, a journalist who went undercover to expose conditions of immigrants working in Germany. Sadly, the movie seems to be as scarce as the soundtrack.

II. The Internet

A great deal of work by TD can be heard on YouTube and other Internet sites. I have to question the legality of much of it, and rationalizing it by saying, "Yeah, but it leads to legitimate sales of the band's music" is the kind of unprincipled pragmatism that my philosophy rejects. So it is with mixed thoughts that I inform you that you will find:

• Concerts, in part or in whole, of wildly varying video and sound quality.
• Individual songs.
• Interviews with band members.

Former TD members

A YouTube or other 'net search will bring info on former members of TD who subsequently produced music on their own or with others. Each undoubtedly learned a great deal from TD founder Edgar Froese, and built upon that gained knowledge. None were content to continue as mere clones of their respected mentor, however; they incorporated their own musical visions and personalities. (That also very much applies to TD's three current members. Some long-time fans are disappointed that they are *not* exact clones of Froese.)

(This list is *not* exhaustive.)
Jerome Froese (son of Edgar)
Johannes Schmoelling
Paul Haslinger
Chris Franke

Enjoy the process of discovery!

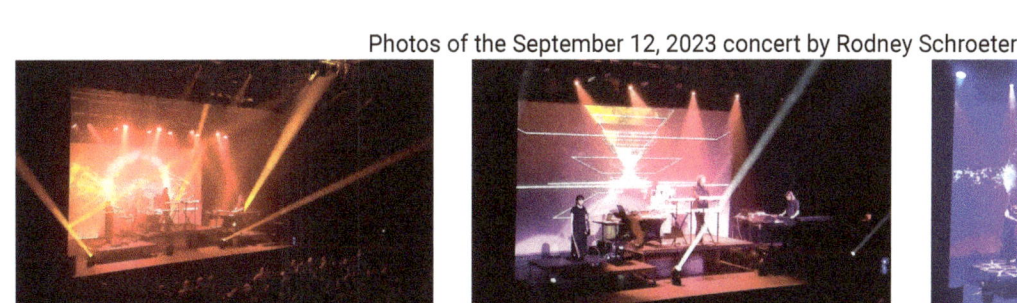

Hoshiko and Thorsten greet fans and sign items. – Photo by Rodney Schroeter

Photos of the September 12, 2023 concert by Rodney Schroeter

Ask a Science Teacher

By Larry Scheckel

Q: What Does "Survival Of The Fittest" Really Mean?

A: When we hear that term, "survival of the fittest," we conjure up images of two bull moose fighting it out until one drops dead or runs away bloodied. The stronger bull wins and survives. Or we might think of a person having a trim body toned by exercise and proper diet. We think that person might live longer than any group of people.

It's helpful to examine the word "fit." At any given time and place, an organism is most likely to survive if it has those traits needed to deal with the current circumstances. For some, it might be brute strength. For others, it may be the ability to hide. Hares that change color in the winter (to white) blend in better with the snow and are less likely to be eaten by predators. Those that do not change color are more likely to be picked off by a bird of prey or a coyote. Chameleons are also great examples of using camouflage. For still others it may be the ability to survive cold, drought, or famine.

When two species are in competition for the same resources, the species that is more fit will survive. But more important is the survival of the fittest within any single species. The individual organisms that make up a species are not all identical. Variation exists among individuals, and each different trait may increase or decrease the odds of survival.

So, the real issue is not really survival, but reproduction, generating offspring. The organisms that are better at surviving are far more likely to have offspring, allowing them to pass along their traits to their offspring. Over time, those traits will spread through the population, becoming more and more common and displacing those traits that reduce fitness.

Our genes are encoded in our DNA, found in the nucleus of our cells. Nearly every cell in our body contains an identical copy of this DNA. The DNA is divided into chromosomes, 23 pairs. A chromosome is a continuous strand of DNA, consisting of a long sequence of base pairs. Four base pairs are possible, abbreviated as G, C, T, and A. In humans, all 23 pairs of chromosomes have been sequenced, an entire human genome, about 3 billion base pairs in all.

Each chromosome contains about a thousand genes and each gene is located on a specific chromosome. Scientists have given individual names to many of these genes. For example, the gene TYK2 is associated with 20 autoimmune diseases.

When two people have different genes, what we really mean is they have different variants, or alleles, of certain genes. A new gene variant can arise due to mutation and most mutations are harmless. The process of culling bad mutations and spreading good mutations is called natural selection.

In really bad movies, the world is terrorized by some monster that arose from a mutation, caused by radiation, cosmic rays, X-rays, or chemical toxins. Occasionally an entire chromosome is replicated. Such is the case with Down's syndrome.

Reviewing the basics: Any species, including humans, is never completely uniform. Individuals possess varying traits. Certain traits increase the odds of survival. Individuals that possess these traits are likely to pass them along to their offspring and such traits spread through the local population. Most of the beneficial traits are influenced by genes. Those genes spread through a local population. Mutations constantly introduce new gene variants. At the same time, certain gene variations, some new and some old, are eliminated from the population. Local conditions, such as climate, change over time and from place to place. These changes have a huge effect in determining which genes are advantageous to a population. In some cases, populations diverge to the point of becoming subspecies and eventually distinct species. That means that new species come into being and old species disappear on a continuous basis. That process has been going on for millions of years. Species that have died out include the dodo bird, saber-toothed cats, mammoths, and ground sloths. Many new species were discovered this past year, including several snakes, frogs, insects, and even a new primate species.

Sources: How Stuff Works, National Geographic, www.livescience.com

A Class Act(or)

Some years ago, Your Editor found a United States address for German actor Jürgen Prochnow. I sent him a blank index card and a stamped, self-addressed envelope, asking for an autograph.

Weeks (months?) later, I received an envelope from Germany, with the photo shown here. Now that's a class act!

Prochnow has acted in many films besides those scored by Tangerine Dream, mentioned on pages 14-15. He was:
• Commander of a German submarine in Das Boot (English title, The Boat) (1981).
• Duke Leo Atreides in the 1984 David Lynch-directed version of Dune.
• Sutter Cane in the John Carpenter-directed nightmare fantasy, In the Mouth of Madness (1994).
• Judge Griffin in the UK Comics-based Judge Dredd (1995), which also starred Sylvester Stallone.
• Major Muller in The English Patient (1996).
• Andre Vernet in The Da Vinci Code (2006).
He is now 82.

The Plymouth Review Current

TAKING YOU PLACES WORTH SEEING
Volume 12 • Issue 11 • October 2023

FREE!

Fine Dining ◆ Movies ◆ Illustration Art
Love in the Leaves

November
2023

Cover image: Love in the Leaves, Disney World, Orlando

Great Movies This Month

Farewell to a Wonderful Magazine (Illustration)

Plymouth Arts Center Events

Astronomical Auction Prices

An Evening with Adam (Seigel, Lupi & Iris, Milwaukee)

PulpArtists by David Saunders: Frank McAleer

The Big Jon and Sparkie Story, by Gavin Callaghan, Author, No School Today

Short Shrifts

Magazines About Movies

Ask a Science Teacher, by Larry Scheckel: What Is a Quarter Horse?

Whatever this guy's trying to do on this 1928 pulp cover (painted by Frank McAleer), it looks somewhat dangerous.

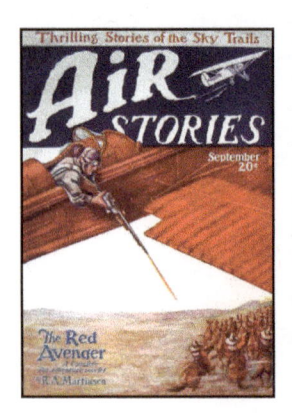

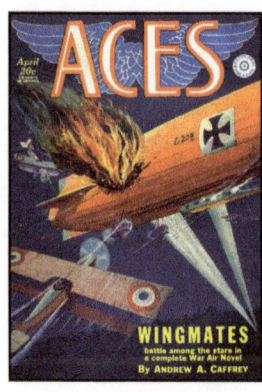

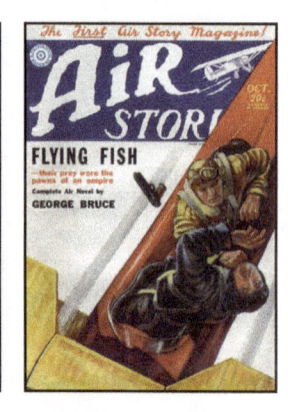

David Saunders' pulpartists.com

Frank McAleer: War & Aviation Artist

(1889-1980)

James Francis McAleer was born on October 18, 1889 in Lowell, Massachusetts. His father, also named James Francis McAleer, was born in 1859 in Ireland, and moved to America in 1879. His mother, Rose Dolan, was born in 1865 in Massachusetts of Irish ancestry. His parents married on June 15, 1887 in Lowell, MA, and had two children, James Francis McAleer (b.1889), and Katherine McAleer (b.1892). The family lived at 22 Chambers Street in Lowell, MA. The father was a barber.

On February 8, 1894 the father, James McAleer, died at the age of thirty-five. After this tragic death, the mother supported her two children by working as a dressmaker.

In 1917 James Francis McAleer was working in New York City as a scenic artist in the theater district. He lived in a hotel at 308 West 42nd Street.

During the Great War James Francis McAleer served in the U.S. Navy from May 22, 1917 until his honorable discharge on April 16, 1918.

On May 17, 1918 he was again summoned to register with the selective service. He identified his marital status as married with a "common law" wife and one child. He also claimed a physical disability, which was not identified on the document.

On August 13, 1918 James Francis McAleer married May McPherson. They moved to Connecticut, where they raised their daughter.

On July 29, 1919 the artist applied for a Seaman's Passport. His application form recorded his as age twenty-nine, five-foot-five, 135 pounds, ruddy complexion, with black hair and blue eyes, and a scar on his abdomen.

In 1925 Frank McAleer began to sell freelance black & white story illustrations to pulp magazines produced by Fiction House. He signed his work "Frank McAleer." His pen-and-ink drawings appeared in *North-West Stories, Fight Stories, Wings, Air Stories,* and *Lariat Story.*

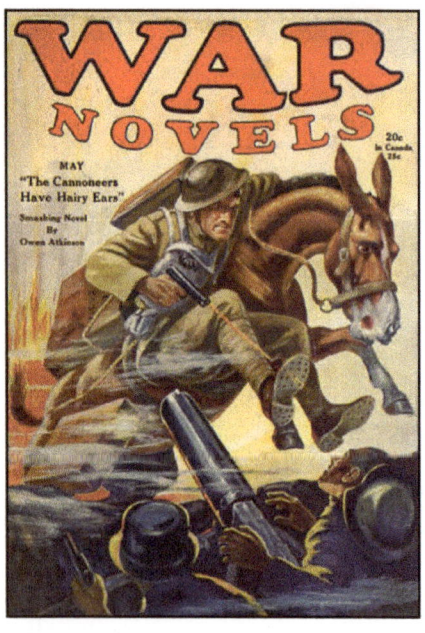

Whose expression is more fierce? The soldier's, or the horse's?

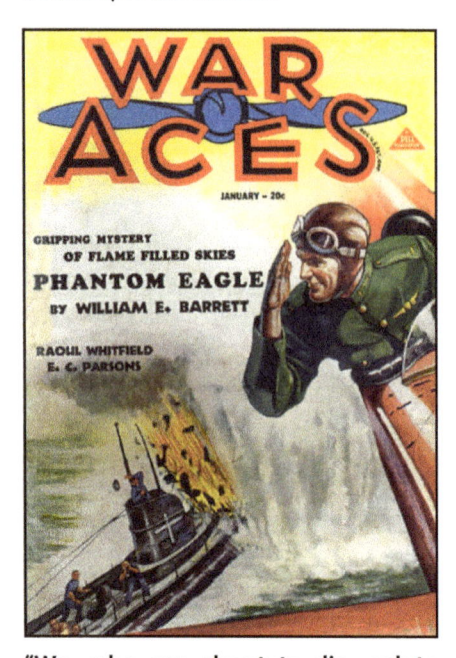

"We, who are about to die, salute you. No, no. You, who are about to die, salute me. No, no. Whatever. Here's a bomb, with my compliments.

In 1927 the artist was listed as "Frank MacAlear, c/o Fiction House, 271 Madison Avenue in NYC" in the professional artist directory, *Advertising Arts & Crafts,* published annually by Lee & Kirby.

By 1928 Frank McAleer had begun to sell painted covers to pulp magazines. His work appeared on *Air Stories, Wings, Sky Riders, Air Stories, War Novels, Western Romances, War Aces, War Birds, Aces,* and the short-lived *Navy Stories.*

After 1934, the work of Frank McAleer no longer appeared in pulp magazines.

In 1936 the artist's mother, Rose (Dolan) McAleer, died at the age of seventy-one in Lowell, MA, and was buried beside her husband in St. Patrick's Cemetery.

By 1942 the artist's daughter had married and moved away from home, after which the artist and his wife left Connecticut and moved to Miami, Florida.

On November 24, 1946 *The Miami Daily News Sunday Magazine* featured "Miami artist Frank McAleer's vision of Miami's Skyline fifty years from now in the year 1996, with electric power supplied by solar energy."

On December 23, 1946 The Miami News reported "Miami Artist Frank McAleer has completed the three glittering stage sets for the annual Orange Bowl Beauty Queen coronation ceremonies."

On January 17, 1970 the artist's unmarried younger sister, Katherine McAleer, died at the age of seventy-seven in Lowell Massachusetts, and was buried beside her mother and father. She spent her entire life as a manual laborer in the local woolen industry.

James "Frank" McAleer died at the age of eighty in Florida on November 13, 1980.

© David Saunders 2018

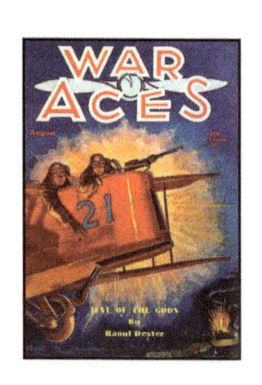

Short Shrifts
Bits and Bytes About This and That

Two YouTube Interviews

I don't often listen to podcasts or watch interviews on YouTube. I spend enough time on the computer, designing books, writing, composing The PRC (I tell people doing that is the closest I've ever come to my childhood goal of being a mad scientist), and keeping up with my correspondence, that I prefer to walk away from the computer after a typical workday, if I'm going to read, listen to, or view something.

So it's kinda ironical that, in the past few months, I was *featured on* two YouTube sessions, both sponsored by the Ayn Rand Centre United Kingdom.

Yes, they someone at ARCUK thought I'd have something interesting to say on two things. For the first, I was approached because someone thought I knew something worth sharing; for the second, I convinced that same person that I knew something worth sharing.

You should be able to find them by searching YouTube with the following titles:

• "The Life and Works of Steve Ditko #777" is about the comics artist who (with Stan Lee) co-created The Amazing Spider-Man in 1962. Much of the podcast is a discussion of Ditko's philosophical work, which he did after leaving Marvel and Spider-Man in 1966.

• In "Eyes Wide Shut: The Master's Masterpiece #802," I talk about the theme of Stanley Kubrick's last film. Since I first saw this *mature-adults-only* film (and believe me, I'm not kidding about that!) in 1999, I've told people it had a very important theme, which is relevant to every person, ever day of his/her life. I wouldn't tell anyone what that theme was; it's most powerful if the viewer sees the film and figures it out on his/her own. It doesn't take a doctorate in philosophy or psychology to figure it out—just a *little bit* of common-sense thinking. (That's a *huge amount* more thinking than many movies require of a viewer.) But on this podcast, I break my 20+ years of silence, and I *tell all,* what I think this film is all about.

For each podcast, I was interviewed by James Valliant, whose work I've enjoyed and admired for years.

I'm happy with the results of these podcasts, and I thank my friend Matthew Humphreys, ARCUK Founder & Director Razi Ginzberg, and James Valliant for making the two experiences possible.

Worth Retweeting

Posted on Twitter, by someone identifying himself only as "Greg": "I wish taco trucks would cruise the neighborhood like ice cream trucks."

Yeah!

If Not a Film Critic, then What?

Watching a documentary on film critics, I realized—that's not what I am.

Just a couple of differences: I believe a critic should give a good idea of the story of a film being reviewed. I often don't give you any idea of the story.

Also, a critic (I think) should cover a film in a thorough, systematic way. Plot. Characterization. Theme. Relate it to the rest of cinema history. (Maybe I'm dreaming, in this view of critics.)

But then, if I'm not a film critic, with all the writing I do about movies, *what am I?*

On our Facebook page, I mentioned a movie. One person responded, "I'd never heard of that one."

That is part of my self-appointed job description. My role is information gatherer. A sifter of all that I am exposed to in the world and history of cinema. And I am here to pass on some highlights to you.

You don't need me to alert you of a new Mission Impossible release, or of the latest film retelling Batman's origin. I'm here to tell you of films you'd likely never know of, otherwise.

Some people travel allllll over the world. They document their discoveries, pass those experiences on to you, and you're able to select one out of any hundred places and say, *"That* sounds like a place I'd like to visit!"

That's my role with movies. Part of my specialization is that I explore the world of film.

And *boy,* do I *ever* explore! While I find some real gems on my prospecting journeys, you'd be aghast at some of the absolute duds that have smacked me in the face. The kind where the director thought it would be *chez* artistic to start the camera rolling, and just follow someone walking through the woods for ten minutes (adding nothing to a non-existent story). The kind where everything ends in despair, because the screenwriter believes human beings are helpless pawns in the "game" of life. The kind where human depravity is considered deep, profound, insightful, interesting; and human dignity an illusion, hopeless, impossible, boring.

And of those gems that I discover? I hope my excitement for them gets *you* excited.

I'm able to only share some of my discoveries, but I do what I can.

What Do I Look For in a Movie?

My film recommendations will *only* be of value to you if we're looking for something similar. One or more of the following are important for a film to be worthwhile to me.

• It tells a *story.* This is important because it assumes an essential aspect of human nature: the presence of free will (or volition). If things "just happen," if the people are smacked around like helpless automatons by "life" or by "society," that story offers nothing relevant to my life.

• Directly related to the previous point: The main characters have chosen to *live* (as opposed to simply avoiding death); they are rational and have a life-affirming, productive purpose. That's my main reason for never watching Bonnie and Clyde (and similar films).

• The story is not one I've seen a hundred (or more) times before. If I can predict what's going to happen, I'm disappointed. That goes especially for twist endings, or "hairpin turn" plot developments. When you expect a twist ending, you can often predict *exactly* how things are going to end.

Now, if you know me at all, you know that I will watch certain films over and over. My running joke about 2001: A Space Odyssey is that I lost count of how many times I'd seen it, somewhere after around the 30th time.

That can be explained with the next point:

• It's *crafted.* There's some style to it. A movie with a generic, made-for-TV style, with banal dialogue and lackluster visuals will deaden my mind into catatonia (and that ain't the same place as Catalina, by any stretch). A crafted movie gives me a feeling that "I'm seeing something new / unique / original / fresh / personal / one-of-a-kind."

I can enjoy a crafted film over and over, for the same reason I can look at the same beautiful work of art many times (I just glanced at my wall, where several James Bama works hang, to prove that point), or listen to a great piece of music over, and over, and over.

Which of these points are important to *you?*

If you and I find the same things important, you might come to trust my recommendations. That's one thing I've tried to accomplish, these past nine years.

OK, communication *should* be a two-way street. But you might feel silly, holding a newspaper and trying to talk to it, so if you have a recommendation for *me,* send it my way by one of the methods described on page 2.

Why TCM?

Several years ago, shortly after assuming editorship of The PRC, I started alerting Readers to a few movies scheduled for Turner Classic Movies (TCM). My reasoning was: Most people get some cable or satellite TV service; TCM is... sometimes/often included in those packages. (That was only a guess. I tried to find out what percentage of households in this part of Wisconsin actually get TCM, but couldn't. If you know that datum, please let me know.)

Whenever I get feedback (mostly in-person) on The PRC, people often remark that they like reading what I write about movies. I'll respond, "Oh, do you get TCM?" And I'll sometimes get: "No, I just like reading what you write about the movies."

!!!

OK, I'll take that compliment with much appreciation.

It's just a little surprising, that's all.

Book I Just Finished This Morning
The Gift of Failure, by Dan Bongino.
Recommended.

This TV / podcast personality tells of several failures he's experienced in his lifetime, and how he learned from them, and made himself better and stronger.

Article I'd Like to Run, but Don't Have Room For:
"Reconsidering Spaceship Earth: The power of human knowledge and technology outweighs the supposed limitations of Earth's resources," by Marian L. Tupy, posted this past July 19 on HumanProgress.org. You can find it searching that website; I also posted a link to it on The PRC's Facebook page (see page 2).

The number of pages in each PRC is determined by the amount of advertising we receive for the issue *(thanks,* advertisers, once again!). And it doesn't seem to matter how *many* pages I have to work with—there's *always* something I have to leave out, for lack of space!

Kind of reminds me of a quote. Publisher Hugh Hefner hired Harvey Kurtzman, the comics writer and artist who originated Mad as a comic book in the 1950s (among his many achievements), to create a magazine. That magazine only lasted a few issues. Hefner later said (supposedly; this might be apocryphal), "I gave Harvey Kurtzman an unlimited budget, and he exceeded it."

You know, if the advertising revenue ever justifies a 64-page issue of The PRC (the highest number of pages our printer will handle), I'll bet you I *still* won't have enough room for all the wonderful content I want to stuff into that issue.

That's it for now!

Paul Bransom's work appears in Illustration Magazine #83. How good was Paul Bransom? *This* good. – HA.com

This suit was used in the making of the 1968 film, 2001: A Space Odyssey. It sold at Heritage Auctions for $447,000. – HA.com

The Plymouth Review Current

Taking you places worth seeing

Volume 13 • Issue 1 • December 2023

FREE!

Equality • Outbid Again! • Fine Art
Rockets and Barns • Bridge of Enchantment

The publication that respects your intelligence • Human Flourishing • Whimsies • Witticisms • Oddities

December 2023

Cover image: The Bellagio, Las Vegas
Great Movies This Month
Why Mr. Beast's Humanitarian Efforts Actually Work—and Why His Critics Hate Him for It
Outbid Again!
What Technique?
Ask a Science Teacher, by Larry Scheckel: Why is Otzi, the Iceman, in the News Again?
PulpArtists by David Saunders: Manning de V. Lee
Plymouth Arts Center Events
And Here It Is...
Equality and the American Dream, by C. Bradley Thompson
This Could Have Been Our Front Cover...
More Visionary Artwork from Bryan Larson...

Jon Wos (bottom painting), meet Bryan Larsen (top painting; acquired recently).
Bryan Larsen, meet Jon Wos.
From Your Editor's office.

377

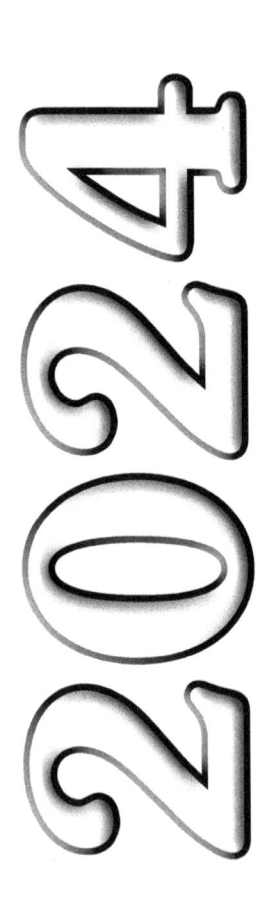

2024

The Plymouth Review Current

Taking You Places Worth Seeing
Volume 13 · Issue 2 · January 2024

Movies • Art • Culture
When Lightning Strikes Planes
White Truffles

January 2024

Cover photo: White Truffle Dinner at Lupi & Iris
Great Movies This Month
White Truffles
Plymouth Arts Center Events
PulpArtists by David Saunders: Doris Stanley
Don't Let 'em Get You!
Young People Aren't Reading
Classic Books: 3 Reasons Why That's a Problem, by C.G. Jones, IntellectualTakeout.org
Teaching Your Child to Read: The Gateway to All Learning, by Heather Carson, IntellectualTakeout.org
Five Things You Should Know Before Getting a Credit Card, by Jon Miltimore FEE.org
Alexander Botts: "I'm a Natural-Born Salesman!"
Ask a Science Teacher by Larry Scheckel: What Happens When an Airplane Gets Struck by Lightning?

Q: What Happens When an Airplane Gets Struck by Lightning?

By Larry Scheckel

A: Lightning strikes on aircraft are quite common, but also quite harmless. According to the FAA (Federal Aviation Administration), on average, every airliner gets hit once a year. Of course, some planes get hit more than once, and some not at all. Yes, indeed, that adds up to a lot of struck planes.

Geography has a lot to do with it. Thunderstorms and lightning are more prevalent near the equator because of convection currents created by warm air. There's an average of 100 thunderstorms a day in Florida, but only 10 on the West Coast.

Aircraft are most frequently struck by lightning just after take-off and just before landing. In order words, when the plane is close to the ground and between 5,000 and 15,000 foot altitude. Planes are rarely struck above 25,000 feet or at cruising altitudes in the 30,000 feet and higher range. Almost all strikes occur when the aircraft is in clouds.

Planes are made of aluminum, which is a very good conductor of electricity. The lightning flows over the skin of the plane and off into the air. Lightning could damage very sensitive electronic instruments on board, so built-in lightning protection systems are required.

Lightning most often hits planes in a protruding part, such as the nose or wingtip. When flying, you might see those metal rods sticking out of the trailing edge of the wing. These static wicks dissipate charges caused by lightning during a flight.

More and more aircraft these days are made of a mix of composite materials and aluminum. The Boeing 787 Dreamliner is 50 percent composite by weight, including the fuselage. The Airbus A350 is a tad more than 50 percent composite. Those carbon fiber laminate composites do not conduct electricity. The manufacturers take extra measures to protect strike-prone areas.

The last time a commercial airplane crash was blamed on lightning was in 1962, when lightning struck a Boeing 707 that was in a holding pattern over Elkton, Maryland. The lightning spark ignited vapors in a fuel tank, causing an explosion and killing eighty-one people on board. The very next week suppressors were installed in aircraft.

In 1967, 23 people died when a Lockheed jet flown by the Iranian Air Force was brought down by lightning. The probable cause was listed as "lightning-induced ignition of the fuel/air mixture in the no. 1 reserve fuel tank with resultant explosive disintegration of the left outer wing and loss of control."

Pilots do try to avoid thunderstorms, not only because of

lightning, but because the high shear winds (updrafts and downdrafts) can tear an aircraft apart. Also, if a jet engine ingests a huge amount of water, the engine will quit (flame out). In addition, an airplane flying into a cloud that has built up an electric charge can actually trigger a lightning stroke.

A Boeing 777 carrying British Prime Minister Tony Blair to a meeting with President Bush in March 2003 was hit by a lightning bolt as it approached Andrews Air Force Base outside Washington, D.C. Lightning hit the left wing. There was no damage to the plane or passengers.

Please send comments and questions to: lscheckel@charter.net

David Saunders' pulpartists.com

DORIS STANLEY: GHOST PAINTER

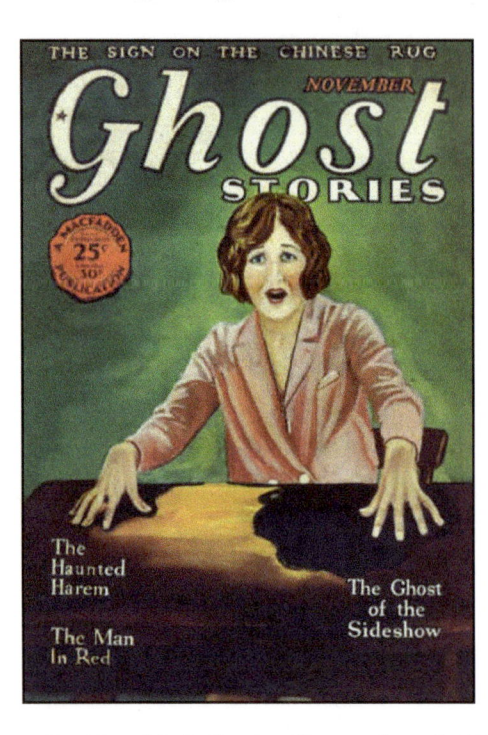

(1907-1965)

Ada Mae Doris Stanley was born on January 29, 1907 in Boston, Massachusetts. Her father, Garnett Wolseley Stanley, was born in 1882 in Moncton, New Brunswick, Canada. Her mother, Agnes Mary Wallace, was born in 1888 in Massachusetts. Her parents were married in Boston on April 20, 1905. She was their only child. The family lived at 32 Sudan Street. The father was an auditor at the American Express Company of Boston.

On April 2, 1914, when Doris was seven years old, her mother died of Tuberculosis at the age of twenty-six. After this tragic loss the father sent Doris to a Catholic girls boarding school, the Academy of the Assumption, in Wellesley Hills, MA, while he became a traveling salesman for the American Seedless Raisin Company of Boston.

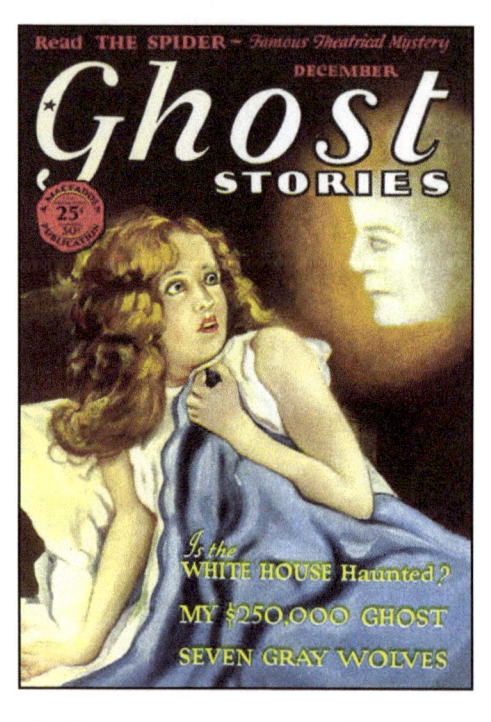

On February 22, 1919 Garnett Wolseley Stanley married his second wife, Alma Marie Snyder. She was born in 1898 in Virginia.

In June of 1920 Doris Stanley, age thirteen, completed the eighth grade at the Catholic boarding school, after which she left schooling and moved in with her paternal grandparents, James Lawrence Stanley (b.1855) and Ada Mae Doris Kinraide Stanley (b.1861). They lived at 735 Tremont Street in West Boylston, Massachusetts.

Her paternal grandfather was a printer with a Boston newspaper, where Doris found work was as a typist. While working at the print shop she became interested in a career as a commercial artist and began to take art weekend lessons at the Boston Museum of Fine Art.

On February 22, 1923 her paternal grandfather, James Lawrence Stanley, died at the age of sixty-eight. After this loss, Doris left her widowed paternal grandmother, Ada Mae Doris Kinraide Stanley, and moved in with her widowed maternal grandmother, Mary Clancy Wallace DeCrow, who was born in 1868 in MA, and lived in East Orange, New Jersey.

In 1925 Doris Stanley lived at 333 Seventh Avenue in New York City, where she listed her employer as Macfadden Publications. The company was run by Bernarr Macfadden (1868-1955), who produced *True Confessions, True Detective, Physical Culture, Dance Magazine,* and *Ghost Stories.* An associate editor at Macfadden Publications at that time was Harold Hersey (1893-1956).

In 1928 Doris Stanley contributed illustrations to *Ghost Stories* from Macfadden Publications. Other artists who worked for the same publisher at that time were Dalton Stevens, Carl Pfeufer (1910-1980), Wilson Stuart Leech (1902-1982), and Delos Palmer.

In 1929 Harold Hersey started Good Story Publishing Company with financial support from Bernarr Macfadden and distributors, Warren Angel and Paul Sampliner, who co-owned Eastern Distributing. Advertising was handled by their affiliate, Henry Dwight Cushing. One of Harold Hersey's first periodicals was the pulp magazine *Ghost Stories.* This magazine continued the numbering sequence of the same title from when it had been a Macfadden publication.

The 1930 Census listed Doris Stanley, age twenty three, at 149 Harrison Street in East Orange, NJ, where she lived with her twice-widowed maternal grandmother, Mary Clancy Wallace DeCrow, age sixty-two.

On March 8, 1932 her paternal grandmother, Ada Mae Doris Kinraide Stanley, died at the age of seventy-one.

On February 13, 1933 her father, Garnett Wolseley Stanley, died at the age of fifty-nine in Boston.

In 1934 Doris Stanley married Theodore Buchanan Welsh of East Orange, NJ. He was born on December 23, 1904 in Oakmont, Pennsylvania. The husband was age twenty-nine and the wife was age twenty-seven. They lived at 214 Glenwood Avenue in East Orange, NJ. He worked as a salesman at the Gulf Oil Corporation at 17 Battery Park Place in Lower Manhattan.

In 1945 the husband and wife left East Orange, NJ, and moved to Pittsburgh, PA, where they lived at 7136 McPherson Street. They had two sons, Theodore Buchanan Welsh (b.1945), and David Stanley Welsh (b.1947). The artist's maternal grandmother, Mary Clancy Wallace DeCrow, also left New Jersey and moved to Pittsburgh to live with the family.

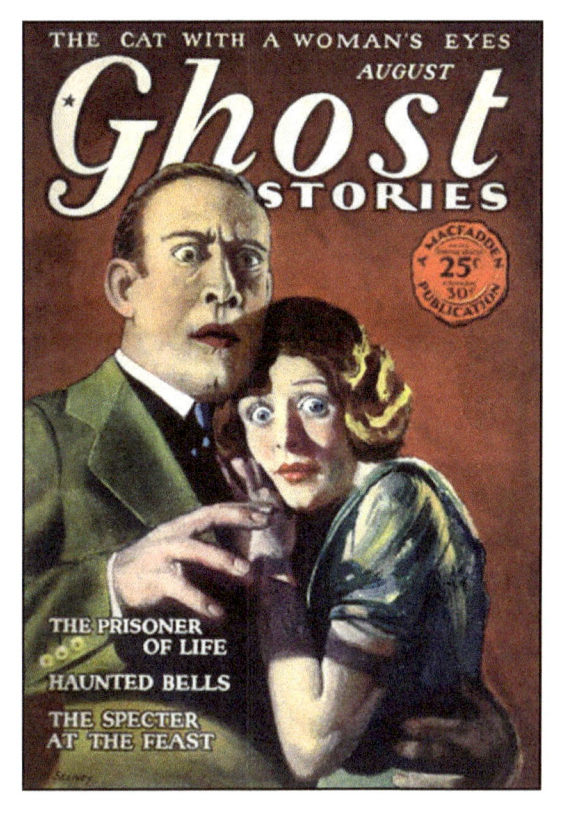

On May 19, 1959 the artist's maternal grandmother died at the age of ninety-one in Pittsburgh.

On May 11, 1962 the artist's husband, Theodore Buchanan Welsh, died at the age of fifty-eight in Pittsburgh.

In 1963 Doris Stanley Welsh married her second husband, Theodore John Bechtold. He was born in 1900 in Pittsburgh. He was a truck driver and was also a widower.

Doris Stanley Welsh Bechtold died in Pittsburgh at the age of fifty-eight on October 12, 1965.

© David Saunders
2020

Don't Let 'em Get You!

At a recent family gathering, someone brought up how helpful spell-checking software is on our word-processing software, especially for the many of us who are not perfect spellers.

I said spell-checkers could be considered a type of "artificial intelligence," one that's been around for awhile. But I also made a point that one type of punctuation has eluded the programmers who build the intelligence into such AI programs; that, until this deficiency is taken care of, the well-informed writer is fully justified in smiling contemptuously when the app makes this mistake, with the realization that, "The human mind is still far, far superior to what passes for 'artificial intelligence.'"

I'll demonstrate with the phrase of this article's title:

Don't let 'em get you!

The above is **JPW** (Just Plain Wrong).

Because? An apostrophe indicating dropped letters *always points to the left.* Always. **Always.**

But when you key this slangy short form of "them," your word-processor app evaluates the situation (in its little non-existent word-processing mind) as such: "**Observation:** A space. Then an apostrophe. Then letter(s). **Conclusion:** This is a single quote." And when you key the apostrophe, the app automatically puts out:

'em

It points the apostrophe to the right. It's not intelligent enough to understand that this is JPW.

But you are.

How then do you fix this? How do you confront this app's ignorance in this matter (while graciously recognizing the many ways in which the app truly makes your writing easier and better), and come out triumphant over that ignorance?

Type the whole thing (or any portion that works for you) like this:

Don't let'em get you!

See that? If you don't type a space before the apostrophe, it will point in the right direction!

You then get in there, position the cursor before the apostrophe, and insert a space:

Don't let 'em get you!

And you have it corrected.

Here's another example, which I see ***all over:***

For Sale:
'59 Chevy-Ford Convertible Hardtop

All right, I don't know much about cars; is there any such thing? It's just an example. An egregiously JPW example. Here's the corrected version:

For Sale:
'59 Chevy-Ford Convertible Hardtop

Yes, when leaving the century off a year, the rule for the apostrophe is the same. ***It points leftward:***

She is certainly a child of the '60s.
The '30s saw hard economic times.
Most pulps were gone by the '50s.

Now here's something different. Which of the following are correct?

Rock n' Roll
Rock n Roll
Rock 'n' Roll

Answer: None of the above. ***JPW,*** every one. (You know that by now, don't you?)
The middle word "and" has a letter dropped at both beginning and ending, so the correct form is:

Rock 'n' Roll

Finally—and I know you're going to find this hard to believe—one of the area's most honored, prestigious newspapers contained something like this in a recent headline:

the '23-'24 school year

JPW. The correct version:

the '23-'24 school year

Now, perhaps you're wondering, "Is it worth the extra second it takes to do it the right way?"
That's your call. We all set our own personal standards for what's important.
When I work on The PRC, ***my*** standards kick up into ultra-high mode. Even then, to my disgust, I ***still*** sometimes make mistaks.

February
2024

Cover photo: History in Photos, Thriller Villa, Las Vegas
Great Movies This Month
Ask a Science Teacher by Larry Scheckel: What Causes a Wheel that Comes off a Moving Car to Roll out ahead of the Car?
PulpArtists by David Saunders: Leighton Budd
IJ Helps WI
Plymouth Arts Center Events
The Liberace Museum Collection at Thriller Villa

David Saunders' pulpartists.com

Leighton Budd: Puckish Animator

(1872-1962)

Roy Leighton Budd was born on December 12, 1872 in Elyria, Ohio. His father, James H. Budd, was born 1845 in New York of Irish ancestry.

The father's family had moved to Ohio in 1860 to start a business supplying animal hides to an eastern manufacturer. During the American Civil War the father served as a private in Company G of the 101st Ohio Infantry, and was wounded in battle.

After the war the father returned to his family business, where he worked until 1871, when he married Helen A. Deney. She was born 1854 in Ohio, and was also of Irish ancestry. They had one child, Roy "Rollo" Leighton Budd (b.1872). The father then left his family business, and instead became a restaurant keeper. They lived at 244 Third Street in Elyria, Ohio.

In 1886, at the age of fourteen, Roy Leighton Budd completed the Eighth Grade, after which he left schooling and entered the work force. He worked in the printing department of *The Elyria Reporter* newspaper, where he became interested in a career as a commercial artist. The older artists on the staff gave him free instruction in basic art skills.

In September of 1892, at the age of nineteen, Roy Leighton Budd left his home in Elyria and moved to New York City to study at the Art Students League.

On July 1, 1893 the "Local News" section of *The Elyria Reporter* announced, "Roy Budd, who has been attending an Eastern Art School, is home for his summer vacation."

In 1894 Roy Leighton Budd was employed as a full-time staff artist at *The New York Herald.*

On May 31, 1895, the father, James H. Budd, died at the age of fifty in Ohio. After this death the mother received a government stipend as a Civil War widow. She earned extra income as a local dressmaker, and advertised her service in the local newspaper.

In 1900 R. Leighton Bud, age twenty-seven, was listed in the U.S. Census as a resident at 34 West 30th Street in New York City. His occupation was identified as an "artist illustrator."

On December 5, 1900 *The Elyria Reporter* announced, "Mr. Roy Budd of New York City is visiting his mother, Mrs. H. A. Budd, of Third Street for two weeks over the holidays."

In 1901 Roy Leighton Budd became a regular contributor to the humor magazine, *Puck.*

In 1906 "The Tumble Brothers" by Leighton Budd became a syndicated newspaper comic strip in *The New York Herald,* where it appeared at the same time as Winsor McCay's "Little Nemo In Slumberland."

The 1905 New York State Census listed Leighton Budd as age thirty-two, residing at 18 West 30th Street. He was employed as an art instructor at the Art Students League.

Over the next ten years he was a regular contributor to *Judge, The Century, Harper's Magazine,* and *Scribner's Magazine.* His work also appeared in *St. Nicholas,* the juvenile magazine. At that time the art editor at *St. Nichola*s was Norman Rockwell.

In 1916 Leighton Budd began to work as an art director at Bray Studios, located at 23 East 26th Street in Manhattan. It was one of the world's first motion picture studios that only produced animated cartoons. Bray Studios employed Louis M. Glackens (1866-1933), Johnny Gruelle (1880-1938), Max Fleischer (1883-1972), Pat Sullivan (1885-1933), Paul Terry (1887-1971), Milt Gross (1895-1953), Jack King (1895-1958), and Walter Lantz (1899-1994).

In 1916 the U.S. Army fought the Mexican Border War. The National Guard was activated for Federal service and stationed along the Mexican border to defend against raiding parties from Pancho Villa (1878-1923), the Mexican revolutionary commander. In support of this national crisis, the Bray Studios produced a series of patriotic animated movies, three of which were created by Leighton Budd. The movies were widely popular and distributed by Paramount.

How many names from the **Bray Studios** do you recognize?

From 1917 to 1919, during the Great War, the Bray Studios again produced patriotic movies. This time Leighton Budd made eleven short animated cartoons of patriotic themes. He also produced training and educational films for the U.S. Army. In 1918 Roy Leighton Budd reported for draft registration. He was recorded to have been age forty-four, and employed at Bray Studios to produce special cartoons for "the U.S. Government."

During the roaring twenties Leighton Budd illustrated advertising that appeared in newspapers and magazines.

In 1930 Leighton Budd (age fifty-eight) lived with his mother (age seventy-five) in Brooklyn at 156 Elliott Place. He never married.

In 1935 Major Malcolm Wheeler-Nicholson (1890-1968) produced some of the earliest American comic books to feature original material, such as *New Fun* and *More Fun.* The artists who drew the features included

383

Adolphe Barreaux, Henry C. Kiefer, Cole Brigham, Lyman Anderson, Ray Wardell, Joe Archibald, and Clem Gretter. The publishing company was named National Allied Publications, and was located at 49 West 45th Street. August 1935 was the cover date of *New Fun Comics* #5, which included "Midsummer Day's Dream" by Leighton Budd. The four-panel strip was actually not original. It was a reprint of a 1906 appearance of the Tumble Brothers."

On December 18, 1935 Albert Stevens Crockett wrote and published "Old Astoria Bar Days," which featured cocktail recipes, witty historic anecdotes, and humorous illustrations by Leighton Budd.

In 1937 the artist's mother, Helen A. Budd, died at the age of eighty-two in Brooklyn.

On April 26, 1938 Leighton Budd was granted a patent for a device that helped artists to depict characters. Two years later he received a second patent for an improved version of his device.

On November 3, 1939 *The New York Sun* gossip columnist Malcolm Johnson reported that "For authentic flavor of old England, combining the mellow charm of the ancient English tavern with the lusty cuisine of the red-faced, hearty, medieval beef-eaters, we recommend the Boar's Head Inn, at forty-seventh street and Lexington Avenue, which was opened recently by August Janssen, one of New York's best known restaurateurs. He has done everything he could, in decor, cuisine and service, to provide a nostalgic spot for lovers of the old-fashioned English Inn. Leighton Budd, whose drawings appeared in *Puck* for many years, and who has been associated with Mr. Janssen for ages, has been in charge of the restoration of the Boar's Head Inn and has painted a four-panel mural depicting a boar hunt and feast in the legendary days of Robin Hood."

On August 6, 1941 *The New York Post* dining columnist, Richard Manson, reported that "The Boar's Head Inn at Lexington and 47th Street was an English chop house, with a cafe bar and mezzanine dining room. Heraldic shields, stained glass windows, antique mugs, and murals by Leighton Budd of a boar hunt make up the decorations. There's also poetry on the walls, affording plenty of atmosphere. Dinners begin at $1.25 and run to $1.80. Specialties of the house are broiled English Mutton chop with a baked potato, $1.75. Prime ribs of beef with Yorkshire pudding $1.30. Steak and kidney pie, $1. Drinks are 35 cents and up."

On May 1, 1953 nationwide newspapers reported, "This week Leighton Budd of New York City patented a Headrest For Cosmetic Mask. The plan is for the beauty seeker to lie on her tummy with her face on a small blanket that is supported by a framework with a hole for her mouth and nose. Mr. Budd explains his boon to the fairer sex thus, 'In massaging the face to aid age-sagging facial tissue, the flesh is moved upward smoothly with the finger tips to its youthful place. Afterwards it is necessary that the tissues be held in the raised position for a length of time.' The Budd invention 'will enable the person to relax and be refreshed for activities while the corrected facial tissues mend in the position the massage has placed them."

Roy Leighton Budd died at the age of eighty-nine in Brooklyn, on October 5, 1962.

© David Saunders 2017

Q: What Causes a Wheel that Comes off a Moving Car to Roll out ahead of the Car?

By Larry Scheckel

Ask a Science Teacher

A: Reminds one of "you picked a fine time to leave me loose wheel," a play on Kenny Rogers' 1977 song, "You picked a fine time to leave me Lucille."

There are two things to consider: why does the wheel fall off and why does it roll on ahead of the car.

The wheel has a certain amount of kinetic energy when moving down the highway. That kinetic energy is composed of both linear (translational or forward) and rotational energy. When the wheel comes off, it still has the same linear forward motion that the car had. But that extra rotational energy is what propels the wheel ahead of the car.

Imagine having a rotating or spinning wheel mounted a few inches above the ground or pavement and on some kind of frame, but not on a car. All the energy is in rotation, with no linear or forward energy. Release the wheel and when it hits the pavement, its spin or rotation will propel it forward.

One driver reported that a rear wheel came off while tooling down the Interstate highway. In fact, seeing the wheel rolling down the road in front of the car was the first indication that anything had happened. He successfully got out of the fast lane and onto the hard shoulder before attempting to slow down. The car stayed in its "normal" position until the speed had dropped to about 10 mph. There was no damage or injuries to anything except the car itself, and that was repairable.

Another driver reported, "I was rotating the wheels when my brother had a medical emergency and I had to take him to a hospital. In a rush, I overlooked that I only had one of four nuts on one wheel. While stopping at a streetlight, I heard a metal noise and saw a wheel passing by us spinning forward. I thought, 'What idiot has lost a wheel?' just before realizing that it was me. It took me a minute to put it back, so a happy ending, but in the meanwhile my car was down to the ground and would not drive on three wheels."

Tom and Ray Magliozzi on Car Talk said, "Generally, there are two things that cause wheels to fall off: One, they're not put on correctly. The lug nuts are either not tightened, or they're overtightened, causing the wheel bolts to break. Or the ball joints fail. Ball joint failure is very rare. So, I'm leaning toward human error. If the lug nuts are severely overtightened, that stretches and weakens the wheel bolts, which are then subject to failure. Even if only one bolt snaps, the pressure then increases on the others because now four are doing the job of five, and before long, another weak one gives out, and the rest fail more quickly. This happens on cars where the tires have been rotated frequently over a long period of time, and when the mechanic overtightens the lug nuts time after time."

Note: The Magliozzi Brothers were known as Click and Clack: The Tappet Brothers on NPR radio. They also had a newspaper column. Tom Magliozzi passed away in 2014.

The wheel falling off while driving can cause an accident. There's the possibility of the driver losing control. In these situations, severe and costly injuries are possible. Additionally, the wheel and tire can cause injuries by running into something or someone.

If you lose a front wheel on a front wheel drive car, you will lose the power to the other front wheel because the differential will just spin the wheel-less axle. This may also over-rev the engine and cause some other damage.

Sources: www.cartalk.com and autoily.com.

Send comments and questions to: lscheckel@charter.net

The Liberace Museum Collection
at Thriller Villa

Something different.

That's what we searched for, planning our November 2023 trip to Las Vegas.

While preparing for previous Las Vegas trips over the years, I regretted hearing that an elaborate Liberace museum had once existed, but was now closed. It had opened in 1979 with Liberace's financial support, but closed in 2010. It sounded like it had been quite an impressive place. Comments in articles said attendance numbers had dropped dramatically, because newer generations weren't familiar with Liberace. (No, I'm still not giving up on Kids Nowadays. Some of my Best Friends are Kids.)

But wait! We found that the museum's contents are now housed in Thriller Villa, a 27,000-sq ft Las Vegas residence. Its name comes from the fact that Michael Jackson lived there from 2007 to his death in 2009. (And if you still believe Michael Jackson was a child molester, search the 'net with "Michael Jackson Objective Standard justice" for an article, "Justice for Michael Jackson" by Tim White, which sets *that* record straight.)

This Liberace tour is not open to the public. We made an appointment for a private tour. Jonathan Warren, Chairman of the Liberace Foundation, was to conduct it. Weeks before our visit, he sent me several links. I read many background stories written by Warren, about Liberace's interaction with other show business celebrities, and historical accounts about the Las Vegas area. (Our Facebook page (see page 2) has links to *several* articles related to what you're reading here. If Facebook isn't your thing, search the 'net with "Jonathan Warren Liberace Collection" and you'll find *plenty* of interesting material.)

My wife and I were the only two on the tour that day. Warren arranged for an Uber to pick us up and transport us to Thriller Villa, where we learned a lot in the next three hours.

After giving us some history on the building, Warren seated us at a bar. Photos covered the walls (see our front page). Each had a story, about events in Liberace's life, or interactions with other entertainment talents. Hearing how he'd encouraged and nurtured the careers of several others, I said it seemed Liberace was not threatened by talent in someone else; rather, he wanted to see others refine and develop their talents, to succeed in their own show business careers. Warren agreed with my observation.

Warren is the right person to host this tour. His knowledge of Liberace and his place in Las Vegas history is phenomenal.

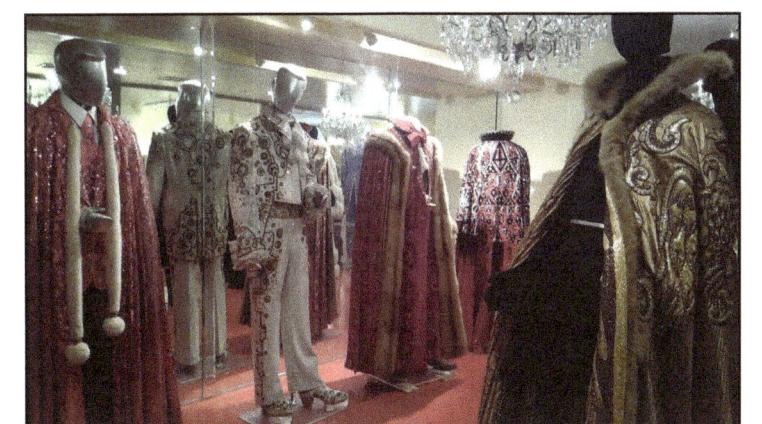

My mind was nearly reaching overload after three hours of visual and anecdotal stimulation. A few highlights:

• Michael Jackson was one of many entertainers Liberace became friends with. Early in his career, Jackson speculated on how he could use glitz and glamor to attract more attention. Jackson thought maybe he should emulate Liberace's over-the-top costumes. Liberace advised against that, because people might dismiss Jackson as a simple Liberace imitator. Liberace suggested that Jackson use just one thing for emphasis. Jackson's choice: The sparkling glove.

• Elvis, too, took advice from Liberace, when he amped up his wardrobe for performances.

• We'd recently seen an old Jack Benny TV program, with Liberace as a guest. My wife mentioned Benny playing a violin with a tiny candelabra attached. Warren smiled and pointed to a cabinet. There it was!

• I vaguely recall that Liberace was a villain on the 1960s Batman TV show. (As someone who takes comics very seriously, I turn red with embarrassment and anger when I accidentally see portions of reruns while changing channels.) He played Chandell (after "chandelier"—get it? get it?), a twin-brother duo. I will find that episode, grit my teeth, and watch it.

• The many costumes are fantastic. Warren described some of the materials that went into making them, and some of the people who designed them. My wife asked if the beads were faceted; Warren said they were.

• I asked how many albums Liberace had been released. There have been so many, Warren replied, that the true number is not known. (Sounds like an interesting project for some collector out there.) There are **many** (vintage vinyl and CD) available on eBay; many at attractive prices; I found a still-sealed 1974 LP for under $10, including shipping.

Looking for something different in Las Vegas? Something personal and stunningly unforgettable? A tour of the Liberace Collection at Thriller Villa is *It.*

This portrait of Michael Jackson is on display at Thriller Villa, which he called home for the last two years of his life.

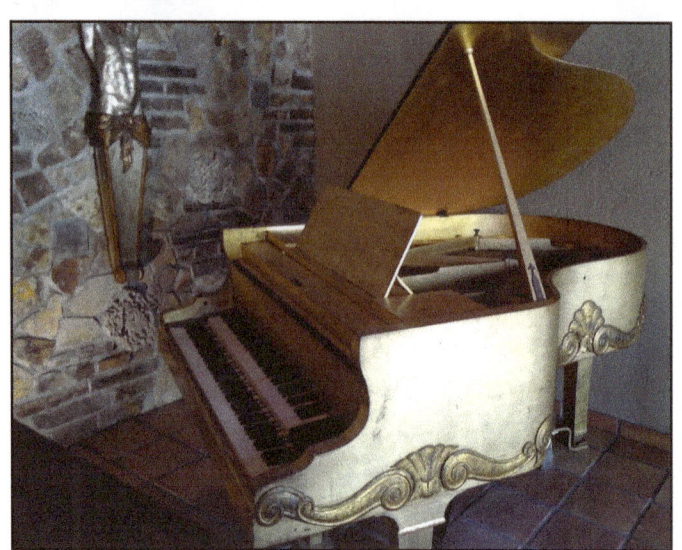

The Plymouth Review Current

TAKING YOU PLACES WORTH SEEING
Volume 13 • Issue 4 • March 2024

FREE!

Movies • Art • Progress • Books • Ideas
Ready to Work!

The publication that respects your intelligence • Human Flourishing • Whimsies • Witticisms • Oddities

March 2024

Cover photo: Ready to Work at MJ Equipment, Inc., Cedar Grove
Great Movies This Month
Illustration Art
Ask a Science Teacher by Larry Scheckel: Why Doesn't a Woodpecker Get a Headache?
Plymouth Arts Center Events
Introducing An Upcoming Book, Heroes of Progress, HumanProgress.org
The Power of Film: All 6 Episodes
An Absolute Masterpiece! (Guillermo del Toro's Pinocchio)
And Here's Another Great Movie! (Polite Society)
PulpArtists by David Saunders: John Clymer
The Bama Covers
Books Recently Read
Abundant Resources for the Laurel & Hardy Fanatic
Start to Finish

James Bama paperback cover painting.
— HA.com

Other books from The Silver Creek Press

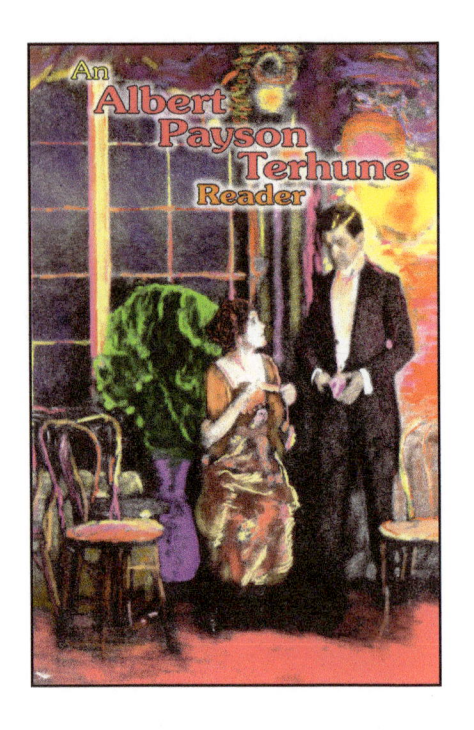

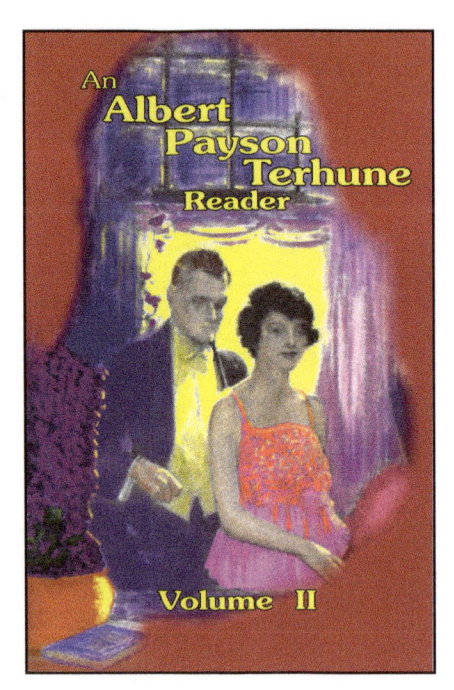

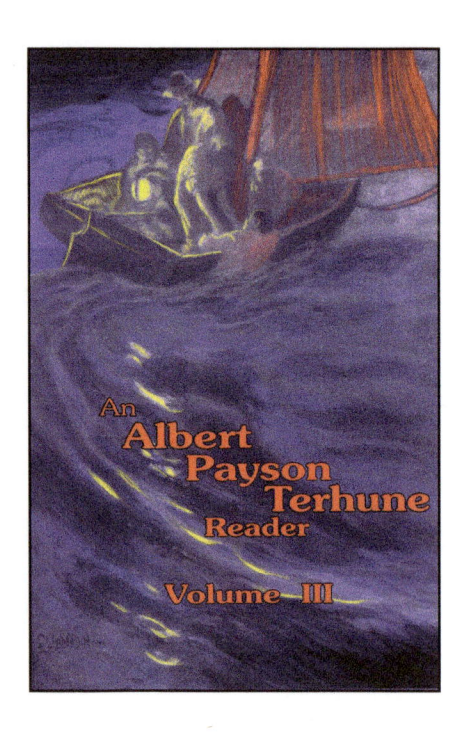

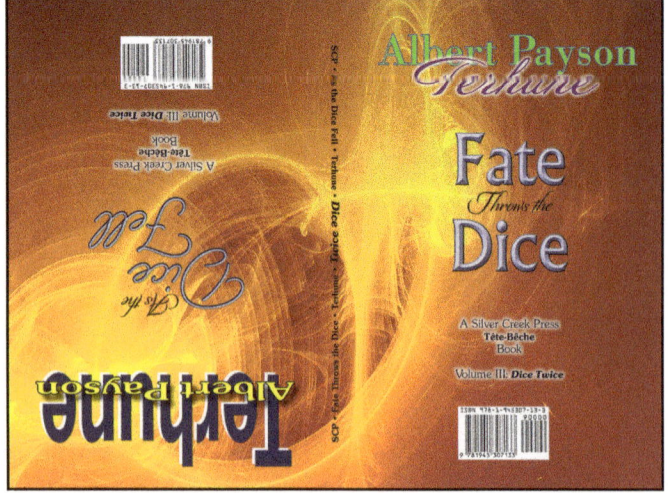

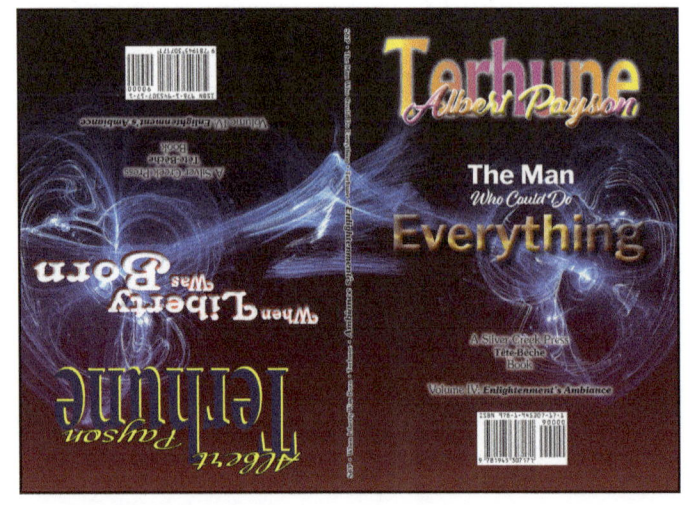

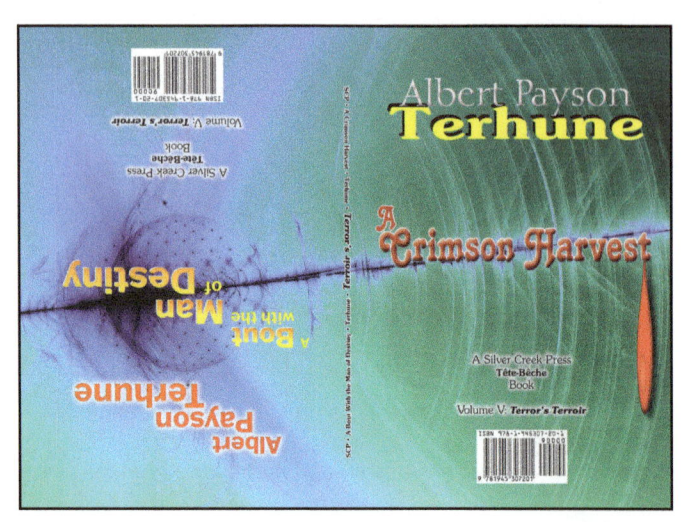

388

Other books from The Silver Creek Press

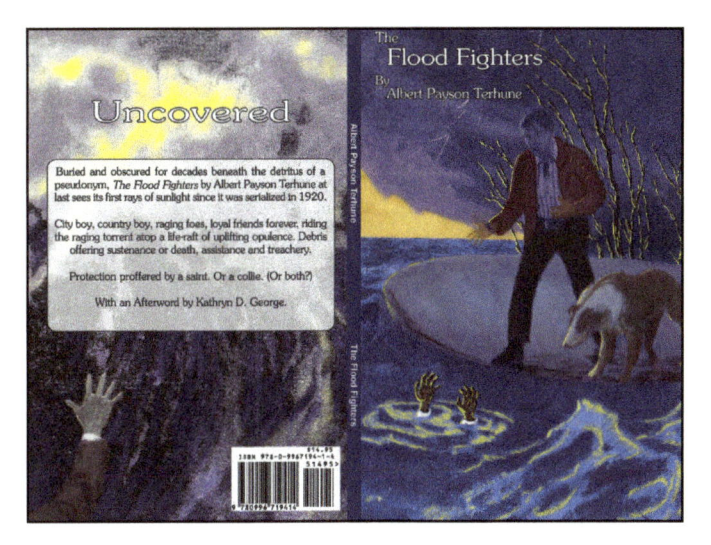

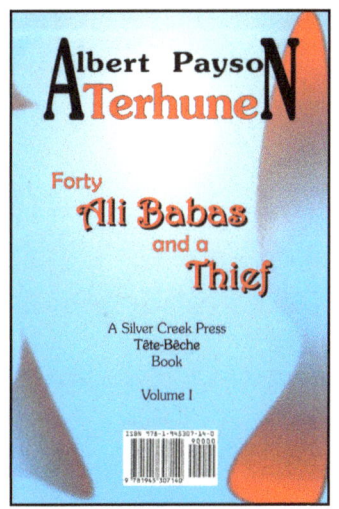

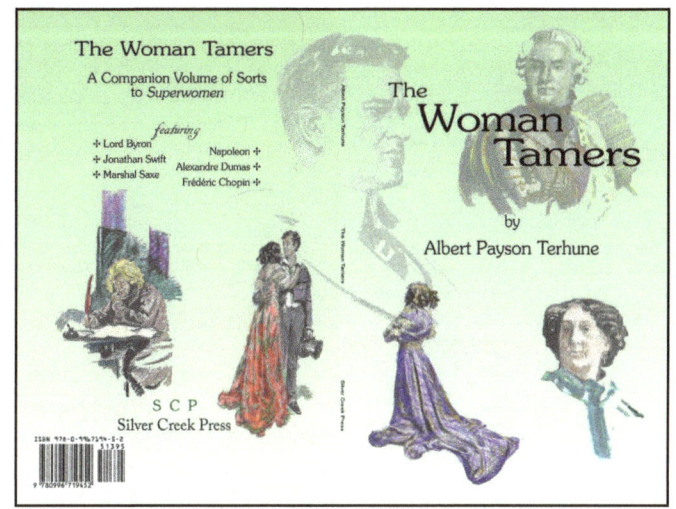

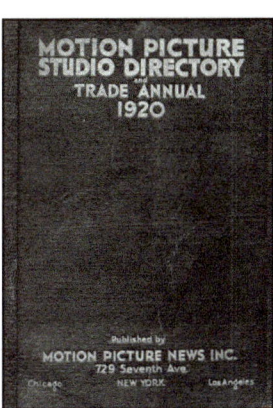

For awhile, one task I had at the Plymouth Review was to design ads. Between assignments from clients, I scanned our clipart service for images that would trigger a useful thought. Staring at this graphic, the text came to me so naturally that a philosophically less-sophisticated person might think "It almost wrote itself." It didn't happen that way.

Milton Keynes UK
Ingram Content Group UK Ltd.
UKHW050407010424
440357UK00003B/52